FOLLOW
OUR LEAD

Wherever you're exploring, we've got
the insider insight on the world's best
destinations.

 TIMEOUT.COM/
NEWYORK/TRAVEL

New York City Subway
with bus and railroad connections

TRANSPORT MAP

Contents

Introduction

'The city seen from the Queensboro Bridge is always the city seen for the first time, in its first wild promise of all the mystery and the beauty in the world,' wrote F Scott Fitzgerald in *The Great Gatsby*. From the gritty glamour of the downtown demimonde to the razzle-dazzle of Broadway, New York has an outsize mythology that entices more than 65 million visitors a year at last count. Yet its compact core, Manhattan, is surprisingly small: a mere 13.4 miles long and 2.3 miles across at its widest point. Like an overstuffed deli sandwich, the slender island packs in numerous distinct neighbourhoods shaped by diverse ethnic and cultural influences.

While many iconic sights remain essentially the same, New York is in a constant state of self-reinvention, adding skyscrapers, attractions, restaurants, parks and developments to its inventory. And, in contrast to Fitzgerald's day, some of the most exciting nightlife, food and arts are now to be found on the other side of the East River, in Brooklyn and Queens. The city's ceaseless pace and its boundless possibilities can be overwhelming, so let this book guide you through our exhilarating, shape-shifting metropolis.

ABOUT THE GUIDE

This is one of a series of Time Out guidebooks to cities across the globe. Written by local experts, our guides are thoroughly researched and meticulously updated. They aim to be inspiring, irreverent, well-informed and trustworthy.

Time Out New York is divided into five sections: Discover, Explore, Experience, Understand and Plan.

Discover introduces the city and provides inspiration for your visit.

Explore is the main sightseeing section of the guide and includes detailed listings and reviews for sights and museums; restaurants & cafés ⑩; bars ⑩; and shops & services ⑩, all organised by area with corresponding street maps for the key areas. To help navigation, each area of New York has been assigned its own colour.

Experience covers the cultural life of the city in depth, including festivals, film, LGBT, music, nightlife, theatre and more.

Understand provides in-depth background information that places New York in its historical and architectural context.

Plan offers practical visitor information, including accommodation options and details of public transport.

Hearts

We use hearts ♥ to pick out venues, sights and experiences in the city that we particularly recommend. The very best of these are featured in the Top 20 (*see p10*) and receive extended coverage in the guide.

Maps

A detachable fold-out map can be found on the inside back cover. There is also an overview map (*see p8*) and individual street maps for each of the key areas of the city. The venues featured in the guide have been given a grid reference so that you can find them easily on the maps and on the ground.

Prices

All our **restaurant listings** are marked with a dollar symbol category from budget to blow-out (**$-$$$$**), indicating the price you should expect to pay for a standard main course: **$** = under $15; **$$** = $15-$30; **$$$** = $30-$45; **$$$$** = over $45.

A similar system is used in our **Accommodation** chapter based on the hotel's standard prices for one night in a double room: budget = under $150; moderate = $150-$300; expensive = $300-$500; luxury = over $500.

Discover

St Patrick's Cathedral and Atlas Statue *p186*

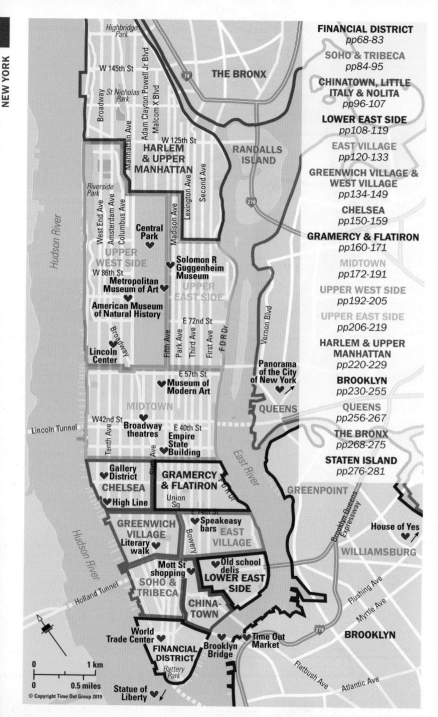

Highbridge Park
W 145th St
St Nicholas Park
Adam Clayton Powell Jr Blvd
Malcom X Blvd
Broadway
St Nicholas Ave
THE BRONX
W 125th St
HARLEM & UPPER MANHATTAN
Manhattan Ave
Lexington Ave
Second Ave
RANDALLS ISLAND
Riverside Park
West End Ave
Amsterdam Ave
Columbus Ave
Madison Ave
Central Park ♥
UPPER WEST SIDE
W 86th St
Solomon R Guggenheim Museum ♥
UPPER EAST SIDE
Metropolitan Museum of Art ♥
American Museum of Natural History ♥
Broadway
E 72nd St
Fifth Ave
Park Ave
Third Ave
First Ave
FDR Dr
Vernon Blvd
Lincoln Center ♥
E 57th St
Museum of Modern Art ♥
Panorama of the City of New York ♥ ↗
QUEENS
MIDTOWN
W 42nd St
Broadway theatres ♥
E 40th St
Tenth Ave
Sixth Ave
Empire State Building ♥
East River
Lincoln Tunnel
Gallery District ♥
FDR Dr
GREENPOINT
CHELSEA
GRAMERCY & FLATIRON
High Line ♥
Union Sq
E 14th St
GREENWICH VILLAGE
Speakeasy bars ♥
EAST VILLAGE
Bowery
Literary walk ♥
Brooklyn Queens Expressway
House of Yes ♥ ↗
WILLIAMSBURG
Hudson River
Mott St shopping ♥
Old school delis ♥
SOHO & TRIBECA
LOWER EAST SIDE
Holland Tunnel
Flushing Ave
Myrtle Ave
CHINA-TOWN
World Trade Center ♥
Time Out Market ♥
278
BROOKLYN
FINANCIAL DISTRICT
Brooklyn Bridge
Battery Park
Flatbush Ave
Atlantic Ave
Statue of Liberty ♥ ↙

0 ___ 1 km
0 ___ 0.5 miles
© Copyright Time Out Group 2019

NEW YORK
CityPASS

Your Ticket to New York City's Top Attractions

SAVE 42%
OR MORE AT
TOP ATTRACTIONS

ENJOY FOR
9 DAYS

Buy
Here

NEW YORK CITYPASS INCLUDES:

Empire State Building, American Museum of Natural History,
The Metropolitan Museum of Art,
Top of the Rock® Observation Deck OR Guggenheim Museum,
Ferry Access to Statue of Liberty & Ellis Island OR Circle Line Sightseeing Cruises,
9/11 Memorial & Museum OR Intrepid Sea, Air & Space Museum

Spend Less
Experience More.

citypass.com

Pricing and programs subject to change; visit citypass.com for details.

Top 20

City essentials, from skyscrapers and museums to massive sandwiches

01

Empire State Building *p182*

King Kong recognised the Empire State's skyscraper supremacy when he commandeered the iconic tower. It may no longer be the city's tallest building, but it has more than 85 years of movie cameos. Brave the crowds to escape the urban jungle and get a pigeon's-eye panorama of the metropolis and beyond.

02

Central Park *p196*

Frederick Law Olmsted and Calvert Vaux's 843-acre green space draws millions of visitors in all seasons: sunbathers and picnickers in summer, ice-skaters in winter, and bird-watchers in spring and autumn. It's also an idyllic venue for beloved cultural events such as Shakespeare in the Park and the New York Philharmonic's annual open-air performances.

03

Statue of Liberty *p73*

Symbolic and surreal, Lady Liberty was a beacon to millions of immigrants who subsequently shaped the city, and America. Impressive viewed from land, up close she is an immense marvel. A climb to the crown affords an exhilarating view of New York Harbor and the chance to see the literal nuts and bolts of Frédéric Auguste Bartholdi's creation.

04

Metropolitan Museum of Art
p214

Not only does this massive institution preserve such treasures as a c15 BC Egyptian temple, but it's also in a state of constant self-improvement. Case in point: a multi-year upgrade of the skylights illuminating its renowned European paintings collection. And a ticket also grants you entry to the Cloisters medieval outpost.

05

High Line *p156*

Where else can you walk through a field of wildflowers with taxis zooming beneath you? As you stroll along the linear park built on an abandoned railway track, keep an eye out for iconic sights, such as the Chrysler Building, and intriguing art installations.

06

Broadway theatres *p340*

The epicentre of American theatre for more than a century, the Great White Way offers new musical spectacles, big-budget revivals and explosive contemporary plays. No small part of the pleasure of seeing a show on Broadway comes from the elegance and opulence of its early 20th-century theatres.

07

Museum of Modern Art *p185*

In 2019, MoMA completed an expansion that added 40,000 square feet of exhibition space, including free street-level galleries and a dedicated performance venue. The multi-faceted institution reinstalled its permanent collection, which showcases iconic works by Picasso, Van Gogh and other modern masters, but also design, film, photography and more.

08

Old-school delis *p114*

New York may be known for its delis, but these kosher canteens are a dying breed. The granddaddy of them all is Katz's Delicatessen on the Lower East Side. Plastered with shots of famous noshers, the cafeteria delivers on its history, with hand-carved, tender smoked meat wedged into overstuffed sandwiches.

09

World Trade Center *p77*

It's impossible not to feel moved as you gaze at the waterfalls cascading down the vast chasms where the Twin Towers stood. Above you, 1 World Trade Center serves as a reminder that this town never stays down for long, while below ground, the 9/11 Memorial Museum documents the tragedy.

09

10

Brooklyn Bridge *p237*

No mere river crossing, this span is an elegant reminder of New York's history of architectural innovation. When it opened in 1883, the Brooklyn Bridge was the longest suspension bridge in the world. Stride along its wood-planked promenade for views of New York Harbor, the Statue of Liberty and downtown skyscrapers.

11

11

House of Yes *p312*

For a truly spectacular night out, this cavernous Brooklyn warehouse delivers time and again with variety shows and arty, frequently risqué extravaganzas complete with aerialists, DJs and immersive performances. Be sure to check the website for the theme of each party and arrive appropriately costumed.

12

Speakeasy bars *p49*

Secret drinking dens are hardly a new feature of the nightlife scene, but New Yorkers have a seemingly unquenchable thirst for hidden watering holes, whether tucked behind a fortune-teller front, or accessed via an unmarked staircase in a fast-food joint. Even better than the novelty thrills are the top-notch drinks.

13

Lincoln Center *p332*

Construction of this celebrated institution began in 1959 with the help of John D Rockefeller III, largely to provide new stomping grounds for the Metropolitan Opera, the New York Philharmonic and the Juilliard School. Today the complex encompasses 11 world-class cultural organisations and a staggering array of theatre, music, dance and film.

14

Solomon R Guggenheim Museum *p217*

When it was completed in 1959, Frank Lloyd Wright's curved concrete edifice caused a stir on the Upper East Side. Today, the iconic spiral – Wright's only building in Manhattan – is considered as much a work of art as the paintings it houses, which include masterpieces by Picasso, Chagall and Kandinsky.

15

Chelsea gallery district *p154*

We're not suggesting you skip the essential museums on our list, but in west Chelsea's contemporary art mecca you can often catch museum-calibre shows without spending a dime. The former industrial buildings have been converted into more than 300 galleries, from sleek blue-chip salons to densely packed warrens of smaller art spaces.

13

16

Greenwich Village literary walk *p137*

No matter how packed your itinerary, leave space to explore the leafy streets and quaint pubs of the Village, a magnet for 20th-century artists and writers. To give your stroll some focus, follow in the footsteps of figures from Henry James to Dylan Thomas on a literary ramble.

17

American Museum of Natural History *p199*

From the towering Tyrannosaurus rex in the peerless dinosaur halls to glittering gems and minerals, AMNH inspires awe and fascination regardless of age or interests. The vintage dioramas depicting American mammals in their native habitats are the next best thing to trips to the Wyoming prairie or the Alaska Peninsula coast.

18

Panorama of the City of New York *p265*

On the grounds of two World's Fairs, the Queens Museum holds one of Gotham's most intriguing curiosities: a 9,335-square-foot scale model of New York, created for the 1964 exposition. Walk around the Little Apple to spot Lilliputian landmarks such as the Empire State Building and Yankee Stadium.

17

17

19

Mott Street shopping *p104*

With some of the best independent boutiques in the city and plenty of chic refuelling options, Nolita offers a relaxed alternative to Soho, downtown's main retail area. Mott Street features buzzed-about openings while retaining an old-school vibe, with iconic Italian purveyors and colourful Asian markets along its length.

20

Time Out Market New York
p45

Hip food courts may be sprouting up across the city, but *Time Out New York*'s culinary collective on the Dumbo waterfront is more than just a multi-vendor dining destination; it offers gastronomic experiences hand-picked by *TONY* editors. In addition to the food, there are free gigs and a rooftop bar with thrilling Manhattan skyline views.

AND ALL THAT JAZZ
CHICAGO
THE MUSICAL
AMBASSADOR THEATRE · 49TH STREET AT BROADWAY
CHICAGOTHEMUSICAL.COM

Itineraries

Make the most of every New York minute with a tailored travel plan

ESSENTIAL WEEKEND

New York in two days
Budget $375-$550 per person
Getting around Walking, subway, bus, taxi

▶ *Budgets include transport, meals and admission prices, but not accommodation and shopping.*

DAY 1

Morning

Boost your calorie intake for some serious sightseeing with a hearty breakfast sandwich or house-baked pastry from Meatpacking District gem **High Street on Hudson** (*see p148*), before heading to the **Whitney Museum of American Art** (*see p147*) in Renzo Piano's striking asymmetrical structure overlooking the southernmost stretch of the High Line. If you've booked in advance online, you'll sail through without waiting in the ticket line. If you don't want to make the time commitment, you can check out the free lobby gallery without a ticket. The **High Line** (*see p156*), a disused freight-train track reborn as a public park-cum-promenade, is one of the most popular spots in the city for both visitors and locals. Stroll north, keeping an eye out for iconic structures such as the Statue of Liberty and the Empire State Building.

Hudson Yards

Whitney Museum of American Art

Afternoon

In the warmer months, you can stop for light eats (sandwiches, salads, charcuterie and cheese plates) and a tipple on the High Line between 15th and 16th Streets, at seasonal open-air offshoot of East Village restaurant **Hearth** (*see p126*). For a more substantial meal, exit at 23rd Street for one of two choices: seasonal New American restaurant **Cookshop** (*see p155*) or the restored 1940s **Empire Diner** (*see p156*).

Now you're ready for more cultural sustenance. The city's main contemporary gallery district is between Tenth and Eleventh Avenues from 18th to 29th Streets (for our picks, *see p154*). And if you want to pick up a souvenir, stop by arty bookshop **Printed Matter** (*see p159*).

Your art tour isn't over when you resume your High Line perambulation: the park has a dedicated curator of temporary site-specific work, so keep an eye out along its length, especially at the Spur, an open section that juts out over Tenth Avenue at 30th Street. Here, changing installations are displayed on the High Line Plinth. Past the Spur, the High Line links to the first completed phase of mega-development Hudson Yards. You can check out the huge climbable honeycomb-like sculpture anchoring the plaza and browse in the glossy **Shops & Restaurants at Hudson Yards** (*see p181*).

Evening

You could quite easily make a night of it in Hudson Yards, by dining at one of the mall's celebrity-chef restaurants and catching a cutting-edge performance at multidisciplinary arts centre the **Shed** (*see p179*). But seeing a Broadway show is an unmissable New York City experience, especially for first-time visitors (*see p340* Broadway theatres). Hop on the 7 train at 34th Street-Hudson Yards station and take the subway two stops to the heart of Times Square. Around 5pm or 6pm, when the initial crowds have thinned out, is a good time to score cut-price Broadway tickets at **TKTS** (*see p339*). Tickets in hand, if you have time, walk west or jump in a cab to contemporary food court **Gotham West Market** (*see p180*), a great pre-theatre pitstop that will keep everyone happy with a choice of casual eats, from ramen to pizza.

Broadway

DAY 2

Morning

A short break in the Big Apple involves some tough choices: the Upper East Side's Museum Mile alone is lined with more than half a dozen world-class institutions. Fortify yourself with Bavarian ham and eggs and exquisite coffee at **Café Sabarsky** (*see p218*) as you mull over your itinerary. If you opt for the **Metropolitan Museum of Art** (*see p214*), you can either take a brisk two-hour essentials tour or forget the rest of the itinerary entirely – the vast museum is home to more than two million objects. Don't miss the famed European Paintings Galleries, the Ancient Egyptian Temple of Dendur and the Costume Institute among the many highlights. The Iris & B Gerald Cantor Roof Garden has a view over Central Park, as well as a new installation each year, and is open in the warmer months. Afterwards, even if you decide you can't manage another Museum Mile institution, walk a few blocks north to the **Guggenheim** (*see p217*) to admire the curvaceous lines of its Frank Lloyd Wright-designed exterior.

Central Park

The Pool

The Grill

Afternoon

Take a detour east to the cinematically perfect retro luncheonette **Lexington Candy Shop** (*see p218*) at Lexington Avenue and 83rd Street. Nab a booth or a spot at the counter and tuck into old-school classics such as burgers topped with a pat of butter, tuna melts and egg creams.

It's time to clear your art-saturated head with a stroll in **Central Park** (*see p196*). Enter at 79th or 76th Street and walk south to admire the picturesque Conservatory Water, or cross East Drive and try to snag a table at the outdoor bar at the Loeb Boathouse to gaze at the lake over drinks. Then, grab a bus or taxi on Fifth Avenue (or walk through the park) to the **Museum of Modern Art** (*see p185*), for iconic art and design from the 19th and 20th centuries.

Evening

If you want to splash out on what promises to be a truly memorable meal, a pair of restaurants in the iconic Four Seasons space, **The Grill** and **The Pool** (*see p189*), feature glamorous nods to classic New York City dining, including a theatrically wheeled-out prime rib. If your budget won't quite stretch to that, head downtown for a bite at contemporary Mexican restaurant **Atla** (*see p124*) before hitting one of our favourite speakeasy bars (*see p49*) in the East Village or Lower East Side.

BUDGET BREAK

Get the most bang for your buck
Budget $60-$70 per person
Getting around Ferry, walking, subway

Morning

It's no secret that the **Staten Island Ferry** (*see p70*) provides thrilling panoramas of New York Harbor and the Statue of Liberty during its brief crossing. Before you embark on this free mini cruise, stop for breakfast at Brookfield Place, north along the Hudson River. A collection of inexpensive eateries in the **Hudson Eats** food court (*see p79*) includes Black Seed, where you can get an egg and cheese bagel for little more than a fiver. New York has several fine free museums, including the **National Museum of the American Indian** (*see p70*) near the ferry terminal (others include the Museum at FIT in Chelsea and the American Folk Art Museum on the Upper West Side).

Afternoon

Take the subway to Canal Street. Here, Chinatown is packed with countless cheap restaurants serving dim sum, noodles and other eastern specialities. We particularly recommend **Nom Wah Tea Parlor** (*see p100*) for its old-school vibe and freshly made classics such as pork buns and egg rolls. Asian markets on eclectic **Mott Street** (*see p104*) overflow with bargain exotic produce and snacks.

Be sure to swing by **Mmuseumm** (*see p93*), exhibiting eccentric collections in an elevator shaft in nearby Tribeca. The free micro-museum keeps limited hours, but even when it's not open you can get a glimpse through peepholes in the door. Also near Chinatown, the Lower East Side has dozens of art galleries that cost nothing to peruse (for our picks, *see p110*).

Evening

Together with the nearby East Village, the area is overflowing with excellent cheap eats, from Jewish knishes and Venezuelan arepas to gourmet veggie burgers. The Lower East Side retains a number of cramped, bare-bones clubs such as **Rockwood Music Hall** (*see p321*), where you can listen to emerging bands for free or a small charge.

If comedy is more your thing, catch the subway from 8th Street-NYU or Union Square to premier alternative-comedy club **Upright Citizens Brigade Theater** (*see p315*) in Hell's Kitchen. The laughs are either on them or under ten bucks for many shows, including the late-night Sunday performance of popular ASSSSCAT 3000, frequently featuring celebrity guests.

FAMILY DAY OUT

The Big Apple for the little ones
Budget $500-$600 for a family of four
Getting around Walking, subway

Central Park

Morning

Set the kids up for the day with porridge, pancakes, or scones in flavours such as pumpkin or ham and cheese, at Wonderland-themed café **Alice's Tea Cup** on the Upper West Side (102 West 73rd Street, at Columbus Avenue, 1-212 799 3006, www.alicesteacup.com) or Upper East Side (156 East 64th Street, at Lexington Avenue, 1-212 486 9200). **Central Park** (*see p196*) is truly a garden of delights for kids, with playgrounds, Central Park Zoo with its penguins and snow leopards, and seasonal attractions including an antique carousel and an ice-skating rink.

American Museum of Natural History

Afternoon

The nearby **American Museum of Natural History** (*see p199*), with its spectacular dinosaur specimens, animal dioramas and planetarium, is a must for a family visit to NYC. A handy location of burger chain **Shake Shack** (*see p202*) close to the museum is a good spot for lunch, though it can get busy at peak periods so it's a good idea to arrive early.

If you have any energy left, catch the subway from the station outside the museum to the 42nd Street-Port Authority stop to check out Times Square family attraction, **Gulliver's Gate** (*see p178*), an amazing scale-model microcosm representing 50 countries.

Gulliver's Gate

Evening

Although many Broadway shows are great for all ages, the **New Victory Theater** (*see p344*) stages international kid-centric productions, from opera and dance to circus-skills spectaculars. There's no shortage of fast-food options in the vicinity, but for some of the best pizza in the city that will appeal to connoisseurs and fussy children alike, walk a few blocks north to **Don Antonio** (*see p180*).

TWO BOROUGHS IN ONE DAY

A scenic river crossing and two hip hoods
Budget $180-$220 per person
Getting around Walking, subway or taxi

▶ *To explore another fascinating New York neighbourhood, check out our Greenwich Village walk (see p139).*

Morning

No longer the preserve of diehard urban explorers, an excursion to Brooklyn is now an essential element of any NYC visit, and one of the nicest ways to get there is on foot. Start on the Lower East Side, which was home to the world's largest Jewish community in the early 20th century. In homage to the old country, start your day with the Shtetl sandwich – smoked sable and goat's milk cream cheese on a bialy – at **Russ & Daughters Cafe** (*see p119*). For a window into how locals lived and worked in the 19th and early 20th centuries, visit the **Tenement Museum** (*see p112*). If you'd rather contemplate the provenance of impeccably selected vintage wares, head to **Edith Machinist** (*see p119*) and **David Owens Vintage** (*see p119*).

Tenement Museum

Afternoon

Before you cross to Brooklyn, you'll want to stop for a pastrami sandwich at cavernous no-frills canteen **Katz's Delicatessen** (*see p114*). When the Williamsburg Bridge was completed in 1903, it was the longest suspension bridge in the world. Soon after, it became known as the 'Jews' Highway' because it provided an exodus for Lower East Side residents into Brooklyn. Hoof it uphill on the two-way bike- and footpath straight up the centre, and you'll get an expansive Financial District skyline vista.

Like its counterpart across the East River, Williamsburg has a mix of indie boutiques, vintage shops and glossier businesses. But the neighbourhood is best known for its music scene. From the bridge, head north to browse vinyl and maybe catch a free show at NYC's outpost of music emporium **Rough Trade** (*see p250*).

Evening

There's no shortage of dinner options in the area, but the pasta at **Lilia** (*see p251*) is particularly divine. If you can still move after this bi-borough odyssey, end the night at one of the many music venues or catch the L train to nearby Bushwick for a burlesque show or an artsy, immersive club night at the **House of Yes** (*see p312*).

House of Yes

When to Visit

New York by season

With its wealth of varied attractions, both indoors and out, New York City can be enjoyed year-round. Each season has its own set of pros and cons, not to mention specific events and festivals on the city's busy cultural calendar (*see pp284–293* Events).

Spring

Early spring is often chilly, and the season can be rainy, but it starts to warm up in late April and May. Green spaces such as Central Park (*see p196*), the Brooklyn Botanic Garden (*see p243*) and the New York Botanical Garden (*see p273*) are frothy with blossom, especially in April. Moderate weather, before the summer heat and humidity sets in, makes this a good time to explore the city on foot. It's also a busy time in the art world, with art fairs and events surrounding Armory Week. Seasonal flea markets open for business, along with other warm-weather staples such as Governors Island (*see p75*).

Summer

Early summer typically brings blue skies and pleasantly warm temperatures, but late July and August can be uncomfortably hot and humid, although air-conditioning is ubiquitous. Since many wealthier residents escape to nearby resort areas such as the Hamptons, the city is quieter, especially on weekends, and it may be easier to score sought-after theatre tickets and restaurant reservations. There are usually good deals on accommodation too.

The season brings a roster of free outdoor music and theatre festivals, including SummerStage, Shakespeare in the Park, the River to River Festival and Lincoln Center

Brooklyn Botanic Garden

Out of Doors, plus alfresco film screenings in several parks. On several Saturdays in August, the city closes a section of Park Avenue and other streets to traffic for strolling, biking and other activities (www.nyc.gov/summerstreets). Those seeking traditional summer pleasures should head to Rockaway Beach (*see p267*) for sea and sand, or Coney Island (*see p255*) for thrill rides and boardwalk amusements.

Coney Island

Village Halloween Parade

calendar, with new show openings on Broadway, blockbuster museum exhibitions, New York Fashion Week and prominent festivals such as the Brooklyn Academy of Music's Next Wave Festival and the New York Film Festival. At the end of October, Halloween is a big event in NYC, when the streets are populated with costumed revellers and families going door to door with trick-or-treating children. Autumn is the high season for hotels, so be sure to book accommodation well in advance if you're planning a trip during this time.

Winter

As you'd expect, the main shopping thoroughfares, such as Fifth and Madison Avenues, are bustling in the run-up to Christmas, with festive lights, elaborate displays in department store windows and a giant tree at Rockefeller Center. Seasonal ice-skating rinks and outdoor holiday bazaars scattered around the city add to the festive atmosphere. Temperatures can be frigid and snow is fairly common, especially in January and February. The white wonderland is picturesque, particularly in Central Park and other large green spaces, though it quickly becomes dirty and slushy. A slew of holiday-themed shows, from traditional offerings such as the New York City Ballet's *Nutcracker* to Yuletide burlesque, hits the city, culminating in a whirl of (generally expensive) New Year's Eve events and parties. Although hotel rates tend to be high in December and early January, you may be able to get a bargain in late January or February.

Autumn

Warm weather typically lasts into September, but October brings cooler days, as well as vivid foliage in the city's streets and parks. Autumn is an important time on the cultural

Central Park

New York Today

Can a city built on outsize dreams attain the sweet spot between idealism and economic growth?

In many ways, contemporary New York City is a model of a safe and prosperous metropolis. The past few years have seen the lowest crime rates since the 1950s; residential and commercial development is robust across the city, and huge swathes of waterfront have been transformed into user-friendly green spaces. Yet tension is bubbling beneath the surface. The gleaming towers redefining the skyline add more multi-million-dollar apartments to an already inflated market, exacerbating the housing crisis. Meanwhile, the city's homeless population has grown to numbers not seen since the Great Depression.

53 West 53 *p370*

Many of the biggest local news stories boil down to gentrification and the issues that surround it. After more than 100 cities submitted bids to Amazon to host the online mega-retailer's secondary HQ (drawing comparisons with America's biggest sporting championship, the Super Bowl), Long Island City, Queens, was declared joint winner with Crystal City, Virginia in autumn 2018. This victory was no doubt aided by subsidies and tax incentives totalling almost $3 billion. Governor Andrew Cuomo and Mayor Bill de Blasio, who rarely concur on issues, both backed the deal, which would have created more than 25,000 jobs. But local activists cited the spectre of rising rents and the misallocation of government money. One of the loudest voices belonged to congresswoman Alexandria Ocasio-Cortez (AOC), whose district includes parts of Queens and the Bronx. In February 2019, Amazon backed out of the deal.

Protests against a new Amazon HQ in Queens. Local activists cited the spectre of rising rents and the misallocation of government money.

The city vs Trump

Sworn into office in January 2019, Ocasio-Cortez has quickly grabbed the national spotlight as a poster child for the progressive left and an outspoken critic of Trump's immigration policies. She, in turn, has been attacked by the President, along with a few other radical-leaning Democrats. In some ways, the conflict can be seen as a clash between new and old New York. The millennial AOC, who is of Puerto Rican descent and grew up in the Bronx, embraces the multiculturalism of her district, which includes the famously immigrant-rich borough of Queens. Ironically, this is the birthplace of Donald Trump, who has adopted protectionist, anti-immigration policies.

Trump's outsized personality, fortune and politics were shaped during a specific era – namely, the period from the mid-1970s to early '90s, when New York was seen as a

US Congresswoman Alexandria Ocasio-Cortez speaks at the third annual Women's March in Manhattan on 19 January 2019.

crumbling wasteland awash in civic chaos. His political outlook was forged by the racially fuelled backlash against New York's crime wave of the 1970s and '80s – a reaction embodied by 'subway vigilante' Bernhard Goetz and the *Death Wish* movies starring Charles Bronson. In 1989, Trump took out a full-page ad in the *New York Times* demanding the death penalty for the so-called Central Park Five, a group of African-American teenagers accused of raping a white woman jogging through the park. Though they were later exonerated, Trump nevertheless reaffirmed his belief in their guilt while running for president.

Having a native New Yorker in the White House has narrowed the gap between national and local news. In October 2018, the *New York Times* published a special investigation into the origins of Donald Trump's wealth. Not only did the findings refute the 45th president's claims that he is a self-made billionaire, they revealed that he, along with his siblings, were the beneficiaries of decades-long dodgy tax dealings by their father, Fred, a prominent construction mogul, through schemes that made his own children his 'landlords'. The report also brought to light President Trump's fraudulent tax dealings in the 1990s.

Having a native New Yorker in the White House has narrowed the gap between national and local news

31

Local Democratic lawmakers have been pushing for Trump's recent tax returns to be released ever since he took office in 2017; in July 2019, Governor Cuomo passed a law requiring tax officials to hand them over to Congress. Claiming 'presidential harassment', Trump fired back with a lawsuit against New York State's Attorney General, the Commissioner of the New York State Department of Taxation & Finance and the House Ways & Means Committee to maintain his privacy, citing the lack of 'a legitimate legislative purpose'. Mayor Bill de Blasio's is another critic of Trump; his opposition to the President's immigration policies, among other issues, predates the latter's tenure in the White House. In May 2019, the Mayor held a rally in Trump Tower, demanding that the building, along with seven other Trump properties, comply with the carbon-emission standards set out in the city's Green New Deal by 2030, or face hefty fines. Around the same time, in a video promoting his own bid for the Democratic candidacy in the run-up to the 2020 Presidential election, de Blasio stressed he'd be a worthy opponent for Trump: "I'm a New Yorker. I've known Trump's a bully for a long time," he said. "I know how to take him on." However, the reception in his own party has been lukewarm at best, and he's unlikely to remain in the race for long.

Governor Andrew Cuomo participating in the 2019 NYC Pride March.

Mayor Bill de Blasio and his wife, Chirlane McCray.

Seeking sanctuary

While Trump populism may have gained traction in many parts of the country, New York remains a bastion of progressive politics, multiculturalism and inclusiveness. The metropolis is a 'sanctuary city', which means it has laws to curb aggressive tactics by immigration authorities. De Blasio, Cuomo, AOC and other liberal politicians were among the five million people who attended WorldPride in summer 2019, which coincided with the 50th anniversary of the historic Stonewall riots, sparked by a clash between West Village bargoers and police and credited with igniting the gay rights movement. The city's cultural landscape is increasingly diverse, with a strong LGBTQ presence in recent Broadway offerings, and women and artists of colour outnumbering their male and white counterparts in the 2019 Whitney Biennial. MoMA's post-renovation inaugural exhibitions skew towards Latin-American and black artists, including a multi-year collaboration with Harlem's temporarily closed Studio Museum.

Rising skyscrapers – and prices

Visitors to the city won't fail to notice the ubiquity of partially built skyscrapers, giant cranes and so-called 'sidewalk sheds' on pavements alongside construction sites. The metropolis is constantly revising its streetscape, even in congested areas such as Midtown Manhattan. In recent years, a series of supertall towers have risen on 57th Street, including a couple under construction that will exceed the city's previous tallest residential building on the same street. This so-called 'Billionaire's Row' has stirred up controversy, not only for its incongruously outsized architecture, but also for the fact that many of the apartments, which have sky-high price tags

The metropolis is a 'sanctuary city', which means it has laws to curb aggressive tactics by immigration authorities

When complete, Central Park Tower on 57th Street's 'Billionaire's Row' will be the city's tallest residential building – but for how long?

to match, are owned by investors who hardly ever set foot in their luxury pads. In January 2019, a hedge fund honcho with multiple abodes around the world bought a spanking-new penthouse on nearby Central Park South for a staggering $238 million – the highest price ever paid for a US home (yes, even surpassing beyond-luxe Hollywood mansions).

Yet, the majority of New Yorkers are struggling to pay their rent. According to a report released in June 2019 by the New York City Comptroller (the city's elected chief financial officer and auditor), the gap between income and expenses has significantly widened since 2005 for single New Yorkers, with more than 43 percent of income now going to housing and utilities. De Blasio has promised to make affordable housing a priority, adding an unprecedented 34,160 affordable homes in 2018, but has faced criticism that he's not doing enough to stem the crisis. The city has more than 60,000 homeless – the highest number of people sleeping rough or in shelters in the country. A state-wide increase of the minimum wage to $15 per hour, which has been gradually coming into effect, should help residents of its biggest city cope with the high cost of living.

In 2019, the city had more than 60,000 homeless – the highest number of people sleeping rough or in shelters in the country.

The luxe life

Thanks to recent changes to city zoning rules, many residential developments are required to offer a certain number of affordable apartments to lower-income New Yorkers, and some complexes come with public facilities attached; for example, the redevelopment of the old Domino Sugar Factory in Brooklyn's trendy Williamsburg features a cool waterfront park that incorporates salvaged industrial equipment such as cranes and syrup tanks.

So far, however, Hudson Yard's Public Square & Gardens has proved a bit underwhelming as a public space – more of a plaza than a 'forest' as the promotional materials proclaim – although there are plans for more than 200 mature trees and thousands of plants in the five-acre space. The massive residential and commercial project, perched over MTA rail yards on the far West Side, finally debuted its first phase in spring 2019 after nearly seven years of construction. But the purpose-built 'neighbourhood' has largely been dismissed by critics, and many citizens, as a luxuriously bland, 'un-New York' environment. To be fair, its mall, the Shops & Restaurants at Hudson Yards, has some unique draws, including the city's first Neiman Marcus department store; a sprawling, swanky Dallas-imported boutique, Forty Five Ten, and a new restaurant, Tak Room, from lauded chef Thomas Keller of Per Se. The real standout feature is The Shed, a multidisciplinary arts centre that will draw locals with its truly original programming. However, the climbable sculpture, once hyperbolically compared to Paris's Eiffel Tower, seems to have little point beyond an Instagram post.

Malls, once a rarity in Manhattan, have been proliferating, including a complex on the South Street Seaport's Pier 17 that is largely devoted to upscale restaurants from influential local chefs, including Jean-Georges Vongerichten

Many residential developments are required to offer a certain number of affordable apartments to lower-income New Yorkers

Hudson Yards' climbable sculpture, once hyperbolically compared to Paris's Eiffel Tower, seems to have little point beyond an Instagram post.

and David Chang. Positioned in areas that draw tourists with popular attractions, these retail behemoths are guaranteed plenty of foot traffic, but the rise of online shopping has proved damaging not only to beloved small 'mom and pop' shops, but also to seemingly bulletproof businesses. A stroll along swanky Madison Avenue on the Upper East Side will take you past several vacant storefronts. News hit in July 2019 that iconic department store Barneys New York may face bankruptcy after the rent on its flagship nearly doubled.

South Street Seaport's dining-focused Pier 17 is one of several upscale complexes sprouting up in the city.

An app for that

Technology is changing the city in sometimes unexpected ways. NYC has long been the place where you could get virtually anything, from a McDonald's hamburger to a bottle of aspirin, delivered to your door, and these days the streets are teeming with fleets of electric-bike couriers feeding New Yorkers' cravings for ramen, poke and pulled-pork via numerous app-based delivery services that bring myriad restaurants within swiping distance. With an urban obstacle course including everything from pedestrian mobile-phone zombies to Amazon delivery trucks and unexpected taxi-door openings, it's a dangerous job. By summer 2019, the death toll for cyclists had climbed to 17 (compared to a total of 10 for the entire previous year), prompting de Blasio to lay out a plan for 80 miles of new dedicated bike lanes by 2021. At the same time, the city's bike-sharing scheme, which launched in 2013, has proved hugely popular with both residents and tourists and is set to triple in capacity to nearly 40,000 bikes over the next five years thanks to a partnership with Lyft.

Such partnerships highlight the long-standing co-dependency of culture and commerce. The city is renowned as both a percolator of progressive ideas and an unabashed centre of capitalism, drawing innovators and self-starters who want to 'make it here'. The confluence of dynamic creative forces stokes commercialism, while the constant generation of wealth maintains the impressive perks that make New York one of the greatest cities in the world.

The city's bike-sharing scheme, which launched in 2013, is set to triple in capacity to nearly 40,000 bikes by 2024.

Eating & Drinking

The ultimate melting pot

While cities such as San Francisco and Houston present serious culinary competition, it will be some time yet before New York is unseated as the leader of American dining culture. Rising rents and shifting trends keep the scene in a constant state of flux, but one thing has always remained true: New Yorkers can be pretty zealous in their pursuit of good food, whether it's the three-dollar bagels they have for breakfast or the Michelin-starred *omakase* they enjoy at dinner.

Uncle Boons p103

The growth of social media and the meteoric rise of food culture has made insider dining accessible to all. Nowadays, greasy spoon diners and hole-in-the-wall pizzerias are described with the same level of excitement as celebrity chef-run Mexican newcomers and white-tablecloth palaces of Chinese fine dining. On the bar front, the city has entered a post-Cocktail Revolution golden age, with experimental mixology dens and, more recently, a new wave of relaxed Japanese cocktail bars joining numerous Prohibition-inspired speakeasies. It's never clear where we're headed next, but one thing is certain: there's never a dull moment when you're dining in New York City. And we can all raise a glass to that.

Toques of the town

The ever-spinning twister of rookie restaurants is grounded by time-honoured dining rooms that are local landmarks in their own right, and for every century-old café, there's a hip newcomer in Brooklyn's latest It

❤ Best blowout restaurants

Aska *p248*
Michelin-starred
Scandinavian tasting-menu.

Atomix *p191*
Sophisticated multi-course
Korean fine dining.

Le Coucou *p88*
Glamorously nostalgic
French restaurant.

Daniel *p210*
Empire-building chef Daniel
Boulud's elegant flagship.

Eleven Madison Park *p166*
Progressive tasting menus
in a grand art deco dining
room.

The Grill/The Pool *p189*
Reinvention of the iconic
Four Seasons site serving
luxe classics like prime rib
and lobster Newburg.

Atomix

The Grill

Le Coucou

neighbourhood. The same goes for the chefs behind them. Every year, a freshman class of toques – think Simone Tong of **Little Tong** (*see p128*) or Junghyun Park of **Atomix** joins the city's varsity-level chefs and restaurateurs like fine-dining Mexican boss Enrique Olvera (Cosme, Atla) and Momofuku kingpin David Chang.

The big-name power players behind NYC's most established restaurant empires aren't resting on their laurels either. Chang, for example, has remained prolific in the decade and a half since launching the game-changing contemporary Asian eaterie **Momofuku Noodle Bar** (*see p129*). Following his Italian-Korean hybrid **Momofuku Nishi** (*see p156*) and fast-casual fried-chicken joint **Fuku** (eatfuku.com), he opened too-new-to-review restaurant Kāwi in the **Shops & Restaurants at Hudson Yards** (*see p181*), soon to be followed by a Japanese-influenced bar at South Street Seaport's **Pier 17** (www.pier17ny.com). It joins a seafood restaurant from celebrity chef Jean-Georges Vongerichten and a forthcoming Italian chop house from Andrew Carmellini.

Andrew Carmellini already has a considerable empire with partners Josh Pickard and Luke Ostrom, including some of Manhattan's best restaurants, such as **Locanda Verde** (*see p94*) and **The Dutch** (*see p88*).

Major Food Group – the restaurant group overseen by chefs Rich Torrisi and Mario Carbone, and business partner Jeff Zalaznick – has made serious headway in diversifying its portfolio, which already included red-sauce clubhouse **Carbone** (*see p138*) and coastal Italian charmer **Santina** (*see p149*), among others. The trio has further solidified its standing in the city's power dining scene with three distinct new concepts housed in the landmark Seagram Building: American chophouse **The Grill**, Japanese brasserie **The Lobster Club**, and seafood stunner **The Pool**.

**In the know
Price categories**

All our restaurant listings are marked with a dollar symbol category, indicating the price you should expect to pay for a standard main course. Bear in mind, however, that prices of individual dishes can vary widely on restaurant menus, and the final bill will of course depend on the number of courses and drinks consumed.

$ = under $15

$$ = $15-$30

$$$ = $30-$45

$$$$ = over $45

JG Melon

♥ **Best NYC classics**

Di Fara Pizza *p46*
For a classic Brooklyn pie.

Grand Central Oyster Bar & Restaurant *p189*
For Long Island oysters (since 1913).

JG Melon *p211*
For diner-style cheeseburgers.

Katz's Delicatessen *p114*
For pastrami or corned beef on rye.

Peter Luger *p251*
For on-site dry-aged steaks.

Russ & Daughters Cafe *p114*
For bagels and lox.

Where to eat & drink

Spread across five boroughs, New York is a complex patchwork of distinctive neighbourhoods, each with its own food and drink scene. Some culinary hubs are nearly as famous as the city they're in: these include the Bronx's **Arthur Avenue**, which lays claim to the title of New York's 'real Little Italy'; the soul-food stronghold of **Harlem**, and the restaurant-packed **Chinatowns** in Manhattan and Flushing, Queens.

Other neighbourhoods have been expanding and intensifying their restaurant and bar offerings. **Soho** has long been a fashionable-dining bubble, with high-profile options such as **Le Coucou** (*see p88*) – the graceful, James Beard Award-winning French spot from chef Daniel Rose and prolific restaurateur Stephen Starr (Buddakan, Morimoto) – and **The Dutch** (*see p88*), Andrew Carmellini's buzzy American eaterie. But its eastern neighbour, **Nolita** has been coming into its own. Highlights include **Pasquale Jones** (*see p103*), the pizza-loving sibling to Ryan Hardy, Grant Reynolds and Robert Bohr's jaunty, wine-charged Soho spot **Charlie Bird** (www.charliebirdnyc.com); Michelin-starred Thai favourite **Uncle Boons**, and **Estela** (*see p102*), a Mediterranean-accented neo-bistro.

Slightly north, the **Gramercy/Flatiron** area has also seen a restaurant resurgence in recent years, with newcomers like Korean stunner **Atomix** (*see p191*) and modern Indian canteen **Gupshup** (*see p171*) joining essential neighbourhood eateries, including Michelin-starred **Eleven Madison Park** (*see p166*) from chef/restaurateur duo Daniel Humm and Will Guidara, and **Maialino** (*see p171*) in the stable of long-established restaurateur Danny Meyer. A few years ago, Humm and Guidara introduced **Made Nice** (*see p166*), a counter-service concept where diners can taste more affordable salads and hot dishes from the celebrated team.

♥ Best international dining

Atla *p124*
Sleek spot for health-conscious Mexican fare and creative mescal cocktails.

Nur *p166*
Retooled Middle Eastern dishes and delectable bread from a top Tel Aviv toque and an artisanal baker.

Red Rooster Harlem *p225*
An upbeat international spin on soul food.

Time Out Market *p45*
The best of NYC's global cuisine under one roof.

Uncle Boons *p103*
Hip Thai spot for charcoal-grilled snacks, rotisserie chicken and Bangkok-style beer slushes.

Via Carota *p145*
Simple, soulful Italian fare in a lively dining room and bar.

Red Rooster Harlem

Meyer, similarly, added a fast-casual concept to his more formal Gramercy venues with **Daily Provisions** (*see p167*), which serves pastries and sandwiches on house-baked bread. The bakery-café adjunct is next door to Meyer's relocated flagship, **Union Square Cafe** (*see p167*), which has retained original appeal in nostalgic design touches as well as staple dishes.

The **Lower East Side** is also a lively destination for stellar food-and-drink options. Along with Ivan Orkin's namesake noodle house **Ivan Ramen** (*see p115*) and the double punch of **Contra** and **Wildair** (for both, *see p116*) from innovative young guns Jeremiah Stone and Fabián von Hauske Valtierra, the downtown neighbourhood is home to some of the city's finest bars. You can enjoy artful Asian tweaks to classic cocktails at Kenta Goto's **Bar Goto** and impeccable end-of-the-evening drinks at **Nitecap** (for both, *see p118*). Eclectic bars and a vast array of inexpensive eateries are also conveniently close together in the **East Village**. Recently, contemporary Asian canteens **Little Tong** (*see p128*) and **Hanoi House** (*see p126*) have added innovative twists on Chinese and Vietnamese cuisines to the area's already thriving Little Tokyo.

You can't talk foodie neighbourhoods without delving into **Williamsburg** in Brooklyn,

♥ **Best for brunch**

Clinton Street Baking Company *p113*
Renowned for biscuits and pancakes.

Cookshop *p155*
Seasonal dishes and indulgent pastries, handy for a post-brunch stroll on the High Line.

High Street on Hudson *p148*
Airy all-day eatery spotlighting local produce, house-baked breads and killer breakfast sandwiches.

Jack's Wife Freda *p89*
A cosy, laid-back choice for comfort dishes like shakshuka and quinoa breakfast bowls.

Miss Ada *p246*
Meze with fluffy pita and heavenly Yemeni pastries at this laid-back Mediterranean eatery in Brooklyn.

Nom Wah Tea Parlor *p100*
Cooked to order dim sum in vintage surroundings.

Prune *p129*
Be prepared to queue for creative twists on breakfast at this enduringly popular weekend destination.

Jack's Wife Freda

a name that has seen a near-meteoric rise in culinary clout in recent years. There, you'll find **Lilia** and **Misi** (for both, *see p251*), airy pasta parlours from acclaimed A Voce vet Missy Robbins, and **Aska** (*see p248*), the Michelin-starred Scandinavian kitchen helmed by Swedish wunderkind chef Fredrik Berselius. The culinary buzz has spread to nearby Greenpoint and Bushwick, the latter home to pioneering locavore pizzeria **Roberta's** (*see p252*).

Contemporary food courts

Even neighbourhoods more traditionally known for lofty skyscrapers and ubiquitous business suits are getting serious culinary cred these days. The lowly food court has seen much advancement in Midtown, an area once plagued by its dearth of quality food options. Inside Grand Central Terminal, Claus Meyer (co-founder of the world-shaking Copenhagen dining room Noma) launched **Great Northern Food Hall** a 5,000-square-foot marketplace adjacent to his Scandinavian tasting-menu restaurant **Agern** (*see p189*) that features Nordic-inspired food pavilions peddling everything from fresh-baked pastries to *smørrebrød* topped with smoked fish or house-cured meats.

Close by, **Urbanspace Vanderbilt** (*see p190*) changed the workaday lunch game near Park Avenue with snacks by grade-A Brooklyn purveyors such as Roberta's, among other vendors. In Hell's Kitchen, **Gotham West Market** (*see p180*) is a worthy pre- or post-theatre stop with cult eats such as Ivan Ramen Slurp Shop, where noodle guru Ivan Orkin offers his famed *shio*, shoyu and chilli-sesame varieties.

Downtown near the new World Trade Center, fast-casual food hall **Hudson Eats** (*see p79*) and **Le District** (*see p80*) – a 30,000-square-foot market that's divided into a bakery-café, meat and cheese stalls, an open-

Clinton Street Baking Company *p113*

In the know
Essentials

Restaurants are generally open for lunch between 11.30am and 3pm and in the evening from 5pm until 11pm (though some may close as early as 9 or 10pm, and other kitchens stay open as late as midnight or 1am). Bars generally close between 2am and 4am, though it varies considerably. Most restaurants, apart from some small or cheap eateries, accept credit cards. It's common to tip 15%-20%, or more if service is exceptional. NYC sales tax is 8.875%, so an easy way to calculate tip is to double the tax. Some restaurants, such as those in restaurateur Danny Meyer's stable, have done away with tipping altogether and include it in the pricing. If this is the case, it will be clearly stated on the menu.

❤ Time Out Market New York $$

*Empire Stores, 55 Water Street, between Main Street & Old Dock Street, Dumbo Brooklyn (1-917 810 4855, www.timeoutmarket.com/newyork). Subway A, C to High Street; F to York Street. **Open** 8am-11pm Mon-Thur, Sun; 8am-midnight Fri, Sat (varies for some bars & restaurants). **Map** p232 G32.*

In 2014, the editors of *Time Out Lisbon* revitalised a neglected 19th-century market hall in the city by bringing in vendors that had been awarded top ratings by *Time Out* critics. Within six months of opening, it had become one of Lisbon's most-visited attractions. Following its overwhelming popularity, the concept has gone global, with markets open in several North American cities, and London and Dubai debuting over the next few years. But this is no cookie-cutter roll-out – each location spotlights uniquely essential food and drink experiences, hand-picked by editors who know their beat inside out. In New York, this translates to a tightly curated snapshot of a sometimes overwhelming gastronomic scene under one roof.

As in Lisbon, the building itself, a restored 19th-century warehouse complex in Dumbo, Brooklyn, has important links to local history (there's even an outpost of the Brooklyn Historical Society in the building if you want to learn more about Dumbo's waterfront legacy). Time Out Market New York isn't the first hip multi-dining destination in the city, but there are several things that set it apart, in addition to impeccable food-scene expertise: the communal tables are paired with leather chairs; the meals are all served on proper china with metal cutlery, and staff will clear away plates – no bussing your own table required. The challenge is deciding what to order. Among the highlights of the market's 21 eateries are pizza from legendary local dough slinger Patsy Grimaldi; sashimi-topped rice cakes courtesy of Bessou's Emily Yuen; master meat purveyor Pat LaFrieda's prime sandwiches; critically lauded couscous from Meir Adoni of Nur; and Clinton Street Baking Company's popular pancakes. Three bars pour local beer and signature cocktails from Time Out Bar Award winners. Then, there are the non-culinary draws. From the fifth-floor rooftop terrace, you can take in a sweeping, panoramic vista of the Manhattan skyline, Brooklyn and Manhattan bridges, and catch free weekend gigs on the rooftop stage, from neo-soul singers to rock bands and DJs.

air grocery shop, bars and sit-down restaurants – helped up-class food-court eating when they opened inside Brookfield Place several years ago. At **Mercado Little Spain**, in the Shops & Restaurants at Hudson Yards (*see p181*), find Spanish street food, epicurean goods and even fine dining courtesy of celebrity chef and activist José Andrés.

Hooked on classics

Even in an era of quick neighbourhood turnover and flavour-of-the-week restaurant buzz, NYC has a wealth of old-school eating establishments still kicking it with the young'uns. For delicious proof, head downtown to the Lower East Side, which was a veritable Jewish Plymouth Rock in the late 19th and early 20th centuries when immigrants from Eastern Europe flooded the area. Though the neighbourhood's Yiddish accent has softened in more recent decades, you can still sample its culinary history at three long-time Houston Street stalwarts. Grab a fluffy, golden potato knish at **Yonah Schimmel Knish Bakery** (*see p116*), which has been doling out Jewish-American comfort foods since 1910; pick up some old-world pickled herring at **Russ & Daughters** (*see p114*) down the street (the 'appetising' institution has been selling the stuff since its pushcart beginnings in 1914); and cap off the tour with a sandwich stop at the iconic **Katz's Delicatessen** (*see p114*), where smoky pastrami has been hand-sliced since 1888.

Pizza is another rich NYC culinary legacy. Study the classics with a trip to Brooklyn's southern tip, which boasts some of the borough's most acclaimed and time-honoured pie operations. Beat the lines by arriving early at Midwood's **Di Fara Pizza** (1424 Avenue J, at E 15th Street, 1-718 258 1367, www.difarapizzany.com), opened by Italian immigrant Dom De Marco in 1964. You may even see the

In the know
Reservations

No-reservation restaurants have become increasingly common in recent years, but if you show up, most will take your name and mobile phone number and call you when a table is available, so you can spend the wait time sightseeing or in a nearby bar. Others, including most Momofuku locations and Major Food Group eateries, can only be reserved online.

Katz's Delicatessen

Rockaway Brewing Company *p267*

octogenarian pizza legend behind the counter, snipping fresh basil onto his world-class Neapolitan pies. If you're not up for making the trek to the original, there's now a less out-of-the-way outpost in Williamsburg's **North 3rd Street Market** (103 North 3rd Street, between Berry Street & Wythe Avenue, 1-929 294 9464). Alternatively, seek out the thin-crusted, char-pocked Margherita pies at **Totonno's** (*see p255*), a Coney Island institution since 1924.

Many visitors will want to get their teeth into a traditional New York steak. At **Peter Luger** (*see p251*) in Brooklyn's Williamsburg, waistcoat-wearing waiters had been serving beautifully rosy porterhouses for decades before the hipsters moved into the area. In the equally historic Midtown chophouse **Keens** (*see p174*), you can tuck into its signature gargantuan mutton chops under a massive collection of churchwarden pipes, each of which was once owned by a Keens regular, such as Teddy Roosevelt, Babe Ruth and Albert Einstein.

What's brewing?

In the late 19th century, Brooklyn was the hub of New York's – and much of the nation's

BlackTail *p79*

– beer industry. In recent years, the taps have started flowing again across all five boroughs. Brooklyn makes a strong showing, with such additions as Carroll Gardens' IPA-driven **Other Half Brewing** (www.otherhalfbrewing.com), **Threes Brewing** (www.threesbrewing.com) in Gowanus and brewery-distillery hybrid **Interboro Spirits and Ales** (interboro.nyc) in East Williamsburg joining local staples such as **Brooklyn Brewery** (*see p247*) and Red Hook's **Sixpoint Brewery** (sixpoint.com). But Staten Island boasts **Flagship Brewery** (www.flagshipbrewery.nyc), the borough's first since Piels closed its plant in the 1960s, and the Bronx welcomed back brewing after 50 years with the debut of **Gun Hill Brewing Company** (www.gunhillbrewing.com). Queens is loaded with hoppy options, from **SingleCut Beersmiths** (www.singlecut.com) in Astoria to **Finback Brewery** (www.finbackbrewery.com) in Ridgewood, and **Big Alice Brewing** (www.bigalicebrewing.com) in Long Island City to the beachside enterprise of **Rockaway Brewing Company** (*see p267*).

Apart from tasting rooms in the breweries themselves, the most dependable spots to sample local offerings are hops-head havens such as West Village microbrew staple **Blind Tiger Ale House** (*see p145*) and Greenpoint's **Tørst** (*see p253*), a rare-beer taproom from Scandinavian brew rock star Jeppe Jarnit-Bjergsø (Evil Twin Brewing) that offers a more sophisticated pint experience.

Cocktail culture

With all due respect to everywhere else on the planet, New York is the cocktail capital of the world. After all, how can you argue when confronted with the sheer breadth and impeccable quality of the city's drinks scene? Audrey Saunders's second-floor Soho sanctum, **Pegu Club** (*see p89*), begat many of today's standard-bearers, including **Death & Co.**

❤ Best beer and wine

Blind Tiger Ale House *p145*
Lively brew-geek clubhouse.

Bohemian Hall & Beer Garden *p263*
European draughts in a traditional, tree-shaded setting.

The Four Horsemen *p252*
Unstuffy wine bar co-owned by a rock star.

Tørst *p253*
Minimalist rare-brew temple with a hidden tasting restaurant.

Tørst

The Pool *p189*

♥ Speakeasy bars

Speakeasies were all the rage in 1920s NYC. The New-York Historical Society estimates that as many as 100,000 illegal drinking spots could have operated during the Prohibition era. The booze laws have changed since then, but New Yorkers still have a thirst for hidden barrooms. Although the trend kicked off around the millennium, it's still going strong.

First on NYC's neo-speakeasy scene was Milk & Honey, the iconic Lower East Side bar from late cocktail legend Sasha Petraske, known for its off-the-cuff creations as well as its 'house rules' (no name-dropping, no hooting). The bar has since closed, but longtime M&H bartenders Sam Ross and Michael McIlroy relaunched the original space as **Attaboy** (*see p116*) in 2013. The intimate spot retains the clandestine vibe – you have to ring a buzzer at the entrance, which is marked with a neon A – and bespoke protocol of its forebear, with ad hoc concoctions to suit each customer's preference.

These days, watering holes are disguised in myriad ways. You can access a highly respectable cocktail bar by picking up a phone in a vintage phone booth inside a hot-dog joint (**PDT**, *see p130*) or passing through a psychic's storefront (**Employees Only**, *see p145*). Sniff around a West Village location of the Five Guys burger chain and you'll find the clandestine stairway that leads to laid-back hangout the **Garret** (296 Bleecker Street, at Barrow Street, www.garretnyc. com). Taking the concept even further, tour guide Matt Levy and his photographer wife Jennifer Macfarlane host small groups by advance reservation at the **Covert Cocktail Club** (www.covertcocktailclub.com) in their home in Bushwick, Brooklyn.

Some establishments, such as convincing 1920s replica saloon the **Back Room** (*see p118*), have bona fide historical ties to the period. After being closed for almost a decade, landmark West Village speakeasy **Chumley's** (*see p145*) – once frequented by the likes of William Faulkner and ee cummings – was restored and resurrected.

Of course, these are just a few of the places on our radar. In a city as storied and saturated as New York, there's no telling how many hush-hush watering holes lie behind closed doors.

PDT

Attaboy

(*see p129*) and **PDT** (*see p130*). More recently, Sean Muldoon and Jack McGarry – the world-renowned duo behind time-capsule cocktail bar the **Dead Rabbit** (*see p76*) – introduced **BlackTail** to the historic Pier A Harbor House complex, which channels Prohibition-era Cuba with a meticulously researched menu of retro drinks and servers sporting straw fedoras.

Across the East River in Brooklyn, you can find thoughtful cocktails at **Maison Premiere** (*see p253*) – the impeccably styled, sumptuously romantic Williamsburg boîte brought French Quarter charm and the city's largest absinthe archive to the bar-heavy neighbourhood, as well as polished service. Further south in Cobble Hill, the **Long Island Bar** (*see p240*) is a retro-fitted cocktail spot from legendary barman Toby Cecchini, credited with creating the modern Cosmo at the Odeon in 1987. Carroll Gardens' **Clover Club**, the standard-bearing cocktail parlour from mixology matriarch Julie Reiner, is known for its regal crystal bowls of punch and finely wrought drinks. Reiner also pulls double duty at neighbour **Leyenda** (*see p239*), her pan-Latin follow-up with Clover Club cohort Ivy Mix, where tropically minded drinks can be enjoyed in a breezy, tree-filled patio out back.

❤ Best cocktails

Attaboy *p116*
Bespoke cocktails in an intimate, tucked-away space.

The Aviary NYC *p202*
Spectacular creations featuring smoke and changing colours vie with the dazzling views.

Bar Goto *p118*
Chilled-out spot for Eastern-influenced concoctions.

BlackTail *p79*
Homage to pre-revolution Cuba with retro drinks.

Clover Club *p239*
Victorian-style cocktail parlour with nostalgic creations to match.

Pegu Club *p89*
Sophisticated spirits den recalling a colonial club.

DINE OUT NEW YORK

We've got the inside track on the city's hottest restaurants, so book with us and be ahead of the culinary curve.

Shopping

Designer bargains, vintage finds and classic department stores

NYC has long been a world-class consumer destination for international visitors toting extra suitcases, but these days, the links between tourism and commerce are tighter than ever. Popular sights, such as the High Line and the National September 11 Memorial & Museum, are adjacent to glossy shopping complexes, while fashionable neighbourhoods such as Soho have essentially morphed into urban malls. As America's fashion capital, and the site of the prestigious Fashion Institute of Technology and other high-profile art colleges, the metropolis is a magnet for creative young designers from around the country. This ensures boutiques and markets are stuffed with unique finds, and it also means that the Garment District is a hotbed of open-to-the-public showroom sales. Whether you want to stock up on cut-price clothing, splash out in Madison Avenue's luxury flagships, or find curated vintage and vinyl in Brooklyn, you won't go home empty-handed.

Feng Sway *p253*

Make it here

Many of the country's most popular designers are based in New York, from long-established names such as Diane von Furstenberg and Marc Jacobs to contemporary stars such as Alexander Wang, Ulla Johnson and Sies Marjan's Sander Lak. Made-in-NYC items – jewellery by **Thea Grant** (*see p238*) or **Doyle & Doyle** (*see p149*), **Mast Brothers** chocolate (*see p254*), cards printed at **Bowne & Co** (*see p82*) or even stitched-on-site jeans at **3x1** (*see p90*) – are chic souvenirs. Stores that stock items by local designers, among other merchandise, include **American Two Shot**, **Opening Ceremony**, **Artists & Fleas** (*see p158*) and, for interior items, **The Future Perfect** (*see p132*). There are also opportunities to buy goods direct from emerging designers at popular weekend markets such as the **Brooklyn Flea** (*see p287*). Some budding shopkeepers test the waters by opening pop-ups, which, if successful, put down permanent roots, such as Hell's Kitchen men's accessories trove **Fine and Dandy** (*see p181*). Likewise, digital marketplaces are opening bricks-and-mortar locations, such as **Depop Space NY** (*see p104*), which provides IRL exposure to a rotating selection of vintage and indie designers from its app-based 'community'.

❤ Best fashion

American Two Shot *p90*
Cool-kid labels and curated vintage garb.

Barneys New York *p211*
The city's trendiest department store.

Dear: Rivington *p132*
Avant-garde Japanese fashion and pristine vintage accessories in a stage-set space.

Modern Anthology *p240*
Clothing, grooming products and design gear for discerning dudes.

Opening Ceremony *p91*
Sprawling multi-level mega-boutique spanning streetwear, contemporary brands and quirky one-offs.

Oroboro *p106*
A stylist's selection of ethically made indie-designer lines.

Oroboro

Shopping Hotspots

The best places to spend it

Soho *p90*

Once a gritty enclave of artists' lofts and galleries, Soho has been heavily commercialised. The old factory buildings and former department stores now feature rows of storefronts for large fashion retailers, such as J.Crew, Madewell and Nike, luxury designer names like Chanel and Prada, and everything in between. It's not all chains, though – you can still find interesting independent shops, especially in the area's southern section, on **Grand** and **Howard Streets**. Urban fashion abounds on **Lafayette Street**, while **Broome Street** is an enclave for chic home design. On the area's eastern fringes, **Nolita** (*see p104*) has been colonised by contemporary boutiques, especially along **Mott** and **Mulberry Streets**.

Lower East Side *p118*

Once the centre of the rag trade, the Lower East Side is home to an ever-shifting array of small shops selling everything from vintage clothing and streetwear to locally made design items and gifts. **Orchard**, **Ludlow** and **Rivington Streets** are good places to start. Storefront art galleries are dotted around the area, plus a few longstanding survivors, such as **Russ & Daughters**, which has sold smoked fish and Jewish delicacies in the neighbourhood for more than a century.

East Village *p131*

Offbeat vintage shops, tattoo parlours and secondhand record stores are scattered throughout this former countercultural bastion. **Great Jones Street**, in the area bordering Greenwich Village known as **Noho,** is a pocket of iconoclastic fashion and interiors stores.

Greenwich Village & West Village

A few years ago, the quaint storefronts of Bleecker Street in the **West Village** (*see p146*) and the former industrial buildings of the **Meatpacking District** (*see p149*) were bursting with designer flagships. While both still have their share of big names (**Cynthia Rowley** and **Paul Smith** on Bleecker Street, for example; **DVF** and the lofty labels of **Jeffrey** department store in the Meatpacking District), many have departed, with mid-range retailers filling the void. A handful of characterful traditional food stores remain in **Greenwich Village** (*see p142*), including old-school coffee purveyor **Porto Rico Importing Co** and decades-old **Murray's Cheese**.

Chelsea & Flatiron District *p158, p168*

Once fertile ground for bargain hunters, these neighbouring areas still have a few exceptional antiques emporiums, including **Mantiques Modern**, a cluttered trove of furniture and fascinating objects, and the sprawling, four-floor **Showplace Antique & Design Center**, with stalls selling everything from vintage designerwear to old radios and Chinese vases. The area is known for furniture stores, including the expansive **ABC Carpet & Home**, which also sells a range of covetable fashion, gifts and beauty products.

Midtown *p176, p181 & p186*

Many of the city's department stores, including New York original **Bergdorf Goodman**, can be found on **Fifth Avenue** between 38th and 59th Streets, in the company of chain stores and premium-designer flagships; the latter also line up on the eastward stretch of **57th Street**. To the south, massive **Macy's** presides over Herald Square. A few indie gems selling men's fashion and hand-crafted homewares can be found nearby in the **Garment District** and **Hell's Kitchen**.

Upper East Side *p211, p218*

Madison Avenue mixes international designer names with more mainstream mall-level brands, and you'll see some of the same names here as on Fifth Avenue. Recently, contemporary labels more associated with a downtown vibe, such as **Veronica Beard** and **Acne** (no.926, www.acnestudios.com), have opened on the luxe uptown strip. Two of the city's most popular department stores, **Barneys New York** and **Bloomingdale's**, are also in the vicinity.

Brooklyn

Trendy **Williamsburg** (*see p253*) has a heady mix of large resale stores and more curated vintage shops, eclectic fashion boutiques, arty home emporiums and, yes, a few clothing chains. Further north, funky **Greenpoint** is a destination for vintage clothing and vinyl hunters. Other neighbourhoods, such as **Dumbo** (*see p238*) and the cheek-by-jowl enclaves **Cobble Hill**, **Carroll Gardens** and **Boerum Hill** (*see p240*), have clusters of independent clothing, furnishings and gift shops, but businesses tend to come and go, so be prepared for new openings.

In response to environmental concerns, trendsetters gravitate towards sustainable 'slow fashion' labels, such as those found at **Oroboro** (*see p106*), and trendy vintage shops like **Feng Sway**. An antidote to the detached experience of online commerce, concept stores are making a comeback. Milan's trailblazing **10 Corso Como** opened an offshoot (*see p82*), complete with an art gallery and a restaurant, in the former fashion desert of the South Street Seaport. **Roman and Williams Guild** showcases the hip NYC design firm's furniture line alongside a global array of contemporary artisan-made home goods, and includes a chic café. At serene boutique **Hesperios** (*see p104*), you can browse knitwear and art books, or chill out with coffee and freshly baked bread plates.

One-stop shopping

Of course, many visitors to New York will simply be looking to make the most of the incredible variety of big brands on offer in the city. For young, casual and streetwear labels, head to Lafayette Street and Broadway in Soho. Fifth Avenue heaves with a mix of designer showcases and mall-level megastores. Madison Avenue is more consistently posh, though contemporary designers (Acne, L'Agence, Maje, Iro, Alice + Olivia and more) have joined the line-up of deluxe labels like Alexander McQueen, Balenciaga, Lanvin and Ralph Lauren.

If you prefer to do all your shopping under one roof, famous department stores **Macy's** (*see p176*; good for mid-range brands), **Bloomingdale's** (*see p212*; a mix of mid-range and designer), **Barneys** (*see p211*; cutting-edge and high-fashion) and **Bergdorf Goodman** (*see p186*; luxury goods and international designer, plus some quirky one-off shops within a shop) are all stuffed with desirable items.

The city recently gained a couple of new department stores: **Nordstrom** opened a pair of men's and women's stores in Midtown (225 & 235

❤ Best design

ABC Carpet & Home *p168*
Stylish four-floor emporium showcasing furniture, home accessories, gifts, jewellery and beauty products.

Fishs Eddy *p169*
Clever NYC-themed glasses, mugs and plates.

The Future Perfect *p132*
Limited-edition, artist-made pieces.

Roman and Williams Guild *p92*
Far-flung artisan goods curated by a top NYC design firm.

Roman and Williams Guild

Spark Pretty

W 57th Street, 1-212 843 5100, shop.nordstrom. com), while **Neiman Marcus** anchors the Shops and Restaurants at Hudson Yards (*see p181*), which opened in spring 2019. New York City was never much of a mall destination, but suddenly large mixed-use complexes combining shops and restaurants with offices or apartments seem to be everywhere, from the rebuilt **World Trade Center** (*see p80*), which features a sprawling underground Westfield shopping centre, to Essex Crossing, home to the transplanted vendors of **Essex Street Market** (*see p112*) and, coming soon, clothing boutiques and art galleries.

Sniffing out sales

New York is fertile bargain-hunting territory. The traditional seasonal sales (which usually start just after, or sometimes even before, Christmas and in early to mid June) have given way to frequent markdowns throughout the year. Keep an eye out for sale racks in boutiques, chains and department stores.

Numerous designer studios and showrooms give rise to a weekly spate of sample sales (*see p176* **In the know**). The best are listed at www.timeout.com/newyork. The most popular

❤ Best vintage and antiques

Erie Basin *p241*
Exquisite, hand-selected jewellery.

Feng Sway *p253*
Hip space stuffed with exotic plants, flamboyant pieces and quirky finds.

Mantiques Modern *p159*
A browse-friendly jumble of eccentric objects and 20th-century design.

Obscura Antiques & Oddities *p133*
Bizarre items from medical relics and taxidermy to creepy dolls.

Showplace Antique & Design Center *p169*
Four floors of eclectic dealers.

Spark Pretty *p133*
Customised '80s denim and campy pop-culture T-shirts.

designers draw long queues, so it's a good idea to arrive early for the best selection of merchandise, though some sales are held over several days and are restocked during their run. To avoid the crowds, it's best to skip the lunch hour and early evening. While some sample sales accept credit cards, others don't so it's best to bring plenty of cash. We also suggest wearing decent underwear since fitting rooms, if provided, are likely to be communal.

Chief among the permanent sale stores is discount department store **Century 21** (*see p80*). It's beloved of rummagers, but detested by those with little patience for sifting through less than fabulous merchandise for the prize finds. There's a smaller Manhattan location on the Upper West Side that's a bit less frenetic, but we recommend braving the original for breadth of stock and, sometimes, deeper discounts. Department store cut-price offshoots **Nordstrom Rack (**with Manhattan locations in Union Square and 865 Sixth Avenue, at 31st Street, www.nordstromrack. com), **Bloomingdale's Outlet** (*see p212*) and **Saks Fifth Avenue Off Fifth** (*see p187*) are all worth checking out too. New York City's first premium outlet mall, **Empire Outlets** (www.empireoutletsnyc.com) opened on Staten Island in 2019.

Magpie

♥ **Best gifts and souvenirs**

Aedes Perfumery *p118*
Unusual and NYC-created fragrances.

Bowne & Co Stationers *p82*
Nostalgic hand-printed cards and more.

Hesperios *p104*
Exquisite knitwear, design tomes and ceramics.

Magpie *p203*
A variety of handmade goods sourced by a former museum-shop buyer.

Uniqulee *p102*
One-of-a-kind vintage finds and locally designed accessories.

Hesperios

**In the know
Essentials**

In general, local shops are open from 10am or 11am to 7pm or 8pm Monday to Saturday and noon to 5pm or 6pm on Sunday, though it varies widely. Many large retailers and book and record stores stay open later. Hours may also change seasonally or during sales. Most stores accept credit cards, apart from some smaller shops, sample sales and market vendors.

Consumer culture

Although some of its branches have closed in recent years, chain retailer **Barnes & Noble** (www.barnesandnoble.com) still dominates the city's bricks-and-mortar book scene. Serious competition has arrived, however: **Amazon** now operates two stores, including one in the **Shops at Columbus Circle** (*see p203*), featuring crowd-sourced ratings and reviews. Well-loved independents, such as the **Strand Book Store**, have been holding their own for years. **Housing Works Bookstore Café** (*see p91*) doubles as a popular Soho hangout. For art books, there are a couple of excellent indies in the heart of the gallery district in **Chelsea** (*see p154*). Museum shops are another great resource. The **Metropolitan Museum of Art** (*see p214*), the **New Museum of Contemporary Art** (*see p113*) and **MoMA** (*see p185*) all have excellent bookstores. The latter also has two standalone design stores, one across the street from the museum at 44 W 53rd Street, the other in Soho (81 Spring Street, between Broadway & Crosby Street, 1-646 613 1367, store.moma.org). At either location, you can pick up design classics such as a George Nelson wall clock, cool tech and kitchen gadgets. The **Museum of Arts & Design** (*see p200*) is a great source of handmade items, including a wide range of jewellery.

While some of the city's best-loved record stores closed in recent years, there are notable survivors, including the **Downtown Music Gallery**, tucked away in a Chinatown basement. Brooklyn has a huge flagship of UK indie retailer **Rough Trade** and smaller record shops are thriving in the borough, especially in Williamsburg and neighbouring Greenpoint – making the area a prime place for casual music lovers and serious vinyl collectors to spend an afternoon.

❤ **Best books and music**

Downtown Music Gallery *p101*
Torch bearer for the avant-garde.

McNally Jackson *p106*
Appealing store with an excellent reading series.

Printed Matter *p159*
Artists' books, in the heart of the Chelsea gallery district.

Rough Trade *p250*
Massive NYC flagship of the London label, hosting in-store gigs.

Strand Book Store *p133*
Indie institution with an encyclopedic selection.

Printed Matter

Explore

Brooklyn Bridge p237

Getting Started

Plan, pre-book and orientate yourself before you start exploring

New York City is made up of five boroughs. Taking our cues from its original development, we start our journey at the bottom of Manhattan island, where 17th-century Dutch settlers founded New Amsterdam. Just as the metropolis expanded upwards, so this guide journeys north through the downtown neighbourhoods that swelled with successive waves of immigration, to the midtown and uptown areas laid out in the 1811 grid plan, and beyond.

Once a separate city, Brooklyn officially became part of Greater New York in 1898, along with Queens, the Bronx and Staten Island, which then comprised towns and rural land. Manhattan continues to be the main focus of attention for tourists but, increasingly, the other boroughs are enticing savvy visitors to venture further afield.

♥ Best views

Brooklyn Bridge *p237*
The city's most scenic pedestrian crossing.

Brooklyn Heights Promenade *p234*
Postcard-worthy views from this riverside strip.

Empire State Building *p182*
No longer the highest viewpoint, but still the top.

One World Observatory *p79*
Whizz up the western hemisphere's tallest tower.

Rockefeller Center *p184*
Take in the cityscape – including the Empire State Building – from the Top of the Rock.

Times Square *p177*
Climb the TKTS steps for a 360-degree light show.

❤ Best family attractions

Bronx Zoo *p273*
Go wild with thousands of animals.

Central Park *p196*
Year-round fun, from puppets to ice-skating.

Gulliver's Gate *p178*
Marvellous scale-model microcosm.

Museum of Natural History *p199*
Dinosaur skeletons and stuffed critters.

Metropolitan Museum of Art *p214*
Egyptian temple, mummies and armour.

New York Hall of Science *p266*
Interactive science playground.

New York City overview

On Manhattan's tip, the **Financial District** (*see p68*) contains the seat of local government, City Hall, and the country's epicentre of capitalism, Wall Street. It's also the site of the rebuilt World Trade Center, with the National September 11 Memorial & Museum (*see p78*). The Statue of Liberty (*see p73*) stands in New York Harbor.

To the north, the former industrial districts of **Soho & Tribeca** (*see p84*) are now prime shopping and dining destinations. **Little Italy** has shrunk in recent years, crowded out by ever-expanding **Chinatown** (*see p96*), with its myriad inexpensive Asian eateries, and boutique-riddled **Nolita** (*see p102*).

Nearby, erstwhile immigrant neighbourhood the **Lower East Side** (*see p108*) is now bursting with trendy bars, boutiques and galleries, but you can still see how the other half lived in the painstakingly researched and recreated apartments and businesses of the Tenement Museum.

With Washington Square Park at its heart, former bohemian stomping ground **Greenwich Village** (*see p134*) still resounds with cultural associations, but is far more affluent today – with the restaurants to prove it. The leafy, winding streets of the **West Village** give way to the Meatpacking District's warehouses, now colonised by shops, eateries and nightspots. Here, the southern foot of the High Line elevated promenade (*see p156*) and the Whitney Museum of American Art attract large crowds of locals and visitors. The once-radical **East Village** (*see p124*) draws foodies, bar-hoppers and vintage shoppers.

Just north of the Meatpacking District, **Chelsea** (*see p150*) contains New York's main contemporary-gallery enclave (*see p154*) while its eastern neighbours the

Flatiron District (*see p162*), named after the distinctive building of the same name, and **Gramercy Park** offer some of the city's best upscale restaurants. Union Square hosts New York's biggest farmers' market.

Midtown (*see p172*) is home to the electronic spectacle that is Times Square and the historic theatres of Broadway (*see p340*). To the west, Hell's Kitchen is the site of Hudson Yards, the city's largest private real-estate development since Rockefeller Center.

Several major attractions, such as the Empire State Building (*see p182*) and the Museum of Modern Art (*see p185*), are in the vicinity of Midtown's Fifth Avenue. The busy commercial stretch is also home to some of the city's poshest stores.

Uptown, bucolic Central Park (*see p196*), with its picturesque lakes, expansive lawns and famous zoo, is the green divider between the affluent **Upper West Side** (*see p192*) and the equally well-heeled **Upper East Side** (*see p206*). Between them, they contain a wealth of cultural institutions: the UWS has the Metropolitan Opera, the New York Philharmonic and the New York City Ballet at Lincoln Center (*see p332*), while the UES claims a world-class collection of museums, especially the massive Metropolitan Museum of Art (*see p214*) and the Solomon R Guggenheim Museum (*see p217*) on Fifth Avenue's Museum Mile. Further north, **Harlem** (*see p220*) offers a vibrant restaurant scene, soul food and plenty of cultural history.

These days, a trip to NYC isn't complete without crossing the East River to **Brooklyn** (*see p230*), which is at the centre of the city's more adventurous food and arts scenes. Head across Brooklyn Bridge (*see p237*) to waterside Dumbo for Brooklyn Bridge Park, cutting-edge theatre at St Ann's Warehouse and foodie treats at the new Time Out Market (*see p45*). To the south-east, visit the thriving culture district of Fort Greene, bucolic Prospect Park and the excellent Brooklyn Museum. In the north-east, Williamsburg and Bushwick have buzzing music and nightlife scenes, exemplified by House of Yes (*see p312*).

Queens also has worthwhile cultural assets, especially progressive art centre MoMA PS1 and the Queens Museum (*see p266*). But gastronauts also venture further to areas such as **Astoria**, **Flushing** and **Jackson Heights** for authentic Greek, Chinese, Indian and other international eats.

Separated from upper Manhattan by the Harlem River, the **Bronx** is home to the Yankee Stadium and the New York Botanical Garden. A ferry ride from lower Manhattan, the frequently overlooked borough of **Staten Island** offers quirky museums and exhilarating views.

COME
HERE, YOU

Museums

Most visitors are aware of New York's massive **Metropolitan Museum of Art** (*see p214*) – at two million square feet, it houses more than that number of objects. But you may not have heard about a much smaller cultural institution. Launched by a trio of filmmakers, the 60-square-foot cabinet of curiosities known as **Mmuseumm** (*see p93*) occupies a Tribeca elevator shaft, plus a nearby cupboard-sized annex. In between, there are institutions of all sizes devoted to just about everything you can think of, from public transport (**New York Transit Museum**, *see p235*) to sex (**Museum of Sex**, *see p164*). Many offer fascinating insights into city history, including the **Tenement Museum** (*see p112*) and the **New-York Historical Society** (*see p200*), which has high-tech displays that bring its extraordinary trove of artefacts, art and documents to vivid life. The **National September 11 Museum** (*see p78*) serves a threefold function as memorial tribute, historical record and mind-boggling evocation of the immense scale of the disaster. The **American Museum of Natural History** (*see p199*), which has an impressive dinosaur collection and classic wildlife dioramas, is an itinerary essential for families.

Visitors with an interest in art may be frustrated by the sheer volume of must-see institutions in the city, necessitating tough choices on shorter visits. Several of the city's world-class art museums, including the Met and the **Guggenheim** (*see p217*), are clustered on the Upper East Side's Museum Mile, but you'll have to trek to Midtown for the peerless art and design collections of the **Museum of Modern Art (MoMA)** (*see p185*). The **Whitney Museum of American Art** (*see p147*), now settled in its Hudson River-hugging Renzo Piano-designed building in the Meatpacking District, is also essential viewing. Together with the **New Museum of Contemporary Art** (*see p113*), a striking off-kilter structure built on the Bowery less than a decade earlier, it represents a considerable culture shift downtown.

If time allows, there are several worthwhile museums in the outer boroughs, especially the **Brooklyn Museum** (*see p243*), which has a notable Egyptian collection and a section devoted to feminist art. In Queens, check out MoMA's cutting-edge affiliate, **MoMA PS1** (*see p258*) and the eclectic **Queens Museum** (*see p266*). The latter occupies a former World's Fair building and contains the remarkable scale model of the metropolis, the **Panorama of the City of New York**.

Because the city's museums are privately funded, admission prices can be steep. However, they usually include entry to

Central Park *p196*

temporary shows as well as the permanent collections, and many institutions offer one day or evening a week when admission fees are either waived or switched to a voluntary donation. Be warned that some museums are closed on Mondays, except on certain holidays, such as Columbus Day and Presidents' Day.

Getting around

Manhattan is a mere 13.4 miles long and 2.3 miles across at its widest point, and once you've mastered the grid, it's easy to find your way (although it gets a little trickier in downtown neighbourhoods that pre-date the grid system). The best way to see the city is by **walking**, and you'll be able to tackle clusters of sights on foot. To get from one area of the metropolis to the next, it's hard to beat the **subway**, which is highly efficient and runs 24 hours a day. It's fairly easy to navigate, but bear in mind that on most lines some numbered or lettered trains go local (stopping at every stop) while others are express and skip stops. Adding to potential confusion, on some lines this changes at weekends and late at night – for example the local W service is replaced by the usually express N. We've provided weekday transport information in our listings and on the maps, so be sure to check www.mta.info for weekend updates. The subway system is almost comprehensive, but one drawback is the lack of crosstown options uptown. This is where **buses** come in handy. The extensive bus system can be a pleasant way to travel, especially outside of rush hours, but routes through traffic-heavy parts of town are often slow. **Taxis** are usually plentiful, apart from during bad weather, but can also get stuck in traffic, bumping up prices. We don't recommend the pedicabs that congregate in Central Park and other tourist-heavy areas because the rates, usually charged per minute, rack up quickly. In recent years, the **ferry** service has expanded, offering affordable, convenient and picturesque routes to parts of Brooklyn and Queens. For more information, *see p384* Getting Around.

Information

The city's official marketing organisation, **NYC & Company** (www.nycgo.com), operates a visitor centre in Macy's department store, offering maps and information on tours, shows, hotels and attractions. You can also purchase tour tickets and discount passes on-site.

Prices and discounts

Many top attractions and museums offer cheaper admission prices if you purchase tickets in advance on their website. If you're planning to visit a number of attractions during your stay, it's worth considering one of a trio of package-deal cards. The following details are correct for current deals, but check the websites as they're subject to change. The **New York CityPASS** (www.citypass.com) gives pre-paid queue-jumping access to six big-ticket attractions, among them the Empire State Building and the Met. The pass is valid for nine consecutive days and costs $132 ($108 reductions). A three-sight option is also available ($84; $64 reductions). If you're determined to pack in as much as possible during a trip, the **New York Pass** (www.newyorkpass.com) grants admission to more than 100 museums, sights and tours. The card is time-tied: it costs from $134 ($99 reductions) for a one-day pass up to $469 ($299 reductions) for ten days. The **New York Explorer Pass** (www. smartdestinations.com) lets you spread out your sightseeing over 30 days, with the option of bundling from three to ten attractions (from $94; $70 reductions).

Guided tours

If you don't mind moving in a pack, guided tours can provide a time-saving overview of the city, or expert insights into a specific aspect of an area's history. **Gray Line** (1-212 445 0848, www.grayline.com/newyork) offers several options, from a basic hop-on, hop-off bus ride ($49) to multi-day passes that also include cruises and admission to attractions.

Circle Line Cruises (1-212 563 3200, www.circleline.com) is known for its guided circumnavigation of Manhattan ($44; $37 reductions), which takes two and a half hours. It's a great way to get your bearings and see many of the city's sights as you pass under its iconic bridges, but the company also has a roster of shorter tours.

New York was known as the Big Onion before it became the Big Apple. The guides of **Big Onion Walking Tours** (1-888 606 9255, www.bigonion.com) will explain why, and they should know. All guides hold advanced degrees in history or a related field. Among the offerings ($20-$40) is the 'Official Gangs of New York Tour' and a 'Multi-Ethnic Eating Tour' that explores the history of the Lower East Side, Chinatown and Little Italy with a little cuisine sampling along the way. The **Municipal Art Society**'s excellent walking tours (1-212 935 3960, www.mas.org/tours; $30), led by architects, art historians and others, reflect the society's focus on contemporary architecture, urban planning and historic preservation. Other niche-interest operators include **Urban Adventures** (1-347 878 8444, www.newyorkcityurbanadventures. com), which primarily focuses on gastro-centric tours. Expeditions include 'Brewed in Brooklyn', which illuminates the borough's suds-making legacy, and a 'Tenements, Tales and Tastes' tour of the Lower East Side ($89 and $79 respectively, including food and drink).

Boroughs of the Dead (1-917 409 8533, boroughsofthedead.com), founded by Andrea Janes, author of *Boroughs of the Dead: New York City Ghost Stories*, offers guided rambles that explore the dark side of various neighbourhoods ($25-$30), plus a spine-tingling tour of Brooklyn's Green-Wood Cemetery.

If you prefer a faster pace, **City Running Tours** (1-877 415 0058, www. cityrunningtours.com) has a variety of four-mile guided group jogs ($40-$45), or opt for a personalised private tour from three to 26 miles (starting at $60). The licensed guides of **Unlimited Biking** (1-212 749 4444, www. unlimitedbiking.com) lead cyclists through historic and newly hip hoods. Some of the many choices ($95-$99 including bicycle & helmet rental) include the Harlem-bound 'Sensational Park and Soul' tour, 'Secret Streets – From High Finance to Hidden Chinatown', and a twilight ride across the Brooklyn Bridge.

Financial District

Commerce has been the backbone of New York's prosperity since its earliest days as a Dutch colony. The southern tip of Manhattan quickly evolved into the Financial District because, in the days before telecommunications, banks established their headquarters near the port. The oldest part of the city, lower Manhattan is the city's financial, legal and political powerhouse; but as the arrival point for the 19th-century influx of immigrants, it played another vital role in the city's evolution.

As more than a decade of construction nears completion, the new World Trade Center is both a potent 9/11 memorial and a busy downtown shopping hub, home to the One World Observatory, the city's highest vantage point. And the South Street Seaport is being transformed from a touristy eyesore into a waterfront destination with bars, shops and areas for outdoor lounging that are also a hit with locals.

❤ **Don't miss**

1 Statue of Liberty *p73*
Ascend to the crown for a breathtaking vista.

2 World Trade Center *p77*
Dramatic 21st-century architecture, the 9/11 Memorial & Museum (*see p78*) and the vertiginous One World Observatory (*see p79*).

3 Governors Island *p75*
A tranquil retreat minutes from Manhattan.

National September 11 Memorial *p78*

BATTERY PARK TO WALL STREET

▶ *Subway A, C, J, Z, 2, 3, 4, 5 to Fulton Street; J, Z to Broad Street; 2, 3, 4, 5 to Wall Street. R, W to Whitehall Street-South Ferry; 1 to South Ferry; 4, 5 to Bowling Green.*

It's easy to forget that Manhattan is an island – what with all those gargantuan skyscrapers obscuring your view of the water. Until, that is, you reach the southern point, where salty ocean breezes are reminders of the millions of immigrants who travelled on steamers in search of prosperity, liberty and a new home. This is where they landed, after passing through Ellis Island's immigration and quarantine centres.

On the edge of Battery Park, **Castle Clinton** was one of several forts built to defend New York Harbor against attacks by the British in the War of 1812 (others included Castle Williams on Governors Island, Fort Gibson on Ellis Island and Fort Wood, now the base of the Statue of Liberty). After serving as an aquarium, immigration centre and opera house, the sandstone fort is now a visitors' centre and ticket booth for **Statue of Liberty** and **Ellis Island** tours.

Joining the throngs making their way to Lady Liberty, you'll head south-east along the shore, where several ferry terminals jut into the harbour. Among them is the **Whitehall Ferry Terminal**, the boarding place for the **Staten Island Ferry**. Constructed in 1907, the terminal was severely damaged by fire in 1991, but was completely rebuilt in 2005. More than 75,000 passengers take the free, 25-minute journey to Staten Island each day; most are commuters but many are tourists, taking advantage of the views of the Manhattan skyline and the Statue of Liberty. Before the Brooklyn Bridge was completed in 1883, the **Battery Maritime Building** (10 South Street, between Broad & Whitehall Streets) served as a terminal for the ferry services between Manhattan and Brooklyn. Now, it's the launch point for a ferry to tranquil **Governors Island** (*see p75*). On the park's northern waterfront, the 1886 **Pier A Harbor House** (www.piera.com), once the HQ for the harbour police, has been reinvented as a massive dining and drinking destination.

Just north of Battery Park you'll find the triangular **Bowling Green**, the city's oldest park and a popular lunchtime spot for Financial District workers; it's also the front lawn of the 1886 **Alexander Hamilton US Custom House**, now home to the **National Museum of the American Indian**.

Dwarfed by the surrounding architecture, the **Stone Street Historic District** is a small pocket of restored 1830s buildings on the eponymous winding cobblestoned lane, also encompassing South William and Pearl Streets and Coenties Alley. Office workers and tourists frequent its restaurants and bars, including the boisterous **Ulysses' Folk House** (95 Pearl Street, between Coenties Alley & Hanover Square, 1-212 482 0400, www.ulyssesnyc.com) and **Stone Street Tavern** (52 Stone Street, between Coenties Alley & Hanover Square, 1-212 785 5658, www.stonestreettavernnyc.com).

Although the neighbourhood is bisected vertically by the ever-bustling Broadway, it's the east–west **Wall Street** (or 'the Street' in trader lingo) that's synonymous with the world's greatest den of capitalism. The name derives from a defensive wooden wall built in 1653 to mark the northern limit of New Amsterdam, and despite its huge

---

❤ Time to eat & drink

Artisanal coffee with a twist
Jack's Stir Brew Coffee *p82*

Varied lunch options
Hudson Eats *p79*

Fine dining and dazzling views
Manhatta *p76*

Historic tipples
BlackTail *p79*, Dead Rabbit Grocery & Grog *p76*

❤ Time to shop

Bargains galore
Century 21 *p80*

Iconic Milan concept store offshoot
10 Corso Como New York *p82*

Quaint shop for hand-printed cards and more
Bowne & Co Stationers *p82*

In the know
The bull's balls

On Bowling Green's northern side stands a three-and-a-half-ton bronze sculpture of a bull (symbolising the bull, or rising, share market). The statue was deposited without permission outside the Stock Exchange by guerrilla artist Arturo di Modica in 1989 and has since been moved by the city to its current location. The bull's enormous balls are often rubbed for good luck by tourists (and perhaps the occasional broker).

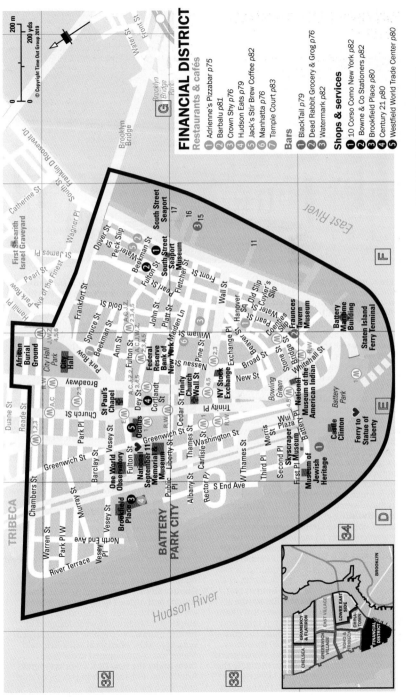

FINANCIAL DISTRICT

Restaurants & cafés

1. Adrienne's Pizzabar p75
2. Barbalu p81
3. Crown Shy p76
4. Hudson Eats p79
5. Jack's Stir Brew Coffee p82
6. Manhatta p76
7. Temple Court p83

Bars

1. BlackTail p79
2. Dead Rabbit Grocery & Grog p76
3. Watermark p82

Shops & services

1. 10 Corso Como New York p82
2. Bowne & Co Stationers p82
3. Brookfield Place p80
4. Century 21 p80
5. Westfield World Trade Center p80

© Copyright Time Out Group 2019

National Museum of the American Indian

significance, the thoroughfare is less than a mile long. At its western intersection with Broadway, you'll find the Gothic Revival spire of **Trinity Church Wall Street**. The original church burned down in 1776, and a second was demolished in 1839; the current version became the island's tallest structure when it was completed in 1846. **St Paul's Chapel**, the church's older satellite, is one of the finest Georgian structures in the US.

A block to the east of Trinity Church is the **Federal Hall National Memorial** (26 Wall Street, at Nassau Street, 1-212 825 6990, www.nps.gov/feha, closed Sat Sept-May, Sun), an august Greek Revival building and – in a previous incarnation – the site of George Washington's first inauguration. It was along this stretch that corporate America made its first audacious architectural statements; a walk eastwards offers much evidence of what money can buy. Structures include the **Bankers Trust Building** at 14 Wall Street (at Broad Street), completed in 1912 and crowned by a seven-storey pyramid modelled on the Mausoleum of Halicarnassus; **40 Wall Street** (between Nassau & William Streets), which battled the Chrysler Building in 1929 for the title of world's tallest building (the Empire State trounced them both in 1931); and the former **Merchants' Exchange** at 55 Wall Street (between Hanover & William Streets), with its stacked rows of Ionic and Corinthian columns. Back round the corner is the **Equitable Building** (120 Broadway, between Cedar & Pine Streets), whose greedy use of vertical space helped to instigate the zoning laws that now govern skyscrapers – stand across the street from the building

to get the best view. Nearby is the **Federal Reserve Bank of New York**, with its huge gold vault.

The nerve centre of the US economy is the **New York Stock Exchange** (11 Wall Street, between Broad & New Streets, www.nyse. com). For security reasons, the Exchange is no longer open to the public, but the street outside offers an endless pageant of brokers, traders and their minions.

Sights & museums

Alexander Hamilton US Custom House/National Museum of the American Indian

1 Bowling Green, between State & Whitehall Streets (1-212 514 3700, www.nmai.si.edu). Subway R, W to Whitehall Street-South Ferry; 1 to South Ferry; 4, 5 to Bowling Green. **Open** *10am-5pm Mon-Wed, Fri-Sun; 10am-8pm Thur.* **Admission** *free.* **Map** *p71 E33.*

Cass Gilbert's magnificent Beaux Arts Custom House, completed in 1907, was home to the Customs Service until 1973, when the federal government moved it to the newly built World Trade Center complex. Four monumental figures by Lincoln Memorial sculptor Daniel Chester French – representing Asia, America, Europe and Africa – flank the impressive entrance. The panels surrounding the elliptical rotunda dome were designed to feature murals, but the plan wasn't realised until the 1930s, when local artist Reginald Marsh was commissioned to decorate them under the New Deal's Works Progress Administration; the paintings depict a ship entering New York Harbor.

❤ Statue of Liberty

*Liberty Island (1-212 363 3200, www.nps.gov/ stli). Subway R, W to Whitehall Street-South Ferry; 1 to South Ferry; 4, 5 to Bowling Green. Then take Statue of Liberty ferry (1-877 523 9849, www.statuecruises.com), departing roughly every 30mins from gangway 4 or 5 in southernmost Battery Park. **Open** ferry runs 9.30am-3.30pm daily (extended hrs in summer; see website). Purchase tickets online, by phone or at Castle Clinton in Battery Park.* **Admission** *$18.50; $9-$14 reductions; free under-4s.*

The sole occupant of Liberty Island, Liberty Enlightening the World stands 305ft tall from the bottom of her base to the tip of her gold-leaf torch.

Intended as a gift from France on America's 100th birthday, the statue was designed by Frédéric Auguste Bartholdi (1834-1904). Construction began in Paris in 1874, her skeletal iron framework crafted by Gustave Eiffel (the man behind the Tower), but only the arm with the torch was finished in time for the centennial in 1876. In 1884, the statue was finally completed – only to be taken apart to be shipped to New York, where it was unveiled in 1886. It served as a lighthouse until 1902, and as a welcoming beacon for millions of immigrants. These 'tired... poor... huddled masses' were evoked in Emma Lazarus's poem 'The New Colossus', written in 1883 to raise funds for the pedestal and engraved inside the statue in 1903.

With a free pass, available only with ferry tickets reserved in advance, you can enter the pedestal and view the interior through a glass ceiling. Access to the crown costs an extra $3 and must be reserved in advance.

A new museum on the island features a multimedia show about the statue's history, exhibits about its design and construction, and the original torch, removed in 1984.

A half-mile across the harbour from Liberty Island is the 32-acre Ellis Island, gateway for over 12 million people who entered the country between 1892 and 1954. In the National Museum of Immigration (a former check-in depot), three floors of photos, interactive displays and exhibits pay tribute to the hopeful souls who made the voyage.

In 1994, the National Museum of the American Indian's George Gustav Heye Center, a branch of the Smithsonian, moved into the first two floors of the building. On the second level, the life and culture of Native Americans are illuminated in three galleries radiating out from the rotunda. In addition to a roster of changing shows, the permanent exhibition, 'Infinity of Nations', displays 700 of the museum's wide-ranging collection of Native American art and objects, from decorated baskets to elaborate ceremonial headdresses, organised by geographical region. On the ground floor, the Diker Pavilion for Native Arts & Culture is the city's only dedicated showcase for Native American performing arts. The imagiNATIONs Activity Center offers hands-on exhibits introducing kids to Native contributions to areas such as medicine and agriculture.

Federal Reserve Bank of New York

*Visitors' entrance: 44 Maiden Lane, between Nassau & William Streets (www.ny.frb.org/aboutthefed/visiting.html). Subway 2, 3, 4, 5 to Wall Street. **Open** Tours vary (reservations required). **Admission** Free. **Map** p71 E33.*

It's no surprise that tours of this important financial institution must be booked in advance on the website (up to a month ahead) and an official photo ID, such as a US driver's licence or a passport, presented before admission. Descend 80ft below street level and you'll find the world's largest known supply of monetary gold (approximately 500,000 bars, worth more than $240 billion), stored in a gigantic vault that rests on the solid bedrock of Manhattan Island. Visitors learn about the New York Fed's safeguarding of the precious metal, and the responsibilities and actions of the Federal Reserve.

Fraunces Tavern Museum

*2nd & 3rd Floors, 54 Pearl Street, at Broad Street (1-212 425 1778, www.frauncestavernmuseum.org). Subway J, Z to Broad Street; 4, 5 to Bowling Green. **Open** noon-5pm Mon-Fri; 11am-5pm Sat, Sun. **Admission** $7; $4 reductions; free under-5s. **Map** p71 E33.*

True, George Washington slept here, but there's little left of the original 18th-century tavern he favoured during the Revolution. Fire-damaged and rebuilt in the 19th century, it was reconstructed in its current Colonial Revival style in 1907. Step into a period recreation of the Long Room, where Washington took tearful farewell of his troops after the British had been defeated and vowed to retire from public life. (Luckily, he had a change of heart six years later and became the country's first president.) The museum also contains a collection of 8,000 Revolutionary War objects, including muskets, prints and such Washington relics as a lock of his hair. And you can still raise a pint in the bar and restaurant, which is run by Dublin's Porterhouse Brewing Company.

💜 Governors Island
*1-212 440 2000, www.govisland.com. Subway R, W to Whitehall Street-South Ferry; 1 to South Ferry; 4, 5 to Bowling Green. Then take ferry from Battery Maritime Building at Slip no.7. **Open** May-Oct 10am-6pm Mon-Fri; 10am-7pm Sat, Sun (extended hrs in summer; see website for ferry schedule). **Admission** Ferry $3 round trip; $1 reductions; free under-12s. Free 10-11.30am Sat, Sun.*

A 172-acre chunk of prime waterside real estate that can never be developed into luxury condos, Governors Island is a secluded anomaly a scant 800 yards from lower Manhattan. The verdant commons and stately red-brick buildings evoke an Ivy League campus by way of a colonial New England village, but today the former military post is occupied by cultural organisations and urban farms.

The island was initially a seasonal fishing and gathering ground for the Lenape Indians, but its strategic position cemented its future as a military base (by the late 19th century it was the army's headquarters for the entire eastern US), and it retains 19th-century officers' residences, Fort Jay, started in 1776, and Castle Williams, completed in 1812. Such legendary figures as Generals Ulysses S Grant and Douglas MacArthur had stints on the island.

Today, as well as providing a peaceful setting for cycling (bring a bike, or rent one on arrival), the island hosts a programme of events, including the popular Jazz Age

Lawn party (*see p287*) and art exhibitions. Sprawling green spaces include the Hammock Grove for shady reclining, and the Hills, constructed from the debris of demolished buildings. The tallest hill offers harbour panoramas from its 70ft summit. Food and drink options include pop-up beer gardens, and oyster and pizza vendors.

Trinity Church Wall Street & St Paul's Chapel
*__Trinity Church Wall Street__ 75 Broadway, at Wall Street (1-212 602 0800, www. trinitywallstreet.org). Subway R, W, 1 to Rector Street; 2, 3, 4, 5 to Wall Street. **Open** 7am-6pm daily (churchyard closes at 4pm Oct-Mar). **Admission** free. **Map** p71 E33.*

*__St Paul's Chapel__ 209 Broadway, between Fulton & Vesey Streets (1-212 602 0800, www. trinitywallstreet.org). Subway A, C, J, Z, 2, 3, 4, 5 to Fulton Street. **Open** 10am-6pm daily. **Admission** free. **Map** p71 E32.*

Trinity Church was the island's tallest structure when it was completed in 1846 (the original burned down in 1776; a second was demolished in 1839). A set of gates on Broadway allows access to the surrounding cemetery, where cracked and faded tombstones mark the final resting places of dozens of past city dwellers, including such notable New Yorkers as founding father Alexander Hamilton and steamboat inventor Robert Fulton.

Six blocks to the north, Trinity's satellite, St Paul's Chapel, is more important architecturally. The oldest public building in New York still in continuous use (it dates from 1766), it is one of the nation's most valued Georgian structures.

▶ For Trinity's free concert series, see p329.

Restaurants & cafés

Adrienne's Pizzabar $
*54 Stone Street, between Coenties Alley & Mill Lane (1-212 248 3838, www.adriennespizza. com). Subway R, W to Whitehall Street-South Ferry; 1 to South Ferry; 2, 3 to Wall Street. **Open** 11.30am-midnight Mon-Sat; 11.30am-10pm Sun. **Map** p71 F33 ❶ Pizza*

This bright, modern pizzeria on quaint Stone Street provides a pleasant break from the Financial District's crowded thoroughfares. The kitchen prepares nicely charred pies with delectable toppings such as the rich *quattro formaggi*. If you're in a hurry, you can eat at the 12-seat bar, otherwise opt for the sleek, wood-accented dining room to savour small plates and main courses such as potato gnocchi and ravioli al *formaggio*. There are tables outside from April to November.

Governors Island

Crown Shy $$$

70 Pine Street, between Pearl & William
Streets (1-212 517 1932, www.crownshy.nyc).
Subway J, Z to Broad Street; 2, 3, 4, 5 to Wall
Street. **Open** *5.30-10pm Mon-Wed, Sun; 5.30-*
11pm Thur-Sat. **Map** *p71 F33* ❸ *American*

Set in a posh art deco residential building,
Crown Shy has a kitchen helmed by James
Kent, longtime chef de cuisine at Michelin-
starred Eleven Madison Park. But down-to-
earth prices for the seasonally changing à la
carte menu of snacks, small plates and mains
mean you can dine like a banker without
breaking the bank. Cavatelli with chicken
liver ragu was given an unexpected kick of
horseradish, and a perfectly tender grilled
pork chop was punctuated by carefully
placed cubed Asian pears and mustard. If
you can't snag a reservation, try to grab a seat
at the bar.

❤ Manhatta $$$

60th Floor, 28 Liberty Street, at William Street
(1-212 230 5788, www.manhattarestaurant.
com). Subway A, C, J, Z, 2, 3, 4, 5 to Fulton
Street; J, Z to Broad Street; 2, 3, 4, 5 to Wall
Street. **Open** *11.30am-2pm, 5-9.30pm Mon-*
Wed, Sun; 11.30am-2pm, 5-10pm Thur-Sat.
Map *p71 E33* ❻ *American*

Perched on the 60th floor of a skyscraper, this
restaurant has a stellar lower Manhattan view
from every seat (even if your back is to the
window, a mirror positioned over the kitchen
allows you to see the skyline). The seasonal,
French-influenced food is beautifully
executed, though not revolutionary: delicate
fish dishes under a veil of creamy sauce, for
example, or expertly seasoned Wagyu steak.
Combined with those dazzling views, the $88
three-course prix fixe, (including service)
is a steal.

Manhatta

Bars

❤ Dead Rabbit Grocery & Grog

30 Water Street, at Broad Street (1-646 422
7906, www.deadrabbitnyc.com). Subway R,
W to Whitehall Street-South Ferry; 1 to South
Ferry. **Open** *11am-4am Mon-Fri; 10am-3am*
Sat, Sun. **Map** *p71 E33* ❷

At this time-capsule nook, you can drink
like a boss – Boss Tweed, that is. Belfast
bar vets Sean Muldoon and Jack McGarry
have conjured up a rough-and-tumble
19th-century tavern in a red-brick landmark.
Resurrecting long-forgotten quaffs is nothing
new in NYC, but the Dead Rabbit's sheer
breadth of mid 19th-century libations eclipses
the competition, spanning 60-odd bishops,
fixes, nogs and smashes. The ever-changing
cocktail selection makes good use of seasonal
produce and esoteric ingredients.

WORLD TRADE CENTER & BATTERY PARK CITY

▶ *Subway A, C, 1, 2, 3 to Chambers Street; A,*
C, J, Z, 2, 3, 4, 5 to Fulton Street; E to World
Trade Center; R, W to Cortlandt Street; 1 to
WTC Cortlandt; 2, 3 to Park Place; 4, 5 to
Bowling Green.

On a date now etched into our collective
memory, the worst attack on US soil took
nearly 3,000 lives and left a gaping hole
where the Twin Towers had once helped to
define the New York skyline. But as you walk
through the World Trade Center's busy, tree-
shaded memorial plaza, it's hard to believe
that this area was a disaster zone, then a
fenced-off construction site, for the better
part of a decade. The **National September
11 Museum** serves a threefold function
as memorial tribute, historical record and
mind-boggling evocation of the immense
scale of the disaster. In addition to marking
the tragedy, the rebuilt World Trade Center
(*see opposite* Explore the New World
Trade center) has more impressive visitor
attractions than its previous incarnation.

Overlooking the Hudson River, granite-
and-glass corporate/retail/dining complex
Brookfield Place abuts **Battery Park City**,
a 92-acre planned community devised in the
1950s to replace decaying shipping piers with
new apartments, green spaces and schools.
It's a man-made addition to the island,
built on soil and rocks excavated from the
original World Trade Center construction
site and sediment dredged from New York
Harbor. Visitors can enjoy its esplanade,
a favoured route for bikers, skaters and
joggers, and a string of parks that runs north
along the Hudson River from Battery Park.

💙 Exploring the World Trade Center

In a city known for its sky-high aspirations, Ground Zero – a deep crater in the middle of downtown Manhattan – was a potent symbol of grief. Although plans for the site's redevelopment were announced in 2003, construction of the new World Trade Center, including office towers and the National September 11 Memorial & Museum (*see p78*), was plagued by infighting, budget overruns and missed deadlines. For most of the decade following the Twin Towers' fall, those who made the pilgrimage were confronted by an impenetrable fence. Yet, as the tenth anniversary of the attacks loomed, construction surged and the memorial opened on 11 September 2011, followed by the museum in 2014. Today, most of the site's planned elements have been completed, and the tree-shaded memorial plaza is bustling with commuters and office workers, as well as visitors gazing into the vast monumental waterfalls where the towers once stood. While the rebuilt World Trade Center offers a space to reflect on the tragedy, it has also boosted the area's attractions, and food

and shopping options. In the old WTC era, the Financial District was a weekend dead zone and local establishments were largely limited to cheap takeout places, raucous stockbroker bars and power-lunch spots. Now, sightseers can whizz up to the 102nd floor of the 1,776-ft 1 World Trade Center, which counts media giant Condé Nast among its tenants, to the city's highest observation deck (*see p79*). The adjacent Oculus, a dramatic bird-like structure designed by starchitect Santiago Calatrava, is the centrepiece of a multi-level Westfield shopping and dining complex – larger than six football fields – spread across the WTC site. From the main hall, with its soaring ribbed steel and glass ceiling, futuristic white passageways, some lined with shops, connect to the Fulton Street subway station, the PATH commuter rail to New Jersey, a branch of Italian-food mecca Eataly at 4 World Trade Center, and Brookfield Place, another massive mall. While it may seem crass to some that a large part of the site is dedicated to consumerism, this is New York City, after all.

Oculus at the World Trade Center

Providing expansive views of the Statue of Liberty and Ellis Island at its southernmost reaches, the stretch is dotted with monuments and sculptures. Close by the marina is the 1997 **Police Memorial** (Liberty Street, at South End Avenue), a granite pool and fountain that symbolically trace the lifespan of a police officer through the use of moving water, with names of the fallen etched into the wall. The **Irish Hunger Memorial** (Vesey Street, at North End Avenue) is here too, paying tribute to those who suffered during the famine from 1845 to 1852. Designed by artist Brian Tolle and landscape architect Gail Wittwer-Laird, the quarter-acre memorial incorporates vegetation, soil and stones from Ireland's 32 counties, and a reproduction of a 19th-century Irish cottage.

To the north, **Nelson A Rockefeller Park** (north end of Battery Park City, west of River Terrace) attracts sun worshippers, kite flyers and soccer players in the warm-weather months. Look out for Tom Otterness's whimsical sculpture installation, *The Real World*. Just east is **Teardrop Park** (between Warren & Murray Streets, east of River Terrace), a two-acre space designed to evoke the bucolic Hudson River Valley, and to the south are the inventively designed **South Cove** (on the Esplanade, between First & Third Place), with its quays and island, and **Robert F Wagner Jr Park** (north of Historic Battery Park, off Battery Place), where an observation deck offers fabulous views of both the harbour and the Verrazano-Narrows Bridge; below it, Louise Bourgeois' *Eyes* gaze over the Hudson from the lawn. The **Museum of Jewish Heritage**, Gotham's memorial to the Holocaust, is on the edge of the green. Across the street at the **Skyscraper Museum**, you can learn about the buildings that have created the city's iconic skyline.

Sights & museums

Museum of Jewish Heritage: A Living Memorial to the Holocaust

Edmond J Safra Plaza, 36 Battery Place, at First Place (1-646 437 4202, www.mjhnyc. org). Subway 4, 5 to Bowling Green. Open 10am-9pm Mon-Thur, Sun; 10am-5pm Fri (10am-3pm Nov-Mar); 10am-3pm eve of Jewish hols. Admission $8; $5 reductions (special exhibitions cost extra); free under-13s. Free 4-8pm Wed, Thur. Map p71 E34.

This museum explores Jewish life before, during and after the Nazi genocide. The permanent collection includes more than 40,000 photographs, documents, films and artefacts – many of them donated by Holocaust survivors and their families –

Battery Park

which are displayed on rotation. Special exhibitions tackle historical events or themes. The Memorial Garden features English artist Andy Goldsworthy's Garden of Stones: 18 fire-hollowed boulders embedded with dwarf oak saplings.

❤ National September 11 Memorial & Museum

Various entry points on Greenwich, Liberty & West Streets (1-212 312 8800, www.911memorial.org). Subway A, C, 1, 2, 3 to Chambers Street; A, C, J, Z, 2, 3, 4, 5 to Fulton Street; E to World Trade Center; R, W to Cortlandt Street; 1 to WTC Cortlandt; 2, 3 to Park Place. Open Memorial plaza 7.30am-9pm daily. Museum 9am-8pm Mon-Thur, Sun; 9am-9pm Fri, Sat (hrs vary seasonally; see website for updates). Admission Memorial plaza free. Museum $26; $15-$20 reductions; free under-7s, 9/11 family members, rescue workers & US military. Free 5-8pm Tue. Map p71 E32.

Surrounded by a tree-shaded plaza, the memorial, Reflecting Absence, created by architects Michael Arad and Peter Walker, comprises two one-acre 'footprints' of the destroyed towers, with 30-ft man-made waterfalls cascading down their sides. Bronze parapets round the edges are inscribed with the names of the 2,983 victims of the 2001 attacks at the World Trade Center, the Pentagon and the passengers of United Flight 93, as well as those who lost their lives in the bombing on 26 February 1993.

The museum pavilion, designed by Oslo-based firm Snøhetta, rises between the pools. Its web-like glass atrium houses two steel trident-shaped columns salvaged from the base of the Twin Towers. Visitors descend to the vast spaces of the WTC's original foundations alongside a remnant of the Vesey Street staircase known as the Survivors' Stairs, which was used by hundreds of people escaping the carnage. Massive pieces of twisted metal and a fallen segment of the North Tower's radio/TV antenna bring home the enormous scale of the disaster.

Around 1,000 artefacts, plus images, documents and oral histories chronicle events leading up to the attacks, commemorate the victims and document how the world changed after 9/11. Items vividly evoke individual stories, from private voicemails left by people in the towers to the East Village's Ladder Company 3 fire truck, dispatched with 11 firefighters who died during the rescue effort. The Memorial Exhibition pays tribute to each victim with a portrait, bio and audio remembrances.

❤ One World Observatory
One World Trade Center, 285 Fulton Street, at Vesey & West Streets (1-844 696 1776, https:// oneworldobservatory.com). Subway A, C, 1, 2, 3 to Chambers Street; A, C, J, Z, 2, 3, 4, 5 to Fulton Street; E to World Trade Center; R, W to Cortlandt Street; 1 to WTC Cortlandt; 2, 3 to Park Place. Open hrs vary seasonally; usually 9am-9pm daily. Admission $35; $29-$33 reductions; free under-6s, 9/11 family members and 9/11 rescue and recovery workers. Map p71 E32.

Perched on floors 100 to 102 of the tallest skyscraper in the western hemisphere, One World Observatory has surpassed the Empire State Building as the highest observation deck in the city. Getting up there is an experience in itself – Sky Pod elevators, featuring a lightning-fast floor-to-ceiling simulation of New York City's development, whisk visitors to the top of the building in a mere minute. When you arrive on the 102nd floor, a high-tech two-minute video presentation whets your appetite for the main attraction before screens rise to reveal the panoramic view. Two levels down, those not prone to vertigo can step onto the Sky Portal, a 14ft-wide circular disc displaying an HD real-time image of the street below. On the middle level, a restaurant, casual café and bar let you relax and take in the incredible vistas over a snack, cocktails or a full meal.

Skyscraper Museum
39 Battery Place, between Little West Street & 1st Place (1-212 968 1961, www.skyscraper. org). Subway 4, 5 to Bowling Green. Open noon-6pm Wed-Sun. Admission $5; $2.50 reductions. Map p71 E34.

In contrast to its modest space, this unique institution explores high-rise buildings as objects of design, products of technology, real-estate investments and places of work and residence. With a mirrored ceiling giving the illusion of height, the single gallery is largely devoted to temporary exhibitions. A substantial chunk of the permanent collection relates to the World Trade Center,

including original models of the Twin Towers and 1 World Trade Center. Other highlights are large-scale photographs of lower Manhattan's skyscrapers from 1956, 1976 and 2004, and a 1931 silent film documenting the Empire State Building's construction.

▶ *For more on New York's skyscrapers, see p369 Race to the Top.*

Restaurants & cafés

❤ Hudson Eats $
Brookfield Place, 230 Vesey Street, between West Street & the Hudson River (1-212 978 1698, www.brookfieldplaceny.com). Subway A, C, 1, 2, 3 to Chambers Street; A, C, J, Z, 2, 3, 4, 5 to Fulton Street; E to World Trade Center; R, W to Cortlandt Street; 1 to WTC Cortlandt; 2, 3 to Park Place. Open 8am-9pm Mon-Sat; 8am-7pm Sun. Map p71 D32 ❹ *Eclectic*

Carved out from the second floor of a monster retail complex, the glossy, 600-seat dining terrace upgrades food-court schlock with white-marble counters, 17ft-high windows offering gobsmacking waterfront views and over 14 chef-driven kiosks, including branches of Mighty Quinn's (*see p128*) for Texas-meets-Carolina 'cue, Dos Toros for tacos and burritos, Num Pang for Cambodian sandwiches, and lox-and-bagel purveyor Black Seed (*see p102*).

Bars

❤ BlackTail
Pier A Harbor House, 22 Battery Place, between Little West Street & Hudson River Greenway (1-212 785 0153, www.blacktailnyc. com). Subway 4, 5 to Bowling Green. Open 5pm-2am daily. Map p71 E34 ❶

It's only a whiskey stone's throw away from the Dead Rabbit – Sean Muldoon and Jack McGarry's Irish tavern-style cocktail bar on Water Street – but the sequel from the renowned team couldn't be further away in terms of theme. Located inside the Pier A Harbor House complex, BlackTail channels Prohibition-era Cuba. A statue of Cuban lit hero José Martí stands at the bar, where the stools are modelled after those in Ernest Hemingway-frequented joints in balmy Havana, and the expansive menu is loaded with more than 40 cocktails – contemporary takes on drinks from the classic 1920s to '50s era. Cuban standards such as daiquiris and mojitos are made with the bar's proprietary 'Cuban Rum Blend' (Bacardi Heritage, Barbancourt White Rhum, Caña Brava and Banks 5 Island). Servers outfitted in straw fedoras and bright *guayaberas* weave between wicker chairs and potted palms with dishes such as a Cuban sandwich with braised pork.

Shops & services

Brookfield Place

*230 Vesey Street, between West Street &
the Hudson River (1-212 978 1673, www.
brookfieldplaceny.com). Subway A, C, 1, 2,
3 to Chambers Street; A, C, J, Z, 2, 3, 4, 5 to
Fulton Street; E to World Trade Center; R, W
to Cortlandt Street; 1 to WTC Cortlandt; 2,
3 to Park Place.* **Open** *10am-8pm Mon-Sat;
noon-6pm Sun (hrs vary for some shops and
restaurants).* **Map** *p71 D32* ❸ *Mall*

Directly across West Street from the World
Trade Center, this sprawling office, retail and
dining complex has the distinction of being
the only mall with a view of the Statue of
Liberty. Anchored by a men's outpost of Saks
Fifth Avenue, it caters to the WTC's stylish
tenants (the likes of Condé Nast) with a mix
of luxe designer names such as Gucci, Bottega
Veneta and Burberry, contemporary fashion
brands including Bonobos and Vince, plus
cool Tribeca-born kids' shop Babesta and a
30,000sq ft French-food market, Le District.
Refuelling options include chic food court
Hudson Eats (*see p79*). Brookfield Place also
hosts numerous free arts events in its Winter
Garden atrium and waterfront plaza (see
online calendar), which overlooks a marina.

♥ Century 21

*22 Cortlandt Street, between Broadway &
Church Street (1-212 227 9092, www.c21stores.
com). Subway A, C, J, Z, 2, 3, 4, 5 to Fulton Street;
E to World Trade Center; R, W to Cortlandt
Street; 1 to WTC Cortlandt.* **Open** *7.45am-9pm
Mon-Wed; 7.45am-9.30pm Thur, Fri; 10am-9pm
Sat; 11am-8pm Sun.* **Map** *p71 E32* ❹ *Fashion*

An Alexander McQueen shirt for less than
$100? Jimmy Choo flats for $172? No, you're
not dreaming – you're shopping at Century
21. You may have to rummage to unearth a
treasure, but with savings of up to 65% off
regular prices, it's worth it. In our experience,
the smaller, more upscale, less chaotic Upper
West Side location doesn't yield as many
steals as the original. **Other locations** 1972
Broadway, between 66th & 67th Streets,
Upper West Side (1-212 518 2121); 472 86th
Street, between Fourth & Fifth Avenues, Bay
Ridge, Brooklyn (1-718 748 3266); 445 Albee
Square, between Willoughby & Gold Streets,
Downtown Brooklyn (1-718 246 2121).

Westfield World Trade Center

*185 Greenwich Street, between Dey & Fulton
Streets (1-212 284 9982, www.westfield.com).
Subway A, C, 1, 2, 3 to Chambers Street; A, C, J,
Z, 2, 3, 4, 5 to Fulton Street; E to World Trade
Center; R, W to Cortlandt Street; 1 to WTC
Cortlandt; 2, 3 to Park Place.* **Open** *10am-8pm
Mon-Sat; 11am-7pm Sun (hrs vary for some
shops and restaurants).* **Map** *p71 E32* ❺ *Mall*

This sprawling shopping complex contains
stores around the perimeter of the Oculus, the
dramatic, light-suffused main hall of Santiago
Calatrava's Transportation Hub, and adjacent
concourses, plus other World Trade Center
towers. The list of shops and restaurants
includes a two-level Apple Store in the
Oculus, fashion from John Varvatos, Kate
Spade and COS, and beauty brands Aesop and
Kiehl's. At 4 World Trade Center, the second
NYC location of Italian food mecca, Eataly
(*see p169*), has a massive in-house bakery
and several eateries serving regional cuisine,
pizza and pasta. Some tables directly overlook
the 9/11 Memorial.

SOUTH STREET SEAPORT

▶ *Subway A, C, J, Z, 2, 3, 4, 5 to Fulton Street.*

New York's fortunes originally rolled in on
the swells that crashed into its harbour. The
city was perfectly situated for trade
with Europe and, after 1825, goods from
the Western Territories arrived via the
Erie Canal and the Hudson River. By 1892,
New York was also the point of entry for
millions of immigrants. The **South Street
Seaport** is the best place to appreciate this
port heritage.

If you enter the Seaport area from Water
Street, the first thing you're likely to spot
is the whitewashed **Titanic Memorial
Lighthouse**. It was originally erected on top
of the Seaman's Church Institute (Coenties
Slip & South Street) in 1913, the year after the
great ship sank, but was moved to its current
location at the intersection of Pearl and
Fulton Streets in 1976.

When New York's role as a vital shipping
hub diminished during the 20th century,
the South Street Seaport area fell into disuse,
but a massive redevelopment project in
the mid 1980s saw old buildings converted
into restaurants, bars, chain stores and the
South Street Seaport Museum. The area
took a battering from Hurricane Sandy in
2012, but a subsequent revitalisation plan
has restored the Fulton Market building,
now home to a luxurious iPic cinema and
an outpost of Milan concept store 10 Corso
Como. Other designer shops, including a
flagship for Sarah Jessica Parker's shoe line
SJP, and a Big Gay Ice Cream Shop (*see p125*)
are also populating the area.

Pier 17 once supported the famous
Fulton Fish Market. However, the market
relocated to Hunts Point in the Bronx in
2005. Its former home, the early-20th-
century Tin Building, is being converted
into a food hall helmed by prominent
chef Jean-Georges Vongerichten. The
pier's 1980s mall has been replaced with
a glassy complex housing restaurants by

10 Corso Como New York *p82*

Vongerichten and other buzzed-about chefs such as David Chang and Andrew Carmellini, opening as this guide went to press. An expansive rooftop space with views of iconic landmarks such as the Statue of Liberty hosts a hip summer concert series and an ice-skating rink in winter. Below it, the Heineken Riverdeck has a drinks kiosk and seats facing the dramatic spans of the Brooklyn and Manhattan Bridges. The South Street Seaport Museum's historic ships are docked at Pier 16. Nearby, **Pier 15** has been transformed into a bi-level lounging space, comprising a lawned viewing deck above the **Watermark**, a stylish glass-enclosed bar.

tours of the 1907 lightship *Ambrose* and the 19th-century cargo ship *Wavertree*. From late May through October, visitors can book excursions in New York Harbor on the 1885 schooner Pioneer and the WO Decker, a locally built 1930 tugboat (see website for prices and schedule). The museum also encompasses Bowne & Co, a printing business established in the Seaport in 1775. An ongoing exhibition at the print shop (209 Water Street) traces the importance of the industry in the former maritime hub and includes printing demos using a 19th-century iron hand press. Next door is the museum's gift shop, Bowne & Co Stationers, *see p82*.

Sights & museums

South Street Seaport Museum
12 Fulton Street, between South & Water Streets (1-212 748 8600, https:// southstreetseaportmuseum.org). Subway A, C, J, Z, 2, 3, 4, 5 to Fulton Street. **Open** *11am-5pm Wed-Sun.* **Admission** *$20; $14 reductions; free under-8s.* **Map** *p71 F32.*

Founded in 1967, the South Street Seaport Museum celebrates the maritime history of New York City's 19th-century waterfront. In addition to rotating exhibitions, the institution has a fleet of historic vessels at Pier 16. The admission price includes

Restaurants & cafés

Barbalu $$
225-227 Front Street, between Beekman Street & Peck Slip (1-646 918 6565, www. barbalu.com). Subway A, C, J, Z, 2, 3, 4, 5 to Fulton Street. **Open** *11am-10.30pm Mon-Thur; 11am-11pm Fri, Sat; 11am-10pm Sun.* **Map** *p71 F32* ❷ *Italian*

After their restaurant, Barbarini Alimentari, was destroyed by Hurricane Sandy, husband-and-wife owners Stefano Barbagallo and Adriana Luque opened this contemporary-rustic Italian eatery at the same location. In the spacious bar area, you can order charcuterie and cheese plates to accompany the Italian wine. Slide into a brown banquette in the skylighted dining room for classics such as mozzarella-and-eggplant caponatina, black linguine with shrimp and tomatoes, and chocolate and almond cake.

♥ Jack's Stir Brew Coffee $

*222 Front Street, between Beekman Street & Peck Slip (1-212 227 7631, www.jacksstirbrew. com). Subway A, C, J, Z, 2, 3, 4, 5 to Fulton Street. **Open** 7.30am-5pm Mon-Fri; 8am-5pm Sat, Sun. **Map** p71 F32* ⑤ *Café*

Java fiends convene at this award-winning caffeine spot that offers organic, shade-grown beans and a homey vibe. Coffee is served by espresso artisans with a knack for oddball concoctions, such as the super-silky Mountie latte, infused with maple syrup. **Other locations** throughout the city.

Bars

Watermark

*Pier 15, between Fletcher Street & Maiden Lane (1-212 742 8200, www.watermarkny. com). Subway A, C, J, Z, 2, 3, 4, 5 to Fulton Street; 2, 3 to Wall Street. **Open** Apr-Nov noon-10pm Mon-Wed, Sun; noon-11pm Thur-Sat. Closed Dec-Mar. **Map** p71 F33* ③

Sip beer or cocktails accompanied by casual bites such as guacamole and burgers at this contemporary waterfront bar – the skyline views through the floor-to-ceiling windows are spectacular.

Shops & services

♥ 10 Corso Como New York

*1 Fulton Street, at Front Street (1-212 265 9500, www.10corsocomo.nyc). Subway A, C, J, Z, 2, 3, 4, 5 to Fulton Street. **Open** Store 11am-7pm Mon-Sat (extended hrs in summer); noon-6pm Sun. Restaurant 11.30am-9pm Mon; 11.30am-10pm Tue-Fri; 11am-10pm Sat; 11am-9pm Sun. **Map** p71 F32* ❶ *Fashion & homewares*

The arrival of 10 Corso Como New York, an outpost of fashion editor and gallerist Carla Sozzani's pioneering Milan concept store, is one of the clearest signals of the Seaport's evolution from tourist trap to stylish retail and dining district. The sprawling space also houses a contemporary Italian restaurant and a gallery, but the eye-catching retail displays have the feel of an art exhibition. Browse designer clothing and accessories by international avant-garde heavyweights such as Azzedine Alaïa, Comme des Garçons, Junya Watanabe and Maison Margiela, alongside rising NYC fashion-scene names such as Sies Marjan and Eckhaus Latta.

Homewares include iconic Memphis design pieces, while cult beauty and fragrances from around the world and art books round out the stock. Pop-ups and limited-edition collaborations ensure an ever-changing selection, and the store's signature logo adorns everything from disposable lighters to Birkenstocks.

♥ Bowne & Co Stationers

*211 Water Street, between Fulton & Beekman Streets (1-646 315 4478). Subway A, C, J, Z, 2, 3, 4, 5 to Fulton Street. **Open** 11am-7pm daily. **Map** p71 F32* ❷ *Gifts & stationery*

The South Street Seaport Museum's quaint gift shop sits next door to a recreation of a historic letterpress printer, where small-batch jobs are hand-set using some of the museum's collection of more than 30 19th- and early 20th-century presses. At both locations, you can buy cards and prints turned out on the premises, featuring images such as the museum's ships or an 1835 map of lower Manhattan. The old-fashioned shop displays an eclectic jumble of stationery and knick-knacks, such as journals, books, rubber stamps, magnets and tote bags.

CIVIC CENTER & CITY HALL PARK

▶ *Subway J, Z to Chambers Street; R, W to City Hall; 2, 3 to Park Place; 4, 5, 6 to Brooklyn Bridge-City Hall.*

The business of running New York takes place in the grand buildings in and around **City Hall Park**, an area that formed the budding city's northern boundary in the 1700s.

At the park's southern end, a granite 'time wheel' tracks its history. In the opposite section, **City Hall** houses the mayor's office and the chambers of the City Council. When City Hall was completed in 1812, its architects were so confident that the city would grow no further north that they didn't bother to put any marble on its northern side. Nevertheless, the building is a beautiful blend of Federalist form and French

> **In the know**
> **The ghost subway station**
>
> If you take the 6 train to its last downtown stop, Brooklyn Bridge-City Hall, ignore the recorded instructions to get off. Stay aboard while the train makes its U-turn loop before heading uptown and you'll get a glimpse of the original 1904 City Hall Station (out of use since 1945) and its brass chandeliers, vaulted ceilings, tile mosaics and skylights.

Renaissance detail. Overlooking the park from the west is Cass Gilbert's **Woolworth Building** (233 Broadway, between Barclay Street & Park Place), the tallest building in the world when it opened in 1913. The neo-Gothic skyscraper's grand spires, gargoyles, vaulted ceilings and church-like interior earned it the moniker 'the Cathedral of Commerce'.

Behind City Hall, on Chambers Street, is the 1872 Old New York County Courthouse; it's popularly known as the **Tweed Courthouse**, after William 'Boss' Tweed (*see p357*), leader of the political machine Tammany Hall, who pocketed some $10 million of the building's $14 million construction budget. What he didn't steal bought a beautiful edifice, with exquisite Italianate detailing. These days, it houses the city's Department of Education and a New York City public school. To the east, other civic offices and services occupy the one million square feet of office space in the 1914 **Manhattan Municipal Building** at 1 Centre Street. This landmark limestone structure, built by McKim, Mead & White, also contains New York City's official gift shop, **CityStore** (www.nyc.gov/citystore, closed Sat, Sun).

The houses of crime and punishment are located in the **Civic Center**, near Foley Square, once the site of the city's most notorious 19th-century slum, Five Points. These days, you'll find the State Supreme Court in the **New York County Courthouse** (60 Centre Street, at Pearl Street), a hexagonal Roman Revival building; the rotunda is decorated with a mural called *Law Through the Ages*. The **Thurgood Marshall United States Courthouse** (40 Centre Street on Foley Square, between Duane & Pearl Streets) is a Corinthian temple crowned with a golden pyramid.

A couple of blocks from the imposing art deco **Criminal Courts Building** (100 Centre Street, between Leonard & White Streets), the **Manhattan Detention Complex** (125 White Street, between Centre & Baxter Streets) is known as 'the Tombs'. Nearby, the **African Burial Ground** was officially designated a National Monument in 2006.

Sights & museums

African Burial Ground National Monument
Visitor centre: 290 Broadway, between Duane & Reade Streets (1-212 637 2019, www.nps. gov/afbg). Subway J, Z to Chambers Street; R, W to City Hall; 4, 5, 6 to Brooklyn Bridge-City Hall. Open Apr-Oct 10am-4pm Tue-Sat (weather permitting). Closed Nov-Mar. Visitor centre year-round 10am-4pm Tue-Sat. Admission free. Map p71 E31.

The African Burial Ground is a small remnant of a 6.6-acre unmarked gravesite where between 10,000 and 20,000 enslaved and free Africans were buried. The burial ground, which closed in 1794, was unearthed during the construction of a federal office building in 1991 and later designated a National Monument. In 2007, a stone memorial, designed by architect Rodney Leon, was erected; the tall, curved structure draws heavily on African architecture and contains a spiral path leading to an ancestral chamber.

City Hall
City Hall Park, from Vesey to Chambers Streets, between Broadway & Park Row (no phone, www.nyc.gov/cityhalltours). Subway J, Z to Chambers Street; R, W to City Hall; 2, 3 to Park Place; 4, 5, 6 to Brooklyn Bridge-City Hall. Open Tours (individuals) noon Wed, 10am Thur; (groups) 10.30am Mon, Tue. Reservations required. Admission free. Map p71 E32.

Designed by French émigré Joseph François Mangin and John McComb Jr, the fine, Federal-style City Hall was completed in 1812. Tours take in the rotunda, with its splendid coffered dome, the City Council Chamber and the Governor's Room, with its collection of American 19th-century political portraits and historic furnishings (including George Washington's desk). Tours must be booked in advance on the website.

Restaurants & cafés

Temple Court $$$
5 Beekman Street, between Naussau Street & Theatre Alley (1-212 658 1848, www. templecourtnyc.com). Subway A, C, J, Z, 2, 3, 4, 5 to Fulton Street; J, Z to Chambers Street; 4, 5, 6 to Brooklyn Bridge-City Hall. Open 6.30-11am, noon-3pm, 6-10pm Mon-Fri; 6.30am-4pm, 6-10pm Sat, Sun. Bar 6.30am-midnight Mon-Thur, Sun; 6.30am-1am Fri, Sat. Map p71 E32 ❼
American

Helmed by prominent chef Tom Colicchio, Temple Court is less fanciful and luminous than Augustine, its French-accented neighbour on the other side of the Beekman Hotel's grand atrium. But it's visually impressive nonetheless (and has better food). The handsome brick-walled room is fitted with mohair-velvet banquettes, stained-glass wall panels and large custom chandeliers. The kitchen doesn't employ any highfalutin theatrics. Instead it offers polished, straightforward, seasonal American food that's informed by the past but without any schmaltzy kitsch, such as lamb wellington or rabbit schnitzel.

Soho & Tribeca

In the 1960s and '70s, artists colonised what had become a post-industrial wasteland south of Houston Street, squatting in abandoned warehouses. Eventually, they worked with the city to rezone and restore them. Others followed suit in the Triangle Below Canal, which was once the site of the city's main produce market.

Today, many of the area's well-preserved factory buildings are occupied by designer stores and high-end restaurants, and those once-spartan loft spaces are among the most desirable real estate in the city. But you can still find pockets of experimental culture in this consumer paradise, in the form of scattered art galleries and Off-Off Broadway theatres.

♥ **Don't miss**

1 Drawing Center *p86*
Pushing the medium's boundaries.

2 Mmuseumm *p93*
A mini masterpiece.

3 Film Forum *p296*
For serious cinephiles.

4 Soho Rep *p347*
Audacious Off Broadway theatre.

STOP

Staple Street, Tribeca

SOHO

▶Subway A, C, E, 1 to Canal Street; C, E, 6 to Spring Street; R, W to Prince Street; 1 to Houston Street.

Now a retail mecca, Soho was once a hardscrabble manufacturing zone with the derisive nickname 'Hell's Hundred Acres'. In the 1960s, it was earmarked for destruction by over-zealous urban planner Robert Moses, but its signature cast-iron warehouses were saved by the artists who inhabited them as cheap live-work spaces. The **King** and **Queen of Greene Street** (respectively, 72-76 Greene Street, between Broome & Spring Streets, and 28-30 Greene Street, between Canal & Grand Streets) are both fine examples of the area's beloved architectural landmarks. The most celebrated of Soho's cast-iron edifices, however, is the five-storey **Haughwout Building**, at 488-492 Broadway, at Broome Street. Designed in 1857, it featured the world's first hydraulic lift.

After landlords sniffed the potential for profits in converting old loft buildings, Soho morphed into a playground for the young, beautiful and rich. It can still be a pleasure to stroll around the cobblestoned side streets, and there are some standout shops in the area, but the large chain stores and sidewalk-encroaching street vendors along Broadway create a shopping-mall-at-Christmas crush on weekends. Although many of the galleries that made Soho an art capital in the 1970s and '80s decamped to Chelsea and the Lower East Side, a few excellent art spaces remain, including the expanded **Drawing Center**.

Sights & museums

♥ Drawing Center

35 Wooster Street, between Broome & Grand Streets (1-212 219 2166, www.drawingcenter. org). Subway A, C, E, 1 to Canal Street. **Open** *noon-6pm Wed, Fri-Sun; noon-8pm Thur.* **Admission** *$5; $3 reductions; free under-12s. Free 6-8pm Thur. Map p87 E30.*

Established in 1977, the Drawing Center showcases the broadly defined art form in its three galleries. The non-profit standout assembles shows of museum-calibre legends such as Philip Guston, James Ensor and Willem de Kooning, but also 'Selections' surveys of newcomers. Art stars such as Kara Walker and Chris Ofili received some of their earliest NYC exposure here.

New York City Fire Museum

278 Spring Street, between Hudson & Varick Streets (1-212 691 1303, www.nycfiremuseum. org). Subway C, E to Spring Street; 1 to Houston Street. **Open** *10am-5pm daily.* **Admission** *$10; $5-$8 reductions. Map p87 D30.*

An active firehouse from 1905 to 1959, this museum is filled with all manner of life-saving gadgetry, from late 18th-century hand-pumped fire engines to present-day equipment.

The New York Earth Room & The Broken Kilometer

The New York Earth Room 141 Wooster Street, between Prince & Houston Streets. The Broken Kilometer 393 West Broadway, between Broome & Spring Streets. (Both 1-212 989 5566, www.diaart.org.) Subway C, E to Spring Street. **Open** *early Sept-early June noon-3pm, 3.30-6pm Wed-Sun.* **Admission** *free. Map p87 E29 & E30.*

♥ Time to eat & drink

Buzzy brunch
Jack's Wife Freda *p89*

Mid-shopping pastries
Dominique Ansel Bakery *p90*

Old-school French dining
Le Coucou *p88*,
Frenchette *p93*

Updated American classics
The Dutch *p88*

Intimate nightcap
Pegu Club *p89*,
Weather Up *p95*

♥ Time to shop

Eclectic 'It' labels
American Two Shot *p90*,
Opening Ceremony *p91*

Effortlessly cool womenswear
Nili Lotan *p95*, Rachel Comey *p92*

An NYC design duo's flagship
Roman and Williams Guild *p92*

Unique denim
3x1 *p90*

Greene Street

SOHO & TRIBECA

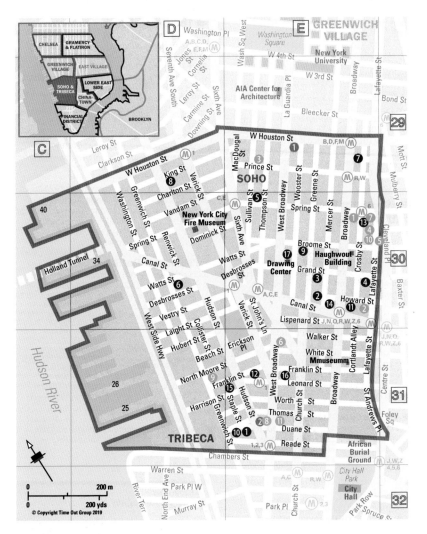

SOHO & TRIBECA

Restaurants & cafés

1. Balthazar *p88*
2. Le Coucou *p88*
3. The Dutch *p88*
4. Ed's Lobster Bar *p88*
5. La Esquina *p89*
6. Frenchette *p93*
7. Jack's Wife Freda *p89*
8. Khe-Yo *p93*
9. Locanda Verde *p94*
10. Osteria Morini *p89*
11. Tiny's and the Bar Upstairs *p94*

Bars

1. Pegu Club *p89*
2. Weather Up *p95*

Shops & services

1. 180 The Store *p95*
2. 3x1 *p90*
3. Alexander Wang *p90*
4. American Two Shot *p90*
5. Dominique Ansel Bakery *p90*
6. La Garçonne *p95*
7. Housing Works Bookstore Cafe *p91*
8. Jacques Torres Chocolate *p91*
9. Kirna Zabête *p91*
10. Nili Lotan *p95*
11. Opening Ceremony *p91*
12. Patron of the New *p95*
13. Rachel Comey *p92*
14. Roman and Williams Guild *p92*
15. Shinola *p95*
16. Steven Alan *p95*
17. What Goes Around Comes Around *p92*

The spirit of Soho before hedge-fund managers and pop stars chased the artists out is preserved in these two installations by the renowned American sculptor Walter De Maria, both of which have been lovingly attended to by the Dia Art Foundation since the late 1970s. *The New York Earth Room* is exactly what it sounds like – a 3,600-square-foot room covered in almost two feet of rich topsoil – while *The Broken Kilometer* consists of five rows of 100 polished brass rods, which would cover the titular distance if all 500 segments were placed end to end. They're testaments to a time when Soho was still a frontier, and art provided the wide open spaces.

Restaurants & cafés

Balthazar $$$
80 Spring Street, between Broadway & Crosby Street (1-212 965 1414, www.balthazarny. com). Subway R to Prince Street; 6 to Spring Street. Open 7.30-11.30am, noon-midnight Mon-Thur; 7.30-11.30am, noon-1am Fri; 8am-4pm, 5.30pm-1am Sat; 8am-4pm, 5.30pm-midnight Sun. Map p87 E30 ❶
French

At dinner, this iconic eatery is perennially packed with rail-thin lookers dressed to the nines. But it's more than simply fashionable – the kitchen rarely makes a false move and the service is surprisingly friendly. The four-tiered seafood platter casts an impressive shadow, and the roast chicken with garlic mashed potatoes for two is *délicieux*.

♥ Le Coucou $$$
138 Lafayette Street, between Canal & Howard Streets (1-212 271 4252, www. lecoucou.com). Subway J, N, Q, R, Z, 6 to Canal Street. Open 7-10.30am, 11.30am-2pm, 5-11pm Mon-Fri; 7-10am,11am-2pm, 5-11pm Sat; 7-10am, 11am-2pm, 5-10pm Sun. Map p87 E30 ❷ *French*

With its vaulted ceilings, hand-blown chandeliers, gold-trimmed plates and 12-inch candles set at each table, the lively stateside debut of lauded Chicago-born chef Daniel Rose is more luxurious than his Parisian flagship, Spring. That's the handiwork of the Roman and Williams design company's power couple, Robin Standefer and Stephen Alesch, who created a dreamy, grown-up dining room. Borrowing from Gallic restaurants of years past, particularly long-gone fine-dining great Lutèce, Rose is less concerned with tweaking French classics (which won him praise in Paris) than with cooking the rich-sauced fare outright: sweetbreads spooned with *crème de tomate*; airy pike quenelles in frothy sauce *américaine*; and halibut bathed in *beurre blanc*.

♥ The Dutch $$$
131 Sullivan Street, at Prince Street (1-212 677 6200, www.thedutchnyc.com). Subway C, E to Spring Street. Open 11.30am-3pm, 5.30-11pm Mon-Thur; 11.30am-3pm, 5.30-11.30pm Fri; 10am-3pm, 5.30-11.30pm Sat; 10am-3pm, 5.30-11pm Sun. Map p87 E29 ❸ *American*

From the moment it opened, Andrew Carmellini's rollicking Soho eaterie seemed destined to join the ranks of neighbourhood classics. The virtuoso chef offers diners an exuberant gastro-tour of the American melting pot, including mini fried-oyster sandwiches on house-made buns and superb dry-aged steaks. That everything tastes good and somehow works well together explains why reservations are hard to come by. Wait for your table in the airy oak bar (with adjacent oyster room) with one of the extensive selection of American whiskeys.

Ed's Lobster Bar $$
222 Lafayette Street, between Kenmare & Spring Streets (1-212 343 3236, www. lobsterbarnyc.com). Subway 6 to Spring Street. Open 11.45am-10.30pm Mon-Thur; 11.45am-11.30pm Fri; 11am-11.30pm Sat; noon-9.30pm Sun. Map p87 E30 ❹ *Seafood*

If you secure a place at the 25-seat marble seafood bar or one of the few tables in the narrow, whitewashed space, expect superlative raw-bar eats, delicately fried clams and lobster served every which way: steamed, grilled, broiled, stuffed into a pie and – the crowd favourite – the lobster roll. Here, it's a buttered bun stuffed with premium chunks of meat and a light coating of mayo.

In the know
Soho's Italian legacy

Just west of West Broadway, tenement- and townhouse-lined streets contain remnants of the Italian community that once dominated the area, such as **St Anthony of Padua Roman Catholic Church** (154 Sullivan Street, at Houston Street), dedicated in 1888. You'll still find old-school neighbourhood flavour at **Pino's Prime Meat Market** (149 Sullivan Street, between Houston & Prince Streets, 1-212 475 8134, closed Sun). The iconic Vesuvio Bakery is now occupied by **Birdbath Neighborhood Green Bakery** (160 Prince Street, between Thompson Street & West Broadway, 1-646 556 7720, www.thecitybakery.com), which has kept the old-fashioned façade intact.

Le Coucou

La Esquina $-$$

114 Kenmare Street, between Cleveland Place & Lafayette Street (1-646 613 7100, www. esquinanyc.com). Subway 6 to Spring Street. **Open** *Taqueria 11am-1am Mon-Thur, Sun; 11am-1.30am Fri, Sat. Café noon-1am Mon-Fri; 11am-1am Sat, Sun. Restaurant 6pm-2am daily.* **Map** *p87 E30* ⑤ *Mexican*

La Esquina comprises three dining and drinking areas: first, a street-level taqueria, serving a short-order menu of tacos and Mexican *tortas*. Round the corner is a 30-seat café, its shelves stocked with books and old vinyl. Lastly, there's a dungeonesque restaurant and lounge accessible through a back door of the taqueria (by reservation only). It's worth planning ahead: a world of Mexican murals, fine tequilas, chicken mole enchiladas and grilled octopus *tostadas* awaits.

❤ Jack's Wife Freda $$

224 Lafayette Street, between Kenmare & Spring Streets (1-212 510 8550, www. jackswifefreda.com). Subway 6 to Spring Street. **Open** *8.30am-11pm Mon-Wed; 8.30am-midnight Thur-Sat; 8.30am-10pm Sun.* **Map** *p87 E30* ⑦ *Café*

Keith McNally protégé Dean Jankelowitz (Balthazar, Schiller's Liquor Bar) helms this charming café. Decked out with dark-green leather banquettes, brass railings and marble counters, the classic yet cosy spot serves homey fare such as Jankelowitz's grandmother's matzo ball soup made with duck fat, or skirt steak sandwich with hand-cut fries. In a prime shopping area, between Soho and Nolita, it's also a great brunch spot. **Other location** 50

Carmine Street, between Bedford & Bleecker Streets, West Village (1-646 669 9888); 116 Eighth Avenue, between W 15th & 16th Streets, Chelsea (1-646 454 9045).

Osteria Morini $$$

218 Lafayette Street, between Broome & Spring Streets (1-212 965 8777, www. osteriamorini.com). Subway 6 to Spring Street. **Open** *noon-11pm Mon; noon-10.30pm Tue-Thur; noon-11.30pm Fri; 11.30am-11.30pm Sat; 11.30am-10pm Sun.* **Map** *p87 E30* ⑩ *Italian*

Michael White has several successful restaurants in the city (and beyond), and this terrific downtown homage to a classic Bolognese *trattoria* is among his most accessible. White spent seven years cooking in Italy's Emilia-Romagna region, and his connection to the area surfaces in the restaurant's rustic food. Handmade pastas are fantastic across the board, while superb meat dishes might include porchetta with crisp, crackling skin and potatoes bathed in pan drippings.

Bars

❤ Pegu Club

2nd Floor, 77 W Houston Street, at West Broadway (1-212 473 7348, www.peguclub. com). Subway B, D, F, M to Broadway-Lafayette Street; R, W to Prince Street. **Open** *5pm-2am Mon-Thur, Sun; 5pm-4am Fri, Sat.* **Map** *p87 E29* ①

It's easy to miss the discreet entrance of this bar, which was inspired by a British officers' club in Burma. Once you've found it, you'll be glad you persevered. The sophisticated second-floor destination, helmed by cocktail maven Audrey Saunders, focuses on classics culled from decades-old booze bibles. Gin is the key ingredient – these are serious drinks for grown-up tastes.

Shops & services

Soho's converted warehouses are packed with just about every major fashion brand you can think of, from budget and mid-priced international chains such as H&M and COS to contemporary stars **Alexander Wang** and **Rachel Comey**, and A-list designer labels like Balenciaga, Chanel and Prada, plus stores selling home goods, cosmetics, food and more. Listed below is a selection of our favourite independent shops.

❤ 3x1

15 Mercer Street, between Howard & Grand Streets (1-212 391 6969, www.3x1.us). Subway A, C, E, J, N, Q, R, Z, 1, 6 to Canal Street. **Open** *11am-7pm Mon-Sat; noon-6pm Sun.* **Map** *p87 E30* ❷ *Fashion*

Featuring a wall of fabric samples, some of them extremely rare, and an on-site studio separated by glass, 3x1 is a temple for denim worshippers, creating limited-edition styles sewn in the store. Designer Scott Morrison, who previously launched Paper Denim & Cloth and Earnest Sewn, fills the large, gallery-like space with a variety of jeans (prices start at around $200 for women, $245 for men) and other denim pieces such as shorts and rompers. Or go for the ultimate splurge with a bespoke pair of jeans.

Alexander Wang

103 Grand Street, between Greene & Mercer Streets (1-212 977 9683, www.alexanderwang. com). Subway J, N, Q, R, Z, 6 to Canal Street. **Open** *11am-7pm Mon-Sat; noon-6pm Sun.* **Map** *p87 E30* ❸ *Fashion*

Anna Wintour-approved designer Alexander Wang has amassed a cult-like following of vogueish downtown types. He launched his eponymous line in 2007, and was propelled to fashion royalty in 2008, after scoring a Council of Fashion Designers of America award. With chalky-white marble display pedestals and overstuffed leather couches, his luxurious and spacious flagship boutique offers the wunderkind's chic-but-casual men's and women's clothing, handbags and showstopping shoes, plus the lower-priced T by Alexander Wang line.

❤ American Two Shot

135 Grand Street, between Crosby & Lafayette Streets (1-212 925 3403, www. americantwoshot.com). Subway J, N, Q, R, Z, 6 to Canal Street. **Open** *11am-7.30pm Mon-Fri; 11am-7pm Sat; noon-6pm Sun.* **Map** *p87 E30* ❹ *Fashion*

A whitewashed brick wall, neon signs and a retro collage create a cool, DIY aesthetic in this laid-back boutique for men and women owned by pals Stephanie Krasnoff and Olivia Wolfe. On the racks are indie NYC and international labels such as Chinatown Market, Lazy Oaf and Rachel Antonoff (who happens to be a friend of *Girls'* Lena Dunham), plus '90s- and early-2000s-focused vintage clothing courtesy of Babemania (www.babemania.nyc). An array of cards and small gift items at the front of the store contributes to the eclectic vibe, and you can hang out over organic juices and snacks from Brooklyn's Grass Roots Juicery.

❤ Dominique Ansel Bakery

189 Spring Street, between Sullivan & Thompson Streets (1-212 219 2773, www. dominiqueansel.com). Subway C, E to Spring Street. **Open** *8am-7pm Mon-Sat; 9am-7pm Sun.* **Map** *p87 E30* ❺ *Food & drink*

Dominique Ansel honed his skills as executive pastry chef at Daniel for six years before opening this innovative patisserie. In 2013, his croissant-doughnut hybrid, the Cronut, created a frenzy in foodie circles and put his ingenious creations into the spotlight. If you can't get your hands on a Cronut, which sell out early, try the DKA – a caramelised, flaky take on the croissant-like Breton speciality *kouign amann*. And his cotton-soft mini cheesecake, an ethereally light gâteau with a brûléed top, leaves the dense old New York classic sputtering in its dust.

▶ For the dessert wizard's latest venture, see p144.

In the know
Neighbourhood portmanteaus

Soho and Tribeca are early examples of an NYC phenom: catchy, contracted neighbourhood names largely driven by real estate agents trying to generate buzz. Recent inventions include NoMad (North of Madison Square Park), Dumbo (Down Under the Manhattan Bridge Overpass) and even Rambo (Right Around the Manhattan Bridge Overpass).

Housing Works Bookstore Cafe

126 Crosby Street, between Houston & Prince Streets (1-212 334 3324, www.housingworks. org). Subway B, D, F, M to Broadway-Lafayette Street; R, W to Prince Street; 6 to Bleecker Street. Open 9am-9pm Mon-Fri; 10am-5pm Sat, Sun. Map p87 E29 **7** *Books*

This popular two-level store – which stocks literary fiction, non-fiction, rare books and collectibles – is also a peaceful spot for a coffee (or wine) break. All proceeds go to providing support services for people living with HIV/AIDS. Emerging writers and the literati take the mic at the regular readings.

Jacques Torres Chocolate

350 Hudson Street, between Charlton & King Streets, entrance on King Street (1-212 414 2462, www.mrchocolate.com). Subway 1 to Houston Street. Open 8.30am-7pm Mon-Fri; 10am-7pm Sat; 10.30am-5pm Sun. Map p87 D29 **8** *Food & drink*

Jacques Torres's Hudson Street flagship sells assortments, truffles and bars, plus more unusual delicacies such as chocolate-covered Cheerios and blueberries, made by hand from raw cocoa beans at his Brooklyn factory. The shop has plenty of seating for enjoying other rich treats, such as chocolate-chip cookies and steamed-to-order hot chocolate. **Other locations** throughout the city.

Kirna Zabête

477 Broome Street, between Greene & Wooster Streets (1-212 941 9656, www.kirnazabete. com). Subway R, W to Prince Street; 6 to Spring Street. Open 11am-7pm Mon-Sat; noon-6pm Sun. Map p87 E30 **9** *Fashion*

Former fashion editor Beth Buccini showcases around 100 labels in her 10,000sq ft boutique. Although the stock leans towards pricey designer wares – Euro heavyweights such as Alaïa, Gucci, Saint Laurent and Valentino, new American classics including Proenza Schouler and Altuzarra, plus newer names like New York-based Rosie Assoulin and Monse – this is no hushed fashion temple. The playful, colourful interior is decorated with six-foot wooden 'chandeliers', black-and-white striped hardwood floors and neon signs displaying quirky mantras, including 'Life is short, buy the shoes'. Unusual jewellery and accessories, plus coffee-table books, stationery and novelties provide plenty of scope for style-minded gifts.

♥ Opening Ceremony

33-35 Howard Street, between Broadway & Lafayette Street (1-212 219 2688, www. openingceremony.com). Subway J, N, Q, R, Z, 6 to Canal Street. Open 11am-8pm Mon-Sat; noon-7pm Sun. Map p87 E30 **11** *Fashion*

The Olympics-referencing name reflects Opening Ceremony's multinational approach

Kirna Zabête

to fashion. The mega-concept store sprawls over two storefronts and four floors, with eye-catching installations and eclectic stock. The constantly rotating mix of labels veers from experimental to refined, and under-the-radar to iconic. You'll find the popular Opening Ceremony collection, including its limited-edition collaborations with other brands, and big names such as Kenzo and Vans, but also some you might not recognise – for example, Adam Selman, who created sensational outfits for Rihanna before launching his own line; HVN, a line of vintage-looking print dresses designed by DJ Harley Viera-Newton, and Lorod, a classics-inspired brand. Cult shoes and accessories bump up the browse factor.

▶ *There's an additional OC outpost at the Ace Hotel, see p379.*

❤ Rachel Comey

95 Crosby Street, between Prince & Spring Streets, 1-212 334 0455, www.rachelcomey. com). Subway R, W to Prince Street; 6 to Spring Street. **Open** *11am-7pm Mon-Sat; noon-6pm Sun.* **Map** *p87 E30* **⓭** *Fashion*

A certain arty, indie sensibility in this NYC designer's output can be traced to her fine arts background and a stint creating stage gear for downtown bands. Comey has amassed a devoted following, and fans flock to this Soho flagship in a strikingly renovated former mechanic's garage. The store showcases the complete collection of vintage-inspired women's clothing and the hugely popular footwear.

❤ Roman and Williams Guild

53 Howard Street, at Mercer Street (1-212 852 9099, www.rwguild.com). Subway J, N, Q, R, Z, 6 to Canal Street. **Open** *10am-7pm daily.* **Map** *p87 E30* **⓮** *Homewares*

If you're smitten by the decor at some of the city's most fashionable restaurants and hotels, such as Le Coucou and the Ace Hotel, this is the place to get your hands on a piece of the signature style of the design duo behind it, Robin Standefer and Stephen Alesch of Roman and Williams. At the heart of the sprawling emporium is a showroom for the designers' own vintage-inspired furniture line, as well as glassware, ceramics and other accessories made by artisans from around the world. Also on site are a flower shop, a French-style café and a basement library of art and design books, all for sale.

What Goes Around Comes Around

351 West Broadway, between Broome & Grand Streets (1-212 343 1225, www. whatgoesaroundnyc.com). Subway A, C, E, 1 to Canal Street. **Open** *11am-8pm Mon-Sat; noon-7pm Sun.* **Map** *p87 E30* **⓱** *Fashion*

A favourite among the city's fashion cognoscenti, this downtown vintage destination sells highly curated stock alongside its own retro label. Style mavens particularly recommend it for 1960s, '70s and '80s rock T-shirts, pristine Alaïa clothing and vintage fur coats. **Other location** 21 E 67th Street, between Fifth & Madison Avenues, Upper East Side (1-646 762 4417).

Roman and Williams Guild

TRIBECA

▶ *Subway A, C, E, 1 to Canal Street; A, C, 1, 2, 3 to Chambers Street; 1 to Franklin Street.*

In just two decades, the Triangle Below Canal Street morphed from an isolated, run-down corner to a wealthy enclave with a family- and celebrity-heavy demographic. Robert De Niro played a major role in the area's transformation. In 1988, he and producer Jane Rosenthal founded the **Tribeca Film Center** (375 Greenwich Street, at Franklin Street, www.tribecafilmcenter. com), which contains the industry magnet **Tribeca Grill** (1-212 941 3900). More than a decade later, the pair launched the Tribeca Film Festival (*see p299*) to help stimulate downtown growth after the devastation of 9/11.

The preponderance of large, hulking former industrial buildings gives Tribeca an imposing profile, but fine, small-scale cast-iron architecture still stands along White Street and the parallel thoroughfares. Upscale eateries and, increasingly, shops cater to the well-heeled locals.

Sights & museums

♥ Mmuseumm

Cortlandt Alley, between Franklin & White Streets (no phone, www.mmuseumm.com). Subway J, N, Q, R, Z, 6 to Canal Street. **Open** *11am-6pm Fri-Sun, or by appointment.* **Admission** *Suggested donation $5.* **Map** *p87 E31.*

Institutions such as the Metropolitan Museum of Art are home to thousands of treasures. At the other end of the spectrum, there's Mmuseumm, a 60-square-foot repository in an abandoned Tribeca freight elevator. The walk-in-closet-size space, founded by indie filmmakers Alex Kalman, Josh Safdie and Benny Safdie, showcases a mishmash of found objects and artefacts donated by hobbyists. Exhibits typically

In the know
Where there's smoke...

Despite the strict city-wide smoking ban, you can still indulge your habit in a few places: establishments that were able to prove that a percentage of their income came from selling tobacco products when the ban was enforced. If you enjoy a cigarette, or even a cigar, with your cocktail, stop by the Soho Cigar Bar (32 Watts Street, between Sixth Avenue & Thompson Street, 1-212 941 1781, www.sohocigarbar.com).

change annually, and have included such varied ephemera as religious objects catering to contemporary consumers (a gluten-free holy communion wafer, for example), Donald Trump-branded merchandise, fake vomit from around the world, and part of a collection charting the evolution of the coffee-cup lid, amassed by two architects. Although Mmuseumm is only open at weekends, viewers can also get a peek at the space when it's closed – look for the small peepholes in a metal door on the narrow throughway between Franklin and White Streets. Two doors up, another hole-in-the-wall space dispenses espresso, snacks and souvenirs.

Restaurants & cafés

♥ Frenchette $$$

241 W Broadway, between Walker & White Streets (1-212 334 3883, www.frenchettenyc. com). Subway A, C, E to Canal Street; 1 to Franklin Street. **Open** *11.30am-11pm Mon-Fri; 10am-3pm, 5.30-11pm Sat, Sun.* **Map** *p87 E31* ⑥ *French*

Before opening this modern Parisian-style brasserie, Riad Nasr and Lee Hanson worked for prolific restaurateur Keith McNally, as the launch chefs at Balthazar and Minetta Tavern, among other ventures. As with those two NYC dining institutions, Frenchette doesn't try to reinvent the French wheel, but drives home classics in a more refined way than your average bistro. Thinly sliced mortadella over toasted brioche revives the childhood memory of a bologna sandwich, without the paper bag, and a perfectly rendered duck breast is served alongside a generous pile of golden frites. You won't have any gustatory revelations, but you will have a virtually flawless experience, from the plush leather booths to the attentive waitstaff.

Khe-Yo $$

157 Duane Street, between Hudson Street & West Broadway (1-212 587 1089, www.kheyo. com). Subway A, C, 1, 2, 3 to Chambers Street. **Open** *11.30am-2.30pm, 5.30-9.45pm Mon-Thur; 11.30am-2.30pm, 5.30-10.15pm Fri; noon-3pm, 5.30-10.15pm Sat; noon-3pm, 5.30-9.15pm Sun.* **Map** *p87 E31* ⑧ *Laotian*

For all the diversity in New York's rich dining landscape, there remains a small pocket of cuisines that are still hard to come by, one of which being the spice-forward, fish-sauced fare of Laos. Khe-Yo, which translates to 'green', is run by a team including megawatt chef Marc Forgione and his longtime cohort, Soulayphet 'Phet' Schwader. Tear-jerking heat is more prevalent in the first half of the menu, which is divided into a selection of

Mmuseumm *p93*

snacky small plates and larger dishes. The latter nod to the tradition of family-style meals anchored around whole fish, while also including familiar alternatives, such as a pitch-perfect upgrade to garden-variety *pad-see-ew* with plump chunks of lobster. Take the edge off the spicy food with fruity, Southeast Asian-inflected cocktails.

In the know
NY sea

The *Sherman Zwicker*, an elegant 1940s schooner home to seasonal oyster bar Grand Banks (Apr-Oct, 1-212 660 6312, www.grandbanks.org), blows trashy party-boat clichés about plastic chairs and beer-swilling masses out of the water. Docked at Tribeca's Pier 25, the elegant vessel has an out-to-sea feel, but with views of the World Trade Center and Statue of Liberty, both illuminated at night. Two brass-tapped bars flank the ship's bow and mizzen-mast, offering prime seating even without reservations, and waitstaff in navy striped shirts deliver a changing selection of oysters, lobster rolls and daily cocktail specials.

Locanda Verde $$$
377 Greenwich Street, at North Moore Street (1-212 925 3797, www.locandaverdenyc.com). Subway 1 to Franklin Street. **Open** *7-11am, 11.30am-3pm, 5.30-11pm Mon-Thur; 7am-11am, 11.30am-3pm, 5.30-11.30pm Fri; 8am-3pm, 5.30-11.30pm Sat; 8am-3pm, 5.30-11pm Sun.* **Map** *p87 D31* 9 *Italian*

This buzzy eaterie in Robert De Niro's Greenwich Hotel features bold family-style fare that's best enjoyed as a bacchanalian banquet. Waygu beef *tartara piedmontese* with hazelnuts and truffles won't last long in the middle of the table. Nor will the 'grandmother's' ravioli, stuffed with veal, pork and beef. This is one of those rare Italian restaurants with exceptional desserts, including decadent confections for two.

Tiny's and the Bar Upstairs $$
135 West Broadway, between Duane & Thomas Streets (1-212 374 1135, www.tinysnyc.com). Subway A, C, 1, 2, 3 to Chambers Street. **Open** *8am-11pm Mon-Thur; 8am-midnight Fri; 9am-midnight Sat; 9am-10pm Sun.* **Map** *p87 E31* 11 *American*

Restaurateur and nightlife impresario Matt Abramcyk teamed up with siblings Ana and Jack for this bi-level American eaterie in an early-19th-century townhouse. Take a seat at the pressed-copper bar upstairs for a classic cocktail or one of several NYC-brewed beers. The space below is divided into a white-tiled room with a bar in front and a back dining room with brick walls and a fireplace, serving everything from breakfast eggs and pancakes to lunchtime sandwiches and salads, and locally sourced meats with seasonal sides at dinner.

Bars

🖤 Weather Up
*159 Duane Street, between Hudson Street & West Broadway (1-212 766 3202, www. weatherupnyc.com). Subway 1, 2, 3 to Chambers Street. **Open** 5pm-1am Mon-Sat; 5-10pm Sun. **Map** p87 E31* ❷

At Kathryn Weatherup's sleek, subway-tiled Manhattan drinkery, a spin-off of her popular Prospect Heights bar, the well-balanced cocktail list features a regularly rotating mix of classics and original quaffs. Pair the booze with smart snacks such as oysters and beef tartare. **Other location** 589 Vanderbilt Avenue, between Bergen & Dean Streets, Prospect Heights, Brooklyn (no phone).

Shops & services

180 The Store
*180 Duane Street, between Greenwich & Hudson Streets (1-212 226 5506, www. 180thestore.com). Subway 1, 2, 3 to Chambers Street. **Open** 11am-7pm Mon-Sat, noon-5pm Sun. **Map** p87 E31* ❶ *Fashion/homewares*

Design and fashion PR Denise Williamson is behind this expansive, white-walled warehouse space highlighting a rotating selection of clothing for men and women, plus lifestyle lines. The eclectic stock spans the likes of cult Brandblack trainers, smock-like dresses by French label École de Curiosités, and patched and embellished military garb by Atelier & Repairs, alongside handcrafted homewares such as pottery and glassware.

La Garçonne
*465 Greenwich Street, at Watts Street (1-646 553 3303, www.lagarconne.com). Subway 1 to Canal Street. **Open** 11am-7pm Mon-Sat; noon-6pm Sun. **Map** p87 D30* ❻ *Fashion*

After nine years as an online boutique, La Garçonne opened this chic bricks-and-mortar version. The minimal, refined aesthetic is reflected in both the space and the stock, which includes such labels as Comme des Garçons, Marni, Jil Sander, Lemaire and the in-house collection, La Garçonne Moderne, alongside newer names. While catering mainly to women, there is a smaller selection of menswear.

🖤 Nili Lotan
*188 Duane Street, between Greenwich & Hudson Streets (1-212 219 8794, www. nililotan.com). Subway 1, 2, 3 to Chambers Street. **Open** 11am-7pm Mon-Sat; noon-6pm Sun. **Map** p87 E31* ❿ *Fashion*

The sparsely hung women's garments in Israeli designer Nili Lotan's airy, all-white store and studio look like art pieces on display in a gallery. Perfectly cut, largely monochrome wardrobe staples such as silk camisoles and dresses, oversized cashmere sweaters, boy-cut trousers and crisply tailored menswear-inspired shirts appeal to minimalists with a penchant for luxury. **Other location** 1186 Madison Avenue, between 86th & 87th Streets, Upper East Side (1-212 840 2432).

Patron of the New
*151 Franklin Street, between Hudson & Varick Streets (1-212 966 7144, patronofthenew.com). Subway A, C, E to Canal Street; 1 to Franklin Street. **Open** noon-7pm Mon-Sat; noon-6pm Sun. **Map** p87 E31* ⓬ *Fashion*

This avant-garde fashion emporium showcases a collection of unique guys' and gals' fashion and home items from both illustrious and under-the-radar designers, including Off-White, Greg Lauren and Fear of God. Goods are pricey, but there are some affordable accessories, jewellery and gifts such as soaps and candles.

Shinola
*177 Franklin Street, between Greenwich & Hudson Streets (1-917 728 3000, www.shinola. com). Subway A, C, E to Canal Street; 1 to Franklin Street. **Open** 11am-7pm Mon-Sat; noon-6pm Sun. **Map** p87 E31* ⓯ *Fashion*

Detroit-based brand Shinola is a Motor City success story. Peruse the range of American-manufactured watches, bicycles, leather goods and other items, all with a sturdy, mid-century aesthetic, in the industrial-edged NYC flagship. You can have many items monogrammed or engraved in-store. **Other location** 49 Water Street, at Dock Street, Dumbo, Brooklyn (1-929 395 0099).

Steven Alan
*103 Franklin Street, between West Broadway & Church Street (1-212 343 0692, www. stevenalan.com). Subway 1 to Franklin Street. **Open** 11am-7pm Mon-Sat; noon-6pm Sun. **Map** p87 E31* ⓰ *Fashion*

Known for well-crafted cotton shirts in an array of stripes, checks and solid colours, Steven Alan also assembles cultish brands for men and women in its flagship store. In addition to the house label, browse knitwear by NYC label Demylee and Saint James Breton shirts, plus handbags and shoes. **Other locations** throughout the city.

Chinatown, Little Italy & Nolita

Take a walk in the area south of Broome Street and east of Broadway, and you'll feel as though you've entered a different continent. The streets of Manhattan's Chinatown are packed with exotic produce stands, herb emporiums, cheap jewellers, snack vendors and, of course, restaurants. As the densely populated Asian community continues to grow, it merges with neighbouring Little Italy. Squeezed between Chinatown's sprawl and the multiplying boutiques and hotspots of Nolita (North of Little Italy), the historically Italian district has long been shrinking, but you can still get a taste of the old neighbourhood in its classic (and neo-classic) cafés and red-sauce eateries.

❤ Don't miss

1 Mott Street *p104*
Shop for jewellery, fashion and gifts.

2 Museum of Chinese in America *p100*
The Chinese-American story, stylishly told.

3 Dim sum *p100*
Try it at Nom Wah Tea Parlor.

Chinatown

CHINATOWN

▶ *Subway F to East Broadway; J, N, Q, R, W, Z, 6 to Canal Street.*

A steady flow of new arrivals keeps this neighbourhood – one of the largest Chinese communities outside Asia – full to bursting, with thousands of residents packed into the area surrounding the eastern stretch of Canal Street. Some eventually decamp to one of NYC's three other Chinatowns, in Sunset Park, Brooklyn, and Flushing and Elmhurst in Queens.

Mott and Grand Streets are lined with fish-, fruit- and vegetable-stocked stands – you might see buckets of live eels and crabs, square watermelons and piles of hairy rambutans. Street vendors sell satisfying snacks such as pork buns and sweet egg pancakes by the bagful. Canal Street glitters with cheap jewellery and gift shops, but beware furtive vendors of (undoubtedly fake) designer goods. Between Kenmare and Worth Streets, Mott Street is packed with restaurants representing the cuisine of virtually every province of mainland China and Hong Kong; the Bowery, East Broadway and Division Street are just as diverse. Adding to the mix are myriad Indonesian, Malaysian, Thai and Vietnamese eateries and shops.

At the engaging **Museum of Chinese in America**, you can learn about the Chinese experience on these shores. The **Eastern States Buddhist Temple of America** (64 Mott Street, between Bayard & Canal Streets, 1-212 966 6229), founded in 1962, is one of the country's oldest Chinese Buddhist temples.

Museum of Chinese in America (MOCA)

♥ Time to eat & drink

Classic dim sum
Nom Wah Tea Parlor *p100*

Fine Thai cuisine in a hip setting
Uncle Boons *p103*

Posh pizza
Pasquale Jones *p103*,
Rubirosa *p103*

Imaginative Med-influenced fare
Estela *p102*

♥ Time to shop

One-of-a-kind souvenirs
Uniqulee *p102*

A world of teas
Sun's Organic Garden *p101*

Serene 'slow fashion' boutiques
Hesperios *p104*, Oroboro *p106*

Literary light
McNally Jackson *p106*

In the know
Manhattan Bridge

It may lack the lore of the Brooklyn and Queensboro bridges, but this sweeping steel suspension bridge, completed in 1909, is among the city's most beautiful. The stone archway, near the junction of Broadway and Canal Street, was designed by New York Public Library architects Carrère and Hastings and modelled on the 17th-century Porte St-Denis in Paris.

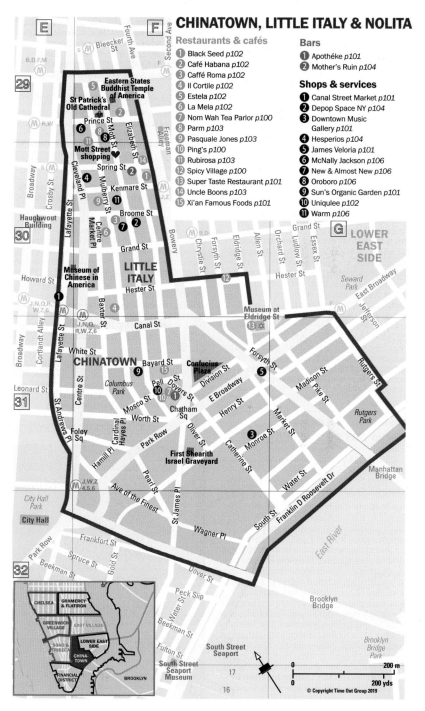

CHINATOWN, LITTLE ITALY & NOLITA

Restaurants & cafés

1. Black Seed *p102*
2. Café Habana *p102*
3. Caffé Roma *p102*
4. Il Cortile *p102*
5. Estela *p102*
6. La Mela *p102*
7. Nom Wah Tea Parlor *p100*
8. Parm *p103*
9. Pasquale Jones *p103*
10. Ping's *p100*
11. Rubirosa *p103*
12. Spicy Village *p100*
13. Super Taste Restaurant *p101*
14. Uncle Boons *p103*
15. Xi'an Famous Foods *p101*

Bars

1. Apothéke *p101*
2. Mother's Ruin *p104*

Shops & services

1. Canal Street Market *p101*
2. Depop Space NY *p104*
3. Downtown Music Gallery *p101*
4. Hesperios *p104*
5. James Veloria *p101*
6. McNally Jackson *p106*
7. New & Almost New *p106*
8. Oroboro *p106*
9. Sun's Organic Garden *p101*
10. Uniquelee *p102*
11. Warm *p106*

© Copyright Time Out Group 2019

CHINATOWN, LITTLE ITALY & NOLITA

Sights & museums

💗 Museum of Chinese in America

215 Centre Street, between Grand & Howard Streets (1-212 619 4785, www.mocanyc.org). Subway J, N, Q, R, Z, 6 to Canal Street. **Open** *11am-6pm Tue, Wed, Fri-Sun; 11am-9pm Thur.* **Admission** *$12; $8 reductions; free under-2s. Free 1st Thur of mth.* **Map** *p99 E30.*

Designed by prominent Chinese American architect Maya Lin, MOCA reopened in an airy former machine shop in 2009. Its interior is loosely inspired by a traditional *siheyuan* residence, with rooms radiating off a central courtyard and, instead of windows, videos projected on glass screens. The core exhibition traces the development of Chinese communities in the US from the 1850s to the present through objects, images and video. Innovative displays (drawers open to reveal artwork and documents, portraits are presented in a ceiling mobile) cover the growth of industries such as laundries and restaurants in New York, Chinese stereotypes in pop culture, and the suspicion and humiliation Chinese-Americans endured during World War II and the McCarthy era. A reconstructed Chinese general store evokes the feel of these multi-purpose spaces, which served as vital community lifelines for men severed from their families under the 1882 Chinese Exclusion Act that restricted immigration. There are also two galleries for special exhibitions.

Restaurants & cafés

💗 Nom Wah Tea Parlor $

13 Doyers Street, between Bowery & Pell Street (1-212 962 6047, www.nomwah.com). Subway J, N, Q, R, W, Z, 6 to Canal Street; J, Z to Chambers Street. **Open** *10.30am-10pm daily.* **Map** *p99 F31* ⑦ *Chinese*

New York's first dim sum house, Nom Wah opened in 1920 and was owned by the same family for more than three decades. The current owner, Wilson Tang, revamped it in a vintage style true to the restaurant's archival photographs. The most important tweaks, though, were behind the scenes: Tang updated the kitchen and did away with the procedure of cooking dim sum en masse. Now, each plate is cooked to order: ultra-fluffy oversized roasted-pork buns, flaky fried crêpe egg rolls and scallion pancakes. The Nolita offshoot has a fresh aesthetic with cartoon dumpling murals, white subway tiles and an open kitchen, serving some Nom Wah staples alongside more contemporary options, such as a vegan noodle soup. **Other location** 10 Kenmare Street, between Bowery & Elizabeth Street, Nolita (1-646 478 8242).

Ping's $$

22 Mott Street, between Mosco Street & Park Row (1-212 602 9988, www.eatatpings. com). Subway J, N, Q, R, W, Z, 6 to Canal Street. **Open** *10.30am-10.30pm Mon-Fri; 9am-10.30pm Sat, Sun.* **Map** *p99 F31* ⑩ *Chinese*

The bank of fish tanks near the entrance suggests the speciality here. Bite-sized pieces of boneless smelt are deep-fried to a golden yellow and served with a mix of Szechuan peppercorns and salt. Big steamed oysters benefit from a splash of Ping's celebrated house-made XO sauce – a spicy condiment made of dried shrimp, scallops and garlic. The sliced sautéed conch is set off by snappy snow peas and a tangy fermented shrimp sauce. Those exotic flavours, plus refinements such as tablecloths, justify prices that are a notch above the Chinatown norm. Dim sum spans staples like pork *shumai* and steamed crab dumplings, subtly enhanced with fragments of leek and coriander (cilantro) and a dab of roe.

Spicy Village $

68B Forsyth Street, between Grand & Hester Streets (1-212 625 8299, www.spicyvillagenyc. com). **Open** *10.30am-11pm Mon-Sat. Subway B, D to Grand Street.* **No cards.** **Map** *p99 F30* ⑫ *Chinese*

A hole-in-the-wall temple to the cuisine of China's Henan heartland, Spicy Village is a pilgrimage site for adventurous eaters and regional cuisine purists. While the illustrated wall-mounted menu boasts noodle soups, dumplings, and, yes, soup dumplings, don't give them a second look.

Nom Wah Tea Parlor

You're really here for the Big Tray Chicken, a red-hot plate of bone-in poultry chunks and potatoes marinated in Budweiser, MSG and a blend of chilli oil, star anise and Szechuan peppercorn. Can't stand the heat? Add an order of the house-made hand-pulled *hui mei* wheat noodles.

Super Taste Restaurant $

26 Eldridge Street, at Canal Street (1-646 283 0999). Subway F to East Broadway. **Open** *10am-10.45pm daily.* **No cards.** **Map** *p99 F31* ⓲ *Chinese*

In a sea of cheap Chinatown noodle bars, Super Taste stands out. Watch the cook hand pull your Lanzhou-style *la mian*, the Chinese relative of Japanese ramen, which is served in a soup with toppings that vary from beef tendon to eel – for less than ten bucks.

Xi'an Famous Foods $

45 Bayard Street, between Bowery & Elizabeth Street (no phone, www.xianfoods. com). Subway J, N, Q, R, W, Z, 6 to Canal Street. **Open** *11.30am-9pm Mon-Thur, Sun; 11.30am-9.30pm Fri, Sat.* **Map** *p99 F31* ⓯ *Chinese*

This cheap NYC Chinese chain highlights the mouth-tingling cuisine of Xi'an, an ancient capital along China's Silk Road. Nosh on spicy noodles or a cumin-spiced burger for around a tenner. **Other locations** throughout the city.

Bars

Apothéke

9 Doyers Street, at Pell Street (1-212 406 0400, www.apothekenyc.com). Subway J, N, Q, R, W, Z, 6 to Canal Street. **Open** *6.30pm-2am Mon-Sat; 8pm-2am Sun.* **Map** *p99 F31* ❶

At this unmarked boîte, the bar is littered with old vials, the cocktails are referred to as 'prescriptions', and the bartenders-cum-mad-scientists are in rare form – note the cinnamon-flambéed Himalayan salt that rims a margarita. Concoctions such as the Tainted Love (gin, beetroot juice, pomegranate shrub and port) and the Sitting Buddha (a vodka and lemongrass elixir with fresh pineapple and ginger) will certainly cure your sobriety.

Shops & services

Canal Street Market

265 Canal Street, between Broadway & Lafayette Street (no phone, www.canalstreet. market). Subway J, N, Q, R, W, Z, 6 to Canal Street. **Open** *11am-7pm Mon-Sat; 11am-6pm Sun.* **Map** *p99 E30* ❶ *Market*

The busy Chinatown thoroughfare is better known for tacky jewellery and souvenir shops, but the design-conscious wares at Canal Street Market are nothing less than tasteful. The sprawling white space houses rotating vendors selling everything from contemporary home accessories to made-in-NYC menswear and Bonsai cultivated in Brooklyn. A mainly Asian-focused food court offers ramen, Chinese steamed rice rolls and other snacks.

Downtown Music Gallery

13 Monroe Street, between Catherine & Market Streets (1-212 473 0043, www. downtownmusicgallery.com). Subway J, Z to Chambers Street; 4, 5, 6 to Brooklyn Bridge-City Hall. **Open** *noon-6pm daily.* **Map** *p99 F31* ❸ *Music*

Many landmarks of the so-called downtown music scene have shuttered, but as long as DMG persists, the community will have a sturdy anchor. The shop stocks the city's finest selection of avant-garde jazz, contemporary classical, progressive rock and related styles.

James Veloria

2nd Floor, 75 East Broadway, under the Manhattan Bridge (1-510 229 2862, www. jamesveloria.com). B, D to Grand Street; F to East Broadway. **Open** *1-7pm daily.* **Map** *p99 F31* ❺ *Fashion*

To access the vintage designer treasures amassed by Collin James Weber and Brandon Veloria Giordano, enter a run-down Asian shopping centre under the Manhattan Bridge, pass the cheap beauty and clothing outlets and head to the second floor, where a few cool shops have taken up residence. On-trend '80s and '90s stock from names such as Jean Paul Gaultier, Vivienne Westwood, Moschino and Comme des Garçons, spans everything from flashy shirts, waistcoats and leather trousers for men to eye-catching print tops and little black dresses for women.

❤ Sun's Organic Garden

79 Bayard Street, between Mott & Mulberry Streets (1-212 566 3260). Subway J, N, Q, R, W, Z, 6 to Canal Street. **Open** *noon-6pm Tue-Fri, Sun; 11.30am-6pm Sat.* **Map** *p99 F31* ❾ *Food & drink*

If you're serious about tea, peruse the well-stocked shelves of this nook, which offers more than a thousand jarred loose-leaf varieties from around the world, available by the ounce. The house-made herbal blends are standouts, in exotic flavours such as holy basil and bilberry.

❤ Uniqulee

36 Mott Street, at Pell Street (1-212 323 2870, www.uniqulee.com). Subway J, N, Q, R, W, Z, 6 to Canal Street. **Open** *11am-8pm Mon-Thur; 11am-8.30pm Fri-Sun (hrs can vary).* **Map** *p99 F31* ❿ *Gifts & accessories*

The antithesis of Chinatown's stock-in-trade cheap gift emporiums, Uniqulee focuses on one-of-a-kind finds. Vintage pieces span immaculately preserved jewellery and evening bags, an array of quirky cufflinks, toy soldiers, antique pocket watches and classic cameras in working order. You'll also find stylish NYC-made ties and pocket squares, plus Homesick soy-wax candles, in scents redolent of 'Books' or 'New York'.

LITTLE ITALY & NOLITA

▶ *Subway B, D, F, M to Broadway-Lafayette Street; J, N, Q, R, W, Z, 6 to Canal Street; J, Z to Bowery; R, W to Prince Street; 6 to Spring Street.*

Abandoning the dismal tenements of the Five Points district (in what is now the Civic Center and part of Chinatown), immigrants from Naples and Sicily began moving to **Little Italy** in the 1880s. The area once stretched from Canal Street to Houston Street, between Lafayette Street and the Bowery, but as families prospered in the 1950s, they moved to the outer boroughs and suburbs. These days, the legacy of that Italian heritage is mainly confined to the blocks immediately surrounding Mulberry Street. Yet ethnic pride remains: Italian-Americans flood in from across the city during the 11-day **Feast of San Gennaro** (*see p291*).

Touristy cafés and restaurants line Mulberry Street between Broome and Canal Streets, but pockets of the past linger nearby. Long-time residents still buy fresh mozzarella from **Di Palo's Fine Foods** (*see p104* Mott Street shopping). Legend has it that the first pizzeria in New York was opened by Gennaro Lombardi on Spring Street in 1905; **Lombardi's** (*see p104* Mott Street shopping) moved down the block in 1994, but still serves its signature clam pies.

Roughly identified as the area between Broome, Houston, Lafayette and the Bowery, **Nolita** became a magnet for independent boutiques and trendy eateries in the 1990s. Elizabeth, Mott and Mulberry Streets, between Houston and Spring Streets, in particular, are home to hip shops (*see p104* Mott Street shopping). Also in Nolita is **St Patrick's Old Cathedral**. Completed in 1809 and restored after a fire in 1868, it was the city's premier Catholic church until it was demoted upon consecration of the Fifth Avenue cathedral of the same name.

Restaurants & cafés

Today, Little Italy's restaurants are largely undistinguished grills and pasta houses, but two reliable choices are **Il Cortile** (125 Mulberry Street, between Canal & Hester Streets, 1-212 226 6060, www.ilcortile. com ❹) and **La Mela** (167 Mulberry Street, between Broome & Grand Streets, 1-212 431 9493, www.lamelarestaurant.com ❻). Drop in for dessert at **Caffè Roma** (385 Broome Street, at Mulberry Street, 1-212 226 8413 ❸), which opened in 1891.

Black Seed $

170 Elizabeth Street, between Kenmare & Spring Streets (1-212 730 1950, www. blackseedbagels.com). Subway J, Z to Bowery. **Open** *7am-5pm daily.* **Map** *p99 F30* ❶ *Café*

At this newfangled Nolita bagelry, from Mile End founder Noah Bernamoff and the Smile impresario Matt Kliegman, the hand-rolled rounds merge two disciplines: they're honey-enhanced à la Bernamoff's native Montreal, but with an eggless, touch-of-salt bite to satisfy NYC-raised Kliegman. Kettle-boiled and wood-fired, the small but mighty bagels are crowned with house-made toppings both classic (scallion cream cheese, silky cold-smoked salmon) and fanciful (salty tobiko caviar, crisp watermelon radishes). **Other locations** throughout the city.

Café Habana $

17 Prince Street, at Elizabeth Street (1-212 625 2001, www.cafehabana.com). Subway R, W to Prince Street; 6 to Spring Street. **Open** *9am-midnight daily.* **Map** *p99 F29* ❷ *Cuban*

Since 1998, this converted corner diner has been drawing crowds for its addictive corn, doused in fresh mayo, chargrilled and generously sprinkled with chilli powder and grated cotija cheese. Other staples include a Cuban sandwich of roasted pork, ham, melted swiss and sliced pickles, and crisp beer-battered catfish tacos.

❤ Estela $$

2nd Floor, 47 E Houston Street, between Mott & Mulberry Streets (1-212 219 7693, www.estelanyc.com). Subway B, D, F, M to Broadway-Lafayette Street; 6 to Bleecker Street. **Open** *5.30-11pm Mon-Thur; 11.30am-3pm, 5.30-11.30pm Fri, Sat; 11.30am-3pm, 5.30-11pm Sun.* **Map** *p99 F29* ❺ *American creative*

The fashionable cookie-cutter decor – exposed brick, globe lights, hulking marble bar – may suggest you've stumbled into yet another bustling rustic restaurant-cum-bar that's not worth the wait. But there's more to this Mediterranean-tinged spot than meets the eye: primarily, the talent of imaginative Uruguayan-born chef Ignacio Mattos. An ever-changing, mostly small-plates menu pivots from avant-garde towards intimate. Highlights might include beef tartare with tart pickled elderberries – with a musty baseline note from fish sauce and crunchy sunchoke (Jerusalem artichoke) chips; egg with gigante beans and cured tuna; and a creamy panna cotta with honey.

Parm $

248 Mulberry Street, between Prince & Spring Streets (1-212 993 7189, www.parmnyc.com). Subway R, W to Prince Street; 6 to Spring Street. Open 11.30am-10pm Mon-Thur, Sun; 11.30am-11pm Fri, Sat. Map p99 F29 ❽ *Italian*

Mario Carbone and Rich Torrisi, two young fine-dining chefs, brought a cool-kid sheen to classic Italian sandwiches and red-sauce plates in 2010, when they debuted now-shuttered Torrisi Italian Specialties, a deli by day and haute eaterie by night. People lined up for their buzzworthy sandwiches. Although the original is no more, the superlative sandwiches, such as herb-rubbed roast turkey, classic cold cuts or chicken parmesan, are still served in these fetching diner digs and its branches. Together with partner Jeff Zalaznick, the duo now has several other restaurants, including the excellent Carbone (*see p138*). **Other locations** 235 Columbus Avenue, between 70th & 71st Streets, Upper West Side (1-212 776 4921); 250 Vesey Street, at North End Avenue, Tribeca (1-212 776 4927).

❤ Pasquale Jones $$

187 Mulberry Street, between Kenmare & Broome Streets (no phone, www. pasqualejones.com). Subway 6 to Spring Street; J, Z to Bowery. Open noon-3.30pm, 5.30-11pm Tue-Sat; noon-3.30pm, 5.30-10pm Sun. Map p99 F30 ❾ *Italian*

This pizzeria with fine-dining aspirations is a sequel to jaunty, wine-charged Soho spot Charlie Bird. Ambitious pies include the destination-making clam pizza, an elemental composition of juicy littlenecks, fire-roasted garlic and a whisper of cream. But Pasquale Jones also offers high-reaching mains such as a gorgeous slow-roasted pork shank for two, and refreshingly out-of-the-box Italian wines served in hand-blown Zalto stems.

❤ Rubirosa $$

235 Mulberry Street, between Prince & Spring Streets (1-212 965 0500, www.rubirosanyc. com). Subway 6 to Spring Street. 11.30am-11pm Mon-Wed, Sun; 11.30am-midnight Thur-Sat. Map p99 F29 ⓫ *Italian*

This family-run restaurant helped usher in Mulberry Street's red-sauce revival, offering simple, thin-crust pizzas and other classic dishes. Rubirosa's crisp yet pliable pies have a delicate char and a small ring of cracker-like crust around the edges. The no-frills vodka rendition is a reliable choice, topped with a layer of creamy, booze-spiked tomato sauce and a gooey patchwork of fresh mozzarella.

❤ Uncle Boons $$

7 Spring Street, between Bowery & Elizabeth Streets (1-646 370 6650, www.uncleboons. com). Subway J, Z to Bowery; 6 to Spring Street. Open 5.30-11pm Mon-Thur, Sun; 5.30pm-midnight Friday, Sat. Map p99 F30 ⓮ *Thai*

One of the city's hippest Thai restaurants, Uncle Boons is part of a riptide of upstarts repackaging homey Asian food – once relegated to holes-in-the-wall or fusty Midtown warhorses – in buzzy, forward-thinking joints. At this dark-wood-panelled rathskeller, you'll find tap wine and Bangkok-style beer slushes, vintage Thai flatware carved from teak and brass, and fine-dining muscle in the kitchen. Husband-and-wife team Matt Danzer and Ann Redding met while cooking at Per Se. Simple snacks from the charcoal grill, such as head-on prawns, are barbecued flawlessly, and succulent roasted chicken (*kai yang muay thai*), from the rotisserie birds spinning near the bar, is another standout dish.

Nearby no-cash spinoff, Uncle Boons Sister, offers more wallet-friendly fare and takeaway. **Other location** 203 Mott Street, between Kenmore & Spring Streets (1-646 850 9480, www.uncleboonssister.com).

Bars

Mother's Ruin

18 Spring Street, between Elizabeth & Mott Streets (no phone, www.mothersruinnyc. com). Subway J, Z to Bowery; 6 to Spring Street. **Open** *11am-4am daily.* **Map** *p99 F30* ❷

A roster of skilled bartenders sling classic and contemporary drinks at this airy, unpretentious Nolita drinkery. The laid-back space – done up with a cream tin ceiling, exposed brick and weathered-wood bar – also has a full menu of globally inflected bites and doubles as a popular brunch spot.

Shops & services

Depop Space NY

168 Mott Street, between Broome & Grand Streets (1-646 609 4311, www.depop.com). Subway B, D to Grand Street; J, Z to Bowery; 6 to Spring Street. **Open** *11-7pm Thur-Sat; noon-6pm Sun.* **Map** *p99 F30* ❷ *Fashion*

NYC's brick-and-mortar manifestation of the buzzed-about DIY e-commerce app offers showroom space to a revolving selection of wares by emerging designers, vintage vendors and reworkers. The space may be small, but the wildly eclectic mix, displayed gallery-like on the walls as well as hanging on a handful of rails, spans pristine designer pieces and wacky hand-painted or hybrid customisations. Regular events include clothing swaps and workshops, and the on-site photo studio can be booked by Depoppers Mon-Wed.

❤ Hesperios

23 Cleveland Place, between Kenmare & Spring Streets (1-212 226 2413, www.hesperios. com). Subway 6 to Spring Street; R, W to Prince Street. **Open** *11am-7pm Mon-Sat; noon-6pm Sun.* **Map** *p99 F30* ❹ *Fashion/ homewares*

An airy space with whitewashed brick walls and serene staff embodies the rarefied world of Hesperios, which encompasses an artsy biannual journal and a knitwear line. Delicate camisoles, pleated skirts and classic pullovers in nostalgic colours and sumptuous materials like cashmere, silk and pima cotton hang on uncluttered racks, or are folded on shelves alongside art and design books and select handmade ceramics. If you want to linger in the tranquil environment, the store doubles as a café serving Irving Farm coffee, House of Waris teas, plus pastries and Nordic-style Meyers Bageri bread with jams and tapenade. There's even a secluded patio garden in the back.

❤ Mott Street shopping

From Houston Street to Pell Street. Subway B, D, F, M to Broadway-Lafayette Street. **Map** *p99.*

While Soho is downtown's undisputed shopping hub, Nolita is perfect for a relaxed browse, combining varied retail pockets with remnants of the old neighbourhood and plenty of craft coffee shops and brunch spots. Recently, Mott Street, in particular, has welcomed hip newcomers without losing its character. A walk south from Houston Street takes in some of the city's best boutiques, old-school Italian institutions and vibrant Chinatown tableaux.

Lined with low-rise red-brick buildings, Mott Street's leafy first blocks recall an earlier NYC streetscape. Israeli-born jeweller **Eli Halili** (no.260, www.elihalili.com) displays his antiquity-inspired creations – some incorporating ancient coins and other

Oroboro

artefacts – in vintage cabinets in a shrine-like space. Showcased in a compact, white-walled shop (no.252, www.wendynicholnyc.com), **Wendy Nichol**'s goth-tinged collections, including silk slip dresses, Victorian-inspired jackets, and gold, leather and gemstone jewellery, are all handmade in NYC. On Fridays, Saturdays and Sundays from March through December, vendors set up from the intersection with Prince Street along the churchyard wall of **St Patrick's Old Cathedral**, selling locally made goods such as jewellery, bags and T-shirts at the **Nolita Market** (www.nolitaoutdoormarket.com). To the south, stylist April Hughes stocks dozens of independent labels from around the world at her serene boutique, **Oroboro** (*see p106*).

For lunch, stop for pizza at **Lombardi's** (32 Spring Street, at Mott Street, 1-212 941 7994), Thai at **Uncle Boon's Sister** (*see p103*) or

a classic NYC sandwich at the early-1900s **Parisi Bakery** (no.198, www.parisibakery.com), once frequented by Frank Sinatra. The simple storefront is now the company's bare-bones deli where staff stuff bread (fresh from newer premises round the corner) with Italian meat and cheese. Sandwiches cost around $10 and are takeaway only, but you can find a bench a couple of blocks west in tiny **Lieutenant Petrosino Square**.

Below Spring Street, the strip is grittier, but dotted with stylish boutiques, including laid-back, indie lifestyle store **Warm** (*see p106*) and lingerie and fashion label **Fleur du Mal** (no.175, www.fleurdumal.com), known for its supermodel-approved bustier tops. The stretch south of Broome is dominated by Chinese herb shops and bakeries, but there are also two stylish vintage spots: **New and Almost New** (*see p106*) and buzzy digital-marketplace spin-off **Depop Space NY** (*see opposite*). Bottles of olive oil and giant wheels of pecorino are displayed in the windows of **Di Palo's Fine Foods** (200 Grand Street, at Mott Street, 1-212 226 1033), a decades-old mainstay for Italian delicacies. Continue into Chinatown, past clusters of busy Asian seafood, meat and vegetable markets spilling onto the pavement, to reach the aptly named gift shop **Uniqulee** (*see p102*).

Depop Space NY

Hesperios *p104*

❤ McNally Jackson

52 Prince Street, between Lafayette & Mulberry Streets (1-212 274 1160, www.mcnallyjackson.com). Subway R, W to Prince Street; 6 to Spring Street. **Open** *10am-10pm Mon-Sat; 10am-9pm Sun.* **Map** *p99 F29* ❻ *Books*

This appealing indie bookstore has one of the city's most thoughtfully curated selections of non-fiction, novels, hard-to-find magazines, children's books and poetry. The on-site café serves espresso drinks, organic tea and light fare. Readings and events – which have included such literary luminaries as Hari Kunzru, Martin Amis and Zadie Smith – take place in the comfortable downstairs space. **Other location** Unit G, 76 North 4th Street, at Wythe Avenue, Williamsburg, Brooklyn (1-718 387 0115).

New & Almost New

171 Mott Street, between Broome & Grand Streets (1-212 226 6677, www.newandalmostnew.com). Subway B, D to Grand Street; J, Z to Bowery; 6 to Spring Street. **Open** *noon-6pm Tue-Sat; 1-5pm Sun.* **Map** *p99 F30* ❼ *Fashion*

Germophobe bargain-hunters will be delighted to find that much of the merchandise at this resale shop is brand new. Owner Maggie Chan hand-selects every piece, ensuring its quality and authenticity, and the stock frequently includes lofty labels such as Prada, Chanel and Hermès. Prices range from as low as $15 up to around $600.

❤ Oroboro

217 Mott Street, between Prince & Spring Streets (1-718 388 4884, www.oroborostore.com). Subway 6 to Spring Street. **Open** *11am-7pm daily (extended hrs in summer).* **Map** *p99 F30* ❽ *Fashion/homewares*

Fashion stylist April Hughes sources stock from independent designers around the world, with an emphasis on hand-crafted and ethically made goods. The carefully selected clothing labels, which tend to be characterised by striking yet simple lines and natural fabrics, include New York's Lauren Manoogian, LA-based Jesse Kamm, Ichi Antiquités from Japan and Belgium's Sofie D'Hoore. Eclectic jewellery ranges from Robin Mollicone's colourful leather and bead cuffs and earrings to understated architectural adornments by Quarry. Standout homewares include unique ceramic and fibre vases with an indigenous-tribal feel by Philadelphia artist Karen Tinney.

Warm

181 Mott Street, between Broome & Kenmare Streets (1-212 925 1200, www.warmny.com). Subway J, Z to Bowery; 6 to Spring Street. **Open** *11.30am-7pm Mon-Sat; noon-6pm Sun.* **Map** *p99 F30* ⓫ *Fashion/accessories*

The husband-and-wife owners of this appealing boutique, Rob Magnotta and Winnie Beattie, bring together an eclectic selection of women's, men's and kids' threads, accessories and home items, all informed by their globe-trotting surfer lifestyle. The laid-back looks include urban boho-chic clothing from the likes of Vanessa Bruno, Forte Forte, the Elder Statesman and the store's own label.

BAG YOURSELF A BARGAIN

Whether it's food, drink, theater or events, we've got exclusive offers and the best tickets in town.

 TIMEOUT.COM/
NEWYORK/OFFERS

THE BEST OF THE CITY

Lower East Side

Once better known for bagels and bargains, the Lower East Side is now brimming with vintage and indie-designer boutiques, fashionable bars and contemporary art galleries. The former slum has been so radically altered by the forces of gentrification that in 2008 it was placed on the National Trust for Historic Preservation's annual list of the 11 most endangered historic places – and there's more development in the works. However, it hasn't yet destroyed the character of this erstwhile centre of immigrant life. You can still explore remnants of the old Jewish neighbourhood that the Marx Brothers and George Gershwin called home, including food purveyors founded more than a century ago, a magnificently restored synagogue and recreated tenement apartments.

❤ **Don't miss**

1 Old-school delis *p114*
Katz is the granddaddy of these NYC institutions.

2 Tenement Museum *p112*
Tour recreated immigrant homes.

3 Museum at Eldridge Street *p113*
Restored synagogue with lavish interior.

4 New Museum of Contemporary Art *p113*
Cutting-edge exhibitions in a cool building.

5 Metrograph *p297*
Boutique cinema with a lively restaurant.

6 Bowery Ballroom *p317*
Prime venue for indie bands.

New Museum of Contemporary Art *p113*

LOWER EAST SIDE

▶ *Subway B, D to Grand Street; F to East Broadway; F to Delancey Street or Lower East Side-Second Avenue; J, Z to Bowery; J, M, Z to Delancey-Essex Streets.*

In the 19th century, tenement buildings were constructed on the Lower East Side, a roughly defined area south of Houston Street and west of the East River, to house the growing number of German, Irish, Jewish and Italian immigrants – by 1900 it was the most populous neighbourhood in the US. The appalling conditions of these overcrowded, unsanitary slums were captured by photographer and writer Jacob Riis in *How the Other Half Lives* in 1890; its publication spurred activists and prompted the introduction of more humane building codes. The dwellings have since been converted or demolished, but you can see how newcomers once lived by visiting the recreated apartments of the **Tenement Museum**.

The neighbourhood was also the focal point of Jewish culture in New York. Between 1870 and 1920, hundreds of synagogues and religious schools thrived alongside Yiddish newspapers, social-reform societies and kosher bakeries. Vaudeville and classic Yiddish theatre also prospered here. Today, most of these places are long gone, but vestiges of Jewish life can be found amid the Chinese businesses spilling over from sprawling Chinatown and the area's ever-multiplying boutiques, restaurants and bars. The magnificent **Eldridge Street Synagogue**, now a museum open to the public, still has a small but vital congregation. The 1912 building on the corner of Orchard and Canal Streets was the premises of the **Sender Jarmulowsky Bank**, which catered to Jewish immigrants until its collapse two years later. It's being converted into a luxury hotel. The **Forward Building** (175 E Broadway, at Canal Street) was once the headquarters of the *Jewish Daily Forward*, a Yiddish-language paper that had a peak circulation of 275,000 in the 1920s; it's now home to multimillion-dollar condominiums. You can sample traditional Jewish delicacies at local institutions **Katz's Delicatessen**, **Russ & Daughters** and **Yonah Schimmel Knish Bakery**.

By the 1980s, when young artists and musicians began moving into the area, the Lower East Side was a patchwork of Asian, Latino and Jewish enclaves. Hipster bars and music venues sprang up on and around Ludlow Street, creating an annex to the East Village. That scene still survives, at spots like the **Mercury Lounge**, but rents have risen dramatically and some stalwarts have closed.

These days, visual art is the Lower East Side's main cultural draw. Dozens of storefront galleries have opened in the vicinity over more than a decade, including boundary-pushing space **Miguel Abreu Gallery** (36 Orchard Street, between Canal & Hester Streets/88 Eldridge Street, between Grand & Hester Streets, 1-212 995 1774, www.miguelabreugallery.com). **Sperone Westwater** (257 Bowery, between E Houston & Stanton Streets, 1-212 999 7337, www.speronewestwater.com), whose high-profile stable includes Bruce Nauman, Susan Rothenberg and William Wegman, occupies a purpose-built showcase designed by starchitect Norman Foster. In 2007, the **New Museum of Contemporary Art** decamped here from Chelsea with a $50-million building on the Bowery.

Indie boutiques haven't yet pushed out the Orchard Street bargain district – a row of shops selling utilitarian goods such as socks, sportswear and luggage, beloved of hagglers. But more mainstream commercial gloss is on the rise. A mega-development, Essex Crossing, is bringing apartments and a massive retail bazaar called the

---

❤ Time to eat & drink

House-baked brunch treats
Clinton Street Baking *p113*

Classic pastrami on rye
Katz's Delicatessen *p114*

Stylish vegetarian dining
Dirt Candy *p113*

Cult noodle bar
Ivan Ramen *p115*

Late-night cocktails
Attaboy *p116*, Bar Goto *p118*, Nitecap *p118*

❤ Time to shop

Fine vintage
David Owens Vintage Clothing *p119*, Edith Machinist *p119*

Glam spot for rare and locally crafted scents.
Aedes Perfumery *p118*

Lox, bagels and history
Russ & Daughters *p119*

NYC street style
Claw & Co *p119*

Lower East Side street art

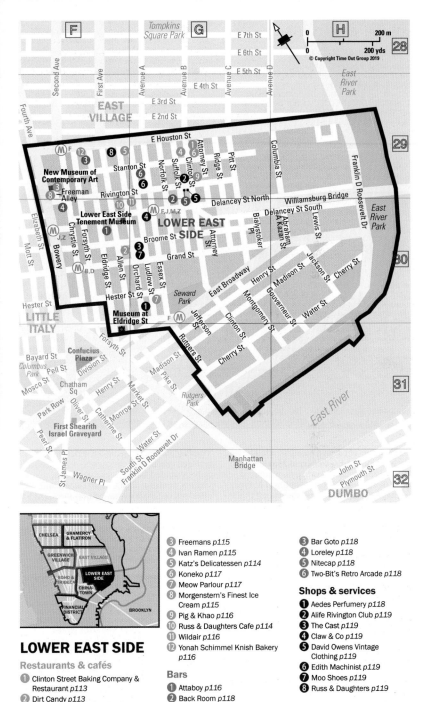

LOWER EAST SIDE

Restaurants & cafés

1 Clinton Street Baking Company & Restaurant *p113*
2 Dirt Candy *p113*
3 Freemans *p115*
4 Ivan Ramen *p115*
5 Katz's Delicatessen *p114*
6 Koneko *p117*
7 Meow Parlour *p117*
8 Morgenstern's Finest Ice Cream *p115*
9 Pig & Khao *p116*
10 Russ & Daughters Cafe *p114*
11 Wildair *p116*
12 Yonah Schimmel Knish Bakery *p116*

Bars

1 Attaboy *p116*
2 Back Room *p118*
3 Bar Goto *p118*
4 Loreley *p118*
5 Nitecap *p118*
6 Two-Bit's Retro Arcade *p118*

Shops & services

1 Aedes Perfumery *p118*
2 Alife Rivington Club *p119*
3 The Cast *p119*
4 Claw & Co *p119*
5 David Owens Vintage Clothing *p119*
6 Edith Machinist *p119*
7 Moo Shoes *p119*
8 Russ & Daughters *p119*

Museum at Eldridge Street

Market Line. The first phase included a new location for **Essex Street Market** (www.essexstreetmarket.com), which originally opened in 1940 as part of Mayor La Guardia's plan to get pushcarts off the streets, and offers high-quality vendors of cheese, produce, fish, meat and sweets. From early 2020, the complex is also home to the International Center of Photography (www.icp.org), which has a museum hosting temporary exhibitions.

Sights & museums

♥ Tenement Museum

Visitors' centre, 103 Orchard Street, at Delancey Street (1-877 975 3786, www. tenement.org). Subway F to Delancey Street; J, M, Z to Delancey-Essex Streets. **Open** *Visitors' centre 10am-6.30pm Mon-Wed, Fri-Sun; 10am-8.30pm Thur. Tours See website for schedule.* **Admission** *$27; $22 reductions.* **Map** *p111 F30.*

This fascinating museum – a series of restored tenement apartments – is accessible only by guided tours. These start at the visitors' centre at 103 Orchard Street, and often sell out, so it's wise to book ahead. At 97 Orchard Street, 'Hard Times' visits the homes of an Italian and a German-Jewish clan; 'Sweatshop Workers' explores the apartments of two Eastern European Jewish families as well as a garment shop where many of the locals would have found employment;

In the know
Grave secrets

Although the gate is usually locked, catch a glimpse of the **First Shearith Israel Graveyard** (55-57 St James Place, between James & Oliver Streets), the final resting place for members of the country's first Jewish community; some gravestones date from 1683, including those of Spanish and Portuguese Jews who fled the Inquisition.

and 'Irish Outsiders' unfurls the life of the Moore family, who are coping with the loss of their child. 'Shop Life' explores the diverse retailers that occupied the building's storefronts, including a 19th-century German saloon. 'Live at the Tenement' lets you interact with actors channelling the original occupants (on select dates; see website). A tour at 103 Orchard Street, 'Under One Roof', tells the stories of later immigrants to the neighbourhood. From mid March to December, the museum also conducts themed daily walking tours of the Lower East Side ($27-$45; $22-$40 reductions).

♥ Museum at Eldridge Street (Eldridge Street Synagogue)
12 Eldridge Street, between Canal & Division Streets (1-212 219 0302, www.eldridgestreet.org). Subway F to East Broadway. **Open** *10am-5pm Mon-Thur, Sun; 10am-3pm Fri.* **Admission** *$14; $8-$10 reductions; free under-5s. Pay what you wish Mon.* **Map** *p111 F31.*

With an impressive façade that combines Moorish, Gothic and Romanesque elements, this opulent house of worship is now surrounded by dumpling shops and Chinese herb stores, but rewind about a century and you would have found delicatessens and *mikvot* (ritual bathhouses). For its first 50 years, the 1887 synagogue had a congregation of thousands and doubled as a mutual-aid society for new arrivals in need of financial assistance, healthcare and employment. But as Jews left the area and the congregation dwindled, the building fell into disrepair. A 20-year, $20-million facelift restored its splendour; the soaring main sanctuary, designed by high-society interior decorators the Herter Brothers, features hand-stencilled walls and a resplendent stained-glass rose window with Star of David motifs. The renovations were completed in 2010, with the installation of a second stained-glass window designed by artist Kiki Smith and architect Deborah Gans. The admission price includes a guided tour (see website for schedule). The downstairs gallery traces the history of the building and Jewish life in the late 19th century through objects, photographs and documents, and hosts changing exhibitions.

♥ New Museum of Contemporary Art
235 Bowery, between Prince & Stanton Streets (1-212 219 1222, www.newmuseum. org). Subway F to Lower East Side-Second Avenue; J, Z to Bowery; R, W to Prince Street; 6 to Spring Street. **Open** *11am-6pm Tue, Wed, Fri-Sun; 11am-9pm Thur.* **Admission** *$18; $12-$15 reductions; free under-19s. Pay what you wish 7-9pm Thur.* **Map** *p111 F29.*

Having occupied various sites for 30 years, New York City's only contemporary art museum got its own purpose-built space in late 2007. Dedicated to emerging media and under-recognised artists, the New Mu also hosts a triennial for young talent. The seven-floor building is worth a look for the architecture alone – it's a striking, off-centre stack of aluminium-mesh-clad boxes designed by the cutting-edge Tokyo architectural firm SANAA. The museum's café is run by the folks behind the area's popular Hester Street Market, offering artisanal eats by a selection of local vendors. At weekends, don't miss the fabulous views from the minimalist seventh-floor Sky Room.

Restaurants & cafés

♥ Clinton Street Baking Company & Restaurant $$
4 Clinton Street, at E Houston Street (1-646 602 6263, www.clintonstreetbaking.com). Subway F to Lower East Side-Second Avenue or Delancey Street; J, M, Z to Delancey-Essex Streets. **Open** *8am-4pm, 5pm-11pm Mon-Fri; 9am-4pm, 5pm-11pm Sat; 9am-6pm Sun.* **No cards** *before 5.30pm.* **Map** *p111 G29* ❶ *Café*

The warm buttermilk biscuits and fluffy plate-size pancakes at this pioneering little eaterie are reason enough to face the brunch-time crowds. If you want to avoid the onslaught, the homey place is just as reliable for both lunch and dinner, and the pancakes are still available. Drop in for the $17 beer and burger special (5.30-11pm Mon-Wed).

♥ Dirt Candy $$
86 Allen Street, between Broome & Grand Streets (1-212 228 7732, www.dirtcandynyc. com). Subway F to Delancey Street; J, M, Z to Delancey-Essex Streets. **Open** *5.30-11pm Tue-Fri; 11am-3pm, 5.30-11pm Sat; 11am-3pm Sun.* **Map** *p111 F30* ❷ *Vegetarian*

Pioneering chef Amanda Cohen creates works of edible art using only vegetables. Emblazoned with a mural of greenery by graffiti artist Noah McDonough, the dining room is focused on the open kitchen at its heart, complete with a chef's counter. Dinner is presented as a tasting menu of five or 10 courses. Each dish is anchored by one vegetable but layers multiple ingredients, such as a portobello-mushroom mousse dish with sautéed Asian pears and cherries. Brunch, which can be ordered à la carte or prix fixe, includes dishes such as the brussels-sprout tacos, served with an array of accompaniments to fold into lettuce wraps.

💙 Old-school delis

There are few things more synonymous with the city than the New York deli, serving dishes from the classic Jewish canon: corn-beef sandwiches, bagels with lox and cream cheese, matzo ball soup, chopped liver and other 'appetising' delicacies. Once the centre of the city's Jewish population, the Lower East Side was the birthplace of these eateries. Today, food-trend-driven diners can feast on everything from brussels-sprout tacos to Tokyo-style *shio* ramen, but you can still get a taste of the old neighbourhood at the granddaddy of all NYC delis. Cavernous, cafeteria-style lunchroom **Katz's** (205 E Houston Street, at Ludlow Street, 1-212 254 2246, www.katzsdelicatessen.com, open 8am-10.45pm Mon-Wed, 8am-2.45am Thur, 8am Fri-10.35pm Sun, *map p111 F29*) opened in 1888. You might get a kick out of the famous faces (from Bill Clinton to Ben Stiller) plastered to the panelled walls, or the spot where Meg Ryan faked it in *When Harry Met Sally*... but the real stars are the

thick-cut pastrami sandwiches and crisp-skinned all-beef hot dogs – the latter still less than five bucks.

Smoked-fish specialist **Russ & Daughters** debuted a café (127 Orchard Street, between Delancey & Rivington Streets, 1-212 475 4881, www.russanddaughterscafe.com, open 9am-10pm Mon-Fri; 8am-10pm Sat, Sun, *map p111 F30*) in its centennial year. The nostalgic yet sleek space takes design cues from the original shop a few blocks away, with tiled floors, clean-lined booths and back-lit art deco signage advertising 'pickles from the barrel' and 'egg cream'. There are some significant upgrades from a traditional nosh spot, however. Seltzer water is dispensed free of charge, but there's also a full bar and you can pair your schmaltz (fat) herring with a shot of vodka. Open-faced sandwich boards let you sample some of the store's famous fish: melt-in-your-mouth sable meets decadent goat's-milk cream cheese on a bagel or bialy in the Shtetl; or

go classic with silky nova, piled high with tomatoes, capers and onions.

Another much-loved family-run old timer, **Barney Greengrass** (*see p201*) was established in 1908, but has occupied its current Upper West Side location since 1929. And from the looks of it, the current wallpaper dates from some two decades later. The self-styled 'Sturgeon King' combines two classic flavours with its pastrami salmon – cured fish with a sharp, peppery edge.

Raised on such neighbourhood landmarks, Upper West Side natives Zach and Alex Frankel (former chef at Jack's Wife Freda and half of Brooklyn synth-pop duo Holy Ghost!, respectively) preserve the traditions of their lox-peddling elders with menschy earnestness at Brooklyn newcomer **Frankel's** (*see p250*). There are no revisionist latkes or molecular-gastro matzo balls here – just the deli staples the brother-owners grew up on, including an excellent pastrami Reuben and a hot brisket sandwich on challah bread.

Katz's Delicatessen

Frankel's

Freemans $$

2 Freeman Alley, off Rivington Street, between Bowery & Chrystie Street (1-212 420 0012, www.freemansrestaurant.com). Subway F to Lower East Side-Second Avenue; J, Z to Bowery. **Open** *11am-4pm, 6-11pm Mon-Fri; 10am-4pm, 6pm-1am Sat, Sun.* **Map** *p111 F29* ❸ *American creative*

Located at the end of a graffiti-marked alley, Freemans, with its colonial-tavern-meets-hunting-lodge style, is an enduring hit with retro-loving New Yorkers. Garage-sale oil paintings and moose antlers serve as backdrops to a curved zinc bar, while the menu recalls a simpler time – devils on horseback (prunes stuffed with stilton cheese and wrapped in bacon), filet mignon and whole grilled local trout. Upstairs, dimly lit Banzarbar serves explorer-themed cocktails in a space that evokes an 18th-century seaside tavern.

❤ Ivan Ramen $$

25 Clinton Street, between E Houston & Stanton Streets (1-646 678 3859, www.ivanramen.com). Subway F to Lower East Side-Second Avenue or Delancey Street; J, M, Z to Delancey-Essex Streets. **Open** *12.30-10pm Mon-Thur, Sun; 12.30-11pm Fri, Sat.* **Map** *p111 G29* ❹ *Japanese*

Ivan Orkin has never been one to play by the rulebook – the brash Long Islander first built his food-world fame 6,000 miles away in Tokyo, where he stirred up Japan's devout ramen congregation with his light, silky slurp bowls in 2007. Seven years later, he opened this narrow slip of a *ramen-ya* on the Lower East Side. The vibrant 65-seat parlour tangles together the noodle virtuoso's all-American roots and Japanophile leanings – a massive papier-mâché mural in front features a kaleidoscope of Dolly Parton, John Wayne, waving lucky cats and Technicolor geishas. Along with his seminal rye-flour noodles (in a choice of broth, including *shio* and *shoyu* varieties), the menu features specials that frequently cross cultures.

Morgenstern's Finest Ice Cream $

2 Rivington Street, between Bowery & Chrystie Street (1-212 209 7684, www.morgensternsnyc.com). Subway J, Z to Bowery; F to Lower East Side-Second Avenue. **Open** *noon-11pm Mon-Thur, Sun; noon-midnight Fri, Sat.* **Map** *p111 F29* ❽ *Ice-cream*

One of the best parts of Nicholas Morgenstern's popular ice-cream parlour, aside from its quirky flavour combos (bourbon vanilla, banana curry), is the late hours. Bustling until midnight on weekends, the scoop shop is a picture-perfect after-dinner retreat, with locals perched at spinning counter seats for behemoth banana splits.

Pig & Khao

Pig & Khao $$

68 Clinton Street, between Rivington & Stanton Streets (1-212 920 4485, www. pigandkhao.com). Subway F to Delancey Street; J, M, Z to Delancey-Essex Streets. **Open** *5-10pm Mon; 5-11pm Tue-Thur; 5pm-midnight Fri; 11am-3.30pm, 5pm-midnight Sat; 11am-3.30pm, 5-10pm Sun.* **Map** *p111 G29* ⑨ *Southeast Asian*

Run by former Top Chef contender Leah Cohen, this mural-splashed joint has a familiar setup, with plenty of canned beer, hot chilies and hip-hop. Chef Leah Cohen has been turning diners on to funky Southeast Asian flavors since 2012 with a pig-centric menu. Enclosed backyard seating is available year-round, and the restaurant offers a weekend brunch with bottomless mimosas.

Wildair $$

142 Orchard Street, between Delancey & Rivington Streets (www.wildair.nyc). Subway F to Delancey Street; J, M, Z to Delancey-Essex Streets. **Open** *6-11pm Mon-Thur, Sun; 6pm-12.30am Fri, Sat.* **Map** *p111 G30* ⑪ *American*

The 45-seat restaurant is a sister to **Contra** (138 Orchard Street, 1-212 466 4633), the understated avant-garde tasting-menu den two doors down, owned by chefs Jeremiah Stone and Fabián von Hauske Valtierra.

Wildair is even more relaxed, with sardine-packed bar tables and neighbourhood affability. And though Wildair's snacky à la carte menu has less sharp-edged experimentation than Contra's, there are low-key innovations at play here. The simple bistro pleasure of breakfast radishes with soft-churned sweet butter are smacked with the briny funk of seaweed, and beef tartare is sultry with smoke courtesy of a haze of hardwood-kissed cheddar, with Brazil nuts adding pops of crunch. Entrée-size options are well-executed – a fat-bordered for-two Wagyu beef with charred Padrón peppers and shallots – but lack the brainy tick of the small plates.

Yonah Schimmel Knish Bakery $

137 E Houston Street, between Eldridge & Forsyth Streets (1-212 477 2858, www. yonahschimmelknish.com). Subway F to Lower East Side-Second Avenue. **Open** *10am-7pm daily (extended hrs in summer).* **Map** *p111 F29* ⑫ *Bakery/café*

Born from the namesake rabbi's pushcart, this neighbourhood stalwart has been doling out its carb-laden goodies since 1910. More than a dozen rotating varieties are available, including blueberry, chocolate-cheese and 'pizza', but traditional potato, kasha and spinach knishes are the most popular.

Bars

♥ Attaboy

134 Eldridge Street, between Broome & Delancey Streets (no phone, www.attaboy. us/nyc). Subway F to Delancey Street; J, M, Z to Delancey-Essex Streets. **Open** *6pm-4am daily.* **Map** *p111 F30* ①

Occupying the former location of Milk & Honey, the seminal cocktail den opened by late mixology pioneer Sasha Petraske, Attaboy is run by alums Sam Ross and Michael McIlroy. The tucked-away haunt

Paws for Coffee

It's 'four legs good' in these pet cafés, if you're a cat person or a dog lover

As a visitor to NYC, it doesn't take long to notice that New Yorkers are pet crazy – shops selling accessories and treats abound, dog runs in parks are plentiful and in many neighbourhoods it seems as if every second person is walking a pooch, from petite Pomeranians to Great Danes that would make the average Manhattan apartment seem cramped. It's hardly surprising, then, that the pet café concept has been a tail-wagging success. While rumours of planned dog-centric eateries had been circulating for years, the trend kicked off with copycat businesses inspired by Tokyo's popular *neko* cafés, and similar establishments in Europe. These feline lairs operate in partnership with rescue groups, which means most of the inhabitants are available for adoption. Visitors must read the rules (no flash photos, no tail pulling) and sign a waiver before admittance.

The first on the scene, **Meow Parlour** (46 Hester Street, between Essex & Ludlow Streets, no phone, www.meowparlour. com; closed Wed) allows the cat-obsessed to commune with around a dozen felines for anything from 30 minutes ($7) to five hours. Co-founded by Christina Ha, who has three cats and a certificate in animal care and handling, it sits next door to her nouveau pâtisserie Macaron Parlour (www. macaronparlour.com). NYC Department of Health regulations prohibit animals on the premises of a facility where food is prepared, but you can have cute cat-shaped cookies, and sometimes kitty-face macarons delivered to you, along with Counter Culture coffee. With high tables for enjoying the treats out of reach of curious paws, the 800-square-foot space – larger than many NYC apartments – was designed with cats in mind. Enclosed beds with glass tops let you observe napping moggies and reach into a side opening to stroke them. There are plenty of dangling toys on hand and a wall of shelving, which residents enjoy scaling, with secret passageways behind it where cats can retreat from attention.

Hot on its paws, **Koneko** (26 Clinton Street, between Houston & Stanton Streets, 1-646 370 5699, www.konekonyc.com; closed Tue) has a distinctly Japanese flavour. In the front is a white-walled café, adorned with artwork such as Shepard Fairey's *Radical Cat*. Founder Benjamin Kalb, who previously cooked in restaurants including Momofuku Noodle Bar, designed the menu of *izakaya* dishes and sake. Stumptown coffee and pastries are also available. Access to the glassed-off cattery ($20 per hour) is in the back. You're asked to leave your shoes at the door (slippers provided) and sanitise your hands before entering. The bi-level space, kitted out with puss-friendly furniture and contemporary bean bags, is home to up to 20 rescued residents. Cats have their own doors out to the enclosed 'catio' featuring a street art-style mural.

In 2018, puppy lovers welcomed the city's first dog café. Unlike the feline versions, **Boris & Horton** (195 Avenue A, at 12th Street, East Village,1-212 510 8986, www. borisandhorton.com) isn't home to the animals, though the namesake pets of the owners are typically on the scene, and the venue hosts adoption nights in collaboration with rescue organisations among its regular events. It's a place where people can hang out and have a bite with their furry pals. Like the cat cafes, however, the venue is divided into two areas to get around the food-safety laws. In the sunny, humans-only side, you can pick up a speciality coffee like the Lassie (a latte with house-made lavender agave) and snacks such as avocado toast or a cheese plate from venerable purveyor Murray's. Then tote them over to the dog-friendly side to consume your purchases with cute canines. A shop sells dog treats and adornments, and there's a photo booth to capture the moment.

Boris & Horton

is lighter and livelier than its forebear, but has kept the same bespoke protocol: at the brushed-steel bar, drinks slingers stir off-the-cuff riffs to suit each customer's preference. Nostalgic boozers can seek solace in Petraske-era standard-bearers, such as Ross's signature Penicillin, a still-inspiring blend of single-malt whisky, honey-ginger syrup and lemon.

Back Room

102 Norfolk Street, between Delancey & Rivington Streets (1-212 228 5098, www.backroomnyc.com). Subway F to Delancey Street; J, M, Z to Delancey-Essex Streets. **Open** *6.30pm-3am Mon-Thur, Sun; 6.30pm-4am Fri, Sat.* **Map** *p111 G30* **2**

Unlike many other ersatz speakeasies, this place has roots in the Prohibition era, when it was the illicit booze-dispensing back room of (now defunct) Ratner's deli. For access, look for a sign that reads 'The Lower East Side Toy Company'. Pass through the gate, down an alleyway and up a metal staircase, and open an unmarked door to find a replica of a 1920s watering hole. Cocktails are poured into teacups, and bottled beer is brown-bagged before being served. Patrons must be 25 or older on Fridays and Saturdays. The dress code is casual, but in a departure from the Jazz Age sensibility, real fur is banned in the bar.

♥ Bar Goto

245 Eldridge Street, between E Houston & Stanton Streets (1-212 475 4411, www.bargoto.com). Subway F to Lower East Side-Second Avenue. **Open** *5pm-midnight Tue-Thur, Sun; 5pm-2am Fri, Sat.* **Map** *p111 F29* **3**

When a sake-and-spirits temple with a Pegu Club-pedigreed barkeep lands on the Lower East Side, there's no avoiding the chorus of cocktail-geek fanfare to follow. Yet take a seat at Kenta Goto's glimmering black-and-gold boîte, lodged away from the Houston Street bedlam, and you'll find the noisy hype storm is curtailed by cool poise, from the hostess's graceful reception to silent servers weaving through tables. In the absence of distractions, focus directs to the well-lit bar, where Goto effortlessly stirs his Far East-whispered creations, drawing on his Japanese heritage as much as his lauded tenure at Audrey Saunders's cocktail trailblazer.

Loreley

7 Rivington Street, between Bowery & Chrystie Street (1-212 253 7077, www.loreleynyc.com). Subway J, Z to Bowery. **Open** *noon-1am Mon-Thur; noon-4am Fri; 10am-4am Sat; 10am-1am Sun.* **Map** *p111 F30* **4**

Perhaps bar owner Michael Momm, aka DJ Foosh, wanted a place where he could spin to his heart's content. Maybe he missed the *biergartens* of his youth in Cologne.

Whatever. Just rejoice that he opened Loreley. Ten imported draughts and eight bottled and canned varieties of Germany's finest brews are available, along with wines from the country's Loreley region and a full roster of spirits.

♥ Nitecap

151 Rivington Street, between Clinton & Suffolk Streets (1-646 490 4338, www.nitecapnyc.com). Subway F to Delancey Street; J, M, Z to Delancey-Essex Streets. **Open** *6pm-2am Mon-Thur, Sun; 6pm-3am Fri, Sat.* **Map** *p111 G29* **5**

The entrance is tricky to find, but the wandering effort is well worth it. A trio of established bar-industry talent stirred up a sultry, cavernous lair that will make you want to linger. Outfitted with retro booths, Nitecap features an inventive, seasonally changing menu that runs the gamut from crisp session cocktails to hefty late-night slugs, plus sections dedicated to bubbly concoctions and shareable punches for groups.

Two-Bit's Retro Arcade

153 Essex Street, between Rivington & Stanton Streets (1-212 477 8161, www.twobitsnyc.com). Subway F to Lower East Side-Second Avenue or Delancey Street; J, M, Z to Delancey-Essex Streets. **Open** *5pm-2am Mon-Fri; 1pm-2am Sat, Sun. p111 G29* **6**

Joystick addicts, take note: this gamer haven offers titles dating back to the 1980s (Pac-Man, Popeye, Final Fight, Donkey Kong), as well as pinball (Fun House, Twilight Zone). After you've grabbed a beer, pause for a moment to admire the video-game-character illustrations inlaid in the bar. One tip: try to make it here by early evening, before the queues to play become three dudes deep.

Shops & services

♥ Aedes Perfumery

16A Orchard Street, between Canal & Hester Streets (1-212 206 8674, www.aedes.com). Subway F to East Broadway. **Open** *noon-8pm Mon-Sat; 1-7pm Sun.* **Map** *p111 G30* **1** *Health & beauty*

After more than two decades in the West Village, Karl Bradl and Robert Gerstner moved their perfume collector's den to the Lower East Side. Decked out like a 19th-century boudoir, with dark walls, stuffed peacocks and vintage cabinets, the space is stocked with ultra-sophisticated scents, plus bath and skincare products. In addition to sleuthing out under-the-radar brands, the couple offer their own glamorously packaged Aedes de Venustas perfumes and candles, and Nomenclature, an ultra-modern, synthetic fragrance line co-created by Bradl, with molecular-inspired packaging.

Alife Rivington Club

158 Rivington Street, between Clinton & Suffolk Streets (1-212 432 7200, www. alifenewyork.com). Subway F to Delancey Street; J, M, Z to Delancey-Essex Streets. **Open** *noon-7pm Mon-Sat; noon-6pm Sun.* **Map** *p111 G29* ❷ *Accessories*

Whether you're looking for simple white trainers or a trendy graphic style, you'll want to gain entry to this 'club', which stocks a wide range of major brands such as Adidas, Puma and Vans. You'll also find lesser-known names including the shop's own label.

The Cast

72 Orchard Street, between Broome & Grand Streets (1-212 228 2020, www.thecast.com). Subway B, D to Grand Street; F to Delancey Street; J, M, Z to Delancey-Essex Streets. **Open** *noon-8pm Mon-Sat; noon-6pm Sun.* **Map** *p111 G30* ❸ *Fashion*

This rock 'n' roll-inspired collection focuses on the trinity of well-cut denim, superior leather jackets based on classic motorcycle styles, and the artful T-shirts that launched the label in 2004. The shop caters to a range of budgets – the Terminal line of jackets for men and women starts around $500, but you'll pay at least $1,500 for a bespoke leather made in NYC. Supple skirts, trousers and a range of accessories are also available, plus vintage boots, accessories and records.

💜 Claw & Co

101 Delancey Street, at Ludlow Street (1-212 995 2440, www.clawandco.com). Subway F to Delancey Street; J, M, Z to Delancey-Essex Streets. **Open** *11am-7pm Mon-Fri; noon-7pm Sat; noon-6pm Sun.* **Map** *p111 G30* ❹ *Fashion/homewares*

Claudia Gold, aka Claw Money, is a graffiti artist and designer who started adorning NYC with her signature claw icon in the late '80s. Inside the hip-hop-inspired shop, expect to find graphic tees and hoodies from her fashion line, trainer collaborations with Nike and Fila, and vintage designer suede and leather jackets and sunglasses from the '70s to the '90s. Dope home decor includes limited-edition denim claw pillows, customised and framed MTA MetroCards and vivid signed prints. You can also pick up inexpensive souvenirs dripping with street cred, such as buttons, badges and key rings.

💜 David Owens Vintage Clothing

161 Rivington Street, between Clinton & Suffolk Streets (1-212 677 3301). Subway F to Lower East Side-Second Avenue. **Open** *11am-7pm daily.* **Map** *p111 G29* ❺ *Fashion*

Specialising in garb from the '40s to the '70s, this small shop is stuffed to the gills with rare pieces for men and women. Possible finds include pristine WWII-era frocks and jackets, '80s DVF dresses, Burberry trench coats and Armani blazers. The accessories selection is strong, with unique buys such as pin-up ties, plus designer bags and scarves by the likes of Gucci, Missoni and Hermès.

💜 Edith Machinist

104 Rivington Street, between Essex & Ludlow Streets (1-212 979 9992, www. edithmachinist.com). Subway F to Delancey Street; J, M, Z to Delancey-Essex Streets. **Open** *noon-6pm Mon, Fri, Sun; noon-7pm Tue-Thur, Sat.* **Map** *p111 G29* ❻ *Fashion/ accessories*

An impeccable, eclectic assemblage of leather bags, shoes and unusual accessories is the main draw of this vintage trove, but you'll also find women's clothing from Italian and French labels.

Moo Shoes

78 Orchard Street, between Broome & Grand Streets (1-212 254 6512, www.mooshoes. com). Subway F to Delancey Street; J, M, Z to Delancey-Essex Streets. **Open** *11.30am-8pm Mon-Sat; 11am-7pm Sun.* **Map** *p111 G30* ❼ *Accessories*

Cruelty-free footwear has come a long way since its days on the unfashionable fringes. This vegan-owned shoe store stocks a variety of brands for men and women, such as Vegetarian Shoes and Novacas, plus styles from independent designers such as Elizabeth Olsen, whose arty OlsenHaus line of high heels and handbags is anything but hippyish.

💜 Russ & Daughters

179 E Houston Street, between Allen & Orchard Streets (1-212 475 4880, www. russanddaughters.com). Subway F to Lower East Side-Second Avenue. **Open** *8am-6pm Mon-Wed, Fri-Sun; 8am-7pm Thur.* **Map** *p111 F29* ❽ *Food & drink*

The daughters in the name have given way to great-grandchildren, but this Lower East Side institution (established 1914) is still run by the same family. Specialising in smoked and cured fish and caviar, it sells about a dozen varieties of salmon, eight types of herring (pickled, salt-cured, smoked and so on) and many other Jewish-inflected Eastern European delectables. Filled bagels such as the amazing Super Heebster (whitefish and baked salmon salad, horseradish cream cheese and wasabi flying-fish roe) are available to take away, but the café (*see p114*) offers a more extensive menu and table service.

East Village

Originally part of the Lower East Side, the East Village developed its distinct identity as a countercultural hotbed in the 1960s. By the dawning of the Age of Aquarius, rock clubs thrived on almost every corner. But in the '70s, the neighbourhood took a dive as drugs and crime prevailed – although that didn't stop the influx of artists and punk rockers. In the early '80s, East Village galleries were among the first to display the work of groundbreaking artists such as Jean-Michel Basquiat and Keith Haring.

The blocks east of Broadway between Houston and 14th Streets may have lost some of their edge, and the former tenements are increasingly occupied by young professionals and trust-fund kids, but humanity in all its guises converges in the parks, bargain restaurants, indie record stores and grungy watering holes on First and Second Avenues and St Marks Place. Chic shops and eateries have taken up residence on Bond and Great Jones Streets in the enclave also known as Noho.

♥ **Don't miss**

1 Merchant's House Museum *p124*
Visit the past via this time capsule.

2 Public Theater *p346*
Ambitious new plays and top cabaret venue Joe's Pub.

3 Danspace Project *p338*
Experimental choreography in a landmark church.

St Marks Place

EAST VILLAGE

▶ *Subway B, D, F, M to Broadway-Lafayette Street; F to Lower East Side-Second Avenue; R, W to 8th Street-NYU; L to First Avenue or Third Avenue; 6 to Astor Place or Bleecker Street.*

From the 1950s to the '70s, **St Marks Place** (E 8th Street, between Lafayette Street & Avenue A) was a hotbed of artists, writers, radicals and musicians, including WH Auden, Abbie Hoffman, Lenny Bruce, Joni Mitchell and GG Allin. The grungy strip still fizzes with energy well into the wee hours, but these days it's packed with cheap eateries, tattoo parlours and shops selling T-shirts, tourist junk and pot paraphernalia.

A short walk north brings you to **St Mark's Church in-the-Bowery** (131 E 10th Street, at Second Avenue, 1-212 674 6377, www.stmarksbowery.org). Built in 1799, the Federal-style church sits on the site of Peter Stuyvesant's farm; the old guy himself, one of New York's first governors, is buried in the adjacent cemetery. Regular services are still held, and the church is home to several cultural organisations, including the Poetry Project and **Danspace Project** (*see p338*).

Cutting between Broadway and Fourth Avenue south of East 8th Street, **Astor Place** is the site of the **Cooper Union**, comprising schools of art, architecture and engineering. It was here, in February 1860, that Abraham Lincoln gave his celebrated Cooper Union Address, which argued for the regulation (though not abolition) of slavery and helped to propel him into the White House.

In the know
Metal landmark

The cover of Led Zeppelin's 1975 album *Physical Graffiti* depicts the apartment buildings at 96 and 98 St Marks Place.

During the 19th century, Astor Place marked the boundary between the slums to the east and some of the city's most fashionable homes. **Colonnade Row** (428-434 Lafayette Street, between Astor Place & E 4th Street) faces the distinguished Astor Public Library building, which theatre legend Joseph Papp rescued from demolition in the 1960s. Today, the old library houses the **Public Theater** (*see p346*), a platform for first-run American plays, and cabaret venue **Joe's Pub** (*see p319*). Nearby, the **Merchant's House Museum** is a perfectly preserved specimen of upper-class domestic life in the 1800s.

Below Astor Place, Third Avenue (one block east of Lafayette Street) becomes the **Bowery**. For decades, the street languished as a seedy strip and the home of missionary organisations aiding the down and out. Although traces of the old flophouses, along with the Gothic Revival headquarters of **Bowery Mission** at no.227 (between Rivington & Stanton Streets), remain, the thoroughfare has been cleaned up and repopulated with high-rise condo buildings, restaurants, nightspots and hotels.

Elsewhere in the neighbourhood, East 7th Street is a stronghold of New York's Ukrainian community, of which the focal

---

♥ Time to eat & drink

Stylish brunch
Lafayette *p127*, Prune *p129*

Quirky sweet treats
Big Gay Ice Cream Shop *p125*, Milk Bar *p132*

Buzzy Asian dining
Hanoi House *p126*, Little Tong *p128*, Momofuku Ssäm Bar *p128*

Historic pub
McSorley's Old Ale House *p130*

Novelty nightcaps
Ghost Donkey *p129*, Mother of Pearl *p130*, PDT *p130*

♥ Time to shop

Back-to-the-80s fashion
Mr Throwback *p133*, Spark Pretty *p133*

Eccentric collectibles
Obscura Antiques & Oddities *p133*

Gender-fluid merch
The Phluid Project *p133*

Japanese labels and vintage goods
Dear: Rivington *p132*

Well-stacked institution
Strand Book Store *p133*

The Phluid Project

EAST VILLAGE

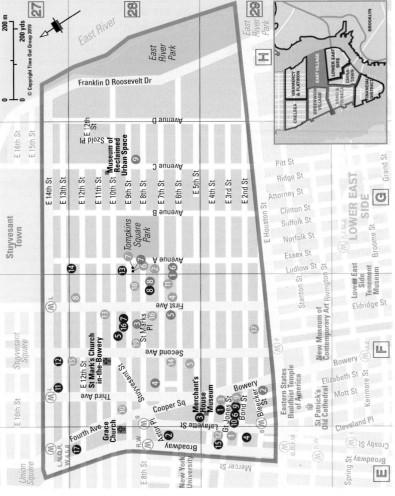

Restaurants & cafés

1. Atla *p124*
2. Big Gay Ice Cream Shop *p125*
3. Bowery Market *p125*
4. Caracas Arepa Bar *p125*
5. Coffee Project New York *p126*
6. Crif Dogs *p126*
7. Hanoi House *p126*
8. Hearth *p126*
9. Il Buco Alimentari & Vineria *p126*
10. Ippudo NY *p127*
11. Kyo Ya *p127*
12. Lafayette *p127*
13. Little Tong *p127*
14. Momofuku Ssäm Bar *p128*
15. Mighty Quinn's *p128*
16. Oiji *p129*
17. Prune *p129*
18. Superiority Burger *p129*
19. Veselka *p129*

1. Mother of Pearl *p130*
2. PDT *p130*
3. Proletariat *p131*
4. Wayland *p131*

Shops & services

1. 3.1 Phillip Lim *p131*
2. Astor Hairstylists *p131*
3. Astor Wines & Spirits *p131*
4. Bond No.9 *p131*
5. Consigliere *p131*
6. Dear: Rivington *p132*
7. Fabulous Fanny's *p132*
8. Fun City Tattoo *p132*
9. The Future Perfect
10. Great Jones Spa
11. Kiehl's
12. Milk Bar
13. Mr Throwback
14. Obscura Antiques & Oddities
15. The Phluid Project
16. Spark Pretty
17. Strand Book Store

Bars

1. Death & Co *p129*
2. Ghost donkey *p129*
3. Holiday Cocktail Lounge *p129*
4. McSorley's Old Ale House *p130*
5. Mister Paradise *p130*

EAST VILLAGE

123

point is the Eastern Catholic **St George's Ukrainian Catholic Church** at no.30. **The Ukrainian Museum** (222 E 6th Street, between Second & Third Avenues, 1-212 228 0110, www.ukrainianmuseum.org, closed Mon, Tue) houses folk and fine art and archival materials from that country. One block over, there's often a long line of loud fraternity types waiting at weekends to enter **McSorley's Old Ale House**. Festooned with aged photos, yellowed newspaper articles and dusty memorabilia, the 1854 Irish tavern is purportedly the oldest continually operating pub in New York, and the spot where Lincoln repaired after giving his Cooper Union Address. **Curry Row** (East 6th Street, between First & Second Avenues) is lined with Indian restaurants that are popular with budget-minded diners.

Alphabet City (which gets its name from its key avenues: A, B, C and D) stretches towards the East River. It was once an edgy Puerto Rican neighbourhood with links to the drugs trade, but its demographic has dramatically shifted over the past 20 years. Avenue C is also known as Loisaida Avenue, a rough approximation of 'Lower East Side' when pronounced with a Hispanic accent. **The Nuyorican Poets Cafe** (236 E 3rd Street, between Avenues B & C, 1-212 780 9386, www.nuyorican.org), a clubhouse for espresso-drinking wordsmiths since 1973, is known for its poetry slams, in which performers wage lyric battles before a score-keeping audience.

Dating from 1834, **Tompkins Square Park** (from 7th to 10th Streets, between Avenues A & B) honours Daniel D Tompkins, governor of New York from 1807 to 1817, and vice-president during the Monroe administration. Over the years, this 10.5-acre park has been a site for demonstrations and rioting. The last major uprising occurred in 1991, when the city evicted squatters from the park and renovated it to suit the influx of affluent residents. Along with mature sycamore and elm trees dating from the 19th century, the landscaped green space has basketball courts, playgrounds and dog runs, and is still a place where bongo beaters, guitarists, multi-pierced teenagers, hipsters, local families and vagrants mingle.

Dotting the surrounding area are remnants of earlier communities: Italian cheese shops; Polish butchers; Russian baths, and a great Italian coffee and cannoli house, **Veniero's** (342 E 11th Street, between First & Second Avenues, 1-212 674 7070, www.venierospastry.com). Indie boutiques and vintage shops are clustered on 9th Street between First and Second Avenues.

Sights & museums

❤ Merchant's House Museum

*29 E 4th Street, between Bowery & Lafayette Street (1-212 777 1089, www.merchantshouse. org). Subway B, D, F, M to Broadway-Lafayette Street; 6 to Bleecker Street. **Open** Jan-Sept noon-5pm Mon, Fri-Sun; noon-8pm Thur. Oct-Dec noon-5pm Mon, Thur-Sun. Guided tours 2pm Mon, Fri-Sun; 2pm, 6.30pm Thur (Jan-Sept only). **Admission** $15; $10 reductions; free under-12s. No international cards. **Map** p123 F29.*

Merchant's House Museum, the city's only fully preserved 19th-century family home, is an elegant, late Federal-Greek Revival property kitted out with the same furnishings and decorations it contained when it was inhabited from 1835 by hardware tycoon Seabury Tredwell and his family. Three years after Tredwell's eighth daughter died in 1933, it opened as a museum. Gertrude Tredwell is said to haunt her home of 93 years (check the website for details of the candlelight ghost tours, held one evening a month Jan-July, sometimes Nov). During regular hours, you can peruse the house and secluded garden at your own pace, following along with the museum's printed guide, or time your visit with a guided tour. Be sure to ascend to the servants' quarters on the fourth floor, and note the original bell that summoned the four Irish maids at the top of the stairs.

Museum of Reclaimed Urban Space

*155 Avenue C, between 9th & 10th Streets (1-646 340 8341, www.morusnyc.org). Subway L to First Avenue. **Open** 11am-7pm Tue, Thur-Sun. **Admission** Suggested donation $5. **Map** p123 G28.*

Co-founded by Bill Di Paola, director of advocacy group Time's Up!, this monument to local activism is housed in C-Squat, a walk-up building that has sheltered activists, down-on-their-luck artists and members of several punk bands (including Leftover Crack, Old Skull and Nausea) from the 1970s to the present. Spread over two floors, documentary-style exhibits show how city residents created, protected and took back community spaces. The museum offers tours of the neighbourhood's historic sites and community gardens (3pm Sat, Sun), and hosts archival film screenings.

Restaurants & cafés

Atla $$

*372 Lafayette Street, between Bond & Great Jones Streets (1-347 662 3522, www.atlanyc. com). Subway B, D, F, M to Broadway-Lafayette Street; 6 to Bleecker Street. **Open** 11am-10pm Mon-Wed, Sun; 11am-11pm Thur-Sat. **Map** p123 F29* ➊ *Mexican*

A cooler, more casual follow-up from Flatiron megahit Cosme, Atla spotlights healthy Mexican fare: chayote squash salad, flax seeds *chilaquiles* and striped bass *aguachile*. There's also a strong emphasis on drinks. At the all-day eatery, you can start the day with *café con leche* or fresh juices, or order evening agave-leaning cocktails. Taking cues from the community-focused restaurants of Mexico City, the sleek spot features black and oak-wood furniture, a white terrazzo bar and vegetation lining the walls.

♥ Big Gay Ice Cream Shop $
*125 E 7th Street, between First Avenue & Avenue A (1-212 533 9333, www. biggayicecream.com). Subway L to First Avenue. **Open** 1-10pm Mon-Thur, Sun; 1-11pm Fri, Sat (hrs vary seasonally). **Map** p123 G28* ❷ *Ice-cream*

Ice-cream truckers Doug Quint and Bryan Petroff now have three bricks-and-mortar shops in NYC dispensing their quirky soft-serve creations. Opt for a simple cone coated in rainbow sprinkles or the signature chocolate dip (with a pinch of salt and cayenne), or try one of the house combos such as the Salty Pimp (vanilla ice-cream, dulce de leche, sea salt and chocolate dip) or Truckers ice-cream sandwiches with rotating flavours and sprinkles. **Other locations** 61 Grove Street, at Seventh Avenue South, West Village (1-212 414 0022); 207 Front Street, between Beekman & Fulton Streets, South Street Seaport.

Bowery Market $
*348 Bowery, between Great Jones & 4th Streets (no phone, www.thebowerymarket. com). Subway B, D, F, M to Broadway-Lafayette Street; 6 to Bleecker Street. **Open** 9am-10pm Mon-Fri; 10am-10pm Sat, Sun (vendors vary). **Map** p123 F29* ❸ *Eclectic*

On the site of a defunct auto-body shop, this all-day, rain-or-shine outdoor marketplace features independent food vendors in corrugated-iron shacks. Options include popular pizza spot Cheska's for creative toppings on a cauliflower or sweet potato crust; *nigiri* operation Sushi on Jones, and Pinks Cantina, serving tacos and other Mexican street food-inspired snacks.

Caracas Arepa Bar $
*91 E 7th Street, between First Avenue & Avenue A (1-212 228 5062, www. caracasarepabar.com). Subway F to Lower East Side-Second Avenue; 6 to Astor Place. **Open** noon-10pm Mon-Thur, Sun; noon-11pm Fri, Sat. **Map** p123 F28* ❹ *Venezuelan*

This endearing spot, with bare-brick walls and tables covered with flower-patterned vinyl, zaps you straight to Caracas. Each *arepa* is made from scratch daily; the pita-like pockets are stuffed with a choice of a dozen fillings, such as the classic beef with black beans, cheese and plantain, or chicken with chorizo and avocado. Top off your snack with a *cocada*, a thick and creamy coconut milkshake made with freshly grated

Merchant's House Museum

cinnamon. **Other location** 291 Grand Street, between Havemeyer & Roebling Streets, Williamsburg, Brooklyn (1-718 218 6050).

Coffee Project New York $

239 E 5th Street, between Bowery & Second Avenue (1-212 228 7888, www.coffeeprojectny. com). Subway 6 to Astor Place. **Open** *7am-6pm Mon-Fri; 8am-6pm Sat; 8am-5.30pm Sun.* **Map** *p123 F28* 5 *Café*

Chi Sum Ngai studied the dark stuff at Portland's American Barista and Coffee School before opening the earth-toned, studio-size café with partner Kaleena Teoh. The drinks menu includes drip and espresso staples made with locally roasted beans, a nitrogen cold brew on tap and a rotating cast of progressive pour 'projects', such as a deconstructed latte flight separating lightly pasteurised milk, espresso and a composed latte into three stemmed glasses to highlight each individual flavour. Beyond coffee, there are teas, hot chocolate and baked goods. **Other location** 78 Rockwell Place, between Fulton Street & Lafayette Avenue, Brooklyn (1-585 888 3153).

Crif Dogs $

113 St Marks Place, between First Avenue & Avenue A (1-212 614 2728, www.crifdogs.com). Subway L to First Avenue; 6 to Astor Place. **Open** *noon-2am Mon-Thur, Sun; noon-4am Fri, Sat.* **Map** *p123 G28* 6 *American*

You'll recognise this place by the giant hot dog outside, bearing the come-on 'Eat me'. Crif offers the best New Jersey-style dogs this side of the Hudson: handmade smoked-pork tube-steaks that are deep-fried until they're bursting out of their skins. While they're served in various guises, among them the Spicy Redneck (wrapped in bacon and covered in chilli, coleslaw and jalapeños), we're partial to the classic with mustard and kraut. If you're wondering why there are so many people hanging around near the public

---

In the know
Rock relics

Pay your respects to the neighbourhood's late, legendary music venues, including the **Dom** (23 St Marks Place, between Second & Third Avenues), where the Velvet Underground headlined – the building is now a condo. CBGB, once the unofficial home of US punk, which fostered the Ramones, Talking Heads and Patti Smith, is now occupied by swanky menswear shop **John Varvatos** (315 Bowery, at Bleecker Street, 1-212 358 0315, www.johnvarvatos.com). The store has preserved a section of the club's flyer-plastered wall behind glass.

phone booth at night, it's because there's a trendy cocktail bar, PDT (*see p130*), concealed behind it. **Other location** 555 Driggs Avenue, at North 7th Street, Williamsburg, Brooklyn (1-718 302 3200).

♥ Hanoi House $$

119 St Marks Place, between Avenue A & First Avenue (1-212 995 5010, www.hanoihousenyc. com) Subway L to First Avenue; 6 to Astor Place. **Open** *5.30-10pm Mon; 5.30-10.30pm Tue-Thur; 5.30-11pm Fri, Sat; noon-3pm, 5.30-10pm Sun.* **Map** *p123 G28* 7 *Vietnamese*

Launched by a couple of alums from Stephen Starr's dining empire, Hanoi House isn't your typical Vietnamese comfort-food canteen. The seasonally changing menu features such elevated fare as coconut-braised octopus dotted with hard-boiled quail eggs, or *banh mi* deconstructed as dainty pâté-slathered toasts crowned with sea urchin and pickled vegetables. But the most effective dish – and its most popular, judging by the steaming bowls that dot the small tables and bar top – is the slow-simmered *pho bac*, with hunks of Black Angus filet mignon and brisket that swim among the slippery rice noodles.

The team recently opened Hanoi Soup Shop a few doors down (115 St Marks Place, 1-646 692 9130), a counter-seated spot catering to the on-the-go lunch crowd.

Hearth $$

403 E 12th Street, at First Avenue (1-646 602 1300, www.restauranthearth.com). Subway L to First Avenue. **Open** *6-10pm Mon-Thur; 6-11pm Fri; 11am-2pm, 6-11pm Sat; 11am-3.30pm, 6-10pm Sun.* **Map** *p123 F28* 8 *American*

Upscale yet relaxed, Hearth skirts food trends with a hearty, health-conscious menu that includes offal, broths, grains and a substantial list of seasonal vegetables. Look for Italian-leaning main courses such as beef-and-ricotta meatballs, polenta with pecorino, and whole roasted wild or sustainably grown fish. There is a small hearth in the restaurant, but the real warmth comes from the staff, who take pains in helping you pick the right dish and are equally interested in finding out afterwards what you thought of it.

Il Buco Alimentari & Vineria $$

53 Great Jones Street, between Bowery & Lafayette Street (1-212 837 2622, www.ilbuco. com). Subway B, D, F, M to Broadway-Lafayette Street; 6 to Bleecker Street. **Open** *8am-11pm Mon-Thur; 8am-midnight Fri; 9am-midnight Sat; 9am-11pm Sun.* **Map** *p123 F29* 9 *Italian*

Il Buco has been a mainstay of the downtown dining scene since the 1990s and a pioneer in

Hanoi House

the sort of rustic Italian food now ubiquitous in the city. Owner Donna Lennard took her sweet time (18 years, to be exact) to unveil her first offshoot, Il Buco Alimentari & Vineria. It was worth the wait: the hybrid bakery, food shop, café and trattoria is as confident as its decades-old sibling, with sure-footed service, the familial bustle of a neighbourhood pillar, and heady aromas of wood-fired short ribs and salt-crusted fish drifting from an open kitchen. If you like the rustic style of the restaurants, you can purchase Italian hand-blown glass, artisan-made kitchenware and vintage finds from the retail shop Il Buco Vita. **Other locations** Il Buco, 47 Bond Street, between Bowery & Lafayette Street, East Village (1-212 533 1932); Il Buco Vita, 57 Great Jones Street, between Bowery & Lafayette Street, East Village (1-917 946 3085).

Ippudo NY $$

*65 Fourth Avenue, between 9th & 10th Streets (1-212 388 0088, www.ippudony.com). Subway 6 to Astor Place. **Open** 11am-3.30pm, 5-11.30pm Mon-Thur; 11am-11.30pm Fri, Sat; 11am-10.30pm Sun. **Map** p123 F28* ⑩ *Japanese*

This sleek outpost of a Japanese ramen chain attracts Nippon natives who queue up for a taste of 'Ramen King' Shigemi Kawahara's *tonkotsu* – a pork-based broth. About half a dozen varieties include the Akamaru Modern, a smooth, buttery soup topped with scallions, cabbage, a slice of roasted pork and pleasantly elastic noodles. Avoid non-soup dishes such as the oily fried-chicken wings.

Long live the Ramen King – just don't ask him to move beyond his speciality. **Other locations** 24 W 46th Street, between Fifth & Sixth Avenues, Midtown (1-212 354 1111); 321 W 51st Street, between Eighth & Ninth Avenues, Hell's Kitchen (1-212 974 2500).

Kyo Ya $$$

*94 E 7th Street, between First Avenue & Avenue A (1-212 982 4140, www.kyoyany. com). Subway 6 to Astor Place. **Open** 6-11.30pm Wed-Sat; 6-10.30pm Sun. **Map** p123 F28* ⑪ *Japanese*

This ambitious Japanese speakeasy is marked only by an 'Open' sign, but in-the-know diners still find their way inside. The food, presented on beautiful handmade plates, includes exquisite renditions of classic dishes, such as *maitake* mushrooms or sweet potato fried in the lightest tempura batter, miso-glazed black cod, and delicate *chawanmushi* (a savoury egg custard dish) with snow crab.

♥ Lafayette $$

*380 Lafayette Street, at Great Jones Street (1-212 533 3000, www.lafayetteny. com). Subway B, D, F, M to Broadway-Lafayette Street; 6 to Bleecker Street. **Open** 8am-10.30pm Mon-Thur; 8am-11pm Fri, Sat; 8am-10pm Sun. **Map** p123 E29* ⑫ *French*

Ace culinary crew Andrew Carmellini, Josh Pickard and Luke Ostrom – the winning team behind blockbusters Locanda Verde and the Dutch – followed up with this souped-up, all-day French bistro, marking Carmellini's

Little Tong

return to his Francophile roots (exemplified by runs at Café Boulud and Lespinasse). The changing menu focuses on the country's rustic south. In the spacious, mahogany-floored eaterie, a zinc-hooded rotisserie twirls roast chicken, while an in-house bakery churns out Provençal staples such as *pain de campagne,* and pretty people gab over their niçoise salads. While some dishes fail to excite, it's a solid choice for brunch.

❤ Little Tong $$
177 First Avenue, at E 11th Street (1-929 367 8664, www.littletong.com). Subway L to First Avenue. **Open** *11.30am-2.30pm, 5.30-11pm Mon-Sat; 11.30am-2.30pm, 5.30-10.30pm Sun.* **Map** *p123 F28* ⑬ *Chinese*

wd~50 alum Simone Tong zooms in on the Yunnanese speciality noodle, *mixian,* and contemporary Chinese dishes at this blond-wood-accented canteen. The slight acidity of the soft, springy rice noodles is best showcased in the lunch menu's porky Little Pot Mixian, laced with pickled mustard seeds and chili vinaigrette, and the Grandma Chicken Mixian, enlivened with the sharp funk of pickled daikon radish, black sesame garlic oil and a savoury tea egg. Spunky small plates include salted cucumber with a nutty tahini-sesame 'bang bang' sauce, and the fresh, fragrant Ghost Chicken Salad (available at lunch), tossed with fermented chilies, pickled red onions and herbs. **Other location** 235 E 53rd Street, between Second & Third Avenues, Midtown East (1-929 383 0465).

Mighty Quinn's $$
103 Second Avenue, at 6th Street (1-212 677 3733, www.mightyquinnsbbq.com). Subway 6 to Astor Place. **Open** *11.30am-11pm Mon-Thur, Sun; 11.30am-midnight Fri, Sat.* **Map** *p123 F28* ⑭ *American*

Drummer-turned-chef Hugh Mangum first hawked his Texalina (Texas spice meets Carolina vinegar) specialities at his immensely popular stand at Smorgasburg (*see p287*). When the operation went bricks-and-mortar, the hungry throngs followed. Lines of customers snake through the steel-tinged joint, watching as black-gloved carvers give glistening meat porn a dash of Maldon salt before slinging it down the assembly line. Dry-rubbed brisket is slow-smoked for 22 hours, and the Jurassic-sized beef rib is so impossibly tender that one bite will quiet the pickiest barbecue connoisseur. **Other locations** throughout the city.

❤ Momofuku Ssäm Bar $$
207 Second Avenue, at 13th Street (no phone, www.momofuku.com). Subway L to First or Third Avenue; L, N, Q, R, W, 4, 5, 6 to 14th Street-Union Square. **Open** *11.30am-3.30pm, 5.30-11.30pm Mon-Thur, Sun; 11.30am-3pm, 5pm-12.30am Fri, Sat.* **Map** *p123 F28* ⑮ *Korean*

Chef David Chang has gone from East Village rebel to awards-circuit veteran, piling up accolades and expanding his empire across the city. Ssäm Bar, his second modern Asian restaurant, shares the pared-down wood decor and utilitarian seating as its nearby predecessor, Momofuku Noodle Bar. Try the wonderfully fatty pork-belly steamed bun with hoisin sauce and cucumbers (on the brunch menu and available by request at lunch and dinner), or one of the ham platters. But you'll need to come with a crowd to sample the house speciality, *bo ssäm* (a slow-roasted pork shoulder that is consumed wrapped in lettuce leaves, with a dozen oysters and other accompaniments); it serves six to ten people and must be ordered in advance. At Momofuku Ko, reserve space at the 19-seat counter to fishbowl-view chef-servers as they prepare the multicourse meal. **Other locations** Momofuku Noodle Bar, 171 First Avenue, between 10th & 11th Streets, East Village; Momofuku Ko, 8 Extra Place, between Bowery & Second Avenue, East Village; Momofuku Nishi, *see p156.*

Oiji $$

119 First Avenue, between 7th Street & St Marks Place (1-646 767 9050, www.oijinyc. com). Subway 6 to Astor Place. **Open** *6-10.30pm Mon-Thur; 6-11pm Fri, Sat; 5-10pm Sun.* **Map** *p123 F28* ⓰ *Korean*

Honey-buttered potato crisps are just one of the instantly craveable takes on cultish South Korean junk food at Oiji, helmed by fine-dining vets Brian Kim and Tae Kyung Ku. Craggy Korean fried chicken is reborn as arguably the most ethereal chicken cutlet ever, trading grease traps of batter for a delicately crisp tapioca coating.

❤ Prune $$

54 E 1st Street, between First & Second Avenues (1-212 677 6221, www. prunerestaurant.com). Subway F to Lower East Side-Second Avenue. **Open** *11.30am-3pm, 5.30-11pm Mon-Fri; 10am-3.30pm, 5.30-11pm Sat, Sun.* **Map** *p123 F29* ⓱ *American creative*

Tiny, well-lit Prune is still as popular as it was the day it opened. Gabrielle Hamilton's French mother developed this fearless chef's palate early on. Expect creative seasonal dishes such as Manila clams with hominy and smoked paprika butter, and rack of lamb with fried mint, fried aubergine (eggplant) and fresh feta. This is the area's go-to brunch spot, so beware: the wait for a table can stretch over an hour.

Superiority Burger $

430 E 9th Street, between Avenue A & First Avenue (1-212 256 1192, www. superiorityburger.com). Subway L to First Avenue. **Open** *11.30am-10pm Mon-Sat; 11.30am-9pm Sun.* **Map** *p123 F28* ⓲ *Vegetarian*

In a white-tiled slip of an East Village eatery, former James Beard Award-winning Del Posto pastry great and erstwhile punk-rock drummer Brooks Headley offers his uberpopular veggie burger. Tofu cabbage wraps, vegetarian sloppy joes and *gelato* are also on the menu, but seating is in short supply.

Veselka $$

144 Second Avenue, at 9th Street (1-212 228 9682, www.veselka.com). Subway L to Third Avenue; 6 to Astor Place. **Open** *24hrs daily.* **Map** *p123 F28* ⓳ *Ukrainian*

When you need food to soak up the mess of drinks you've consumed in the East Village in the early hours, it's worth remembering Veselka – a relatively inexpensive Ukrainian restaurant with plenty of seats, which is open 24 hours a day. Hearty appetites can get a platter of Eastern European grub: *pierogies*, goulash, *kielbasa*, beef stroganoff or *bigos* stew. For dessert, try the *kutya* (traditional Ukrainian pudding made with wheat berries, walnuts, poppy seeds and honey).

Bars

Death & Co

433 E 6th Street, between First Avenue & Avenue A (1-212 388 0882, www. deathandcompany.com). Subway F to Lower East Side-Second Avenue; 6 to Astor Place. **Open** *6pm-2am Mon-Thur, Sun; 6pm-3am Fri, Sat.* **Map** *p123 F28* ❶

The nattily attired mixologists are deadly serious about drinks at this pseudo speakeasy with gothic flair (don't be intimidated by the imposing wooden door). Black walls and cushy booths combine with chandeliers to set a luxuriously sombre mood. The inventive cocktails, including some neat twists on the classics, are matched by a changing selection of top-notch bar bites.

❤ Ghost Donkey

4 Bleecker Street, between Bowery & Elizabeth Street (1-212 254 0350, www.ghostdonkey. com). Subway B, D, F, M to Broadway-Lafayette Street; F to Lower East Side-Second Avenue; 6 to Bleecker Street. **Open** *5pm-2am daily.* **Map** *p123 F29* ❷

Festooned with red lights, this Latin-spirited haunt stacks fun-loving experts behind the bar to mix playful drinks from head bartender Ignacio 'Nacho' Jimenez, such as a mushroom-infused mescal margarita or a mescal Negroni with mole spices. And who wouldn't want to drink out of a ceramic ass? (A donkey, of course.) At this joint, you'll be feeling good way before the tequila shots. The proper accompaniment to the cocktails is a hefty portion of haute nachos, in varieties such as black truffle with white cheddar or mole chicken.

Holiday Cocktail Lounge

75 St Marks Place, between First & Second Avenues (1-212 777 9637, www. holidaycocktaillounge.nyc). Subway L to First Avenue; 6 to Astor Place. **Open** *4pm-4am Mon-Fri; noon-4am Sat, Sun.* **Map** *p123 F28* ❸

Formerly a grungy time capsule, Holiday hosted the likes of Allen Ginsberg, Joey Ramone and Frank Sinatra. Shuttered for three years following the sale of the building, it was reborn, and while the joint has been spruced up – duct-taped booths traded for green banquettes, neon beer signs for gold sconces – it hasn't been scrubbed clean of its charm. The signature horseshoe bar is still the centrepiece, and a harem-girl mural, dating back to the 1920s when the bar was known as Ali Baba Burlesque, has been restored. Dive bar aficionados will revel in the $6 cans of Rolling Rock, but the drinks list encompasses craft beer as well as classic and creative cocktails.

❤ McSorley's Old Ale House

15 E 7th Street, between Second & Third Avenues (no phone, https:// mcsorleysoldalehouse.nyc). Subway F to Lower East Side-Second Avenue. **Open** *11am-1am Mon-Sat; 1pm-1am Sun.* **No cards.** **Map** *p123 F28* ④

Ladies should probably leave the Blahniks at home. In traditional Irish-pub fashion, McSorley's floor has been thoroughly scattered with sawdust to take care of the spills and other messes that often accompany the consumption of large quantities of beer. Established in 1854, McSorley's became an institution by remaining steadfastly authentic and providing only two options: McSorley's Dark Ale and McSorley's Light Ale. A fascinating cast of characters has raised a glass here, from Tammany Hall politicians to purported regular Harry Houdini (look for his handcuffs above the bar).

Mother of Pearl

Mister Paradise

105 First Avenue, between 6th & 7th Streets (no phone, www.misterparadisenyc.com). Subway F to Lower East Side-Second Avenue; 6 to Astor Place. **Open** *5pm-1am Mon-Wed; 5pm-3am Thur, Fri; 2pm-3am Sat; 2pm-1am Sun.* **Map** *p123 F28* ⑤

An emerald-green bar and a wall of undulating sand-tone banquettes give this well-designed watering hole a playful vibe. That cheeky spirit continues with innovative twists on classic drinks. The Dr Angel Face substitutes Japanese shochu for vodka or gin, while the Cafe Disco combines rye whiskey, olive oil, buckwheat, coffee and absinthe for a unique take on an old-fashioned. Bar grub includes fancy riffs on fast food, including French fries with foie gras mousse, and a diner-style burger with caramelised onions and bacon-flavoured American cheese.

❤ Mother of Pearl

95 Avenue A, at 6th Street (1-212 614 6818, www.motherofpearlnyc.com). Subway F to Lower East Side-Second Avenue. **Open** *5pm-1am Mon-Wed; 5pm-2am Thur, Fri; 3pm-2am Sat; 3pm-1am Sun.* **Map** *p123 G28* ⑥

You won't find any standard-issue mai tais at this postmodern take on a tiki bar from Ravi DeRossi (Death & Co). The Shark Eye plays on a Demerara dry float, swapping the usual rum for curaçao and bourbon in a novelty ceramic shark's head cup. The cosy teal-and-white den is rife with time-warp nods to the Pacific isles, including retro floral-patterned banquettes, hand-carved totem pole stools and mother-of-pearl light fixtures. The effect is somewhat dreamlike, enhanced by a lo-fi pop soundtrack ranging from the Velvet Underground to St. Vincent.

❤ PDT

113 St Marks Place, between First Avenue & Avenue A (1-212 614 0386, www.pdtnyc.com). Subway L to First Avenue; 6 to Astor Place. **Open** *6pm-2am Mon-Thur, Sun; 6pm-3am Fri, Sat.* **Map** *p123 G28* ⑦

The word is out about 'Please Don't Tell', the faux speakeasy inside gourmet hot dog joint Crif Dogs (*see p126*), so it's a good idea to reserve a booth in advance (phone line open 3-6pm). Once you arrive, you'll notice people lingering outside an old wooden phone booth near the front. Slip inside, pick up the receiver and the host opens a secret panel to the dark, narrow space. The serious cocktails surpass the gimmicky space entry: try the house old-fashioned, made with bacon-infused bourbon, which leaves a smoky aftertaste.

Proletariat

*102 St Marks Place, between First Avenue & Avenue A (1-212 777 6707, www.proletariatny. com). Subway 6 to Astor Place. **Open** 5pm-2am Mon-Thur; 2pm-2am Fri, Sat; 2pm-midnight Sun. **Map** p123 F28* ❽

Proletariat is a much-deserved look into no-holds-barred beer geekdom, blissfully free of TVs and generic pub grub. With a 12-stool bar, plus a communal table, brewhounds get the type of intimacy usually reserved for the cocktail and wine crowds. The expert servers have a story for every keg they tap, from the newest local brews to German craft ales and deep cuts from the Belgian canon.

Wayland

*700 E 9th Street, at Avenue C (1-212 777 7022, www.thewaylandnyc.com). Subway L to First Avenue. **Open** 4pm-4am Mon-Fri; 11am-4am Sat, Sun. **Map** p123 G28* ❾

East Village bar crawlers have been stumbling further down the alphabet for years, but it's taken Avenue C time to develop the critical mass necessary to attract a late-night buzz. At this fun-loving bar, solicitous staff, a young crowd and the likelihood of a spontaneous singalong round the piano all contribute to a convivial vibe that makes you want to call for another round. An old-fashioned riff called I Hear Banjos (apple pie moonshine, rye whiskey and apple-spice bitters) comes with a ceremonious puff of applewood smoke, captured in an overturned glass that's placed over the drink.

Shops & services

3.1 Phillip Lim

*48 Great Jones Street, between Bowery & Lafayette Street (1-212 334 1160, www.31philliplim.com). Subway B, D, F, M to Broadway-Lafayette; 6 to Bleecker Street. **Open** 11am-7pm Mon-Sat; noon-6pm Sun. **Map** p123 F29* ❶ *Fashion*

The New York-based designer has amassed a devoted international following for his simple yet strong silhouettes and beautifully constructed tailoring with a twist. His spacious, all-white flagship showcases his collections for men and women, alongside accessories, including his highly sought-after handbags.

Astor Place Hairstylists

*2 Astor Place, at Broadway (1-212 475 9854, www.astorplacehairnyc.com). Subway R, W to 8th Street-NYU; 6 to Astor Place. **Open** 8am-8pm Mon; 8am-9pm Tue-Fri; 8am-6.30pm Sat; 9am-6pm Sun. **No cards**. **Map** p123 E28* ❷ *Health & beauty*

The army of barbers at Astor Place tackles everything from neat trims to more complicated and creative shaved designs. Though some stylists take reservations, the decades-old chop shop mainly caters to walk-ins. Be prepared for a wait, especially on weekday evenings. Sunday mornings are usually quieter. Cuts start at $18.

Astor Wines & Spirits

*399 Lafayette Street, at 4th Street (1-212 674 7500, www.astorwines.com). Subway R, W to 8th Street-NYU; 6 to Astor Place. **Open** 9am-9pm Mon-Sat; noon-6pm Sun. **Map** p123 F28* ❸ *Food & drink*

High-ceilinged, wide-aisled Astor Wines is a terrific place to browse for wines of every price, vineyard and year. Sakés and spirits are also well represented.

Bond No.9

*9 Bond Street, between Broadway & Lafayette Street (1-212 228 1732, www.bondno9.com). Subway B, D, F, M to Broadway-Lafayette Street; 6 to Bleecker Street. **Open** 11am-8pm Mon-Fri; 10am-7pm Sat; noon-6pm Sun. **Map** p123 E29* ❹ *Health & beauty*

The Bond No.9 fragrance collection pays olfactory homage to New York City. Choose from more than 60 'neighbourhoods' and 'sensibilities', including Wall Street, Park Avenue, Nuits de Noho, High Line, Brooklyn – even Chinatown (but don't worry, it smells of peach blossoms, gardenia and patchouli, not fish stands). The arty bottles and neat, colourful packaging are particularly gift-friendly. **Other locations** throughout the city.

Consigliere

*220 E 10th Street, between First & Second Avenues (1-212 777 0350, www.shopconsigliere. com). Subway L to First Avenue; 6 to Astor Place. **Open** noon-8pm Mon-Sat; noon-7pm Sun. **Map** p123 F28* ❺ *Male grooming*

The primary focus at this stylish, slender shop is on grooming, stocking mainly American niche brands, including Alder New York, Baxter of California and Ursa Major. The locally made Man Shop house line includes beard balm and oil to tame unruly facial hair while moisturising the skin. Soy-wax candles in such manly fragrances as whiskey, tobacco or woods are available in mini gift sets, and cool accessories such as leather toiletries bags and wallets are also in the mix.

> **In the know**
> **Spin the Alamo**
>
> Astor Place is marked by a steel cube that has occupied a traffic island by the entrance to the 6 train since 1967. With a little elbow grease, the cube, whose proper title is *Alamo*, will spin on its axis.

♥ Dear: Rivington

*37 Great Jones Street, between Bowery &
Lafayette Street (1-212 673 3494, www.
dearrivington.com). Subway B, D, F, M to
Broadway-Lafayette; 6 to Bleecker Street.*
Open *11am-7pm Mon-Sat; noon-6pm Sun.*
Map *p123 F29* **6** *Fashion*

A utilitarian white space provides a stage for
Moon Rhee and Hey Ja Do's installation-like
displays, incorporating industrial furniture,
manufacturing relics and other curios.
Hanging on an assortment of period rolling
racks, the duo's own line of one-of-a-kind
garments is interspersed with select pieces
by the likes of Comme des Garçons and
Yohji Yamamoto; the Dear label combines a
Japanese minimalist aesthetic with Victorian
and 1950s influences, often incorporating
salvaged trimmings such as beaded collars
and lace. Pristine vintage handbags and
accessories are scattered around the store and
arranged in old display cases. The lower level
showcases contemporary ceramics, antique
furnishings and decorative objects.

Fabulous Fanny's

*335 E 9th Street, between First & Second
Avenues (1-212 533 0637). Subway L to First
Avenue; 6 to Astor Place.* **Open** *noon-8pm
daily.* **Map** *p123 F28* **7** *Accessories*

Formerly a Chelsea flea market booth, this
shop is the city's best source of unworn
period glasses, stocking an ever-changing
array of more than 30,000 pairs of spectacles,
from Jules Verne-esque wire rims to 1970s
rhinestone-encrusted Versace shades.

Fun City Tattoo

*94 St Marks Place, between First Avenue &
Avenue A (1-212 353 8282, www.funcitytattoo.
com). Subway R, W to 8th Street-NYU; 6
to Astor Place.* **Open** *noon-10pm daily.* **No
cards.** **Map** *p123 F28* **8** *Tattoo parlour*

Jonathan Shaw started inking locals from his
apartment in the mid-1970s (when tattooing
was illegal) before opening this store in 1989.
The legendary figure has retired, but his New
York City institution – which has served the
likes of Johnny Depp, Jim Jarmusch, Dee
Dee Ramone and Sepultura's Max Cavalera
– continues its operations. Fun City's artists
can do most anything, from lettering and
Japanese to American traditional.

The Future Perfect

*55 Great Jones Street, between Bowery
& Lafayette Street (1-212 473 2500, www.
thefutureperfect.com). Subway 6 to Bleecker
Street.* **Open** *10am-6pm Mon-Fri; by appt
Sat, Sun.* **Map** *p123 F29* **9** *Homewares*

Championing avant-garde interior design, this
innovative store specialises in artist-made,
limited-edition and one-of-a-kind pieces. The
Future Perfect is the exclusive US stockist
of Dutch designer Piet Hein Eek's elegant
woodwork and pottery, but it also showcases
local talent. Look out for beautifully simple
hand-thrown and -glazed bowls by Jason
Miller and spare gold jewellery and branching
metal light fixtures by Lindsey Adelman.

Casa Perfect, a West Village townhouse
where furnishings and objects are displayed
in situ, is accessed by appointment only (the
address is revealed once you've booked on
the website or by phone).

Great Jones Spa

*29 Great Jones Street, at Lafayette Street
(1-212 505 3185, www.gjspa.com). Subway 6 to
Astor Place.* **Open** *9am-10pm daily.* **Map** *p123
F29* **10** *Health & beauty*

Harnessing the wellbeing-boosting
properties of water, Great Jones is outfitted
with a popular wet lounge complete with
subterranean pools, saunas, steam rooms
and a three-storey waterfall. Access to the
15,000sq ft paradise is complimentary with
spa services over $100 – treat yourself to
a divinely scented body scrub, a massage
or one of the many indulgent packages.
Alternatively, a three-hour pass costs $55.

Kiehl's

*109 Third Avenue, between 13th & 14th Streets
(1-212 677 3171, www.kiehls.com). Subway L
to Third Avenue; N, Q, R, W, 4, 5, 6 to 14th
Street-Union Square.* **Open** *10am-9pm Mon-
Sat; 11am-7pm Sun.* **Map** *p123 F27* **11** *Health
& beauty*

The apothecary founded on this site in 1851
has morphed into a major skincare brand,
but the products, in their minimal packaging,
are still good value and effective. Lip balms
and the thick-as-custard Creme de Corps
have become cult classics. **Other locations**
throughout the city.

♥ Milk Bar

*251 E 13th Street, at Second Avenue (1-646
692 4154, www.milkbarstore.com). Subway
L to First or Third Avenue; L, N, Q, R, W,
4, 5, 6 to 14th Street-Union Square.* **Open**
*9am-midnight Mon-Thur, Sun; 9am-1am Fri,
Sat.* **Map** *p123 F27* **12** *Food & drink*

Pastry wizard Christina Tosi conjures up
inventively homey sweets at this lauded
bakery across the street from Momofuku
Ssäm Bar (*see p128*). East Village hipsters,
foodies and in-the-know visitors come for
the cultish goodies, including the house pie
with an addictively buttery filling, Cereal
Milk soft serve and Compost Cookies made
with pretzels, potato chips, coffee, oats,
butterscotch and chocolate chips. **Other
locations** throughout the city.

Spark Pretty

♥ Mr Throwback

*437 E 9th Street, between First Avenue &
Avenue A (1-917 261 7834, www.mrthrowback.
com). Subway L to First Avenue. Open
noon-8pm Mon-Sat; noon-6pm Sun. Map p123
G28* ⓭ *Fashion*

Rappers and celebs, such as Kid Cudi and
Scarlett Johansson, are fans of this sports-
centric vintage trove, specialising in '80s
and '90s major league gear. Pick up an
original New York Knicks champion jersey
or a Mets satin starter jacket, or choose from
dozens of other teams. You'll also find caps,
trainers and the store's own line of T-shirts
and hoodies featuring players and other era-
appropriate icons.

♥ Obscura Antiques & Oddities

*207 Avenue A, between 12th & 13th Streets
(1-212 505 9251, www.obscuraantiques.
com). Subway L to First Avenue. Open
12.45pm-8pm Mon-Fri; noon-8pm Sat; noon-
7pm Sun (hrs can vary). Map p123 G28* ⓮
Gifts & souvenirs/homewares

Housed inside a former funeral home, this
eccentric shop, immortalised in a Science
Channel reality TV series, specialises in
bizarre items such as medical and scientific
antiques, human skulls and taxidermied
animals dating from the 19th century. Owners
Evan Michelson and Mike Zohn scour flea
markets, auctions and even museums for rare
artefacts such as anatomical prints, jarred
piranhas and Victorian memorial artwork
made from the deceased's hair.

♥ The Phluid Project

*684 Broadway, at Great Jones Street (1-212
655 0551, www.thephluidproject.com).
Subway B, D, F, M to Broadway-Lafayette
Street; 6 to Bleecker Street; R, W to 8th
Street-NYU. Open 11am-8pm Mon-Sat; noon-
6pm Sun. Map p123 E29* ⓯ *Fashion/gifts &
souvenirs*

Founded by a former fashion-industry
executive after an epiphany on a jungle
retreat, the city's first gender-free store-
hangout has a welcoming, upbeat vibe.
The expansive space offers a coffee bar
and regular events such as poetry readings
and talks, as well as apparel, accessories,
cosmetics and gifts. The diverse fashion
aesthetic spans everything from basic denim
and hoodies from well-known brands to
flamboyant shirts and caftans by emerging
NYC designers, plus T-shirts with slogans
like 'Ask me my pronouns' and 'New York
Phucking City'.

♥ Spark Pretty

*333 East 9th Street, between First & Second
Avenues (1-646 850 0327, www.sparkpretty.
com). Subway L to First Avenue; 6 to Astor
Place. Open noon-8pm Mon-Sat. Map p123
F28* ⓰ *Fashion*

Enter a world of MTV, troll dolls and
Baywatch posters in this colourful, kitsch
homage to the '80s and '90s (with a bit of '70s
glam-rock edge thrown in). Run by a pair
of former stylists to punky designer Betsey
Johnson, the vintage boutique is bursting
with clubtastic animal-print and glittery
get-ups; crystal-encrusted, hand-painted
denim jackets; and shredded acid-wash jeans,
plus pins, tees and sweatshirts emblazoned
with nostalgic pop-culture images from
Rick Springfield and Nirvana to Barbie, the
Chippendales and stars of *Dallas*.

♥ Strand Book Store

*828 Broadway, at 12th Street (1-212 473 1452,
www.strandbooks.com). Subway L, N, Q,
R, W, 4, 5, 6 to 14th Street-Union Square.
Open 9.30am-10.30pm daily. Map p123
E28* ⓱ *Books*

Established in 1927, the Strand has a
mammoth collection of more than 2.5
million discount volumes (both new and
used), and the store is made all the more
daunting by its chaotic, towering shelves and
sometimes crotchety staff. You can find just
about anything here, from that out-of-print
Victorian book on manners to the kitschiest
of sci-fi pulp. Note that the rare book room
upstairs closes at 6.15pm. There are also
Strand kiosks on the edge of Central Park at
Fifth Avenue and 60th Street, and in Times
Square on 43rd Street between Broadway &
Seventh Avenue (weather permitting).

Greenwich Village & West Village

Anchored by New York University, Greenwich Village, along with its western adjunct the West Village, is one of the most picturesque parts of the city. The stomping ground of the Beat Generation is no longer a cheap-rent bohemian paradise, but it's still a pleasant place for idle wandering, dining in excellent restaurants and hopping between bars and cabaret venues. The Meatpacking District, which over the past three decades has evolved from gritty industrial zone to gay cruising spot to hedonistic consumer playground, has a flashier feel. But the 2015 opening of the Whitney Museum brought a welcome injection of culture to the neighbourhood.

❤ **Don't miss**

1 Greenwich Village literary walk *p139*
Follow in the footsteps of novelists, playwrights and poets.

2 Whitney Museum of American Art *p147*
Huge riverside art temple.

3 Washington Square Park *p136*
The heart of Village life.

4 Comedy Cellar *p314*
You never know who might drop by...

5 Village Vanguard *p324*
Iconic jazz bar.

Street performers in Washington Square Park

GREENWICH VILLAGE

▶Subway A, B, C, D, E, F, M to W 4th Street; L, N, Q, R, W, 4, 5, 6 to 14th Street-Union Square; R, W to 8th Street-NYU; 1 to Christopher Street-Sheridan Square.

Stretching from Houston Street to 14th Street, between Broadway and Sixth Avenue, **Greenwich Village** has been inspiring bohemians for more than a century. Now that it has become one of the most expensive neighbourhoods in the city, you need a lot more than a struggling artist's or writer's income to inhabit its leafy streets. Follow in the footsteps of some of the Village's literary greats on our walk around the neighbourhood (*see p139*).

Great for people-watching, **Washington Square Park** attracts a disparate cast of characters that takes in hippies, students, chess players and street musicians. Skateboarders clatter near the base of the Washington Arch, a modestly sized replica of Paris's Arc de Triomphe. Built in 1895 to honour George Washington, it leads to the park's large central fountain.

In the 1830s, the wealthy began building handsome townhouses around the square. A few of those properties are still privately owned and occupied, but many others have become part of the ever-expanding NYU campus. The university also owns the Washington Mews, a row of charming 19th-century former stables that line a tiny cobblestoned alley just to the north of the park between Fifth Avenue and University Place. Several famed literary figures, including Henry James (author of the celebrated novel that took its title from the square), Herman Melville, Edith Wharton, Edgar Allan Poe and Eugene O'Neill, lived on or near the square. In 1871, the local creative community founded the **Salmagundi Club** (47 Fifth Avenue, between 11th & 12th Streets, 1-212 255 7740, www.salmagundi.org), one of America's oldest artists' clubs. Now situated north of Washington Square on Fifth Avenue, it has galleries that are open to the public.

Greenwich Village continues to change with the times, for the better and for the worse. In the 1960s, **8th Street** was the closest New York got to San Francisco's hippie magnet, Haight Street; Jimi Hendrix's **Electric Lady Studios** is still at 52 West 8th Street, between Fifth & Sixth Avenues. For years, the run-down strip was a procession of piercing parlours, smoke shops and shoe stores, but it's been smartened up with the arrival of upscale cafés, bars and restaurants, including **Stumptown Coffee Roasters** and **Loring Place**.

Once the dingy but colourful domain of Beat poets and folk and jazz musicians, the well-trafficked section of **Bleecker Street** between LaGuardia Place and Sixth Avenue is now an overcrowded stretch of poster shops, cheap restaurants and music venues for the college crowd. Renowned hangouts such as **Le Figaro Café** (184 Bleecker Street, at MacDougal Street), Kerouac's favourite, are no more, but a worthy alternative is **Caffe Reggio**, the oldest coffeehouse in the village. Although 1960s hotspot **Cafe Wha?** (115 MacDougal Street, between Bleecker & W 3rd Streets, 1-212 254 3706, cafewha.

❤ Time to eat & drink

Morning coffee
Caffe Reggio *p138*, Stumptown Coffee Roasters *p141*

Pastries and sandwiches
Dominique Ansel Kitchen *p144*, High Street on Hudson *p148*

New-classic dining
Carbone *p138*, Via Carota *p145*, Bistro Pierre Lapin *p143*

Seasonal-cuisine standouts
Blue Hill *p138*, Loring Place *p140*

Historic watering holes
Dante *p141*, White Horse Tavern *p146*

❤ Time to shop

Antique and heirloom-inspired jewellery
Doyle & Doyle *p149*

Boho-chic fashion
Fairlight/Alix of Bohemia *p146*

Perfect for Washington Square Park picnics
Murray's Cheese *p142*

Venerable apothecary
CO Bigelow *p142*

Washington Square Park

GREENWICH VILLAGE & WEST VILLAGE

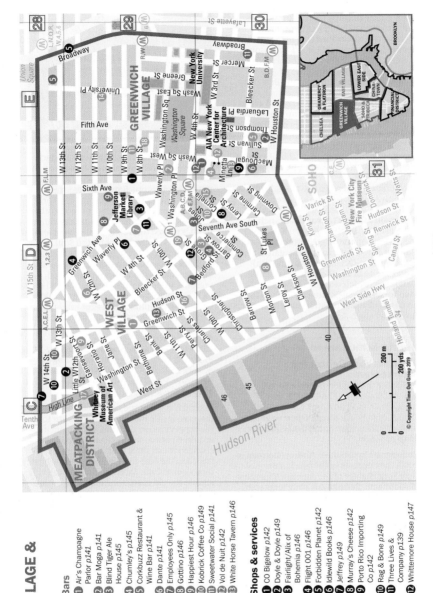

Restaurants & cafés

1. Bistro Pierre Lapin p143
2. Blue Hill p138
3. Buvette p143
4. Caffe Reggio p138
5. Carbone p138
6. Corner Bistro p144
7. Dominique Ansel Kitchen p144
8. EN Japanese Brasserie p144
9. High Street on Hudson p148
10. Kesté Pizza & Vino p144
11. Loring Place p140
12. Mamoun's Falafel p140
13. Minetta Tavern p140
14. Nix p140
15. Pearl Oyster Bar p144
16. RedFarm p144
17. Santina p149
18. Stumptown Coffee Roasters p141
19. Via Carota p145

Bars

1. Air's Champagne Parlor p141
2. Bar Moga p141
3. Blind Tiger Ale House p145
4. Chumley's p145
5. Corkbuzz Restaurant & Wine Bar p141
6. Dante p141
7. Employees Only p145
8. Gottino p146
9. Happiest Hour p146
10. Kobrick Coffee Co p149
11. Sweetwater Social p141
12. Vol de Nuit p142
13. White Horse Tavern p146

Shops & services

1. CO Bigelow p142
2. Doyle & Doyle p149
3. Fairlight/Alix of Bohemia p146
4. Flight 001 p146
5. Forbidden Planet p142
6. Idlewild Books p146
7. Jeffrey p149
8. Murray's Cheese p142
9. Porto Rico Importing Co p142
10. Rag & Bone p149
11. Three Lives & Company p139
12. Whittemore House p147

com) is now running on the fumes of its illustrious past, it has a decent house band. Nearby, the **Bitter End** (147 Bleecker Street, between LaGuardia Place & Thompson Street, 1-212 673 7030, www.bitterend.com) has proudly championed the singer-songwriter – including a young Bob Dylan – since 1961.

The famed Village Gate jazz club at the corner of Bleecker and Thompson Streets – which staged performances by Miles Davis, Nina Simone and John Cage – closed in 1993. However, in 2008, **Le Poisson Rouge** (*see p321*) opened on the site with a similar mission to present diverse genres under one roof.

Not far from here, in the triangle formed by Sixth Avenue, Greenwich Avenue and 10th Street, you'll see the Gothic-style **Jefferson Market Library** (a branch of the New York Public Library). Next to it, the lovingly maintained **Jefferson Market Garden** (www.jeffersonmarketgarden. org; open Apr-Oct 9am-dusk Tue-Sun) is on the site of the Women's House of Detention, which was torn down in 1974. Mae West did a little time there in 1926, on obscenity charges stemming from her Broadway show *Sex*.

Sights & museums

AIA New York Center for Architecture

536 LaGuardia Place, between Bleecker & W 3rd Streets (1-212 683 0023, www. centerforarchitecture.org). Subway A, B, C, D, E, F, M to W 4th Street. **Open** *9am-8pm Mon-Fri; 11am-5pm Sat.* **Admission** *free.* **Map** *p137 E30.*

Redesigned by architect Andrew Berman in 2003, the Center is in the headquarters of the New York chapter of the American Institute of Architects. Berman cut away large slabs of flooring at the street and basement levels, converting underground spaces into light, museum-quality galleries. Exhibitions focus on both local and international themes. AIA New York also offers architectural walking and boat tours.

Restaurants & cafés

♥ Blue Hill $$$

75 Washington Place, between Washington Square West & Sixth Avenue (1-212 539 1776, www.bluehillfarm.com). Subway A, B, C, D, E, F, M to W 4th Street. **Open** *5-11pm Mon-Sat; 5-10pm Sun.* **Map** *p137 E29* ❷
American creative

More than a mere crusader for sustainability, Dan Barber is also one of the most talented

Blue Hill

cooks in town, building his menu around whatever's at its peak on the family farm in Great Barrington, Massachusetts, and the not-for-profit Stone Barns Center for Food and Agriculture in Westchester, New York (home to a sibling restaurant), among other suppliers. The tastefully understated dining room is tucked discreetly on the lower level of a townhouse just off Washington Square Park. Choose from the ever-changing four-course daily menu or six-course tasting menu. The evening may begin with a sophisticated seasonal spin on a pig's liver terrine and move on to a sweet slow-roasted parsnip 'steak' with creamed spinach and beet ketchup, or grass-fed lamb. Wine pairings are available.

♥ Caffe Reggio $

119 MacDougal Street, at W 3rd Street (1-212 475 9557, www.caffereggio.com). Subway A, B, C, D, E, F, M to W 4th Street. **Open** *9am-3am Mon-Thur, Sun; 9am-4am Fri, Sat.* **Map** *p137 E30* ❹ *Café*

Legend has it that the original owner of this classic café introduced Americans to the cappuccino in 1927 and, apart from its acquired patina, we bet the interior hasn't changed much since then. Although it's traded in the coal-fuelled espresso machine for a sleeker Caffe Sacco model, you can still admire the old custom chrome-and-bronze contraption on the bar. Sip espresso and tuck into a house-made tiramisu under the Italian Renaissance-style paintings.

♥ Carbone $$$

181 Thompson Street, between Bleecker & Houston Streets (no phone, www. carbonenewyork.com). Subway C, E to Spring Street. **Open** *5.30-11.30pm Mon; 11.45-2pm, 5.30-11.30pm Tue-Fri; 11.45-2pm, 5-11.30pm Sat, Sun.* **Map** *p137 E30* ❺ *Italian*

Red sauce revivalists Rich Torrisi and Mario Carbone honour Gotham's legendary Italian joints (Rao's, Bamonte's) with their high-profile revamp of historic Rocco's Ristorante. Suave, tuxedo-clad waiters – Bronx accents intact, but their burgundy threads designed by Zac Posen – tote an avalanche of complimentary extras: chunks of chianti-

💜 Greenwich Village literary walk

As the rich migrated uptown following World War I, free thinkers and artists – most notably writers – from all over the world began to move into Greenwich Village, taking advantage of the cheap rents and large apartments. In the 1950s, the Beat poets made the area their own. Start your literary ramble with an espresso at **Caffe Reggio** (*see opposite*), which opened in 1927 and served as a hangout for Beats including Jack Kerouac and native Villager Gregory Corso. Heading north, you'll pass the **Provincetown Playhouse** (133 MacDougal Street, between 3rd & 4th Streets, www.steinhardt.nyu.edu), where the Provincetown Players (1916-29) premiered the works of the troupe's leading member, Eugene O'Neill, among others. Now run by NYU Steinhardt's Department of Music and Performing Arts Professions, with a façade restored to its 1940 appearance, it hosts mainly free storytelling shows and concerts.

The stately townhouses along the northern fringe of **Washington Square** evoke the august world of Henry James's novel of that name, although the setting that inspired it – his grandmother's home at no.14 – has not survived. However, 21 Washington Square North was used as Jennifer Jason Leigh's house in the 1997 film remake. James himself lived at no.1, as did – at different points – Edith Wharton and the literary critic William Dean Howells. Diagonally across the square, at 38 Washington Square South, Eugene O'Neill consecrated his first New York residence by having an affair with journalist Louise Bryant, while her husband, John Reed (author of *Ten Days That Shook the World*) was in hospital.

Leave the square via Fifth Avenue and turn left on to 10th Street, where Mark Twain lived in 1900 in the elegant, reputedly haunted brownstone at no.14. At the corner of Sixth Avenue is the landmark **Jefferson Market Library**, next to the **Jefferson Market Garden** (*see opposite*), with its flowerbeds and fish pond, where you can rest your feet. Just behind the library lies **Patchin Place**, once home to some of New York's literary pantheon. This cul-de-sac lined with mid-19th-century brick houses is off limits to the public, but through the gate you can make out no.4, where the poet, and foe of capitalisation, ee cummings resided from 1923 to 1962, and no.5, where Djuna Barnes, author of *Nightwood*,

lived from 1940 to 1982. Ezra Pound and Theodore Dreiser are among those who passed through.

Head west on 10th to quaint bookshop **Three Lives & Company** (no.154, www.threelives.com) to browse such classic paeans to the city as EB White's *Here is New York*, chronicling a 1940s stroll around Manhattan.

Continue west until you get to Hudson Street, then hang a right to the **White Horse Tavern** (*see p146*), favourite watering hole of self-destructive Welsh poet Dylan Thomas, and also frequented by Kerouac, James Baldwin and Norman Mailer. Solemnly raise a glass to Thomas, who had his last drink in the pub, then make your way a block east to head down Bleecker Street. Either turn right at Grove Street to reach the legendary literary bar **Chumley's** (*see p145*) or continue south, taking a left at Carmine Street on to Minetta Lane. At the corner of MacDougal is revived hotspot **Minetta Tavern** (*see p140*), once the haunt of literati including Ernest Hemingway and F Scott Fitzgerald, as well as the famously blocked Joe Gould, whose dry spell was recounted in Joseph Mitchell's *Joe Gould's Secret*.

Jefferson Market Library

infused parmesan, olive-oil-soaked 'Grandma Bread' and rotating cured meats, such as slivers of smoky prosciutto. Follow updated renditions of classic pasta, including a spicy, über-rich rigatoni vodka, with mains such as sticky cherry-pepper ribs and lavish takes on tiramisu for dessert.

♥ Loring Place $$
21 W 8th Street, between Fifth & Sixth Avenues (1-212 388 1831, www.loringplacenyc. com). Subway A, B, C, D, E, F, M to W 4th Street. **Open** *noon-2.30pm, 5.30-9.45pm Mon; noon-2.30pm, 5.30-10.30pm Tue-Thur; noon-2.30pm, 5.30-11pm Fri; 11am-3pm, 5.30-11pm Sat; 11am-3pm, 5.30-9.45pm Sun.* **Map** *p137 E29* ⑪ *American creative*

Dan Kluger's vibrant farmers' market riffs not only earned ABC Kitchen (*see p164*) a James Beard Award in 2011 but also a legion of locavore followers who have seemingly tailed the chef downtown to his solo dining room, a split-level expanse of whitewashed walls and sleek neutrals. A well-heeled crowd populates the pine-wood tables, dipping seasonal vegetable 'fries' in lemony parmesan dressing and sharing wholewheat pizzas with creative toppings. The chef's acclaimed layering techniques – finding harmony in a clang of sweet, sour and salt – are showcased in plates such as crispy bulbs of Indian-spiced cauliflower brightened with a tart swipe of Meyer lemon jam, and a hyper-seasonal grain salad with a shifting array of vegetables.

Mamoun's Falafel $
119 MacDougal Street, between Bleecker & W 3rd Streets (no phone, www.mamouns.com). Subway A, C, E, B, D, F, M to W 4th Street. **Open** *11am-5am daily.* **No cards.** **Map** *p137 E30* ⑫ *Middle Eastern*

Favoured by famous foodies and late-night bar-hoppers alike, this cheap-eats stalwart has been serving quality Middle Eastern food since 1971. The falafel is served in a pita with lettuce, tomato and tahini, and you'd be well advised to add houmous or baba ganoush. Seating is severely limited in the cramped, counter-service space, so be prepared to tackle the messy, overstuffed snack standing up. Sweet pastries such as baklava and knafe – shredded filo dough with pistachios – leave you satisfied and ready for bed.

Minetta Tavern $$$
113 MacDougal Street, between Bleecker & W 3rd Streets (1-212 475 3850, www. minettatavernny.com). Subway A, B, C, D, E, F, M to W 4th Street. **Open** *5.30pm-midnight Mon, Tue; noon-3pm, 5.30pm-midnight Wed; noon-3pm, 5.30pm-1am Thur, Fri; 11am-3pm, 5.30pm-1am Sat; 11am-3pm, 5.30pm-midnight Sun.* **Map** *p137 E30* ⑬ *Eclectic*

Restaurateur Keith McNally brought the buzz back to this erstwhile literati hangout once frequented by Hemingway and Fitzgerald. In line with the spot-on restoration of its vintage interior, the big-flavoured bistro fare includes classics such as roasted bone marrow, trout meunière topped with crabmeat, and an airy Grand Marnier soufflé. But the most illustrious thing on the menu is the Black Label burger. You might find the price tag a little hard to swallow (starting at $30 at lunch), but the superbly tender sandwich – essentially chopped steak smothered in caramelised onions in a bun – is worth every penny.

▶ *For less expensive but equally acclaimed burgers, see Corner Bistro (p144), Shake Shack (p202) and JG Melon (p211).*

Nix $$
72 University Place, between 10th & 11th Streets (1-212 498 9393, www.nixny.com). Subway L, N, Q, R, W, 4, 5, 6 to 14th Street-Union Square. **Open** *5.30-11pm Mon-Thur; 5-11pm Fri; 10.30am-2.30pm, 5-11pm Sat; 10.30am-2.30pm, 5-10pm Sun.* **Map** *p137 E29* ⑭ *Vegetarian*

Nix is the first veg-only restaurant from Michelin-starred chef John Fraser, who dipped his toe in the genre with Meatless Mondays at now-shuttered Dovetail and his blogger-luring rotisserie beets at Narcissa. But you'll find no #cleaneating diatribes

Dante

at this California-chic spot. The dishes are defined more by decadence than discipline, having no qualms about drenching any bulb, leaf or stalk in dairy or fryer oil. Tempura-fried florets of cauliflower, pickle chips and whipped tofu are loaded into Chinese-style steamed buns, while an intensely creamy dish of boiled eggs shellacked in habanero mayo and tangles of potato crisps is the devilled egg of Paula Deen's dreams.

❤ Stumptown Coffee Roasters $
30 W 8th Street, at MacDougal Street (1-855 711 3385, www.stumptowncoffee.com). Subway A, B, C, D, E, F, M to W 4th Street. **Open** *7am-8pm daily.* **Map** *p137 E29* ⑱
Café

The lauded Portland, Oregon, outfit expanded its New York holdings – which include a branch inside the Ace Hotel (*see p379*) – with this stand-alone café. The wood-panelled counter and old-fashioned cabinetry nod to classic coffee houses, but purists can savour single-origin espresso from a La Marzocco GS3 machine and slow brews prepared via java-geek speciality drips. The low-key hangout offers a wide selection of seasonal coffees, plus pastries and sandwiches. **Other location** 212B Pacific Street, between Boerum Place & Court Street, Cobble Hill, Brooklyn (1-347 416 6741).

Bars

Air's Champagne Parlor
127 MacDougal Street, between 3rd & 4th Streets (1-212 420 4777, www. airschampagneparlor.com). Subway A, B, C, D, E, F, M to W 4th Street. **Open** *5pm-midnight Tue, Wed; 5pm–1am Thur-Sat.* **Map** *p137 E30* ①

Air's founder Ariel Arce is trying to bring bubbly down to earth. Although a glass can still run more than $20, the fizz-focused bar also offers bottles under $50. The small space evokes a Gatsby-style cabana, complete with a marble-slab bar, brass-accented stools, gilded geometric mirrors and potted palm fronds – a fitting setting to kick off a glam night out.

Bar Moga
128 W Houston Street, between Sullivan & Thompson Streets (1-929 399 5853, www. barmoga.com). Subway A, B, C, D, E, F, M to W 4th Street; 1 to Houston Street. **Open** *5pm-midnight Mon-Thur, Sun; 5pm-2am Fri, Sat.* **Map** *p137 E30* ②

Inspired by *mogas*, independent-minded women from 1920s Japan who listened to jazz and dressed in Westernised fashions, this Japanese-accented cocktail bar is decked out with tin ceilings, vintage chandeliers and walls dotted with retro advertisements. The menu balances both East and West with *yōshoku*-style food and cocktails stirred with ingredients from both hemispheres and plenty of shochu.

Corkbuzz Restaurant & Wine Bar
13 E 13th Street, between Fifth Avenue & University Place (1-646 873 6071, www. corkbuzz.com). Subway L, N, Q, R, W, 4, 5, 6 to 14th Street-Union Square. **Open** *4pm-midnight Mon-Thur, Sun; 4pm-1am Fri, Sat.* **Map** *p137 E28* ⑤

This intriguing and elegant hybrid bar, restaurant and educational centre was created by master sommelier, Laura Maniec, as an unintimidating space for wine appreciation and enjoyment. Staff preach the Maniec gospel to patrons as they navigate more than 50 by-the-glass options and around 250 bottles. **Other location** Chelsea Market, 75 9th Avenue, between 15th & 16th Streets, Chelsea (1-646 237 4847).

❤ Dante
79-81 MacDougal Street, between Bleecker & Houston Streets (1-212 982 5275, www. dante-nyc.com). Subway A, B, C, D, E, F, M to W 4th Street; 1 to Houston Street. **Open** *10am-midnight daily.* **Map** *p137 E30* ⑥

Come for an aperitivo, stay for the vibe and just move right in for the pasta. That's the simple, pleasure-seeking ideology that embodies Dante, the beloved Italian café turned small plates restaurant and cocktail bar in 2015. After a century as a staple in the once predominantly Italian neighbourhood, the original owners sold the name to an Australian hospitality group who revamped both the decor and menu, but preserved the history through prized Negronis and pre-dinner sips such as the refreshingly simple Garibaldi (Campari and orange juice).

Sweetwater Social
643 Broadway, at Bleecker Street (1-212 253 0477, www.drinksweetwater.com). Subway B, D, F, M to Broadway-Lafayette Street; 6 to Bleecker Street. **Open** *5pm-midnight Mon-Wed; 5pm-2am Thur-Sat.* **Map** *p137 E30* ⑪

In the know
Dylan's village

Bob Dylan resided at 94 MacDougal Street (on a row of historic brownstones near Bleecker Street) through much of the 1960s, performing in Washington Square Park and at clubs such as **Café Wha?** and the **Bitter End** (for both, *see p136*).

Channelling a 1980s basement rec room, cocktail-world vets Tim Cooper and Justin Noel concoct a lively playground of game-hall amusements and well-executed quaffs at this throwback bar. The Ivan Drago, for example, named after the Soviet opponent in *Rocky IV*, updates a classic Moscow mule with aromatic cardamom, clove and cinnamon. Leather-jacketed gents and off-duty suits huddle over foosball tables unearthed from Cooper's own childhood basement or test their skills at Ms. Pac-Man and Jenga.

Vol de Nuit
*148 W 4th Street, between Sixth Avenue & MacDougal Street (1-212 982 3388, www. voldenuitbar.com). Subway A, B, C, D, E, F, M to W 4th Street. **Open** 4pm-midnight Mon-Thur, Sun; 4pm-2am Fri, Sat. Map p137 E29* ⑫

Duck through an unmarked doorway and find yourself in a red-walled Belgian bar that serves brews exclusively from the motherland. Clusters of European grad students knock back glasses of Lindemans Framboise – just one of more than a dozen beers on tap and 25 by the bottle. Frites – served with a choice of a dozen sauces – are available most nights.

Shops & services

❤ CO Bigelow
*414 Sixth Avenue, between 8th & 9th Streets (1-212 533 2700, www.bigelowchemists.com). Subway A, B, C, D, F, M to W 4th Street; 1 to Christopher Street-Sheridan Square. **Open** 7.30am-9pm Mon-Fri; 8.30am-7pm Sat; 8.30am-5.30pm Sun. Map p137 D29* ❶ *Health & beauty*

Established in 1838, Bigelow is the oldest apothecary in the US. Its appealingly old-school line of toiletries includes such tried-and-trusted favourites as Mentha Lip Shine, Rose Salve and Bay Rum After-Shave Balm. The spacious, chandelier-lit store is packed with natural remedies, organic skincare products and drugstore essentials – and the place still fills prescriptions.

Forbidden Planet
*832 Broadway, between 12th & 13th Streets (1-212 473 1576, www.fpnyc.com). Subway L, N, Q, R, W, 4, 5, 6 to 14th Street-Union Square. **Open** 9am-10pm Mon, Tue; 8am-midnight Wed; 9am-midnight Thur-Sat; 10am-10pm Sun. Map p137 E28* ❺ *Books*

Embracing pop culture and the cult underground, Forbidden Planet takes comics very seriously. You'll also find graphic novels, manga, action figures, DVDs and more.

❤ Murray's Cheese
*254 Bleecker Street, between Sixth & Seventh Avenues (1-212 243 3289, www.murrayscheese. com). Subway A, B, C, D, E, F, M to W 4th Street. **Open** 8am-9pm Mon-Sat; 9am-7pm Sun. Map p137 D30* ❽ *Food & drink*

For the last word in curd, New Yorkers have been flocking to Murray's since 1940 to sniff out the best international and domestic cheeses. The helpful staff will guide you through hundreds of stinky, runny, washed-rind and aged comestibles.

▶ *Murray's also has an outpost in Grand Central Terminal, plus a Cheese Bar at 264 Bleecker Street.*

Porto Rico Importing Co
*201 Bleecker Street, between Sixth Avenue & MacDougal Street (1-212 477 5421, www. portorico.com). Subway A, B, C, D, E, F, M to W 4th Street. **Open** 8am-9pm Mon-Fri; 9am-9pm Sat; noon-7pm Sun. Map p137 E30* ❾ *Food & drink*

This small, family-run store, established in 1907, has earned a large following for its terrific range of coffee beans, including its own prepared blends. Prices are reasonable, and the selection of teas also warrants exploration. **Other locations** 40½ St Marks Place, between First & Second Avenues, East Village (1-212 533 1982); Essex Market, 88 Essex Street, at Delancey Street, Lower East Side (1-212 677 1210); 636 Grand Street, between Manhattan Avenue & Leonard Street, Williamsburg, Brooklyn (1-718 782 1200).

WEST VILLAGE

▶ *Subway A, C, E, 1, 2, 3 to 14th Street; L to Eighth Avenue; 1 to Christopher Street-Sheridan Square.*

In the early 20th century, the **West Village** was largely a working-class Italian neighbourhood. These days, it's a highly desirable enclave, reflected in the property prices, but a low-key, everyone-knows-everyone feel remains. One of the oldest parts of the Village, the area west of Sixth Avenue to the Hudson River, from 14th Street to Houston Street, retains a street layout based on the original settlers' horse paths. Only here could West 10th Street cross West 4th Street, and Waverly Place cross... Waverly Place.

Locals and visitors crowd bistros along Seventh Avenue and Hudson Street, and patronise the high-rent boutiques on this stretch of Bleecker Street. The area's bohemian population may have dwindled

Townhouses in the West Village

years ago, but a few old landmarks, such as the **White Horse Tavern**, remain. On and just off Seventh Avenue South are jazz and cabaret clubs, including the **Village Vanguard** (*see p324*).

The West Village is also a historic gay neighbourhood, although the current scene has mostly migrated north to Hell's Kitchen. The **Stonewall Inn** (*see p304*), on Christopher Street, was the site of the 1969 riots that marked the birth of the modern gay-rights movement. The street's pivotal role is commemorated in **Christopher Park**, which faces the bar, by George Segal's *Gay Liberation*, a piece comprising plaster sculptures of two same-sex couples.

Restaurants & cafés

♥ Bistro Pierre Lapin $$$

99 Bank Street, at Greenwich Street (1-212 858 6600, www.pierresnyc.com). Subway A, C, E, 1, 2 to 14th Street; L to Eighth Avenue. **Open** *5-10pm Mon, Tue; 5-11pm Wed-Sat; 11am-3pm, 5-9pm Sun.* **Map** *p137 C29* ❶ *French*

Once you finally find the restaurant's elusive entrance, floral wallpaper and red-velvet booths (along with a giant portrait of the namesake rabbit) create the illusion of being tucked away in the Marais district of Paris. A generous bread basket of warm baguette with pâté, house-made butter, olives and cheese ushers in this Francophile's dream. Chef Harold Moore perfects brasserie classics, such as a cheesy croque-madame with crisp frites, or a whole roast chicken with velvety potato purée and foie gras-laden bread stuffing.

Buvette $$

42 Grove Street, between Bedford & Bleecker Streets (1-212 255 3590, www.ilovebuvette. com). Subway 1 to Christopher Street-Sheridan Square. **Open** *7am-2am daily.* **Map** *p137 D30* ❸ *French*

Chef Jody Williams has filled every nook of tiny, Gallic-inspired Buvette with old picnic baskets, teapots and silver trays, among other vintage ephemera. The food is just as thoughtfully curated – Williams's immaculate renditions of coq au vin, duck rillettes or

143

intense, lacquered wedges of tarte tatin arrive on tiny plates, in petite jars or in miniature casseroles.

Corner Bistro $

331 W 4th Street, at Jane Street (1-212 242 9502, www.cornerbistrony.com). Subway A, C, E to 14th Street; L to Eighth Avenue. **Open** *11.30am-4am Mon-Sat; noon-4am Sun.* **No cards.** *Map p137 D29* ⑥ *American*

There's one compelling reason to come to this legendary pub: it serves what some New Yorkers say are the city's best burgers – plus the beer is just $5 for a mug of McSorley's. The patties are no-frills and served on a flimsy paper plate. To get one, you may have to queue for a good hour, especially on weekend nights; if the wait is too long for a table, try to slip into a space at the bar. **Other location** 47-18 Vernon Boulevard, at 47th Road, Long Island City, Queens (1-718 606 6500).

▶ *For other top-ranking burgers, see Minetta Tavern (see p140), Shake Shake (p202) and JG Melon (p211).*

❤ Dominique Ansel Kitchen $

137 Seventh Avenue South, between Charles & W 10th Streets (1-212 242 5111, www. dominiqueanselkitchen.com). Subway A, B, C, D, E, F, M to W 4th Street; 1 to Christopher Street-Sheridan Square. **Open** *9am-9pm daily.* *Map p137 D29* ⑦ *Café*

Dominique Ansel's innovative second NYC spot gives new meaning to the term 'freshly baked'. Pastries, desserts and savoury snacks, such as flaky croissants, madeleine cookies, tarts, chocolate mousse and a croque monsieur, are made while you wait. Order at the counter in the white-subway-tiled café space, then take a seat at one of the marble-topped tables while chefs prepare your treats in the open kitchen. Dessert diehards can take part in themed nighttime tastings at a 12-seat table upstairs called UP (short for 'Unlimited Possibilities'), which pairs cocktails and wine with exclusive sweet and savoury creations that aren't available in the shop below.

EN Japanese Brasserie $$

435 Hudson Street, at Leroy Street (1-212 647 9196, www.enjb.com). Subway 1 to Houston Street. **Open** *noon-2.30pm, 5.30-10.30pm Mon-Thur; noon-2.30pm, 5.30-11.30pm Fri; 11am-2.30pm, 5.30-11.30pm Sat; 11am-2.30pm, 5.30-10.30pm Sun.* **Map** *p137 D30* ⑧ *Japanese*

The owners of this popular spot aim to evoke a sense of Japanese living in the multilevel space. As well as the spacious main dining room, tatami-style rooms and recreations of a Meiji-era living room, dining room and library can be booked (for an extra charge)

for large groups. Highlights of chef Abe Hiroki's menu include freshly made scooped tofu served with *wari-joyu* sauce (a mix of soy sauce and *dashi*, a fish broth); miso-marinated, grilled Alaskan black cod; and Black Angus washugyu short rib cooked on a hot stone at the table. Try the Japanese whisky, saké and shochu flights.

Kesté Pizza & Vino $$

271 Bleecker Street, between Cornelia & Jones Streets (1-212 243 1500, www.kestepizzeria. com). Subway 1 to Christopher Street-Sheridan Square. **Open** *4.30-10pm Mon-Wed; 11.30am-3.30pm, 4.30-10pm Thur; 11.30am-11.30pm Fri, Sat; 11.30am-10pm Sun.* *Map p137 D30* ⑩ *Pizza*

If anyone can claim to be an expert on Neapolitan pizza, it's Kesté's Roberto Caporuscio: as president of the US branch of the Associazione Pizzaiuoli Napoletani, he's the top dog for the training and certification of *pizzaioli*. At his intimate space, it's all about the crust – blistered, salty and elastic, it could easily be eaten plain. Add ace toppings such as sweet-tart San Marzano tomato sauce, milky mozzarella and fresh basil, and you have one of New York's finest pies. **Other location** 66 Gold Street, at Ann Street, Financial District (1-212 693 9030).

▶ *Roberto Caporuscio also owns superior Theater District pizza place, Don Antonio (see p180).*

Pearl Oyster Bar $$

18 Cornelia Street, between Bleecker & W 4th Streets (1-212 691 8211, www.pearloysterbar. com). Subway A, B, C, D, E, F, M to W 4th Street. **Open** *noon-2.30pm, 5.30-10.30pm Mon-Thur; noon-2.30pm, 6-11pm Fri; 6-11pm Sat.* *Map p137 D30* ⑮ *Seafood*

There's a good reason this convivial, no-reservations, New England-style fish joint always has a queue – the food is outstanding. Signature dishes include the lobster roll (sweet, lemon-scented meat laced with mayonnaise on a toasted, buttered bun) and a contemporary take on bouillabaisse: a briny lobster broth packed with mussels, cod, scallops, shrimp and clams, topped with an aïoli-smothered croûton.

RedFarm $

529 Hudson Street, between Charles & W 10th Streets (1-212 792 9700, www. redfarmnyc.com). Subway 1 to Christopher Street-Sheridan Square. **Open** *5-11pm Mon-Wed; 5-11.30pm Thur, Fri; 11am-2.30pm, 5-11.30pm Sat; 11am-2.30pm, 5-11pm Sun.* *Map p137 D29* ⑯ *Chinese*

The high-end ingredients and whimsical plating at Ed Schoenfeld's interpretive Chinese restaurant have helped to pack the dining room since opening night. Chef Joe Ng is known for his dim sum artistry, including pastrami-stuffed egg rolls and shrimp dumplings decorated with 'eyes' and pursued on the plate by a sweet-potato Pac-Man. **Other location** 2170 Broadway, between 76th & 77th Streets, Upper West Side (1-212 724 9700).

❤ Via Carota $$
51 Grove Street, between Bleecker Street & Seventh Avenue South (no phone, www.viacarota.com). Subway 1 to Christopher Street-Sheridan Square. **Open** *11am-midnight Mon-Wed, Sun; 11am-1am Thur-Sat.* **Map** *p137 D29* ⑲ *Italian*

The soulful Italian plates served at this glass-fronted gastroteca, the first joint effort from chef power couple Jody Williams and Rita Sodi, prove that simple food can be anything but basic. Pastas are satisfying but safe – what really stands out is *verdure*. The seasonally changing selection might include fuss-free provincial stunners such as *barbabietola*, a toss of tender beets and pickled apples flecked with fragrant thyme and tangy pebbles of goat's-milk feta. You can make an excellent meal here on vegetable dishes alone, but then you'd miss out on the house *svizzerina*, a bunless, hand-chopped round of New York strip steak that arrives flash-seared and nearly naked, save a few husk-on garlic cloves and a salty, rosemary-licked pool of fat. The chefs operate with an unflappable disregard for 'cool' that nearly borders on subversive – the knick-knacky room is garnished with more bowls of fruit than a Nancy Meyers movie kitchen.

Bars

Blind Tiger Ale House
281 Bleecker Street, at Jones Street (1-212 462 4682, www.blindtigeralehouse.com). Subway A, B, C, D, E, F, M to W 4th Street; 1 to Christopher Street-Sheridan Square. **Open** *11.30am-4am daily.* **Map** *p137 D29* ❸

Brew geeks descend on this hops heaven for boutique ales and more than two dozen daily rotating, hard-to-find drafts. The clubby room features windows that open on to the street. Late afternoons and early evenings are ideal for serious sippers enjoying plates of charcuterie and cheese, while the after-dark set veers dangerously close to Phi Kappa society territory.

Chumley's
86 Bedford Street, between Barrow & Grove Streets (1-212 675 2081, chumleysnewyork. com). Subway 1 to Christopher Street-Sheridan Square. **Open** *5.30-10.15pm Mon-Thur; 5.30-10.30pm Fri, Sat.* **Map** *p137 D30* ❹

Chumley's

Behind a heavy, unmarked wooden door – the same one that once welcomed New York literati such as William Faulkner, ee cummings and Edna St Vincent Millay – lies the landmark speakeasy that social activist Leland Stanford Chumley opened back in 1922. Following a chimney collapse in 2007, the bar was in limbo for the better part of a decade before Sushi Nakazawa restaurateur Alessandro Borgognone partnered with longtime owner Jim Miller and revamped the historic space. Brown-spirit cocktails are as cosy as the dimly lit, wood-panelled environs, and the menu touts the bar's history: a towering double cheeseburger stacked with crispy shallots and smeared with bone marrow, is dubbed the 86'd Burger, after lore that the term was born at Chumley's. Police would warn bartenders to '86' drunken guests through the front entrance – 86 Bedford Street – before coming through the alley door during Prohibition-era raids.

Employees Only
510 Hudson Street, between Christopher & W 10th Streets (1-212 242 3021, www. employeesonlynyc.com). Subway 1 to Christopher Street-Sheridan Square. **Open** *6pm-4am daily.* **Map** *p137 D29* ❼

This Prohibition-themed bar cultivates an exclusive vibe, but there's no cover and no hassle at the door. Pass by the palm reader in the window (it's a front) and you'll find an amber-lit art deco interior where formality continues to flourish: servers wear custom-designed frocks and bartenders are in waitstaff whites. But the real stunners are cocktails such as the West Side, a lethal mix of lemon vodka, lemon juice and fresh mint.

Gottino
52 Greenwich Avenue, between Charles & Perry Streets (1-212 633 2590, www.gottino. nyc). Subway 1 to Christopher Street-Sheridan Square. Open 11am-2am daily. Map p137 D29 ⑧

Jockey for a seat at this narrow enoteca – there are just five tables, plus a long marble bar. It's worth the crush. The all-Italian wine list is complemented by a menu of choice salumi, cheese and delectable prepared bites. There's also a small, casual back garden.

Happiest Hour
121 W 10th Street, at Greenwich Avenue (1-212 243 2827, www.happiesthournyc.com). Subway 1 to Christopher Street-Sheridan Square. Open 5pm-midnight Mon, Tue; 5pm-2am Wed; 5pm-3am Thur, Fri; 2pm-3am Sat; 2pm-midnight Sun. Map p137 D29 ⑨

A 1960s pop soundtrack sets the mood at this retro-kitted tiki lounge crammed with mid-century curios. Renowned barman Jim Kearns (Pegu Club, the NoMad) mans the horseshoe-shaped bar, offering a clever list of cocktails that can be customised with a choice of spirits. The breezy vibe attracts an eclectic young crowd: off-hours suits sipping scotch on the rocks, bubbly girl groups clinking wine glasses, polo-clad bros glugging Miller High Life and couples getting cosy in the half-moon booths.

❤ White Horse Tavern
567 Hudson Street, at 11th Street (1-212 989 3956 , www.whitehorsetavern1880.com). Subway 1 to Christopher Street-Sheridan Square. Open 11am-2am daily (hrs vary seasonally). Map p137 D29 ⑬

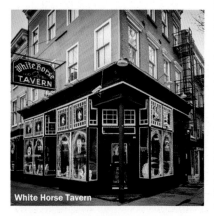
White Horse Tavern

Popular lore tells us that in 1953, Dylan Thomas knocked back 18 straight whiskies here before expiring in his Chelsea Hotel residence – a portrait of him hangs in the middle room, above his favourite table in the corner. Now the old-school bar and its adjacent outdoor patio play host to a yuppie crowd and clutches of tourists, drawn by the outdoor seating, a fine selection of beers – and the legend.

Shops & services

❤ Fairlight/Alix of Bohemia
13 Christopher Street, between Greenwich Avenue & Waverly Place (1-212 924 9200, www.fairlightnyc.com, www.alixofbohemia. com). Subway A, B, C, D, E, F, M to W 4th Street; 1 to Christopher Street-Sheridan Square. Open noon-7pm Tue-Sat; noon-6pm Sun. Map p137 D29 ❸ *Fashion*

With an appealingly makeshift vibe in line with the Village's boho past, this down-to-earth space is two indie boutiques in one. Kelly Colasanti sells vintage fashion alongside cool clothing labels such as Caron Callahan and Alexa Stark, plus hand-crafted jewellery, under the name Fairlight. Rising designer Alix Verley-Pietrafesa creates exquisitely tailored jackets, some featuring elaborate embroidery and other embellishments, peasanty print dresses and floaty shirts inspired by historical free spirits such as the Bloomsbury group.

Flight 001
96 Greenwich Avenue, between Jane & W 12th Streets (1-212 989 0001, www.flight001.com). Subway A, C, E to 14th Street; L to Eighth Avenue. Open 11am-7pm Mon-Sat; noon-6pm Sun. Map p137 D29 ❹ *Travel*

As well as a tasteful selection of luggage, this one-stop shop carries everything for the chic jet-setter. The range of fun and functional travel products includes novelty printed eye masks and luggage tags, emergency tote bags that squash down to pocket size, adapters and battery backups for your gadgets.

Idlewild Books
170 Seventh Avenue S, at Perry Street (1-212 414 8888, www.idlewildbooks.com). Subway A, B, C, D, E, F, M W 4th Street; 1, 2, 3 to 14th Street. Open noon-8pm Mon-Thur; noon-6pm Fri-Sun. Map p137 D29 ❻ *Books*

Opened by a former United Nations press officer, Idlewild stocks travel guides to around 200 countries and all 50 states, which are grouped with related works of fiction and non-fiction. It also has a selection of works in French, Spanish and Italian. Fun fact: Idlewild was the original name for JFK Airport.

Whittemore House

45 Grove Street, at Bleecker Street (1-212 242 8880, www.whittemorehousesalon.com). Subway 1 to Christopher Street-Sheridan Square. **Open** *10am-8pm Tue, Fri; noon-7pm Wed; 10am-9pm Thur; 10am-6pm Sat.* **Map** *p137 D29* ⓬ *Health & beauty*

Victoria Hunter and Larry Raspanti, who each spent more than 15 years at Bumble & Bumble, opened their own hair salon in an 1830s mansion. The decor features faux-decayed stencilled walls and boudoir chairs. Cuts (from $120) and natural-looking colour – including the salon's signature non-damaging Hair Paint lightening technique – come courtesy of some of New York's best stylists.

MEATPACKING DISTRICT

▶ *Subway A, C, E to 14th Street; L to Eighth Avenue.*

The north-west corner of the West Village has been known as the **Meatpacking District** since the area was dominated by the wholesale meat industry in the early 20th century. As business waned, gay fetish clubs took root in derelict buildings and the area was a haunt for transsexual prostitutes. In the 1990s, however, hip eateries and designer boutiques started to move in. Frequent mentions on *Sex and the City*, along with the arrival of swanky hotel **Gansevoort Meatpacking NYC** in the noughties, cemented the area's reputation as a mainstream consumer playground. Large, party-centric chain restaurants and nightspots, such as **Le Bain** (*see p310*), continue to draw after-dark pleasure seekers.

The 2009 opening of freight-track-turned-park the **High Line** (*see p156*) brought even bigger crowds to the area, and, since 2015, the attractions have been boosted by the **Whitney Museum of American Art**. Slick style hotel the **Standard** straddles the elevated park at West 13th Street, and its Biergarten, nestled beneath it, is a great spot for a pint.

Sights & museums

♥ Whitney Museum of American Art

99 Gansevoort Street, between Washington & West Streets (1-212 570 3600, www.whitney.org). Subway A, C, E to 14th St; L to Eighth Avenue. **Open** *10.30am-6pm Mon, Wed, Thur, Sun; 10.30am-10pm Fri, Sat. Closed Tue Sept-June.* **Admission** *$25; $18 reductions; free under-19s. Pay what you wish 7-10pm Fri.* **Map** *p137 C29.*

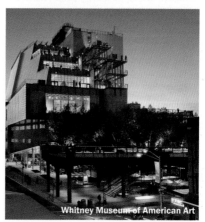

Whitney Museum of American Art

High Street on Hudson

Founded by sculptor and art patron Gertrude Vanderbilt Whitney in 1931, the museum holds more than 24,000 works created by more than 3,500 American artists during the 20th and 21st centuries, including Willem de Kooning, Edward Hopper, Jasper Johns, Georgia O'Keeffe and Claes Oldenburg.

The nine-storey, steel-and-glass building, designed by Renzo Piano at the southern foot of the High Line, and completed in 2015, includes spacious galleries spotlighting selections from the permanent collection, including such iconic works as Alexander Calder's *Circus*, Hopper's *Early Sunday Morning* and Johns' *Three Flags*, alongside temporary shows such as the prestigious and controversial Whitney Biennial, a survey of contemporary American art held in odd-numbered years.

An 8,500-square-foot public plaza beneath the High Line leads to the cantilevered glass entrance. Inside, you'll find a ground-floor restaurant helmed by dining guru Danny Meyer (plus a café with seasonal outdoor seating on the eighth floor), a gift shop and a free-admission lobby gallery.

The art isn't restricted to the museum's interior. The dramatic, asymmetrical structure features a series of outdoor terraces that rise like steps above the High Line. On the fifth, sixth and seventh floors you can take in alfresco sculptures and installations while admiring views of the Hudson River and city landmarks, including the Empire State Building and 1 World Trade Center.

Restaurants & cafés

❤ High Street on Hudson $$

637 Hudson Street, at Horatio Street (1-917 388 3944, www.highstreetonhudson.com). Subway A, C, E to 14th Street; L to Eighth Avenue. **Open** *8am-10pm Mon-Thur, Sun; 8am-10.30pm Fri, Sat.* **Map** *p137 C29* ❾
American

Bread is no mere afterthought at the day-to-night sibling to Philadelphia's lauded restaurant, High Street on Market. Beautiful loaves – potent New World ryes, hearty German-style *einkorn rugbrod*, and *anadama miche* enriched with molasses – are for sale, along with equally great baked goods, near the eaterie's street-facing windows. During the day, a buttery biscuit, popping with black pepper and subdued with sage, hugs a cloud-soft egg, malted sausage and melty aged cheddar in the kitchen's gorgeous send-up of a breakfast sandwich. When the lights dim, sandwiches and pastries make way for composed dishes spotlighting local produce.

Santina $$

820 Washington Street, between Gansevoort & Little West 12th Streets (1-212 254 3000, www.santinanyc.com). Subway A, C, E to 14th Street; L to Eighth Avenue. **Open** *11.45am-10pm Mon-Thur; 11.45am-midnight Fri; 10am-midnight Sat; 10am-10pm Sun.* **Map** *p137 C29* ⑰ *Italian*

Major Food Group (Carbone, The Grill and others) brings the flavours of the Italian coast to this Hudson-hugging locale. A Renzo Piano-designed glass cube under the High Line, next to the Whitney Museum, is decked out with Murano-glass chandeliers and seascape paintings crafted from ceramic plates. Bread service, a trope of Italian-American eating, is replaced by *cecina*, thin chickpea crêpes served with a choice of filling, the best and boldest of which is a tuna tartare charged with capers and Calabrian chile. Fish and vegetables feature prominently on the menu – carpaccio, for example, trades beef for weightless, sunset-orange petals of squash, dotted with pumpkin seeds, honey *agrodolce* and crème fraîche.

Bars

Kobrick Coffee Co

24 Ninth Avenue, between 13th & 14th Streets (1-212 255 5588, www.kobricks.com). Subway A, C, E to 14th Street; L to Eighth Avenue. **Open** *7am-4am Mon-Fri; 8am-4am Sat, Sun.* **Map** *p137 C28* ⑩

Fourth-generation Kobricks, Scott and Niki, put a boozy twist on the family business (great-grandad Samuel Kobrick established the roastery and distributor Kobrick Coffee Co in 1920). The siblings teamed up with Hella Bitters founder Tobin Ludwig for an all-day coffeeshop/cocktail bar hybrid that will give you all kinds of buzz. You won't find any espresso martinis here. Modern coffee-spiked quaffs include the aromatic Mexican Jumping Bean, a blend of Kobrick's full-bodied Tiger Stripe ristretto shot, tequila and the citrusy China-China amer liqueur. Non-coffee cocktails are also available. Settle onto stools at the front bar or head to the cosy back room, which has tufted chairs, velvet-backed banquettes and candlelit tables. And if you're starting to feel the java jitters, there's a menu of light snacks and small plates.

Shops & services

❤ Doyle & Doyle

412 W 13th Street, between Ninth Avenue & Washington Street (1-212 677 9991, www.doyledoyle.com). Subway A, C, E to 14th Street; L to Eighth Avenue. **Open** *noon-7pm Mon-Wed, Fri-Sun; noon-8pm Thur.* **Map** *p137 C29* ❷ *Accessories*

Meatpacking District

Whether your taste is art deco or nouveau, Victorian or Edwardian, Elizabeth and Irene Doyle are bound to have that one-of-a-kind piece you're looking for, including engagement and eternity rings. The gemologist sisters, who specialise in vintage and antique jewellery, have also launched their own collection of new heirlooms.

Jeffrey

449 W 14th Street, between Ninth & Tenth Avenues (1-212 206 1272, www.jeffreyusa.com). Subway A, C, E to 14th Street; L to Eighth Avenue. **Open** *10am-8pm Mon-Fri; 10am-7pm Sat; noon-6pm Sun.* **Map** *p137 C28* ❼ *Fashion*

Jeffrey Kalinsky, a former Barneys shoe buyer, was a Meatpacking District pioneer when he opened his namesake store in 1999. Designer clothing abounds here – by Saint Laurent, Givenchy and Christopher Kane, among others. The centrepiece is the shoe salon, which features the work of Manolo Blahnik, Christian Louboutin and Gianvito Rossi, as well as newer names.

Rag & Bone

425 W 13th Street, at Washington Street (1-212 249 3331, www.rag-bone.com). Subway A, C, E to 14th Street. **Open** *11am-8pm Mon-Sat; 11am-7pm Sun.* **Map** *p137 C28* ⑩ *Fashion*

This large downtown outpost of the enduringly hip brand, which began as a denim line in 2002, was once a meat factory, and it retains much of that industrial vibe, with unfinished concrete floors, brick walls and an original Dave's Quality Veal sign. Sip a latte from the in-store Jack's Stir Brew Coffee before or after browsing the impeccably cut jeans, classic T-shirts, luxurious knitwear and well-tailored jackets for men and women. **Other locations** throughout the city.

Chelsea

Formerly a working-class Irish and Hispanic neighbourhood, the corridor between 14th and 29th Streets west of Sixth Avenue emerged as the nexus of New York's queer life in the 1990s. Due to rising housing costs and the protean nature of the city's cultural landscape, it's since been eclipsed by Hell's Kitchen to the north (just as Chelsea overtook the West Village), but you'll still find bars, restaurants and shops catering to the once-ubiquitous 'Chelsea boys'.

The cityscape shifts from leafy side streets lined with pristine 19th-century brownstones to an array of striking industrial and contemporary architecture on the far west side. In recent years, the local buzz has moved to the previously neglected Hudson-hugging strip that has evolved into the city's main gallery district. But it's the transformation of a disused elevated freight train track snaking through the area into one of the city's most popular parks that's really drawing crowds to this patch.

❤ Don't miss

1 High Line *p156*
Insanely popular elevated park with views, art and sunbathing spots.

2 Chelsea gallery district *p154*
More than 300 art spaces in just over ten blocks.

3 Museum at FIT *p153*
A must for fashion-conscious folk – and it's free.

4 The Kitchen *p338*
Long-standing experimental arts space.

CHELSEA

▶Subway A, C, E, 1, 2, 3 to 14th Street; C, E, 1 to 23rd Street; L to Eighth Avenue; 1 to 18th Street or 28th Street; 7 to 34th Street-Hudson Yards.

In the 1990s, many of New York's contemporary galleries left Soho for the once-desolate western edge of Chelsea (*see p154* Chelsea gallery district). Today, internationally recognised spaces such as **Gagosian Gallery**, **Luhring Augustine** and **Gladstone Gallery**, as well as numerous less exalted names, attract swarms of art aficionados. The **High Line** (*see p156*) has brought even more gallery-goers to the area as it provides a verdant pathway from the shop- and restaurant-rich Meatpacking District to the art enclave. Traversing the elevated promenade, you'll pass through the old loading dock of the former Nabisco factory, where the first Oreo cookie was made in 1912. This conglomeration of 18 structures, built between the 1890s and the 1930s, now houses **Chelsea Market** (75 Ninth Avenue, between 15th & 16th Streets, www.chelseamarket.com). The ground-floor food arcade offers artisanal bread, wine, baked goods and freshly made ice-cream, among other treats. The complex houses bars, restaurants and the **Artists & Fleas** designer/vintage/craft market.

Swanky apartment buildings have sprung up alongside the park, including a curvy, futuristic structure at 28th Street designed by the late Zaha Hadid. Also among the area's notable industrial architecture is the **Starrett-Lehigh Building** (601 W 26th Street, at Eleventh Avenue). The stunning 1929 structure was left in disrepair until the dot-com boom of the late 1990s, when media companies, photographers and designers snatched up its loft-like spaces.

Stretching along the waterfront, the Chelsea section of Hudson River Park (www. hudsonriverpark.org) incorporates once-derelict piers that served as terminals for grand ocean liners. It's home to mega sports centre **Chelsea Piers**. Just north, Pier 62 (between 22nd & 23rd Streets) includes a garden, carousel and skate park, while Pier 64 (at 24th Street) is now a grassy, tree-lined green space.

To get a glimpse of how Chelsea looked back when it was first developed in the 1880s, stroll along **Cushman Row** (406-418 W 20th Street, between Ninth & Tenth Avenues) in the Chelsea Historic District. Just to the north is the block-long **General Theological Seminary of the Episcopal Church** (440 W 21st Street, between Ninth & Tenth Avenues). The seminary's land was part of the estate known as Chelsea, owned by poet Clement Clarke Moore, author of 'A Visit from St Nicholas' (more commonly known as ''Twas the Night Before Christmas'), and the guest wing has been converted into the **High Line Hotel**.

A hostelry with a more notorious history is nearby. The **Chelsea Hotel** (222 West 23rd Street, between Seventh & Eighth Avenues) has been a magnet for creative types since it first opened in 1884; Mark Twain was an early guest. The list of those who have stayed here reads like an international *Who's Who* of the artistic elite: Sarah Bernhardt (who slept in a coffin), William Burroughs (who wrote *Naked Lunch* here), Dylan Thomas, Janis Joplin and Jimi Hendrix, to name a few. In the 1960s, it was the stomping ground of Andy Warhol's coterie of superstars, and the location of his 1966 film *The Chelsea Girls*. It gained punk-rock notoriety on 12 October 1978, when Sex Pistol Sid Vicious stabbed girlfriend Nancy Spungen to death in Room 100. Though some long-term tenants remain, the hotel portion of the property is closed for renovations. These have dragged on for years due to various setbacks and change of ownership, but it is expected to reopen eventually.

The weekend **flea markets** in the area have shrunk in recent years (casualties of development), but you'll still find one on West 25th Street, between Sixth Avenue and Broadway (www.annexmarkets.com).

♥ Time to eat & drink

Brunch with the art world
Cookshop *p155*

Celebrated chef's outpost
L'Atelier de Joël Robuchon *p155*

Cocktail-sipping and singalongs
Sid Gold's Request Room *p158*

♥ Time to shop

Arty tomes
192 Books *p158*; Printed Matter *p159*

Atmospheric trove of unique objects
Mantiques Modern *p159*

Museum at FIT

Not far from here, the Fashion Institute of Technology, on 27th Street, between Seventh and Eighth Avenues, counts Calvin Klein, Nanette Lepore and Michael Kors among its alumni. The school's **Museum at FIT** mounts free exhibitions.

Sights & museums

❤ Museum at FIT

*Building E, Seventh Avenue, at 27th Street (1-212 217 4558, www.fitnyc.edu/museum). Subway 1 to 28th Street. **Open** noon-8pm Tue-Fri; 10am-5pm Sat. **Admission** free. **Map** p153 D26.*

The Fashion Institute of Technology owns one of the largest and most impressive clothing collections in the world, with some 50,000 garments and accessories dating from the 18th century to the present. Under the directorship of fashion historian Dr Valerie Steele, the museum showcases a rotating selection from the permanent collection, and hosts a programme of temporary exhibitions focusing on individual designers or spotlighting fashion from cultural angles.

Rubin Museum of Art

*150 W 17th Street, at Seventh Avenue (1-212 620 5000, www.rubinmuseum.org). Subway A, C, E to 14th Street; L to Eighth Avenue; 1 to 18th Street. **Open** 11am-5pm Mon, Thur; 11am-9pm Wed; 11am-10pm Fri; 11am-6pm Sat, Sun. **Admission** $19; $14 reductions; free under-13s. Free 6-10pm Fri. **Map** p153 D27.*

Dedicated to the art of the Himalayan region, the Rubin is a very stylish museum – a fact that falls into place when you learn that the six-storey space was once occupied by

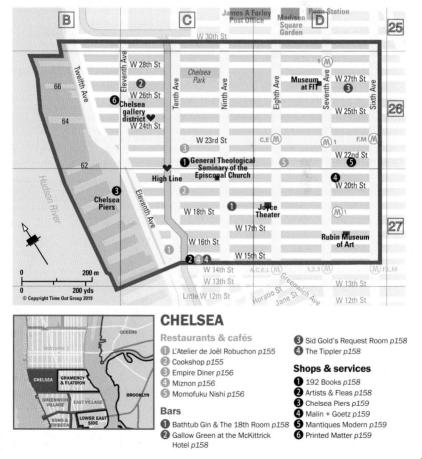

CHELSEA

Restaurants & cafés

1. L'Atelier de Joël Robuchon *p155*
2. Cookshop *p155*
3. Empire Diner *p156*
4. Miznon *p156*
5. Momofuku Nishi *p156*

Bars

1. Bathtub Gin & The 18th Room *p158*
2. Gallow Green at the McKittrick Hotel *p158*
3. Sid Gold's Request Room *p158*
4. The Tippler *p158*

Shops & services

1. 192 Books *p158*
2. Artists & Fleas *p158*
3. Chelsea Piers *p159*
4. Malin + Goetz *p159*
5. Mantiques Modern *p159*
6. Printed Matter *p159*

❤ Chelsea gallery district

From West 18th Street to West 29th Street, mainly between Tenth and Eleventh Avenues, converted industrial buildings are crammed with more than 300 art spaces. Here, you'll find group shows by up-and-comers, blockbuster exhibitions from big names and a slew of provocative work.

The highest concentration of major art-world players is on W 24th Street, including the mammoth showroom of early Chelsea adopter **Larry Gagosian** (No.555, 1-212 741 1111, www.gagosian.com), which opened in 1999. The renowned dealer also has a space a few blocks south, at 552 W 21st Street. **Luhring Augustine** (No. 531, 1-212 206 9100, www.luhringaugustine.com) has an impressive index of artists, including Rachel Whiteread, Christopher Wool and Pipilotti Rist. **Matthew Marks Gallery** (No. 523, 1-212 243 0200, www.matthewmarks. com), which opened in 1991, was a driving force behind Chelsea's transformation into an art destination (there's a second location at 522 W 22nd Street). Also on this stretch, **Metro Pictures** (519 W 24th Street, 1-212 206 7100, www.metropictures.com) is best known for representing art-world superstar Cindy Sherman, along with big names such as Pictures Generation artists Louise Lawler and Robert Longo. Blue-chip **Gladstone Gallery** (No.515, 1-212 206 9300, www.gladstonegallery.com) focuses on daring conceptual art.

Around the corner, **Yossi Milo** (245 Tenth Avenue, between 24th & 25th Streets, 1-212 414 0370, www.yossimilo. com) has an impressive roster of camera talent encompassing emerging and established photographers.

A few blocks south, on W 22nd Street, the outdoor art installation *7000 Oaks* by German artist Joseph Beuys comprises 37 pairings of basalt stones and trees. The piece was spin-off of a five-year international effort, begun in 1982 at Germany's 'Documenta 7' exhibition, to enact social and environmental change by planting 7,000 trees. It's maintained by powerhouse foundation Dia (www.diaart.org).

The elegant **Tanya Bonakdar Gallery** (521 W 21st Street, 1-212 414 4144, www. tanyabonakdargallery.com) represents such prominent names as *New York City Waterfalls* maestro Olafur Eliasson. Nearby, long-running **303 Gallery** (no.555, 1-212 255 1121, www.303gallery.com) has fostered the careers of critically acclaimed artists including photographer Stephen Shore and painters Mary Heilmann and Karen Kilimnik. **David Zwirner** has spaces at 525 W 19th Street (1-212 727 2070, www. davidzwirner.com) and 537 W 20th Street

Gladstone Gallery

CHELSEA

(1-212 727 2070), mixing museum-quality shows of historical figures with a head-turning array of contemporary artists.

Note that galleries are generally closed or operate on an appointment-only basis on Mondays, and are open 10am-6pm Tuesday to Saturday. In summer, however, many keep different hours and close at weekends. Some may shut up shop for two weeks or a month at a stretch in July or August, so call before visiting.

Luhring Augustine

fashion store Barneys. The ground-floor Indian- and Tibetan-inflected café used to be the accessories department, and retail lives on in the colourful gift shop. In the galleries, rich-toned walls are classy foils for the serene statuary and intricate, multicoloured textiles. Rotating selections from the permanent collection of more than 3,000 pieces from the second century to the present day are highlighted in 'Gateway to Himalayan Art'. A recreation of a Tibetan Buddhist shrine room lets visitors see sculptures, paintings, textiles, furnishings and ritual objects in context. The Rubin's temporary shows often extend beyond the museum's primary focus to contemporary art and photography.

Restaurants & cafés

❤ L'Atelier de Joël Robuchon $$$$
85 Tenth Avenue, at 15th Street (1-212 488 8885, www.joelrobuchonusa.com). Subway A, C, E to 14th Street; L to Eighth Avenue. **Open** *6-10pm Mon-Thur; 5.30-10pm Fri, Sat.* **Map** *p153 C27* ❶ *French*

French chef Joël Robuchon has collected more than 30 Michelin stars and mentored Gordon Ramsay and Éric Ripert. When his Midtown outpost closed in 2012, New York was left as one of the only major food cities worldwide without his presence. Now Robuchon is back, on the far West Side, with a choice of à la carte or seasonal prix fixe menus, including a vegetarian option. Choose the Wagyu rib eye for quantity, the foie gras-stuffed quail for quality – dish upon dish offers a varied sensory overload. It's food that transcends fine dining to become an absolute, unfettered joy.

❤ Cookshop $$
156 Tenth Avenue, at 20th Street (1-212 924 4440, www.cookshopny.com). Subway C, E to 23rd Street. **Open** *8am-11pm Mon-Fri; 10am-11pm Sat; 10am-10pm Sun.* **Map** *p153 C27* ❷ *American creative*

Chef Marc Meyer and his wife Vicki Freeman want their restaurant to be a platform for sustainable ingredients from independent farmers. True to this mission, the ingredients are consistently top-notch, and the menu changes daily. While organic ingredients alone don't guarantee a great meal, Meyer knows how to let the flavours speak for themselves, and Cookshop scores points for getting the house-made ice-cream to taste as good as Ben & Jerry's. The buzzing art world favourite is always packed for its excellent weekend brunch.

Empire Diner $

210 Tenth Avenue, at 22nd Street (1-212 335 2277, www.empire-diner.com). Subway C, E to 23rd Street. **Open** *8am-11pm Mon-Thur, Sun; 8am-midnight Fri, Sat.* **Map** *p153 C26* ❸ *American*

This iconic 1940s Fodero dining car – immortalised by Woody Allen in the 1979 movie *Manhattan* – has changed hands several times in recent years. Inside the restored vintage digs, chef John DeLucie serves classic American cuisine, including macaroni and cheese with Black Diamond cheddar and parmesan breadcrumbs, a double-patty burger with herbed French fries, and sourdough-pretzel fried chicken with chilli-mustard sauce.

Miznon $

Chelsea Market, 435 W 15th Street, at Ninth Avenue (1-646 490 5871, www.miznonnyc. com). Subway A, C, E to 14th Street; L to Eighth Avenue. **Open** *11am-9pm Mon, Sun; 11am-10pm Tue, Wed; 11am-11pm Thur-Sat.* **Map** *p153 C27* ❹ *Israeli*

This heralded Israeli pita shop in Chelsea Market is a key player in the renaissance of Middle Eastern cuisine in NYC. The menu is split between in-a-pita and out-of-the-pita, although you're going to want to get a sampling of both (especially the whole roasted baby cauliflower). The folded cheeseburger pita will make you question everything you thought you knew about a great burger. **Other location** 161 W 72nd Street, between Amsterdam & Columbus Avenues, Upper West Side.

Momofuku Nishi $$

232 Eighth Avenue, between 21st & 22nd Streets (1-646 518 1919, nishi.momofuku. com). Subway C, E to 23rd Street. **Open** *5.30-11pm Mon-Fri; noon-3pm, 5.30-11pm Sat, Sun.* **Map** *p153 D26* ❺ *Eclectic*

David Chang's first West Side eatery (the name means 'west' in Japanese) has the same spare aesthetic as his restaurants across town. In the blonde-wood canteen, myriad culinary influences are at play. The kitchen's update of Rome's elemental *cacio e pepe* is a flawless study in simplicity, but instead of the classic salty pecorino romano, it's made with a smooth house chickpea *hozon* fermented for six months, imbuing the sweet, nutty twirl of *bucatini* pasta with an I-can't-believe-it's-not-butter richness. At lunchtime, limited numbers of the convincingly meaty, Silicon Valley-engineered, plant-based Impossible Burger have been known to draw queues. Taken together, the eatery's sundry culinary influences don't register as Italian or Korean or American. There's really only one word for it all: Chang-ian.

❤ High Line

1-212 500 6035, www.thehighline.org. **Open** *usually 7am-10pm daily (hrs vary seasonally; see website for updates).*

Back in the early days of the 20th century, the West Side had something in common with the Wild West. When freight-bearing trains competed with horses, carts and pedestrians on Tenth Avenue, the thoroughfare was so treacherous it earned the moniker 'Death Avenue'. In an attempt to counteract the carnage, mounted men known as 'West Side Cowboys' would ride in front of the train, waving red flags to warn of its imminent approach. These urban cowboys lost their jobs when the West Side Improvement Project finally raised the railway off street level and put it up on to an overhead trestle – the High Line – in 1934. Originally stretching from 34th Street to Spring Street, the line fell into disuse after World War II as trucks replaced trains. A southern chunk was torn down beginning in the 1960s, and, after the last train ground to a halt in 1980, local property owners lobbied for its destruction. However, thanks to the efforts of railroad enthusiast Peter Obletz and, later, the Friends of the High Line, which

CHELSEA

was founded by local residents Joshua David and Robert Hammond, the industrial relic was saved. A decade after the group began advocating for its reuse as a public space, the first phase of New York's first elevated public park opened in summer 2009.

Running from Gansevoort Street in the Meatpacking District, next to the Whitney Museum, through Chelsea's gallery district to 34th Street and Eleventh Avenue, the slender, sinuous green strip was designed by landscape architects James Corner Field Operations and architects Diller Scofidio + Renfro. As well as trees, flowers and landscaped greenery, the High Line has several interesting features along the way, plus a programme of public art with its own dedicated curator. Commanding an expansive river view, the 'sun deck' between 14th and 15th Streets features wooden deck chairs on the original tracks, plus a water feature with benches for cooling your feet. Nearby, the promenade cuts through the former loading dock of the old Nabisco factory, now home to Chelsea Market (*see p152*).

At 17th Street, steps descend into a sunken amphitheatre with a glassed-over 'window' in the steel structure overlooking the avenue. As you head north, look out for the Empire State Building rising above the skyline to the east. After cutting through Chelsea's gallery district, the park skirts the under-construction mixed-use complex Hudson Yards. The first phase, which debuted in spring 2019, includes a luxury shopping centre and multidisciplinary arts centre The Shed. The Spur, a block-long section extending over the avenue at 30th Street contains the park's largest open space. It features the High Line Plinth, inspired by the Fourth Plinth in London's Trafalgar Square and showcasing temporary art installations.

In the know
Vino alfresco

From around late April until late October, food vendors set up on the High Line, and you can stop for a tipple at seasonal open-air café **Hearth on the High Line**, between 15th & 16th Streets, which serves local beer, wine and snacks courtesy of Hearth restaurant (see p126).

Bars

Bathtub Gin & The 18th Room

132 Ninth Avenue, between 18th & 19th Streets (1-646 559 1671, www.bathtubginnyc. com). Subway A, C, E to 14th Street; L to Eighth Avenue; 1 to 18th Street. **Bathtub Gin** *5pm-2am Mon-Wed; 5pm-3am Thur; 5pm-4am Fri; 4pm-4am Sat; 4pm-2am Sun.* **The 18th Room** *6pm-2am Tue-Thur; 6pm-3am Fri, Sat.* **Map** *p153 C27* ❶

Yes, it's another speakeasy-style bar, this one showcasing an Instagram-candy copper bathtub. True to its name, the drinks list is heavy on gin, in cool twists on G&Ts, martinis and other classic cocktails, although brown spirits, bubbly and punches also get a look-in. Weekly jazz and burlesque shows foster a period-appropriate party vibe. The neighbouring 18th Room (134 Ninth Avenue, www.the18throom.com) is the latest Prohibition-themed den from the same team. Step through a faux coffee shop to perch at the marble-top bar or slink into a velvet banquette for intricate seasonal quaffs.

Gallow Green at the McKittrick Hotel

542 W 27th Street, between Tenth & Eleventh Avenues (1-212 564 1662, www. mckittrickhotel.com/gallow-green). Subway C, E to 23rd Street; 7 to 34th Street-Hudson Yards. **Open** *5pm-midnight Mon-Wed; 5pm-1am Thur, Fri; 10am-1am Sat; 10am-midnight Sun.* **Map** *p153 C26* ❷

Evoking a vintage train station and a lush country garden gone to seed, this verdant bar sits atop a warehouse known as the McKittrick Hotel, the vast multi-level venue for immersive theatre experience *Sleep No More*. In contrast to the view of gleaming West Side buildings, weathered wooden tables sit beneath vine-covered trellises – a summery spot for evening cocktails with pizza or lobster rolls, or an indulgent weekend brunch buffet. In winter, the space transforms into the Lodge, a cosy ski-cabin-style retreat, with comfort food and drinks to match.

❤ Sid Gold's Request Room

165 W 26th Street, between Sixth & Seventh Avenues (1-212 229 1948, www.sidgolds.com). Subway C, E to 23rd Street; 1 to 28th Street. **Open** *5pm-2am Mon-Sat.* **Map** *p153 D26* ❸

The campy joint effort of Beauty Bar proprietor Paul Devitt and Loser's Lounge founder (and Psychedelic Furs ivory tickler) Joe McGinty, Sid's has the kind of downtown clout that draws New York notables (Parker Posey, Andrew Rannells), without the velvet-rope snootiness. Instead, a pink-bow-tied gent cheerfully ushers you through the velvet curtains separating the tamer front bar from the razzly-dazzly clubhouse in the back, an anything-goes sanctuary of Hemingway daiquiris and Celine Dion belt-alongs. At 9pm nightly (except for Thursdays and Fridays, when Happy Hour Karaoke starts at 6pm) game guests flip through karaoke-style songbooks, decamp from lowly lit half-moon booths and take to the stage, accompanied by a pianist on a Baldwin baby grand. The bar's Monday-night series brings in a rotating cast of performers.

The Tippler

Chelsea Market, 425 W 15th Street, between Ninth & Tenth Avenues (no phone, www. thetippler.com). Subway A, C, E to 14th Street; L to Eighth Avenue. **Open** *4pm-1am Mon-Thur, Sun; 4pm-3am Fri, Sat.* **Map** *p153 C27* ❹

Even at its most packed, there's still a fair amount of room to manoeuvre in this expansive lounge, so you won't have too much trouble accessing the long marble bar. The menu includes draft and bottled beers, and wine, but the ever-changing selection of cocktails, incorporating unusual ingredients such as infused spirits and house-made shrub, is the main attraction.

Shops & services

❤ 192 Books

192 Tenth Avenue, between 21st & 22nd Streets (1-212 255 4022, www.192books.com). Subway C, E to 23rd Street. **Open** *11am-7pm daily.* **Map** *p153 C26* ❶ *Books*

In an era when many an indie bookshop has closed, 192, open since 2003, is proving that quirky boutique booksellers can make it after all. Owned by art dealer Paula Cooper and her husband, editor Jack Macrae, the store offers a strong selection of art books and literature, as well as tomes on history, current affairs, music, science and nature. A programme of events highlights top authors, poets and artists of the calibre of Colm Tóibín, Anne Waldman and Sophie Calle.

Artists & Fleas

88 Tenth Avenue, at 15th Street (1-917 488 0044, www.artistsandfleas.com). Subway A, C, E to 14th Street; L to Eighth Avenue. **Open** *10am-9pm Mon-Sat; 10am-8pm Sun.* **Map** *p153 C27* ❷ *Accessories/gifts & souvenirs*

Every weekend, a rotating selection of around 100 vendors, including local craftspeople, designers and artists, sets up shop in a Williamsburg warehouse. The Chelsea Market outpost is smaller, but it's oh so convenient and open seven days a week. The browsable mix includes everything from original T-shirts and handmade jewellery to home-decor

Artists & Fleas

items and vinyl. **Other locations** 70 North 7th Street, between Kent & Wythe Avenues, Williamsburg, Brooklyn (1-917 488 4203); 568 Broadway, at Prince Street, Soho (1-917 767 6965).

Chelsea Piers
*Piers 59-62, W 17th to 23rd Streets, at Twelfth Avenue (1-212 336 6666, www.chelseapiers. com). Subway C, E to 23rd Street. **Open** hrs vary. **Map** p153 B26* ❸ *Sport*

Chelsea Piers is the most impressive all-in-one athletic facility in New York. Between the ice rink (Pier 61, 1-212 336 6100), the bowling alley (between Piers 59 & 60, 1-212 835 2695), the driving range (Pier 59, 1-212 336 6400) and scads of other choices, there's an activity for everyone. The Field House (between Piers 61 & 62, 1-212 336 6500) has a climbing wall, a gymnastics centre, batting cages and basketball courts. At the fitness centre (Pier 60, 1-212 336 6000), you'll find classes covering everything from boxing to triathlon training in the pool, as well as a gym with comprehensive weight deck and cardiovascular machines.

Malin + Goetz
*177 Seventh Avenue, between 20th & 21st Streets (1-212 727 3777, www.malinandgoetz. com). Subway 1 to 18th or 23rd Street. **Open** 10am-8pm Mon-Fri; 11am-8pm Sat; 11am-6pm Sun. **Map** p153 D26* ❹ *Health & beauty*

Matthew Malin and Andrew Goetz's modern apothecary, one of four Manhattan locations, showcases their full line of natural, locally manufactured skin and hair products. The no-nonsense packaging has unisex appeal, and popular items include grapefruit face cleanser, bergamot body wash, sage styling cream and aluminium-free eucalyptus deodorant. Also in store are candles and fragrances in unusual scents. **Other locations** 235 Elizabeth Street, Nolita (1-646 694 9655); 455 Amsterdam Avenue, Upper

West Side (1-212 799 1200); 1270 Madison Avenue, between 90th & 91st Streets, Upper East Side (1-212 328 9347).

❤ Mantiques Modern
*146 W 22nd Street, between Sixth & Seventh Avenues (1-212 206 1494, www. mantiquesmodern.com). Subway 1 to 23rd Street. **Open** 10.30am-6.30pm Mon-Fri; 11am-7pm Sat, Sun. **Map** p153 D26* ❺ *Gifts & souvenirs/homewares*

Walking into this two-level shop is like stumbling on the private collection of a mad professor. Specialising in industrial and modernist art, objects, furnishings and accessories from the 1880s to the 1980s, it's a fantastic repository of beautiful and bizarre items, from kinetic sculptures and early 20th-century wooden artists' mannequins to a Soviet World War II telescope. Pieces by famous designers such as Hermès sit side by side with natural curiosities. Skulls (in metal or Lucite), crabs, animal horns and robots are recurring themes.

❤ Printed Matter
*231 Eleventh Avenue, at 26th Street (1-212 925 0325, www.printedmatter.org). Subway C, E to 23rd Street; 7 to 34th Street-Hudson Yards. **Open** 11am-7pm Mon-Wed, Sat; 11am-8pm Thur, Fri; noon-6pm Sun. **Map** p153 B26* ❻ *Books*

This non-profit organisation is devoted to artists' books – from David Shrigley's deceptively naïve illustrations to provocative photographic self-portraits by Matthias Herrmann. Works by little-known talents share shelf space with those by veterans such as Edward Ruscha, Richard Prince and Gilbert & George, including rare and out-of-print pieces. There's also an extensive array of contemporary and vintage art and underground magazines, plus posters and random objects. **Other location** Swiss Institute, 38 St Marks Place, at Second Avenue, East Village (1-646 590 3247).

Gramercy & Flatiron

Lying east of Chelsea, the Gramercy and Flatiron neighbourhoods contain some of the city's most distinctive architecture – including the famous wedge-shaped building that gave the Flatiron District its name – and several inviting green spaces. Unfortunately, you'll probably only get tantalising over-the-gate glimpses of pretty Gramercy Park, which remains the exclusive preserve of residents of the surrounding buildings. But in recent years, the attractions for visitors have multiplied in this part of town, with the arrival of new museums and shops, including the country's first Museum of Mathematics and Italian food mecca Eataly. Some of the city's best eateries, from contemporary taverns to decadent fine dining rooms, have taken root here, cementing the area's reputation as a gastronomic hotspot.

❤ **Don't miss**

1 Flatiron Building *p162*
The striking structure that gave the nabe its name.

2 Madison Square Park *p162*
A pretty patch with an adventurous public-art programme.

3 Museum of Sex *p164*
Eye-opening exhibits.

Please
Do Not Block

FLATIRON DISTRICT & UNION SQUARE

▶Subway F, M to 14th Street; L, N, Q, R, W, 4, 5, 6 to 14th Street-Union Square; L to Sixth Avenue; R, W, 6 to 23rd Street or 28th Street.

Taking its name from the distinctive wedge-shaped **Flatiron Building**, this district extends from 14th to 29th Streets, between Sixth and Lexington Avenues. (However, as with many NYC neighbourhoods, the borders are disputed and evolving – NoMad is slowly catching on as the new name for the blocks north of Madison Square Park.) The area was once predominantly commercial, home to numerous toy manufacturers and photography studios – it's still not uncommon to see models and actors strolling to and from their shoots. However, in the 1980s, the neighbourhood became more residential, as buyers were drawn to its 19th-century brownstones and early 20th-century industrial architecture. Clusters of restaurants and shops soon followed. By the turn of the millennium, many internet start-ups had moved to the area, earning it the nickname 'Silicon Alley'.

There are two major public spaces in the locale: Madison Square Park and Union Square. Opened in 1847, **Madison Square Park** (from 23rd to 26th Streets, between Fifth & Madison Avenues) is the more stately of the two. In the 19th century, the square was a highly desirable address. Winston Churchill's grandfather resided in a magnificent but since-demolished mansion at Madison Avenue and 26th Street; Edith Wharton also made her home in the neighbourhood and set many of her high-society novels here. By the 1990s, the park had become a decaying no-go zone given over to drug dealers and the homeless, but it got a much-needed makeover in 2001 thanks to the efforts of the Madison Square Park Conservancy (www.madisonsquarepark.org), which has created a programme of cultural events, including Mad Sq Art, a year-round 'gallery without walls', featuring sculptural, video and installation exhibitions from big-name artists. A further lure is the original Shake Shack, the burger stand that spawned the popular chain (for a review of the large Upper West Side location, *see p202*); it still attracts a perpetual queue.

The square is surrounded by illustrious buildings. Completed in 1909, the **Metropolitan Life Tower** (1 Madison Avenue, at 24th Street) was modelled on the Campanile in Venice's Piazza San Marco (an allusion as commercial as it was architectural, for Met Life Insurance wanted to remind people that it had raised funds for the Campanile after its fall two years earlier). It's now home to the luxurious New York Edition Hotel. The **Appellate Division Courthouse** (35 E 25th Street, at Madison Avenue) features one of the most beautiful pediments in the city, while Cass Gilbert's **New York Life Insurance Company Building** (51 Madison Avenue, at 26th Street) is capped by a golden pyramid that's one of the skyline's jewels.

The most famous of all Madison Square's edifices, however, lies at the southern end. The **Flatiron Building** (175 Fifth Avenue, between 22nd & 23rd Streets) was the world's first steel-frame skyscraper, a 22-storey Beaux Arts structure clad conspicuously in white limestone and glazed terracotta. But it's the unique triangular shape that has drawn sightseers since it opened in 1902. Legend has it that a popular 1920s catchphrase originated at this corner of 23rd Street –

♥ Time to eat & drink

Vintage diner fare
Eisenberg's Sandwich Shop
p165

Hot chocolate and cookies
City Bakery *p165*

Elevated spins on street food
Cosme *p165*, Nur *p166*

Classy NYC dining
Eleven Madison Park *p166*, Union Square Cafe *p167*

Time-travel tipples
Old Town Bar *p168*, Pete's Tavern *p171*, Raines Law Room *p168*

♥ Time to shop

Eclectic indoor market
Showplace Antique & Design Center *p169*

Far more than furnishings
ABC Carpet & Home *p168*

Locally made foodstuffs
Union Square Greenmarket *p169*

Witty NYC-themed crockery
Fishs Eddy *p169*

Metropolitan Life Tower

police would give the '23 skidoo' to ne'er-do-wells trying to peek at ladies' petticoats as the unique wind currents that swirled around the building blew their dresses upward. Speaking of rampant libidos: the nearby **Museum of Sex** houses an impressive collection of salacious ephemera.

In the 19th century, the neighbourhood went by the moniker of Ladies' Mile, thanks to the ritzy department stores that lined Broadway and Sixth Avenue. These retail palaces attracted the 'carriage trade', wealthy women who bought the latest imported fashions and household goods. By 1914, most of the department stores had

moved north, leaving their proud cast-iron buildings behind. Today, the area is peppered with chain clothing stores and tasteful home-furnishing shops such as **ABC Carpet & Home**.

The Flatiron District's other major public space, **Union Square** (from 14th to 17th Streets, between Union Square East & Union Square West) is named after neither the Union of the Civil War nor the labour rallies that once took place here, but simply for the union of Broadway and Bowery Lane (now Fourth Avenue). Even so, it does have its radical roots: from the 1920s until the early '60s, it was a favourite spot for tub-

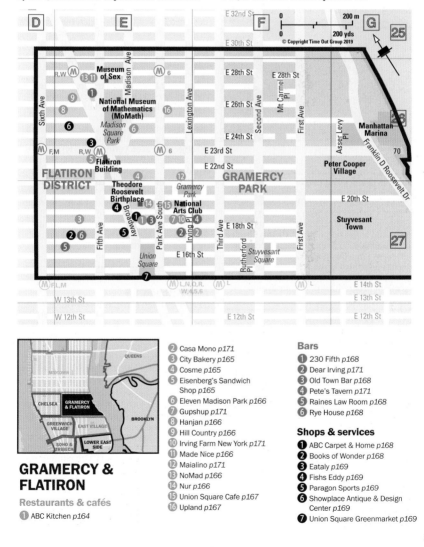

GRAMERCY & FLATIRON

Flatiron Building

thumping political oratory. Following 9/11, the park was home to candlelit vigils and became a focal point for the city's grief; more recently it was the site of anti-Trump and immigrants' rights rallies. Formerly grungy, the park has been refreshed by a rolling renovation project started in the 1980s and is the home of the **Union Square Greenmarket**. The square is flanked by a variety of large businesses, including a **Barnes & Noble** bookstore (www. barnesandnoble.com) that hosts an excellent programme of author events.

Sights & museums

♥ Museum of Sex

233 Fifth Avenue, at 27th Street (1-212 689 6337, www.museumofsex.com). Subway R, W, 6 to 28th Street. **Open** *10.30am-11pm (last entry 9pm) Mon-Thur, Sun; 10.30am-midnight (last entry 10pm) Fri, Sat.* **Admission** *$20.50; $17.50 reductions. Under-18s not admitted.* **Map** *p163 E26.*

Situated in the former Tenderloin district, which was bumping and grinding with dance halls and brothels in the 1800s, the Museum of Sex explores its subject within a cultural context. In the three-level space, rotating highlights of the collection of more than 20,000 objects range from the tastefully erotic to the outlandish. You may see kinky art courtesy of Picasso and Keith Haring, one of Hugh Hefner's smoking jackets or a highly

uncomfortable-looking 1890s anti-onanism device. The permanent installation 'Jump for Joy' lets you frolic in a 'Bouncy Castle of Breasts', and the changing exhibitions have covered such subjects as hardcore porn and 'The Sex Lives of Animals'. The large gift shop stocks books and arty sex toys.

National Museum of Mathematics (MoMath)

11 E 26th Street, between Fifth & Madison Avenues (1-212 542 0566, www.momath. org). Subway R, W, 6 to 23rd Street. **Open** *10am-5pm daily (10am-2.30pm 1st Wed of each mth).* **Admission** *$19; $16 reductions.* **Map** *p163 E26.*

Designed for visitors of all ages, the country's first Museum of Mathematics replaces lectures and textbooks with more than 40 eclectic, interactive exhibits covering such topics as algebra and geometry. Think a ride on a square-wheeled trike could never be smooth? Find out just how bump-free it can be when you take said tricycle over a sunflower-shaped track, where the petals create strategically placed catenaries – curves used in geometry and physics – that make a level ride possible. Elsewhere, you can pass 3D objects (or even your own body) through the laser-light 'Wall of Fire', and the lasers will display the objects as two-dimensional cross-sections (a cone becomes a triangle and circle, for instance). Or collaborate with a pair of fellow visitors to pan, zoom and rotate your own video cameras to create a single composite image, which can be manipulated into a bevy of interesting 'Feedback Fractals' (or fragmented shapes).

Restaurants & cafés

ABC Kitchen $$

35 E 18th Street, between Broadway & Park Avenue South (1-212 475 5829, www. abckitchennyc.com). Subway L, N, Q, R, W, 4, 5, 6 to 14th Street-Union Square. **Open** *noon-3pm, 5.30-10.30pm Mon-Wed; noon-3pm, 5.30-11pm Thur; noon-3pm, 5.30-11.30pm Fri; 11am-3pm, 5.30-11.30pm Sat; 11am-3pm, 5.30-10pm Sun.* **Map** *p163 E27* ❶ *Eclectic*

The *haute* green cooking at Jean-Georges Vongerichten's artfully decorated restaurant at premier interior store ABC Carpet & Home is based on the most gorgeous ingredients from up and down the East Coast. The local, seasonal bounty finds its way into dishes like a mushroom pizza, topped with parmesan, oregano and a farm egg, or roasted black sea bass infused with chillies and herbs. A signature sundae of salted caramel ice-cream, candied peanuts and popcorn with chocolate sauce reworks the kids' classic to thrill a grown-up palate. ABC delivers one message

Museum of Sex

overall: food that's good for the planet needn't be any less flavourful or stunning to look at. The store is also home to the team's Latin-accented ABC Cocina, and vegetable-focused ABCV restaurant.

♥ City Bakery $

*3 W 18th Street, between Fifth & Sixth Avenues (1-212 366 1414, www.thecitybakery. com). Subway L, N, Q, R, W, 4, 5, 6 to 14th Street-Union Square. **Open** 7.30am-6pm Mon-Fri; 8am-6pm Sat; 9am-6pm Sun (hrs vary). **Map** p163 E27* ③ *Café*

Pastry genius Maury Rubin's loft-size City Bakery is jammed with shoppers loading up on creative baked goods and seasonal salad bar choices. There's also a small selection of hot dishes. But never mind all that: the thick, incredibly rich hot chocolate with fat house-made marshmallows is justly famed, and the moist 'melted' chocolate-chip cookies are divinely decadent.

♥ Cosme $$

*35 E 21st Street, between Broadway & Park Avenue South (1-212 913 9659, www. cosmenyc.com). Subway 6 to 23rd Street. **Open** noon-2.30pm, 5.30-11pm Mon-Thur; noon-2.30pm, 5.30pm-midnight Friday; 11.30am-2.30pm, 5.30pm-midnight Sat; 11.30am-2.30pm, 5.30-11pm Sun. **Map** p163 E26* ④ *Mexican*

Enrique Olvera is the megawatt talent behind acclaimed Mexico City restaurant Pujol. The elegant, high-gear small plates served at his first stateside debut – a bare-concrete dining room – are pristine, pricey and market-fresh. Tacos make an appearance on the menu in a generous portion of duck *carnitas*, cooked to the sinful midpoint of unctuous fat and seared flesh. Single-corn tortillas pop up frequently, from a complimentary starter of crackly blue-corn tortillas with chilli-kicked pumpkin-seed butter to dense, crispy tostadas dabbed with bone-marrow salsa and creamy tongues of sea urchin. But it's the face-melting, savoury-sweet, Instagrammed-to-death husk meringue, with its fine hull giving way to a velvety, supercharged corn mousse, that cements Olvera's status as a premier haute-Mex ambassador.

♥ Eisenberg's Sandwich Shop $

*174 Fifth Avenue, at 22nd Street (1-212 675 5096, www.eisenbergsnyc.com). Subway R, W to 23rd Street. **Open** 7.30am-6pm Mon-Fri; 9am-5pm Sat; 10am-3pm Sun. **Map** p163 E26* ⑤ *Deli*

Since 1929, this slender Flatiron joint has dished out diner fare such as hamburgers and egg creams with the kind of (earned) swagger unique to New York's restaurant institutions. Workers from nearby offices and visitors sidle up to the counter for retro classics. The corned beef and chopped liver sandwich and the spectacularly cheesy Reuben belong in the pantheon of the city's deli stalwarts.

❤ Eleven Madison Park $$$$

11 Madison Avenue, at 24th Street (1-212 889 0905, www.elevenmadisonpark.com). Subway R, W, 6 to 23rd Street. **Open** *5.30-10pm Mon-Wed; 5.30-10.30pm Thur; noon-1pm, 5.30-10.30pm Fri-Sun.* **Map** *p163 E26* ⑥ *American creative*

Michelin-starred chef Daniel Humm and impresario Will Guidara helm this vast art-deco jewel, which began life as a brasserie before evolving into one of the city's most rarefied and progressive eateries. The service is famously mannered, and the room among the city's most grand. But the heady, epic seasonal tasting menus that pay homage to NYC history are the true heart of Eleven Madison Park, a format that spotlights Humm's auteur instincts.

Hanjan $$

36 W 26th Street, between Broadway & Sixth Avenue (1-212 206 7226, www.hanjan26. com). Subway R, W to 28th Street. **Open** *noon-2.30pm, 5-10.30pm Mon-Wed; noon-2.30pm, 5-11.30pm Thur-Sat.* **Map** *p163 E26* ⑧ *Korean*

Hanjan is a shining example of a *joomak*, the Korean equivalent of the English gastropub. Expect a barrage of deeply satisfying dishes: glutinous rice cakes licked with spicy pork fat; crispy spring onion pancakes studded with local squid; and skewers of fresh chicken thighs that you can swab with *ssamjang* (a spicy sauce). Each plate packs its own surprises, but the whole feast is tied together by a soulful bass note melding sweetness, spice and just the right amount of fishy funk.

Hill Country $$

30 W 26th Street, between Broadway & Sixth Avenue (1-212 255 4544, www.hillcountryny. com). Subway R, W to 28th Street. **Open** *11.30am-10pm Mon-Wed, Sun; 11.30am-11pm Thur-Sat.* **Map** *p163 E26* ⑨ *American barbecue*

Owner Marc Glosserman's grandfather was the mayor of Lockhart, a Texas town known for its barbecue, and the cooking here is true to the restaurant's namesake region. Dishes feature sausages imported from barbecue stalwart Kreuz Market and two options for brisket: go for the 'moist' (read: fatty) version for succulence. Beef shoulder emerges from the smoker in 20lb slabs, and hefty tips-on pork ribs have just enough fat to imbue them with proper flavour. Daily rotating desserts, such as jelly-filled cupcakes with peanut butter frosting, live out some kind of *Leave It to Beaver* fantasy, though June Cleaver wouldn't approve of the dozens of tequilas and bourbons on offer. Regular live music in the downstairs bar includes country, folk and roots acts.

Made Nice $

8 W 28th Street, between Broadway & Fifth Avenue (no phone, www.madenicenyc. com). Subway R, W to 28th Street. **Open** *11am-10pm Mon-Thur; 11am-9pm Fri; noon-9pm Sat; noon-10pm Sun.* **Map** *p163 E26* ⑪ *American*

Daniel Humm and Will Guidara, the duo behind Eleven Madison Park and the NoMad, are responsible for this nearby counter-service concept. The tight menu includes creative salads and hot dishes such as roast chicken with lemon parmesan stuffing and rosemary fries. Single-digit-priced glasses of wine are available, as well as local beer and house-made sodas. The bright, casual space, with a mural by street artist Shepard Fairey and disposable plates and cutlery, may lack ambience for an evening meal, but makes a great quick lunch stop.

NoMad $$$

Nomad Hotel, 1170 Broadway, at 28th Street (1-212 796 1500, www.thenomadhotel.com). Subway R, W to 28th Street. **Open** *7-10am, noon-2pm, 5.30-10.30pm Mon-Thur; 7-10am, noon-2pm, 5.30-11pm Fri; 7-10am, 11am-2.30pm, 5.30-11pm Sat; 7-10am, 11am-2.30pm, 5.30-10pm Sun.* **Map** *p163 E26* ⑬ *American*

With plush armchairs around well-spaced tables, Daniel Humm and Will Guidara's restaurant in the NoMad Hotel is a stylish return to three-course dining. The food, like the space, exudes unbuttoned decadence, with over-the-top starters such as one built on a slow-cooked egg. And while there are plenty of rich-man roast chickens for two in New York, the amber-hued bird here – with a foie gras, brioche and black truffle stuffing under the skin – is surely the new gold standard, well worth its $98 price tag. For the leaner of wallet, the elegant NoMad Bar serves lofty pub grub and smart cocktails.

❤ Nur $$$

34 E 20th Street, between Park Avenue South & Fifth Avenue (1-212 505 3420, www.nurnyc. com). Subway 6 to 23rd Street. **Open** *5-10pm Mon-Thur; 5-10.30pm Fri; 11am-1.30pm, 5-10.30pm Sat; 11am-1.30pm, 5-10pm Sun.* **Map** *p163 E27* ⑭ *Middle Eastern*

Nur is the forward-thinking pan-Middle Eastern restaurant from Israeli-Moroccan celebu-toque Meir Adoni (of Tel Aviv's acclaimed Blue Sky and Lumina) and Breads Bakery founder Gadi Peleg. Adoni, one in a growing line of chefs who are retooling Israeli eating in New York, stretches beyond comfort dishes to pull influences from all over the Levant, from Jewish and Arab traditions to his own North African roots. Save pieces of the excellent bread to drag through the sauces and dressings of plates such as a lovely carpaccio of fire-roasted eggplant with feta, pistachios and sweet date syrup, or plump, pan roasted octopus warmed with black and white tahinis.

♥ Union Square Cafe $$$
*101 E 19th Street, at Park Avenue South (1-212 243 4020, www.unionsquarecafe. com). Subway L, N, Q, R, W, 4, 5, 6 to 14th Street-Union Square. **Open** 11.30am-10pm Mon-Thur; 11.30am-11pm Fri; 11am-11pm Sat; 11am-10pm Sun. **Map** p163 E27* 15
American creative

The original Union Square Cafe, the beloved flagship of the formidable Danny Meyer empire, opened on East 16th Street in 1985, long before a Shake Shack patty ever sizzled on a griddle top. A rent spike prompted a move three blocks north to a two-storey space that's nearly double the size. The light and lofty setting, designed by architect David Rockwell, features little nods to the original: cherry-wood service stations, dark-green wainscotting, and quirky, colourful paintings lining the walls. The service is as well trained and personable as ever and a warm, convivial spirit still dominates the dining room. New dishes fit effortlessly with familiar favourites such as ricotta gnocchi and lunchtime tuna burgers, and farmers' market produce is still very much in evidence.

Next door, **Daily Provisions** (103 E 19th Street, between Irving Place & Park Avenue South, 1-212 488 1505, www. dailyprovisionsnyc.com) is a casual, quick-service annex, serving sandwiches such as a club-sandwich riff on USC's herb-rubbed rotisserie chicken, plus house-baked pastries, Joe coffee, beer and wine, at marble counters or to take away.

Upland $$
*345 Park Avenue South, at 26th Street (1-212 686 1006, www.uplandnyc.com). Subway 6 to 28th Street. **Open** 11.30am-3pm, 5-11pm Mon-Fri; 10am-2.45pm, 5-11pm Sat; 10am-2.45pm, 5-10pm Sun. **Map** p163 E26* 16 *American*

A Golden State glow radiates throughout Upland, a glossy tribute to chef Justin Smillie's hometown nestled at the foot of the San Gabriel Mountains. The big, buzzing room is damn near SoCal-sunny on a drab stretch of Park Avenue South. That good-looking gleam extends to the copper and oak shelves stocked with uplit wine bottles and jars of preserved Moroccan lemons, the lacquered ceilings and the affluent diners sitting beneath them, suit jackets tossed behind their chairs as they tuck into sausage and kale pizza and crispy, *yuzu kosho*-smacked duck wings.

Union Square Cafe

Bars

230 Fifth

230 Fifth Avenue, at 27th Street (1-212 725 4300, www.230-fifth.com). Subway R, W to 28th Street. **Open** *2pm-2am Mon-Fri; 10am-4am Sat, Sun.* **Map** *p163 E26* ❶

Perched atop an anonymous office building, the 14,000sq ft roof garden dazzles with spectacular views, including a close-up of the Empire State Building. While the sprawling outdoor space gets mobbed on sultry nights, it's less crowded during the cooler months when heaters and transparent igloos make it a winter hotspot. For those who prefer to drink indoors, there's a glitzy lounge below, with plush sofas and floor-to-ceiling windows.

❤ Old Town Bar

45 E 18th Street, between Broadway & Park Avenue South (1-212 529 6732, www. oldtownbar.com). Subway L, N, Q, R, W, 4, 5, 6 to 14th Street-Union Square. **Open** *11.30am-1am Mon-Fri; noon-1am Sat; 1pm-midnight Sun (hrs can vary).* **Map** *p163 E27* ❸

Amid the swank food and drink sanctums around Park Avenue South, this classic tavern remains a shrine to unchanging values. Grab a sweet wooden booth or belly up to the long bar and drain a few pints alongside the regulars who gather on stools 'south of the pumps' (their lingo for taps). If you work up an appetite, skip the much-praised burger in favour of the chilli dog: a grilled and scored all-beef hot dog with spicy house-made beef-and-red-kidney-bean chilli. (Note that the kitchen closes at 11.30pm Monday to Saturday and 10pm on Sunday.)

❤ Raines Law Room

48 W 17th Street, between Fifth & Sixth Avenues (no phone, www.raineslawroom. com). Subway F, M to 14th Street; L to Sixth Avenue. **Open** *5pm-2am Mon-Wed; 5pm-3am Thur-Sat; 5pm-1am Sun.* **Map** *p163 E27* ❺

There's no bar at this louche lounge. In deference to its name (which refers to an 1896 law that was designed to curb liquor consumption), drinks are prepared in a half-hidden back room resembling a kitchen, surrounded by gleaming examples of every tool and gizmo a barkeep could wish for. From this gorgeous tableau comes an austere cocktail list. Kick back in the plush, upholstered space to sip classics, and variations thereof. **Other location** The William, 24 E 39th Street, between Madison & Park Avenues (1-646 922 8600, www. thewilliamnyc.com).

Rye House

11 W 17th Street, between Fifth & Sixth Avenues (1-212 255 7260, www.ryehousenyc. com). Subway F, M to 14th Street; L to Sixth Avenue. **Open** *noon-midnight Mon, Sun; noon-1am Tue, Wed; noon-2am Thur-Sat.* **Map** *p163 E27* ❻

As the name suggests, American spirits, such as bourbons and ryes, are the focus of this contemporary-classic bar, though there's also a selection of whiskies from other parts of the world, notably Scotland and Japan. As well as single pours, you can sample some of the offerings in flights or mixed into cocktails such as the Wake-up Call, made with jalapeño-infused bourbon. While the focus is clearly on drinking, there's excellent upscale pub grub, such as truffle grilled cheese or potato pierogi.

Shops & services

❤ ABC Carpet & Home

888 Broadway, at 19th Street (1-212 473 3000, www.abchome.com). Subway L, N, Q, R, W, 4, 5, 6 to 14th Street-Union Square. **Open** *10am-7pm Mon-Wed, Fri; 10am-8pm Thur; 11am-6pm Sun.* **Map** *p163 E27* ❶ *Homewares*

Founded in 1897, this stylish emporium packs more than just homewares into four sprawling levels. Browse everything from hand-embroidered cushions, contemporary ceramics and Tibetan crafts to jewellery and natural skincare on the bazaar-style ground floor. The upper floors showcase sleek modern and vintage furniture, and exquisite one-off rugs, including antique and colour-saturated silk. Bed and bath linens are in the basement. The outlet store in Brooklyn's Industry City complex offers reduced-price rugs and furnishings. **Other location** 3906 Second Avenue, between 39th & 41st Street, Sunset Park, Brooklyn (1-347 415 8874).

Books of Wonder

18 W 18th Street, between Fifth & Sixth Avenues (1-212 989 3270, www.booksofwonder. com). Subway F, M to 14th Street; L to Sixth Avenue; 1 to 18th Street. **Open** *10am-7pm Mon-Sat; 11am-6pm Sun.* **Map** *p163 E27* ❷ *Books*

This large independent children's bookstore sells rare and out-of-print editions as well as new titles, plus a special collection of Oz books. The store also always has a good stock of signed books and children's book art. **Other location** 217 W 84th Street, between Amsterdam Avenue & Broadway, Upper West Side (1-212 989 1804).

Eataly

*200 Fifth Avenue, between 23rd & 24th Streets (1-212 229 2560, www.eataly.com). Subway F, M, R, W to 23rd Street. **Open** Market 9am-11pm daily. Café 7am-11pm daily. Restaurants 11.30am-11pm daily. **Map** p163 E26* ❸ *Food & drink*

The first Stateside spin-off of an operation by the same name in Turin, this massive foodie destination sprawls across 42,500sq ft. The Italian gastro-complex encompasses six sit-down restaurants, including a rooftop beer garden. Adjacent retail areas offer gourmet provisions, including artisanal breads baked on the premises, fresh mozzarella, salumi and a vast array of olive oils. **Other location** 3rd Floor, 4 World Trade Center, 101 Liberty Street, Financial District (1-212 897 2895).

ABC Carpet & Home

❤ Fishs Eddy

*889 Broadway, at 19th Street (1-212 420 9020, www.fishseddy.com). Subway R, W to 23rd Street. **Open** 10am-9pm Mon-Sat; 10am-8pm Sun. **Map** p163 E27* ❹ *Homewares*

Penny-pinchers frequent this barn-like space for sturdy dishware and glasses – surplus stock from restaurants, ocean liners and hotels (plain white side plates start at a mere $1.99). But there are plenty of affordable, freshly minted goods too, many with novelty patterns. Add spice to mealtime with glasses adorned with male or female pole-dancers. Dinnerware and mugs printed with the Manhattan skyline, or sugar and butter dishes with Brooklyn-accented labels ('shuguh', 'buttah'), make excellent NYC souvenirs.

Paragon Sports

*867 Broadway, at 18th Street (1-212 255 8036, www.paragonsports.com). Subway L, N, Q, R, W, 4, 5, 6 to 14th Street-Union Square. **Open** 10am-8.30pm Mon-Fri; 10am-8pm Sat; 11am-7pm Sun. **Map** p163 E27* ❺ *Sports equipment*

Established in 1908, Paragon offers three floors of equipment and clothing for almost every activity, from the everyday (workout-wear and trainers) to the more niche (croquet sets, boxing accessories).

❤ Showplace Antique & Design Center

*40 W 25th Street, between Fifth & Sixth Avenues (1-212 633 6063, www.nyshowplace. com). Subway F, M to 23rd Street. **Open** 10am-6pm Mon-Fri; 8.30am-5.30pm Sat, Sun (individual vendors vary). **Map** p163 E26* ❻ *Fashion/homewares*

Set over four expansive floors, this indoor market houses more than 250 high-quality dealers. The warren of stalls specialises in everything from classical antiquities and Asian art to vintage toys, early-20th-century radios, designer clothing and collectable handbags. The top floor has a more open layout showcasing furniture as well as decorative objects, jewellery and accessories. Note that some dealers may knock off early, so it's best not to visit at the end of the day.

❤ Union Square Greenmarket

*From 16th to 17th Streets, between Union Square East & Union Square West (1-212 788 7476, www.grownyc.org/greenmarket). Subway L, N, Q, R, 4, 5, 6 to 14th Street-Union Square. **Open** 8am-6pm Mon, Wed, Fri, Sat. **Map** p163 E27* ❼ *Market*

Shop elbow-to-elbow with top chefs for locally grown produce, handmade breads and baked goods, preserves and cheeses at the city's flagship farmers' market on the periphery of Union Square Park. From around mid November until Christmas, a holiday market sets up shop here too.

GRAMERCY PARK

▶ *Subway L to Third Avenue; L, N, Q, R, 4, 5, 6 to 14th Street-Union Square; R, W, 6 to 23rd Street.*

A key to **Gramercy Park**, the tranquil, gated square at the bottom of Lexington Avenue, between 20th and 21st Streets, is one of the most sought-after treasures in all the five boroughs. For the most part, only residents of the beautiful surrounding townhouses and apartment buildings have access to the park, which was developed in the 1830s to resemble a London square. The park is flanked by two private clubs. The **Players Club** (16 Gramercy Park South, between Park Avenue South & Irving Place, 1-212 475 6116, www.theplayersnyc.org) was inspired by London's Garrick Club. It's housed in an 1847 brownstone formerly owned by Edwin Booth, the celebrated 19th-century actor and brother of John Wilkes Booth, Abraham Lincoln's assassin. Next door at no.15 is the Victorian Gothic Revival Samuel Tilden Mansion, which houses the **National Arts Club** (1-212 475 3424, www.nationalartsclub.org, closed Sat, Sun & July, Aug). The busts of literary greats (Shakespeare, Dante) along the façade were chosen to reflect Tilden's library, which, along with his fortune, helped to create the New York Public Library. The NAC's galleries are open to non-members, but call before visiting as they may close for private events or between shows.

Leading south from the park to 14th Street, Irving Place is named after author Washington Irving (although he never lived here). Near the corner of 15th Street sits music venue **Irving Plaza** (closed for renovation at time of writing). A block west of the park is the **Theodore Roosevelt Birthplace**, a national historic site.

The largely residential area bordered by 23rd and 30th Streets, Park Avenue and the East River is known as **Kips Bay** after Jacobus Kip, whose farm covered the area in the 17th century. Third Avenue is the district's main thoroughfare, and a locus of restaurants representing a variety of eastern cuisines, including Afghan, Tibetan and Turkish.

Sights & museums

Theodore Roosevelt Birthplace National Historic Site

*28 E 20th Street, between Broadway & Park Avenue South (1-212 260 1616, www. nps.gov/thrb). Subway 6 to 23rd Street. **Open** 9am-5pm Wed-Sun. Tours hourly 10am-4pm (except noon). **Admission** free. **Map** p163 E27.*

The brownstone where the 26th President of the United States was born and raised until the age of 14 was demolished in 1916. But it was recreated after his death in 1919, complete with authentic period furniture (some from the original residence). The house

Gupshup

can only be explored on the first come, first served guided tours. A 25-minute film about Teddy's childhood is screened in the ground-floor exhibition gallery.

Restaurants & cafés

Casa Mono $$
*52 Irving Place, at 17th Street (1-212 253 2773, www.casamononyc.com). Subway L to Third Avenue; N, Q, R, W, 4, 5, 6 to 14th Street-Union Square. **Open** noon-11pm Mon, Tue, Sun; noon-midnight Wed-Sat. **Map** p163 F27* ② *Spanish*

Reserve a table or squeeze into a space at the bar in this compact spot to feast on adventurous Spanish fare such as mussels with chorizo and cava, fried sweetbreads with fennel, foie gras with *cinco cebollas* (five types of onion), and fried duck egg with black truffles. For a slightly cheaper option, the attached Bar Jamón (125 E 17th Street, open 5pm-2am Mon-Fri, noon-2am Sat, Sun) offers tapas, Ibérico hams and Spanish cheeses.

Gupshup $$
*115 E 18th Street, between Irving Place & Park Avenue South (1-212 518 7313, www.gupshupnyc.com). Subway L, N, Q, R, W, 4, 5, 6 to 14th Street-Union Square. **Open** 11.30am-2.30pm, 5-10pm Mon-Wed; 11.30am-2.30pm, 5-11pm Thur, Fri; 11am-3pm, 5-11pm Sat; 11am-3pm, 5-10pm Sun. **Map** p163 E2* ⑦ *Indian*

Chef Gurpreet Singh, an alum of New Delhi's posh Indian Accent, presides over bilevel digs that resemble a colourful mansion in 1970s Bombay, with black-and-white chequered floors and green velvet-cushioned booths. Singh ventures deep into fusion territory with small plates – think fluffy, street-style *puchkas* nestled in a curd-rice mousse flecked with nubs of lightly smoked salmon, or a Mumbai-meets-Mexico City guacamole served with strips of spiced chips baked with chickpea flour. Fewer liberties are taken with the main dishes, such as a succulent grilled lobster tail soaked in a rich coconut-milk *moilee* sauce.

Irving Farm New York $
*71 Irving Place, between 18th & 19th Streets (1-212 206 0707 ext 71, www.irvingfarm.com). Subway L, N, Q, R, 4, 5, 6 to 14th Street-Union Square. **Open** 7am-8pm Mon-Fri; 8am-8pm Sat, Sun. **Map** p163 E26* ⑩ *Café*

Irving Farm's beans are roasted in a 100-year-old carriage house in the Hudson Valley. The rural connection is reflected in the rustic feel of this café, set within a stately brownstone. Breakfast, baked goods, sandwiches and salads accompany the excellent java. **Other locations** throughout the city.

Maialino $
*Gramercy Park Hotel, 2 Lexington Avenue, at 21st Street (1-212 777 2410, www.maialinonyc.com). Subway 6 to 23rd Street. **Open** 7.30-10am, noon-2pm, 5.30-10pm Mon-Wed; 7.30-10am, noon-2pm, 5.30-10.30pm Thur, Fri; 10am-2.30pm, 5.30-10.30pm Sat; 10am-2.30pm, 5.30-10pm Sun. **Map** p163 E26* ⑫ *Italian*

Danny Meyer's full-fledged foray into Italian cuisine is a dedicated homage to the neighbourhood trattorias that kept him well fed as a 20-year-old tour guide in Rome. In the wood-beamed dining room, the menu offers facsimiles of dishes specific to Rome, such as spaghetti alla carbonara and suckling pig, while the encyclopedic Italian wine list reaches across the country with rotating regional selections by the glass and more than 1,000 bottles. The lively bar caters to walk-in diners, and also serves salumi, cheeses and creative small plates between set mealtimes.

Bars

Dear Irving
*55 Irving Place, between 17th &18th Streets (no phone, www.dearirving.com). Subway L, N, Q, R, W, 4, 5, 6 to 14th Street-Union Square. **Open** 5pm-2am Mon-Sat; 5pm-1am Sun. **Map** p163 E27* ②

All golden-age yearning and space-time shuffling, this dapper Gramercy lounge is from the team behind Raines Law Room. The railroad space is divided into period-piece quarters, including a tufted Victorian parlour and an ashtray-dotted hooch den worthy of Don Draper. Spend an hour at this luxe oasis sipping tried-and-true classics (Gibson, Rusty Nail) and house creations, and you'll completely lose track of time. **Other location** 40th Floor, Aliz Hotel, 310 W 40th Street, between Eighth & Ninth Avenues, Hell's Kitchen (1-646 609 5122).

❤ Pete's Tavern
*129 E 18th Street, at Irving Place (1-212 473 7676, www.petestavern.com). Subway L, N, Q, R, W, 4, 5, 6 to 14th Street-Union Square. **Open** 11am-2.30am Mon-Wed, Sun; 11am-3am Thur; 11am-4am Fri, Sat. **Map** p163 F27* ④

According to history buffs, in 1904, O Henry wrote his sentimental short story 'The Gift of the Magi' in what was then a quiet Gramercy pub. Today it's three deep at the bar, and O Henry would have a hard time parking it anywhere. Although Pete's – a Civil War-era survivor – draws its share of tourists, you'll also rub shoulders with neighbourhood types who slide into the wooden booths to snack on affordable Italian-inflected eats accompanied by the hoppy house ale in frosty mugs.

Midtown

Soaring office towers, crowded pavements and taxi-choked streets – that's the image most people have of the busy mid-section of Manhattan. It's home to some of the city's best-known landmarks, including iconic skyscrapers such as the Empire State Building and the Chrysler Building, the dazzling electronic spectacle that is Times Square, and Rockefeller Center with its picturesque seasonal ice-skating rink. Fifth Avenue, the dividing line between Midtown West and Midtown East, is continuously clogged with shoppers from all over the world. But closer to the rivers, more residential neighbourhoods such as Hell's Kitchen and Murray Hill are less frenetic and offer worthwhile restaurants and shops. On the far West Side, the development of Hudson Yards means the character of this area will continue to evolve.

❤ **Don't miss**

1 Empire State Building *p182*
The world's most famous skyscraper.

2 Museum of Modern Art (MoMA) *p185*
A new vision for the iconic institution.

3 Broadway theatres *p340*
Take in a top show in an opulent early 1900s setting.

4 The Shed *p179*
Cutting-edge visual and performing arts in an equally innovative building.

5 Gulliver's Gate *p178*
See the whole world in miniature.

Atlas statue at Rockefeller Center *p182 and p184*

HERALD SQUARE & GARMENT DISTRICT

▶ *Subway A, C, E, 1, 2, 3 to 34th Street-Penn Station; B, D, F, M, N, Q, R, W to 34th Street-Herald Square.*

Seventh Avenue, aka Fashion Avenue, is the main drag of the **Garment District** (roughly from 34th to 40th Streets, between Broadway & Eighth Avenue). Although manufacturing in the area has decreased, it's still where designers – and their fitters, machinists and assistants – feed America's multi-billion-dollar clothing industry. Delivery trucks and workers pushing racks of clothes clog streets lined with wholesale trimming, button and fabric shops. Many showrooms hold sample sales (*see p176*).

Taking up an entire city block, from 34th Street to 35th Street, between Broadway and Seventh Avenue, is the legendary **Macy's** (*see p176*). With more than two million square feet of space spread across 11 floors, it's one of the biggest department stores in the world. Facing Macy's, at the intersection of Broadway, 34th Street and Sixth Avenue, is **Herald Square**, named after a long-gone newspaper, the *New York Herald*. The lower section is known as **Greeley Square** after editor and reformer Horace Greeley, owner of the *Herald*'s rival, the *New York Tribune* (the two papers merged in 1924). Once seedy, the square now offers bistro chairs and tables that get crowded with shoppers and lunching office workers in the warmer months. To the east, the spas, restaurants and karaoke bars of small enclave **Koreatown** line 32nd Street, between Broadway and Fifth Avenue.

Located not in Madison Square but on Seventh Avenue, between 31st and 33rd Streets, **Madison Square Garden** (*see p316*) is home to the Knicks basketball and Rangers ice hockey teams, and has welcomed rock icons from Elvis to Lady Gaga. The massive arena is actually the fourth building to bear that name (the first two were appropriately located in the square after which they were named) and opened in 1968, replacing the grand old Pennsylvania Station, razed four years earlier. This brutal act of architectural vandalism spurred the creation of the city's Landmarks Preservation Commission, which has saved many other edifices from a similar fate.

Beneath Madison Square Garden stands **Penn Station**, a claustrophobic catacomb serving thousands of Amtrak, Long Island Rail Road (LIRR) and New Jersey Transit passengers daily and the busiest train station in America. A proposal to relocate the Amtrak and LIRR ticket counters and waiting areas across the street to the stately **James A Farley Post Office** (421 Eighth Avenue, between 31st & 33rd Streets) was championed by the late Senator Patrick Moynihan in the early 1990s. The project stalled over the years, but Moynihan Station is expected to be completed in 2021.

Restaurants & cafés

Keens Steakhouse $$$
72 W 36th Street, at Sixth Avenue (1-212 947 3636, www.keens.com). Subway B, D, F, M, N, Q, R, W to 34th Street-Herald Square. **Open** *11.45am-10.30pm Mon-Fri; 5-10.30pm Sat; 5-9.30pm Sun.* **Map** *p175 D25* ⑩
Steakhouse

❤ **Time to eat & drink**

Pastries, cookies and coffee
Amy's Bread *p181*

Pedigree pizza near Broadway
Don Antonio *p180*

A classic for seafood and cocktails
Grand Central Oyster Bar *p189*

Classy dining, reimagined
Atomix *p191*, The Grill/The Pool *p189*

A nightcap with live jazz
The Rum House *p180*, Fine & Rare *p191*

❤ **Time to shop**

Chic shopping complex
The Shops & Restaurants at Hudson Yards *p181*

Essentials for dapper gents
Fine and Dandy *p181*, JJ Hat Center *p187*

Fifth Avenue icons
Bergdorf Goodman *p186*, FAO Schwarz *p187*

Global home goods
Domus *p181*

NYC's Comme concept store
Dover Street Market *p191*

Dover Street Market

Restaurants & cafés

1. Agern & Great Northern Food Hall *p189*
2. Atomix *p191*
3. Benoit *p186*
4. Don Antonio *p180*
5. Gotham West Market *p180*
6. Grand Central Oyster Bar & Restaurant *p189*
7. The Grill/The Pool *p189*
8. Kajitsu *p191*
9. Kashkaval Garden *p180*
10. Keens Steakhouse *p174*
11. Mandoo Bar *p176*
12. Monkey Bar *p190*
13. Quality Meats *p186*
14. Urbanspace Vanderbilt *p190*

Bars

1. Ardesia *p180*
2. Dutch Fred's *p180*
3. Fine & Rare *p191*
4. Middle Branch *p191*
5. The Rum House *p180*

Shops & services

1. Amy's Bread *p181*
2. B&H *p176*
3. Bergdorf Goodman *p186*
4. Domus *p181*
5. Dover Street Market New York *p191*
6. FAO Schwarz *p187*
7. Fine and Dandy *p181*
8. JJ Hat Center *p187*
9. Macy's *p176*
10. Nepenthes New York *p176*
11. Saks Fifth Avenue *p187*
12. Sam Ash Music *p176*
13. The Shops & Restaurants at Hudson Yards *p181*

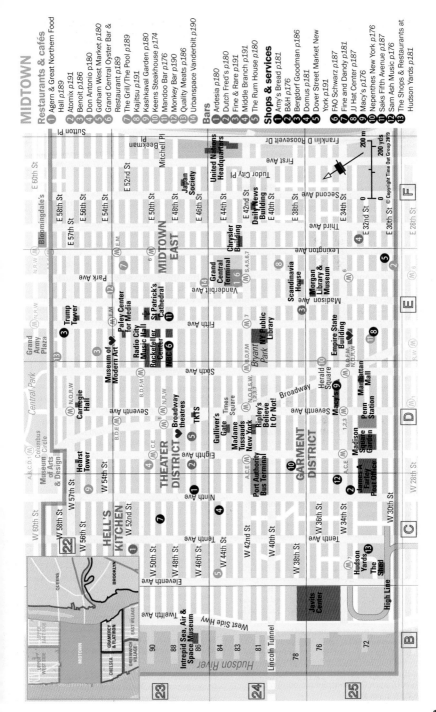

MIDTOWN

The ceiling and walls are hung with pipes, some from such long-ago Keens regulars as Babe Ruth, JP Morgan and Teddy Roosevelt. Even in these non-smoking days, you can catch a whiff of the restaurant's history. Bevelled-glass doors, two working fireplaces and a forest's worth of dark wood suggest a time when 'Diamond Jim' Brady piled his table with bushels of oysters, slabs of seared beef and troughs of ale. Established in 1885, Keens still offers a three-inch-thick mutton chop, and the porterhouse (for two or three) holds its own against any steak in the city.

Mandoo Bar $

2 W 32nd Street, between Fifth Avenue & Broadway (1-212 279 3075, www.mandoobar. net). Subway B, D, F, M, N, Q, R, W to 34th Street-Herald Square. Open 11.30am-10pm daily. Map p175 E25 ⑪ *Korean*

If the staff members filling and crimping dough squares in the front window don't give it away, we will – this wood-wrapped industrial-style spot elevates *mandoo* (Korean dumplings) above mere appetiser status. Several varieties of the tasty morsels are filled with such delights as subtly piquant kimchi, juicy pork, succulent shrimp and vegetables. Try them miniaturised, as in the Baby Mandoo, swimming in a soothing beef broth or atop soupy ramen noodles.

Shops & services

B&H

420 Ninth Avenue, at 34th Street (1-212 444 6615, www.bhphotovideo.com). Subway A, C, E to 34th Street-Penn Station; 7 to 34th Street-Hudson Yards. Open 9am-7pm Mon-Thur; 9am-2pm Fri; 10am-6pm Sun. Map p175 C25 ❷ *Electronics & photography*

In the know
Sample sales

Home to numerous designer studios and showrooms, New York's Garment District (see p174) hosts a weekly spate of sample sales. The best are listed in the Shopping & Style section of *Time Out New York* magazine and www.timeout.com/newyork. A good bet is **Clothingline** (1-212 947 8725, www.clothingline.com), which holds regular sales for a variety of labels – from R13 and Tory Burch to Helmut Lang and Rag & Bone, at its showroom (Second Floor, 261 W 36th Street, between Seventh & Eighth Avenues). Another prime hunting ground, **260 Sample Sale**, holds sales for the likes of DVF, Current Elliott and Phillip Lim in the Flatiron District (260 Fifth Avenue, between 28th & 29th Streets, 1-212 725 5400, www.260samplesale.com) plus locations in Soho.

This huge store is the ultimate one-stop shop for all your photographic, video and audio needs. Adding to the character of the place, goods are transported from the stock room via an overhead conveyor belt. Note that due to the largely Hasidic Jewish staff, it's closed on Saturdays and Jewish holidays.

Macy's

151 W 34th Street, between Broadway & Seventh Avenue (1-212 695 4400, www. visitmacysusa.com). Subway B, D, F, M, N, Q, R, W to 34th Street-Herald Square; 1, 2, 3 to 34th Street-Penn Station. Open 10am-10pm Mon-Sat; 11am-9pm Sun (hrs vary). Map p175 D25 ❾ *Department store*

It may not be as glamorous as New York's other famous stores, but for sheer breadth of stock, the 34th Street behemoth is hard to beat. Mid-price fashion for all ages, big beauty names and housewares have traditionally been the store's bread and butter, but it has since upped its game aand now hosts luxury boutiques including Gucci and Burberry, plus an Apple outpost featuring watches, on the main floor. A cool concept store, the brainchild of New Yorker Rachel Shechtman, has been introduced; Story brings together gift-friendly goods and experiences, selected according to a regularly changing theme, such as 'colour'.

▶ *If you need tourist guidance, stop by the store's Official NYC Information Center.*

Nepenthes New York

307 W 38th Street, between Eighth & Ninth Avenues (1-212 643 9540, www.nepenthesny. com). Subway A, C, E, 1, 2, 3 to 34th Street-Penn Station. Open noon-7pm Mon-Sat; noon-5pm Sun. Map p175 D24 ❿ *Fashion*

Well-dressed dudes with an eye on the Japanese style scene will already be familiar with this Tokyo fashion retailer. The narrow Garment District shop – its first US location – showcases the house menswear labels. These include Daiki Suzuki's American-produced Engineered Garments, known for sturdy, expertly crafted pieces, such as workwear-inspired jackets and rustic shirts, and Needles, which is designed and made in Japan with vintage and pop-culture influences. There is also a small selection of women's clothing.

Sam Ash Music

333 W 34th Street, between Eighth & Ninth Avenues (1-212 719 2299, www.samashmusic. com). Subway A, C, E to 34th Street-Penn Station. Open 11am-8pm Mon-Thur; 10am-8pm Fri, Sat; 11am-7pm Sun. Map p175 C25 ⑫ *Music*

Established in Brooklyn in 1924, this musical instrument emporium moved from Times Square's now-silent 'music row' in 2013. The

Times Square

30,000sq ft store offers new, vintage and custom guitars among other instruments, along with amps, DJ equipment, drums, keyboards, recording equipment, turntables and an array of sheet music.

THEATER DISTRICT & HELL'S KITCHEN

▶ *Subway A, C, E to 42nd Street-Port Authority; C, E, 1 to 50th Street; N, R, W to 49th Street; N, Q, R, S, W, 1, 2, 3, 7 to 42nd Street-Times Square; 7 to 34th Street-Hudson Yards.*

Times Square's evolution from a traffic-choked fleshpot to a tourist-friendly entertainment hub has accelerated in the past several years. Not only has 'the Crossroads of the World' gained an elevated viewing platform atop the TKTS discount booth, from which visitors can admire the surrounding light show, this stretch of Broadway is closed to cars. The Times Square 'Bowtie' features six pedestrian plazas of varying sizes, designed by National September 11 Museum architects Snøhetta and outfitted with granite benches.

Originally Longacre Square, the junction of Broadway and Seventh Avenue, stretching from 42nd to 47th Streets, was renamed after the *New York Times* moved here in the early 1900s. The first electrified billboard graced the district in 1904, on the side of a bank at 46th and Broadway. The same year, the inaugural New Year's Eve party in Times Square doubled as the paper's housewarming party in its new HQ. Today, about a million people gather here to watch an illluminated Waterford Crystal ball descend every 31 December.

The *Times* left the building only a decade after it had arrived (it now occupies a Renzo Piano-designed tower on Eighth Avenue,

between 40th and 41st Streets). However, it retained ownership of its old headquarters until the 1960s, and erected the world's first scrolling electric news 'zipper' in 1928. The readout, now sponsored by Dow Jones, still trumpets the latest breaking stories.

Times Square is also the gateway to the **Theater District**, the zone between 41st Street and 53rd Street, from Sixth Avenue to Ninth Avenue, where extravagant shows are put on six days a week (Monday is the traditional night off). While numerous venues stage first-rate productions in the area, only 41 are officially Broadway theatres (*see p340*).The distinction is based on size rather than location or quality – Broadway theatres must have more than 500 seats.

The Theater District's transformation from the cradle of New York's sex industry began in 1984, when the city condemned properties along 42nd Street ('Forty Deuce', or 'the Deuce' for short), between Seventh and Eighth Avenues. A change in zoning laws meant adult-oriented venues must now subsist on X-rated videos rather than live 'dance' shows; the square's sex trade is now relegated to short stretches of Seventh and Eighth Avenues, just north and south of 42nd Street.

The streets to the west of Eighth Avenue are filled with eateries catering to theatregoers, especially the predominantly tourist-oriented, pricey places along **Restaurant Row** (46th Street, between Eighth and Ninth Avenues). Locals tend to walk west to Ninth Avenue – in the 40s and 50s, the Hell's Kitchen strip is tightly packed with inexpensive restaurants serving a variety of ethnic cuisines.

Recording studios, record labels, theatrical agencies and other entertainment and media companies reside in the area's office buildings. The **Brill Building** (1619 Broadway, at 49th Street) was once a hive of music publishers and producers; such

In the know
Desperate characters

Following complaints that costumed street performers in Times Square were hassling visitors a bit too aggressively for tips, Spider-Man, Elmo and even the now-famous Naked Cowboy must remain within designated 'activity' zones indicated by teal-painted areas in the pedestrian plazas.

luminaries as Jerry Lieber, Mike Stoller and Carole King wrote and auditioned their hits here. Flashy attractions and huge retail stores strive to outdo one another in hopes of snaring the tourist throngs.

West of the Theater District lies **Hell's Kitchen**. The precise origins of the name are unclear, but are no doubt connected to its emergence as an Irish-mob-dominated neighbourhood in the 19th century. In the 1950s, clashes between Irish and recently arrived Puerto Rican factions were dramatised in the musical *West Side Story*. It was a particularly violent incident in 1959, in which two teenagers died, that led to an attempt by local businesses to erase the stigma associated with the area by renaming it Clinton (taken from a park named after one-time mayor DeWitt Clinton). The new name never really took, and gang culture survived until the 1980s.

The area has become a gay nightlife hotspot, and, with the construction of **Hudson Yards** – a massive residential and commercial development – in its southern fringes, it's still evolving. The development's eastern section, which debuted in spring 2019, includes a sleek, seven-floor shopping mall, architecturally innovative arts centre **The Shed** (*see p179*) and a huge climbable sculpture by Thomas Heatherwick. The honeycomb-like structure, which features 154 interconnecting staircases, offers views of the Hudson River and plentiful Instagram opportunities. It's open 10am-9pm daily and admission is free, but visitors need to reserve a time slot online (www.hudsonyardsnewyork.com) or at the site. However, the vantage point will pale into insignificance in 2020, with the opening of an outdoor observation ledge jutting out from the super-tall 30 Hudson Yards tower, 1,100 feet above the ground. Just north, new apartment blocks have sprung up in the former wasteland near the Hudson River, dominated by the massive, black-glass **Jacob K Javits Convention Center** (Eleventh Avenue, between 34th & 39th Streets). A couple of major draws are also here: the Circle Line Terminal (*see p384*), at Pier 83, the departure point for the cruise company's three-hour circumnavigation of

Manhattan Island; and the **Intrepid Sea, Air & Space Museum**, a retired aircraft carrier-cum-naval museum.

Sights & museums

♥ Gulliver's Gate
216 West 44th Street, between Seventh & Eighth Avenues (no phone, gulliversgate.com). Subway A, C, E to 42nd Street-Port Authority; N, Q, R, S, 1, 2, 3, 7 to 42nd Street-Times Square. Open 10am-8pm daily Admission $36; $27 reductions. Map p175 D24.

This interactive miniature world spans an entire city block and comprises more than 300 incredibly detailed scale models (1:87). Representing 50 nations, the scenes were created (roughly) in the region they depict, so the mini NYC – complete with landmarks such as Times Square itself with tiny LED billboards – was built in Brooklyn, while Europe was made in Rimini, Italy. The exhibition covers the iconic global attractions you'd expect – Niagara Falls, the Taj Mahal, the Eiffel Tower, the Parthenon, the Great Wall of China – but there's plenty of humour across the displays, too (mummies on the attack in Egypt, for instance, and the Loch Ness Monster in Scotland). Geography and time periods are a bit fluid. Kids will delight in the many moving elements, including animals and vehicles – there are more than 1,000 trains, 10,000 cars and trucks, plus an entire working airport. Visitors can even have themselves scanned and 3D printed to become 'model citizens', as well as peer into the command centre to see the inner workings of the computer-controlled microcosm.

Intrepid Sea, Air & Space Museum
USS Intrepid, Pier 86, Twelfth Avenue & 46th Street (1-212 245 0072, www.intrepidmuseum.org). Subway A, C, E to 42nd Street-Port Authority, then M42 bus to Twelfth Avenue or 15min walk; 7 to 34th Street-Hudson Yards, then 15min walk. Open Apr-Oct 10am-5pm Mon-Fri; 10am-6pm Sat, Sun. Nov-Mar 10am-5pm daily. Admission $33; $24-$31 reductions; free under-5s, active & retired US military. Map p175 B23.

Commissioned in 1943, this 27,000-ton, 898-ft aircraft carrier survived torpedoes and kamikaze attacks in World War II, served during the Vietnam War and the Cuban Missile Crisis, and recovered two space capsules for NASA. It was decommissioned in 1974, then resurrected as a museum. On its flight deck and portside aircraft elevator are top-notch examples of American military might, including the US Navy F-14 Tomcat (as featured in *Top Gun*), an A-12 spy plane and a fully restored Army AH-1J Sea Cobra gunship

The Shed

helicopter. Visitors can board a 1950s guided-nuclear-missile submarine, or experience flight simulators (for an extra charge). The Space Shuttle Pavilion houses the prototype NASA orbiter Enterprise (OV-101), along with related artefacts, photos and video.

Madame Tussauds New York
234 W 42nd Street, between Seventh & Eighth Avenues (1-212 512 9600, www.madametussauds.com/newyork). Subway A, C, E to 42nd Street-Port Authority; N, Q, R, S, 1, 2, 3, 7 to 42nd Street-Times Square. **Open** *hrs vary; usually 9am-10pm daily* **Admission** *$37; $33 reductions.* **Map** *p175 D24.*

With roots in 18th-century Paris and founded in London in 1802, the world's most-famous wax museum now draws celebrity-hungry crowds to more than 20 locations worldwide. At the New York outpost, you can get a stalker's-eye view of a regularly updated array of paraffin doppelgängers of political, sports, film and pop stars, from Donald Trump and Carmelo Anthony to Lady Gaga and the Kardashians. Check the website for online booking discounts.

Ripley's Believe It or Not!
234 W 42nd Street, between Seventh & Eighth Avenues (1-212 398 3133, www.ripleysnewyork.com). Subway A, C, E to 42nd Street-Port Authority; N, Q, R, S, 1, 2, 3, 7 to 42nd Street-Times Square. **Open** *10am-11pm Mon-Wed, Sun (last entry 10pm); 10am-1am Thur-Sat (last entry midnight).* **Admission** *$32; $24 reductions; free under-4s.* **Map** *p175 D24.*

Times Square might be a little whitewashed these days, but you can get a feel for the old freak show at this repository of the eerie and uncanny. Marvel at such bizarre artefacts as antique torture devices, a six-legged cow and the world's largest collection of shrunken heads.

♥ The Shed
545 W 30th Street, between Tenth & Eleventh Avenues, Hudson Yards (1-646 455 3494, www.theshed.org). Subway 7 to 34th Street-Hudson Yards. **Open** *hrs vary; exhibitions typically 11am-6pm Tue-Wed, Sun; 11am-8pm Thur-Sat.* **Admission** *varies.* **Map** *p175 C25.*

The cultural centrepiece of mega-development Hudson Yards, this non-profit multi-disciplinary arts centre is programmed by an international team led by Alex Poots, a champion of groundbreaking work as former artistic director of the Park Avenue Armory and founder of the Manchester International Festival. The organisation's Bloomberg Building features a 20,000sq ft open-air plaza, which transforms into its flexible main hall, the 'McCourt', via an eight-million-pound retractable steel shell that extends across the courtyard on wheels. The building's vast, flexible theatre and gallery spaces host concerts, dance and theatrical productions and exhibitions that blur the distinction between visual and performing arts. Highlights of the 2019 opening year included a contemporary opera by Björk, a collaborative multimedia musical installation by composer Steve Reich and artist Gerhard

MIDTOWN

In the know
Rise above it

After you've queued to score cheap theatre tickets at the **TKTS** in Duffy Square (Broadway, at 47th Street; *see p339*), ascend the ticket booth's red glass structural steps for an eye-popping panorama of the Great White Way. The glowing staircase, which debuted in 2008, was the brainchild of Australians John Choi and Tai Ropiha, who won a globe-spanning competition for a new design.

Richter, and a thrilling, cross-discipline showcase of emerging NYC talent. It's best to buy tickets at the venue if possible since phone and online booking incurs a fee.

Restaurants & cafés

❤ Don Antonio $$

*309 W 50th Street, between Eighth & Ninth Avenues (1-646 719 1043, www. donantoniopizza.com). Subway C, E to 50th Street. **Open** 11.30am-3.30pm, 4.30-11pm Mon-Thur; 11.30am-11pm Fri, Sat; 11.30am-10.30pm Sun. **Map** p175 D23* ❹ *Italian/pizza*

It may not be trendy, but this pedigreed eaterie, a collaboration between Kesté's (*see p144*) talented Roberto Caporuscio and his decorated Naples mentor, Antonio Starita, is the real deal for pizza aficionados. Start with tasty bites like the *fritattine* (a deep-fried spaghetti cake oozing prosciutto cotto and mozzarella sauce). The main event should be the habit-forming Montanara, which gets a quick dip in the deep fryer before hitting the oven to develop its puffy, golden crust. Topped with tomato sauce, basil and intensely smoky buffalo mozzarella, it's a worthy addition to the pantheon of classic New York pies.

Gotham West Market $-$$

*600 Eleventh Avenue, between 44th & 45th Streets (1-212 582 7940, www. gothamwestmarket.com). A, C, E to 42nd Street-Port Authority. **Open** 8am-10pm Mon-Thur, Sun; 8am-11pm Fri, Sat. **Map** p175 C24* ❺ *Eclectic*

This hip take on a food court is perfect for lunch or a quick pre-theatre bite. The 15,000sq ft retail-dining mecca features varied eateries as well as a full-service NYC Velo bike shop. Dine-in or take-out options include Ivan Ramen Slurp Shop, where Tokyo noodle guru Ivan Orkin offers his famed *shio*, *shoyu* and other varieties; Orkin's latest venture, Corner Slice, serving pizza with exceptionally light crust; Seamore's for sustainable seafood platters and cocktails; and ultra-popular Brooklyn ice-cream shop Ample Hills Creamery. Seating is at chefs' counters or communal tables.

Kashkaval Garden $-$$

*852 Ninth Avenue, between 55th & 56th Streets (1-212 245 1758, www. kashkavalgarden.com). Subway C, E to 50th Street. **Open** noon-midnight Mon, Tue; noon-1am Wed; noon-2am Thur, Fri; 11am-2am Sat; 11am-midnight Sun (closed Sun in summer). **Map** p175 C22* ❾ *Mediterranean*

This charming tapas and wine bar evokes fondue's peasant origins, with deep cast-iron pots and generous baskets of crusty bread. We suggest steering clear of the bland and rubbery kashkaval (a Balkan sheep's-milk cheese) and opting instead for the gooey gruyère and truffle. Or choose from the selection of tangy Mediterranean spreads – such as asparagus houmous and beetroot skordalia – and the impressive roster of skewers.

Bars

▶ *For gay bars in Hell's Kitchen, see p306.*

Ardesia

*510 W 52nd Street, between Tenth & Eleventh Avenues (1-212 247 9191, www.ardesia-ny. com). Subway C, E to 50th Street. **Open** 4pm-midnight Mon-Wed; 4pm-2am Thur, Fri; 2pm-2am Sat; 2-11pm Sun. **Map** p175 C23* ❶

Le Bernardin vet Mandy Oser's iron-and-marble gem offers superior wines in a relaxed setting, including a 36-seat summer patio. The selection of around 100 international bottles is a smart balance of Old and New World options that pair beautifully with the artisanal cheeses, charcuterie, salads and a constantly changing choice of small plates, such as the daily selection of croquettes and house-made NYC-style pretzels. One for the serious oenophile.

Dutch Fred's

*307 W 47th Street, between Eighth & Ninth Avenues (1-646 918 6923, dutchfreds.com). Subway N, R, W to 49th Street; C, E, 1 to 50th Street. **Open** 4pm-4am Mon; 11am-4am Tue-Sun. **Map** p175 D23* ❷

With mosaic tile floors and flat screens showing black-and-white films, this spacious bar taps into the Prohibition era of its namesake, a local policeman who – according to one origin story at least – coined the term Hell's Kitchen. Period-piece drinks have names that nod to neighbourhood history and Broadway past and present, such as the Kiss Kiss Bang Bang (gin, blackberry purée and champagne), plus there are 24 craft beers on tap.

❤ The Rum House

*228 W 47th Street, between Broadway & Eighth Avenue (1-646 490 6924, www. therumhousenyc.com). Subway N, R, W to 49th Street. **Open** noon-4am daily. **Map** p175 D23* ❺

Not long ago, the rakish, 1970s vintage piano bar in the Edison Hotel seemed destined to go the way of the Times Square peep show. But the team behind Tribeca mixology den Ward III ushered in a second act, introducing key upgrades (including serious cocktails) while maintaining the charmingly offbeat vibe. Sip dark, spirit-heavy tipples, such as a funky old-fashioned riff that showcases a sultry aged rum, while listening to live music (9.30pm until late nightly).

Shops & services

💗 Amy's Bread

*672 Ninth Avenue, between 46th & 47th Streets (1-212 977 2670, www.amysbread. com). Subway C, E to 50th Street; N, R, W to 49th Street. **Open** 7am-9pm Mon; 7am-10pm Tue-Fri; 8am-10pm Sat; 8am-9pm Sun. The Pantry 7.30am-2.30pm Mon-Fri; 8am-2.30pm Sun. **Map** p175 C23* ❶ *Food & drink*

Whether sweet (oversized chocolate-chip and black-and-white cookies) or savoury (black olive bread twists), Amy's never disappoints. The bakery-café serves breakfast and snacks such as grilled cheese sandwiches (made with New York State cheddar and spicy chipotle-pepper purée). The adjacent Pantry sells cheese, charcuterie, confectionery, jams and other products handmade in NYC and nearby regions. In addition to the other locations listed below, there are café outposts in the New York Public Library's Stephen A Schwarzman Building (*see p388*) and Library for the Performing Arts at Lincoln Center (*see p195*), plus the Museum of the City of New York (*see p216*). **Other locations** Chelsea Market, 75 Ninth Avenue, between 15th & 16th Streets, Chelsea (1-212 462 4338); 311 Henry Street, between Atlantic Avenue & State Street, Brooklyn Heights (1-929 276 3108).

💗 Domus

*413 W 44th Street, at Ninth Avenue (1-212 581 8099, www.domusnewyork.com). Subway A, C, E to 42nd Street-Port Authority. **Open** noon-8pm Tue-Sat; noon-6pm Sun. **Map** p175 C24* ❹ *Homewares*

Scouring the globe for unusual design products is nothing new, but owners Luisa

In the know
Listen up

Steal a moment of relative quiet amid the clamour of one of NYC's busiest intersections and experience sound in the name of art. Rising from a metal subway grate on Broadway, between 45th and 46th Streets, a 1977 sound installation by Max Neuhaus titled *Times Square* often competes with – but also depends upon – its environment. The surrounding architecture and a series of underground spaces amplify the piece, which evokes ringing church bells.

Cerutti and Nicki Lindheimer take the concept a step further; each year they visit a far-flung part of the world to forge links with and support co-operatives and individual craftspeople. The beautiful results, such as vivid pillows screen-printed in Morocco or handwoven bath towels from Tunisia and South Africa, reflect a fine attention to detail and a sense of place. It's a great place to pick up gifts, including NYC-made porcelain mugs and artisan jewellery from the US, Bali, Thailand, Ecuador and more.

💗 Fine and Dandy

*445 W 49th Street, between Ninth & Tenth Avenues (1-212 247 4847, www. fineanddandyshop.com). Subway C, E to 50th Street. **Open** noon-8pm Mon-Sat; 1-8pm Sun. **Map** p175 C23* ❼ *Accessories*

Decked out with collegiate memorabilia, vintage barware and rare books (also for sale), this Hell's Kitchen shop is a prime location for the modern gent to score of-the-moment retro accoutrements such as bow ties, pocket squares, suspenders (braces) and spats. House-label printed ties are hung in propped-open vintage trunks, and patterned socks are displayed in old briefcases. A line of made-to-measure shirts is also available, plus fun souvenirs such as a mock college pennant emblazoned with 'Hell's Kitchen'.

💗 The Shops & Restaurants at Hudson Yards

*20 Hudson Yards, Tenth Avenue, between 31st & 33rd Streets (1-646 954-3100, www. hudsonyardsnewyork.com). Subway 7 to 34th Street-Hudson Yards. **Open** 10am-9pm, Mon-Sat; 11am-7pm Sun (hrs vary for some shops, bars & restaurants). **Map** p175 C25* ⓭ *Mall*

Anchored by Dallas-born luxury department store Neiman Marcus, making its NYC debut, this seven-level complex houses more than 100 shops and restaurants, plus Snark Park, with interactive art installations that change three times each year. Retail runs the gamut from budget-friendly garb and homewares at Madewell and Muji to designer wares at another Dallas export, Forty Five Ten, which showcases men's and women's clothing and accessories, design objects and and vintage fashion in several spaces on the fifth level. Numerous eateries cater to all wallets, with fried chicken at Momofuku offshoot **Fuku** and the elegant **Tak Room** from renowned toque Thomas Keller among the highlights. **Mercado Little Spain**, a food hall created by celebrity chef José Andrés in collaboration with Spanish siblings Ferran and Albert Adrià, has three full-service restaurants, plus 15 kiosk offering everything from *jamón* and *queso* to *churros* and hot chocolate.

FIFTH AVENUE & AROUND

▶ *Subway B, D, F, M, N, Q, R, W to 34th Street-Herald Square; B, D, F, M to 42nd Street-Bryant Park; B, D, F, M to 47-50th Streets-Rockefeller Center; E, M to Fifth Avenue-53rd Street; 7 to Fifth Avenue.*

The city's central thoroughfare is the main route for public processions, such as the **St Patrick's Day Parade** *(see p286)*, the **LGBT Pride March** *(see p288)* and many others. But even without floats or marching bands, the sidewalks are generally teeming with shoppers and sightseers. The most famous skyscraper in the world also has its entrance on Fifth Avenue: the **Empire State Building** *(see right)*, located smack-bang in the centre of Midtown.

A pair of impassive stone lions, which were dubbed Patience and Fortitude by Mayor Fiorello La Guardia during the Great Depression, flank the steps of the beautiful Beaux Arts humanities and social sciences branch of the **New York Public Library** at 42nd Street (officially named the Stephen A Schwarzman Building). Just behind the library is **Bryant Park**, a manicured lawn that hosts a popular outdoor film series in summer and an ice-skating rink in winter.

The former American Radiator Building on 40th Street now houses the luxury Bryant Park Hotel. Designed by architect Raymond Hood in the mid 1920s, the structure is faced with near-black brick and trimmed in gold leaf. Alexander Woollcott, Dorothy Parker and her 'vicious circle' held court and traded barbs at the nearby **Algonquin** (59 W 44th Street, between Fifth & Sixth Avenues, 1-212 840 6800, www.algonquinhotel.com); though it's been renovated, you can soak up vestiges of the old vibe in the lobby bar.

Step off Fifth Avenue into **Rockefeller Center** and you'll find yourself in an interlacing complex of 19 buildings housing corporate offices, retail space and Rockefeller Plaza. After plans for an expansion of the Metropolitan Opera on the site fell through in 1929, John D Rockefeller Jr set about creating the 'city within a city' to house radio and television corporations. Designed by Raymond Hood and many other prominent architects, Rock Center grew over the decades, with each new building conforming to the original master plan and art deco design. On weekday mornings, a crowd gathers at the NBC network's glass-walled, ground-level studio (where the *Today* show is shot), at the south-west corner of Rockefeller Plaza and 49th Street. The complex is also home to art auction house **Christie's** (20 Rockefeller Plaza, 49th Street, between Fifth & Sixth Avenues, 1-212 636 2000, www.christies.

♥ Empire State Building

*350 Fifth Avenue, between 33rd & 34th Streets (1-212 736 3100, www.esbnyc.com). Subway B, D, F, M, N, Q, R to 34th Street-Herald Square. **Open** 8am-2am daily (last elevator 1.15 am). **Admission** 86th floor $36; $31-$35 reductions; free under-6s. 102nd floor call or see website for information. **Map** p175 E25.*

Financed by General Motors executive John J Raskob at the height of New York's skyscraper race, the Empire State Building sprang up in little more than a year, weeks ahead of schedule. Since opening in 1931, the Indiana limestone and granite tower has been immortalised in countless photos

and films, from the original *King Kong* to *Sleepless in Seattle*. The building contains 2.7 million sq ft of office space, and has more than 130 antennas powering the region's broadcasting industry. But for NYC visitors, it's all about the view. At 1,454ft from its base to the top of its spire, the iconic skyscraper is the city's second-tallest building. Its enclosed 102nd-floor observatory is 1,250ft above the street, just a few feet lower than One World Observatory at the World Trade Center, and the roomier panoramic deck on the 86th floor offers an outdoor lookout point at 1,050ft. On a clear day, the view extends past the five boroughs to surrounding states

New Jersey, Pennsylvania, Connecticut and Massachusetts. The building's marble-clad lobby features a faithful aluminium-and-gold reproduction of the art deco ceiling mural, depicting the sky with industrial-themed celestial bodies. After dark, the tower is illuminated with flashy LEDs. The colour scheme often honours holidays, charities or special events.

▶ *To cut down waiting time, purchase tickets online and visit between 8am and 10am or after 9pm. Alternatively, springing for an express pass ($69-$74 for the 86th floor) allows you to cut to the front of the line.*

com; closed Sat, Sun); pop into the lobby to admire a mural by conceptualist Sol LeWitt.

When it opened on Sixth Avenue (at 50th Street) in 1932, **Radio City Music Hall** (*see p321*) was designed as a showcase for high-end variety acts, but the death of vaudeville led to a quick transition into what was then the world's largest movie house. Today, the art deco jewel hosts concerts and the traditional *Christmas Spectacular* featuring renowned precision dance troupe the Rockettes. Visitors can get a peek backstage, and meet one of the high-kicking dancers, on the Stage Door tour (every 30mins, 9.30am-5pm daily; $30, $26 reductions; see www.radiocity.com/tours for details).

Facing Rockefeller Center is the beautiful **St Patrick's Cathedral**. Famous couples from F Scott and Zelda Fitzgerald to Liza Minnelli and David Gest have tied the knot here; funeral services for such notables as Andy Warhol and baseball legend Joe DiMaggio were held in its confines. A few blocks north is the **Museum of Modern Art** (MoMA; *see opposite*) and the **Paley Center for Media**.

The stretch of Fifth Avenue between Rockefeller Center and Central Park South (59th Street) showcases retail palaces bearing names that were famous long before the concept of branding was developed. Along with Madison Avenue uptown, this is the centre of high-end shopping in New York. During the frenetic Christmas shopping season, when a huge Christmas tree towers above Rockefeller Plaza, the elaborate window displays are worth a look even if you're not buying. A block from the park, Grand Army Plaza is presided over by a gilded statue of General William Tecumseh Sherman. To the west stands the Plaza, the 1907 French Renaissance-style landmark hotel. Stretching north is **Central Park** (*see p196*).

Sights & museums

New York Public Library

476 Fifth Avenue, at 42nd Street (1-917 275 6975, www.nypl.org). Subway B, D, F, M to 42nd Street-Bryant Park; 7 to Fifth Avenue. **Open** *Sept-June 10am-6pm Mon, Thur-Sat; 10am-8pm Tue, Wed; 1-5pm Sun. July, Aug 10am-6pm Mon, Thur-Sat; 10am-8pm Tue, Wed (see website for gallery times).* **Admission** *free.* **Map** *p175 E24.*

Guarded by the marble lions Patience and Fortitude, this austere Beaux Arts edifice, designed by Carrère and Hastings, was completed in 1911. The building was renamed in honour of philanthropist Stephen A Schwarzman in 2008, but Gothamites still know it as the New York Public Library

(although the city-wide library system comprises 92 locations). Free hour-long tours (11am, 2pm Mon-Sat; 2pm Sun, except July & Aug) take in the Rose Main Reading Room on the third floor, which at 297ft long and 78ft wide is almost the size of a football field. Specialist departments include the Map Division, containing some 433,000 maps and 20,000 atlases and books, and the Rare Books Division boasting Walt Whitman's personal copies of the first (1855) and third (1860) editions of *Leaves of Grass*. The library also stages major exhibitions and events, including an excellent series of talks from big-name authors and thinkers (see the website for the schedule). Renovations are opening more space to the public in late 2020, including a rotating display of treasures in the Gottesman Exhibition Hall, such as a handwritten draft of the Declaration of Independence by Thomas Jefferson and a letter opener made from the paw of Dickens's cat, Bob.

Paley Center for Media

25 W 52nd Street, between Fifth & Sixth Avenues (1-212 621 6800, www.paleycenter. org). Subway B, D, F, M to 47-50th Streets-Rockefeller Center; E, M to Fifth Avenue-53rd Street. **Open** *noon-6pm Wed, Fri-Sun; noon-8pm Thur.* **Admission** *Suggested donation $10; $5-$8 reductions.* **No cards.** **Map** *p175 E23.*

Nirvana for telly addicts and pop-culture junkies, the Paley Center houses an immense archive of more than 150,000 radio, TV and online shows and commercials. Head to the fourth-floor library to search the system for your favourite episode of *Seinfeld*, *Mad Men*, or rarer fare, and watch or listen to it on your assigned console. A theatre on the concourse level is the site of frequent screenings, premières and high-profile panel discussions.

Rockefeller Center

From 48th to 51st Streets, between Fifth & Sixth Avenues (tours & Top of the Rock 1-212 698 2000, www.rockefellercenter. com). Subway B, D, F, M to 47-50th Streets-Rockefeller Center. **Open** *Tours roughly every 30mins 10am-7.30pm. Observation deck 8am-midnight daily (last elevator 11pm).* **Admission** *Tours $25 (under-6s not admitted). Observation deck $38; $32-$36 reductions; free under-6s.* **Map** *p175 E23.*

Constructed under the aegis of industrialist John D Rockefeller in the 1930s, this art deco complex is inhabited by NBC, Simon & Schuster and other large companies, as well as Radio City Music Hall, Christie's auction house, and an underground shopping arcade. Guided tours of the entire complex are available daily, and there's a separate

💙 Museum of Modern Art (MoMA)

11 W 53rd Street, between Fifth & Sixth Avenues (1-212 708 9400, www.moma.org). Subway E, M to Fifth Avenue-53rd Street. **Open** *10am-5.30pm Mon-Thur, Sat, Sun; 10am-9pm Fri (& 1st Thur of mth).* **Admission** *(incl admission to film programmes) $25; $14-$18 reductions; free under-17s & 5.30-9pm Fri.* **Map** *p175 E23.*

In an interview in 1964, MoMA's founding director, Alfred Barr, described what it was that distinguished his institution from other NYC art museums: '[MoMA] is a torpedo moving through time, its head the ever-advancing present, its tail the ever-receding past of 50 to 100 years ago.' His statement reflected the prevailing mid-century view that modernism represented a progressive chronicle in which the torch of important art was passed from Europe to the United States. And indeed, after opening in 1929, MoMA became key to spreading the gospel of modern art over the course of the 20th century, positioning itself as a kind of temple for only the most dedicated aficionados. Today, that approach has largely been discarded in favour of a more inclusive programme that features women and artists of colour, as well as lesser-known figures from global reaches beyond Europe and the United States. MoMA has become increasingly user-friendly through successive expansions – the most recent of which, in 2019, added 40,000sq ft of new exhibition space, including street-facing galleries free to the public and a dedicated venue for live performances. Amenities include the serene, Philip Johnson-designed sculpture garden and a cinema (*see p299*), as well as a Michelin-starred restaurant (don't worry, there are also less-expensive dining options). MoMA also collaborates on contemporary exhibitions with its Queens-based affiliate MoMA PS1 (*see p258*). Still, it's hard for the institution to completely shake of its legacy; people still come to see famous artists such as Van Gogh, Pollock, Picasso and Matisse, after all. But through repeated renewal and reinvention, MoMA has exceeded its original role as modernism's incubator to become one of NYC's most important – and visited – museums.

MIDTOWN

FAO Schwarz

tour of **NBC Studios** at 30 Rockefeller Plaza (1-212 664 3700; $33, $29 reductions), home to iconic show *Saturday Night Live*.

The buildings and grounds are embellished with works by several well-known artists; look out for Isamu Noguchi's stainless-steel relief, *News*, above the entrance to 50 Rockefeller Plaza, and José Maria Sert's mural *American Progress* in the lobby of 30 Rockefeller Plaza (also known as the GE Building). But the most breathtaking sights are those seen from the 70th-floor **Top of the Rock** observation deck (combined tour/observation deck tickets are available). From around mid-October to April, the Plaza's sunken courtyard, featuring Paul Manship's bronze statue of Prometheus, becomes a picturesque, if crowded, ice-skating rink.

St Patrick's Cathedral
Fifth Avenue, between 50th & 51st Streets (1-212 753 2261, www.saintpatrickscathedral. org). Subway B, D, F, M to 47-50th Streets-Rockefeller Center; E, M to Fifth Avenue-53rd Street. **Open** *6.30am-8.45pm daily.* **Admission** *free.* **Map** *p175 E23.*

One of the largest Catholic churches in America, St Patrick's counts presidents, business leaders and movie stars among its past and present parishioners. The Gothic-style façade features intricate white-marble spires; equally impressive is the interior, including the Louis Tiffany-designed altar, solid bronze baldachin, and the rose window by stained-glass master Charles Connick.

▶ *Further uptown is another awe-inspiring house of worship, the Cathedral Church of St John the Divine; see p204.*

Benoit $$$
60 W 55th Street, between Fifth & Sixth Avenues (1-646 943 7373, www.benoitny. com). Subway E, M to Fifth Avenue-53rd Street; F to 57th Street. **Open** *11.45am-3pm, 5.30-10.30pm Mon-Sat; 11.45-3pm, 5.30-10pm Sun.* **Map** *p175 E22* ❸ *French*

Alain Ducasse's classic brasserie attempts to reclaim 55th Street's former Francophile row. Come for successful, seasonality-snubbing classics such as pâté en croûte and filet mignon with pepper sauce. At the weekend brunch, an all-you-can-eat dessert bar ($19) offers seasonal pastries and tarts, plus a station for crêpes and pancakes.

Quality Meats $$$
57 W 58th Street, between Fifth & Sixth Avenues (1-212 371 7777, www. qualitymeatsnyc.com). Subway N, Q, R, W to 57th Street-Seventh Avenue; F to 57th Street; N, R, W to Fifth Avenue-59th Street. **Open** *11.30am-3pm, 5-10.30pm Mon-Wed; 11.30am-3pm, 5-11.30pm Thur, Fri; 5-11.30pm Sat; 5-10pm Sun.* **Map** *p175 E22* ⓭ *Steakhouse*

Michael Stillman – son of the founder of landmark steakhouse Smith & Wollensky – is behind this highly stylised industrial theme park complete with meat-hook light fixtures, wooden butcher blocks, white tiles and exposed brick. Lespinasse-trained chef Craig Koketsu nails the steaks (including a double-rib steak for two) and breathes new life into traditional side dishes such as airy 'gnocchi & cheese', a clever take on mac and cheese. Dessert options include unusual ice-cream flavours served sundae-style with a choice of sauce.

Bracketed by **Saks Fifth Avenue** and **Bergdorf Goodman**, the prime shopping stretch of Fifth Avenue is chock-a-block with luxury designer flagships (Gucci, Prada, Tiffany & Co, Valentino) and mall-level brands (Abercrombie & Fitch, Gap, Uniqlo), not to mention a 24-hour, subterranean Apple Store (www.apple.com), entered via a 32-foot glass cube. The parade of big names continues east along 57th Street.

❤ Bergdorf Goodman
754 Fifth Avenue, between 57th & 58th Streets (1-212 753 7300, www.bergdorfgoodman.com). Subway E, M to Fifth Avenue-53rd Street; N, R, W to Fifth Avenue-59th Street. **Open** *10am-8pm Mon-Sat; 11am-7pm Sun.* **Map** *p175 E22* ❸ *Department store*

Synonymous with understated luxury, Bergdorf's is known for designer clothes and accessories. On the fourth floor, Linda's is an elegant 'boutique' created by the store's fashion director, Linda Fargo, and stuffed with her personal picks: a mix of fresh-from-the-catwalk designs, vintage pieces and global finds, such as beauty products and handmade items. The fifth floor is dedicated to younger, trend-driven labels. It's also worth venturing to the seventh floor for Kentshire's amazing cache of vintage designer jewellery. In the basement, the wide-ranging beauty department includes unusual fragrance lines such as Roja, created by renowned perfumer Roja Dove and including an exclusive Bergdorf scent. The men's store is across the street at 745 Fifth Avenue.

♥ FAO Schwarz

30 Rockefeller Plaza, at 49th Street (1-800 326-8638, www.faoschwarz.com). Subway B, D, F, M to 47-50th Streets-Rockefeller Center. **Open** *9am-9pm Mon-Thur; 9am-10pm Fri, Sat; 9am-8pm Sun.* **Map** *p175 E23* ❻ *Toys*

Parents and other New Yorkers with treasured childhood memories of visiting FAO Schwarz were shocked when the iconic toy store closed in 2015. Three years later it returned, in smaller premises in Rockefeller Center. The downsized space isn't quite as spectacular as the original, but it still packs in a veritable Noah's Ark of Steiff animals as well as fun interactive experiences across three floors, plus a mezzanine. After being welcomed by door staff in bright-red 'toy soldier' uniforms, kids can work with a mechanic to create their own customised remote-control racing car, adopt a baby doll complete with a certificate, or line up to take a turn on the famed dance-on piano.

♥ JJ Hat Center

310 Fifth Avenue, between 31st & 32nd Streets (1-212 239 4368, www.jjhatcenter.com). Subway B, D, F, M, N, Q, R, W to 34th Street-Herald Square. **Open** *10am-7pm Mon-Fri; 10am-6pm Sat; noon-5pm Sun.* **Map** *p175 E25* ❽ *Accessories*

Traditional hats may currently be back in fashion, but this venerable shop, in business

since 1911, is oblivious to passing trends. Dapper gents sporting the shop's wares will help you choose from thousands of fedoras, pork pies, caps and other styles in the splendid, chandelier-illuminated, wood-panelled showroom. Prices start at around $45 for a wool cap.

Saks Fifth Avenue

611 Fifth Avenue, between 49th & 50th Streets, (1-212 753 4000, www.saksfifthavenue.com). Subway E, M to Fifth Avenue-53rd Street. **Open** *10am-8.30pm Mon-Sat; 11am-7pm Sun.* **Map** *p175 E23* ⓫ *Department store*

Although Saks has more than 40 locations nationwide, the Fifth Avenue flagship is the original, established in 1924 by New York retailers Horace Saks and Bernard Gimbel. A massive, multi-stage overhaul moved the beauty hall to the second floor, with mini outposts of luxury makeup and fragrance brands such as Gucci and Guerlain, and treatment rooms for skincare lines including Chanel, Clé de Peau Beauté and Sisley Paris. Linked by an iridescent escalator designed by Rem Koolhaas, the ground level is largely given over to handbags, lined with boutiques for Prada, Celine and many more. The redesign also brought a new-look contemporary designer realm, with of the moment brands such as LoveShackFancy and L'Agence, plus the Philippe Starck-designed L'Avenue at Saks, an offshoot of the fashionable Paris restaurant. **Other locations** The Men's Store, 250 Vesey Street, Brookfield Place, Financial District (1-646 344 6300); Saks Fifth Avenue Off 5th, 125 E 57th Street, between Lexington & Park Avenues, Midtown (1-212 634 0730).

MIDTOWN EAST

▶ *Subway E, M to Lexington Avenue-53rd Street; S, 4, 5, 6, 7 to 42nd Street-Grand Central; 6 to 51st Street.*

The area east of Fifth Avenue is home to several iconic architectural landmarks. The 1913 **Grand Central Terminal** is the city's most spectacular point of arrival, although these days it welcomes only commuter trains from Connecticut and upstate New York. Looming behind the terminal, the **MetLife Building** (formerly the Pan Am Building) was the world's largest office tower when it opened in the 1960s. Other must-see buildings in the vicinity include **Lever House** (390 Park Avenue, between 53rd & 54th Streets), the **Seagram Building** (375 Park Avenue, between 52nd & 53rd Streets), the slanted-roofed **Citigroup Center** (from 53rd Street to 54th Street, between Lexington & Third Avenues) and

In the know
Recharge, no charge

A growing number of stores, including Saks Fifth Avenue and Bloomingdale's (see above), offer free mobile phone-charging lockers (look for them near the public toilets). Once you've connected your device, your phone number serves as a code to secure the compartment while you shop.

the stunning art deco skyscraper that anchors the corner of Lexington Avenue and 51st Street, formerly the General Electric Building (and before that, the RCA Victor Building).

East 42nd Street has a wealth of architectural distinction, including the Romanesque Revival hall of the former **Bowery Savings Bank** (no.110) and the art deco details of the **Chanin Building** (no.122). Completed in 1930 by architect William Van Alen, the gleaming **Chrysler Building** (at Lexington Avenue) is a pinnacle of the art deco style, paying homage to the automobile with vast radiator-cap eagles in lieu of traditional gargoyles and a brickwork relief sculpture of racing cars complete with chrome hubcaps. The **Daily News Building** (no.220), another art deco gem designed by Raymond Hood, was immortalised in the *Superman* films. Although the namesake tabloid no longer has its offices here, the lobby still houses its giant globe and weather instruments.

To the east lies the literally elevated **Tudor City** (between First & Second Avenues, from E 41st to E 43rd Streets), a pioneering 1925 residential development with buildings that resemble high-rise versions of England's Hampton Court Palace. If you need respite from the traffic in Midtown East, this peaceful residential enclave features a charming park where you can rest your feet. Head for the development's east-facing terrace for an impressive view of (and steps leading down to) the **United Nations Headquarters**. Not far from here is the **Japan Society**, an officially designated landmark.

MIDTOWN

Sights & museums

Grand Central Terminal

From 42nd to 44th Streets, between Vanderbilt & Lexington Avenues (audio tours 1-917 566 0008, www.grandcentralterminal. com). Subway S, 4, 5, 6, 7 to 42nd Street-Grand Central. **Open** *5.30am-2am daily (hrs vary for shops, bars & restaurants).* **Map** *p175 E24.*

Each day, the world's largest rail terminal sees around 750,000 people shuffle through its Beaux Arts threshold – many of them sightseers. Designed by Warren & Wetmore and Reed & Stern, the gorgeous transport hub opened in 1913 with lashings of Botticino marble and staircases modelled after those of the Paris opera house. After mid-century decline, the terminal underwent extensive restoration and is now a destination in itself, with shops, restaurants and bars, including a ground-level food market with an outpost of Murray's Cheese (*see p142*), a sprawling Apple

Grand Central Terminal

Store (1-212 284 1800) on the East Balcony, and the Campbell (1-212 297 1781), a watering hole in the former office-cum-pied-à-terre of 1920s financier John Campbell.

The opulent ceiling mural in the main concourse, by French painter Paul Helleu, depicts the October zodiac in the Mediterranean sky, complete with 2,500 LEDs, though the constellations are backwards. Visit the website for information about self-guided audio tours ($12; $10-$11 reductions) or guided tours ($30; $20 reductions), or download the $5 smartphone app.

▶ *For trains from Grand Central, see p382; for dining highlights in the terminal, see opposite.*

Japan Society

333 E 47th Street, between First & Second Avenues (1-212 832 1155, www.japansociety. org). Subway E, M to Lexington Avenue-53rd Street; 6 to 51st Street. **Open** *hrs vary. Gallery noon-7pm Tue-Thur; noon-9pm Fri; 11am-5pm Sat, Sun.* **Admission** *$12; $10 reductions; free 6-9pm Fri.* **Map** *p175 F23.*

Founded in 1907, the Japan Society moved into its current home in 1971. Designed by Junzo Yoshimura, it was the first contemporary Japanese building in New York, complete with a waterfall and bamboo garden. The gallery mounts temporary exhibitions on such diverse subjects as specific themes in woodblock prints, decorative crafts and works by prominent contemporary artists.

United Nations Headquarters

Visitors' entrance: First Avenue, at 46th Street (tours 1-212 963 8687, visit.un.org). Subway S, 4, 5, 6, 7 to 42nd Street-Grand Central. **Open** *Visitor centre 9am-4.45pm Mon-Fri; 10am-4.30pm Sat, Sun. Tours 9.30am-4.45pm Mon-Fri.* **Admission**

Tours $20; $11-$13 reductions (under-5s not admitted on tours). **Map** *p175 F24.*

The UN has undergone extensive renovations to its complex and Le Corbusier's Secretariat building is gleaming. Roughly hour-long tours discuss the history and role of the UN, and visit the Security Council Chamber and the General Assembly Hall (when they're not in session). Artworks on view include Norman Rockwell's mosaic *The Golden Rule*, and José Vela Zanetti's epic, 64ft-long 1953 mural *Mankind's Struggle for a Lasting Peace*. Note that while tickets may be available on site (cash only), it's advisable to book online. All visitors 18 and older must have government-issued photo ID (see website for security guidelines). The UN is closed for two weeks in September for the General Debate, and during high-level meetings (check the website for alerts).

Restaurants & cafés

Agern $$$

Grand Central Terminal, 89 E 42nd Street, between Park & Lexington Avenues (1-646 568 4018, agernrestaurant.com). Subway S, 4, 5, 6, 7 to 42nd Street-Grand Central. **Open** *11.30am-2.30pm, 5.30-10pm Mon-Fri; 5.30-10pm Sat.* **Map** *p175 E24* ❶ *Scandinavian*

Escape the commuter clamour of Grand Central in the Scandinavian stillness of the terminal's formal Nordic dining room, a happily incongruous project from Noma co-founder Claus Meyer. The clean-lined space is as blond as a Swede, matched with black-leather banquettes, brass pendant lights and pops of pea-green chevron tiles. In the kitchen, Gunnar Gíslason, the Icelandic chef behind acclaimed Reykjavík restaurant

Dill, takes now-familiar Scandi sensations – a sweet beet, freshly cracked out of a salt-baked hull; a tartare of beef heart, fragrant with dill – and executes them exceptionally well.

For a less expensive taste of Meyer's cuisine, the adjacent **Great Northern Food Hall** (www.greatnorthernfood.com) occupies the stately former waiting room Vanderbilt Hall. Several Nordic-inspired eateries include the Grain Bar serving sweet and savoury porridges in the morning, segueing to hot dogs, pretzels and craft beers in the evenings, and Open Rye featuring a rotating selection of *smørrebrød*, Danish open sandwiches, built with house-cured meats and fish.

❤ Grand Central Oyster Bar & Restaurant $$

Grand Central Terminal, Lower Level, 42nd Street, at Park Avenue (1-212 490 6650, www. oysterbarny.com). Subway S, 4, 5, 6, 7 to 42nd Street-Grand Central. **Open** *11.30am-9.30pm Mon-Sat.* **Map** *p175 E24* ❻ *Seafood*

The legendary Grand Central Oyster Bar has been a fixture since 1913. The sometimes surly countermen at the mile-long bar (the best seats in the house) are part of the charm. We suggest avoiding the more complicated fish concoctions and playing it safe with a reliably awe-inspiring platter of iced, just-shucked oysters (the selection sometimes exceeds 30 varieties, including many from nearby Long Island).

❤ The Grill/The Pool $$$$

99 E 52nd St, between Park & Lexington Avenues (1-212 375 9001, www. thegrillnewyork.com, www.thepoolnewyork. com). Subway E, M to Lexington Avenue-53rd Street; 6 to 51st Street. **The Grill** *11.45am-2pm, 5-11pm Mon-Fri; 5-11pm Sat.* **The Pool** *11.45am-2pm, 6-11pm Mon-Fri; 6-11pm Sat.* **Map** *p175 E23* ❼ *American/ Seafood*

From 1959 to 2016, the Four Seasons was the city's most exclusive supper club, a veritable village green for New York's wealthy, famous and powerful. So it's no small feat that Major Food Group's remake of the famed Grill Room dazzles. Inspired by mid-century menus from Delmonico's and the 21 Club, chef Mario Carbone deftly reconstructs continental classics such as filet mignon, lobster Newburg and three iterations of Dover sole. The party trick is the prime rib that's wheeled out on a silver-domed service trolley by tuxedo-clad waiters.

In contrast to the Grill's rollicking ambience, the Pool, occupying the original restaurant's main dining room with its iconic marble pool, is almost hushed. The fish-focused menu swells to a luxurious

In the know
Public art

While you're walking around Midtown, keep an eye out for famous pieces of public art, such as Robert Indiana's 12-foot-high, red-and-blue *LOVE* (Sixth Avenue at 55th Street) and Alexander Calder's red, mobile-like yet static *Saurien* (Madison Avenue at 57th Street). Next to Grand Central Terminal, the Grand Hyatt (109 E 42nd Street, 1-212 883 1234, www.grandhyattnewyork.com) has two ethereal marble heads by Barcelona-based artist Jaume Plensa. Other intriguing works, hidden within office buildings, need to be sleuthed out, such as the life-size nude sculpture between the revolving doors of 747 Third Avenue (between 46th & 47th Streets) – you get a surreal double-take glimpse as you pass through.

crescendo, from East Coast oysters or caviar with blinis and duck fat-roasted potatoes to crisp-skinned grilled whole fish. The mezzanine bar dispenses 'poolside-inspired' cocktails mixed with summery ingredients and small seafood plates.

Monkey Bar $$$
Hotel Elysée, 60 E 54th Street, between Madison & Park Avenues (1-212 288 1010, www.monkeybarnewyork.com). Subway E, M to Lexington Avenue-53rd Street; 6 to 51st Street. Open 11.30am-1am Mon-Fri; 5.30pm-1am Sat (kitchen closes at 10pm). Map p175 E22 ⑫ *American*

After the repeal of Prohibition in 1933, this one-time piano bar in the swank Hotel Elysée became a boozy clubhouse for the glitzy artistic figures of the age, among them Tallulah Bankhead, Dorothy Parker and Tennessee Williams. The Monkey Bar is now owned by publishing titan Graydon Carter, who brought new buzz to the historic space. Perch at the bar for cocktails such as a Monkey Gland (gin and absinthe with pomegranate), or get a table for classic dishes like lobster bisque and New York strip steak.

Urbanspace Vanderbilt $-$$
45th Street, at Vanderbilt Avenue (1-646 747 0810, www.urbanspacenyc.com/urbanspace-vanderbilt). Subway S, 4, 5, 6, 7 to 42nd Street-Grand Central. Open 6.30am-9pm Mon-Fri (some vendors until 10pm Wed-Fri); 9am-5pm Sat, Sun. Map p175 E23 ⑭ *Food court*

This sprawling food court from Urbanspace, the team behind seasonal street-side pop-up food markets such as Mad Sq Eats and Broadway Bites, includes such cult delicacies as Roberta's wood-fired pizza and handmade doughnuts from Dough, plus tacos, ramen and more.

Shops & services

▶ *For our pick of the department stores on Fifth Avenue, see p186.*

MURRAY HILL

▶ *Subway S, 4, 5, 6, 7 to 42nd Street-Grand Central; 6 to 51st Street; 6 to 33rd Street.*

Murray Hill spans 30th to 40th Streets, between Third and Fifth Avenues. Townhouses of the rich and powerful were once clustered around Madison and Park Avenues, including the home of Pierpont Morgan; his private library is now the **Morgan Library & Museum**, which houses some 500,000 rare books, prints,

manuscripts and objects. These days, the neighbourhood is populated mostly by young professionals, and only a few streets retain their former elegance. One is **Sniffen Court** (150-158 E 36th Street, between Lexington & Third Avenues), an unspoiled row of 1864 carriage houses located within earshot of the Queens Midtown Tunnel's ceaseless traffic.

Sights & museums

Morgan Library & Museum
225 Madison Avenue, at 36th Street (1-212 685 0008, www.themorgan.org). Subway 6 to 33rd Street. Open 10.30am-5pm Tue-Thur; 10.30am-9pm Fri; 10am-6pm Sat; 11am-6pm Sun. Admission $22; $14 reductions; free under-13s; free 7-9pm Fri. Map p175 E25.

This Madison Avenue institution began as the private library of financier Pierpont Morgan, and is his cultural gift to the city. Building on the collection Morgan amassed in his lifetime, the museum houses first-rate works on paper, including drawings by Michelangelo, Rembrandt and Picasso; three Gutenberg Bibles; a copy of *Frankenstein* annotated by Mary Shelley; manuscripts by Dickens, Poe, Twain, Steinbeck and Wilde; sheet music handwritten by Beethoven and Mozart; and an original edition of Dickens's *A Christmas Carol* that's displayed every Yuletide. A massive renovation and expansion orchestrated by Renzo Piano brought more natural light into the building and doubled the available exhibition space. This was followed by the restoration of the interior and exterior of the original 1906 building, designed by McKim, Mead & White. The imposing neoclassical structure includes Morgan's private study and the spectacular East Room, with its 30ft-high book-lined walls and murals by Henry Siddons Mowbray (who also painted the ceiling of the restored Rotunda).

Scandinavia House – The Nordic Center in America
58 Park Avenue, at 38th Street (1-212 779 3587, www.scandinaviahouse.org). Subway S, 4, 5, 6, 7 to 42nd Street-Grand Central. Open hrs vary. Gallery noon-6pm Tue, Thur-Sat; noon-7pm Wed. Admission varies (usually free). Map p175 E24.

One of the city's top cultural centres, Scandinavia House serves as a link between the US and the Scandinavian nations, and offers a full schedule of film screenings, lectures and book talks, concerts and art exhibitions. An outpost of Smörgås Chef (open 11am-9pm Mon-Sat, 11am-4pm Sun), serves tasty Swedish meatballs, and the shop is a showcase for chic Scandinavian design.

Restaurants & cafés

♥ Atomix $$$$

*104 East 30th Street, at Park Avenue South (no phone, www.atomixnyc.com). Subway 6 to 28th Street. **Open** Restaurant seatings 6pm & 9pm. Bar 5.30pm-midnight Tue-Sat. **Map** p175 E25* ② *Korean*

Hidden in the basement of a walk-up apartment building, Atomix is a Korean fine-dining experience like no other. Seated at one of the 14 grey-suede chairs at the U-shaped, black-granite counter overlooking the immaculate kitchen, you'll collect a series of cards throughout the multi-course, $205-per-person tasting menu. These describe meticulously the components of each nuanced dish (the likes of deep-fried langoustine with creamed uni, grilled and braised turbot, and scorched rice pudding), alongside a little nugget of history or culinary knowledge. On the ground floor, a no-reservations bar with geometric couches offers cocktails and snacks.

Kajitsu $$$

*2nd Floor, 125 E 39th Street, between Park & Lexington Avenues (1-212 228 4873, www. kajitsunyc.com). Subway S, 4, 5, 6, 7 to 42nd Street-Grand Central. **Open** 5.30-9pm Tue-Sun. **Map** p175 E24* ⑧ *Japanese/ vegetarian*

There's no shortage of cheap ramen joints in postgrad mecca Murray Hill, but house-made soba crowned with shaved black truffles? That's only at Kajitsu. The minimalist, Michelin-starred den displays a devotion to produce, influenced by the monk-approved *shojin-ryori* (vegetarian) tradition. The sublime fare has made it a cult favourite among top-notch toques like Momofuku's David Chang. In the small, bare dining room or at the eight-seat chef's counter, choose from two ever-changing menus of ten or eight courses. Drink pairings with sake or tea are available.

Downstairs, casual sibling Kokage serves non-vegetarian dishes such as house-made noodles and Kyoto-style *saba* (mackerel) sushi, and is open most days for lunch and dinner (see website for hours).

Bars

♥ Fine & Rare

*9 E 37th Street, between Fifth & Madison Avenues (1-212 725 3866, www.fineandrare. nyc). Subway 6 to 33rd Street. **Open** 5pm-midnight Mon; noon-2.30pm, 5pm-midnight Tue; noon-2.30pm, 5pm-1am Wed, Thur; noon-2.30pm, 5pm-2am Fri; 11am-3.30pm, 5pm-2am Sat; 11am-3.30pm, 5pm-midnight Sun. **Map** p175 E23* ③

Set on a quiet street near the Morgan Library & Museum, this sophisticated spirits den oozes retro glam, with tufted leather banquettes, an oversized fireplace, art deco wallpaper, and vintage teller windows sourced from nearby Grand Central Terminal. Jazz acts croon a playlist that pulls from the 1930s, '40s and '50s. Novel takes on classic cocktails include an old-fashioned with a rye or scotch base and a choice of smoke, including hickory, applewood or cherrywood. The drinks list also highlights pricey, hard-to-find bottles, accessed via library-style rolling ladders.

Middle Branch

*154 E 33rd Street, between Lexington & Third Avenues (1-212 213 1350). Subway 6 to 33rd Street. **Open** 5pm-2am daily. **Map** p175 F25* ④

Middle Branch plants a flag for artisanal cocktails in post-frat epicentre Murray Hill. Unlike its forebear Little Branch, this is no sly speakeasy, hidden from the masses with a windowless façade and an unmarked entrance: the bi-level drinkery, sporting French doors that offer a glimpse inside, practically beckons passersby to come in. Its focus is on classic cocktails and riffs thereon, built with hand-cut ice and superior spirits. **Other location** Little Branch, 20 Seventh Avenue South, at Leroy Street, West Village (1-212 929 4360).

Shops & services

♥ Dover Street Market New York

*160 Lexington Avenue, at 30th Street (1-646 837 7750, newyork.doverstreetmarket. com). Subway 6 to 28th or 33rd Street. **Open** 11am-7pm Mon-Sat; noon-6pm Sun. **Map** p175 E25* ⑤ *Fashion/accessories*

In late 2013, Comme des Garçons designer Rei Kawakubo brought her quirky, upscale interpretation of a London fashion market to the former New York School of Applied Design, complete with an outpost of the cult Paris eaterie, Rose Bakery. One of five offspring of the original location on Mayfair's Dover Street in London (the others are in Tokyo, Beijing, Singapore and LA), DSMNY is a multilevel store that blurs the line between art and commerce. A transparent elevator whisks shoppers through the seven-floor consumer playground. Three pillars running through six of the levels have been transformed into art installations: a stripey patchwork knitted sheath by Magda Sayeg, London Fieldworks' miniature wooden metropolis, and 3D collages by 'junk sculptor' Leo Sewell. In addition to all of the Comme lines, the store stocks luxury labels such as Balenciaga and Gucci, newer names such as Simone Rocha, Kiko Kostadinov and Melitta Baumeister, streetwear brands NikeLab and Supreme among others, and the latest emerging talent.

Upper West Side

In the late 19th century, lavish apartment buildings sprang up alongside newly completed Central Park, luring well-heeled New Yorkers north. And in the decades that followed, immigrants brought diverse shops and eateries to the neighbourhood's avenues. While a few character-filled institutions survive, the arrival of new real estate and chain stores has had a homogenising effect. But the four-mile-long stretch between the park and the Hudson River is still culturally rich and cosmopolitan. The area is home to the American Museum of Natural History, the New-York Historical Society and venerated performing-arts complex Lincoln Center.

❤ **Don't miss**

1 Central Park *p196*
New York City's bucolic back yard.

2 Lincoln Center *p332*
Home of the city's premier performing-arts institutions.

3 American Museum of Natural History *p199*
Nature comes to life at this revitalised classic.

4 New-York Historical Society *p200*
Bringing the past into the present.

5 Cathedral Church of St John the Divine *p204*
An awe-inspiring building.

Bow Bridge, Central Park

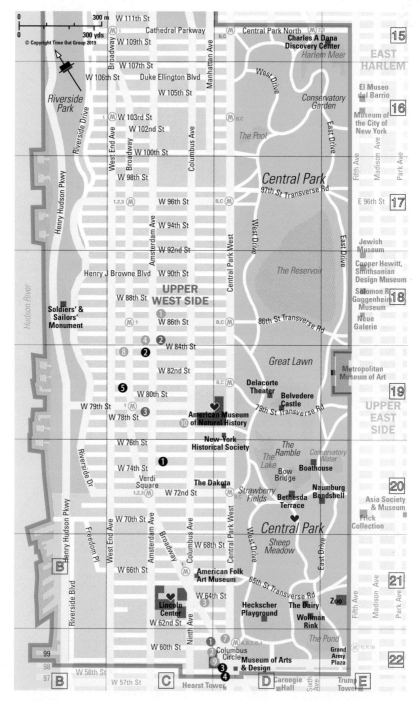

UPPER WEST SIDE

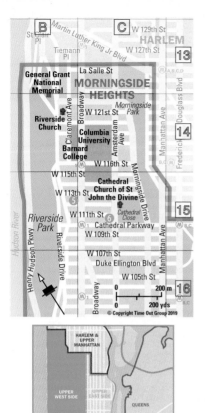

UPPER WEST SIDE

Restaurants & cafés

1. Barney Greengrass *p201*
2. Bouchon Bakery & Café *p201*
3. Boulud Sud *p201*
4. Celeste *p201*
5. Community Food & Juice *p205*
6. Hungarian Pastry Shop *p205*
7. Jean-Georges *p201*
8. Maison Pickle *p202*
9. Per Se *p202*
10. Shake Shack *p202*

Bars

1. The Aviary NYC *p202*
2. Jacob's Pickles *p203*
3. Manhatten Cricket Club *p203*

Shops & services

1. Levain Bakery *p203*
2. Magpie *p203*
3. The Shops at Columbus Circle *p203*
4. TurnStyle *p203*
5. Zabar's *p204*

UPPER WEST SIDE

▶ *Subway A, B, C, D, 1 to 59th Street-Columbus Circle; B, C to 72nd Street, 81st Street-Museum of Natural History, 86th Street, 96th Street or 103rd Street; 1, 2, 3 to 72nd Street or 96th Street; 1 to 66th Street-Lincoln Center, 79th Street, 86th Street or 103rd Street.*

The gateway to the Upper West Side is **Columbus Circle**, where Broadway meets 59th Street, Eighth Avenue, Central Park South and Central Park West – a rare roundabout in a city of right angles. The architecture round it could make anyone's head spin. At the entrance to Central Park, a 700-ton statue of Christopher Columbus is dwarfed by the skyscrapers across the street, housing the Shops at Columbus Circle, a luxury hotel and Jazz at Lincoln Center's stunning **Frederick P Rose Hall** (*see p323*). The first five levels of the enormous glass complex are filled with high-end retailers and restaurants, such as **Per Se**. On the south side of the circle is the **Museum of Arts & Design**.

A few blocks north, **Lincoln Center** (*see p332*), a complex of concert halls and auditoriums built in the early 1960s, is the home of the New York Philharmonic, the New York City Ballet, the Metropolitan

---

💜 Time to eat & drink

Bagels and lox
Barney Greengrass *p201*

Superior classic cookies
Bouchon Bakery & Café *p201*,
Levain Bakery *p203*

New York craft beers
Jacob's Pickles *p203*

Blow-the-budget dining
Per Se *p202*, Jean-Georges *p201*

Dazzling cocktails and views
The Aviary NYC *p202*

💜 Time to shop

Hand-crafted gifts
Magpie *p203*

New York food institution
Zabar's *p204*

Posh shopping mall
The Shops at Columbus Circle *p203*

❤ Central Park

In 1858, the newly formed Central Park Commission chose landscape designer Frederick Law Olmsted and architect Calvert Vaux to turn 750 acres of rocky swampland into a rambling oasis of lush greenery. Inspired by the great parks of London and Paris, the Commission imagined a place that would provide city dwellers with respite from the crowded streets. It was a noble thought, but one that required the eviction of 1,600 mostly poor or immigrant inhabitants, including residents of Seneca Village, the city's oldest African-American settlement. Still, clear the area they did. When completed in 1873, it was the first major man-made public park in the US.

Although it suffered from neglect at various points in the 20th century (most recently in the 1970s and '80s, when it gained a reputation as a dangerous spot), the park has been returned to its green glory thanks largely to the Central Park Conservancy. Since this not-for-profit civic group was formed in 1980, it has been instrumental in the park's restoration and maintenance.

The 1870 Victorian Gothic **Dairy** (mid-park at 65th Street, 1-212 794 6563, www.centralparknyc.org) houses one of Central Park Conservancy's five visitor centres and a gift shop; there are additional staffed information booths dotted around the park.

The southern section abounds with family-friendly diversions, including the **Central Park Zoo** (enter at Fifth Avenue & 64th Street, 1-212 439 6500, www.centralparkzoo.org), known for its penguins and snow leopards. The Tisch Children's Zoo is home to kid-friendly species, such as pot-bellied pigs and goats. The roving characters on the George Delacorte Musical Clock – perched atop a brick arcade between the two zoos – delight little ones every half-hour. There are 21 playgrounds in Central Park, but the **Heckscher Playground**, in the south-west corner, is the largest, sprawling over more than an acre

and a half. It has an up-to-date adventure area, a water feature and handy restrooms.

The **Wollman Rink** (between 62nd & 63rd Streets 1-212 439 6900, www.wollmanskatingrink.com; open late Oct-Mar) doubles as a small children's amusement park, **Victorian Gardens** (1-212 982 2229, www.victoriangardensnyc.com), in the warmer months. Central Park's classic **Carousel** (mid-park at 64th Street, open daily Apr-Oct, call 1-212 439 6900 for out-of-season hours) was built in 1908. It's the fourth merry-go-round on the site since 1871 (the first was operated by a mule or horse hidden under the floorboards). Found in a Coney Island warehouse, the current model belts out pop organ music for riders of its 57 steeds.

Come summer, kites, Frisbees and soccer balls seem to fly every which way across **Sheep Meadow**, the designated quiet zone that begins at 66th Street. Sheep did indeed graze here until 1934, but they've since been replaced by sunbathers. **Tavern on the Green** (Central Park West, at 67th Street, 212-877-8684, www.tavernonthegreen.com), the landmark restaurant housed in the former shepherd's residence has been relaunched with a rustic, seasonal focus. East of Sheep Meadow, between 66th and 72nd Streets, is the **Mall**, an elm-lined promenade that attracts street performers and in-line skaters. And just east of the Mall's Naumburg Bandshell is **Rumsey Playfield** – the main venue of the annual **SummerStage** series (*see p287*), an eclectic roster of free and benefit concerts in the city's parks.

One of the park's most popular meeting places (and loveliest spots) is north of here, overlooking the lake: the grand **Bethesda Fountain & Terrace**, near the midpoint of the 72nd Street Transverse Road. *Angel of the Waters*, the sculpture in the centre of the fountain, was created by Emma Stebbins, the first woman to be granted a major public art commission in New York City. Be sure to admire the Minton-tiled ceiling of the ornate passageway that connects the plaza around the fountain to the Mall – after years of neglect in storage, the tiles, designed by Jacob Wrey Mould, were restored and reinstated in 2007. Mould also designed the intricately carved ornamentation of the stairways leading down to the fountain.

Just north is the **Loeb Boathouse** (mid-park, between 74th & 75th Streets, 1-212 517 2233, www.thecentralparkboathouse.com). From here, you can take a rowing boat or a gondola out on the lake, which is crossed by the elegant Bow Bridge. The Loeb houses a restaurant and bar (closed dinner Nov-Mar), and lake views make it a lovely place for brunch or drinks.

To the east, near the 72nd Street and Fifth Avenue entrance to the park is **Conservatory Water**. The small pond is a mecca for model-yacht racers in summer. Kids can't resist climbing on the bronze rendering of Lewis Carroll's Alice, the Mad Hatter and the White Rabbit north of the pond, while the Hans Christian Andersen statue is a gathering point for free Saturday-morning storytelling sessions in summer (early June-Sept 11am-noon, www.hcastorycenter.org).

West of the Bethesda Fountain, near the W 72nd Street entrance, sits **Strawberry Fields**, which memorialises John Lennon, who lived in, and was shot in front of, the nearby Dakota Building. It features a mosaic of the word 'imagine' that was donated by the city of Naples. Tucked just inside the western boundary of the park near 81st Street is a curiously incongruous old wooden structure. Designed as a schoolhouse, the building was Sweden's entry in the 1876 Centennial Exposition in Philadelphia (it was moved to NYC a year later). Inside the **Swedish Cottage** is one of the best-kept secrets in town: a tiny marionette theatre with regular shows. It's best to book tickets in advance (1-212 639 1697, www.cityparksfoundation.org). From the cottage, rustic stone steps lead up to the **Shakespeare Garden**, with winding paths bordered by plants mentioned in the Bard's works. The nearby Delacorte Theater hosts **Shakespeare in the Park** (*see p287*), a summer run of free open-air performances of plays by the Bard and others. Perched above the park's second-highest peak, the popular **Belvedere Castle**, a restored Victorian folly, overlooks the Turtle Pond. Just north is the **Great Lawn** (mid-park, between 79th & 85th Streets), a sprawling stretch of grass that doubles as a rallying point for political protests and a concert spot for just about any act that can attract six-figure audiences. At other times, it's used by seriously competitive soccer, baseball and softball teams. East of the Great Lawn, behind the **Metropolitan Museum of Art** (*see p214*), is the **Obelisk**, a 69-foot hieroglyphics-covered granite monument dating from around 1500 BC, which was given to the US by the Khedive of Egypt in 1881.

In the mid 1990s, the **Reservoir** (mid-park, between 85th & 96th Streets) was renamed in honour of the late Jacqueline Kennedy Onassis, who used to jog round it. A turn here gives great views of the skyscrapers rising above the park; in spring, the cherry trees that ring the reservoir path and the bridle path below it make it particularly beautiful.

In the northern section, the exquisite **Conservatory Garden** (entrance on Fifth Avenue, at 105th Street) comprises formal gardens inspired by English, French and Italian styles. At the top of the park, next to the Harlem Meer, the **Charles A Dana Discovery Center** (entrance at Malcolm X Boulevard/Lenox Avenue, at 110th Street, 1-212 860 1370) operates a roster of activities, events and exhibitions.

▶ *Near the Sheep Meadow, mid-park at 69th Street, you'll find an outpost of popular café Le Pain Quotidien in the former mineral springs (which once served health-giving water to park-goers). Indoor and outdoor seating is available for coffee, pastries, salads or the chain's signature tartines.*

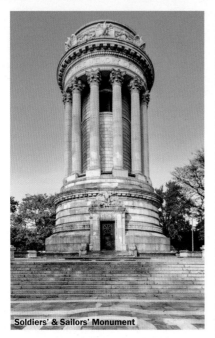

Soldiers' & Sailors' Monument

73rd & 74th Streets). Over the years, Enrico Caruso, Babe Ruth and Igor Stravinsky have lived in this Beaux Arts masterpiece; it was also the site of the Continental Baths, the gay bathhouse and cabaret where Bette Midler got her start, and Plato's Retreat, a swinging 1970s sex club.

After Central Park was completed, magnificently tall residential buildings rose up along **Central Park West** to take advantage of the views. The first of these great apartment blocks was the **Dakota** (at 72nd Street), allegedly named because its location was considered remote when it was built in 1884. The fortress-like building is known as the setting for *Rosemary's Baby* and the site of John Lennon's murder in 1980 (Yoko Ono still lives there); other residents have included Judy Garland, Rudolph Nureyev, Lauren Bacall and Boris Karloff – but not Billy Joel, Cher, or Madonna, who were rejected by the building's board. You might recognise **55 Central Park West** (at 66th Street) from the movie *Ghostbusters*. Built in 1930, it was the first art deco building on the block. Heading north on Central Park West, you'll spy the massive twin-towered **San Remo Apartments** (at 74th Street), which also date from 1930. Rita Hayworth, Steven Spielberg, Tiger Woods and U2's Bono have been among the building's many celebrity residents.

A few blocks to the north, the **New-York Historical Society** is the city's oldest museum, founded in 1804. Across the street, at the **American Museum of Natural History** (*see right*), dinosaur skeletons, a planetarium and an IMAX theatre lure visitors of all ages.

To see West Siders in their natural habitat, queue at the perpetually jammed gourmet market **Zabar's**. The legendary (if scruffy) restaurant and delicatessen **Barney Greengrass**, the self-styled 'Sturgeon King', has specialised in smoked fish, knishes and what may be the city's best chopped liver since 1908.

Riverside Park, a sinuous stretch of riverbank along the Hudson from 59th Street to 155th Street, was originally designed by Central Park's Frederick Law Olmsted, and subsequently extended. You'll probably see yachts, along with several houseboats, berthed at the **79th Street Boat Basin**. Several sites provide havens for quiet reflection. The **Soldiers' & Sailors' Monument** (89th Street, at Riverside Drive), built in 1902 by French sculptor Paul EM Duboy, honours Union soldiers who died in the Civil War; and a 1913 memorial (100th Street, at Riverside Drive) pays tribute to fallen firemen.

Opera and a host of other notable arts organisations. The big circular fountain in the central plaza is a popular gathering spot. Lincoln Center's visitor centre, the **David Rubenstein Atrium** (Broadway, between W 62nd & W 63rd Streets), was conceived as a contemporary interior garden with lush planted walls. It stages free genre-spanning concerts and events and has a box office selling discounted tickets (see www.lincolncenter.org for details). It's also the starting point for guided tours of the complex (1-212 875 5350, $25, $20 reductions, free under-7s), which contains several notable artworks, including Henry Moore's *Reclining Figure* in the plaza near Lincoln Center Theater, and two massive music-themed paintings by Marc Chagall in the lobby of the Metropolitan Opera House. Nearby is the **New York Public Library for the Performing Arts** (40 Lincoln Center Plaza, at 65th Street, 1-917 275 6975, www.nypl.org, closed Sun); alongside its extraordinary collection of films, letters, manuscripts, videos and sound recordings, it stages concerts and lectures.

Around Sherman and Verdi Squares (from 70th to 73rd Streets, where Broadway and Amsterdam Avenue intersect), classic early 20th-century buildings stand cheek-by-jowl with newer high-rises. The jewel is the 1904 **Ansonia Hotel** (2109 Broadway, between

❤ American Museum of Natural History

Central Park West, at 79th Street (1-212 769 5100, www.amnh.org). Subway B, C to 81st Street-Museum of Natural History. **Open** *10am-5.45pm daily.* **Admission** *Suggested donation $23; $13-$18 reductions.* **Map** *p194 C19.*

The American Museum of Natural History's fourth-floor dino halls are home to the largest and arguably most fabulous collection of dinosaur fossils in the world. Nearly 85% of the bones on display are original, but during the museum's mid 1990s renovation, several specimens were remodelled to incorporate later discoveries. The Tyrannosaurus rex, for instance, was once believed to have walked upright, Godzilla-style; it now stalks prey with its head lowered and tail raised parallel to the ground.

The Hall of North American Mammals has undergone an extensive restoration of its formerly faded 1940s dioramas. A life-size model of a blue whale hangs from the cavernous ceiling of the Hall of Ocean Life, while in the Hall of Meteorites the focal point is Ahnighito, the largest iron meteorite on display in any museum, weighing in at 34 tons. Other halls explore human origins, world ecosystems and environmental preservation.

The spectacular Rose Center for Earth & Space offers insight into recent cosmic discoveries via shows in the Hayden Planetarium and a simulation of the origins of the Universe in the Big Bang Theater. The museum also screens digital nature films in 3D, and the roster of temporary exhibitions is thought-provoking for all ages.

UPPER WEST SIDE

American Folk Art Museum

2 Lincoln Square, Columbus Avenue, at 66th Street (1-212 595 9533, www.folkartmuseum. org). Subway 1 to 66th Street-Lincoln Center. **Open** *11.30am-7pm Tue-Thur, Sat; noon-7pm Fri; noon-6pm Sun.* **Admission** *free.* **Map** *p194 C19.*

The small space is misleading – the American Folk Art Museum's unparalleled holdings of folk art include roughly 8,000 works dating from the late 18th century to the present. Changing exhibitions explore the work of self-taught and outsider artists, as well as showing traditional folk such as quilts and needlework, and other decorative objects. You can purchase original handmade pieces in the large gift shop, and the museum regularly hosts free musical performances and other events. For the museum's Self-Taught Genius Gallery in Queens, *see p260.*

Museum of Arts & Design

2 Columbus Circle, at Broadway (1-212 299 7777, www.madmuseum.org). Subway A, B, C, D, 1 to 59th Street-Columbus Circle. **Open** *10am-6pm Tue, Wed, Fri-Sun; 10am-9pm Thur.* **Admission** *$16; $12-$14 reductions; free under-19s. Pay what you wish 6-9pm Thur.* **Map** *p194 D22.*

This institution celebrates creative practice with thematic exhibitions that bring together contemporary objects created in a wide range of media – including clay, glass, wood, metal and cloth – with a strong focus on materials and process. The permanent collection of more than 3,000 objects from 1950 to the present includes porcelain ware by Cindy Sherman, stained glass by Judith Schaechter and tapestries by Judy Chicago. Before moving into Edward Durell Stone's austere 1964 Columbus Circle landmark in 2008, MAD redesigned the ten-storey building. Four floors of exhibition space include the Tiffany & Co Foundation Jewelry Gallery, and you can also watch resident artists create works in studios on the sixth floor. The ninth-floor bistro has views over the park.

♥ New-York Historical Society

170 Central Park West, at 77th Street (1-212 873 3400, www.nyhistory.org). Subway B, C to 81st Street-Museum of Natural History. **Open** *10am-6pm Tue-Thur, Sat; 10am-8pm Fri; 11am-5pm Sun.* **Admission** *$21; $6-$16 reductions; free under-5s. Pay what you wish 6-8pm Fri.* **Map** *p194 D19.*

Founded in 1804 by a group of prominent New Yorkers that included Mayor DeWitt Clinton, the New-York Historical Society is the city's oldest museum, originally based at City Hall. Over the past several years, the society has transformed the interior of its stately 1904 building to make the collection more accessible to a 21st-century audience,

---

In the know
New-York, New-York

The name of the New-York Historical Society (*see above*) is itself a historical preservation – placing a hyphen between 'New' and 'York' was common in the early 19th century. In fact, according to the Society, the *New York Times*, the paper of record, maintained the convention until 1896.

New-York Historical Society

using technology such as touch-screen monitors to offer insight into artwork and documents. A piece of the ceiling mural from Keith Haring's Pop Shop (the artist's Soho store, which closed after his death in 1990) is on view in the Robert H and Clarice Smith New York Gallery of American History, where rotating displays highlight New York's place in American history. In the auditorium, an 18-minute film traces the city's development. On the fourth floor, objects from the permanent collection chronicle various strands of New York history, such as slavery, the Hudson River School artists and 9/11. A striking glass-accented space showcases 100 Tiffany lamps, while a small gallery focuses on original watercolours from Audubon's *Birds of America*. The Center for Women's History features artefacts such as tennis gear donated by Billie Jean King and changing exhibitions, while downstairs, the DiMenna Children's History Museum engages the next generation.

Restaurants & cafés

♥ Barney Greengrass $-$$

*541 Amsterdam Avenue, between 86th & 87th Streets (1-212 724 4707, www. barneygreengrass.com). Subway B, C, 1 to 86th Street. **Open** Shop 8am-6pm Tue-Sun. Restaurant 8.30am-4pm Tue-Fri; 8.30am-5pm Sat, Sun. **No cards** on weekends. **Map** p194 C18* ① *American*

Despite decor that Jewish mothers might call 'schmutzy', this legendary deli is a madhouse at breakfast and brunch. Enormous egg platters come with a choice of smoked fish (such as sturgeon or Nova Scotia salmon). Prices are on the high side, but portions are large, and that goes for the sandwiches too. Soup – matzo-ball or cold pink borscht – is a less costly option.

♥ Bouchon Bakery & Café $-$$

*3rd Floor, 10 Columbus Circle, at Broadway (1-212 823 9366, www.thomaskeller.com). Subway A, B, C, D, 1 to 59th Street-Columbus Circle. **Open** 8am-8pm Mon-Sat; 8am-7pm Sun. **Map** p194 D22* ② *Café*

Thomas Keller's café, in the same mall as his lauded fine-dining room Per Se (*see p202*), lacks ambience, and the menu (soups, tartines, salads, sandwiches) is basic. But it offers the chance to sample the chef's cuisine at much more palatable prices. Several items, such as a croque madame with sauce Mornay are under $20. Baked goods, including Keller's takes on American classics like Oreo cookies, are the highlights. **Other locations** 1 Rockefeller Plaza, at 49th Street, Midtown (1-212 782 3890); 5th Floor, 20 Hudson Yards, Hell's Kitchen (1-929 450 4001).

Boulud Sud $$$

*20 W 64th Street, between Broadway & Central Park West (1-212 595 1313, www.bouludsud. com). Subway 1 to 66th Street-Lincoln Center. **Open** 11.30am-2.30pm, 5-10.30pm Mon; 11.30am-2.30pm, 5-11pm Tue-Fri; 11am-3pm, 5-11pm Sat; 11am-3pm, 5-10pm Sun. **Map** p194 C21* ③ *Mediterranean*

At his most international restaurant yet, superchef Daniel Boulud highlights the new French cuisine of melting-pot cities such as Marseille and Nice. With his executive chef, Ulises Olmos, he casts a wide net – looking to Egypt, Turkey and Greece. Diners can build a full tapas meal from shareable snacks like octopus à la plancha, with marcona almonds and arugula (rocket). Heartier dishes combine Gallic finesse with polyglot flavours: sweet-spicy chicken tagine with harira soup borrows from Morocco. Desserts – such as grapefruit givré stuffed with sorbet, sesame mousse and rose-scented nuggets of Turkish delight – take the exotic mix to even loftier heights.

Celeste $

*502 Amsterdam Avenue, between 84th & 85th Streets (1-212 874 4559). Subway 1 to 86th Street. **Open** 5-10.30pm Mon-Thur; 5-11pm Fri; noon-3pm, 5-11pm Sat; noon-3pm, 5-10pm Sun. **No cards**. **Map** p194 C18* ④ *Italian*

This popular spot, offering pizza and other Italian fare in a rustic setting, doesn't take reservations so a wait is to be expected. Once you're in, start with *carciofi fritti*: fried artichokes that are so light, they're evanescent. House-made pastas include a standout tagliatelle with shrimp, cabbage and pecorino. Those who can manage a few more bites are advised to try the *pastiera*, a grain-and-ricotta cake flavoured with candied fruit and orange-blossom water.

♥ Jean-Georges $$$$

*1 Central Park West, at Columbus Circle (1-212 299 3900, www.jean-georgesrestaurant.com). Subway A, B, C, D, 1 to 59th Street-Columbus Circle. **Open** 11.45am-2.30pm, 5.30-10pm Mon-Thur, Sun; 11.45am-2.30pm, 5-11pm Fri, Sat. **Map** p194 D22* ⑦ *French*

Unlike some of its vaunted peers, the flagship of celebrated chef Jean-Georges Vongerichten has not become a shadow of itself: the top-rated food is still breathtaking. Velvety foie gras terrine is coated in a thin brûlée shell; other signature dishes include ginger-marinated yellowfin tuna ribbons with avocado and spicy radish. Inventive desserts comprise several mini portions on a flavour theme, such as chocolate or orchard fruit. The more casual onsite eatery, Nougatine, is less expensive, but offers a taste of its big brother, plus terrace seating.

The Aviary NYC

Maison Pickle $$
2315 Broadway, between 83rd & 84th Streets (1-212 496 9100, www.maisonpickle.com). Subway 1 to 86th Street. **Open** *11am-11pm Mon-Wed, Sun; 11am-midnight Fri; 9am-midnight Sat. Bar until 2am Mon-Thur, Sun & 4am Fri, Sat.* **Map** *p194 C19* ⑧
American

It may be named after briny cukes, but the central focus of this retro-luxe bar and eaterie from Jacob Hadjigeorgis – the Jacob of Jacob's Pickles (*see p203*) – is on French-dip sandwiches and cocktails. The kitchen turns out four varieties of the iconic American sandwich, from a classic beef with horseradish aioli to 'royale' with seared foie gras, but the menu also extends to seafood, steaks and indulgent dishes such as fried chicken with French toast.

❤ Per Se $$$$
4th Floor, 10 Columbus Circle, at 60th Street (1-212 823 9335, www.perseny.com). Subway A, B, C, D, 1 to 59th Street-Columbus Circle. **Open** *5.30-9.30pm Mon-Thur; noon-1pm, 5.30-9.30pm Fri-Sun.* **Map** *p194 D22* ⑨
French

Expectations are high at Per Se – and that goes both ways. You're expected to wear the right clothes (jackets are required for men) and pretend you aren't eating in a shopping mall. The restaurant, in turn, is expected to deliver one hell of a tasting menu for $355 (including service). And it does. Dish after dish is flawless, beginning with Thomas Keller's signature Oysters and Pearls (a sabayon of pearl tapioca with oysters and caviar). An all-vegetable version is also available.

Shake Shack $
366 Columbus Avenue, at 77th Street (1-646 747 8770, www.shakeshack.com). Subway B, C to 81st Street-Museum of Natural History; 1 to 79th Street. **Open** *10.30am-11pm daily.* **Map** *p194 C19* ⑩ *American*

The spacious offspring of Danny Meyer's wildly popular Madison Square Park concession stand is now one of many locations across the city and beyond, but this spacious location is particularly convenient for the American Museum of Natural History. Shake Shack is still a contender for New York's best burger. Patties are made from fresh-ground, all-natural Angus beef, and the franks are served Chicago-style on potato buns and topped with secret ShackSauce. Frozen-custard shakes hit the spot, and there's beer and wine if you want something stronger. **Other locations** throughout the city.

Bars

❤ The Aviary NYC
Mandarin Oriental New York, 80 Columbus Circle, at 60th Street (1-212 805 8800, www. aviarynyc.com). Subway A, B, C, D, 1 to 59th Street-Columbus Circle. **Open** *11am-midnight daily.* **Map** *p194 D22* ①

Chicago import The Aviary NYC, stationed on the 35th floor of the Mandarin Oriental, brings the same attention to detail and sense of wonder as the original location. The impressive space looks like Don Draper art-directed *The Jetsons*. Break out your camera, as every cocktail on the seasonally changing list is an interactive spectacle, with smoke, fire, changing colours, or some combination

UPPER WEST SIDE

of the three, as in the aptly named Science AF, a pyrotechnic spin on a Penicillin.

♥ Jacob's Pickles

*509 Amsterdam Avenue, between 84th & 85th Streets (1-212 470 5566, www. jacobspickles.com). Subway 1 to 86th Street. **Open** 10am-2am Mon-Thur; 10am-4am Fri; 9am-4am Sat; 9am-2am Sun. **Map** p194 C18* ❷

This craft-beer-and-biscuit-slinging gastropub shochorns a grab bag of tippling memes – Dixieland grub, house-made bitters, local rosé on tap – into one rustic barroom. There's plenty for brew geeks to get excited about, with more than two dozen taps offering an all-domestic lineup. The list is broken down by state, with a stable of New York breweries complemented by a constantly rotating roster of cross-country favourites. If you're feeling peckish, go for the namesake pickles or the biscuits in sausage gravy (note that the kitchen typically closes 90 minutes before the bar).

Manhattan Cricket Club

*226 W 79th Street, between Amsterdam Avenue & Broadway (1-646 823 9252, www. mccnewyork.com). Subway 1 to 79th Street. **Open** 6pm-1am Mon-Thur; 6pm-2am Fri, Sat. **Map** p194 C19* ❸

Upstairs from Australian bistro Burke & Wills, this gold-brocaded, cricket-inspired cocktail parlour is a polished upgrade from the shrimp-on-the-barbie kitsch that often plagues Aussie efforts. Summit Bar founder Greg Seider created pricey but potent quaffs inspired by cricket hubs such as India and South Africa. The I'll Have Another jolts a dark-and-stormy base of sweet rum and shaved ginger with the spice-heavy bite of garam masala-infused agave, while the kafir lime's sweetness tempers a smoky spritz of campfire essence in the vodka-based Bonfire of the Calamities.

Shops & services

♥ Levain Bakery

*167 W 74th Street, between Amsterdam & Columbus Avenues (1-212 874 6080, www. levainbakery.com). Subway 1 to 79th Street. **Open** 8am-7pm Mon-Sat; 9am-7pm Sun. **Map** p194 C20* ❶ *Food & drink*

Levain sells bread, muffins, brioche and other delectable baked goods, but we're crazy about the cookies. A full 6oz each, the massive mounds stay gooey in the middle. The lush, brownie-like double-chocolate variety, made with extra-dark French cocoa and semi-sweet chocolate chips, is a truly decadent treat. **Other locations** throughout the city.

♥ Magpie

*488 Amsterdam Avenue, between 83rd & 84th Streets (1-212 579 3003, www.magpienewyork. com). Subway 1 to 86th Street. **Open** 11am-7pm Mon-Sat; 11am-6pm Sun. **Map** p194 C19* ❷ *Homewares*

Sylvia Parker worked as a buyer at the American Folk Art Museum gift shop before opening this eco-friendly boutique. The slender space is packed with locally made, handcrafted, sustainable and fair-trade items. Finds include hand-embellished cushions and ceramics, attractively packaged soaps and candles and jewellery created from recycled or found materials, such as resin, wood and Hudson River sea glass.

♥ The Shops at Columbus Circle

*10 Columbus Circle, at 59th Street (1-212 823 6300, www.theshopsatcolumbuscircle. com). Subway A, B, C, D, 1 to 59th Street-Columbus Circle. **Open** 10am-9pm Mon-Sat; 11am-7pm Sun (hrs vary for some shops, bars & restaurants). **Map** p194 D22* ❸ *Mall*

This classy shopping centre features upscale stores alongside more mid-range mall staples. Notable tenants include Coach and Cole Haan for accessories and shoes, London shirtmaker Thomas Pink, Bose home entertainment, cult candle maker Diptyque, French confectioner La Maison du Chocolat, fancy kitchenware purveyor Williams-Sonoma and organic grocer Whole Foods. Some of the city's top restaurants (including Thomas Keller's gourmet destination Per Se, *p202*, and his Bouchon Bakery & Café, *p201*) have made it a dining destination that transcends the stigma of eating at the mall.

▶ *The Museum of Arts & Design next door has a gift shop selling handcrafted jewellery and design items; see p200.*

TurnStyle

*Columbus Circle, at Eighth Avenue & 57th Street (www.turn-style.com). Subway A, B, C, D, 1 to 59th Street-Columbus Circle. **Open** 8am-9pm daily (hrs vary for some shops & restaurants). **Map** p194 D22* ❹ *Mall*

The first major private development inside an NYC subway station, TurnStyle occupies an underground passageway from 57th Street and Eighth Avenue to the train platforms at 59th Street-Columbus Circle. Designed with glass storefronts, porcelain floor tiles and white steel columns, the subterranean mall houses commuter-friendly eateries such as Taiwanese dumpling and noodle house Yong Kang Street, vegan favourite Blossom du Jour and a second outpost of Chelsea Market's Doughnuttery. Ample seating and tables create a sidewalk café atmosphere. Small speciality stores include an outpost of sweet-tooth mecca Dylan's Candy Bar and local accessories chain Mulberry & Grand.

♥ Zabar's

*2245 Broadway, at 80th Street (1-212 787 2000, www.zabars.com). Subway 1 to 79th Street. **Open** 8am-7.30pm Mon-Fri; 8am-8pm Sat; 9am-6pm Sun. **Map** p194 C19* ❺ *Food & drink*

Zabar's is more than a shop – it's a New York City landmark. It began life in 1934 as a tiny storefront specialising in Jewish 'appetising' delicacies, and has gradually expanded to take over half a block of prime Upper West Side real estate. What never cease to surprise, however, are the reasonable prices – even for high-end foods. Besides the famous smoked fish and traditional treats such as rugelach pastries, Zabar's has fabulous bread, cheese, olives and coffee, plus kitchenwares.

MORNINGSIDE HEIGHTS

▶ *Subway B, C, 1 to 110th Street-Cathedral Parkway; 1 to 116th Street.*

Morningside Heights runs from 110th Street (also known west of Central Park as Cathedral Parkway) to 125th Street, between Morningside Park and the Hudson River. The campus of **Columbia University** exerts a considerable influence over the surrounding neighbourhood, while the Cathedral Church of St John the Divine draws visitors from all over the city.

One of the oldest universities in the US, Columbia was initially chartered in 1754 as King's College (the name changed after the Revolutionary War). It moved to its present location in 1897. If you wander into Columbia's campus entrance at 116th Street, you won't fail to miss the impressive **Low Memorial Building**, modelled on Rome's Pantheon. The former library, completed in 1897, is now an administrative building. The list of illustrious graduates includes Alexander Hamilton, Allen Ginsberg and Barack Obama.

Thanks to the large student population of Columbia and its sister school, Barnard College, the area has an academic feel, with bookshops, inexpensive restaurants and coffeehouses lining Broadway between 110th and 116th Streets. The façade of **Tom's Restaurant** (2880 Broadway, at 112th Street, 1-212 864 6137, www.tomsrestaurant.net) will be familiar to *Seinfeld* aficionados, but the interior doesn't resemble Monk's Café, which was created on a studio set for the long-running sitcom.

The **Cathedral Church of St John the Divine** is the seat of the Episcopal Diocese of New York. Subject to a series of

Cathedral Church of St John the Divine

construction delays and misfortunes, the enormous cathedral (larger than Paris's Notre Dame) is on a medieval schedule for completion, although work has wrapped up for the time being. Just behind is the green expanse of **Morningside Park** (from 110th to 123rd Streets, between Morningside Avenue & Morningside Drive).

North of Columbia, **General Grant National Memorial** (aka Grant's Tomb), the mausoleum of former president Ulysses S Grant, is located in Riverside Park. Across the street stands the towering Gothic-style **Riverside Church** (490 Riverside Drive, at 120th Street, 1-212 870 6700, www.theriversidechurchny.org), built in 1930. The tower contains the world's largest carillon: 74 bronze bells, played every Sunday at 10.15am and 3pm.

Sights & museums

♥ Cathedral Church of St John the Divine

*1047 Amsterdam Avenue, at 112th Street (1-212 316 7540, www.stjohndivine.org). Subway B, C, 1 to 110th Street-Cathedral Parkway. **Open** 9am-5pm Mon-Sat; 12.30-2.30pm Sun. **Admission** $10, $8 reductions. Tours $14-$20; $12-$18 reductions. **Map** p195 C15.*

Construction of this massive house of worship, affectionately nicknamed St John the Unfinished, began in 1892 following a Romanesque-Byzantine design by George Heins and Christopher Grant LaFarge. In 1911, Ralph Adams Cram took over with a Gothic Revival redesign. Work came to a halt in 1941, when the US entered World War II. It resumed in earnest in 1979, but a fire in 2001, which destroyed the church's gift shop and damaged two 17th-century Italian tapestries, further delayed completion. It's still missing a tower and a north transept, among other things, but the nave has been restored and the entire interior reopened and rededicated. No further work is planned... for now. In addition to Sunday services, the cathedral hosts concerts and tours (the Vertical Tour, which takes you to the top of the building, is a revelation). It bills itself as a place for all people – and it certainly means it. Annual events include both winter and summer solstice celebrations, the Blessing of the Animals during the Feast of St Francis, which draws pets and their people from all over the city, and even a Blessing of the Bikes every spring.

General Grant National Memorial

Riverside Drive, at 122nd Street (1-646 670 7251, www.nps.gov/gegr). Subway 1 to 125th Street. **Open** *Visitor centre 9am-5pm Wed-Sun.* **Admission** *free.* **Map** *p195 B14.*

Although he was born in Ohio, Civil War hero and 18th president Ulysses S Grant lived in New York for the last five years of his life. More commonly referred to as Grant's Tomb, the neoclassical granite and marble mausoleum was completed in 1897; his wife, Julia, is also laid to rest here. Start at the

visitor centre, which offers exhibits and a video about Grant, before visiting the tomb, which closes for short periods throughout the day (see website for schedule).

Restaurants & cafés

Community Food & Juice $$

2893 Broadway, between 112th & 113th Streets (1-212 665 2800, www.communityrestaurant. com). Subway 1 to 110th Street-Cathedral Parkway. **Open** *8am-3.30pm, 5-9.30pm Mon-Thur; 8am-3.30pm, 5-10pm Fri; 9am-3.30pm, 5-10pm Sat; 9am-3.30pm, 5-9.30pm Sun.* **Map** *p195 B15* **5** *American*

Clinton Street Baking Company's UWS sibling is a neighbourhood brunch destination, but there's more to eating here than eggs and pancakes. Chef-co-owner Neil Kleinberg's dinner menu of global comfort food includes the popular rice bowls and a top-notch grass-fed burger with caramelised onions and Vermont cheddar. Vegetarians will be pleased by a range of creative dishes.

Hungarian Pastry Shop $

1030 Amsterdam Avenue, between 110th & 111th Streets (1-212 866 4230). Subway 1 to 110th Street-Cathedral Parkway. **Open** *7.30am-11pm Mon-Fri; 8.30am-11pm Sat; 8.30am-10pm Sun.* **No cards.** **Map** *p195 C15* **6** *Café*

A Columbia University neighbourhood institution. The java is strong enough to make up for the erratic array of pastries, and the Euro feel is enhanced by the view of the cathedral from outdoor tables.

Columbia University

Upper East Side

Luxurious pre-war apartments owned by blue-blooded socialites, soigné restaurants filled with Botoxed ladies-who-lunch, exclusive designer boutiques... This is the clichéd image of the Upper East Side, and you'll see lots of supporting evidence on Fifth, Madison and Park Avenues. Although Manhattan's super-rich now live all over town, the air of old money is most palpable in the area east of Central Park. Drawn to the freshly landscaped green space in the late 19th century, the city's more affluent residents began building mansions and townhouses along Fifth Avenue. Many of these buildings now house foreign consulates and some of the world-class institutions that draw hordes of visitors and New Yorkers to Museum Mile.

❤ **Don't miss**

1 Metropolitan Museum of Art *p214*
The globe- and era-spanning behemoth.

2 Solomon R Guggenheim Museum *p217*
Impressive exhibitions in a stunning Frank Lloyd Wright building.

3 Cooper Hewitt, Smithsonian Design Museum *p216*
A fresh look at design in a historic mansion.

4 Park Avenue Armory *p210*
Boundary-pushing arts and period rooms in a massive former military space.

5 Museum of the City of New York *p216*
The ultimate New York City starter pack.

SOLOMON R GUGGENHEIM

Solomon R Guggenheim Museum

LENOX HILL

▶ *Subway F to Lexington Avenue-63rd Street; 6 to 68th Street-Hunter College or 77th Street.*

The swathe between Fifth and Lexington Avenues in the 60s and 70s, Lenox Hill encapsulates the classic Upper East Side. Along Fifth, Madison and Park, stately mansions and townhouses rub shoulders with deluxe apartment buildings guarded by uniformed doormen. The 1916 limestone structure at 820 Fifth Avenue (at 63rd Street) was one of the earliest luxury apartment buildings on the avenue, and still has just one residence per floor. And further north, Stanford White designed 998 Fifth Avenue (at 81st Street) in the image of an Italian Renaissance *palazzo*. The neighbourhood's gilded past is also reflected in the impressive 1881 **Park Avenue Armory**.

If you head east on 59th Street, you'll eventually reach the **Ed Koch Queensboro Bridge**, which was renamed in 2011 to honour the former mayor, and links to Queens. Nearby, admire the handsome stone façade of the **Mount Vernon Hotel Museum & Garden** (421 E 61st Street, between First & York Avenues, 1-212 838 6878, www.mvhm.org; closed Mon). The 1799 carriage house, which operated as a bucolic retreat in the early 19th century, is open for guided tours of eight period rooms. At Second Avenue you can catch the overhead tram to **Roosevelt Island**. The two-mile-long isle between Manhattan and Queens is largely residential. However, from 1686 to 1921, it went by the name of Blackwell's Island, when it was the site of an insane asylum, a smallpox hospital and

a prison. Notable inmates included Mae West, who served eight days here after being moved from the Women's House of Detention in Greenwich Village, and Emma Goldman, the anarchist, feminist and political agitator. In 2012, **Franklin D Roosevelt Four Freedoms Park** (www.fdrfourfreedomspark.org; closed Tue) opened on the island's southern tip, 40 years after Mayor John Lindsay and Governor Nelson A Rockefeller announced the memorial. The plans languished until 2005, when an exhibition at Cooper Union revived interest in the project. Commemorating the 32nd President's famous 'four freedoms' speech, the park offers postcard-worthy skyline views.

Sights & museums

Asia Society & Museum

725 Park Avenue, at 70th Street (1-212 288 6400, www.asiasociety.org). Subway 6 to 68th Street-Hunter College. **Open** *July, Aug 11am-6pm Tue-Sun. Sept-June 11am-6pm Tue-Thur, Sat, Sun; 11am-9pm Fri.* **Admission** *$12; $7-$10 reductions; free under-16s (must be accompanied by an adult). Free 6-9pm Fri.* **Map** *p209 E20.*

The Asia Society sponsors study missions and conferences while promoting public programmes in the US and abroad. The headquarters' striking galleries host exhibitions of art from dozens of countries and time periods (from ancient India and medieval Persia to contemporary Japan); some are assembled from public and private collections, including the permanent Mr and Mrs John D Rockefeller III collection of Asian art. You can break for sushi or dim sum at the atrium-like pan-Asian café.

❤ Time to eat & drink

Old-school breakfast
Lexington Candy Shop *p218*

Coffee and cake
Café Sabarsky *p218*

Lunch with a pint
Earl's Beer & Cheese *p218*,
JG Melon *p211*

Elegant dining
Daniel *p210*, Rôtisserie
Georgette *p211*

Classy cocktails
Bar Pleiades *p211*,
Bemelmans Bar *p211*

❤ Time to shop

Chic department store
Barneys New York *p211*

Eclectic fashion under one roof
Fivestory *p212*

Ethical luxury label
Gabriela Hearst *p212*

Glam baubles
Alexis Bittar *p218*

Preppy chic
Veronica Beard *p213*

In the know
Roosevelt Island tram

Suspended on a cable, the tram to Roosevelt Island reaches a height of 250 feet on its brief journey. The fare is the same as a subway ride – MetroCards are accepted – and the views are spectacular.

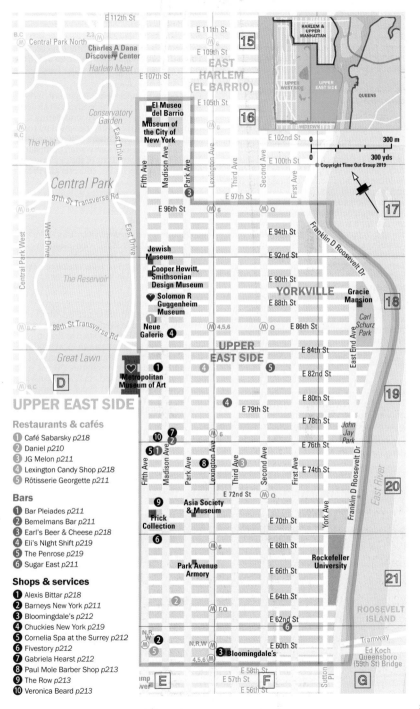

UPPER EAST SIDE

Restaurants & cafés

1. Café Sabarsky p218
2. Daniel p210
3. JG Melon p211
4. Lexington Candy Shop p218
5. Rôtisserie Georgette p211

Bars

1. Bar Pleiades p211
2. Bemelmans Bar p211
3. Earl's Beer & Cheese p218
4. Eli's Night Shift p219
5. The Penrose p219
6. Sugar East p211

Shops & services

1. Alexis Bittar p218
2. Barneys New York p211
3. Bloomingdale's p212
4. Chuckies New York p219
5. Cornelia Spa at the Surrey p212
6. Fivestory p212
7. Gabriela Hearst p212
8. Paul Mole Barber Shop p213
9. The Row p213
10. Veronica Beard p213

Frick Collection

1 E 70th Street, at Fifth Avenue (1-212 288 0700, www.frick.org). Subway 6 to 68th Street-Hunter College. **Open** *10am-6pm Tue-Sat; 11am-5pm Sun.* **Admission** *(under-10s not admitted) $22; $12-$17 reductions. Pay what you wish 2-6pm Wed. Free 6-9pm 1st Fri of the mth (except Jan & Sept).* **Map** *p209 E20.*

Industrialist, robber baron and collector Henry Clay Frick commissioned this opulent mansion with a view to leaving his legacy to the public. Designed by Thomas Hastings of Carrère & Hastings (the firm behind the New York Public Library) and built in 1914, the building was inspired by 18th-century British and French architecture.

In an effort to preserve the feel of a private residence, labelling is minimal, but you can opt for a free audio guide, download the app or pay $2 for a booklet. Works spanning the 14th to the 19th centuries include masterpieces by Rembrandt, Vermeer, Whistler, Gainsborough, Holbein and Titian, and exquisite period furniture, porcelain and other decorative objects. Aficionados of 18th-century French art will find two rooms especially enchanting: the panels of the Boucher Room (1750-52) depict children engaged in adult occupations; the Fragonard Room contains the artist's series *Progress of Love* – four of the paintings were commissioned (and rejected) by Louis XV's mistress Madame du Barry. A gallery in the enclosed garden portico is devoted to decorative arts and sculpture. It's advisable to check before visiting in 2020 and beyond since the museum is planning a major expansion of its exhibition spaces.

▶ *For the Frick's excellent concert series, see p331.*

❤ Park Avenue Armory

643 Park Avenue, between 66th & 67th Streets (1-212 616 3930, www.armoryonpark.org). Subway 6 to 68th Street-Hunter College. **Open** *during events; see website for details.* **Admission** *Tours $15; $10 reductions.* **Map** *p209 E21.*

Once home to the Seventh Regiment of the National Guard, this impressive 1881 structure contains a series of period rooms dating from the late 19th century, designed by such luminaries as Louis Comfort Tiffany and the Herter Brothers. The vast Wade Thompson Drill Hall has become one of the city's premier alternative spaces for art, concerts and theatre.

Restaurants & cafés

❤ Daniel $$$

60 E 65th Street, between Madison & Park Avenues (1-212 288 0033, www.danielnyc.com). Subway F to Lexington Avenue-63rd Street; 6 to 68th Street-Hunter College. **Open** *5-10.30pm Mon-Sat.* **Map** *p209 E21* ②
French

The cuisine at Daniel Boulud's elegant fine-dining flagship, designed by Adam Tihany, is rooted in French technique with contemporary flourishes such as fusion elements and an emphasis on local produce. Although the menu changes seasonally, it usually includes a few signature dishes, such as the chef's oven-baked black sea bass with Syrah sauce, or the duo of beef – a sumptuous pairing of Black Angus short ribs and seared Wagyu tenderloin. **Other locations** Café Boulud, 20 E 76th Street, between Fifth & Madison Avenues, Upper East Side (1-212 772 2600); Bar Boulud, 1900 Broadway, at 64th Street, Upper West Side (1-212 595 0303); DB

Park Avenue Armory

Bistro Moderne, 55 West 44th Street, between Fifth & Sixth Avenues, Midtown West (1-212 391 2400).

▶ *For Boulud Sud, see p201.*

♥ JG Melon $

1291 Third Avenue, at 74th Street (1-212 744 0585). Open 11.30am-2.30am Mon-Sat; 11.30am-1am Sun. Subway Q to 72nd Street, 6 to 77th Street. No cards. Map p209 F20 ❸
American

This classic bar and eatery, with its nostalgic neon sign, green-and-white checked tablecloths and tie-sporting staff, is constantly packed with a preppy local crowd and visitors eager to try the headlining burger. The plump, loosely packed round is made with a hush-hush beef blend from Master Purveyors, the same source for the choice cuts found at legendary steakhouses such as Peter Luger and Keens. Veiled with melty American cheese, the juicy, griddle-cooked beaut is served on a modest Arnold bun with red onions and crinkled pickle chips.

♥ Rôtisserie Georgette $$$

14 E 60th Street, between Fifth & Madison Avenues (1-212 390 8060, www.rotisserieg. com). Subway N, R, W to Fifth Avenue-59th Street. Open noon-2.30pm, 5.45-10pm Mon; noon-2.30pm, 5.45-11pm Tue-Fri; 5.45-11pm Sat; noon-3pm, 5.45-10pm Sun (closed Sun Jul, Aug). Map p209 E22 ❺ *French/American*

Georgette Farkas, who was Daniel Boulud's publicist for nearly two decades, opened this 90-seat rotisserie, furnished with caramel-coloured banquettes and showcasing spit-fired roasts, including beef, lamb, poultry and whole fish. The menu also includes seasonal starters, salads and sides, such as pancetta-studded brussels sprouts and three takes on potatoes (traditional roasted, au gratin with Gruyère, or baked with apples and tarragon). The wine list showcases lesser-known French producers.

Bars

♥ Bar Pleiades

The Surrey, 20 E 76th Street, between Fifth & Madison Avenues (1-212 772 2600, www. barpleiades.com). Subway 6 to 77th Street. Open noon-midnight Mon-Thur, Sun; noon-1am Fri, Sat. Map p209 E20 ❶

Designed as a nod to Coco Chanel, Daniel Boulud's chic bar in the Surrey hotel is framed in black lacquered panels that recall an elegant make-up compact. The luxe setting and moneyed crowd might seem a little stiff, but the seasonally rotating cocktails are so exquisitely executed you probably won't mind. Light eats are provided by Café Boulud next door.

♥ Bemelmans Bar

The Carlyle, 35 E 76th Street, at Madison Avenue (1-212 744 1600, www.thecarlyle. com). Subway 6 to 77th Street. Open noon-12.30am Mon, Sun; noon-1am Tue-Thur; noon-1.30am Fri, Sat. Map p209 E19 ❷

The Plaza may have Eloise, but the Carlyle has its own children's book connection – the wonderful 1947 murals of Central Park by *Madeline* creator Ludwig Bemelmans in this, the quintessential classy New York bar. A pianist adds to the atmosphere in the early evening and a jazz trio takes up residence later (9pm Mon, Sun; 9.30pm Tue-Sat), when a $15-$35 cover charge kicks in.

Sugar East

1125 First Avenue, at 62nd Street (1-212 832 4610, www.sugareast.com). Subway N, R, W to Lexington Avenue-59th Street; F, Q to Lexington Avenue-63rd Street. Open 5pm-2am daily. Map p209 F21 ❻

Adorned with dark leather banquettes, wood-panelled walls and working fireplaces, this underground speakeasy feels like a seductive bachelor pad from the 1960s. The simple cocktail menu lists each drink by its foremost ingredient, such as coconut or carrot. The decor isn't the only thing that recalls the Mad Men era – a grandfathered cigar licence from the space's former resident, Merchants NY Cigar Bar, makes this a rare destination for legal indoor cigarette smoking.

Shops & services

Madison Avenue, between 57th and 86th Streets, is packed with international designer names: Alexander McQueen, Balenciaga, Derek Lam, Golden Goose, Iro, Prada, Lanvin, Ralph Lauren, Tom Ford, Valentino and many more.

♥ Barneys New York

660 Madison Avenue, at 61st Street, Upper East Side (1-212 826 8900, www.barneys.com). Subway N, R, W to Fifth Avenue-59th Street; 4, 5, 6 to 59th Street. Open 10am-8pm Mon-Wed; 10am-8.30pm Thur-Sat; 11am-7pm Sun. Map p209 E22 ❷ *Department store*

Barneys has a reputation for spotlighting more independent designer labels than other upmarket department stores, and it also has its own trend-driven collection. The ground floor showcases luxe accessories, and cult beauty and fragrance brands are in the basement. Head to the seventh and eighth floors for contemporary designer and denim lines. **Other locations** 101 Seventh Avenue, at 16th Street, Chelsea (1-646 264 6400); 194 Atlantic Avenue, at Court Street, Cobble Hill, Brooklyn (1-718 637 2234).

Bloomingdale's

1000 Third Avenue, at 59th Street (1-212 705 2000, www.bloomingdales.com). Subway N, R, W to Lexington Avenue-59th Street; 4, 5, 6 to 59th Street. **Open** *10am-8.30pm Mon-Sat; 11am-7pm Sun (hrs vary).* **Map** *p209 F22* ❸ *Department store*

Ranking among the city's top tourist attractions, Bloomie's is a gigantic, glitzy department store stocked with everything from handbags to home furnishings. The dynamic beauty section includes mini shops such as Wellchemist for natural brands, and an outpost of globe-spanning apothecary Space NK. Huge, artist-decorated high heels dot the extensive women's footwear department, dubbed 'Shoe York'. You can get a mid-shopping sugar fix at the on-site Magnolia Bakery. The compact Soho outpost concentrates on contemporary fashion and cosmetics, and there's a discount outlet. **Other locations** 504 Broadway, between Broome & Spring Streets, Soho (1-212 729 5900); Bloomingdale's Outlet, 2085 Broadway, Upper West Side (1-212 634 3190).

Cornelia Spa at the Surrey

2nd Floor, 20 E 76th Street, between Fifth & Madison Avenues (1-646 358 3600, www.corneliaspaatthesurrey.com). Subway 6 to 77th Street. **Open** *10am-8pm Mon-Fri; 9am-7pm Sat, Sun.* **Map** *p209 E20* ❺ *Health & beauty*

Tucked inside an upscale hotel, this intimate yet luxurious oasis is designed to make you feel as if you're lounging in your own living space, complete with post-treatment savoury and sweet bites and herbal teas. Splurge on the Reparative Caviar and Oxygen Quench facial ($325), or a customised signature massage ($195 for an hour), which combines

various techniques such as deep-tissue, Swedish and shiatsu.

♥ Fivestory

18 E 69th Street, between Fifth & Madison Avenues (1-212 288 1338, www.fivestoryny.com). Subway 6 to 68th Street-Hunter College. **Open** *10am-6pm Mon-Fri; noon-6pm Sat, Sun (closed Sun in summer).* **Map** *p209 E21* ❻ *Fashion*

At just 26 (with a little help from her fashion-industry insider dad), Claire Distenfeld opened this glamorous, grown-up boutique, which sprawls over several spaces in – yes – a five-storey townhouse. The hand-selected stock spans big-name and lesser-known American and European labels and eclectic styles, from urban-casual pieces by Alexander Wang and sleek tailored designs by Brandon Maxwell to boho-chic looks from Ulla Johnson. Jewellery is showcased in a devoted room, and a discreet elevator whisks you up to a glam wing with evening dresses and a designer shoe salon.

♥ Gabriela Hearst

985 Madison Avenue, between 76th & 77th Streets (1-212 433 4499, www.gabrielahearst.com). Subway 6 to 77th Street. **Open** *10am-6pm Mon-Sat; noon-5pm Sun.* **Map** *p209 E19* ❼ *Fashion*

Married into the storied media clan, Gabriela Hearst designs simple clothes that exude understated luxury: slouchy, minimalist suits, crisp cotton dresses with well-placed pleats and oversized sweaters handknit by a women's cooperative in her native Uruguay. The elegant flagship is your best bet for getting your hands on one of the sculptural bags, such as the popular Nina, without joining a waiting list. It's also the exclusive NYC stockist of French apothecary line Buly, in gift-friendly old-fashioned packaging.

Third Avenue

there's also a small men's line. Even if you can't quite stretch to the one-percenter price tags, it's worth checking out the art peppering the space by the likes of Keith Haring, Andy Warhol and Isamu Noguchi.

♥ Veronica Beard

988 Madison Avenue, at 77th Street (1-646 930 4746, www.veronicabeard.com). Subway 6 to 77th Street. **Open** *10am-7pm Mon-Sat; noon-6pm Sun.* **Map** *p209 E19* ❿ *Fashion*

Launched by two sisters-in-law who share the name, the Veronica Beard label combines urban cool with classic American preppy. At the centre of the collection are blazers that can be customised with removable hoodie or turtleneck dickeys. Browse racks of ruched shirt dresses and well-tailored trousers in a laid-back space decorated with Turkish kilim rugs from ABC Carpet & Home (*see p168*) and leopard-print sofas. Much of the art on the walls, courtesy of the Upper East Side's Voltz Clarke Gallery, can also be purchased. **Other location** 78 Greene Street, between Broome & Spring Streets, Soho (1-646 655 0895).

MUSEUM MILE & CARNEGIE HILL

▶ *Subway 4, 5, 6 to 86th Street; 6 to 96th Street or 103rd Street.*

Philanthropic gestures made by the moneyed classes over the past 130-odd years have helped to create an impressive cluster of art collections, museums and cultural institutions on the Upper East Side. Indeed, Fifth Avenue from 82nd to 105th Streets is known as **Museum Mile**, and for good reason: it's lined with more than half a dozen celebrated institutions, including the **Metropolitan Museum of Art** (*see p214*) and the **Solomon R Guggenheim Museum** (*see p217*).

Carnegie Hill, the northern blocks of the Upper East Side between Fifth and Lexington Avenues, takes its name from early resident Andrew Carnegie. The Scottish philanthropist bought a large chunk of then-rural land in 1898 to build a 64-room mansion, which is now home to the **Cooper Hewitt, Smithsonian Design Museum**.

Veronica Beard

Paul Molé Barber Shop

1034 Lexington Avenue, at 74th Street (1-212 535 8461). Subway 6 to 77th Street. **Open** *7.30am-7.30pm Mon-Fri; 7.30am-5.30pm Sat; 8am-4.30pm Sun.* **Map** *p209 E20* ❽ *Health & beauty*

Best known for its precise shaves, this nostalgic barber shop has been grooming men since 1913 (John Steinbeck used to be a customer). As well as its signature Deluxe Staight Razor Shave ($42), you can get a haircut ($42) and other services such as a scalp massage ($10).

The Row

17 E 71st Street, between Fifth & Madison Avenues (1-212 755 2017, www.therow.com). Subway 6 to 72nd Street. **Open** *10am-6pm Mon-Wed, Fri, Sat; 10am-7pm Thur.* **Map** *p209 E20* ❾ *Fashion*

The flagship of Ashley and Mary-Kate Olsen's luxurious yet understated label occupies a discreet townhouse. Its elegant, pared-down interior provides the perfect foil for the impeccably tailored pieces in sumptuous fabrics and a muted colour palette. Exquisitely crafted classic loafers and heels are showcased in a separate room, and

In the know
Night at the museum

Most of the city's major museums are free or pay what you wish one evening (usually Thursday or Friday) or afternoon of the week. Some enhance the experience with musical and other performances.

UPPER EAST SIDE

💙 Metropolitan Museum of Art

1000 Fifth Avenue, at 82nd Street (1-212 535 7710, www.metmuseum.org). Subway 4, 5, 6 to 86th Street. **Open** *10am-5.30pm Mon-Thur, Sun; 10am-9pm Fri, Sat.* **Admission** *(incl same-day admission to the Met Breuer & the Met Cloisters) $25; $12-$17 reductions; free under-12s.* **Map** *p209 E19.*

The Met, which opened in 1880, now occupies 13 acres of Central Park. Its original Gothic Revival building was designed by Calvert Vaux and Jacob Wrey Mould, but is now almost hidden by subsequent additions. The encyclopedic globe- and millennia-spanning holdings include fine and decorative art, arms and armour, musical instruments and ancient artefacts. The first floor's north wing contains the collection of ancient Egyptian art and the glass-walled atrium housing the Temple of Dendur, moved en masse from its original Nile-side setting and now overlooking a reflective pool.

In the north-west corner is the American Wing with its grand Engelhard Court, flanked by the salvaged façade of Wall Street's Branch Bank of the United States and a stunning loggia designed by Louis Comfort Tiffany for his Long Island estate. The centrepiece of the wing's Galleries for Paintings, Sculpture and Decorative Arts is Emanuel Gottlieb Leutze's iconic 1851 painting *Washington Crossing the Delaware*.

In the southern wing are the halls housing Greek and Roman art. Turning west brings you to the Arts of Africa, Oceania and the Americas collection, slated for major renovation in late 2020. It was donated by Nelson Rockefeller as a memorial to his son Michael, who disappeared while visiting New Guinea in 1961. A wider-ranging bequest, the two-storey Robert Lehman Wing, is at the western end of the floor. This eclectic collection is housed in a recreation of the Lehman family townhouse and features works by Botticelli, Bellini, Ingres and Rembrandt, among others. At ground level, the Costume Institute is the site of the Met's blockbuster fashion exhibitions.

Upstairs, the central western section is dominated by the European Paintings galleries, which hold an amazing reserve of old masters, including Rembrandt, Rubens, Vermeer, Velázquez and Goya. To the south, the 19th-century European galleries contain

some of the Met's most popular works – in particular the two-room Monet holdings and a colony of Van Goghs that includes his oft-reproduced *Irises*.

Walk eastward and you'll reach the galleries of the Art of the Arab Lands, Turkey, Iran, Central Asia and Later South Asia. In the north-east wing of this floor, you'll find the sprawling collection of Asian art; be sure to check out the ceiling of the Jain Meeting Hall in the South Asian galleries. You can rest your feet in the Astor Court, a tranquil recreation of a Ming Dynasty garden, or head up to the Iris & B Gerald Cantor Roof Garden (usually open May-Oct).

As per a temporary agreement, the Met hosts exhibitions spotlighting its stellar collection of 20th- and 21st-century art in the Met Breuer, the former home of the Whitney Museum of American Art, designed by Hungarian architect Marcel Breuer. From summer 2020 onwards, it's advisable to call or check the website before visiting the Met Breuer (945 Madison Avenue, at 75th Street, 1-212 731 1675). For the **Cloisters**, which houses the Met's medieval art collection, *see p229.*

💗 Cooper Hewitt, Smithsonian Design Museum

*2 E 91st Street, at Fifth Avenue (1-212 849 8400, www.cooperhewitt.org). Subway 4, 5, 6 to 86th Street. **Open** 10am-6pm Mon-Fri, Sun; 10am-9pm Sat. **Admission** $18; $9-$12 reductions; free under-19s. Pay what you wish 6-9pm Sat. **Map** p209 E18.*

The museum began as a collection created for students of the Cooper Union for the Advancement of Science and Art by the Hewitt sisters – granddaughters of the institution's founder, Peter Cooper – and opened to the public in 1897. Part of the Smithsonian since the 1960s, the Cooper Hewitt is the only museum in the US solely dedicated to historic and contemporary design. In 1976, it took up residence in the former home of steel magnate Andrew Carnegie.

Thanks to a three-year renovation, completed in 2014, historic spaces such as the Teak Room, with its intricately carved wall panelling and cabinets, have been painstakingly restored.

Each visitor receives a hi-tech pen, allowing them to 'collect' objects, explore them and even create their own designs on high-definition screens on tables. The second floor showcases objects from the permanent collection, with textiles, product design, decorative arts, drawings, prints and graphic design, organised by theme. Items from different eras and geographical areas are attractively grouped together, creating interesting juxtapositions and revealing links. The varied holdings include oil sketches by Hudson River School painter Frederic Church (1826-1900) and a 1996 concept design for the Air Jordan XIII sneaker by the shoe's original designer, Tinker Hatfield. The digital Immersion Room lets you fully experience the institution's impressive collection of wallcoverings – the largest in the US.

Rotating exhibitions include the excellent Selects series, in which a prominent artist, designer, architect or other tastemaker curates their favourite items from the collection.

In the know
Refined taste

Of course, there's always Central Park, but for a civilised alfresco break on Museum Mile, enter the **Cooper Hewitt** (see above) via the back garden and pick up a coffee or snack at the café. No ticket is required to linger at an outdoor table and get a taste of how one of New York's richest men, Andrew Carnegie, once lived.

El Museo del Barrio

*1230 Fifth Avenue, at 104th Street (1-212 831 7272, www.elmuseo.org). Subway 6 to 103rd Street. **Open** 11am-6pm Wed-Sat; noon-5pm Sun. **Admission** Suggested donation $9; $5 reductions; free under-12s; free over-65s Wed. **Map** p209 E16.*

Founded in 1969 by the artist and former MoMA curator Rafael Montañez Ortiz, El Museo del Barrio takes its name from its East Harlem locale (though this stretch of Fifth Avenue is an extension of the Upper East Side's Museum Mile). Housed in a 1921 Beaux Arts building, El Museo is dedicated to the art and culture of Puerto Ricans and Latin Americans all over the US. Renovated galleries provide a polished, contemporary showcase for the diversity and vibrancy of Hispanic art. Rotating exhibitions spotlight selections from the museum's holdings of more than 6,500 pieces, from pre-Columbian artefacts to contemporary installations.

Jewish Museum

*1109 Fifth Avenue, at 92nd Street (1-212 423 3200, www.thejewishmuseum.org). Subway 4, 5, 6 to 86th Street; 6 to 96th Street. **Open** 11am-5.45pm Mon, Tue, Sat, Sun; 11am-8pm Thur; 11am-5.45pm Fri (11am-4pm Nov-Mar). Closed some Jewish holidays. **Admission** $18; $8-$12 reductions; free under-19s. Free Sat. **Map** p209 E18.*

The Jewish Museum is housed in a magnificent 1908 French Gothic-style mansion – the former home of the financier, collector and Jewish leader Felix Warburg. Inside, the centrepiece exhibition 'Scenes from the Collection' presents rotating selections of the museum's cache of around 30,000 works of art, artefacts and media installations from antiquity to the present day. The excellent temporary shows, which spotlight Jewish artists or related themes, appeal to a broad audience. You can nosh on bagels, knishes and other delicacies at an outpost of famed Lower East Side purveyor, Russ & Daughters (see p119).

▶ *The Museum of Jewish Heritage: A Living Memorial to the Holocaust (see p78) and the Museum at Eldridge Street (see p113), both downtown, further explore Jewish culture.*

💗 Museum of the City of New York

*1220 Fifth Avenue, between 103rd & 104th Streets (1-212 534 1672, www.mcny.org). Subway 6 to 103rd Street. **Open** 10am-6pm daily. **Admission** Suggested donation $18; $12 reductions; free under-20s. **Map** p209 E16.*

This institution provides a great introduction to NYC. The entire first floor is devoted to 'New York at its Core', a permanent exhibition chronicling the city's 400-year history, from its beginnings as a Dutch colony to the urban force

💙 Solomon R Guggenheim Museum

1071 Fifth Avenue, between 88th & 89th Streets (1-212 423 3500, www.guggenheim. org). Subway 4, 5, 6 to 86th Street. **Open** *10am-5.30pm Mon, Wed-Fri, Sun; 10am-8pm Tue, Sat.* **Admission** *$25; $18 reductions; free under-12s. Pay what you wish 5-8pm Sat.* **Map** *p209 E18.*

While its winding cantilevered curves have become as integral to New York's architectural landscape as the spire of the Chrysler Building or the arches of the Brooklyn Bridge, the Solomon R Guggenheim Museum caused quite a stir when it debuted in 1959. Many felt its appearance clashed with the rest of staid Fifth Avenue, while Willem de Kooning and Robert Motherwell complained that their art was not best appreciated from the museum's interior ramps. Some critics suggested the building was less a museum than a monument to its architect, Frank Lloyd Wright, who died six months before its completion.

These criticisms were of little concern to Wright. When someone complained that the walls wouldn't be high enough to display certain paintings, he retorted that the canvases should be cut in half. The skylight that imbued the space with natural light proved damaging to certain works, and the glass was replaced with thermal panes in the 1980s.

In 1992, the addition of a ten-storey tower provided space for additional galleries, a café and an auditorium. Today, the museum also has a more upscale restaurant, appropriately named the Wright. The Rotunda is devoted to large-scale changing exhibitions.

Solomon R Guggenheim's original founding collection, amassed in the 1930s, includes works by Kandinsky, Chagall, Picasso, Franz Marc and others. The Solomon R Guggenheim Foundation's holdings have since been enriched by subsequent bequests, including the Thannhauser Collection, with paintings by Impressionist and post-Impressionist Masters such as Manet, Cézanne and Gaugin, and the Panza di Biumo Collection of American minimalist and conceptual art from the 1960s and '70s.

The fact that the Guggenheim is the sole major building by one of America's greatest 20th-century architects in its most iconic architectural city isn't so surprising. (There's also a house designed by Wright in the Lighthouse Hill section of Staten Island that isn't open to the public.) Wright wasn't really an urban architect. Most of his designs were for private homes in rural or suburban sites, and he was initially reluctant to take on the Guggenheim project. But his Gotham swansong is probably his most famous creation.

UPPER EAST SIDE

it is today. In addition to hi-tech interactive displays, which allow you to virtually 'meet' key players from the past, the hundreds of objects include a 17th-century Lenape war club, a ceremonial shovel from the groundbreaking of the first subway, a Studio 54 guest list from the nightclub's heyday, and Milton Glaser's original concept sketch for the 1976 'I Heart New York' campaign. A 28-minute film, *Timescapes*, which also illuminates the growth of Gotham, is shown free with admission every 40 minutes from 10.20am to 5pm. But the museum's jewel is the amazing Stettheimer Dollhouse, created in the 1920s by Carrie Stettheimer, whose artist friends reinterpreted their masterpieces in miniature to hang on the walls. Look closely and you'll spy a tiny version of Marcel Duchamp's *Nude Descending a Staircase*. Temporary shows, on such varied subjects as gay culture and social activism, spotlight the metropolis from different angles.

Neue Galerie

1048 Fifth Avenue, at 86th Street (1-212 628 6200, www.neuegalerie.org). Subway 4, 5, 6 to 86th Street. **Open** *11am-6pm Mon, Thur-Sun; 11am-9pm 1st Fri of the mth.* **Admission** *(under-12s not admitted) $22; $12-$16 reductions. Free 6-9pm 1st Fri of the mth.* **Map** *p209 E18.*

Set within a refined 1914 mansion designed by New York Public Library architects Carrère & Hastings, the elegant Neue Galerie showcases German and Austrian fine art, objects and furnishings from the late 19th and early 20th centuries in several exquisitely restored rooms. The creation of the late art dealer Serge Sabarsky and cosmetics mogul Ronald S Lauder, it has the largest concentration of works by Gustav Klimt and Egon Schiele outside of Vienna, including Klimt's gilded portrait of Adele Bloch-Bauer, which was returned to the subject's family (and subsequently purchased by the Neue Galerie) after being stolen by the Nazis in World War II. Factor in a stop at the chic Café Sabarsky (*see below*) for coffee and ravishing Viennese pastries, or something more substantial.

Restaurants & cafés

♥ Café Sabarsky $$

Neue Galerie, 1048 Fifth Avenue, at 86th Street (1-212 288 0665, www.neuegalerie.org/cafes/sabarsky). Subway 4, 5, 6 to 86th Street. **Open** *9am-6pm Mon, Wed; 9am-9pm Thur-Sun.* **Map** *p209 E18* ❶ *Austrian/café*

Purveyor of indulgent pastries and whipped cream-topped *einspänner* coffee for Neue Galerie patrons by day, this sophisticated, high-ceilinged restaurant, inspired by a classic Viennese *kaffeehaus*, is helmed by chef Kurt Gutenbrunner of modern Austrian restaurant

Wallsé. Appetisers are most adventurous – the creaminess of the *spätzle* noodles a perfect base for peas, tarragon and wild mushrooms – while main course specials, such as wiener schnitzel tartly garnished with lingonberries, are capable yet ultimately feel like the calm before the *Sturm und Drang* of dessert. Try the *klimttorte*, which masterfully alternates layers of hazelnut cake with chocolate. Note: the eaterie is closed on Tuesdays.

♥ Lexington Candy Shop $

1226 Lexington Avenue, at 83rd Street (1-212 288 0057, www.lexingtoncandyshop.net). Subway 4, 5, 6 to 86th Street. **Open** *7am-7pm Mon-Fri; 8am-7pm Sat; 8am-6pm Sun.* **Map** *p209 E19* ❹ *American*

You won't find much candy for sale at this well-preserved vintage lunchroom, which opened in 1925. The extensive menu lists old-fashioned diner fare, such as burgers (including one topped with a pat of butter) and soda fountain treats, such as egg creams and milkshakes. If you come for breakfast, order the doorstop slabs of french toast.

Bars

♥ Earl's Beer & Cheese

1259 Park Avenue, between 97th & 98th Street (1-212 289 1581, www.earlsny.com). Subway 6 to 96th Street. **Open** *11am-midnight Mon-Thur, Sun; 11am-2am Fri, Sat.* **Map** *p209 E17* ❸

Tucked into the no-man's land between the Upper East Side and Spanish Harlem, this craft-beer cubby hole has the sort of community-hub vibe that makes you want to settle in. The well-priced, rotating selection of American craft brews and slapdash set-up appeal to a neighbourhood crowd, but the madcap bar menu makes it destination-worthy. Try the NY State Cheddar – a grilled cheese sandwich with braised pork belly, fried egg and house-made kimchi. (Be advised that the kitchen closes at 11pm.)

Shops & services

♥ Alexis Bittar

1100 Madison Avenue, between 82nd & 83rd Streets (1-212 249 3581, www.alexisbittar.com). Subway 4, 5, 6 to 86th Street. **Open** *10am-6pm Mon-Sat; noon-5pm Sun.* **Map** *p209 E19* ❶ *Accessories*

Alexis Bittar started out selling his jewellery from a humble Soho street stall, but now the designer has three NYC shops in which to show off his flamboyant line. Typical pieces include sculptural Lucite cuffs, oversized pendant necklaces and dramatic drop earrings. The elegant grey-toned space is lined with accessible display cases and staff encourage

UPPER EAST SIDE

shoppers to try on items. **Other locations** 465 Broome Street, between Greene & Mercer Streets, Soho (1-212 625 8340); 353 Bleecker Street, between Charles & 10th Streets, West Village (1-212 727 1093).

Chuckies New York

1169 Madison Avenue, between 85th & 86th Streets (1-212 249 2254, www. chuckiesnewyork.com). Subway 4, 5, 6 to 86th Street. Open 10am-7pm Mon-Sat; noon-6pm Sun. Map p209 E18 ❹ *Accessories*

Only the most exquisite women's footwear gains shelf space in this compact, bi-level shoebox. The finely tuned international stock spans cool contemporary labels such as Alexander Wang and Leoffler Randall and coveted designer lines including Lanvin, Chloé and Balenciaga.

YORKVILLE

▶ *Subway 6 to 77th Street; Q to 86th Street.*

The atmosphere becomes noticeably more rarefied as you walk east from Central Park, with grand edifices giving way to bland modern apartment blocks and walk-up tenements. Not much remains of the old German and Hungarian immigrant communities that once filled **Yorkville**, the neighbourhood above 79th Street between Third avenue and the East River, with delicatessens, beer halls and restaurants. However, one such flashback, open since 1936, is **Heidelberg** (1648 Second Avenue, between 85th & 86th Streets, 1-212 628 2332, www.heidelberg-nyc.com), where dirndl-wearing waitresses serve up steins of Spaten and platters of sausages from the wurst-meisters at butcher shop **Schaller & Weber** a few doors up (1654 Second Avenue, 1-212 879 3047, www.schallerweber.com). Second Avenue in the 70s and 80s throbs with rowdy pick-up bars frequented by preppy, twentysomething crowds, as well as numerous inexpensive eateries from sushi spots to taco joints. Now, craft-beer and cocktail bars bring an indie-cool downtown vibe to the area.

The only Federal-style mansion in Manhattan, **Gracie Mansion** stands at the eastern end of 88th Street. The stately pile has served as New York's official mayoral residence since 1942 (except during Michael Bloomberg's time in office). The mansion is fenced off, but much of the exterior can be seen from surrounding **Carl Schurz Park.**

One block from Gracie Mansion, the **Henderson Place Historic District** (at East End Avenue, between 86th & 87th Streets) contains 24 handsome Queen Anne row houses – commissioned by furrier and noted real-estate developer John C Henderson

as servants' quarters – with their original turrets, double stoops and slate roofs.

Bars

Eli's Night Shift

189 E 79th Street, at Third Avenue (1-212 879 7160, www.elizabar.com). Subway 6 to 77th Street. Open 5pm-2am. Map p209 F19 ❹

A New York food fixture for more than four decades, restaurateur Eli Zabar partnered with his son Oliver to open this drinks-and-nibbles den. The zinc-topped bar offers ten rotating NYC-area brews, poured through nozzles protruding from a menu-scrawled chalkboard, plus wine and cocktails. Elevated comfort-food standards, served until midnight, balance the booze, such as a burger on a brioche or pigs in a blanket: house-made franks rolled in fresh puff pastry. **Other locations** Bar 87, 1291 Lexington Avenue, at 87th Street, Upper East Side (1-212 348 4943); Bar 91, 1270 Madison Avenue, at 91st Street, Upper East Side (1-646 755 3999).

The Penrose

1590 Second Avenue, between 82nd & 83rd Streets (1-212 203 2751, www.penrosebar. com). Subway Q to 86th Street. Open 11am-4am Mon-Fri; 9.30am-4am Sat, Sun. Map p209 F19 ❺

Named for a neighbourhood in Cork, Ireland, where two of the owners grew up, the Penrose stands apart from the Upper East Side's sports bars and fancier joints – its exposed-brick walls, retro decorative touches and curved wooden bar are casually sophisticated. The changing craft-beer selections includes European and American brews (some from New York State). An extensive list of whiskies spans Irish, American and Scotch. The comfort-food-heavy menu includes a thick, juicy Pat LaFrieda blend house burger.

In the know
Underground art

The extension of the Q line between 63rd and 96th Streets has an impressive display of public art in its four stations. At 63rd Street, Jean Shin's tiled murals are based on 1930s and '40s photos of the original elevated trains. At 72nd Street, Vik Muniz has created full-size portraits of New Yorkers waiting for the train. Chuck Close's large-scale mosaics of artists and musicians, such as Alex Katz and Lou Reed, gaze out from the walls at 86th Street, while, at 96th Street, Sara Sze has created a huge abstracted 'landscape', with sheets of paper, scaffolding, birds, trees and foliage that seem caught up in a whirlwind.

Harlem & Upper Manhattan

Harlem is the cultural capital of black America – a legacy of the Harlem Renaissance, the artistic and intellectual movement that spanned the 1920s. During the Jazz Age, white New Yorkers accepted Duke Ellington's famous invitation to 'Take the A Train' uptown to the neighbourhood's celebrated nightclubs, but in the 1960s and '70s, crime and urban decay kept non-residents away. Today, Harlem is seeing a second renaissance. The area isn't packed with sights, but it's worth visiting for its eclectic architecture, theatrical street life, historic churches with exuberant gospel choirs, and a buzzing restaurant and bar scene peppered with live jazz.

❤ **Don't miss**

1 Apollo Theater *p317*
Legendary stage for jazz, soul and R&B.

2 Met Cloisters *p229*
A fairy-tale castle houses the museum's medieval collection.

3 Morris-Jumel Mansion *p229*
George Washington slept in this pre-Revolutionary home.

Apollo Theater

WEST & CENTRAL HARLEM

▶ *Subway A, B, C, D to 125th Street; B, C to 116th Street or 135th Street; 1, 2, 3 to 125th Street.*

The village of Harlem, named by Dutch colonists after their native Haarlem, was annexed by the City of New York in 1873. The extension of the elevated subway two decades later brought eager developers who overbuilt in the suddenly accessible suburb. The consequent housing glut led to cheap rents, and Jewish, Italian and Irish immigrants escaping the tenements of the Lower East Side snapped them up.

Around the turn of the 20th century, black Americans joined the procession into Harlem, their ranks swelled by the Great Migration from the Deep South. By 1914, the black population of Harlem had risen well above 50,000; by the 1920s, Harlem was the country's most populous African-American community. This prominence soon attracted some of black America's greatest artists: writers such as Langston Hughes and Zora Neale Hurston and musicians including Duke Ellington, Louis Armstrong and Cab Calloway. The unprecedented cultural gathering was known as the **Harlem Renaissance**. White New York took notice, venturing uptown – where the enforcement of Prohibition was lax – to enjoy the Cotton Club, Connie's Inn, Smalls Paradise and the Savoy Ballroom, which supplied the beat for the city that never sleeps.

The Depression killed the Harlem Renaissance, and deeply wounded Harlem. By the 1960s, the community had been ravaged by middle-class flight and municipal neglect. Businesses closed, racial tensions ran high, and the looting during the 1977 blackout was among the worst the city had seen. However, as New York's economic standing improved in the mid '90s, investment began slowly spilling into the area, spawning new businesses and the phalanxes of renovated brownstones that draw a racially diverse middle class. This moneyed influx's coexistence with Harlem's long-standing residents can be tense, but it is seldom volatile.

On 125th Street, Harlem's main artery, street preachers and ad hoc vendors of CDs, fragrance oils and jewellery vie for the attentions of the human parade. The celebrated **Apollo Theater** (*see p317*) hosts concerts and the classic Amateur Night every Wednesday – James Brown, Ella Fitzgerald, Michael Jackson and Lauryn Hill are among its starry alumni. A block east, construction is in progress on a new building for the highly regarded **Studio Museum in Harlem**, designed by David Adjaye, architect of the Smithsonian National Museum of African American History & Culture in Washington, DC. The museum continues to offer exhibitions and events that highlight artists of African descent at its temporary **Studio Museum 127** space (429 W 127th Street, between Amsterdam & Convent Avenues; 1-212 864 4500, www.studiomuseum.org) and other locations, such as the Museum of Modern Art (*see p185*). A major player in the small but growing gallery scene is **Gavin Brown's Enterprise** (439 W 127th Street, between Amsterdam & Convent Avenues; 1-212 627 5258, www.gavinbrown.biz; closed Sun, Mon), with three vast exhibition floors in an old warehouse showcasing artists such as Alex Katz and Rob Pruitt.

Lined with spruced-up, Edward Hopper-esque brick apartment buildings, Frederick Douglass Boulevard (Eighth Avenue) is sprinkled with craft-beer pubs, wine bars and coffee shops. Broad Malcolm X Boulevard (Lenox Avenue) buzzes with restaurant- and bar-goers after dark.

While most of the storied jazz clubs have closed, **Minton's Playhouse** (*see p225*) has been revived, and **Showman's** (375 W 125th Street, between St Nicholas & Morningside Avenues, 1-212 864 8941, closed Sun) is a neighbourhood old-timer. The musical legacy is traced at the small but interesting **National Jazz Museum** in Harlem, which also hosts jam sessions and performances.

❤ Time to eat & drink

Cheap Harlem eats
Charles Pan Fried Chicken Restaurant *p225*

Global soul food and a lively scene
Red Rooster Harlem *p225*

Gorgeous late-night cocktails and bites
The Honey Well *p227*, ROKC *p228*

❤ Time to shop

If it's good enough for Jay Z...
Harlem Haberdashery *p226*

Luxe pre-owned labels
Trunk Show Designer Consignment *p226*

Salvaged treasure
Demolition Depot *p227*

7 HARLEM & UPPER MANHATTAN

Restaurants & cafés

1. Amy Ruth's *p225*
2. Charles Pan Fried Chicken Restaurant *p225*
3. The Grange Bar & Eatery *p227*
4. Minton's Playhouse & The Cecil Steakhouse *p225*
5. Red Rooster Harlem *p225*
6. Taszo Espresso Bar *p229*
7. Teranga *p226*

Bars

1. The Honey Well *p227*
2. ROKC *p228*
3. Shrine *p225*

Shops & services

1. Demolition Depot *p227*
2. Harlem Haberdashery *p226*
3. Trunk Show Designer Consignment *p226*

Mount Morris Historic District

Although modern apartment buildings are scattered throughout the neighbourhood, Harlem has retained many of the buildings that went up around the turn of the century because redevelopers shunned it for so long. Of particular interest, the **Mount Morris Historic District** (from 119th to 124th Streets, between Malcolm X Boulevard/Lenox Avenue & Mount Morris Park West) contains charming brownstones and a collection of religious buildings in a variety of architectural styles.

The section of W 116th Street between Malcolm X Boulevard (Lenox Avenue) and Frederick Douglass Boulevard (Eighth Avenue) is dotted with West African shops and restaurants – the remains of a diminishing **Little Senegal**. East of the domed **Masjid Malcolm Shabazz** (no.102), the mosque of Malcolm X's ministry, is the **Malcolm Shabazz Harlem Market** (no.52), a covered outdoor bazaar with vendors selling traditional clothes, jewellery, musical instruments and other goods.

Further north is **Strivers' Row**, also known as the St Nicholas Historic District. On 138th and 139th Streets, between Adam Clayton Powell Jr Boulevard (Seventh Avenue) and Frederick Douglass Boulevard (Eighth Avenue), these harmonious blocks of brick townhouses were developed in 1891 by David H King Jr and designed by three different architects, one of whom was Stanford White. The enclave is so well preserved that the alleyway sign advising you to 'walk your horses' is still visible.

Harlem's rich history is stored in the archives of the nearby **Schomburg Center for Research in Black Culture**. This branch of the New York Public Library contains millions of documents, artefacts, films and prints relating to the cultures of peoples of African descent, with a strong emphasis on the African-American experience.

Sights & museums

National Jazz Museum in Harlem

58 W 129th Street, between Fifth Avenue & Malcolm X Boulevard (Lenox Avenue) (1-212 348 8300, www.jazzmuseuminharlem.org). Subway 2, 3 to 125th Street. **Open** *11am-5pm Mon, Thur-Sun (other times during events).* **Admission** *Suggested donation $12; free under-12s.* **Map** *p223 E13.*

Occupying a single gallery space, the Smithsonian-affiliated National Jazz Museum in Harlem has its sights on expansion. Exhibits explore the history of jazz through early figures such as composer James Reese Europe, who brought a black orchestra to Carnegie Hall in 1912; photographs and performance clips of Louis Armstrong, Fats Waller and more; plus instruments and ephemera. The centrepiece is Duke Ellington's white 1920s baby grand piano, which is occasionally tinkled during the museum's regular performances.

Schomburg Center for Research in Black Culture

*515 Malcolm X Boulevard (Lenox Avenue), between 135th & 136th Streets (1-917 275 6975, www.nypl.org/locations/schomburg). Subway 2, 3 to 135th Street. **Open** General & gallery 10am-6pm Mon, Thur-Sat; 10am-8pm Tue, Wed. Other departments hrs vary. **Admission** free. **Map** p223 D12.*

Part of the New York Public Library, this institution holds an extraordinary trove of vintage literature and historical memorabilia relating to black culture and the African diaspora, much of which was amassed by notable bibliophile Arturo Alfonso Schomburg, who was curator from 1932 until his death in 1938. (It was posthumously renamed in his honour.) Note that parts of the collection can only be viewed on certain days by appointment; call or refer to the website. The centre also hosts regular exhibitions, concerts, films, lectures and other events.

Restaurants & cafés

Amy Ruth's $-$$

*113 W 116th Street, between Malcolm X Boulevard (Lenox Avenue) & Adam Clayton Powell Jr Boulevard (Seventh Avenue) (1-212 280 8779, www.amyruths.com). Subway 2, 3 to 116th Street. **Open** 8.30am-11pm Mon; 8.30am-11pm Tue-Thur; 8.30am-5.30am Fri; 7.30am-5.30am Sat; 7.30am-11pm Sun. **Map** p223 D14* ❶ *American soul food*

This popular no-reservations spot has a broad menu of classic soul food. Delicately fried okra is delivered without a hint of slime, and the mac and cheese is gooey inside and crunchy-brown on top. Dishes take their names from notable African-Americans, such as the Reverend Al Sharpton (fried chicken and waffle) or the Michelle Obama (fried whiting).

❤ Charles Pan Fried Chicken Restaurant $

*2461 Frederick Douglass Boulevard (Eighth Avenue), at 132nd Street (1-212 281 1800). Subway B, D to 155th Street. **Open** 11am-10.30pm Mon-Thur; 11am-11pm Fri, Sat; noon-10pm Sun. **Map** p223 D12* ❷ *American Southern*

Fried chicken guru Charles Gabriel's no-frills eaterie has hopped around Harlem over the years, but devotees still rave about his speciality's moist flesh and crackly skin. In addition to the poultry, you can feast on barbecued ribs, mac and cheese, collard greens, yams and other Southern favourites.

Minton's Playhouse & The Cecil Steakhouse $$

*206 & 210 W 118th Street, between Adam Clayton Powell Jr Boulevard (Seventh Avenue) & St Nicholas Avenue (Minton's Playhouse 1-212 243 2222, www.mintonsharlem.com; The Cecil Steakhouse 1-212 866-1262, www.thececilharlem.com). Subway B, C to 116th Street. **Minton's Playhouse** hrs vary (see online calendar for shows). **The Cecil Steakhouse** 5pm-midnight Mon-Fri; noon-5pm, 6pm-midnight Sat, Sun (hrs vary in summer). **Map** p223 D14* ❹ *American*

Housed in the restored Cecil Hotel, Minton's Playhouse is a revived version of the historic jazz club where Thelonious Monk served as house pianist and Dizzy Gillespie invented Bebop. On weekend nights, plus Sunday brunch and select weeknight spots, jazz acts take to the stage anchored by a 1948 mural of Hot Lips Page. You can order dishes such as baked clams, porterhouse, pasta and more from the menu shared by the Cecil Steakhouse, in the same building. Or if you prefer, start the night with cocktails and dinner at Cecil's before the show.

❤ Red Rooster Harlem $$

*310 Malcolm X Boulevard (Lenox Avenue), between 125th & 126th Streets (1-212 792 9001, www.redroosterharlem.com). Subway 2, 3 to 125th Street. **Open** 11.30am-10.30pm Mon-Thur; 11.30am-11pm Fri; 10am-11pm Sat; 10am-10pm Sun. Bar until 2am Mon-Thur, Sun & 3am Fri, Sat. **Map** p223 D13* ❺ *American*

With its hobnobbing bar scrum, potent cocktails and lively jazz, this buzzy eaterie serves as a worthy clubhouse for the new Harlem. Superstar Ethiopian-born, Swedish-raised chef Marcus Samuelsson draws on a mix of Southern-fried, East African, Scandinavian and French flavours. At the teardrop-shaped bar, Harlem politicos mix with trendy downtowners, swilling cocktails and gorging on rib-sticking food.

Sprawling basement lounge Ginny's Supper Club (1-212 421 3821, www.ginnyssupperclub.com) is modelled after the Harlem speakeasies of the '20s with eclectic cocktails and a steady line-up of live music.

Bars

Shrine

*2271 Adam Clayton Powell Jr Boulevard (Seventh Avenue), between 133rd & 134th Streets (1-212 690 7807, www.shrinenyc.com). Subway B, C, 2, 3 to 135th Street. **Open** 4pm-3am daily. **Map** p223 D12* ❸

Playfully adapting a sign left over from the previous tenants (the Black United

Harlem Haberdashery

Foundation), the Shrine advertises itself as a 'Black United Fun Plaza'. The interior is tricked out with African art and vintage album covers, and actual vinyl adorns the ceiling. Nightly performances might feature indie rock, jazz, reggae or DJ sets. The cocktail menu aspires to similar diversity with wittily named tipples such as the rum-based Afro Trip.

Shops & services

♥ Harlem Haberdashery
245 Malcolm X Boulevard (Lenox Avenue), between 122nd & 123rd Streets (1-646 707 0070, www.harlemhaberdashery.com). Subway 2, 3 to 125th Street. **Open** *noon-8pm Mon-Fri; 1-8pm Sat; hrs vary Sun.* **Map** *p223 D14* ❷ *Fashion*

File this under 'If it's good enough for Jay Z'. Harlem Haberdashery was founded by the folks behind clothing label 5001 Flavors, which dressed the rapper for his 'Empire State of Mind' video. In addition to locally made urban-meets-preppy clothes for men and women, there are graphic T-shirts and flashy accessories such as gold-plated flasks. Fun fact: the boutique is housed in a brownstone where Malcolm X once lived.

♥ Trunk Show Designer Consignment
275-277 W 113th Street, between Adam Clayton Powell Jr Boulevard (Seventh Avenue) & Frederick Douglass Boulevard (Eighth Avenue) (1-212 662 0009, www. trunkshowconsignment.com). Subway B, C to 110th Street-Cathedral Parkway. **Open** *by appointment 1-8pm Tue-Fri; 12.30-7.30pm Sat; 12.30-6pm Sun.* **Map** *p223 D15* ❸ *Fashion*

Modelling agent Heather Jones graduated from hosting oversubscribed pop-up trunk shows to co-opening this small Harlem storefront. Men's and women's threads and accessories range from Madison Avenue labels (Gucci, Chanel, Céline, Saint Laurent) to edgier brands (Margiela, Rick Owens, Vetements), with in-season items marked down between 20% and 70%. Although the shop welcomes walk-ins, it's mainly open on an appointment basis, so it's best to call before making a special trip.

EAST HARLEM

▶ *Subway 6 to 110th Street or 116th Street.*

East of Fifth Avenue is **East Harlem**, commonly called Spanish Harlem but also known to its primarily Puerto Rican residents as El Barrio. The traditional southern boundary with the Upper East Side is 96th Street, but is becoming increasingly blurred as gentrification creeps northward. Its main east–west cross street, East 116th Street, shows signs of an influx of Mexican immigrants. The **Graffiti Hall of Fame**, a vivid, evolving street art display, adorns inside and outside walls of a schoolyard at 106th Street and Park Avenue. Be sure to check out the nearby **El Museo del Barrio** (*see p209*), too. Facing Central Park's northeast corner, the recently opened **Africa Center** (1280 Fifth Avenue, at 110th Street; 1-212 444 9795, www. theafricacenter.org, closed Mon) offers exhibitions, performances and other events, plus a contemporary counter-service pan-African eaterie.

Restaurants & cafés

▶ *For bars on the border of the Upper East Side and East Harlem, see p218.*

Teranga $
1280 Fifth Avenue, at 109th Street (no phone, www.itsteranga.com). Subway 2, 3 to Central Park North; 6 to 110th Street. **Open** *8am-7pm Tue-Fri; 9am-7pm Sat, Sun.* **Map** *p223 E15* ❼ *African*

Located in the Africa Center, Teranga – loosely translated from Senegalese to 'good hospitality' – evolves fast-casual dining into something exceptional. The airy, plant-strewn space has a laid-back, homey vibe and playful decorative touches such as a brightly painted fishing boat. West African-born chef Pierre Thiam has created a continent-spanning menu incorporating sustainably grown African ingredients. Diners order at the counter, creating their own 'market plate' by selecting a grain base, such as *attieke* (fermented cassava couscous), adding meat, fish or stew, plus a sauce, then pairing with a side such as plaintain and red palm *fufu*.

Shops & services

❤ Demolition Depot

159-161 E 126th Street, between Lexington & Third Avenues (1-212 860 1138, www. demolitiondepot.com). Subway 4, 5, 6 to 125th Street. **Open** *10am-6pm Mon-Fri; 11am-6pm Sat.* **Map** *p223 F13* ❶ *Homewares*

Even if you're not in the market for, say, a 19th-century zinc frieze with a satyr's mask or vintage elevator doors, it's fascinating to poke around the eclectic period pieces in this quirky emporium. Three floors, plus a garden are stuffed with furniture, fixtures, architectural salvage, signs, ornaments and artwork that make good on the business's goal of reclaiming building elements to preserve architectural history.

HAMILTON HEIGHTS

▶ *Subway A, B, C, D, 1 to 145th Street; 1 to 137th Street.*

Named after founding father Alexander Hamilton, who owned an estate and a farm here, **Hamilton Heights** extends from 125th Street to the Trinity Cemetery at 155th Street, between Riverside Drive and St Nicholas Avenue. Hamilton's 1802 Federal-style house, the **Grange**, now a national memorial, was moved from 287 Convent Avenue round the corner to St Nicholas Park.

The neighbourhood developed after the West Side elevated train was built in the late 19th century; it's notable for the elegant turn-of-the-20th-century row houses in the **Hamilton Heights Historic District**, centred on the side streets off scenic **Convent Avenue** between 140th and 145th Streets – just beyond the Gothic Revival-style campus of the **City College of New York** (Convent Avenue, from 135th to 140th Streets).

Sights & museums

Hamilton Grange National Memorial

St Nicholas Park, 414 W 141st Street, near Convent Avenue (1-646 548 2310, www. nps.gov/hagr). Subway A, B, C, D to 145th Street. **Visitor centre** *9am-5pm Wed-Sun.* **Tours** *10am, 11am, 2pm.* **Admission** *free.* **Map** *p223 C11.*

The Federal-style estate of America's first Secretary of the Treasury was completed two years before he was shot in a duel with Vice President Aaron Burr. Guided tours visit restored period rooms, including Hamilton's study and the parlour, with his daughter's pianoforte. Alternatively, you can peruse the house independently for an hour at noon or

3pm (space permitting; note that guided and self-guided tours are first come, first served). A short film about the founding father's life is shown in the visitor centre.

Restaurants & cafés

The Grange Bar & Eatery $$

1635 Amsterdam Avenue, at 141st Street (1-212 491 1635, www.thegrangebarnyc. com). Subway A, B, C, D to 145th Street; 1 to 137th Street-City College. **Open** *11.30am-4am Mon-Fri; 9.30am-4am Sat, Sun.* **Map** *p223 C11* ❸ *American*

Harlem goes back to its rural roots at this locavore bistro and bar, outfitted with rustic wooden tables, white-oak floors and antique chandeliers. The comfort-food menu is rooted in seasonal New York State produce with seasonal small plates and salads, hearty roast-meat mains, and a sirloin and brisket burger with cornichon remoulade. At the 40ft-long butcher-block bar, the changing selection of cocktails feature unusual flavour combinations and Harlem-referencing names.

Bars

❤ The Honey Well

3604 Broadway, between 148th & 149th Streets (1-646 861 0489, www. thehoneywellnyc.com). Subway 1 to 145th Street. **Open** *5pm-2am daily.* **Map** *p223 C10* ❶

At this sly, effortlessly cool '70s-styled cocktail den, bartenders have torched cocoa butter-topped drinks; stirred red wine ice cubes into a glowing, off-menu lava lamp tipple; and poured sips of wine directly into patrons' mouths from traditional Spanish porrons. While the old-school funk beats,

---

In the know
Hallelujah!

In the 1930s, the **Abyssinian Baptist Church** (132 Odell Clark Place/W 138th Street, between Malcolm X Boulevard/Lenox Avenue & Adam Clayton Powell Jr Boulevard/Seventh Avenue, 1-212 862 7474, www.abyssinian. org) was under the leadership of legendary civil rights crusader Adam Clayton Powell Jr. From the staid gingerbread Gothic exterior, you'd never suspect the energy that charges the church when the gospel choir gets into swing. Visitors are welcome to most 11.30am Sunday services (see website for exclusions). Get there early, and dress respectfully (no shorts, leggings or flip-flops, and shoulders must be covered).

amber lighting, wood panelling, beaded curtains and cheese ball appetisers are decidedly retro, the creative quaffs are utterly current.

♥ ROKC

3452 Broadway, between 140th & 141st Streets (no phone, www.rokcnyc.com). Subway 1 to 137th Street-City College. **Open** *5-11.15pm Mon-Thur, Sun; 5pm-midnight Fri, Sat.* **Map** *p223 C11* ②

Tucked between a neighbourhood bodega and a Latin religious-articles shop, ROKC (ramen, oysters, kitchen and cocktails, FYI) is an unadorned semi-subterranean room, paint cracking on its white walls and a handful of small tables crammed in front of a long wooden bar. But the drinks, courtesy of former Angel's Share cohorts Shigefumi Kabashima and Tetsuo Hasegawa, along with Joji Watanabe (Experimental Cocktail Club), are stunning showpieces. Swapping out a traditional cocktail glass for a lightbulb (yes, a lightbulb) set in a small pot of pebbled ice, the lavender-flecked Flower is floral without tasting like liquid potpourri, thanks to an elegant balance of Japanese barley vodka, elderflower and tart cranberry. The Tomato/ Clam registers like a smoky Bloody Mary, with mescal, a hit of wasabi and copious cracks of black pepper inside a big, beautiful seashell. The kitchen doles out the titular ramen (six varieties), East Coast oysters and Asian snacks.

WASHINGTON HEIGHTS & INWOOD

▶ *Subway A, C, 1 to 168th Street-Washington Heights; A to 175th or 190th Street; A, 1 to 181st Street; C to 163rd Street-Amsterdam Avenue; 1 to 157th or 191st Street.*

The area from West 155th Street to Dyckman (200th) Street is called **Washington Heights**. An ever-growing number of artists, musicians and young families are relocating to these parts, attracted by the spacious pre-war buildings, big parks, hilly streets and (comparatively) low rents.

Washington Heights' main attraction is the Morris-Jumel Mansion, a stunning Palladian-style house that served as a headquarters for George Washington during the autumn of 1776. On Broadway, between 155th & 156th Street, **Audubon Terrace** is a cluster of grand, early-20th-century Italian Renaissance Revival buildings on the site of 19th-century naturalist and illustrator John James Audubon's estate. Once a cultural centre that contained the Museum of the American Indian and the American Geographical Society, among

other institutions, it's still home to the **Hispanic Society of America** (Broadway, between 155th & 156th Streets; 1-212 926 2234, www.hispanicsociety.org), an overlooked gem featuring a surprising collection of masterworks. However, the society's museum is closed for an extensive renovation (see website for updates).

Since the 1920s, waves of immigrants have settled in Washington Heights. In the post-World War II era, many German-Jewish refugees (among them Henry Kissinger and Dr Ruth Westheimer) moved to the western edge of the district. Broadway was once home to a small Greek population – opera singer Maria Callas lived here in her youth. But in the last few decades, the southern and eastern parts of the area have become predominantly Spanish-speaking due to a large population of Dominican settlers.

A trek along Fort Washington Avenue, from about 173rd Street to **Fort Tryon Park**, puts you in the heart of **Hudson Heights** – the posh area of Washington Heights. Start at the **George Washington Bridge**, the city's only bridge across the Hudson River. A pedestrian walkway (also used by cyclists) commands dazzling Manhattan views. Under the bridge on the New York side is a diminutive lighthouse. To see it up close, look for the footpath on the west side of Henry Hudson Parkway below 181st Street, which leads down to the riverside Fort Washington Park and the Hudson River Greenway, a popular route for walkers, joggers and cyclists.

North of the bridge is the beautiful Fort Tryon Park; at the park's northern edge is the **Met Cloisters**, a museum built in 1938 using segments of five medieval cloisters. It houses the Metropolitan Museum of Art's medieval art collection.

Manhattan's northernmost neighbourhood, **Inwood** stretches from Dyckman Street up to Spuyten Duyvil Creek, where the Hudson and Harlem Rivers converge. Dyckman buzzes with street life from river to river, but, north of that, the island narrows considerably and the parks along the western shoreline culminate in the seclusion of **Inwood Hill Park**, another Frederick Law Olmsted legacy. It's believed that this is the location of the legendary 1626 transaction between Peter Minuit and the Native American Lenapes for the purchase of a strip of land called Manahatta – a plaque at the south-west corner of the ballpark near 214th Street marks the purported spot. The 196-acre refuge contains the island's last swathes of virgin forest and salt marsh. Today, you can hike over the hilly terrain, liberally scattered with massive glacier-deposited boulders (called erratics) and picture Manhattan as it was before development.

Morris-Jumel Mansion

Sights & museums

❤ Met Cloisters

*99 Margaret Corbin Drive, Fort Tryon Park
(1-212 923 3700, www.metmuseum.org).
Subway A to 190th Street, then 10min walk.
Open Mar-Oct 10am-5.15pm daily. Nov-Feb
10am-4.45pm daily. **Admission** (incl same-
day admission to Metropolitan Museum of
Art) $25; $12-$17 reductions; free under-12s.
Map Pull-out map B3.*

Set in a lovely park overlooking the Hudson
River, the Cloisters houses the Metropolitan
Museum's medieval art and architecture
collections. A path winds through parkland
to a castle that seems to date from the Middle
Ages; in fact, it was built in the 1930s using
pieces from five medieval French cloisters,
shipped from Europe by the Rockefeller clan.
Highlights include the impressive limestone
apse of the 12th-century Fuentidueña Chapel,
the Unicorn Tapestries and the Annunciation
triptych by Robert Campin.

❤ Morris-Jumel Mansion

*65 Jumel Terrace, between 160th & 162nd
Streets (1-212 923 8008, www.morrisjumel.
org). Subway C to 163rd Street-Amsterdam
Avenue. **Open** 10am-4pm Tue-Fri; 10am-5pm
Sat, Sun. **Admission** $10; $8 reductions; free
under-12s. **Map** p223 C8.*

Constructed in 1765, Manhattan's only
surviving pre-Revolutionary pile was
originally built for British governor
Roger Morris but later served as General
Washington's headquarters in the early
months of the Revolutionary War. Later,
an elderly Aaron Burr lived here after
marrying widow Eliza Brown Jumel in 1833.
(They divorced a year later.) The restored
interior features 19th-century pieces Eliza
commissioned from renowned furniture
designer Duncan Phyfe and a colonial-
era kitchen with the original hearth. The
handsome Palladian-style villa offers
fantastic views. While you're here, check out
its former driveway, Sylvan Terrace, which
has the longest continuous stretch (one
block in total) of old wooden houses in all of
Manhattan.

Restaurants & cafés

Taszo Espresso Bar $

*5 Edward M Morgan Place, between 157th &
158th Streets (1-212 694 8770). Subway 1 to
157th Street. **Open** 7.30am-8pm Mon-Thur;
7.30am-11pm Fri-Sun. **Map** p223 B9* ⑥
Café

At this laid-back café, you can accompany
Brooklyn-roasted Devocíon coffee with cult
baked goods such as Danny Macaroons and
Balthazar Bakery pastries, or pair light eats
such as house-made panini with a craft beer
or a glass of wine. All this, plus occasional
evening sets by local musicians, draws an
eclectic crowd that often spills out on to
the sidewalk. **Other location** 366 Audubon
Avenue, between W 183rd & W 184th Streets.

> ### In the know
> ### Local colour
>
> If you take a stroll along the river in the
> Heights' **Fort Washington Park**, you may
> spot birdlife that's a little more colourful
> than the average NYC pigeon. How a flock of
> wild bright-green monk parakeets got here
> isn't known, but local legend has it the birds'
> ancestors escaped after being shipped from
> Argentina to JFK airport in the 1960s.

Brooklyn

Not long ago, many Manhattanites baulked at the idea of crossing the East River for a day or night out. Times sure have changed. Not only is the second borough a destination in its own right, with a thriving cultural and food scene, but 'Brooklyn' has also become shorthand for a particular brand of indie cool, recognised the world over. Popular areas such as Williamsburg, known for its nightlife, and Dumbo, gateway to the gorgeous Brooklyn Bridge Park, are easily accessible – even on foot.

Settled by the Dutch in the early 17th century, Brooklyn was America's third largest municipality until its amalgamation with the four other boroughs that created New York City in 1898. Its many brownstones are a testament to a large and wealthy merchant class that made its money from the shipping trade. By the end of the 19th century, Brooklyn had become so prosperous, and its view of itself so grandiloquent, that it built copies of the Arc de Triomphe (in Grand Army Plaza) and the Champs-Elysées (Eastern Parkway), and a greensward (Prospect Park) to rival Central Park.

❤ Don't miss

1 Brooklyn Bridge *p237*
Approach the borough on foot for spectacular panoramas.

2 House of Yes *p312*
A multi-faceted venue for all kinds of revelry.

3 Time Out Market *p45*
Hand-picked eateries, plus live music and art.

4 Brooklyn Museum *p243*
The second borough's answer to the Met.

5 Green-Wood Cemetery *p244*
Where the great, the good and the bad are buried.

6 New York Transit Museum *p235*
A moving experience, especially for bus- and train-mad kids.

BROOKLYN PUBLIC LIBRARY

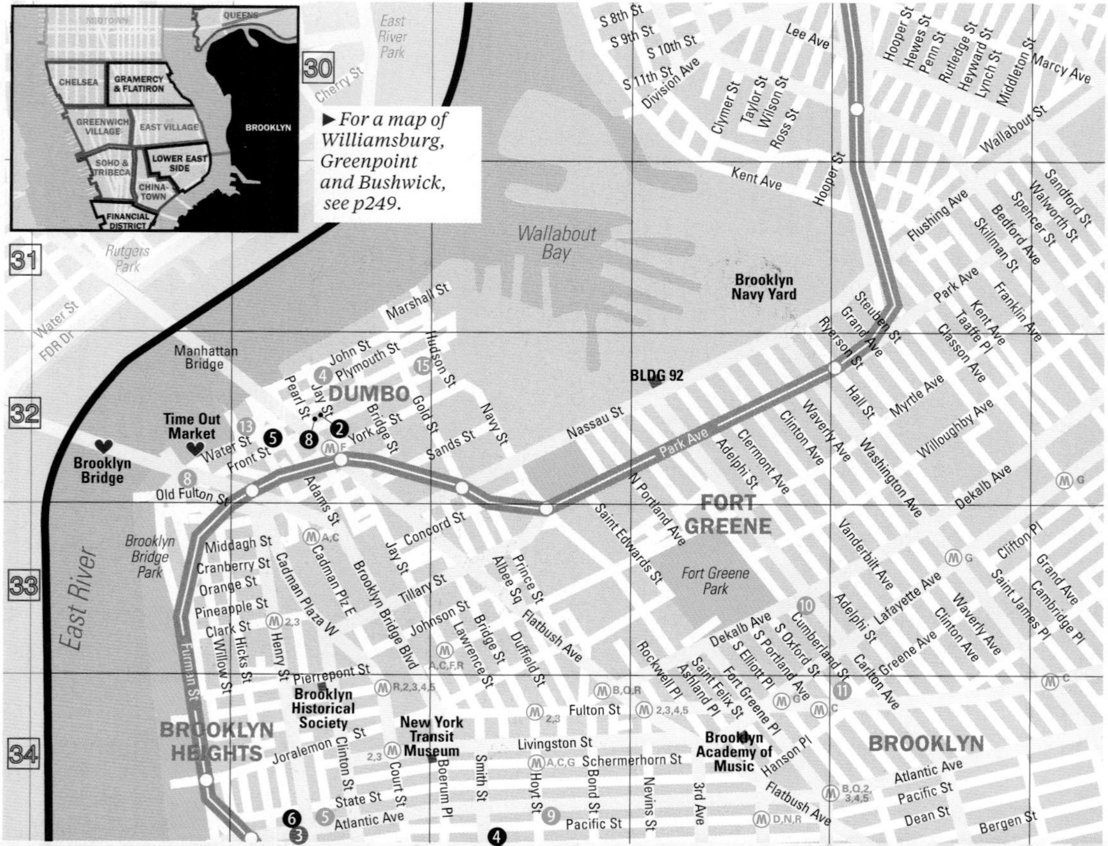

BROOKLYN

Restaurants & cafés

1. Al di Trattoria *p244*
2. Blue Marble Ice Cream *p244*
3. Brooklyn Crab *p240*
4. Brooklyn Roasting Company *p236*
5. Colonie *p236*
6. Four & Twenty Blackbirds *p245*
7. Frankies 457 Spuntino *p239*
8. Juliana's *p236*
9. Mile End *p239*
10. Miss Ada *p246*
11. No. 7 *p246*
12. Olmsted *p245*
13. One Girl Cookies *p236*
14. Ugly Baby *p239*
15. Vinegar Hill House *p236*

Bars

1. Clover Club *p239*
2. Leyenda *p239*
3. Long Island Bar *p240*
4. Seaborne *p241*
5. Sunny's Bar *p241*
6. Union Hall *p245*

Shops & services

1. Brooklyn Superhero Supply Company *p245*
2. Egg *p238*
3. Erie Basin *p241*
4. Modern Anthology *p240*
5. Powerhouse Arena *p238*
6. Salter House *p238*
7. Steve's Authentic Key Lime Pie *p241*
8. Thea Grant *p238*
9. Wooden Sleepers *p241*

▲ *For a map of Williamsburg, Greenpoint and Bushwick, see p249.*

BROOKLYN NAVY YARD

BLDG 92

FORT GREENE

Fort Greene Park

DUMBO

Time Out Market

Brooklyn Bridge

Brooklyn Bridge Park

BROOKLYN HEIGHTS

New York Transit Museum

Brooklyn Historical Society

Brooklyn Academy of Music

Wallabout Bay

East River

East River Park

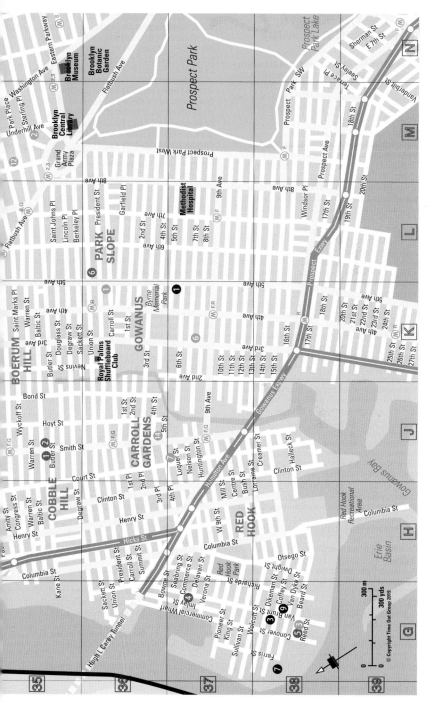

BROOKLYN

233

BROOKLYN HEIGHTS, DOWNTOWN & DUMBO

▶ *Brooklyn Heights & Downtown Brooklyn – Subway A, C, F, R to Jay Street-MetroTech; A, C, G to Hoyt-Schermerhorn; R to Court Street; 2, 3, 4, 5 to Borough Hall; 2, 3 to Clark Street. Dumbo – Subway A, C to High Street; F to York Street.*

Home to well-to-do families and professionals lured by its proximity to Wall Street, **Brooklyn Heights** is where you'll find the idyllic leafy, brownstone-lined streets of Brooklyn legend. Thanks to the area's historic district status, it has retained many Greek Revival and Italianate row houses dating from the 1820s. Take a stroll down the gorgeous tree-lined streets – try Cranberry, Hicks, Pierrepont and Willow – to see the area at its best.

Given its serenity and easy access to Manhattan, it's not surprising that Brooklyn Heights has been home to numerous illustrious (and struggling) writers. Walt Whitman printed the first edition of *Leaves of Grass* at 98 Cranberry Street (in a building since demolished); Truman Capote wrote *Breakfast at Tiffany*'s at 70 Willow Street; and Thomas Wolfe penned *Of Times and the River* at 5 Montague Terrace.

Henry and Montague Streets are peppered with shops, restaurants and bars. At the end of Montague, the **Brooklyn Heights Promenade** offers spectacular waterfront views of lower Manhattan, New York Harbor and the nearby **Brooklyn Bridge**, a marvel of 19th-century engineering.

In the other direction, **Downtown Brooklyn**'s grand **Borough Hall** (209 Joralemon Street, at Court Street), the seat of local government, stands as a monument to Brooklyn's past as an independent municipality. Completed in 1851, but only later crowned with a Victorian cupola, the Greek Revival edifice was renovated in the late 1980s. The building is linked to the **New York State Supreme Court** (360 Adams Street, between Joralemon Street & Tech Place) by Cadman Plaza (from Prospect Street to Tech Place, between **Cadman Plaza** East & Cadman Plaza West).

By the turn of the 19th century, **Dumbo** (Down Under the Manhattan Bridge Overpass) was a thriving industrial district; all kinds of manufacturers, including Brillo and Benjamin Moore, were based here, leaving behind a fine collection of factory buildings and warehouses; the most famous of these, the **Eskimo Pie Building** (100 Bridge Street, at York Street), with its embellished façade, was actually built for the Thomson Meter Company in 1908-09.

In the 1970s and '80s, these warehouses were colonised by artists seeking cheap live/work spaces. But playing out a familiar New York migration pattern, the area is now home to million-dollar apartments and an array of eateries and shops. The spectacular views – taking in the Statue of Liberty, the lower Manhattan skyline and the Brooklyn and Manhattan Bridges – remain the same. The best vantage point is below the Brooklyn Bridge at the **Fulton Ferry Landing**, which juts out over the East River at Old Fulton and Water Streets. It was here that General George Washington and his troops beat a hasty retreat by boat from the Battle of Brooklyn in 1776. It's now a stop on the NYC Ferry service (*see p384*), which links to Manhattan and Queens. Docked at the pier is one of the borough's great cultural jewels: **Bargemusic** (*see p331*), a 100-foot steel barge that was built in 1899 but has staged chamber music concerts since the 1970s.

On both sides of the landing, **Brooklyn Bridge Park** (riverside, from the Manhattan Bridge to Atlantic Avenue) has been redeveloped, with lawns, freshwater gardens, a water fowl-attracting salt marsh and the Granite Prospect, a set of stairs fashioned out of salvaged granite facing the Manhattan

---

❤ Time to eat & drink

On-site roasted morning coffee
Brooklyn Roasting Company *p236*

Laid-back brunch
Colonie *p236*, Miss Ada *p246*, Vinegar Hill House *p236*

Sweet pick-me-up
Blue Marble Ice Cream *p244*, Four & Twenty Blackbirds *p245*, Steve's Authentic Key Lime Pie *p241*

Tipples and bites
Clover Club *p239*, The Four Horsemen *p252*, Maison Premiere *p253*

Destination dinners
Aska *p248*, Olmsted *p245*, Lilia *p251*, Roberta's *p252*

Neighbourhood institutions
Peter Luger *p251*, Sunny's Bar *p241*

❤ Time to shop

Classic homewares (plus a café)
Salter House *p238*

Cool men's gear
Modern Anthology *p240*, Wooden Sleepers *p241*

Massive music store
Rough Trade *p250*

Unique vintage troves
Erie Basin *p241*, Feng Sway *p253*

skyline. But the undoubted centrepiece is the vintage merry-go-round known as **Jane's Carousel** (www.janescarousel.com), which was restored by local artist Jane Walentas over more than two decades and now occupies a Jean Nouvel-designed Plexiglas pavilion in the section of park between Main Street and the Brooklyn Bridge. Along this stretch of riverfront, the post-Civil War cargo warehouse, **Empire Stores**, has been developed into a complex housing shops, a satellite gallery of the **Brooklyn Historical Society** (see p235) and the **Time Out Market** (see p45).

The artists who flocked to the area en masse in the 1970s and '80s maintain a presence in the local galleries, most of which support the work of emerging talent. Dumbo is also home to Off Broadway standout, **St Ann's Warehouse** (see p346).

Head east on Water or Front Street to discover one of Brooklyn's forgotten neighbourhoods. Once a rough and bawdy patch dotted with bars and brothels frequented by sailors and dockworkers, **Vinegar Hill**, between Bridge Street and the Navy Yard, earned the moniker 'Hell's Half Acre' in the 19th century. Only fragments of the enclave remain (parts of it were designated a historic district in the late 1990s), and it's considerably quieter today. Although inhabited, the isolated strips of early-19th-century row houses and defunct storefronts on Bridge, Hudson and Plymouth Streets, and a stretch of Front Street, have a ghost-town quality, heightened by their juxtaposition with a Con Edison generating station. For refreshment, seek out the enclave's tavern-like **Vinegar Hill House** (see p236).

Sights & museums

Brooklyn Historical Society
128 Pierrepont Street, at Clinton Street, Brooklyn Heights (1-718 222 4111, www. brooklynhistory.org). Subway R to Court Street; 2, 3, 4, 5 to Borough Hall. **Open** *Museum noon-5pm Wed-Sun. Gift shop noon-5pm daily. Library 1-5pm Wed-Sat.* **Admission** *Suggested donation $10; $6 reductions; free under-12s, students.* **Map** *p232 H34.*

Founded in 1863, the BHS is based in a landmark Queen Anne-style building, which houses a major photo and research library containing historic maps and newspapers, oral-history interviews, documents and artefacts. The society presents long-term and temporary exhibitions (typically three to four at its main location, plus another at its satellite gallery in Dumbo, open 11am-6pm Tue-Sun) illuminating aspects of borough history, such as public health from colonial times to the present, or the Brooklyn waterfront. **Other location** Empire Stores, 55 Water Street, between Main Street & Old Dock Street, Dumbo, Brooklyn (same phone).

❤ New York Transit Museum
Corner of Boerum Place & Schermerhorn Street, Brooklyn Heights (1-718 694 1600, www.mta.info/mta/museum). Subway A, C, G to Hoyt-Schermerhorn; 2, 3, 4, 5 to Borough Hall. **Open** *10am-4pm Tue-Fri; 11am-5pm Sat, Sun.* **Admission** *$10; $5 reductions; free seniors Wed.* **Map** *p232 J34.*

Located in a historic 1936 IND subway station, this is the largest museum in the United States devoted to urban public transport history. Exhibits explore the social and practical impact of public transport on the development of greater New York; among the highlights is an engrossing walk-through display charting the construction of the city's subway system in the early 1900s, when fearless 'sandhogs' were engaged in dangerous tunnelling. A line-up of turnstiles shows their evolution from the 1894 'ticket chopper' to the current Automatic Fare Card model. But the best part is down another level to a real platform where you can board an exceptional collection of vintage subway and El ('Elevated') cars, some complete with vintage ads. **Other location** New York Transit Museum Gallery Annex & Store, Grand Central Terminal, adjacent to stationmaster's office, main concourse (1-212 878 0106; see p388).

Restaurants & cafés

♥ Brooklyn Roasting Company $
25 Jay Street, between John & Plymouth Streets, Dumbo (1-718 855 1000, www. brooklynroasting.com). Subway A, C to High Street; F to York Street. **Open** *7am-7pm daily.* **Map** *p232 H32* ④ *Café*

Supplier of fair-trade, organic beans to many top NYC spots, Brooklyn Roasting Company serves its coffee and espresso drinks in a spacious, industrial-chic on-site café. Kick back on a sofa and savour the aromas wafting from the fuel-efficient roasting machine. You can accompany your brew with baked goods or a sandwich from local purveyors. **Other locations** throughout the city.

♥ Colonie $$
127 Atlantic Avenue, between Clinton & Henry Streets, Brooklyn Heights (1-718 855 7500, www.colonienyc.com). Subway R to Court Street; 2, 3, 4, 5 to Borough Hall. **Open** *6-10.30pm Mon-Thur; 6-11.30pm Fri; 11am-3pm, 5-11.30pm Sat; 11am-3pm, 5-10.30pm Sun.* **Map** *p232 H34* ⑤ *American*

Four veterans of Nolita's defunct global-cuisine hotspot Public are behind this barnyard-chic American restaurant. Herbs from a vertical garden, on a wall dividing the bar and dining areas, are used in the short, seasonally changing menu of simple fare, such as oysters, cheeses, and small and large plates. In addition to an extensive wine list, there are local beers on tap. The popular weekend brunch features retooled hearty classics such as doughnuts and hash and eggs.

Juliana's $-$$
19 Old Fulton Street, between Front & Water Streets, Dumbo (1-718 596 6700, www.julianaspizza.com). Subway A, C to High Street; F to York Street. **Open** *11.30am-3.15pm, 4-10pm daily.* **Map** *p232 G32* ⑧ *Pizza*

For years, visitors have been making the pilgrimage to famed Dumbo pizza joint Grimaldi's – but they may not be aware that founder Patsy Grimaldi sold the place more than 20 years ago. In 2012, he burst out of retirement to reclaim his shop's first location, along with its original coal oven. This time, Grimaldi – who learned to spin dough at age 13 in his Uncle Patsy Lancieri's Harlem institution – named the spot after his mother. At Juliana's, the menu spotlights iconic red-sauce fare, including classic pizzas, such as sausage and broccoli rabe, though there are nods to modern times with pizza specials incorporating more exotic ingredients such as white truffles or guacamole.

One Girl Cookies $
33 Main Street, at Water Street, Dumbo (1-212 675 4996, www.onegirlcookies.com). Subway A, C to High Street; F to York Street. **Open** *8am-7pm Mon-Fri; 8am-7pm Sat; 9am-7pm Sun.* **Map** *p232 H32* ⑬ *Café*

Dawn Casale started her cookie business out of her Greenwich Village apartment in 2000 (hence the name), before hiring chef David Crofton to help. Now married, they run three bakery-cafés. Pair your tea cookies or a whoopie pie with a cup of Brooklyn-roasted coffee. **Other locations** 68 Dean Street, between Smith Street & Boerum Place, Cobble Hill, Brooklyn (1-212 675 4996); Industry City, Food Hall, 254 36th Street, Sunset Park, Brooklyn (1-212 675 4996).

♥ Vinegar Hill House $$
72 Hudson Avenue, between Front & Water Streets, Dumbo (1-718 522 1018, www. vinegarhillhouse.com). Subway A, C to High Street; F to York Street. **Open** *6-10.30pm Mon-Thur; 6-11pm Fri; 10.30am-3.30pm, 6-11pm Sat; 10.30am-3.30pm, 5.30-10pm Sun.* **Map** *p232 H32* ⑮ *American creative*

A visit to Vinegar Hill House feels like a magical adventure to another time and place. The cosy, tavern-like eatery is virtually hidden in a residential street in the forgotten neighbourhood of Vinegar Hill (now essentially part of Dumbo). The frequently changing menu focuses on eclectic seasonal dishes, many cooked in the restaurant's wood-fired oven. In the warmer months, linger over brunch or dinner in the secluded back garden.

❤ Brooklyn Bridge

Subway A, C to High Street; J to Chambers Street; 4, 5, 6 to Brooklyn Bridge-City Hall. **Map** *p232 G32.*

Every day, thousands of people walk or bike across the wide, wood-planked promenade of the Brooklyn Bridge, taking in views of New York Harbor, the Statue of Liberty and the skyscrapers of lower Manhattan (not to mention the motorists on the car level below). But it was once an even more vital link in New York's infrastructure. Designed by John Roebling, the bridge was built in response to the harsh winter of 1867, when the East River froze over, severing connection between Manhattan and what was then the nation's third most populous city. When it opened in 1883, the 5,989ft-long structure was the world's longest bridge, and the first in the world to use steel suspension cables.

Construction began on the Brooklyn side. To lay the foundation on bedrock 44ft below, workers in airtight containers chipped away at the riverbed. More than 100 were paralysed with the bends, caused by the change in air pressure when they surfaced. When the Manhattan side was built, chief engineer Washington Roebling – John Roebling's son – got the bends too. He wasn't the only family casualty: John died in 1869 after his foot was crushed by a docking ferry. Washington spent the next decade watching the bridge's progress through a telescope and relaying directions through his wife, Emily. (A plaque on the Brooklyn tower honours her.) Fearing more deaths on the Manhattan tower, he stopped construction before it reached the 100ft-deep bedrock. To this day, the tower rests on sand and hardpan.

Brooklyn Heights

Shops & services

Egg
72 Jay Street, between Front & Water Streets, Dumbo (1-347 356 4097, www.egg-baby.com). Subway A, C to High Street; F to York Street. **Open** *10am-6pm daily.* **Map** *p232 H32* ❷ *Children*

Set in the old HQ of the Grand Union Tea Company, designer Susan Lazar's NYC store has a retro garment-factory vibe. Among her seasonally changing creations for babies and children you might find adorable patterned baby rompers, unique print dresses for girls, and classic blazers for boys. While the bulk of the collection is for kids aged eight and under, select styles go up to age ten or 12. **Other location** 104 Franklin Street, between West Broadway & Church Street, Tribeca (1-646 780 1915).

Powerhouse Arena
28-32 Adams Street, between Front & Water Streets, Dumbo (1-718 666 3049, www. powerhousearena.com). Subway A, C to High Street; F to York Street. **Open** *10am-7pm daily (hrs vary in summer).* **Map** *p232 H32* ❺ *Books*

Also serving as a gallery and performance space, the Powerhouse Arena is the cavernous retail arm of Powerhouse Books, which produces coffee-table books on such diverse subjects as retro NYC music flyers, celebrity dogs and the Brooklyn Navy Yard. In addition

to lifestyle, design and photography tomes, the store stocks fiction and children's books. **Other location** Powerhouse on 8th, 1111 Eighth Avenue, between 11th & 12th Streets, South Slope, Brooklyn (1-718 801 8375).

♥ Salter House
119 Atlantic Avenue, at Henry Street, Brooklyn Heights (1-347 987 4675, www. salter.house). Subway R to Court Street; 2, 3, 4, 5 to Borough Hall. **Open** *8am-6pm daily.* **Map** *p232 H34* ❻ *Homewares*

Owned by the same couple as next-door art gallery Picture Room, Salter House combines a shop selling aesthetically appealing, sustainable homewares and a café in one light-suffused space. Displayed in wooden cupboards or on the walls, goods include walnut or maple spoons hand-carved in Brooklyn, Indian woven jute bags, wood-handled washing-up brushes, linen aprons, embroidered nightdresses, children's clothing and nostalgic toys like spinning tops. Perch on a cushioned window seat to sip La Colombe coffee or one of the small-batch Leaves and Flowers teas – also available for purchase.

Thea Grant
63B Pearl Street, between Front & Water Streets, Dumbo (1-917 330 9258, www. theagrant.com). Subway A, C to High Street; F to York Street. **Open** *noon-7pm Wed-Sat; 11am-6pm Sun.* **Map** *p232 H32* ❽ *Accessories*

Married jewellers Thea Grant and Nico Bazzani showcase their collections in this small, antiques-cluttered shop set within a Dumbo warehouse. Old-fashioned cabinets hold the couple's vintage finds as well as creations based on them and crafted from recycled metals. At the workbench in the front, simple brass, copper or silver bracelets, as well as brass pendants, money clips and key rings, are customised with words or letters using antique hand-carved stamps.

BOERUM HILL, CARROLL GARDENS & COBBLE HILL

▶ *Subway A, C, F to Jay Street-MetroTech; F, G to Bergen Street or Carroll Street; 2, 3, 4, 5 to Borough Hall.*

These blurry-boundaried 'hoods, which go by the convenient if annoying real estate agents' portmanteau BoCoCa, are a prime example of gentrification at work. The mile-long stretch of Atlantic Avenue between Henry and Nevins Streets, most of which falls under **Boerum Hill**, was once crowded with Middle Eastern restaurants and markets. Only a few remain, including the sprawling **Sahadi's** (no.187, between Clinton & Court Streets, Cobble Hill, 1-718 624 4550, sahadis.com, closed Sun), a neighbourhood institution that sells olives, spices, cheeses, nuts and other gourmet treats. Antique and modern furniture stores are clustered alongside small, local-designer clothing boutiques between Bond and Hoyt Streets.

The stretch of Smith Street that runs from Atlantic Avenue to the Carroll Street subway stop is lined with restaurants and bars, interspersed with upscale clothing stores.

West of Smith Street, **Cobble Hill** has a palpable small-town feel. Here, **Court Street** is dotted with cafés and shops.

Further south, you'll cross into **Carroll Gardens**, which retains a few traditional Italian-American food stores, such as **Caputo Bakery** (329 Court Street, between Sackett & Union Streets, 1-718 875 6871) and **G Esposito & Sons** butchers (357 Court Street, between President & Union Streets, 1-718 875 6863; closed Sun in summer), plus a handful of browse-worthy shops among the restaurants and bars.

Restaurants & cafés

Frankies 457 Spuntino $$

457 Court Street, between Lucquer Street & 4th Place, Carroll Gardens (1-718 403 0033, www.frankies457.com). Subway F, G to Carroll Street. Open 11am-11pm Mon-Thur, Sun; 11am-midnight Fri, Sat. Map p232 J37 ❼ *Italian*

This casual Italian eatery was an instant classic when it debuted in Carroll Gardens in 2004. The mavericks behind the place – collectively referred to as 'the Franks' Castronovo and Falcinelli – went on to become neighbourhood pillars, opening German-leaning steakhouse Prime Meats down the block. Their flagship remains as alluring as ever, turning out an impressive selection of cheeses, antipasti and cured meats, distinctive salads and exceptional pastas to a mostly local crowd. Cavatelli with hot sausage and browned sage butter is a staple, as are the flawless meatballs – feather-light orbs stuffed into a sandwich or served solo. **Other location** Frankies 570 Spuntino, 570 Hudson Street, at 11th Street, West Village (1-212 924 0818).

Mile End $-$$

97A Hoyt Street, between Atlantic Avenue & Pacific Street, Boerum Hill (1-718 852 7510, www.mileenddeli.com). Subway A, C, G to Hoyt-Schermerhorn; 2, 3 to Hoyt Street. Open 8am-10pm Mon-Fri; 10am-10pm Sat, Sun. Map p232 J34 ❾ *Deli*

New Yorkers have pastrami, Montrealers have smoked meat – luscious brisket that's been dry-rubbed, cured, smoked, steamed and hand cut, resulting in flavourful, delicious slices bound for mustard-slathered rye. This Montreal-style deli serves the sandwiches in old-school fashion, along with other regional specialities – like the excellent poutine (including a smoked-meat riff) and a killer hash.

Ugly Baby $$

407 Smith Street, between 4th & 5th Streets, Carroll Gardens (1-347 689-3075, www.uglybabynyc.com). Subway F, G to Carroll Street. Open 5-10.30pm Mon-Fri; noon-3.30pm, 5-10.30pm Sat, Sun. Map p232 J36 ⓮ *Thai*

It may not be scientifically proven, but spicy food is addictive – especially at this small eatery tucked on a quiet stretch of Smith Street. Whether you're ordering the 'stay-away spicy' Udon Thani duck salad or the khao soi, a northern curry noodle soup with beef shank, the servers will warn you over and over to be careful. You'll go against their advice and end up begging for more of the cooling cucumbers to ward off the heat. But the sweat and tears are worth it because the food is so good.

Bars

❤ Clover Club

210 Smith Street, between Baltic & Butler Streets, Cobble Hill (1-718 855 7939, www.cloverclubny.com). Subway F, G to Bergen Street. Open 4pm-2am Mon-Thur; 4pm-4am Fri; 10.30am-4am Sat; 10.30am-1am Sun. Map p232 J35 ❶

Classic cocktails are the signature tipples at Julie Reiner's Victorian-styled cocktail parlour. Royales, fizzes, punches and cobblers all get their due at the 19th-century mahogany bar. Highbrow snacks (fried oysters, steak tartare) accompany drinks like the eponymous Clover Club (with gin, raspberry syrup, egg whites, dry vermouth and lemon juice).

Leyenda

221 Smith Street, between Baltic & Butler Streets, Cobble Hill (1-347 987 3260, leyendabk.com). Subway F, G to Bergen Street. Open 5pm-2am Mon-Thur; 5pm-3am Fri; noon-3am Sat; noon-1am Sun. Map p232 J35 ❷

True to her name, Ivy Mix stirs an incredible cocktail, which stands to reason since she served as Julie Reiner's head bartender at nearby Clover Club. This pan-Latin follow-up has a mystic-cool space rigged with Indio candles, cathedral-pew booths and a golden tin ceiling imprinted with crosses. Pulling from her time spent living and working in Guatemala, Argentina and Peru, Mix pours South of the Border cocktails that go well beyond tequila. Grab one of her more tropically minded numbers – like the Tia Mia, a riff on a mai tai made with mescal, rum, lime, orgeat and curaçao – and head for the breezy, tree-filled, salsa-soundtracked patio out back. Latin eats include tacos and larger plates such as Grandma Torres's *pernil con mofongo*, starring a pork shoulder braised for 48 hours that shreds with the single swipe of a fork and is served with garlicky smashed green plantains.

Long Island Bar

110 Atlantic Avenue, at Henry Street, Cobble Hill (1-718 625 8908, thelongislandbar. com). Subway F, G to Bergen Street; 2, 3, 4, 5 to Borough Hall. Open 5.30pm-midnight Mon-Thur, Sun; 5.30pm-2am Fri, Sat. Map p232 H34 ❸

A revivalist spirit is at the core of this retro-fitted bar from cocktail vet Toby Cecchini, which was formerly a mid-century greasy spoon. The menu swaps the tortas that once powered neighbourhood blue-collars for Cecchini's fine-tuned list of seven bedrock quaffs. Here you'll find a biting but balanced rye-and-Campari Boulevardier and a tart gimlet, given a fiery kick from ginger grated into the lime cordial. The iconic signage and old-line interior – terrazzo floors, Formica walls – have been preserved with an almost religious reverence, down to the faded cigarette burns that still cheetah-spot the gleaming art deco bar.

Shops & services

❤ Modern Anthology

123 Smith Street, between Dean & Pacific Streets, Boerum Hill (1-929 250 2880, www. modernanthology.com). Subway F, G to Bergen Street. Open 11am-7pm Mon-Thur; 11.30am-7.30pm Fri, Sat; 11am-6pm Sun. Map p232 J35 ❹ *Fashion/homewares*

Becka Citron and John Marsala, who helped create the *Man Caves* TV series, are behind this lifestyle shop attached to their interior design studio, bringing together vintage and contemporary homewares, clothing, accessories and grooming products. Understatedly stylish dudes can update their wardrobes with well-made shirts, sweaters and jeans from independent labels such as Save Khaki, Corridor, Umber & Ochre and Raleigh Denim. Hip furnishings skew industrial or mid-century, including sleek leather seating and decor items such as retro pennants emblazoned with Brooklyn neighbourhood names.

RED HOOK

▶ *Subway A, C, F, R to Jay Street-MetroTech, then B57 bus; F, G to Smith-9th Streets, then B61 bus; NYC Ferry from Wall Street-Pier 11.*

To the south-west of Carroll Gardens, beyond the Brooklyn-Queens Expressway, the formerly rough-and-tumble industrial locale of **Red Hook** has long avoided urban renewal. In recent years, however, the arrival of gourmet mega-grocer Fairway, Swedish furniture superstore IKEA and several new restaurants have served notice that gentrification is moving in.

Luckily for its protective residents, the Hook still feels secluded, tucked away on a peninsula. While the area continues to evolve, its time-warp charm is still evident, and its decaying piers make a moody backdrop for old warehouses and trucks clattering over cobblestone streets. The lack of public transport has thus far prevented it from becoming overdeveloped. From the Smith-9th Streets subway stop, it's either a half-hour walk south or a transfer to the B61 bus. However, a new, low-cost ferry service from downtown Manhattan has boosted the transportation options (*see p384*).

The area offers singular views of the Statue of Liberty and New York Harbor from **Valentino Pier**, and has an eclectic selection of bars, eateries and artists' studios. To see local creative output, seek out **Kentler International Drawing Space** (353 Van Brunt Street, between Wolcott & Dikeman Streets, 1-718 875 2098, www. kentlergallery.org, closed Mon-Wed & Jan, Aug) or check the website of **Brooklyn Waterfront Artists Coalition** (481 Van Brunt Street, 1-718 596 2506/7, www.bwac. org) for details of its large group shows at weekends in spring, summer and autumn.

Restaurants & cafés

Brooklyn Crab $$

24 Reed Street, between Conover & Van Brunt Streets (1-718 643 2722, www.brooklyncrab. com). Subway F, G to Smith-9th Streets, then B61 bus. Open Mid Mar-mid Oct 11.30am-10pm Mon-Thur, Sun; 11.30am-11pm Fri, Sat. Mid Oct-mid Mar 11.30am-10pm Wed, Thur, Sun; 11.30am-11pm Fri, Sat. Map p232 G38 ❸ *Seafood*

Channelling Maine's minigolf clam shacks, this hulking 250-seat spot brings games and seaside flavours to Red Hook's waterfront. Elevated on stilts, the three-storey stand-alone restaurant is done up with wharf-themed flourishes: lobster traps, fishing rods and a mounted shark's head. Gather friends

In the know
The truck stops here

At weekends from May through October, Latin American food trucks descend on the corner of Bay and Clinton Streets, adjacent to the Red Hook Ball Fields, to serve up some of the best street food in the city, including Ecuadorean ceviche, Salvadoran *papusas*, and Mexican tacos and *huaraches*. Originally catering to soccer players, the vendors now attract foodies from all over. For more info, see www.redhookfoodvendors.com or their Facebook or Twitter page.

for a round of minigolf or cornhole (beanbag toss) outdoors, then grab a picnic table and dig into simple coastal fare, such as peel-and-eat shrimp, and steam pots brimming with crabs and lobster. Drinkers can sip margaritas and piña coladas or split a mixed bucket of five beers on the open-air roof deck, with views of New York's Upper Bay.

Bars

Seaborne
228 Van Brunt Street, at Commerce Street (1-718 852 4888). Subway F, G to Smith-9th Streets, then B61 bus. **Open** *5pm-3am daily.* **Map** *p232 G37* ❹

When pioneering drinks legend Sasha Petraske died unexpectedly at the age of 42 in 2015, cocktail-loving New York mourned the loss of one of its most influential barkeeps. Following Petraske's passing, his erstwhile protégé and Middle Branch partner Lucinda Sterling, along with longtime cohort John Bonsignore, sought to carry out his final act, seeing through the construction of this snug boîte, with only a few crimson leather-padded booths and barstools. Sterling taps into Petraske's mantra of harmony in cocktails with expertly balanced drinks such as the bar's pisco sour, a textbook example of the Peruvian classic with shaken egg white providing a wonderful froth to tame the rustic bite of grape brandy.

❤ Sunny's Bar
253 Conover Street, between Beard & Reed Streets (1-718 625 8211, www.sunnysredhook.com). Subway F, G to Smith-9th Streets, then B61 bus. **Open** *5pm-midnight Mon; 4pm-2am Tue; 4pm-4am Wed; 3pm-4am Thur, Fri; 11am-4am Sat; 11am-midnight Sun.* **No cards.** **Map** *p232 G38* ❺

This treasured time-warp watering hole has been passed down in the same family since 1890. After the death of octogenarian owner Sunny Balzano in 2016, its future seemed shaky, but thanks to the bar's many fans, his widow was able to raise the necessary funds to ensure its survival. The eclectic, convivial crowd brings together hard-drinking regulars, local artists and hip millennials soaking up the dimly lit, Old World vibe, with its hodge podge of folk art, knick-knacks from the 1940s and perfect location just off New York Harbor. A local music hub, Sunny's holds bluegrass jamborees every Saturday at 9pm (bring an instrument and join in!), and other nights feature everything from sultry jazz singers to blues bands.

Shops & services

❤ Erie Basin
388 Van Brunt Street, at Dikeman Street (1-718 554 6147, eriebasin.com). Subway F, G to Smith-9th Streets, then B61 bus. **Open** *hrs vary; usually noon-6pm Wed-Sat.* **Map** *p232 G38* ❸ *Accessories*

For a one-of-a-kind keepsake, check out Russell Whitmore's finely honed collection of jewellery dating from the 18th century to the 1970s. The striking stock spans everything from unusual fin de siècle earrings, lockets and brooches to art deco cocktail rings. Vintage engagement and wedding rings are a speciality. Whitmore often incorporates antique gems in his EB line of fine jewellery, which is also available in the shop, alongside a selection of furniture and decorative objects. The hours sometimes vary seasonally, so it's best to call before making a special trip.

❤ Steve's Authentic Key Lime Pie
185 Van Dyke Street, at Ferris Street (1-718 858 5333, www.keylime.com). Subway F, G to Smith-9th Streets, then B61 bus. **Open** *hrs vary; usually noon-6pm Mon-Thur; noon-7pm Fri; 11am-7pm Sat; 11am-6pm Sun.* **Map** *p232 G38* ❼ *Food & drink*

An authentic Florida dessert in Brooklyn? Miami transplant and Key Lime pie purist Steve Tarpin and his crew make small-batch treats using freshly squeezed citrus at this quirky Red Hook institution. In the bakery, you can buy the signature graham-cracker-crusted pies (in ten-inch, eight-inch or single-serving four-inch sizes), filled with a condensed-milk custard laced with zesty lime juice. Also available is the Swingle, a frozen tartlet on a stick, dipped in dark Belgian chocolate.

❤ Wooden Sleepers
395 Van Brunt Street, between Coffey & Van Dyke Streets (1-718 643 0802, wooden-sleepers.com). Subway F, G to Smith-9th Streets, then B61 bus. **Open** *noon-6pm Wed-Sun; by appointment Mon, Tue.* **Map** *p232 G38* ❾ *Fashion*

After running a successful online shop and flea-market booths, Brian Davis found a permanent home for his curated collection of vintage menswear in this appropriately nostalgic storefront in a freestanding clapboard house. Spanning the 1930s to the '90s, the stock is displayed on industrial garment racks and weathered wooden shelves, interspersed with old fishing books, canteens and collegiate memorabilia. The classic American workwear, military and outdoor gear include perfectly aged hunting and field jackets, flannel shirts and athletic team T-shirts.

PARK SLOPE, GOWANUS & PROSPECT HEIGHTS

▶ *Park Slope & Gowanus – Subway F, G to 7th Avenue, 15th Street-Prospect Park; F, G, R to Fourth Avenue-9th Street; R to Union Street. Prospect Heights – Subway B, Q, Franklin Avenue S to Prospect Park; B, Q to Seventh Avenue; 2, 3 to Grand Army Plaza or Eastern Parkway-Brooklyn Museum.*

Bustling with parents pushing baby strollers and herding lively children, **Park Slope** houses hip young families in Victorian brownstones and feeds them organically from the nation's oldest working food co-operative (only open to members). The neighbourhood's intellectual, progressive and lefty political heritage is palpable. Famous residents include literary couple Paul Auster and Siri Hustvedt and actors Maggie Gyllenhaal, Peter Sarsgaard and Patrick Stewart.

Fifth Avenue is Park Slope's strip for restaurants, bars and shops, but in recent years interest has shifted west to **Gowanus**, the post-industrial area hugging the canal of the same name. It might seem baffling that anyone would want to build glitzy condos or big retail shops near a polluted waterway, but that's precisely what's happening. In 2010, the Environmental Protection Agency identified the canal as a hazardous-waste site, and clean-up is expected to continue until at least the early '20s (though there are fears it could be delayed by recent federal budget cuts). All-purpose performance hub the **Bell House** (*see p317*) was among the first hotspots in the area, joined in 2014 by the Miami-esque **Royal Palms Shuffleboard Club** (*see p244*). The arrival of upscale supermarket Whole Foods at the corner of Third Avenue and 3rd Street is a sure signal of rising property prices.

On the western edge of Prospect Park is a section of the **Park Slope Historic District**, graced by brownstones and several fine examples of Romanesque Revival and Queen Anne residences. Particularly charming are the brick edifices that line Carroll Street, Montgomery Place and Berkeley Place. Fans of writer-director Noah Baumbach, who grew up in these parts, may recognise the locale from 2005 hit *The Squid and the Whale*, much of which was set here.

Brooklyn Museum

Central Park may be bigger and far more famous, but **Prospect Park** (main entrance at Grand Army Plaza, Prospect Heights, 1-718 965 8999, www.prospectpark.org) has a more rustic quality. This masterpiece, which designers Frederick Law Olmsted and Calvert Vaux said was more in line with their vision than Central Park, is a great spot for birdwatching, especially with a little guidance from the Prospect Park Audubon Center at the Boathouse. You can pretend you've left the city altogether by hiking along the paths of the Ravine District (park entrances on Prospect Park West, at 3rd, 9th & 15th Streets), a landscape of dense woods, waterfalls and stone bridges in the park's centre.

Children enjoy riding the hand-carved horses at the antique carousel (Flatbush Avenue, at Empire Boulevard) and seeing real animals in the **Prospect Park Zoo** (park entrance on Flatbush Avenue, near Ocean Avenue, Prospect Heights, 1-718 399 7339, www.prospectparkzoo.com). A 15-minute walk from Prospect Park in the Sunset Park neighbourhood is the verdant necropolis of **Green-Wood Cemetery**.

Near the main entrance to Prospect Park sits the massive Civil War memorial arch at **Grand Army Plaza** (intersection of Flatbush Avenue, Eastern Parkway & Prospect Park West) and the imposing art deco central branch of the **Brooklyn Public Library** (10 Grand Army Plaza, Prospect Heights, 1-718 230 2100, www.bklynlibrary.org). Around the corner are the tranquil **Brooklyn Botanic Garden** and the **Brooklyn Museum**. East of here, in the Crown Heights neighbourhood, is the **Brooklyn Children's Museum**, which lays claim to being the first of its kind.

North of the park, on the edge of Downtown Brooklyn, the **Barclays Center** (*see p316*) is a major concert venue and the home of the (rechristened) Brooklyn Nets.

Sights & museums

Brooklyn Botanic Garden
*990 Washington Avenue, at Eastern Parkway, Prospect Heights (1-718 623 7200, www.bbg. org). Subway B, Q to Prospect Park; S to Botanic Garden; 2, 3 to Eastern Parkway-Brooklyn Museum; 2, 3, 4, 5 to Franklin Avenue. **Open** Mar-Oct 8am-6pm Tue-Fri; 10am-6pm Sat, Sun. Nov 8am-4.30pm Tue-Fri; 10am-4.30pm Sat, Sun. Dec-Feb 10am-4.30pm Tue-Sun. **Admission** $15; $8 reductions; free under-12s. See website for free admission days. **Map** p232 N36.*

This 52-acre haven of luscious greenery was founded in 1910. In spring, when Sakura Matsuri, the annual Cherry Blossom Festival,

takes place, prize buds and Japanese culture are in full bloom. Linger in serene spots such as the Japanese Hill-and-Pond Garden, one of the first Japanese-inspired gardens in the US, and the Shakespeare Garden, brimming with plants mentioned in the Bard's works. Start your stroll at the eco-friendly visitor centre, which has a green roof filled with 45,000 plants.

Brooklyn Children's Museum
*145 Brooklyn Avenue, at St Marks Avenue, Crown Heights (1-718 735 4400, www. brooklynkids.org). Subway A, C to Nostrand Avenue; C to Kingston-Throop Avenues; 3 to Kingston Avenue. **Open** 10am-5pm Tue, Wed, Fri; 10am-6pm Thur; 10am-7pm Sat, Sun. **Admission** $11; free under-1s. Pay what you wish 2-6pm Thur; 4-7pm Sun.*

Founded in 1899, the first museum created specifically for kids was retooled for the 21st century with a major renovation in 2008. The star attraction, 'World Brooklyn', is an interactive maze of small mom-and-pop shops based on real-world Brooklyn businesses. 'Neighborhood Nature' puts the spotlight on the borough's diverse ecosystems with a collection of pond critters in terrariums and a tide-pool touch tank. Little ones up to age six will delight in 'Totally Tots', a sun-drenched play space with a water station, sand zone, and a special hub for babies aged 18 months and under.

♥ Brooklyn Museum
*200 Eastern Parkway, at Washington Avenue, Prospect Heights (1-718 638 5000, www. brooklynmuseum.org). Subway 2, 3 to Eastern Parkway-Brooklyn Museum. **Open** 11am-6pm Wed, Fri-Sun; 11am-10pm Thur; 11am-11pm 1st Sat of mth (except Jan & Sept). **Admission** Suggested donation $16; $10 reductions; free under-20s. Some special exhibitions $20-$25; $8-$12 reductions. Free 5-11pm 1st Sat of mth (except Jan & Sept). **Map** p232 M35.*

Among the many assets of Brooklyn's premier institution are the third-floor Egyptian galleries; highlights include the Mummy Chamber, an installation of 170 objects, including human and animal mummies. Also on this level, works by Cézanne, Monet

---

In the know
Arty party

On the first Saturday of each month, the **Brooklyn Museum** (*see above*) stays open until 11pm and puts on music and dance performances, talks, workshops, films and more. Admission is waived from 5pm until closing, but it's a good idea to get there early since events are free but ticketed on a first-come, first-served basis.

Royal Palms Shuffleboard Club
Bringing the sport of seniors to the next generation

The vibe is Florida by way of post-industrial Gowanus at this cavernous, pastel-streaked playground with ten sunken aquamarine courts and black-and-white cabanas. The place isn't a mere posing ground, though, thanks to the genuine passion for shuffleboard of owners Jonathan Schnapp and Ashley Albert (ranked no. four and no. 26 in the world, respectively). In the hangar-like space, bag a first-come, first-served court ($40 an hour). White-clad staff initiate newbies into the rules and lingo – the stick is called the 'tang', the puck is a 'biscuit'. If you're looking for pointers, watch the pros during league nights on Monday and Tuesday, before nabbing a court when they open up at around 10pm. Regular DJs add to the party atmosphere and a rotating line-up of food trucks provides the eats, from Greek souvlaki to pasta, to go with your tropical cocktail or craft beer from the venue's two extra-long bars.

▶ *514 Union Street, between Nevins Street & Third Avenue (1-347 223 4410, www. royalpalmsshuffle.com). Open 6pm-midnight Mon-Thur; 6pm-2am Fri; noon-2am Sat; noon-10pm Sun. Closed Mon July-mid Sept. Subway R to Union Street. Map p249 J26.*

and Degas, part of an impressive European art collection, are displayed in the museum's skylighted Beaux-Arts Court. The Elizabeth A Sackler Center for Feminist Art on the fourth floor is dominated by Judy Chicago's monumental mixed-media installation, *The Dinner Party*. The fifth floor is mainly devoted to American works, including Albert Bierstadt's immense *A Storm in the Rocky Mountains, Mt Rosalie*, and the Visible Storage-Study Center, where paintings, furniture and other objects are intriguingly juxtaposed. It's always worth checking the varied schedule of temporary shows, and the institution is also home to The Norm, a restaurant helmed by Michelin-starred chef Saul Bolton.

❤ Green-Wood Cemetery
Fifth Avenue, at 25th Street, Sunset Park (1-718 210 3080, www.green-wood.com). Subway R to 25th Street. Open Apr-Sept 7am-7pm daily. Oct-Mar 8am-5pm daily. Admission free. Map p232 K39.

Filled with Victorian mausoleums, cherubs and gargoyles, hills and ponds, this lush 478-acre landscape is the resting place of some half-million New Yorkers, among them Jean-Michel Basquiat, Leonard Bernstein, Boss Tweed and Horace Greeley.

Restaurants & cafés
Al di la Trattoria $$
248 Fifth Avenue, at Carroll Street, Park Slope (1-718 783 4565, www.aldilatrattoria.com). Subway R to Union Street. Open noon-3pm, 5.30-10pm Mon-Thur; noon-3pm, 5.30-11pm Fri; 11am-3pm, 5.30-11pm Sat; 11am-3pm, 5-10pm Sun. Map p232 K36 ❶ *Italian*

A fixture on the Slope's Fifth Avenue since 1998, this convivial restaurant, owned by married couple Emiliano Coppa and chef Anna Klinger, is still extremely popular and reservations are only accepted for large groups. It's worth the inevitable wait for Klinger's northern Italian dishes, such as braised rabbit with black olives atop polenta, and superb simple pastas such as house-made tagliatelle *al ragù*. The full menu is also served in the restaurant's bar, which has a separate entrance round the corner on Carroll Street.

❤ Blue Marble Ice Cream $
186 Underhill Avenue, between St Johns & Sterling Places, Prospect Heights (1-718 399 6926, www.bluemarbleicecream. com). Subway 2, 3 to Grand Army Plaza. Open 7am-10pm Mon-Thur; 7am-11pm Fri; 8am-11pm Sat; 8am-10pm Sun. Map p232 M35 ❷ *Ice-cream*

With dozens of rotating seasonal flavours, including tangy strawberry or creamy sea salt caramel, Blue Marble is beloved by locals of all ages. Produced in NYC's only certified-organic ice-cream plant, in Sunset Park's Industry City, it's a cut above standard scoops. **Other location** Industry City, ground floor, 220 36th Street, between Second & Third Avenues, Sunset Park, Brooklyn (1-718 858 5551).

❤ Four & Twenty Blackbirds $
*439 Third Avenue, at 8th Street, Gowanus (1-718 499 2917, www.birdsblack.com). Subway F, G, R to Fourth Avenue-9th Street. **Open** 8am-8pm Mon-Fri; 9am-8pm Sat; 10am-7pm Sun. **Map** p232 K37* ⑥ *Café*

South Dakota-reared Emily and Melissa Elsen learned pie-baking from their grandma, and her expert instruction is evident in varieties such as lemon chess, salted caramel apple and the rich chocolate-and-custard Black Bottom Oat. Settle in at one of the communal tables in the homey space and savour a slice. **Other location** 634 Dean Street, between Carlton & Vanderbilt Avenues, Prospect Heights, Brooklyn (1-347 350 5110).

❤ Olmsted $$
*659 Vanderbilt Avenue, at Park Place, Prospect Heights (1-718 552 2610, www. olmstednyc.com). Subway B, Q to Seventh Avenue; 2, 3 to Grand Army Plaza. **Open** 5.30-10pm Mon-Thur; 5-10.30pm Fri, Sat; 5-9.30pm Sun. **Map** p232 M35* ⑫ *American creative*

It would be eye-roll-inducing if it weren't so goddamned great: a Brooklyn restaurant so zoom-focused on fresh produce that it's outfitted with a working mini-farm in the back, where a live bird squawks in a corner coop as twenty-somethings Instagram their crawfish crackers. But it's what chef Greg Baxtrom does, and all that farm-to-table fuss sets Olmsted apart from like-minded eateries. He cranks out smart, seasonal dishes that are approachable, affordable and downright craveable, such as a tender carrot crêpe filled with plump littleneck clams.

Bars
Union Hall
*702 Union Street, between Fifth & Sixth Avenues, Park Slope (1-718 638 4400, www. unionhallny.com). Subway R to Union Street. **Open** 4pm-4am Mon-Fri; 1pm-4am Sat, Sun. **Map** p232 L36* ⑥

In Union Hall's main space, outfitted with bookshelves, fireplaces, Soviet-era globes and paintings of fez-capped men, bar-goers pair burgers with microbrews before battling it out on the clay bocce courts in the back. Downstairs, the taxidermy-filled basement has a stage for bands, comedians and offbeat events.

Shops & services
Brooklyn Superhero Supply Company
*372 Fifth Avenue, between 5th & 6th Streets, (1-718 499 9884, www.superherosupplies. com). Subway F, G, R to Fourth Avenue-9th Street. **Open** hrs vary; usually noon-6pm Tue-Sun (call before visiting). **Map** p232 K37* ❶ *Gifts & souvenirs*

To unleash your inner superhero, stop by this purveyor of capes, masks, X-ray glasses and gallon tins of Immortality. Just be sure you adhere to the Vow of Heroism you must recite before your purchases are handed over. Proceeds benefit the 826NYC kids' writing centre behind a concealed door in the back of the store, so you can feel super about that, too.

Green-Wood Cemetery

FORT GREENE

▶ *Subway B, Q, R to DeKalb Avenue; B, D, N, Q, R, 2, 3, 4, 5 to Atlantic Avenue-Barclays Center; C to Lafayette Avenue; G to Fulton Street or Clinton-Washington Avenues.*

With its stately Victorian brownstones and other grand buildings, **Fort Greene** has undergone a major revival over the past two decades. It has long been a centre of African-American life and business – Spike Lee, Branford Marsalis and Chris Rock have all lived here. **Fort Greene Park** (from Myrtle to DeKalb Avenues, between St Edwards Street & Washington Park) was conceived in 1846 at the behest of poet Walt Whitman (then editor of the *Brooklyn Daily Eagle*); its masterplan was fully realised by Olmsted and Vaux in 1867. At the centre of the park stands the Prison Ship Martyrs Monument, erected in 1909 (from a design by Stanford White) in memory of 11,000 American prisoners who died on squalid British ships that were anchored nearby during the Revolutionary War.

Despite its name, the 34-floor **Williamsburgh Savings Bank**, at the corner of Atlantic and Flatbush Avenues, is in Fort Greene, not Williamsburg. The 512-foot-high structure was long the tallest in Brooklyn and, with its four-sided clocktower, one of the most recognisable features of its skyline. The 1927 building has been renamed One Hanson Place, and converted into (what else?) luxury condominiums.

Originally founded in Brooklyn Heights, the **Brooklyn Academy of Music** (*see p336*) moved to its current site on Fort Greene's southern border in 1901. America's oldest operating performing-arts centre, BAM was the home of the Metropolitan Opera until 1921; today, it's the heart of a growing cultural district that also includes the **Polonsky Shakespeare Center** (*see p347*). Almost as famous is the cheesecake at nearby **Junior's Restaurant** (386 Flatbush Avenue, at DeKalb Avenue, 1-718 852 5257, www.juniorscheesecake.com).

In addition to some funky shops, a slew of restaurants can be found on or near **DeKalb Avenue**.

In the know
Brooklyn baddie

Alphonse (Al) Capone was born in 1899 in a house that stood just east of the Manhattan Bridge and south of the Brooklyn Navy Yard at 95 Navy Street; before moving to Chicago, he was a member of several local gangs, including the Brooklyn Rippers.

Sights & museums
BLDG 92

63 Flushing Avenue, at Carlton Avenue (1-718 907 5932, www.brooklynnavyyard.org). Subway A, C to High Street, then 20min walk; F to York Street, then 20min walk or B62 bus; A, C, F, R to Jay Street-MetroTech, then B57 bus. Open 11am-6pm Wed-Fri; noon-6pm Sat, Sun. Admission free. Map p232 K32.

The 1850s Marine Commandant's residence on the edge of the Brooklyn Navy Yard is home to a small museum chronicling the mighty history of the former shipbuilding centre, which employed more than 70,000 people at its peak during World War II. Exhibits examine the yard's origins and significance throughout history, but also its new role as a modern manufacturing hub. Businesses include an urban farm, furniture makers and a distillery. BLDG 92 also has a café and rotating exhibitions, and is the starting point for bus, bike and factory tours (see website for information).

Restaurants & cafés
❤ Miss Ada $$

184 DeKalb Avenue, between Carlton Avenue & Cumberland Street (1-917 909 1023, www.missadanyc.com). Subway C to Lafayette Avenue; G to Fulton Street. Open 5.30-10.30pm Tue-Thur; 5.30-11.30pm Fri, Sat; 11am-2.30pm, 5.30-10.30pm Sun. Map p232 K33 ⑩ *Mediterranean*

The name is a playful twist on the phonetic pronunciation of *misada*, the Hebrew word for 'restaurant'. At this relaxed, rustic-chic spot, Israeli-born chef Tomer Blechman combines his Latvian heritage with Mediterranean cooking for smart mezes, fluffy pita and fragrant main-course Middle Eastern plates, best enjoyed on the outdoor terrace.

No. 7 $$

7 Greene Avenue, between Cumberland & Fulton Streets (1-718 522 6370, www.no7restaurant.com). Subway C to Lafayette Avenue; C, G to Clinton-Washington Avenues. Open 5-11pm Tue-Fri; 11am-3pm, 5-11pm Sat; 11am-3pm, 4-9pm Sun. Map p232 L34 ⑪ *Eclectic*

Given the constraints of No. 7's tiny kitchen, chef Tyler Kord's eclectic cuisine – influenced by Asian and Eastern European flavours, among others – is impressively bold. The menu changes frequently but might include such cross-cultural hybrids as crisp broccoli tempura with black-bean houmous, or fish tacos with pickled strawberries, hot mayonnaise and cheddar.

WILLIAMSBURG, GREENPOINT & BUSHWICK

▶ *Williamsburg – Subway G to Metropolitan Avenue; J, M, Z to Marcy Avenue; L to Bedford Avenue or Lorimer Street. Greenpoint – Subway G to Greenpoint Avenue or Nassau Avenue. Bushwick – Subway L to Jefferson Street or Morgan Avenue.*

Known for its thriving music scene, **Williamsburg** gained a reputation as a hip enclave before developers began to transform its waterfront with gleaming new residential towers. However, the area retains many worthwhile clubs, restaurants, laid-back bars and independent shops, plus quirky repository of NYC ephemera, the **City Reliquary**.

Long before the trendsetters invaded, Williamsburg's waterfront location had made it ideal for industry. When the Erie Canal linked the Atlantic Ocean to the Great Lakes in 1825, the area became a bustling port. Companies such as Pfizer and Domino Sugar started here, but businesses had begun to abandon the area's huge industrial spaces by the late 20th century. Today, the site of the old Domino refinery is gradually being populated with apartments. The complex includes recently debuted **Domino Park** (Kent Avenue, between Grand & South 5th Streets, www.dominopark.com), offering killer views of the Williamsburg Bridge. Incorporating salvaged industrial elements in its design, the waterfront space includes an elevated walkway, lawns and a playground, plus volleyball and bocce courts.

Bedford Avenue is the neighbourhood's main thoroughfare. By day, the epicentre of the strip is the **Mini Mall** (no.218, between North 4th & North 5th Streets) – you won't find a Gap or Starbucks here, but vintage clothing shops and **Spoonbill & Sugartown, Booksellers** (1-718 387-7322, www.spoonbillbooks.com). The area has a constantly shifting array of cafés and eateries, but there are some neighbourhood fixtures; south of the Williamsburg Bridge on Broadway, **Marlow & Sons** was a pioneer in the kind of rustic aesthetic and farm-to-table fare that's become the norm in Brooklyn. Nearby, New York institution **Peter Luger** grills some of the best steaks in the city. Another local gem is the **Brooklyn Brewery** (79 North 11th Street, between Berry Street & Wythe Avenue, 1-718 486 7422, www.brooklynbrewery.com), housed in a former ironworks. The tasting room is open daily (5-11pm Mon-Thur; 5pm-midnight Fri; noon-midnight Sat; noon-8pm Sun), with free tours on weekends.

With Williamsburg approaching hipster saturation point and rents rising accordingly, many of its young, creative residents seek cheaper digs nearby – which usually starts the gentrification cycle over again. **Greenpoint**, Williamsburg's northern neighbour, has been quietly undergoing a transformation of its own in the past decade or so. The former Polish stronghold's cachet rose even further as the setting of HBO's *Girls*. **WNYC Transmitter Park** – a 1.6-acre waterfront green space between

Greenpoint Avenue and Kent Street that was once the site of the local public radio station's AM transmitter towers – offers a stellar view of the Manhattan skyline. Young, wealthy residents are moving into the neighbourhood in droves, leading to inevitable tensions between old and new denizens.

Bushwick has also attracted a creative demographic to its industrial spaces. The annual **Bushwick Open Studios** (typically held in autumn, but check www.artsinbushwick.org) gives a glimpse inside hundreds of artists' work spaces, but you'll also see plenty of street art in the vicinity of the Morgan Avenue subway stop. Bounded by Bushwick Avenue to the north-west and Broadway to the south-west, this traditionally Latino neighbourhood has begun to sprout coffee shops, bars and vintage stores over the past several years, not to mention restaurants, such as acclaimed locavore eaterie **Roberta's**.

Sights & museums

City Reliquary

*370 Metropolitan Avenue, at Havemeyer Street, Williamsburg (1-718 782 4842, www. cityreliquary.org). Subway G to Metropolitan Avenue; L to Lorimer Street. **Open** noon-6pm Thur-Sun. **Admission** $7; $5 reductions; free under-13s. **Map** p249 K28.*

This not-for-profit mini-museum of New York history is crammed with fascinating Gotham ephemera. The collection includes memorabilia from both NYC World's Fairs, a shrine to the Brooklyn Dodgers' Jackie Robinson, hundreds of Lady Liberty figurines and such anachronistic objects as subway tokens and seltzer bottles. Other idiosyncratic relics include a vintage barber-shop diorama furnished with a chair from Barber Hall of Famer Antonio Nobile's Bay Ridge, Brooklyn, shop, and a transplanted Chinatown newsstand.

In the know
The L word

If you're visiting before autumn 2020, bear in mind that the L subway line is operating a reduced schedule nights and weekends to allow for essential repairs to the Canarsie Tunnel under the East River, following damage wreaked by Superstorm Sandy. The NYC Ferry (www.ferry.nyc) offers a route linking Williamsburg with Wall Street and 34th Street in Manhattan and other Brooklyn stops along the East River.

City Reliquary

Restaurants & cafés

Allswell $$

*124 Bedford Avenue, at North 10th Street, Williamsburg (1-347 799 2743, www. allswellnyc.com). Subway L to Bedford Avenue. **Open** noon-11pm Mon-Thur; 10am-1am Fri, Sat; 10am-11pm Sun (bar stays open 1hr later). **Map** p249 K27* ⑯ *American*

Chef-owner Nate Smith, who earned his gastropub stripes at the Spotted Pig, broke out on his own with this laid-back tavern, done up with a reclaimed pine bar and brass-hunting-horn chandeliers. The frequently changing menu typically features chefly bar grub such as fried oysters or twists on burgers, salads and heartier dishes, such as steak or roasted chicken with seasonal vegetables. The drinks list takes a locavore slant with small-production wines and craft beers on tap, plus a selection of market-driven cocktails.

♥ Aska $$$$

*47 South 5th Street, between Kent & Wythe Avenues, Williamsburg (1-929 337 6792, askanyc.com). Subway J, M, Z to Marcy Avenue. **Open** 6pm-midnight Tue-Sat. **Map** p249 J29* ⑰ *Nordic*

Basically a Brooklyn version of Copenhagen's Noma, Aska is helmed by Michelin-starred chef Fredrik Berselius. The Swedish wunderkind is known for his inventiveness, impeccable plating and hand-foraged ingredients – evident in such morsels as a barely cooked scallop served in its shell with grilled coral and a tableside spooning of brown butter broth and pickled elderberries. The converted-warehouse dining room has a moody cool, with wooden tables covered in edgy black cloth. Dinner is reservation- and tasting menu-only ($265 for 12 courses, including a non-refundable deposit). A more casual, light-strung garden out back and

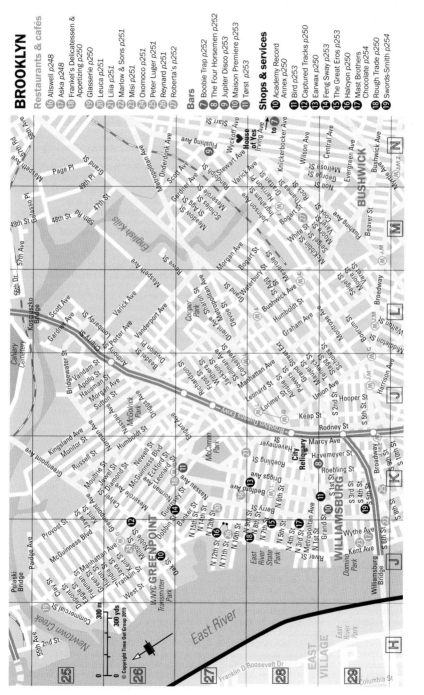

BROOKLYN

Restaurants & cafés

16 Allswell p248
17 Aska p248
18 Frankel's Delicatessen & Appetizing p250
19 Glasserie p250
20 Leuca p251
21 Lilia p251
22 Marlow & Sons p251
23 Misi p251
24 Oxomoco p251
25 Peter Luger p251
26 Reynard p251
27 Roberta's p252

Bars

7 Boobie Trap p252
8 The Four Horsemen p252
9 Jupiter Disco p253
10 Maison Premiere p253
11 Torst p253

Shops & services

10 Academy Record Annex p250
11 Bird p253
12 Captured Tracks p250
13 Earwax p250
14 Feng Sway p253
15 The Great Eros p253
16 Halcyon p250
17 Mast Brothers Chocolate p254
18 Rough Trade p250
19 Swords-Smith p254

On the Record

Embark on a crate-digging crawl of Williamsburg and Greenpoint

Despite ongoing reports of the record store's demise, a number of shops have put down roots in North Brooklyn, making it a prime place for casual music lovers and serious vinyl collectors to spend an afternoon. In late 2013, UK indie retailer **Rough Trade** (64 North 9th Street, between Kent & Wythe Avenues, 1-718 388 4111, www.roughtrade. com. *Map p249 J26* ⓳) opened its first Stateside outpost in a 15,000-square-foot Williamsburg warehouse, complete with in-house café. In addition to tens of thousands of all-new titles – roughly half of them vinyl and half CDs – the megastore sells music books, magazines and equipment, curates rotating art installations, and hosts gigs both ticketed and free by the likes of Television, Will Butler and Kimbra (for schedule and tickets, see www.roughtradenyc.com).

Rough Trade joined old timers such as **Earwax** (167 North 9th Street, between Bedford & Driggs Avenues, Williamsburg, 1-718 486 3771, www.earwaxrecords.net. *Map p249 J26* ⓭), which opened in 1991 at a previous location. Earwax's selection spans genres and decades, from buzzy indie pop to funk, psychedelic and world music, and the insanely knowledgeable staff can be counted on to provide some tuneful inspiration. Dance-music-oriented **Halcyon** (74 Wythe Avenue, at North 12th Street,

1-718 360 0992, www.halcyontheshop.com. *Map p249 J27* ⓰) has a deep selection of beat-heavy titles – including rare house, hip-hop and drum 'n' bass 12-inches – plus a performance space decked out with a lustworthy Funktion-One sound system.

Just a few blocks north, Greenpoint is drawing record stores with cheaper rents than its gentrified neighbour. Case in point is **Academy Record Annex** (85 Oak Street, between Franklin & West Streets, 1-718 218 8200, www.academy-lps.com. *Map p249 J26* ⓾), which moved from its long-time home in Williamsburg to its current sunny digs by the Greenpoint waterfront. Expect serious buyers, reasonable prices and a massive collection of punk, rock 'n' roll, jazz, soul and experimental records.

Nearby is the eponymous flagship of trendsetting label **Captured Tracks** (195 Calyer Street, between Manhattan Avenue & Leonard Street, 1-718 609 0871, www. capturedtracks.com. *Map p249 J26* ⓬). In addition to stocking an ever-changing trove of vinyl, there are lots of cassettes, art books, vintage recording equipment and curation booths from local musicians. Don't be surprised to find yourself browsing alongside artists from the top-shelf Captured Tracks roster, such as DIIV's Zachary Cole Smith.

---

a cellar bar downstairs are open to walk-ins looking for cocktails and an à la carte Nordic snack.

Frankel's Delicatessen & Appetizing $

*631 Manhattan Avenue, between Nassau & Bedford Avenues, Greenpoint (1-718 389 2302, frankelsdelicatessen.com). Subway G to Nassau Avenue. **Open** 8am-4pm daily. **Map** p249 K26* ⓲ *Delicatessen*

Native New Yorkers Zach and Alex Frankel (former chef at Jack's Wife Freda and half of Brooklyn synth-pop duo Holy Ghost!, respectively) pay homage to the Jewish-food landmarks they grew up with, such as Barney Greengrass and Zabar's. What Frankel's gets right is the balanced ratio of its ingredients: ribbons of Irish organic salmon, equal parts oil and silk, have just enough fresh salinity and wood-chip smokiness to stand up to a creamy spread of whitefish salad and capers on a bagel sandwich. The shop's hand-cut, thick-sliced pastrami is a fatty marvel; get it Reuben-style, dressed copiously with sauerkraut, Russian dressing and its own considerable juices on rye

or, more unexpectedly, in an egg-and-cheese sandwich.

Glasserie $$

*95 Commercial Street, between Box Street & Manhattan Avenue, Greenpoint (1-718 389 0640, www.glasserienyc.com). Subway G to Greenpoint Avenue. **Open** 5.30-11pm Mon, Tue; 11.30am-2.30pm, 5.30-11pm Wed, Thur; 11.30am-2.30pm, 5.30pm-midnight Fri; 10am-4pm, 5.30pm-midnight Sat; 10am-4pm, 5.30-11pm Sun. **Map** p249 H25* ⓳ *Eclectic*

Housed in a former glass factory, Glasserie brings a touch of the breezy Mediterranean coast to the gritty Greenpoint waterfront. The whitewashed brick walls are hung with framed glass-catalogue prints from the erstwhile manufacturer and the loading dock has been transformed into a small terrace. The daily changing menu, a mix of small and large plates, reflects Spanish, Greek and Middle Eastern influences in dishes such as harissa rabbit, or squash *kataif* pastry with fresh ricotta and okra. At brunch, the best way to sample everything is by ordering the meze feast of nine small dishes, served with flatbread.

Leuca $$$

William Vale Hotel, 111 North 12th Street, between Berry Street & Wythe Avenue, Williamsburg (1-718 581 5900, www.leuca. com). Subway L to Bedford Avenue. **Open** *7-11am, 11.30am-10pm Mon-Thur; 7-11am, 11.30am-midnight Fri; 7am-10pm Sun.* **Map** *p249 K27* 20 *Italian*

This subterranean spot in the William Vale Hotel is helmed by chef-restaurateur Andrew Carmellini (Locanda Verde, the Dutch) and his NoHo Hospitality team (they also oversee the hotel's rooftop bar Westlight, with its three-borough-spanning views, and the burger-slinging Mister Dips in an Airstream trailer on hotel grounds). The main dining room, decked out in tawny leather, is an attractive, adult addition to the 'hood. The menu, too, is smart and civilised, though largely plays it safe. Carmellini takes inspiration from Italy's south, yielding dishes such as a starter of sheep's-milk ricotta folded with warm honey and toasted garlic. Pastas include the wonderful *mafaldini*, with crimped ribbons that wind round a bitter, earthy broccoli rabe pesto popped with sweet and sour peppers. Of the flame-grilled mains, the beautifully juicy Chicken Rosalina for two makes a lasting impression with its thrum of blistered peppers.

♥ Lilia $$

567 Union Avenue, at North 10th Street, Williamsburg (1-718 576 3095, www. lilianewyork.com). Subway L to Bedford Avenue. **Open** *5.30-11pm Mon-Fri; 5-11pm Sat, Sun.* **Map** *p249 K27* 21 *Italian*

The biggest problem you'll have at acclaimed chef Missy Robbins's airy skylit dining room (apart from scoring a table) is choosing what to eat from an entire menu of destination dishes. Maybe it's Robbins's ricotta gnocchi, delicate cheese dumplings covered in a thatch of vibrant, verdant broccoli-basil pesto studded with pistachios. Dreamboat *agnolotti*, tenderly filled with soft sheep's-milk cheese and stained sunset-yellow from saffron-laced butter, is also a top contender. But, despite Robbins's obvious proficiency with pasta, her signature dish may very well be, of all things, a casual starter of fritters. Rather than usher out yet another plate of voguish *cacio e pepe*, Robbins rejuvenates the ancient recipe as snacky, savoury doughnuts: crispy, fresh-from-the-fryer hulls dusted in parmesan and pepper give way to a cheese-oozing core that recall Italian-festival street food (in a great way). The chef's second Williamsburg spot, **Misi** (329 Kent Avenue, between South 3rd & 4th Streets, 1-347 566 3262 23) features a pasta-making room that's visible to diners and passersby alike.

Marlow & Sons $$

81 Broadway, between Berry Street & Wythe Avenue, Williamsburg (1-718 384 1441, www. marlowandsons.com). Subway J, M, Z to Marcy Avenue. **Open** *8am-10pm Mon-Thur, Sun; 8am-11pm Fri, Sat.* **Map** *p249 J29* 22 *American creative*

In this charming oyster bar, restaurant and café, diners wolf down meze, market-fresh salads and succulent brick chicken. In the back, a shucker cracks open the bivalve catch of the day, while the bartender mixes the kind of potent drinks that helped to make the owners' earlier ventures (including the next-door Diner, a tricked-out 1920s dining car) successes.

Oxomoco $$

128 Greenpoint Avenue, between Franklin Street & Manhattan Avenue, Greenpoint (1-646 688 4180, www.oxomoconyc.com). Subway G to Greenpoint Avenue. **Open** *noon-3pm, 5.30-10pm Mon-Wed; noon-3pm, 5.30-10.30pm Thur; noon-3pm, 5.30-11.30pm Fri; 11am-3pm, 5.30-11.30pm Sat; 11am-3pm, 5.30-10pm Sun.* **Map** *p249 J26* 24 *Mexican*

Michelin-starred Oxomoco focuses on wood-fired dishes, such as a beet 'chorizo' taco, masa-fried cauliflower with black mole, *pepitas*, and butternut squash crema, and chicken al pastor with grilled pineapple. A faint campfire smell spreads throughout the all-white dining room, which is accented only by the green ivy hanging from the skylights. The illuminated bar is lined with beautiful bottles of mescal and tequila, ready to be shaken or stirred into cocktails.

♥ Peter Luger $$$

178 Broadway, at Driggs Avenue, Williamsburg (1-718 387 7400, www. peterluger.com). Subway J, M, Z to Marcy Avenue. **Open** *11.45am-9.45pm Mon-Thur; 11.45am-10.45pm Fri, Sat; 12.45-9.45pm Sun.* **No cards.** **Map** *p249 K29* 25 *Steakhouse*

At Luger's old-school steakhouse, the menu is limited, but the porterhouse is justly famed. Choose from various sizes, from a small single steak to 'steak for four'. Although a slew of Luger copycats have prospered over the years, none has captured the elusive charm of this stucco-walled, beer hall-style eaterie, with worn wooden floors and tables, and waiters in white shirts and bow ties.

Reynard $$

Wythe Hotel, 80 Wythe Avenue, at North 11th Street, Williamsburg (1-718 460 8004, www.reynardnyc.com). Subway L to Bedford Avenue. **Open** *8am-10pm Mon, Sun; 8am-11pm Tue-Thur; 8am-midnight Fri, Sat.* **Map** *p249 J27* 26 *American creative*

The Wythe's restaurant is a Balthazar for Brooklyn, urbane and ambitious, mature and low-key. The spacious dining room serves casual breakfast and lunch to a drop-in crowd, including a terrifically earthy grass-fed burger. The spare menu, which changes often – sometimes daily – becomes much more serious at night, but there are no trendy buzzwords. The thoughtful food, portioned to satisfy and priced to move, mostly speaks for itself.

♥ Roberta's $$

*261 Moore Street, between Bogart & White Streets, Bushwick (1-718 417 1118, www. robertaspizza.com). Subway L to Morgan Avenue. **Open** 11am-4pm, 5pm-midnight Mon-Fri; 10am-4pm, 5pm-midnight Sat, Sun. **Map** p249 M28* ㉗ *Italian*

This sprawling hangout is the unofficial meeting place for Brooklyn's sustainable-food movement. Opened in 2008, Roberta's has its own on-site garden that provides some of the ingredients for its locally sourced dishes. The pizzas – such as the three-cheese Famous Original, topped with mozzarella, caciocavallo and parmesan – are among Brooklyn's finest. Blanca, a sleek spot in the back, showcases chef Carlo Mirarchi's acclaimed evening-only tasting menu (6pm and 9pm Wed-Fri, 5pm and 8pm Sat, $198).

Bars

Boobie Trap

*308 Bleecker Street, at Irving Avenue, Bushwick (1-347 240 9105, www. boobietrapbrooklyn.com). Subway L, M to Myrtle-Wyckoff Avenues. **Open** noon-4am Mon-Sat; noon-midnight Sun. **Map** p249 N28* ❼

Lady lumps abound at this brazen, retro-kitted dive, done up with hot-pink lights and heaps of B-movie camp. The bathroom ceiling is tiled with rubber knockers lit by a chandelier of Barbies, the gold zebra-printed walls are nailed with '90s troll dolls and plastic dinosaurs, and a neon sign boldly proclaims 'f*** off' from behind the bar. But hidden beneath the kitsch is a surprisingly respectable neighbourhood hangout. While you'll find big-name domestic cans such as Bud and Blue Moon at the bar, two draft lines sprouting from a naked mannequin pour one light (Pacífico) and one dark (Negra Modelo) brew.

♥ The Four Horsemen

*295 Grand Street, between Havemeyer & Roebling Streets, Williamsburg (1-718 599 4900, www.fourhorsemenbk.com). Subway G to Metropolitan Avenue; J, M, Z to Marcy Avenue; L to Bedford Avenue. **Open** 5.30pm-midnight Mon-Thur; 5.30pm-1am Fri; noon-4pm, 5.30pm-1am Sat; noon-4pm, 5.30-11pm Sun. **Map** p249 K29* ❽

You could throw a number of superlatives at the Four Horsemen, and they would comfortably stick. For one, it has the best acoustics of any bar in Brooklyn: cedar-slatted ceilings and burlap-covered walls were designed to reduce the auditory assault of clinking glasses and chatter. It's equipped with the borough's hippest co-proprietor, as well: LCD Soundsystem frontman James Murphy. And it's home to some of New York's most ambitious wine-bar eats, such as sea scallops with pickled sunchokes (Jerusalem artichokes) and nori oil, or plum-glazed ribs sprinkled with *togarashi*. But the Four Horsemen could coast on its wine prowess alone. The minimalist bar has done ample work to help embed natural wine – that cloudier, funkier, mouthful-of-barn cousin to your more conventional bottle – into Brooklyn nightlife, with its dozen by-the-glass varieties and comprehensive selection of more than 250 bottles, each of which the savvy staff details without a drop of dogma or dismissal.

Feng Sway

Jupiter Disco

1237 Flushing Avenue, between Harrison Place & St Nicholas Avenue, Bushwick (no phone, www.jupiterdisco.com). Subway L to Jefferson Street. **Open** *6pm-4am daily.* **Map** *p249 N27* **9**

Sure, it has a silly name and proudly touts a mid-century dystopian sci-fi theme, but this industrial, LED-lit bar is more an earnest ode to the science-fiction genre than Instagram-snapping ironic. Inventive, pop culture-nodding cocktails are named after everything from British prog-rock songs to chapters of *The Hobbit*. And with a top-of-the-line sound system that runs through a custom rotary mixer and an alternating line-up of local DJs spinning an assortment of progressive disco, synth and electronic music, the jams, like the digs, are otherworldly too.

♥ Maison Premiere

298 Bedford Avenue, between Grand & South 1st Streets, Williamsburg (1-347 335 0446, www.maisonpremiere.com). Subway L to Bedford Avenue. **Open** *2pm-2am Mon-Wed; 2pm-4am Thur, Fri; 11am-4am Sat, Sun.* **Map** *p249 K29* **10**

Most of NYC's New Orleans-inspired watering holes choose debauched Bourbon Street as their muse, but this gorgeous salon embraces the romance found in the Crescent City's historic haunts. Belly up to the oval, marble-topped bar and get familiar with the twin pleasures of oysters and absinthe: two French Quarter staples with plenty of appeal in Brooklyn. The drinks list includes two dozen international varieties of the mythical anise-flavoured liqueur and a trim list of cerebral cocktails.

Tørst

615 Manhattan Avenue, between Driggs & Nassau Avenues, Greenpoint (1-718 389 6034, www.torstnyc.com). Subway G to Nassau Avenue. **Open** *noon-midnight Mon-Thur, Sun; noon-2am Fri, Sat.* **Map** *p249 K27* **11**

Danish for 'thirst', Tørst is helmed by legendary 'gypsy brewer' Jeppe Jarnit-Bjergsø and chef Daniel Burns, formerly of Noma in Copenhagen. These warriors are laying waste to tired ideas of what a great taproom should be, with a minimalist space that looks like a modernist log cabin, and rare brews from across Europe and North America. The ever-changing, 21-tap draft menu can move faster than a Swedish vallhund, but usually includes selections from Jarnit-Bjergsø's own Evil Twin Brewing. More than 100 bottled beers are also available. Tørst has more in common with a high-end wine bar than with your average local watering hole – well-heeled locals and pilgrimaging brew buffs quietly sip from designer wineglasses at the sleek white marble counter.

Shops & services

Bird

203 Grand Street, between Bedford & Driggs Avenues, Williamsburg (1-718 388 1655, www. shopbird.com). Subway L to Bedford Avenue. **Open** *noon-8pm Mon-Fri; 11am-7pm Sat, Sun.* **Map** *p249 K29* **11** *Fashion*

A former assistant buyer at Barneys, Jen Mankins opened her first Bird boutique in Park Slope in 1999. Now fashion-forward Brooklyn (and Manhattan) residents flock to four locations for local and international designers. The spacious LEED-certified green Williamsburg store stocks clothing and accessories for men and women, with eclectic pieces by well-known and not-so-familiar names rubbing shoulders on the racks, including Rachel Comey, Ulla Johnson, Acne Studios, Our Legacy, No. 6 and Black Crane. **Other locations** 220 Smith Street, at Butler Street, Cobble Hill (1-718 797 3774); 316 Fifth Avenue, between 2nd & 3rd Streets, Park Slope (1-718 768 4940); 85 Lafayette Avenue, between South Elliott Place & South Portland Avenue, Fort Greene (1-718 858 8667).

♥ Feng Sway

86 Dobbin Street, between Meserole & Norman Avenues, Greenpoint (1-917 480 0636, www.fengsway.com). Subway G to Nassau Avenue. **Open** *11am-8pm daily.* **Map** *p249 K27* **14** *Fashion/homewares*

Tucked in a still-industrial patch, Feng Sway surprises with a wonderful jumble of exotic plants, vintage goods, and avant-garde displays incorporating art, religious icons and random kitsch. You might find '80s painted-wood earrings in the shape of guitars or cats and other baubles arranged on a vanity table, with an open drawer revealing socks embroidered with 'First Class Bitch' and 'Slut'. The eclectic stock tends towards colourful and flamboyant – expect the likes of silk kimonos, tropical- and animal-print clothing, hand-woven '70s cushions, antique rugs, rare crystals and Greenpoint-made skincare in the highly browsable mix.

The Great Eros

135 Wythe Avenue, between North 7th & 8th Streets (1-718 384 4072, www.thegreateros. com). Subway L to Bedford Avenue. **Open** *11am-7pm Mon-Sat; noon-6pm Sun.* **Map** *p249 J28* **15** *Lingerie*

Clean, modern lines, luxurious fabrics and styles that cross over from lingerie to loungewear define The Great Eros. Designer Christina Viviani's minimalist shop showcases glamorously sleek bra sets, silk robes and pyjama-like trousers in a classy black, white and neutral colour palette, all exuding laid-back sex appeal. A selection of jewellery and hand-crafted stone 'pleasure wands' and jade eggs complement the line.

Mast Brothers Chocolate

111 North 3rd Street, between Berry Street & Wythe Avenue (1-718 388 2644, www. mastbrothers.com). Subway L to Bedford Avenue. **Open** *11am-7pm daily.* **Map** *p249 J28* **17** *Food & drink*

Michael and Rick Mast started their Brooklyn-based bean-to-bar chocolate company in 2007. Although the exquisite artisan bars can now be found worldwide, the flagship store has exclusive items such as a Brooklyn Collection of six bars featuring ingredients and illustrated packaging inspired by the borough. Hot chocolate, cocoa beer and chocolate chip cookies are served on site.

Swords-Smith

98 South 4th Street, between Bedford Avenue & Berry Street, Williamsburg (1-347 599 2969, www.swords-smith.com). Subway L to Bedford Avenue; J, M, Z to Marcy Avenue. **Open** *noon-8pm Mon-Fri; 11am-8pm Sat; noon-7pm Sun.* **Map** *p249 K29* **19** *Fashion*

Fashion vets Briana Swords (a former womenswear designer for Levi Strauss) and R Smith (a graphic designer whose credits include *Vogue*) are behind this boutique for men and women. The duo offers carefully selected clothing and accessories from more than 80 independent designers in the skylit, minimalist space. Stock is sourced from around the world, including the strong silhouettes and unusual prints of Henrik Vibskov (from Copenhagen), Swedish label Hope and New York-based Rodebjer. Also look out for Buenos Aires designer Martiniano's artisan-crafted shoes.

CONEY ISLAND & BRIGHTON BEACH

▶ *Coney Island – Subway D, F, N, Q to Coney Island-Stillwell Avenue; F, Q to West 8th Street-NY Aquarium. Brighton Beach – Subway B, Q to Brighton Beach.*

Combining old-time fairground attractions, new amusement park rides and traditional seaside pleasures against a gritty urban backdrop, **Coney Island** is a strange hybrid undergoing a revitalisation plan that also includes improvements to the surrounding residential neighbourhood. In its heyday, from the turn of the century until World War II, Coney Island was New York City's playground, drawing millions each year to its seaside amusement parks Dreamland, Luna Park and Steeplechase Park. The first two were destroyed by fire (Dreamland in 1911 and Luna Park in 1944) and not rebuilt, while Steeplechase Park staggered on until 1964. Astroland was built in 1962 in the euphoria leading up to the World's Fair, went up in flames in 1975 and was rebuilt, only to shutter in 2008.

A year later, the city commissioned a new incarnation of **Luna Park** (1000 Surf Avenue, at W 10th Street, 1-718 373 5862, www.lunaparknyc.com, open Apr-Oct). It now has more than 20 rides, including the Thunderbolt, Coney Island's first custom-built rollercoaster since the whiplash-inducing **Cyclone** opened in 1927. A 2020 expansion includes a log flume water ride and zip lines. Nearby is the 1918 **Deno's Wonder Wheel** (www.denoswonderwheel.com), which, like the Cyclone, is a protected landmark.

Brighton Beach

Nostalgic visitors will enjoy a stroll along the three-mile boardwalk, lined with corny carnival games and souvenir shops. The iconic 1939 **Parachute Jump** has been restored and is illuminated at night. Non-profit arts organisation Coney Island USA keeps the torch burning for 20th-century-style attractions at its **Coney Island Museum** with seasonal circus sideshows, as well as kitsch summer spectacle the **Mermaid Parade** (*see p288*). The local baseball team, **Brooklyn Cyclones**, play at the seaside **MCU Park** (www.brooklyncyclones.com).

Walk left along the boardwalk from Coney Island and you'll reach **Brighton Beach**, New York's Little Odessa. Groups of Russian expats (the big hair and garish fashion can be jaw-dropping) crowd semi-outdoor eateries such as **Tatiana** (3152 Brighton 6th Street, at the Boardwalk, 1-718 891 5151, tatianarestaurant.com) – on weekend nights, it morphs into a glitzy club.

Sights & museums

Coney Island Museum

1208 Surf Avenue, at 12th Street, Coney Island (no phone, www.coneyisland.com). Subway D, F, N, Q to Coney Island-Stillwell Avenue. **Open** *Museum Mid June-Aug noon-6pm Wed-Sat; 2-6pm Sun. Sept-mid June noon-6pm Sat; 2-6pm Sun. Shows hrs vary.* **Admission** *Museum $5; $3 reductions. Shows $12-$20; $8 reductions.*

Housed in a 1917 building, the Coney Island Museum acts as both a repository of the district's past and the focus of its current alternative culture. Exhibitions include Coney Island-inspired work by local artists, and artefacts from the permanent collection such as fun-house mirrors and antique postcards. From Easter to the end of September, its venue, Sideshows by the Seashore, showcases

the freaky talents of sword swallowers, snake charmers and fire breathers, while Burlesque at the Beach slinks onto the stage on summer Friday and Saturday nights (see website for the schedule).

New York Aquarium

602 Surf Avenue, at West 8th Street, Coney Island (1-718 265 3474, www.nyaquarium. com). Subway D, F, N, Q to Coney Island-Stillwell Avenue; F, Q to W 8th Street-NY Aquarium. **Open** *Sept-May 10am-4.30pm daily. June-Aug 10am-6 pm daily.* **Admission** *$25-$30; $20-$27 reductions; free under-3s. Pay what you wish after 3pm Fri.*

Get an up-close look at aquatic animals of all shapes and sizes, from Technicolor tropical fish and coral to black-footed penguins and pacific walrus. In the Conservation Hall, kids can stick their hands in a touch tank to hold small marine creatures, and see penguin, otter and walrus feedings throughout the day. 'Ocean Wonders: Sharks!', features NYC's underwater residents – 18 species of sharks and rays as well as other marine wildlife. A glass-walled tunnel lets you walk 'inside' a vivid coral reef inhabited by zebra sharks and blacktip reef sharks, plus exotic fish.

Restaurants & cafés

Nathan's Famous $

1310 Surf Avenue, at Stillwell Avenue, Coney Island (1-718 333 2202, www.nathansfamous. com). Subway D, F, N, Q to Coney Island-Stillwell Avenue. **Open** *9am-1am Mon-Thur, Sun; 9am-2am Fri, Sat. American*

Opened in 1916, the famed frank joint has retained its subway tiles and iconic signage, as well as staples such as crinkle-cut fries and thick-battered corn dogs. At the raw bar, East Coast oysters and littlenecks are shucked over a mountain of ice, served with chowder crackers, lemon wedges, sinus-clearing horseradish and cocktail sauce.

Totonno's $

1524 Neptune Avenue, between 15th & 16th Streets, Coney Island (1-718 372 8606, www. totonnosconeyisland.com). Subway D, F, N, Q to Coney Island-Stillwell Avenue. **Open** *noon-7.30pm Thur-Sun.* **No cards**. *Pizza*

In-the-know pizza lovers make the trek from the beach to this wonderfully old-school table-service pizzeria. Totonno's has been a Coney Island beacon since it opened in 1924. While the purist margherita is superb, the pizza *de résistance* is the top-notch white pie, an off-menu garlicky round covered in gleaming white house-made mozzarella and *pecorino romano*, and leopard-spotted with crispy char marks.

Coney Island

Queens

While Queens is the point of arrival for visitors flying into JFK or LaGuardia airports, the borough hasn't traditionally been on most tourists' must-see list. Now, however, cultural institutions such as MoMA PS1, the Museum of the Moving Image and the Queens Museum are drawing both out-of-towners and Manhattanites across the Ed Koch Queensboro Bridge

Queens is an increasingly popular gastronomic destination. It's one of the country's most diverse urban areas, with almost half its residents hailing from outside the US. Not for nothing is the elevated 7 subway line that serves these parts nicknamed the 'International Express'. Astoria is home to Greek tavernas and Brazilian *churrascarias*; Jackson Heights has Indian, Thai and South American eateries; and Flushing is known for its thriving Chinatown.

❤ **Don't miss**

1 Panorama of the City of New York *p265*
See the entire city in miniature.

2 MoMA PS1 *p258*
Adventurous shows and great summer parties.

3 Noguchi Museum *p262*
A serene sanctuary in industrial Queens.

4 Museum of the Moving Image *p262*
Nirvana for cinephiles.

Gantry Plaza State Park, Long Island City *p258*

LONG ISLAND CITY

► *Subway E, M to Court Square-23rd Street; G, 7 to Court Square; G to 21st Street; N, W, 7 to Queensboro Plaza; 7 to Vernon Boulevard-Jackson Avenue.*

Just across the East River from Manhattan, Long Island City has seen a rapid transformation over the past decade, with shiny modern apartment towers replacing swathes of industrial wasteland. Fronting the main stretch of residential riverside development, **Gantry Plaza State Park** (48th Avenue, at Center Boulevard) commands an impressive panorama of Midtown. The 12-acre park takes its name from the hulking industrial gantries that still stand watch over the piers and which were used to haul cargo from rail barges. Deckchairs offer direct views of the United Nations across the East River.

Vernon Boulevard is the neighbourhood's prime restaurant, retail and bar hub. The cultural jewel is the progressive art institution **MoMA PS1**. In summer months, its courtyard becomes a dance-music hub when it hosts the hugely popular Saturday-afternoon **Warm Up** parties (*see p289*). Other notable art spaces include **SculptureCenter**, housed in a dramatic industrial space, and the **Self-Taught Genius Gallery**, an outpost of the **American Folk Art Museum** (*see p200*). A well-preserved block of 19th-century houses constitutes the **Hunter's Point Historic District** (45th Avenue, between 21st & 23rd Streets).

❤ Time to eat & drink

Morning coffee with serious lift (off)
Sweetleaf *p260*

Quirky takes on classic dishes
M Wells Steakhouse *p260*

Fanciful Chinese fare
Daxi *p267*

Beer and bratwurst
Bohemian Hall & Beer Garden *p263*

Well-crafted nightcap
Dutch Kills *p261*

Sights & museums

► *For the* **Noguchi Museum,** *see p262.*

❤ MoMA PS1

22-25 Jackson Avenue, at 46th Avenue (1-718 784 2084, www.momaps1.org). Subway E, M to Court Square-23rd Street; G, 7 to Court Square; G to 21st Street. **Open** *noon-6pm Mon, Thur-Sun.* **Admission** *Suggested donation $10; $5 reductions; free under-16s.* **Map** *p259 J23.*

MoMA PS1 mounts cutting-edge shows in a distinctive Romanesque Revival building (formerly a public school, hence the name). The contemporary art centre became an affiliate of MoMA in 1999, and the two institutions sometimes stage collaborative exhibitions, such as the quinquennial Greater New York, scheduled for 2020. The DJed summer Warm Up parties are a fixture of the dance-music scene.

SculptureCenter

44-19 Purves Street, at Jackson Avenue (1-718 361 1750, www.sculpture-center.org). Subway E, M to Court Square-23rd Street; E, M, R to Queens Plaza; G, 7 to Court Square. **Open** *11am-6pm Mon, Thur-Sun.* **Admission** *Suggested donation $10; $5 reductions.* **Map** *p259 J22.*

One of the best places to see sculpture by emerging and mid-career artists, this non-profit space is known for its broad definition of the discipline. Exhibition spaces are spread over two levels in an early-1900s trolley-repair shop that was reimagined by acclaimed architect Maya Lin and subsequently expanded, providing a dramatic industrial setting for innovative work.

Self-Taught Genius Gallery *p260*

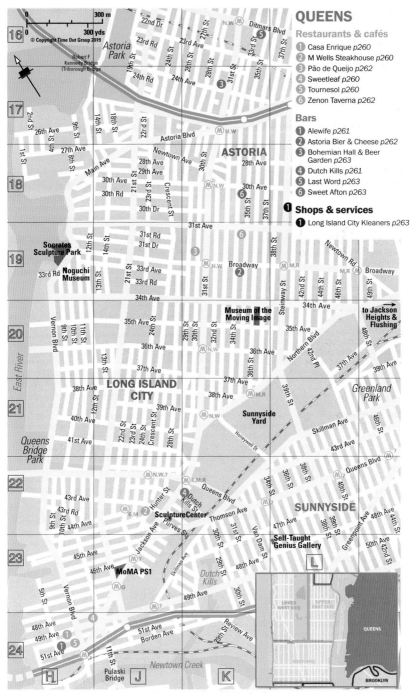

QUEENS

Restaurants & cafés

1. Casa Enrique *p260*
2. M Wells Steakhouse *p260*
3. Pão de Queijo *p262*
4. Sweetleaf *p260*
5. Tournesol *p260*
6. Zenon Taverna *p262*

Bars

1. Alewife *p261*
2. Astoria Bier & Cheese *p262*
3. Bohemian Hall & Beer Garden *p263*
4. Dutch Kills *p261*
5. Last Word *p263*
6. Sweet Afton *p263*

Shops & services

1. Long Island City Kleaners *p263*

MoMA PS1 *p258*

Self-Taught Genius Gallery

*2nd Floor, 47-29 32nd Place, between 47th & 48th Avenues (1-212 595 9533, www. folkartmuseum.org). Subway 7 to 33rd Street-Rawston Street. **Open** 11am-5pm Mon-Thur. **Map** p259 L23.*

Hidden in an industrial corner of Long Island City, this offshoot of the American Folk Art Museum is in the same building as the institution's Collection and Education Center. Ring the bell and climb the stairs to the large, well-lit space, which presents changing, thematic exhibitions highlighting the museum's extensive stash of paintings, photographs, furniture, handicrafts and more.

Restaurants & cafés

Casa Enrique $$

*5-48 49th Avenue, between Vernon Boulevard & 5th Street (1-347 448 6040, www.henrinyc. com/casa-enrique). Subway G to 21st Street; 7 to Vernon Boulevard-Jackson Avenue. **Open** 5-11pm Mon-Fri; 11am-3.30pm, 5-11pm Sat, Sun. **Map** p259 H24* ❶ *Mexican*

With concrete floors and a sleek, gleaming-white interior, this chic eaterie specialises in the regional cuisine of Cintalapa, Chiapas. Brothers Cosme and Luis Aguilar, the chef and GM respectively, pay homage to their late mother with traditional plates, including some based on her recipes, such as chicken mole and cochinito chiapaneco (guajillo-marinated baby pork ribs).

♥ M Wells Steakhouse $$

*43-15 Crescent Street, between 43rd Avenue & 44th Road (1-718 786 9060, www. magasinwells.com). Subway N, W, 7 to Queensboro Plaza. **Open** 5-10pm Mon, Tue, Sun; 5-11pm Wed-Sat. **Map** p259 J22* ❷ *Steakhouse/eclectic*

At Hugue Dufour and Sarah Obraitis's cool spin on a classic steakhouse, hipsters mingle with families in a former auto-body shop for smoky steaks cooked over a wood-fire grill, shellfish and creative takes on Quebecois and American favourites such as poutine and a charred iceberg wedge salad with creamy blue cheese. Long Island trout are fished from a large tank on the edge of the dining room and poached to order.

♥ Sweetleaf $

*10-93 Jackson Avenue, at 11th Street (1-917 832 6726, www.sweetleafcoffee.com). Subway 7 to Vernon Boulevard-Jackson Avenue. **Open** 7am-7pm Mon-Fri; 8am-7pm Sat, Sun. **Map** p259 J24* ❹ *Café*

Long Island City's first speciality coffee shop opened in 2008 in this quaint, tin-ceilinged, antique-furnished space, which has a funky 'record room' in the back featuring a turntable and around 200 albums. There are now four locations serving direct-trade coffee, artisan espresso and mainly house-made pastries. Get a tasty caffeine blast with Rocket Fuel – cold-brewed iced coffee sweetened with maple syrup and milk. The larger Queens location, in a high-rise near the waterfront, also offers cocktails in the evening. **Other locations** 4615 Center Boulevard, between 46th & 47th Avenues, Long Island City (1-347 527 1038); 28-10 Jackson Avenue, between Orchard Street & Queens Boulevard, Long Island City (1-718 361 8000); 159 Freeman Street, between Manhattan Avenue & Franklin Street, Greenpoint, Brooklyn (1-347 987 3732).

Tournesol $$

*50-12 Vernon Boulevard, between 50th & 51st Avenues (1-718 472 4355, www.tournesolnyc. com). Subway 7 to Vernon Boulevard-Jackson Avenue. **Open** 5.30-10.30pm Mon; 11.30am-3pm, 5.30-10.30pm Tue-Thur; 11.30am-3pm, 5.30-11pm Fri; 11am-3.30pm, 5.30-11.30pm Sat; 11am-3.30pm, 5-10pm Sun. **No cards** (except AmEx). **Map** p259 H24* ❺ *French*

While Tournesol is a local favourite for steak frites and *magret de canard*, it's worth making a journey here for beautifully executed southwestern French cuisine at prices you'd be hard-pressed to find across the East River. Squeeze into one of the red banquettes in the intimate tin-ceilinged dining room, and split an appetiser of the obscenely good housemade foie gras terrine.

Bars

Alewife

5-14 51st Avenue, between Vernon Boulevard & 5th Street (1-718 937 7494, www.alewife. beer). Subway 7 to Vernon Boulevard-Jackson Avenue. Open 4-11pm Mon; 4pm-1am Tue-Thur; 4pm-3am Fri; 11am-3am Sat; 11am-1am Sun. Map p259 H24 ❶

A serious craft-beer selection is the draw at this bi-level beer hall. The hops-zealot owners recently launched their own beer, in addition to a worldly list of rotating taps and casks, plus bottles. Suds aficionados can sample weekly 'test brews' created in the on-site single-barrel 'Scullery'. A beer-friendly menu of tacos, burgers and other hearty snacks is available.

❤ Dutch Kills

27-24 Jackson Avenue, at Dutch Kills Street (1-718 383 2724, www.dutchkillsbar.com). Subway E, M, R to Queens Plaza. Open 5pm-2am Mon-Thur, Sun; 5pm-3am Fri, Sat. Map p259 K22 ❹

What separates Dutch Kills from NYC's other mixology temples modelled after vintage saloons is the abundance of elbow room. Settle into one of the deep, dark-wood booths in the front, or head for the back to perch at the bar. Cocktails are mostly creative, seasonal twists on classics, with prices slightly lower than in similar establishments in Manhattan.

In the know
Where the action is

Broadway Danny Rose (1984) and *Do the Right Thing* (1989) are among the movies shot at Long Island City's **Silvercup Studios** (42-22 22nd Street, between 43rd & 44th Avenues, www.silvercupstudios.com), a former bread factory in an industrial section by the Ed Koch Queensboro Bridge. The studios have also been home to some of the most iconic New York-set (and New Jersey-set) TV shows: *Sex and the City* (the series and both spots), *The Sopranos* and *The Deuce*. While you're in the neighbourhood, look out for its massive retro sign, which featured in the rooftop fight scene of 1986 flick *Highlander*.

ASTORIA

▶ *Subway M, R to Steinway Street; N, W to Broadway, 30th Avenue, 36th Avenue or Astoria-Ditmars Boulevard.*

A lively, traditionally Greek and Italian neighbourhood, Astoria has over the last few decades seen an influx of Brazilians, Bangladeshis, Eastern Europeans, Colombians and Egyptians. Gentrification has also moved in. A 15-minute downhill hike from Broadway subway station towards Manhattan brings you to the **Noguchi Museum**, which was created by the visionary sculptor. Nearby lies the **Socrates Sculpture Park** (Broadway, at Vernon Boulevard, www.socratessculpturepark.org), a riverfront art space in an industrial setting with great views of Manhattan.

In the early days of cinema, Astoria was a major celluloid hub. Taking advantage of its proximity to talent-laden Broadway, Famous Players-Lasky (later Paramount Pictures) opened its first studios in the neighbourhood in 1920. Portions of Rudolf Valentino's blockbuster *The Sheikh* (1921) were filmed there, and the studio produced the Marx Brothers' *The Cocoanuts* (1929) and *Animal Crackers* (1930) before Paramount moved its operations west. After years of neglect, the studios were declared a National Historic Landmark in 1976, and, in 1982, developer George S Kaufman bought the site and created **Kaufman Astoria Studios** (34-12 36th Street, between 34th & 35th Avenues, www.kaufmanastoria. com). Scenes for numerous films, including *Birdman* (2014) and *The Bourne Legacy* (2012), were shot here, and the studios are also home to TV shows *Orange Is the New Black* and *Sesame Street*, among others. The **Museum of the Moving Image** is across the street.

Still New York's Greek-American stronghold, Astoria is well known for Hellenic eateries and cafés. You can puff on a *shisha* – a (legal) hookah pipe – with a thick Turkish coffee in the cafés of 'Little Egypt' along Steinway Street, between 28th Avenue and Astoria Boulevard. At the end of the N and W subway lines (Astoria-Ditmars Boulevard), walk west to **Astoria Park** (from Astoria Park South to Ditmars Boulevard, between Shore Boulevard & 19th Street) for its dramatic views of two bridges: the Robert F Kennedy Bridge (formerly the Triborough), Robert Moses's automotive labyrinth connecting Queens, the Bronx and Manhattan; and the 1916 Hell Gate Bridge, a steel single-arch tour de force and template for the Sydney Harbour Bridge. On the area's north-east fringes, you can tour the still-thriving red-brick 1871 piano factory **Steinway & Sons** (1 Steinway Place, between 19th Avenue & Berrian Boulevard, 1-718 721 2600, www.steinway.com/about/factory-tour). The weekly tour, conducted from September to June, must be booked in advance via the website (and typically fills up quickly).

Sights & museums

❤ Museum of the Moving Image

36-01 35th Avenue, at 36th Street (1-718 777 6888, www.movingimage.us). Subway R, M to Steinway Street; N, W to 36th Avenue. **Open** *10.30am-5pm Wed, Thur; 10.30am-8pm Fri; 10.30am-6pm Sat, Sun.* **Admission** *$15; $9-$11 reductions; free under-3s. Free 4-8pm Fri.* **Map** *p259 K20.*

Following a major expansion in 2011, the Museum of the Moving Image became one of the foremost museums in the world dedicated to TV, film and video. The institution's collection, galleries and state-of-the-art screening facilities are housed on the campus of Kaufman Astoria Studios. On the second and third floors, the core exhibition, Behind the Screen, contains approximately 1,400 artefacts – including the super-creepy stunt doll used in *The Exorcist*, with full head-rotating capabilities, and the (surprisingly small) model of the Tyrell Corporation building from *Blade Runner*, alongside interactive displays. A gallery space devoted to Muppets creator Jim Henson showcases sketches, storyboards, scripts, behind-the-scenes clips and 47 puppets, including Kermit the Frog, Miss Piggy and Big Bird.

❤ Noguchi Museum

9-01 33rd Road, at Vernon Boulevard (1-718 204 7088, www.noguchi.org). Subway N, W to Broadway, then 15min walk or Q104 bus to 11th Street; 7 to Vernon Boulevard-Jackson Avenue, then Q103 bus to 10th Street. **Open** *10am-5pm Wed-Fri; 11am-6pm Sat, Sun. May-Sept 10am-8pm 1st Fri of the mth.* **Admission** *$10; $5 reductions; free under-12s. Free 1st Fri of the mth. No pushchairs/strollers.* **Map** *p259 H19.*

When Japanese-American sculptor and designer Isamu Noguchi (1904-88) opened his Queens museum in 1985, he became the first living artist in the US to establish such an institution. The Noguchi Museum occupies a former photo-engraving plant across the street from the studio he had occupied since the 1960s (its location allowed him to be close to stone and metal suppliers along Vernon Boulevard). Noguchi designed the entire building to be a meditative oasis amid its gritty, industrial setting, and the ground floor is largely devoted to sculptures placed by the artist. Upstairs, additional galleries

showcase work such as sculptures, drawings, architectural models, and stage and furniture designs, plus special exhibitions. The serene garden features a minimalist fountain and such works as the megalithic 1978 *Core (Cored Sculpture)* carved from volcanic basalt.

Restaurants & cafés

Pão de Queijo $

31-90 30th Street, between Broadway & 31st Avenue (1-718 204 1979, www.newyorkpaodequeijo.com). Subway N, W to Broadway. **Open** *10am-midnight Mon-Thur; 9am-midnight Fri-Sun.* **Map** *p259 K19* ③ *Brazilian*

This laid-back all-day café is known for its inventive twists on burgers, in combinations layering the likes of banana or smoked sausage, along with corn and potato sticks. The namesake *pão de queijo*, a baked cheese-roll snack, is available with various fillings, such as ham and cheese, guava, or Nutella. Açaí bowls, fresh fruit juices, and Guarana, a popular Brazilian soft drink, complete the Rio-channelling vibe.

Zenon Taverna $$

34-10 31st Avenue, at 34th Street (1-718 956 0133, www.zenontaverna.com). Subway N, W to Broadway. **Open** *noon-10pm Mon-Thur; noon-11pm Fri; 11am-11pm Sat; 11am-10pm Sun.* **No cards. Map** *p259 K19* ⑥ *Greek*

The faux-stone entryway and murals of ancient ruins don't detract from the Mediterranean charm of this humble place that's been run by the same family since the late 1980s. In addition to the signature meze meals, specials rotate daily, embracing all the Greek and Cypriot classics – stuffed grape leaves, *keftedes* (Cypriot meatballs), *spanakopita* (spinach pie) – and less ubiquitous dishes such as plump *loukaniko* (pork sausages). The menu also embraces vegan dishes and sticky house-made sweets.

Bars

Astoria Bier & Cheese

34-14 Broadway, between 34th & 35th Streets (1-718 545 5588, milkandhops.com). Subway M, R to Steinway Street; N, W to Broadway. **Open** *noon-11pm Mon-Thur; noon-midnight Fri, Sat; noon-10pm Sun.* **Map** *p259 K19* ②

Manhattan's hybrid bar-shop trend has crossed the bridge with this quirky curds-and-brew haven. At the marble bar, grab one of the ten rotating seasonal, mostly local drafts. There's also a wide choice of bottles and cans that can be purchased to go or opened on-site for a $2 corking fee. Dozens of cheese selections are available, some of

which are worked into a sit-down menu that includes sandwiches and tasting plates with or without cured meats. **Other location** 5-11 Ditmars Boulevard, between 35th & 36th Streets, Astoria (1-718 255 6982).

🖤 Bohemian Hall & Beer Garden

*29-19 24th Avenue, between 29th & 31st Streets (1-718 274 4925, www.bohemianhall. com). Subway N, W to Astoria Boulevard. **Open** 5pm-1am Mon-Thur; 5pm-3am Fri; noon-3am Sat; noon-midnight Sun. **Map** p259 K17* ❸

This authentic Czech beer garden, established in the early 20th century, features plenty of mingle-friendly picnic tables, where you can sample cheap, robust platters of sausage, goulash and other specialities alongside 14 mainly European drafts. (Note that the kitchen closes at 9.45pm Mon-Thur, Sun; 10.45pm Fri, Sat.) Though the huge, linden-canopied garden is open year-round (in winter, the area is partially tented and heated), summer is prime time to visit.

The Last Word

*31-30 Ditmars Boulevard, between 32nd & 33rd Streets (1-718 440 3378, www. tlwcocktailbar.com). Subway N, W to Astoria-Ditmars Boulevard. **Open** 6pm-1am Tue, Wed, Sun; 6pm-2am Thur; 6pm-3am Fri, Sat. **Map** p259 K16* ❺

Pass through the red-velvet curtains to enter a 1920s-inspired space with vintage tin ceilings, antique furniture and tufted seating. A 16ft marble-and-oak bar gives guests ample room to sip expertly crafted concoctions, such as warm cocktails in winter and The Last Word (gin, chartreuse, lime), elegantly served with a 'sidecar' mini carafe on ice.

Sweet Afton

*30-09 34th Street, between 30th & 31st Avenues (1-718 777 2570, www.sweetaftonbar. com). Subway N, W to 30th Avenue. **Open** 3pm-4am Mon-Fri; 10.30am-4am Sat, Sun. **Map** p259 K18* ❻

Sweet Afton combines an industrial feel – lots of concrete and massive beams – with the dark-wood cosiness of an Irish pub. The smartly curated array of reasonably priced suds includes strong, seasonally rotating selections from craft breweries such as Sixpoint and Ommegang, but the bartender will happily mix a cocktail. The satisfying food menu includes beer-battered and fried McClure's pickles – an epic bar snack.

Shops & services

Long Island City Kleaners

*30-53 Steinway Street, between 30th & 31st Avenues (1-718 606 0540, www.licknyc.com). Subway M, R to Steinway Street; N, W to 30th Avenue. **Open** 11am-8pm Mon-Sat; noon-6pm Sun. **Map** p259 L19* ❶ *Fashion*

This concept store evokes gritty NYC storefronts from the 1980s that posed as dry cleaners but hosted illegal activities. There's nothing sketchy about it, though – in the airy space you'll find T-shirts hanging on the racks in dry-cleaning bags, skating goods and footwear, including the Nike SB range.

JACKSON HEIGHTS

▶ *Subway E, F, M, R to Jackson Heights-Roosevelt Avenue; 7 to 74th Street-Broadway.*

Dizzying even by Queens standards, Jackson Heights' multiculturalism gives it an energy all its own. Little India greets you with a cluster of small shops on 74th Street between 37th Road and 37th Avenue, selling Indian music, Bollywood DVDs, saris and glitzy jewellery. But the main appeal for visitors is culinary. The unofficial HQ of the Indian expat community, **Jackson Diner** serves sumptuous curries. Along with neighbouring Elmhurst and Woodside, Jackson Heights has also welcomed waves of Latin American and South-east Asian immigrants. Fresh, meaty tacos – think broiled beef and steamed tongue – give **Taqueria Coatzingo** (76-05 Roosevelt Avenue, between 76th & 77th Streets, 1-718 424 1977) an edge over the other tempting no-frills joints alongside the 7 train track.

Restaurants & cafés

Jackson Diner $

37-47 74th Street, between 37th Avenue & 37th Road (1-718 672 1232, www.jacksondiner. com). Subway E, F, M, R to Jackson Heights-Roosevelt Avenue; 7 to 74th Street-Broadway. **Open** *11.30am-10pm Mon-Thur, Sun; 11.30am-10.30pm Fri, Sat. Indian*

Harried waiters and Formica-topped tables evoke a diner experience at this spacious meet-and-eat headquarters for New York's Indian expat community. Popular dishes include samosa chat topped with chickpeas, yoghurt, onion, tomato, and a sweet-spicy mix of tamarind and mint chutneys, and tender chicken tikka masala, in a rich tomato and cream sauce. The daily lunch buffet lets you eat as much as you like for less than $15. **Other location** 256-01 Hillside Avenue, at 256th Street, Glen Oaks (1-718 343 7400).

Lhasa Fast Food $

37-50 74th Street, between 37th Avenue & 37th Road (1-347 952 6934). Subway E, F, M, R to Jackson Heights-Roosevelt Avenue; 7 to 74th Street-Broadway. **Open** *11.30am-9.30pm Mon-Fri; 11.30am-10pm Sat, Sun. Nepalese*

Venture into a cramped, bare-bones space beyond a cellphone store for one of the best bets for Himalayan and Tibetan cuisine in Jackson Heights. Feast on spicy noodle soups

or plump steamed momo Tibetan dumplings filled with succulent beef, chicken or chives for less than a tenner. **Other location** 81-09 41st Avenue, between 81st Street & Baxter Avenue, Elmhurst, Queens (1-917 745 0364).

Sripraphai $

64-13 39th Avenue, between 64th & 65th Streets (1-718 899 9599, www. sripraphairestaurant.com). Subway 7 to 61st Street-Woodside. **Open** *11.30am-9.30pm Mon, Tue, Thur-Sun.* **No cards.** *Thai*

Woodside's destination eaterie offers distinctive, traditional dishes such as catfish salad or green curry with beef: a thick, piquant broth filled out with roasted Thai aubergine. The dining areas, which sprawl over two levels and a garden (open in summer), are packed with Manhattanites who can be seen eyeing the plates enjoyed by the Thai regulars, mentally filing away what to order the next time.

FLUSHING

▶ *Subway 7 to Flushing-Main Street, 103rd Street-Corona Plaza, 111th Street or Mets-Willets Point.*

Egalitarian Dutchmen staked their claim to 'Vlissingen' in the 1600s and were shortly joined by pacifist Friends, or Quakers, seeking religious freedom in the New World. The plain wooden **Old Quaker Meeting House** (137-16 Northern Boulevard, between Main & Union Streets), built in 1694, creates a startling juxtaposition to the predominantly Chinese businesses that surround its weathered wooden walls. **Flushing Town Hall** (137-35 Northern Boulevard, at Linden Place, 1-718 463 7700, www.flushingtownhall.org), built during the Civil War in the highly fanciful Romanesque Revival style, showcases local arts groups, and hosts jazz and chamber music concerts. A short walk away, the 1854 landmark **St George's Church** (135-32 38th Avenue, between Main & Prince Streets, 1-718 359 1171) contains two examples of Queens-made Tiffany stained glass.

However, most non-locals come to these parts for the restaurants and dumpling stalls. Flushing's sprawling **Chinatown** has a more affluent demographic than its Manhattan counterpart – a case in point is the gleaming **New World Mall** (136-20 Roosevelt Avenue, at Main Street, 1-718 353 0551, www.newworldmallny.com) and its opulent upstairs restaurants. Downstairs, a vast food court is lined with counters offering everything from Thai curries and Chinese noodles to sushi. At the spacious **Jmart** supermarket, peruse such exotic

💙 Panorama of the City of New York

Queens Museum (for listing, see p266).

Want to see all of New York City's five boroughs in a single day? You can, in a manner of speaking, by visiting its miniature doppelgänger, the Panorama of the City of New York. The extraordinary 9,335sq ft scale model of the metropolis was exhibited at the 1964 World's Fair in the New York City Building, now home to the **Queens Museum**, where it remains to this day. The popular attraction cost 10 cents to visit and was originally viewed from plastic 'helicopter' cars on a track. Today, visitors walk along ramps encircling the model to spot Lilliputian versions of Gotham landmarks, including the Statue of Liberty, the George Washington Bridge, the Cyclone roller coaster at Coney Island and thousands of other buildings and municipal features, all rendered in remarkable detail. The Empire State Building is a mere 15 inches high, while Central Park sprawls over little more than 2ft long and one across. Tiny planes fly over the city and land at LaGuardia Airport every minute.

Dreamed up by powerful urban planner Robert Moses to showcase New York City's infrastructure, the project took 100 workers three years to construct at a cost of around $672,663 (roughly equivalent to $5 million today). It originally included 830,000 buildings, and was updated throughout the 1960s. New buildings have been added sporadically over the years, bringing the total up to around 895,000, but one part of the Panorama remains notably frozen in time: the Twin Towers still stand proudly in lower Manhattan, albeit one twelve-hundredth their actual size.

QUEENS

produce as the formidably prickled durian and the elusive mangosteen, or gawk at tanks of fish and buckets of live frogs.

The most visited site in Queens is rambling **Flushing Meadows Corona Park** (from 111th Street to Van Wyck Expressway, between Flushing Bay & Grand Central Parkway, www.nycgovparks.org), where the 1939-40 and 1964-65 World's Fairs were held. Larger than Central Park, it's home to the **Queens Zoo** (1-718 271 1500, www. queenszoo.com); **Queens Theatre** (1-718 760 0064, www.queenstheatre.org), an indoor amphitheatre designed by Philip Johnson; the **New York Hall of Science** (*see p266*), an acclaimed interactive museum; the **Queens Botanical Garden**, a 39-acre cavalcade of greenery; and the **Queens Museum**. Also here are **Citi Field** (Roosevelt Avenue, near 126th Street, 1-718 507 8499, www.mlb. com/mets/ballpark), the home of the Mets baseball team, and the **USTA Billie Jean King National Tennis Center**. The US Open (*see p290*) raises an almighty racket at summer's end, but the general public can play here the other 11 months of the year. Nearby, the **Louis Armstrong House**, in neighbouring Corona, was home to the musician for nearly 30 years.

Sights & museums

Louis Armstrong House
*34-56 107th Street, between 34th & 37th Avenues, Corona (1-718 478 8274, www. louisarmstronghouse.org). Subway 7 to 103rd Street-Corona Plaza. **Open** 10am-5pm Wed-Fri; noon-5pm Sat, Sun. Tours hourly (last tour 4pm). **Admission** $12; $7-$8 reductions; free under-5s.*

Flushing Meadows Corona Park

Pilgrims to the two-storey house where 'Satchmo' lived from 1943 until his death in 1971 will find a shrine to the revolutionary trumpet player – as well as his wife's passion for wallpaper. Her decorative attentions extended to the interiors of cupboards, closets and even bathroom cabinets. The 40-minute guided tour is enhanced by audio clips of Armstrong that give much insight into the tranquil domesticity he sought in the then suburban neighbourhood. Among the artefacts on display are a detailed life mask of the great musician and the gold-plated horn given to him by King George V in 1933. Across the street, a new cultural centre, scheduled for completion in 2020, will illuminate and celebrate Armstrong's legacy through exhibitions, performances and other programming.

New York Hall of Science
*47-01 111th Street, at 47th Avenue, Flushing Meadows Corona Park, Queens (1-718 699 0005, www.nysci.org). Subway 7 to 111th Street. **Open** 9.30am-5pm Mon-Fri; 10am-6pm Sat, Sun. **Admission** $16; $13 reductions. Free 2-5pm Fri, before 11am Sun. Science playground (open Apr-Nov weather permitting; see website for times) extra $5. Rocket Park Mini Golf (open Apr-Nov weather permitting; see website for times) extra $6; $5 reductions.*

Housed in a 1964 World's Fair pavilion and flanked by rockets from the US space programme, this museum has always been worth a trek for its discovery-based interactive displays. Within the high, undulating walls of the dramatic Great Hall, visitors can explore the six natural habitats and 38ft-high central projected waterfall of the immersive animated exhibition 'Connected Worlds'. The drop-in kids' Design Lab encourages creative thinking through activities such as creating gadgets and structures using everyday materials. From April through November, the 30,000sq ft outdoor Science Playground teaches children the principles of balance, gravity and energy, while a mini-golf course in Rocket Park lets families play outdoors overlooked by refurbished rockets that date from the 1960s space race.

Queens Museum
*New York City Building, Flushing Meadows Corona Park (1-718 592 9700, www. queensmuseum.org). Subway 7 to Mets-Willets Point, then 15min walk. **Open** 11am-5pm Wed-Sun. **Admission** Suggested donation $8; $4 reductions; free under-19s.*

Facing the Unisphere, the 140ft stainless-steel globe created for the 1964 World's

Rock Rock Rockaway Beach

The urban surf hub is a summertime hotspot

Situated on a long peninsula, the 170-acre Rockaway Beach, popular with local surfers, has become a hip summer destination. Part of its appeal is that it's an easy, if lengthy, subway ride from Manhattan: take the A train to Broad Channel, then transfer to the S. Alternatively, a ferry service (www.ferry.nyc) from Wall Street is just as cheap, more scenic and takes about an hour.

Rockaway Beach proper stretches from Beach 3rd Street to Beach 153rd Street. The western stretch of sand, **Jacob Riis Park**, is part of the Gateway National Recreation Area (www.nps.gov/gate) and features a restored art deco bathhouse and a summer 'beach bazaar' with pop-up cult food vendors and weekend live music. Further west, **Fort Tilden Beach** feels more remote.

Over the past few years, eating and drinking options have multiplied on and around the boardwalk, though we favour the ramshackle retro vibe at popular dive **Connolly's** (155 Beach 95th Street/Cross Bay Parkway, between Rockaway Beach Boulevard and Shore Front Parkway, 1-718 474 2374), with its (in)famous frozen piña coladas. For something a little more sophisticated, stop by **Sayra's Wine Bar & Bier Garden** (91-11 Rockaway Beach Boulevard, between Beach 91st & 92nd Streets, 1-347 619 8009), the

brainchild of local surfer Rashida Voorhies and artist Patrick Flibotte. The shoreside drinkerie showcases vino from around the world, alongside bites such as cheese plates, smoked-paprika-rosemary chips and barbecue pulled-pork sandwiches. Out back is a 1,200-square-foot garden fitted with beach rocks and wooden picnic tables. A short walk from the sand, **Rockaway Brewing Company** (415 Beach 72nd Street, between Failing Avenue & Amstel Boulevard, 1-718 482 6528, rockawaybrewco.com) has a taproom set inside an industrial garage space with picnic tables and metal barstools and eight rotating taps.

Fair, in Flushing Meadows Corona Park, the Queens Museum occupies the former New York City Building, which was built to house the Gotham-themed pavilion for the earlier World's Fair in 1939. In the 1940s, the structure was the first home of the United Nations. In 2013, the museum wrapped up a major renovation project that doubled its size and added an airy atrium. The extra space accommodates nine studios for local artists, a café and the World's Fair Visible Storage where more than 900 artefacts from the 1939 and 1964 fairs are on display. As well as changing historical, cultural and art exhibitions, the museum is home to the Neustadt Gallery, showcasing Tiffany glass, and the extraordinary Panorama of the City of New York (*see p265*).

Restaurants & cafés

♥ Daxi $$

2nd Floor, 136-20 Roosevelt Avenue, between Main & Union Streets (1-718 621 9999, www.daxisichuan.com). Subway 7 to Flushing-Main Street. **Open** *11am-11pm daily. Chinese*

On the second floor of the vast New World Mall, this palatial restaurant puts an upscale spin on fiery Sichuan cuisine such as Chengdu-style sautéed pork. Keep a bowl of black fungus salad handy as a refreshing – if sharp – palate cleanser, and wash down the spice with sour plum juice. Theatrical presentation highlights include dry Tibetan pork ribs served in a flowery birdcage.

Fu Run $

40-09 Prince Street, between Roosevelt Avenue & 40th Road (1-718 321 1363, www.furunflushing.com). Subway 7 to Flushing-Main Street. **Open** *11.30am-11pm daily. Chinese*

Thanks to a change in immigration patterns, Flushing has seen an increase in northern Chinese restaurants such as Fu Run, whose owners are from Dongbei (what was once known as Manchuria). They call their justly celebrated dish the 'Muslim lamb chop', but it's more like a half rack of ribs: a platter of bone-in, fatty meat is braised, then battered and deep-fried, the whole juicy slab blanketed with cumin seeds, chilli powder and flakes, and black and white sesame seeds.

The Bronx

The only NYC borough that's physically attached to the mainland, the Bronx seems remote to most visitors – and, indeed, many New Yorkers. Part of this perceived distance is due to the South Bronx's lingering reputation for urban strife, which was at its height in the 1970s. But there's more to the boogie-down borough than gritty cityscapes. In addition to its two best-known visitor attractions, Yankee Stadium and the Bronx Zoo, the area offers striking art deco architecture on the Grand Concourse, an up-and-coming art scene, old-school Italian eateries on Arthur Avenue and some of the most exquisite gardens in the city.

Visitors should note that although many parts of the Bronx are safe to explore, others, such as sections of the South Bronx and the northern swathe of the Grand Concourse, are still rough around the edges.

❤ **Don't miss**

1 Grand Concourse *p271*
A fascinating parade of (somewhat faded) art deco architecture.

2 Bronx Zoo *p273*
Huge family attraction that's home to thousands of animals.

3 New York Botanical Garden *p273*
A sprawling oasis for all seasons.

4 Wave Hill *p275*
Lush gardens with stunning Hudson River views.

5 Mike's Deli *p274*
Essential lunch stop.

6 Mott Haven Bar & Grill *p271*
Bronx-brewed beer and eclectic eats.

7 Dominick's *p273*
Classic Italian-American fare in basic surroundings

New York Botanical Garden

THE SOUTH BRONX

▶ *Subway B, D, 4 to 161st Street-Yankee Stadium; 6 to Hunts Point Avenue or 138th Street-Third Avenue.*

In the 1960s and '70s, the **South Bronx** was so ravaged by post-war 'white flight' and community displacement from the construction of the Cross Bronx Expressway that the neighbourhood became virtually synonymous with urban blight. Crime was rampant and arson became widespread, as landlords discovered that renovating decayed property was far less lucrative than simply burning it down to collect insurance. During a World Series baseball game at Yankee Stadium in 1977, TV cameras caught a building on fire just blocks away. 'Ladies and gentlemen,' commentator Howard Cosell told the world, 'the Bronx is burning.'

These days, the South Bronx is rising from the ashes. In the early 2000s, local government and non-profit organisations laid out plans to revitalise the area, which included transforming vacant lots into green spaces such as **Barretto Point Park** (between Tiffany & Barretto Streets) and **Hunts Point Riverside Park** (at the foot of Lafayette Avenue on the Bronx River). In 2005, Hunts Point became home to the city's **Fulton Fish Market** (1-718 378 2356, www.newfultonfishmarket.com), which moved from the site it had occupied for 180 years at South Street Seaport to a massive modern facility.

New apartment complexes are sprouting up, old warehouses are being redeveloped, once-crumbling tenements are being refurbished and, inevitably, chain stores are moving in. Yet despite developers' hopes for 'SoBro', the area has not quite turned into the Next Big Thing. Yet.

The area is slowly gaining traction as a creative hub. In 1994, a group of artists and community leaders converted an industrial building into **The Point** (940 Garrison Avenue, at Manida Street, 1-718 542 4139, www.thepoint.org, closed Sat, Sun), a mural-splashed community development centre with a much-used performance space and gallery, studios and workshops for neighbourhood children. In **Mott Haven** to the west, **Longwood Art Gallery @ Hostos** (450 Grand Concourse, at 149th Street, 1-718 518 6728, www.bronxarts.org, closed Mon, Sat, Sun), the creation of the Bronx Council on the Arts, mounts top-notch exhibits in a variety of media.

Of course, the vast majority of visitors to the South Bronx are just stopping long enough to take in a game at **Yankee Stadium**, where some of baseball's most famous legends, from Babe Ruth to Derek Jeter, have made history.

Sights & museums

Yankee Stadium

*River Avenue, at 161st Street (1-646 977 8687 tours, www.yankees.com). Subway B, D, 4 to 161st Street-Yankee Stadium. **Open** Tours vary; see website for details. **Admission** Tours $25, $23 reductions, $20 booked online, free under-4s.*

In 2009, the Yankees vacated the fabled 'House that Ruth Built' and moved into their

Yankee Stadium

new $1.3-billion stadium across the street. Monument Park, an open-air museum behind centre field that celebrates the exploits of past Yankee heroes, can be visited as part of a tour, along with the New York Yankees Museum and/or the dugout and the press box.

Bars

♥ Mott Haven Bar & Grill
1 Bruckner Boulevard, at Third Avenue (1-718 665 2001, www.motthavenbar.com). Subway 6 to Third Avenue-138th Street. **Open** *11am-11pm Mon, Tue, Sun; 11am-midnight Wed-Sat.*

In an unlikely industrial setting alongside the Third Avenue Bridge, this popular neighbourhood hangout has eight beers on tap, including Bronx Brewery Pale Ale, plus a wide range of bottled craft beers, and an eclectic menu of bar snacks, sandwiches and main dishes. The local hub hosts DJ brunches and cultural events, and bar-goers enjoy posing by the extensive street-art display just outside.

GRAND CONCOURSE

▶ *Subway B, D, 4 to 167th Street; B, D, 4 to Kingsbridge Road; B, D, 4 to 161st Street-Yankee Stadium.*

A few blocks east of Yankee Stadium runs the four-and-a-half-mile **Grand Concourse**, which begins at 138th Street in the South Bronx and ends at Mosholu Parkway just shy of **Van Cortlandt Park** (*see p274*). Once the most prestigious strip in the Bronx, the Grand Boulevard and Concourse (to give its official title) is still a must for lovers of art deco. Engineer Louis Risse designed the boulevard in 1892, modelling it on Paris's Champs-Elysées, and it opened to traffic in 1909. Following the arrival of a new subway line nearly a decade later, rapid development along the Concourse began in the architectural style so popular in the 1920s and '30s.

Starting at 161st Street and heading south, look for the permanent street plaques that make up the **Bronx Walk of Fame**, honouring famous Bronxites from Stanley Kubrick and Tony Orlando to Colin Powell and hip hop 'godfather' Afrika Bambaataa. Heading north, the buildings date mostly from the 1920s to the early '40s, and constitute the country's largest concentration of art deco housing outside Miami Beach. Erected in 1937 at the corner of 161st Street, **888 Grand Concourse** has a large concave entrance of gilded mosaic and is topped by a curvy metallic marquee.

Inside, the mirrored lobby's central fountain and sunburst-patterned floor could rival those of any hotel on Miami's Ocean Drive. On the south side of **Joyce Kilmer Park**, at 161st Street, is the elegant white-marble Lorelei Fountain, built in 1893 in Germany in homage to Heinrich Heine, who wrote the poem entitled 'Lorelei'. This was intended as the original entrance to the Concourse before it was extended south. The grandest building on the Concourse is the landmark **Andrew Freedman Home** (no.1125, between McClellan & E 166th Streets; 1-718 410 6735, andrewfreedmanhome. org. Closed Sun), a 1924 French-inspired limestone palazzo. Freedman, a millionaire businessman who had a hand in construction of the subway, left the bulk of his $7-million fortune with instructions to build a poorhouse for the rich – that is, those who had lost their fortunes and were suffering an impecunious old age. It's now a venue for art exhibitions and cultural events, and home to the Family Preservation Center (FPC), a community-based social service agency. Across the street, **The Bronx Museum of the Arts** stages cutting-edge exhibitions in a striking contemporary structure.

A couple of blocks north, **1150 Grand Concourse**, at McClellan Place, is a 1937 art deco apartment block commonly referred to as the 'Fish Building' because of the colourful marine-themed mosaic flanking its doors; pause inside the restored lobby for a glimpse of its two large murals depicting pastoral scenes. Near the intersection of Fordham Road, keep an eye out for the Italian rococo exterior of the **Paradise Theater** (2403 Grand Concourse, at 187th Street). Once the largest cinema in the city, it's now occupied by a religious organisation.

Further north to Kingsbridge Road lies the **Edgar Allan Poe Cottage**, a small wooden farmhouse where the writer lived

---

In the know
Hip hop history

DJ Kool Herc's old digs at 1520 Sedgwick Avenue in the West Bronx is the acknowledged birthplace of hip hop, but the area in and around the **Bronx River Houses** (174th Street, between Bronx River & Harrod Avenue) is where Afrika Bambaataa and his Universal Zulu Nation developed it into a phenomenon. The **Universal Hip Hop Museum** (www.uhhm.org), founded by a team including former rappers Kurtis Blow and Ice-T, is expected to open on the Harlem River waterfront in 2023.

Bronx Museum of the Arts

Bronx Zoo

from 1846 to 1849. It was moved to the Grand Concourse from its original spot on Fordham Road in 1913.

Sights & museums

The Bronx Museum of the Arts

1040 Grand Concourse, at 165th Street (1-718 681 6000, www.bronxmuseum.org). Subway B, D to 167th Street; 4 to 161st Street-Yankee Stadium. **Open** *11am-6pm Wed, Thur, Sat, Sun; 11am-8pm Fri.* **Admission** *free.*

With a permanent collection featuring more than 2,000 works, this multicultural art museum presents an eclectic programme of contemporary exhibitions. A particular focus is on 20th- and 21st-century artists who are of African, Asian or Latino ancestry, or have a connection to the Bronx.

Edgar Allan Poe Cottage

2640 Grand Concourse, at Kingsbridge Road (1-718 881 8900, www.bronxhistoricalsociety. org). Subway B, D, 4 to Kingsbridge Road. **Open** *10am-3pm Thur, Fri; 10am-4pm Sat; 1-5pm Sun.* **Admission** *$5; $3 reductions.*

Pay homage to Poe in the early-19th-century house where he spent the last three years of his life and wrote works including *Annabel Lee* and *The Bells*. The cottage has been restored with period furnishings, including the author's rocking chair.

BELMONT & BRONX PARK

▶ *Subway B, D, 4 to Fordham Road, then Bx12 bus; B, D, 4 to Bedford Park Boulevard; 2, 5 to E Tremont-W Farms Square.*

Settled in the late 19th century by Italian immigrants hired to landscape nearby Bronx Zoo, close-knit **Belmont** is centred on Arthur Avenue, lined with delis, bakeries, restaurants and stores selling T-shirts proclaiming the locale to be New York's 'real Little Italy'. Still celebrating Mass in Italian, neoclassical **Our Lady of Mt Carmel Church** (627 E 187th Street, at Hughes Avenue, 1-718 295 3770, ourladymtcarmelbx.org) has been serving the community for more than a century. Aspects of Italian-American history and culture are highlighted in infrequent exhibitions at the **Enrico Fermi Cultural Center** (in the Belmont Branch Library, 610 E 186th Street, between Arthur & Hughes Avenues, 1-718 933 6410).

Food, however, is the main reason to visit. **Arthur Avenue Retail Market** (2344 Arthur Avenue, between Crescent Avenue & E 186th Street) is a covered market built in the 1940s when Mayor Fiorello La Guardia campaigned to get the pushcarts off the street. Inside, you'll find **Mike's Deli**, where you can order enormous sandwiches bursting with Italian cold cuts. For a full meal, try old-school red-sauce joints such as **Mario's**, featured in several *Sopranos* episodes and Mario Puzo's

of an Asian rainforest inside a 37,000sq ft building, while lions, giraffes, zebras and other animals roam the African Plains. Step aboard the Wild Asia Monorail (open May-Oct, admission $6), which tours more than 40 acres of exhibits inhabited by gaur, tigers, elephants and more. The popular Congo Gorilla Forest has turned 6.5 acres into a dramatic central African rainforest habitat. A glass-enclosed tunnel winds through the area, allowing visitors to get close to the dozens of primate families in residence, including the largest troop of western lowland gorillas in North America. Tiger Mountain is populated by Siberian and Malayan tigers, while the Himalayan Highlands features snow leopards and red pandas. There's a dedicated children's zoo (open May-Oct, $6), and kids will also adore Madagascar!, featuring exotic animals from the lush island nation off the eastern coast of Africa, including five species of lemurs, tortoises and hissing cockroaches.

► *For other zoos, see p196, p243 and p266.*

novel *The Godfather*; or bare-bones dining room **Dominick's**.

On the eastern edge of Belmont, within easy walking distance of Arthur Avenue, is **Bronx Park**, home to two of the borough's most celebrated attractions. Opened in 1899 by Theodore Roosevelt, the 265-acre **Bronx Zoo** has expansive habitats, plus rides and other fun features for kids. A 15-minute walk north of the zoo – and still in Bronx Park – brings you to the **New York Botanical Garden**.

Sights & museums

❤ Bronx Zoo

2300 Southern Boulevard (1-718 220 5100, www.bronxzoo.com). Subway 2, 5 to E Tremont-W Farms Square, then walk to the zoo's Asia entrance; or Metro-North (Harlem Line local) from Grand Central Terminal to Fordham, then take the Bx9 bus to 183rd Street & Southern Boulevard. **Open** *Apr-Oct 10am-5pm Mon-Fri; 10am-5.30pm Sat, Sun. Nov-Mar 10am-4.30pm daily.* **Admission** *$23; $15-$21 reductions; pay what you wish Wed. Some rides & exhibitions cost extra.*

The Bronx Zoo shuns cages in favour of indoor and outdoor environments that mimic natural habitats. More than 8,000 animals, representing more than 600 species, live here. Home to monkeys, leopards and tapirs, the lush, steamy Jungle World is a recreation

❤ New York Botanical Garden

Bronx River Parkway, at Fordham Road (1-718 817 8700, www.nybg.org). Subway B, D, 4 to Bedford Park Boulevard, then 20min walk or Bx26 bus to the garden's Mosholu Gate; or Metro-North (Harlem Line local) from Grand Central Terminal to Botanical Garden. **Open** *Jan, Feb 10am-5pm Tue-Sun. Mar-Dec 10am-6pm Tue-Sun.* **Admission** *$23-$28; $10-$25 reductions. Grounds only free Wed, 9-10am Sat.*

The serene 250 acres comprise 50 gardens and plant collections, including the Peggy Rockefeller Rose Garden, the Everett Children's Adventure Garden and the last 50 original acres of a forest that once covered the whole city area. The Azalea Garden features around 3,000 vivid azaleas and rhododendrons, while the wild flowers and trees of the Native Plant Garden attract birds and butterflies. In spring, clusters of lilac, cherry, magnolia and crab apple trees burst into bloom; in autumn you'll see vivid foliage in the oak and maple groves. The grand Enid A Haupt Conservatory, built in 1902, contains A World of Plants, a series of environmental galleries that takes you on an eco-tour through tropical rainforests, deserts and a palm tree oasis.

Restaurants & cafés

❤ Dominick's $$

2335 Arthur Avenue, between Crescent Avenue & E 186th Street (1-718 733 2807). Subway B, D, 4 to Fordham Road, then Bx12 bus. **Open** *noon-9.30pm Mon, Wed-Sat; 1-8.30pm Sun.* **No cards.** Italian

In this basic, pine-accented dining room – one of the most popular on Arthur Avenue – neighbourhood folks, out-of-towners and tracksuited wiseguys feast at long, crowded tables on massive platters of veal *parmigiana*, steaming bowls of mussels marinara and linguine with white clam sauce. The only menu is posted on the wall, but you can trust your waiter's advice.

Mario's $$

*2342 Arthur Avenue, between Crescent Avenue & E 186th Street (1-718 584 1188, www. mariosrestarthurave.com). Subway B, D, 4 to Fordham Road, then Bx12 bus. **Open** noon-9pm Tue-Thur, Sun; noon-10pm Fri, Sat. Italian*

The Migliucci family has stayed in business since 1919 by pleasing the customer; if you don't see what you want on the menu, feel free to ask for embellishments or modifications to the Neapolitan-inspired cuisine. Do as the regulars do and order the signature gnocchi, which arrive perfectly light and plump with a deliciously savoury and tangy sauce. For something more hearty, try the *saltimbocca alla romana* (veal braised in Marsala wine and served over spinach sautéed with prosciutto), or the generous lobster-tail *oreganata*, accompanied by a baked clam.

❤ Mike's Deli $

*Arthur Avenue Retail Market, 2344 Arthur Avenue, between Crescent Avenue & E 186th Street (1-718 295 5033, www.arthuravenue. com). Subway B, D, 4 to Fordham Road, then Bx12 bus. **Open** 7am-7pm Mon-Wed; 7am-9pm Thur-Sat; 9am-7pm Sun. Café/deli*

This venerable delicatessen, butcher and café may leave you paralysed with indecision: the glossy menu lists more than 50 sandwiches, plus platters, pastas, soups, salads, *stromboli* (a kind of cheese turnover) and sides. Try the Yankee Stadium Big Boy hero sandwich, stuffed with prosciutto, soppressata, mozzarella, capicola, mortadella, peppers and lettuce.

Bars

Bronx Beer Hall

*Arthur Avenue Retail Market, 2344 Arthur Avenue, between Crescent Avenue & E 186th Street (1-347 396 0555, www. thebronxbeerhall.com). Subway B, D, 4 to Fordham Road, then Bx12 bus. **Open** 4-11pm Mon; 11am-2am or later Tue-Sat; 11am-8pm Sun.*

Surrounded by the cigar makers and meat and cheese counters of the septuagenarian

Arthur Avenue Market, patrons can sit at BBH's rustic wooden bar and imbibe one of six New York State choices on draft. Some of the grub – like antipasto platters of cheese and sausages served with bread and sides such as hot peppers – is from market purveyors such as Mike's Deli. Late-night pizzas are courtesy of a popular Arthur Avenue restaurant.

RIVERDALE & VAN CORTLANDT PARK

▶ *Subway D to Norwood-205th Street; 1 to 242nd Street-Van Cortlandt Park.*

Riverdale, along the north-west coast of the Bronx, reflects the borough's suburban past; its huge homes perch on narrow, winding streets that meander towards the Hudson River. The only one you can actually visit is **Wave Hill**, an 1843 stone mansion set on a former private estate that has beautiful gardens and a gallery. In the nearby 1,146-acre **Van Cortlandt Park** (entrance on Broadway, at 242nd Street), you can hike through a 100-year-old forest, play golf on the nation's first municipal course or visit the oldest building in the Bronx, the **Van Cortlandt House Museum**. Abutting the park is **Woodlawn Cemetery** (1-718 920 0500, www.thewoodlawncemetery. org), the resting place for such notable souls as Herman Melville, Duke Ellington, Miles Davis, FW Woolworth and Fiorello La Guardia. To help you to pay your respects, maps are available at the main entrance at Webster Avenue and E 233rd Street or you can download a free app. About five blocks south on Bainbridge Avenue, history buffs will also enjoy the **Museum of Bronx History**, set in a 1758 stone farmhouse.

Sights & museums

Museum of Bronx History

*Valentine-Varian House, 3266 Bainbridge Avenue, between Van Cortlandt Avenue East & 208th Street (1-718 881 8900, www. bronxhistoricalsociety.org). Subway D to Norwood-205th Street. **Open** 10am-4pm Sat; 1-5pm Sun. **Admission** $5; $3 reductions.*

Operated by the Bronx County Historical Society, the museum features rotating exhibitions of its collection of documents and photos in the Valentine-Varian House, a Federal-style fieldstone residence built in 1758.

▶ *The society also offers historical tours of the Bronx neighbourhoods.*

Wave Hill

contemporary art shows inspired by nature, and the property is also a venue for concerts and other events.

PELHAM BAY PARK

▶ *Subway 6 to Pelham Bay Park.*

At more than three times the size of Central Park, the 2,765-acre **Pelham Bay Park** (www.pelhambaypark.org), in the borough's north-eastern corner, is NYC's largest green space. Within the park, the 19th-century **Bartow-Pell Mansion Museum** overlooks Long Island Sound. The park's 13 miles of coastline skirt the Hutchinson river to the west and Long Island Sound and Eastchester Bay to the east. In summer, locals hit **Orchard Beach**; developed in the 1930s, this 'Riviera of New York' is that rare beast – a Robert Moses creation (with landfill-fortified sands and a promenade) not universally lamented.

Van Cortlandt House Museum

Van Cortlandt Park, entrance on Broadway, at 246th Street (1-718 543 3344, www. vchm.org). Subway 1 to 242nd Street-Van Cortlandt Park. **Open** *10am-4pm Tue-Fri; 11am-4pm Sat, Sun (hrs vary).* **Admission** *$5; $3 reductions; free under-13s. Pay what you wish Wed.*

Frederick Van Cortlandt began construction of this Georgian-style stone house on his family's wheat plantation in 1748. Later, it was alternately used as headquarters by George Washington and British General Sir William Howe during the Revolutionary War. The rooms are furnished in period style, including the 'Dutch chamber', evoking life in the New Amsterdam colony.

❤ Wave Hill

W 249th Street, at Independence Avenue (1-718 549 3200, www.wavehill.org). Subway 1 to 242nd Street-Van Cortlandt Park or Metro-North (Hudson Line local) from Grand Central Terminal to Riverdale, then free shuttle (see website for details). **Open** *Mid Mar-Oct 9am-5.30pm Tue-Sun. Nov-mid Mar 9am-4.30pm Tue-Sun. Gallery 10am-4.30pm Tue-Sun.* **Admission** *$10; $4-$6 reductions; free under-6s. Free 9am-noon Tue, Sat.*

Laze around in 28 lush acres overlooking the Hudson River at Wave Hill, the setting of a Georgian Revival house that was home at various times to Mark Twain, Teddy Roosevelt and conductor Arturo Toscanini. Now open to the public, the grounds contain exquisite cultivated gardens and woodlands commanding excellent views of the river. The small on-site gallery hosts intriguing

Sights & museums

Bartow-Pell Mansion Museum

895 Shore Road North, at Pelham Bay Park (1-718 885 1461, www. bartowpellmansionmuseum.org). Subway 6 to Pelham Bay Park, then Bee-Line bus 45 (ask driver to stop at Bartow-Pell Mansion). **Museum** *noon-4pm Wed, Sat, Sun.* **Grounds** *8.30am-dusk daily.* **Admission** *$8; $6 reductions; free under-6s.*

The origins of this impressive property, which has been a museum since the 1940s, date from 1654, when Thomas Pell bought the land from the Siwonay Indians. It was Robert Bartow, publisher and Pell descendant, who added the 1842 Greek Revival stone mansion and carriage house. The grounds, with its trails and gardens, can be visited free of charge.

> ### In the know
> #### City Island
>
> It may look like a slightly gritty New England fishing town, but City Island, on the north-west edge of Long Island Sound, is part of the Bronx and accessible by the Bx29 bus from Pelham Bay Park. Two casual eateries on Belden Point, **Johnny's Reef** (2 City Island Avenue, 1-718 885 2086, www.johnnysreefrestaurant.com) and **Tony's Pier Restaurant** (1 City Island Avenue, 1-718 885 1424, www.tonyspiercityisland.com) offer outdoor seating. Grab a couple of beers and a basket of fried clams, sit at one of the picnic tables and watch the boats sail by.

Staten Island

With a largely suburban vibe, abundant parkland and beaches, New York's third largest – but least-populated – borough feels removed from the rest of the city. And, physically, it is. To visitors, Staten Island is best known for its ferry. A vital public-transport link to Manhattan for locals, it just happens to pass by Lady Liberty. If you decide to embark on this free mini cruise, it's worth taking time to stroll along the Esplanade to soak up the Manhattan skyline views. Alternatively, venture further to explore historic structures and quirky museums, or hike in the borough's sprawling green spaces.

❤ Don't miss

1 Staten Island Ferry *p279*
Fabulous views for free.

2 Fort Wadsworth *p279*
Sweeping harbour views from a historic site.

3 Greenbelt *p279*
Miles of woodland and wetland trails.

4 Jacques Marchais Museum of Tibetan Art *p280*
An offbeat shrine to a collector's passion.

5 Snug Harbor Cultural Center & Botanical Garden *p280*
Quirky collections and gardens on an 1800s campus.

Postcards 9/11 memorial *p278*

Staten Island became one of the five boroughs in 1898, but remained a backwater until 1964, when the Verrazano-Narrows Bridge joined the island to Bay Ridge in Brooklyn. Many say that's when small-town Staten Island truly vanished. Still, many quaint aspects remain, not least the free Staten Island Ferry. Next to the St George ferry terminal, NYC's first outlet mall **Empire Outlets** (www.empireoutletsnyc.com) features mid-range and designer retailers, including discount department store Nordstrom Rack. Walk along the **Esplanade**, with its stirring views of lower Manhattan across the harbour, to pay your respects at *Postcards*, a memorial to the 274 Staten Islanders lost on 9/11. The fibreglass wings of the sculpture frame the spot where the Twin Towers used to stand.

Across the street from the ferry terminal is the Borough Hall, with its distinctive clock tower. Walk up Nick Laporte Place alongside it to Hyatt Street for a glimpse of the baroque-style lobby of the **St George Theatre** (35 Hyatt Street, at Central Avenue, 1-718 442 2900, www.stgeorgetheatre.com). The restored 1920s vaudeville venue stages family-friendly fare and concerts with classic rock bands or veteran stars such as Michael Bolton. If you turn right on to St Marks Place, you'll come to the landmark **St George Historic District**. Covering portions of St Marks and Carroll Places, and Westervelt and Hamilton Avenues, it features Queen Anne and Colonial Revival houses, some from the early 1830s.

The island's attractions, such as historic **Fort Wadsworth** and the collection of quirky museums and sprawling grounds of **Snug Harbor Cultural Center & Botanical Garden**, are scattered across the borough.

Sights & museums

Alice Austen House

*2 Hylan Boulevard, at Edgewater Street (1-718 816 4506, www.aliceausten.org). S51 bus to Hylan Boulevard. **Open** Mar-Dec 1-5pm Tue-Fri; 11am-5pm Sat, Sun. Closed Jan, Feb. **Admission** suggested donation $5.*

This restored 17th-century cottage was the home of photographer Alice Austen (1866-1952), known for her pioneering documentary work. A rotating selection of her glass-negative images are on display, as well as changing contemporary photography exhibits. The restored grounds, which have

♥ **Time to eat & drink**

Grandma-made dishes
Enoteca Maria *p281*

Tapas and sangria
Beso *p281*

Traditional beer garden
Killmeyer's Old Bavaria Inn *p281*

Staten Island Ferry

impressive harbour views, often host concerts and events.

Conference House

7455 Hylan Boulevard, at Satterlee Street (1-718 984 6046, www.conferencehouse.org). S78 bus to Craig Avenue & Hylan Boulevard. **Open** *Apr-mid Dec 1-4pm Fri-Sun.* **Admission** *$4; $3 reductions.*

In 1776, Britain's Lord Howe parlayed with John Adams and Benjamin Franklin here, trying to forestall the American Revolution. The stone manor house was built around 1680 by Captain Christopher Billopp, and tours point out 18th-century furnishings, decor and daily objects. The lovely grounds command a terrific view over Raritan Bay, and provide a picturesque setting for free concerts and events.

♥ Fort Wadsworth

210 New York Avenue, on the east end of Bay Street (1-718 354 4500, www.nps.gov/gate/index.htm). S51 bus to Fort Wadsworth. **Open** *dawn-dusk daily. Visitor centre 9am-5pm Wed-Sun. Tours vary; call or see website for information.* **Admission** *free.*

This prime defensive site was established by the Dutch in the 17th century and used by British forces during the Revolutionary War. The current structures were built between the mid-19th and early 20th centuries, including granite Battery Weed (accessible by guided tour), which protected the southern entrance to New York Harbor during the Civil War.

In the know
♥ Getting around

The free **Staten Island Ferry** (1-212 639 9675, www.siferry.com) runs between the Financial District's Whitehall Terminal (4 South Street, at Whitehall Street) and the island's St George Terminal, where you can catch the buses noted in this chapter. The crossing takes 25 minutes. The Staten Island Railway (SIR) has one line running from St George to Tottenville on the southern tip of the island. Fares are the same as the subway and paid with a MetroCard (see p383).

♥ Greenbelt

Greenbelt Nature Center *700 Rockland Avenue, at Brielle Avenue (1-718 351 3450, www.sigreenbelt.org). S61 bus to Forest Hill Road/Rockland Avenue, or SIR to New Dorp, then S57 bus to Rockland Avenue/Brielle Avenue.* **Open** *Apr-Oct 10am-5pm Tue-Sun. Nov-Mar 11am-5pm Wed-Sun.* **Admission** *free.*

High Rock Park *200 Nevada Avenue, at Rockland Avenue. Hike from Greenbelt Nature Center, or S62 bus to Manor Road, then S54 bus to Nevada Avenue.* **Open** *dawn-dusk daily.* **Admission** *free.*

With 2,800 acres of open space, the Greenbelt offers 35 miles of trails through parks and woodland. Start your expedition

Fort Wadsworth p279

at the Nature Center, where you can pick up a copy of the trail map (also on the website). A mile away, at the 90-acre High Rock Park, visitors can hike the Lavender Trail around Loosestrife Swamp, or climb the man-made Moses' Mountain for panoramic treetop views.

Historic Richmond Town

*441 Clarke Avenue, at St Patrick's Place (1-718 351 1611, www.historicrichmondtown. org). S74 bus to Richmond Road/St Patrick's Place. **Open** 1-5pm Wed-Sun. Tours 2pm Wed-Fri; 1.30pm, 3pm Sat, Sun (see website for extended summer hrs). **Admission** $8; $5-$6 reductions; free under-4s.*

The former county seat, Historic Richmond Town evokes Staten Island's rural roots, with a collection of buildings dating as far back as the 1660s. Guided tours take in restored homes and businesses, including a general store and a carpenter's shop, sometimes staffed by period-garbed craftspeople. The on-site historical museum exhibits objects reflecting old-time island life, such as a 19th-century oyster-fishing skiff, locally made baskets and antique toys.

♥ Jacques Marchais Museum of Tibetan Art

*338 Lighthouse Avenue, off Richmond Road (1-718 987 3500, www.tibetanmuseum.org). S74 bus to Lighthouse Avenue. **Open** Mar-Jan 1-5pm Wed-Sun. Feb 1-5pm Sat (weather permitting). **Admission** $6; $4 reductions; free under-6s.*

This small museum, built by collector Jacques Marchais in the 1940s in the style of a Himalayan monastery, contains a formidable Buddhist altar, tranquil meditation gardens and an extensive collection of Tibetan art and artefacts.

National Lighthouse Museum

200 The Promenade, at Lighthouse Point (1-718 390 0040, www.lighthousemuseum.

*org). 6 min walk from St George Ferry Terminal. **Open** Apr-Oct 11am-5pm Tue-Sun; Nov-Mar 11am 4pm Tue-Sun. **Admission** $7; $4-$5 reductions; free under-12s.*

Housed in a 1912 foundry at the former general depot of the United States Lighthouse Service, the museum displays more than 180 model lighthouses, as well as exhibits focusing on light sources and keepers' stories. The institution also runs themed boat tours roughly every month in summer and autumn, exploring nearby lighthouses, ship graveyards and other attractions on New York Harbor and the East and Hudson rivers.

♥ Snug Harbor Cultural Center & Botanical Garden

1000 Richmond Terrace, between Snug Harbor Road & Tysen Avenue (1-718 425 3504, www.snug-harbor.org). S40 bus to Richmond Terrace/North Gate, or S44 bus to Henderson Avenue/South Gate.

Botanical Garden *1-718 425 3504, www. snug-harbor.org. **Open** dawn-dusk daily. Chinese Scholar's Garden Apr-Oct noon-5pm Tue-Fri; 10am-5pm Sat, Sun. Nov noon-4pm Tue-Fri; 10am-4pm Sat, Sun. Dec-Feb 10am-4pm Fri-Sun. Connie Gretz Secret Garden mid June-Aug 10am-4pm. **Admission** Chinese Scholar's Garden $5; $4 reductions; free under-6s. Connie Gretz Secret Garden $3 per child. Grounds & other gardens free.*

Newhouse Center for Contemporary Art *1-718 425 3504, www.snug-harbor.org. **Open** Mar-Dec noon-7pm Thur, Fri; 11am-5pm Sat, Sun. Closed Jan, Feb. **Admission** $5; $4 reductions; free under-6s. Combined ticket with Chinese Scholar's Garden $8; $7 reductions.*

Noble Maritime Collection *1-718 447 6490, www.noblemaritime.org. **Open** noon-5pm Thur-Sun. **Admission** Pay what you wish.*

Staten Island Museum *1-718 727 1135, www. statenislandmuseum.org. **Open** 11am-5pm*

Wed-Sun. **Admission** *Suggested donation $8; $2-$5 reductions.*

Stately Greek Revival structures form the nucleus of this former sailors' retirement home. Dating from 1833, the centre has been restored and converted into an arts complex.

As Staten Island's premier contemporary art venue, the Newhouse Center holds several annual exhibitions featuring international and local sculptors, painters and mixed-media artists.

The Noble Maritime Collection is dedicated to the artist-seaman John A Noble, who had a 'floating studio' moored in the Kill van Kull, between Staten Island and New Jersey. As well as his maritime-themed paintings, Noble's houseboat is on display, restored to its appearance when the artist was featured in *National Geographic* magazine in 1954. The museum also has a collection of model ships and exhibits about life at the former Sailors' Snug Harbor, including a recreated dormitory room, circa 1900.

Founded as a private society of naturalists in 1881, the Staten Island Museum has an eclectic permanent collection spanning everything from fossils and insect specimens to decorative art, photographs and artefacts. The permanent exhibition 'Opening the Treasure Box' showcases some of the globe-spanning holdings, including Egyptian and Roman antiquities, an embroidered dragon robe from Imperial China and intricately beaded Sioux moccasins. Changing shows highlight everything from local artists to borough history.

Outside are more than a dozen themed gardens, including the traditional Chinese Scholar's Garden, with its pavilions, meandering paths and delicate footbridges, and the medieval-style Secret Garden, complete with a 38ft-high castle and a maze.

In addition to the above, the Staten Island Children's Museum (1-718 273 2060, sichildrensmuseum.org, closed Mon), art and music schools and a dance centre are also based here.

Restaurants & cafés

❤ Beso $$
11 Schuyler Street, between Richmond Terrace & Stuyvesant Place (1-718 816 8162, www. besonyc.com). 10 min walk from St George Ferry Terminal. **Open** *11.30am-11pm Mon-Thur; 11.30am-midnight Fri, Sat; noon-10pm Sun. Spanish*

Although Beso is billed as a Spanish tapas bar, the menu at this little spot right by the ferry terminal goes far beyond Iberia (by way of

Cuba, Mexico and Puerto Rico, for starters). Grab a fruity-sweet glass of tequila-spiked sangria and go straight for the house-made guacamole, seafood and chorizo paella, or Bistec Cubano – skirt steak marinated in sherry with herbs and garlic and served with ginger-mojito sauce, fried plantains and Cuban salad.

❤ Enoteca Maria $$
27 Hyatt Street, at Central Avenue (1-718 447 2777, www.enotecamaria.com). 10 min walk from St George Ferry Terminal. **Open** *noon-8.30pm (last seating) Thur-Sun.* **No cards.** *Italian/eclectic*

When Jody Scaravella opened this cosy restaurant in the St George neighbourhood near the ferry terminal, he named it after his mother and hired Italian *nonnas* to cook regional cuisine. In 2015, he broadened the evening repertoire, with globe-spanning guest grandmothers from other parts of Europe, South America and Asia in the kitchen. Choose from daily-changing pastas and traditional Italian meat dishes such as *capuzzelle* – a whole sheep's head stuffed with breadcrumbs, vegetables, rosemary and garlic baked in white wine. Alternatively, try specialities hailing from the likes of Bangladesh, Tokyo or Buenos Aires. Advance booking is recommended, as the restaurant is extremely popular.

Trattoria Romana $$
1476 Hylan Boulevard, at Ben ton Avenue (1-718 980 3113, www.trattoriaromanasi. com). Staten Island Railway to Old Town. **Open** *noon-10pm Tue-Thur; noon-11pm Fri, Sat; 1-9pm Sun. Italian*

This casually elegant eatery owes its popularity to the constant presence of chef-owner Vittorio Asoli as well as to the wood-burning brick oven that cooks everything from pizza to portobellos. The *saltimbocca alla romana* is a classic done right – tender veal scaloppine topped with salty prosciutto and accented with butter and sage.

Bars

❤ Killmeyer's Old Bavaria Inn
4254 Arthur Kill Road, at Sharrotts Road (1-718 984 1202, www.killmeyers.com). S74 bus to Arthur Kill Road/Sharrotts Road. **Open** *11.30am-midnight Mon-Thur; 11.30am-2am Fri, Sat; noon-midnight Sun.*

Semi-industrial Arthur Kill Road is home to this Bavarian bar and eatery with 19th-century roots. Sit in the beer garden (open May-Oct) and enjoy any of 100-plus beers, plus *sauerbraten*, spicy goulash and potato pancakes. Note that the kitchen typically closes a couple of hours before the bar.

Experience

Jazz Age Lawn Party p287

Events

The best annual festivals and happenings on the NYC calendar

New Yorkers hardly struggle to find something to celebrate. In addition to well-known city-wide traditions, numerous offbeat shindigs dot the calendar. Soak up the local vibe at quirky annual events such as Brooklyn's Mermaid Parade or the Jazz Age Lawn Party on Governors Island, and take advantage of free summer concerts and outdoor films and theatre in the city's green spaces, such as Central, Bryant and Madison Square Parks. For more festivals and events, check individual chapters in the Experience section. Before you set out, or plan a trip around an event, it's wise to call or check online first as dates, times and locations are subject to change. Of course, this is only a fraction of what's going on in the great metropolis each season – for the latest listings and more ideas, consult *Time Out New York* magazine or www.timeout.com/newyork.

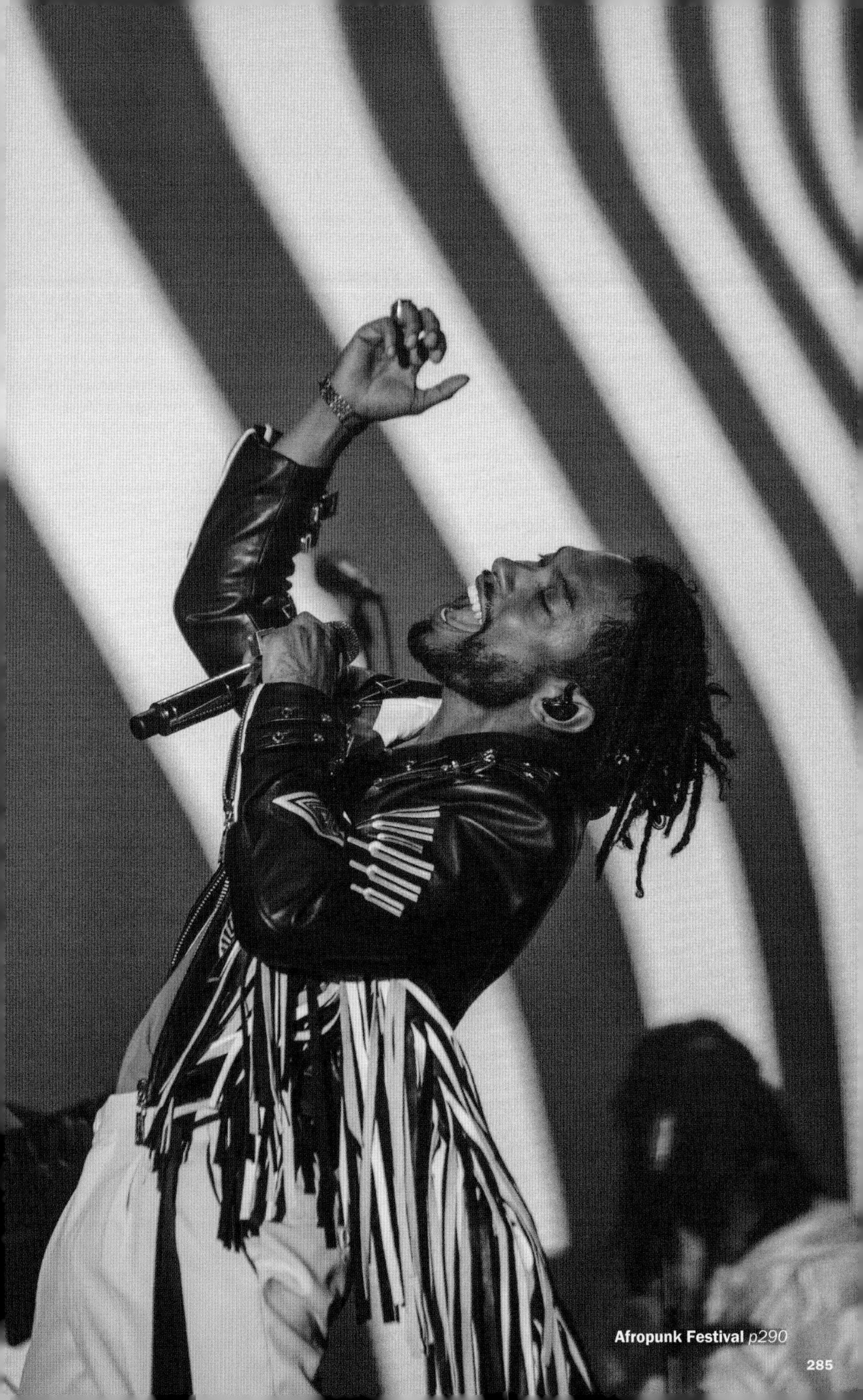

Afropunk Festival *p290*

Spring

Armory Show

Piers 92 & 94, Twelfth Avenue, at 55th Street, Hell's Kitchen (1-212 645 6440, www. thearmoryshow.com). Subway C, E to 50th Street. **Date** *early Mar.*

Although its name pays homage to the 1913 show that introduced avant-garde European art to an American audience, this contemporary international art mart debuted in 1999. It's now held on the Hudson River. In recent years, several other annual art shows have popped up around the city during this period, now known as Armory Week.

St Patrick's Day Parade

Fifth Avenue, from 44th to 79th Streets, Midtown to Upper East Side (www. nycstpatricksparade.org). Subway E, M to Fifth Avenue-53rd Street; N, R, W to Fifth Avenue. **Date** *17 Mar.*

This massive march is even older than the United States – it was started by a group of homesick Irish conscripts from the British army in 1762. If you feel like braving huge crowds and potentially nasty weather, you'll see thousands of green-clad merrymakers strutting to the sounds of pipe bands.

Easter Parade

Fifth Avenue, from 49th to 57th Streets, Midtown. Subway E, M to Fifth Avenue-53rd Street. **Date** *late Mar/early Apr.*

From 10am on Easter Sunday, participants gather to show off elaborately constructed hats – we're talking noggin-toppers shaped like the NYC skyline or the Coney Island Cyclone. Between 49th and 57th Streets, Fifth Avenue becomes a promenade of gussied-up crowds milling around and showing off their extravagant bonnets.

Tribeca Film Festival

Date *Apr.*

See p299 Film festivals.

❤ Sakura Matsuri

For listings, see p243 **Brooklyn Botanic Garden**. *Date late Apr.*

The climax to the cherry blossom season, when more than 200 trees are in flower, the annual Sakura Matsuri celebrates both the blooms and Japanese culture with concerts, traditional dance, cosplay fashion shows, manga exhibitions and tea ceremonies.

Five Boro Bike Tour

Lower Manhattan to Staten Island (1-212 870 2080, www.bikenewyork.org). Subway R, W to Whitehall Street-South Ferry; 1 to South Ferry. **Date** *early May.*

Thousands of cyclists take over the city for a 40-mile, car-free Tour de New York. Advance registration is required if you want to take part. The route begins near Battery Park, moves up through Manhattan and makes a circuit of the boroughs before winding up at Staten Island's Fort Wadsworth for a festival.

Frieze Art Fair New York

Randalls Island Park (www.frieze.com). **Date** *early/mid May.*

The New York edition of the tent-tastic London art fair first arrived on Randalls Island in 2011. A global array of around 200 galleries sets up shop under a temporary structure overlooking the East River, and several contemporary artists are commissioned to create site-specific works.

Washington Square Outdoor Art Exhibit

Various streets surrounding Washington Square Park, from University Place, at 13th Street, to Schwartz Plaza, at 3rd Street, Greenwich Village (1-212 982 6255, www. wsoae.org). Subway A, B, C, D, E, F, M to W 4th Street; R, W to 8th Street-NYU. **Date** *late May/early June & early/mid Sept.*

In 1931, Jackson Pollock and Willem de Kooning propped up a few of their paintings on the pavement near Washington Square

---

❤ Best events

Sakura Matsuri *p286*
The climax of the cherry blossom season.

SummerStage *p287*
Eclectic free performances in city parks.

Jazz Age Lawn Party *p287*
Young hepcats dance and mingle in period attire.

Mermaid Parade *p288*
Creative costumes and aquatic floats.

Midsummer Night Swing *p288*
Outdoor dance parties at Lincoln Center.

Village Halloween Parade *p292*
Spectacular get-ups, bands, dancers and giant puppets fill Sixth Avenue.

New York Film Festival *p299*
Premières and star appearances.

Park and called it a show. A lot has changed since then: now, close to 100 artists and artisans exhibit here. If you miss it in May and June, you'll have another chance to browse in late summer/early autumn.

Summer

Shakespeare in the Park
Date late May-Aug.

See p347.

BRIC Celebrate Brooklyn! Festival
Prospect Park Bandshell, Prospect Park West, at 9th Street, Park Slope, Brooklyn (1-718 683 5600, www.bricartsmedia. org). Subway F to Seventh Avenue. Date June-Aug.

Community arts organisation BRIC launched this series of outdoor performances to revitalise Prospect Park, and now the festival is Brooklyn's premier summer fête. It includes music, dance, film and spoken word acts. A $5 donation is requested and there's an admission charge for some shows.

❤ SummerStage
Rumsey Playfield, Central Park, entrance on Fifth Avenue, at 72nd Street, Upper East Side (1-212 360 2777, www.summerstage.org). Subway 6 to 68th Street-Hunter College. Date June-Sept.

Rockers, world music stars, opera singers, DJs, dance companies and more hit the main stage in Central Park – and green spaces across the five boroughs – for this popular, long-running and mostly free annual series. Show up early or listen from outside the enclosure gates.

❤ Jazz Age Lawn Party
Governors Island, see p75 (www. jazzagelawnparty.com). Date mid June & mid Aug.

Young hepcats in period garb gather on the green lawns of Colonels Row to drink cocktails and look fantastic. Held twice during the summer, the weekend event includes Charleston contests, old-timey swimsuit competitions and a DJ spinning 78rpm records, among other activities.

National Puerto Rican Day Parade
Fifth Avenue, from 44th to 79th Streets, Midtown to Upper East Side (www.nprdpinc. org). Date early/mid June.

This exuberant celebration of the city's largest Hispanic community and its culture draws crowds of more than a million. The march features *vejigantes* (carnival dancers), colourful floats, and live salsa and reggaetón bands.

NYC Flea Markets
Shop and snack at seasonal bazaars

Although traditional antiques and bric-a-brac markets have waned, seasonal bazaars, combining handmade and vintage goods with gourmet food vendors are now an indispensable part of the warm-weather scene. These are a few of the most popular, typically open April to October.

Brooklyn Flea & Smorgasburg
Launched in 2008, the trailblazing Brooklyn Flea offers high-quality crafts, locally designed fashion and gourmet snacks alongside vintage wares. Around 60 vendors gather under the Manhattan Bridge Archway and adjacent Pearl Street in Dumbo, Brooklyn, on Sundays, while a Williamsburg location (North 6th Street, at Kent Avenue) operates on Saturdays. The nosh-only spin-off Smorgasburg (www.smorgasburg.com) is at Williamsburg's East River State Park on Saturdays and Prospect Park on Sundays.

Hester Street Fair
On the site of a former Lower East Side pushcart market (Hester Street, at Essex Street, www.hesterstreetfair.com), this Saturday fixture has around 50 stalls selling wares such as emerging-designer clothing, hand-crafted jewellery and art objects, and often includes themed events, such as an 'ice-cream social' or 'lobster and beer'.

Smorgasburg

Jazz Age Lawn Party *p287*

Egg Rolls, Egg Creams & Empanadas Festival

Museum at Eldridge Street. For listings, see p113. **Date** *mid June.*

Organised by the Museum at Eldridge Street, this block party celebrates the convergence of Jewish, Chinese and Puerto Rican traditions on the Lower East Side, with klezmer and bomba music, acrobats, Chinese opera, tea ceremonies and, of course, plenty of the titular treats.

Governors Ball Music Festival

Randalls Island Park (www. governorsballmusicfestival.com). **Date** *early June.*

A bona fide big-tent music festival, Governors Ball takes over Randalls Island Park with hip-hop chart toppers, tastemaker-approved buzz bands, left-field pop heroes and dance-commanding EDM overlords. The eclectic slate of crowd-pleasers has recently included Tyler, the Creator, the Strokes and Florence + the Machine.

Museum Mile Festival

Fifth Avenue, from 82nd to 110th Streets, Upper East Side (www.museummilefestival. org). Subway 4, 5, 6 to 86th Street; 6 to 96th Street or 103rd Street. **Date** *early/mid June.*

Several of the city's most prestigious art institutions – including the Guggenheim,

the Met and the Museum of the City of New York – open their doors to the public free of charge. Music, dance and children's activities turn this into a celebration stretching for nearly 30 blocks, but you'll have to arrive early to stand a chance of getting into the museums themselves.

New York Philharmonic Concerts in the Parks

Various parks throughout the city (1-212 875 5709, www.nyphil.org). **Date** *mid/late June.*

Thousands of classical music lovers lay their picnic blankets on Central Park's Great Lawn, as well as in other green spaces across the city, for free evening performances. The crowd-pleasing programmes are followed by fireworks.

River to River Festival

Various venues in lower Manhattan and on Governors Island (1-212 219 9401, www.lmcc. net/river-to-river). **Date** *mid-late June.*

Lower Manhattan organisations present dozens of free events – from visual arts to all sorts of performances – at mainly waterfront venues. Past participants have included Yoko Ono, Patti Smith and Laurie Anderson.

❤ Mermaid Parade

Coney Island, Brooklyn (www.coneyisland. com). Subway D, F, N, Q to Coney Island-Stillwell Avenue. **Date** *3rd Sat in June.*

Glitter-covered semi-nude revellers, aquatically adorned floats and classic cruisers fill Surf Avenue for this annual art parade.

❤ Midsummer Night Swing

Damrosch Park at Lincoln Center Plaza, W 62nd Street, between Columbus & Amsterdam Avenues, Upper West Side (1-212 721 6500, www.midsummernightswing. org). Subway 1 to 66th Street-Lincoln Center. **Date** *late June-mid July.*

Lincoln Center's Damrosch Park is turned into a giant dancefloor as bands play salsa, Cajun, swing and other music. For three weeks (Tue-Sat), each night's party is devoted to a dance style, and is preceded by lessons. Beginners are welcome, of course.

NYC LGBT Pride March

From Fifth Avenue, at 26th Street, to Christopher Street, West Village (route varies) (1-212 807 7433, www.nycpride.org). **Date** *late June.*

NYC's Pride parade, in commemoration of the 1969 Stonewall Riots, paints Fifth Avenue all the colours of the rainbow, with floats, drag queens and hundreds of marching organisations. Parties, performances and street festivals at various venues bookend the event.

Warm Up

For listings, see p258 MoMA PS1.
***Date** July-Aug.*

Thousands of dance-music fanatics and alt-rock enthusiasts make the pilgrimage to Long Island City on summer Saturdays to drink and dance in MoMA PS1's courtyard. The sounds range from spiritually inclined soul to full-bore techno or dubstep, sometimes on the same day. Each season brings massive, Burning Man-worthy site-specific outdoor art, plus installations inside the museum that rotate during the course of the festival. There are lots of local food stands as well.

Macy's Fourth of July Fireworks

Various waterfront locations (1-212 494 4495, www.macys.com/fireworks).
***Date** 4 July.*

At NYC's main Independence Day attraction, fireworks are launched from barges on the East or Hudson River. The pyrotechnics start at around 9pm, but you'll need to scope out your vantage point much earlier. Spectactors are packed like sardines at prime spots.

Panorama

Randalls Island Park (www.panorama.nyc).
***Date** late July.*

Goldenvoice, organiser of California's Coachella music festival, launched this East Coast counterpart held over three days. The sprawling multi-stage affair attracts some of the biggest names in hip hop, indie rock, pop and beyond, such as Janet Jackson, the Weeknd, Migos and the Killers.

Midsummer Night Swing

Harlem Week

Various Harlem locations (1-212 862 8477, www.harlemweek.com). Subway B, C, 2, 3 to 135th Street. ***Date** late July-late Aug.*

Get into the groove at this massive culture fest, which began in 1974 as a one-day event. Harlem Day is still the centrepiece, but

Mermaid Parade

New York Burlesque Festival

'Harlem Week' is now a misnomer; besides the street fair serving up music, art and food along W 135th Street, between Fifth & St Nicholas Avenues, concerts, films, dance performances, fashion and sports events are on tap for around a month.

Summer Restaurant Week
www.nycgo.com/restaurant-week.
Date *late July/early Aug.*

Twice a year, for two weeks or more at a stretch, some of the city's finest restaurants dish out three-course prix-fixe lunches for under $30; most also offer dinner for little more than $40. For the full list of participating restaurants, visit the website. Make reservations well in advance.

Lincoln Center Out of Doors
For listings, see p332 Lincoln Center.
Date *late July-mid Aug.*

Free dance, music, theatre, opera and more make up the programme over the course of three weeks at this ambitious and family-friendly festival.

Battery Dance Festival
Robert F Wagner, Jr Park, Battery Park City (batterydance.org). Subway 4, 5 to Bowling Green. **Date** *mid Aug.*

During one summer week, the waterside park comes to life with dozens of free dance performances against the backdrop of New York Harbor at sunset. The programme mixes local and international companies, offering everything from contemporary premières to classical Indian Kuchipudi.

Afropunk Festival
Commodore Barry Park, Fort Greene, Brooklyn (www.afropunk.com). Subway F to York Street, then 15min walk. **Map** *p232 J32.* **Date** *late Aug.*

This two-day festival celebrates black power and creative expression, showcasing some of the most influential artists in the music industry, such as Lauryn Hill, Tierra Whack and Leon Bridges. You'll also find food trucks, art displays, a cool craft market and serious fashion inspiration among the crowds.

US Open
USTA Billie Jean King National Tennis Center, Flushing Meadows Corona Park, Queens (1-718 760 6200, www.usopen.org).

Subway 7 to Mets-Willets Point.
Date *late Aug-mid Sept.*

For two weeks every summer, Flushing, Queens, becomes the centre of the tennis universe when it hosts the final Grand Slam event of the year.

Autumn

West Indian American Day Carnival
Eastern Parkway, from Schenectady Avenue to Flatbush Avenue, Crown Heights, Brooklyn (1 718 467 1797, www. wiadacarnival.org). Subway 2, 3 to Grand Army Plaza or Eastern Parkway-Brooklyn Museum; 3, 4 to Crown Heights-Utica Avenue. **Date** *early Sept.*

This annual Caribbean parade is never short on costumed stilt dancers, floats blaring soca and calypso music, and plenty of flags from Caribbean countries such as Trinidad & Tobago, Jamaica and elsewhere. Look out for vendors stationed along Eastern Parkway selling island eats including jerk chicken, curry goat and oxtail.

Electric Zoo
Randall's Island (www.electriczoo.com). **Date** *early Sept.*

Don your Day-Glo shades and head for this three-day outdoor rager. The festival has become an unmissable attraction on the EDM circuit, featuring a wide range of artists, both top name and underground. Diplo, Eric Prydz and a collaboration between Skrillex and Boyz Noise were among the recent headliners.

Feast of San Gennaro
Mulberry Street, between Canal & Houston Streets; Grand Street, between Baxter & Mott Streets; Hester Street, between Baxter & Mott Streets, Little Italy. Subway B, D, F, M to Broadway-Lafayette Street; J, N, Q, R, W, Z, 6 to Canal Street. **Date** *mid-late Sept.*

Celebrate the martyred third-century bishop and patron saint of Naples at this 11-day festival that fills the streets of Little Italy every year. In the evenings, there's live music at the festival stage, sparkling lights arch over Mulberry Street and the smells of frying *zeppole* (custard- or jam-filled fritters) and sausages hang in the sultry air. On the official feast day, a statue of San Gennaro is carried in a Grand Procession outside the Most Precious Blood Church.

Brooklyn Book Festival
Brooklyn Borough Hall & Plaza, 209 Joralemon Street, at Court Street, Downtown Brooklyn

(www.brooklynbookfestival.org). Subway 2, 3, 4, 5 to Borough Hall. **Date** *mid-late Sept.*

The city's largest (and free) literary fest takes over Brooklyn Borough Hall and Plaza every autumn for a full day of panels and readings, bibliophile swag and inordinate book buying. Related city-wide events lead up to the festival and there's a separate children's day.

Next Wave Festival
For listings, see p330 Brooklyn Academy of Music. **Date** *Sept-Dec.*

The festival is among the most highly anticipated of the city's autumn culture offerings, as it showcases only the very best in avant-garde music, dance, theatre and opera. Legends such as John Cale, Meredith Monk and Steve Reich are among the many luminaries the festival has hosted.

Atlantic Antic
Atlantic Avenue, from Fourth Avenue to Hicks Street, Brooklyn (1-718 875 8993, www. atlanticave.org). Subway B, D, N, Q, R, 2, 3, 4, 5 to Atlantic Avenue-Barclays Center. **Date** *late Sept.*

More than 500 food and craft vendors and a dozen stages close down a busy Brooklyn artery for the annual Atlantic Antic. Spanning ten blocks and cutting through four neighbourhoods, it's billed as NYC's largest street fair, and features local bands and cult Brooklyn food and drink.

New York Burlesque Festival
Various venues (www.thenewyork burlesquefestival.com). **Date** *late Sept.*

Co-produced by performer Angie Pontani, the 'Italian Stallionette', NYC's annual burlesque fest brings an international line-up of tassel twirlers, boylesque artists and circus-skills acts to several venues over four days. The centrepiece is the Saturday Spectacular, a retro supper club extravaganza, and the festival closes with the Golden Pastie Awards.

❤ New York Film Festival
Date *late Sept-mid Oct.*

See p299 Film festivals.

New York Comic Con
Javits Center, 655 West 34th Street, at Eleventh Avenue, Hell's Kitchen (1-888 608 6059, www.newyorkcomiccon.com). Subway 7 to 34th Street-Hudson Yards. **Map** *p175 B24.* **Date** *early Oct.*

Pop culture devotees don elaborate costumes to transform themselves into Wonder Woman, Thor, Captain America and more for this massive convention. Extending beyond comics to genres such as graphic novels, anime, video games and cosplay (and, of course, screen adaptations), the four-day event offers panel discussions, workshops and the chance to meet creators and actors.

Open House New York Weekend
1-212 991 6470, www.ohny.org.
Date *mid Oct.*

More than 250 of the city's coolest and most exclusive architectural sites, private homes and landmarks open their doors during a weekend of urban exploration. Behind-the-scenes tours and educational programmes are also on offer.

New York City Wine & Food Festival
Various locations (www.nycwff.org).
Date *mid Oct.*

The Food Network's epicurean fête offers four belt-busting days of tasting events and celebrity-chef demos.

Tompkins Square Park Halloween Dog Parade
East River Park Amphitheater, between Grand & Jackson Streets, Lower East Side (www.tompkinssquaredogrun.com/ halloween). Subway F to E Broadway, then 15min walk. **Date** *late Oct.*

To see a plethora of puppies in adorable outfits, head to this canine costume parade, which still bears the name of the East Village park where it was held for more than 25 years (and where it may return in the future). The get-ups are remarkably elaborate and conceptual and have included the band members of Kiss, ET and one of the sandworms from *Beetlejuice.* Enterprising owners win prizes if their dog is selected Best in Show.

❤ Village Halloween Parade
Sixth Avenue, from Spring to 16th Streets, Greenwich Village (www.halloween-nyc. com). Subway C, E to Spring Street; A, B, C, D, E, F, M to W 4th Street-Washington Square; F, L, M to 14th Street. **Date** *31 Oct.*

The sidewalks at this iconic Village shindig are always packed with spectators so be sure to snag your space well before the 7pm start time. Each year brings a different theme, with dancers, bands, puppets, floats and ordinary folks in spectacularly arty, gruesome and jokey costumes. For the best vantage point, register to dress up and experience it from within the parade.

New York Comedy Festival
Various venues (www.nycomedyfestival. com). **Date** *early-mid Nov.*

This seven-day laugh fest features both big names (Jo Koy, Marc Maron, Jerry Seinfeld and Amy Schumer in recent years) and up-and-comers.

New York City Marathon
Staten Island side of the Verrazano-Narrows Bridge to Tavern on the Green in Central Park (www.tcsnycmarathon.org).
Date *early Nov.*

More than 50,000 runners hotfoot it through all five boroughs over a 26.2-mile course. For a good view, we recommend staking out a spot on First Avenue between 60th and 96th Streets or Fifth Avenue, between 90th and 105th Streets on the Upper East Side, or Fourth Avenue in Park Slope, Brooklyn, though there are many other options.

Macy's Thanksgiving Day Parade & Balloon Inflation
Central Park West, at 77th Street, to Macy's, Broadway, at 34th Street, Upper West Side

Macy's Thanksgiving Day Parade

to Midtown (1-212 494 4495, www.macys. com/parade). Subway A, B, C to 72nd Street; 1, 2, 3 to 34th Street-Penn Station. **Date** late Nov.

At 9am on Thanksgiving Day, the stars of this nationally televised parade are the gigantic balloons, the elaborate floats and good ol' Santa Claus. The evening before, New Yorkers brave the cold night air to watch the rubbery colossi take shape at the inflation area around the Museum of Natural History (beginning at 79th Street & Columbus Avenue).

Winter

Rockefeller Center Christmas Tree Lighting Ceremony
Rockefeller Center, Fifth Avenue, between 49th & 50th Streets, Midtown (1-212 332 6868, www.rockefellercenter.com). Subway B, D, F, M to 47th-50th Streets-Rockefeller Center. **Date** late Nov/early Dec.

Proceedings start at 7pm, but this festive celebration is always mobbed, so it's a good idea to get there early. Most of the event , which runs between two and three hours, is devoted to celebrity performances, then the roughly 50,000 energy-efficient LEDs covering the massive evergreen are switched on.

Unsilent Night
Washington Square Arch, Fifth Avenue, at Waverly Place, to Tompkins Square Park, Greenwich Village to East Village (www. unsilentnight.com). Subway A, B, C, D, E, F, M to W 4th Street. **Date** mid Dec.

This trippy musical performance piece, dreamed up by composer Phil Kline, is downtown's arty, secular answer to Christmas carolling. Boom-box-toting participants gather under the Washington Square Arch, where they're given a cassette of one of four different atmospheric tracks; you can also download the Unsilent Night app and sync up via smartphone or stream via SoundCloud. Everyone then presses play at the same time and marches through the streets of New York, blending their music and filling the air with a beautiful, echoing 45-minute piece.

New Year's Eve in Times Square
Times Square, Theater District (1-212 768 1560, www.timessquarenyc.org). Subway N, Q, R, S, W, 1, 2, 3, 7 to 42nd Street-Times Square. **Date** 31 Dec.

Get together with a million others and watch the giant illuminated Waterford Crystal ball descend from 1 Times Square,

at 43rd Street, amid a blizzard of and cheering. Arrive as early as p (by 3pm at the latest) to stake out a in the 'Bowtie' formed by the crossi of Broadway and Seventh Avenue an be prepared to stay put. There are no public restrooms or food vendors, and leaving means giving up your spot. You endurance will be rewarded with celebr performances held across two stages, beginning at 6pm. Forget toasting the new year with champagne, though: public drinking is illegal in NYC.

New Year's Day Marathon Reading
Poetry Project at St Mark's Church, 131 E 10th Street, at Second Avenue (1-212 674 0910, www.poetryproject.org). Subway L to Third Avenue; 6 to Astor Place. **Date** 1 Jan.

More than 140 of the city's best poets, artists and performers gather at St Mark's Church in-the-Bowery and, one after another, recite their work to a hall full of listeners. Big-name bohemians such as Penny Arcade, Anne Waldman and Patti Smith have stepped up to the mic during this spoken-word spectacle, organised by the Poetry Project.

No Pants Subway Ride
www.improveverywhere.com. **Date** early/mid Jan.

The name says it all. Improv Everywhere's annual bare-legged expedition began in January 2002 with a handful of operatives in one car on the downtown 6 train, but it's grown into a well-publicised mass event. No longer a mildly subversive, playful prank, it's now a chance for New Yorkers to perform a cheeky feat while being supported by thousands of fellow residents. For unsuspecting visitors, it's a surreal spectacle.

Winter Restaurant Week
www.nycgo.com/restaurant-week. **Date** late Jan/early Feb.

The Winter Restaurant Week provides yet another opportunity to sample delicious gourmet food at highly palatable prices.

Chinese New Year
Around Chinatown (www.betterchinatown. com). Subway J, N, Q, R, W, Z, 6 to Canal Street. **Date** late Jan/Feb.

Gung hay fat choy!, the greeting goes. Chinatown is charged with energy and colour during the two weeks of the Lunar New Year. The key events are the parade down Mott Street and the firecracker ceremony, which is usually held in Sara D Roosevelt Park and includes lion dances and food and craft vendors as well as the pyrotechnics.

Film

Plug yourself into New York's non-stop movie scene

Even if this is your first visit to NYC, chances are the cityscape will feel familiar. Virtually every corner of the metropolis has been immortalised on celluloid, whether it's Woody Allen's vision of the Upper East Side, Martin Scorsese's Midtown street scenes or Spike Lee's take on Bedford-Stuyvesant, Brooklyn. It's easy to feel as if you've walked on to a massive movie set, especially when photogenic landmarks such as the Empire State Building pan into view. You might even stumble on an actual shoot, as the local film industry, largely based in Queens, is thriving.

When it comes to going to the pictures, cinephiles are in their element. The city's superb indie screens have been boosted by cinemas offering top-notch food and drink as well.

CINEMAS

Few cities offer the film-lover as many options as New York. If you insist, you can check out the blockbusters at the multiplexes on 42nd Street and dotted throughout the city; but Gotham's gems are its arthouses, museums and other film institutions. For current movie listings, consult *Time Out New York* magazine or www.timeout.com/newyork.

Angelika Film Center

18 W Houston Street, at Mercer Street, Greenwich Village (1-212 995 2570, www.angelikafilmcenter.com). Subway B, D, F, M to Broadway-Lafayette Street; R, W to Prince Street; 6 to Bleecker Street. **Tickets** *$17; $15 reductions.* **Map** *p87 E29.*

When it opened in 1989, the Angelika immediately became a player in the then-booming Amerindie scene, and the six-screen cinema still puts the emphasis on edgier fare, both domestic and foreign. The complex is packed at weekends, so come extra early or visit the website to buy advance tickets.

BAM Rose Cinemas

Brooklyn Academy of Music, 30 Lafayette Avenue, between Ashland Place & St Felix Street, Fort Greene, Brooklyn (1-718 636 4100, www.bam.org). Subway B, D, N, Q, R, 2, 3, 4, 5 to Atlantic Avenue-Barclays Center; C to Lafayette Avenue; G to Fulton Street. **Tickets** *$16; $11 reductions.* **Map** *p232 K34.*

With four screens, Brooklyn's premier art-film venue does double duty as a repertory house for well-programmed classics on 35mm and as a first-run multiplex for indie films. June's annual BAMcinemaFest is an excellent showcase of new American work.

❤ Best cinemas

Film Forum *p296*
Long-standing non-profit cinema with superb programming.

Film at Lincoln Center *p296*
Host of the prestigious New York Fim Festival.

IFC Center *p297*
Indie fare with frequent director Q&As.

Metrograph *p297*
Retro-chic movie house with a buzzing eaterie and bars.

Cinema Village

22 E 12th Street, between Fifth Avenue & University Place, Greenwich Village (1-212 924 3363, www.cinemavillage.com). Subway L, N, Q, R, W, 4, 5, 6 to 14th Street-Union Square. **Tickets** *$12; $8 reductions.* **Map** *p137 E29.*

A classic cinema that charmed Noah Baumbach long before he made *The Squid and the Whale*, this three-screener specialises in indie flicks, cutting-edge documentaries and foreign films.

❤ Film Forum

209 W Houston Street, between Sixth Avenue & Varick Street, Soho (1-212 727 8110, www.filmforum.org). Subway 1 to Houston Street. **Tickets** *$15, $9 reductions.* **No cards** *(except for online purchases).* **Map** *p137 D30.*

The city's leading taste-making venue for independent new releases and classic movies, Film Forum is programmed by festival-scouring staff who take their duties as seriously as a Kurosawa samurai. Born in 1970 as a makeshift screening space with folding chairs, Film Forum is still one of the few non-profit cinemas in the United States. The latest renovation added a fourth screen and comfortable new seats as well as improving sight lines.

❤ Film at Lincoln Center

144 & 165 W 65th Street, between Broadway & Amsterdam Avenue, Upper West Side (1-212 875 5600, www.filmlinc.org). Subway 1 to 66th Street-Lincoln Center. **Tickets** *$15; $12 reductions.* **Map** *p194 C21.*

Founded in 1969, as the Film Society of Lincoln Center, the recently renamed organisation hosts the prestigious New York Film Festival, among other annual fests, in addition to presenting diverse programming

King Kong (1933)

throughout the year. Film series are usually thematic, with an international perspective, or focused on a single auteur. The contemporary Elinor Bunin Munroe Film Center, which opened in 2011, houses two plush cinemas that host frequent post-screening Q&As. Together, these state-of-the-art screens and the Walter Reade Theater across the street add up to a small multiplex.

♥ IFC Center

323 Sixth Avenue, at W 3rd Street, Greenwich Village (1-212 924 7771, www. ifccenter.com). Subway A, B, C, D, E, F, M to W 4th Street. **Tickets** *$16; $13 reductions.* **Map** *p137 D30.*

In 2005, the long-darkened 1930s Waverly was reborn as a five-screen arthouse cinema, showing the latest indie hits, along with choice midnight cult items and occasional foreign classics. You may come face to face with directors or actors, as many introduce their work on opening night and stick around for post-screening Q&As. The annual DOC NYC festival brings hundreds of documentary films, plus filmmakers and celebrities, each November.

Leonard Nimoy Thalia

Symphony Space, 2537 Broadway, at 95th Street, Upper West Side (1-212 864 5400, www.symphonyspace.org). Subway 1, 2, 3 to 96th Street. **Tickets** *$15-$18; $12-$14 reductions.* **Map** *p194 C17.*

The famed Thalia arthouse, which featured in *Annie Hall* (when it was screening *The Sorrow and the Pity*), is now part of multidisciplinary arts venue Symphony Space (*see p334*). The cinematic fare is an eclectic mix of international, arthouse, documentary and classic films, plus HD screenings of plays and operas.

♥ Metrograph

7 Ludlow Street, between Canal & Hester Streets, Lower East Side (1-212 660 0312, www.metrograph.com). Subway B, D to Grand Street; F to East Broadway. **Tickets** *$15; $12 reductions.* **Map** *p111 G30.*

Founded in 2016 by filmmaker and designer Alexander Olch, this retro-chic bi-level movie house has two theatres outfitted with comfortable seats fashioned out of reclaimed wood from Williamsburg's old Domino Sugar Refinery. And they're reserved at purchase, eliminating the need to arrive early to nab your preferred spot. The complex also contains a film bookstore and a posh candy shop. Upstairs, a full-service restaurant, the Commissary (featuring a menu inspired by Hollywood's old-time studio cafeterias), serves breakfast, lunch and dinner, plus a late-night menu. It also has two bars. But more important is the standout programming,

Spike Lee on set of 'Crooklyn'

which includes inspired retrospectives and imaginatively framed series.

Nitehawk Cinema

188 Prospect Park West, at 14th Street, Park Slope, Brooklyn (1-929 282 4300, www. nitehawkcinema.com). Subway F, G to 15th Street-Prospect Park. **Tickets** *$13; $10 reductions.* **Map** *p232 M38.*

A pioneer of the dine-in movie trend, Nitehawk followed up its sleek Williamsburg location by transforming a grimy 1928 theatre into an elegant take on a multiplex. Nearly triple the size of its predecessor, the 650-seat complex houses seven screens, plus a second-floor bar with Prospect Park views. Four of the theatres have 35mm reel-to-reel capacity to accommodate rare celluloid in its eclectic programme of classic films, indie new releases and Hollywood blockbusters. **Other location** 136 Metropolitan Avenue, between Berry Street & Wythe Avenue, Williamsburg, Brooklyn.

Quad

34 W 13th Street, between Fifth & Sixth Avenues, Greenwich Village (1-212 255 2243, www.quadcinema.com). Subway F, M to 14th Street; L to Sixth Avenue. **Tickets** *$16; $13 reductions.* **Map** *p137 E31.*

The Quad was Manhattan's first multiplex when it opened in 1972. A major renovation

Dinner at the Movies

Gastro-cinemas are thinking outside the popcorn box

The latest wave of New York cinemas offers the classic date-night dinner and a movie combination under one roof, with exceptional on-site eateries and in-seat dining. Downtown cinephile clubhouse, **Metrograph** (*see p297*), has a buzzy full-service restaurant equipped with two bars and a late-night menu, for pre- or post-viewing socialising. Uptown, the Film at Lincoln Center's sleek **Elinor Bunin Monroe Film Center** (*see p333*) contains upscale-casual café Indie Food and Wine, where movie-goers can stop in for market-driven salads, sandwiches and mains. Brooklyn's **Nitehawk Cinema** (*see p297*) takes the concept further. At both locations of the hip cinema-restaurant-bar hybrid, theatre seats are arranged in pairs with tables, and you can order during the film on a slip of paper to be collected by a server. The comfort food menu includes a tasty burger, but the real highlights are the fancy variations on concession-stand staples, such as popcorn tossed with truffle butter. Best of all, you can sip beer, wine or cocktails – including movie tie-in specials – in your seat.

Austin-born dine-in movie chain **Alamo Drafthouse** has an outpost in Downtown Brooklyn (445 Albee Square West, between Willoughby & Gold Streets, drafthouse.com/nyc, 1-718 513 2547), offering such mid-feature bites as gourmet flatbreads and hot dogs, plus tipples like the PG-13-rated Dude's White Russian (G-rated non-alcoholic drinks and stiff R cocktails are also available) or New York State-brewed draughts. Two additional NYC locations are in the works.

There's no gleaming 1930s-style marquee beckoning you through the doors of **Syndicated** (40 Bogart Street, between Grattan & Moore Streets, 1-718 386 3399, syndicatedbk.com), housed in a former warehouse in Brooklyn's arty Bushwick neighbourhood. Instead, art deco touches can be found in the 70-seat main dining room, anchored by a four-sided marble-topped bar, packed with moviegoers guzzling craft cocktails before catching indie or throwback flicks. The cinema-cum-restaurant is popular for its cheap movie tickets ($7 across the board) and seasonal American fare. Snacks, sandwiches and main dishes such as cheesy waffle fries, pulled pork sliders and fish tacos – along with 'adult milkshakes', beer or wine – can be delivered while you watch.

a few years ago brought luxurious seats, state-of-the-art projection facilities and a bar serving organic wine and craft beer as well as coffee, tea and snacks. The varied programming includes themed retrospectives, LGBT favourites and post-show discussions with directors and critics.

Other institutions

Anthology Film Archives
32 Second Avenue, at 2nd Street, East Village (1-212 505 5181, www.anthologyfilmarchives. org). Subway F to Lower East Side-Second Avenue; 6 to Bleecker Street. **Tickets** *$12; $7-$9 reductions.* **Map** *p124 F29.*

This red-brick former courthouse feels a bit like a fortress – and, in a sense, it is one, protecting the legacy of NYC's fiercest film experimenters. Featuring two screens, Anthology is dedicated to the preservation, study and exhibition of independent, avant-garde and artist-made work. An expansion will add a café and rooftop terrace, among other enhancements, so call before visiting in 2020 in case of temporary closure.

Maysles Documentary Center
343 Malcolm X Boulevard (Lenox Avenue), between 127th & 128th Streets, Harlem (www. maysles.org). Subway A, B, C, D, 2, 3 to 125th Street. **Tickets** *Suggested donation $12.* **Map** *p223 D13.*

The documentary centre founded by late cinema *vérité* legend Albert Maysles contains the intimate Maysles Cinema. Socially conscious docs, naturally, make up the bulk of the programming, but you're also likely to catch funky series of music-related films and plenty of uptown-centric flicks.

Museum of Modern Art
For listings, see p185. **Tickets** *$12; $8-$10 reductions; free under-17s; free with museum admission.* **Map** *p175 E22.*

Renowned for its superb programming of art films and experimental work, MoMA draws from a vast vault. Film-goers have to

buy or collect tickets purchased online at the museum's main lobby information desk (see www.moma.org/visit/film or call 1-212 708 9480 for more information). Note that while museum admission includes the day's film programme, a film ticket doesn't include admission to the museum galleries – although it can be applied towards the cost within 30 days.

Museum of the Moving Image
For listings, see p262. **Tickets** *$15; $9-$11 reductions.* **Map** *p259 K20.*

Housed in the Astoria Studios complex, the museum screens a broad range of international new releases and restored archival films in its state-of-the-art 267-seat cinema.

Foreign-language specialists

You can catch the latest foreign-language flicks at art and revival houses, but the city has a wealth of specialist venues as well, including the **French Institute Alliance Française** (22 E 60th Street, 1-212 355 6100, www.fiaf.org), the **Japan Society** (*see p188*) and **Scandinavia House** (*see p190*). The **Asia Society & Museum** (*see p208*) screens works from Asian countries plus Asian-American productions.

FILM FESTIVALS

From late September to mid October, **Film at Lincoln Center** (*see p296*) hosts the city's biggest event for film fans and industry folk alike. The **New York Film Festival** offers more than two weeks of premières, features and short flicks from around the globe. Another autumn offering is NewFest's annual **New York LGBT Film Festival** (www.newfest.org).

Film at Lincoln Center offers the popular **Film Comment Selects** in collaboration with Lincoln Center's *Film Comment* magazine, showcasing films that have yet to be distributed in the United States. January brings the annual **New York Jewish Film Festival** (www.nyjff.org) to Lincoln Center's Walter Reade Theater (*see p333*).

In early spring, the **New York International Children's Film Festival** (1-212 349 0330, nyicff.org) kicks off four weekends of anime, shorts and features made for kids and teens. Also in spring, the Museum of Modern Art and Film at Lincoln Center sponsor the highly regarded **New Directors/New Films** series, presenting works by on-the-cusp filmmakers. And each April, Robert De Niro's **Tribeca Film Festival** (1-212 941 2400, www.tribecafilm.com) draws more than 140,000 fans to screenings of independent movies and other events. Summer takes the action outdoors with several outdoor film festivals (*see left* In the know).

FILM

In the know
Alfresco films

Each summer, outdoor film series return to city parks, including **Bryant Park** (www. bryantpark.org) and **Central Park** (see p196). Arrive early to claim a prime patch of grass in front of the big screen. From May through August, **Rooftop Films** (www.rooftopfilms.com) show over 40 new independent films against an urban backdrop at more than a dozen locations.

LGBT

The inside scoop on where to be out

Ever since the 1969 Stonewall riots gave birth to the modern gay rights movement, New York has been a beacon for LGBT folks from all corners of the globe. The constant influx of new blood keeps the scene vital, from buzzing bars to activist events and cutting-edge performances. Even as LGBT culture permeates the mainstream, NYC remains a bastion of the wonderfully weird and uniquely queer. The scene often revolves around two major gaybourhoods: the West Village, home of the Stonewall National Monument, the many bars of Christopher Street and the AIDS Memorial; and Hell's Kitchen, a Broadway-adjacent hotbed of bars and nightlife. But a diverse queer network also thrives in the East Village, in Brooklyn's Williamsburg and Bushwick neighbourhoods and in Jackson Heights in Queens.

Bushwig *p305*

THE QUEER CALENDAR

NYC Pride (www.nycpride.org), New York's biggest queer event, takes place in mid to late June, bringing a whirl of parties and performances. Although the route has varied in recent years, the **NYC LGBT Pride March** includes a stretch of Fifth Avenue and the West Village, birthplace of the gay rights movement. Pride weekend now packs plenty of events beyond the march, including the star-studded music festival Pride Island. Film fans might like the offerings at summer's **New York LGBT Film Festival** (www.newfest.org). As the temperature soars, the social scene extends to scenic **Fire Island**, home to the neighbouring beach resorts of Cherry Grove and the Pines (about a 90-minute train and ferry ride from Manhattan). August's **Flame Con** (www.flamecon.org) allows the city's queer comic fans to let their freak flags fly. Witness gender-switched costumes of your favourite comic book and video games; head to panels with gay writers, illustrators and editors; and pace yourself for costume-clad dance parties and drag shows. Autumn in gay New York kicks off with the **Bushwig** and **Wigstock festivals** (*see p305*) where the drag scene celebrates itself. **Halloween** (*see p292*) is a major to-do, with bars and clubs packed with costumed revellers. Culture buffs can check out summer's annual **Hot!** (dixonplace.org/hot-festival) festival at Dixon Place, offering a wide variety of queer art, theatre, dance and comedy events.

INFORMATION, MEDIA & CULTURE

To find out what's going on, refer to *Time Out New York* magazine or www.timeout.com/newyork. *Gay Cities* (www.gaycities.com) provides regularly updated LGBT-oriented event listings. The monthly *Go!* (www.gomag.com), 'a cultural road map for city girls', gives the lowdown on the lesbian nightlife and travel scene. *Gay City News* (www.gaycitynews.com) provides feisty political coverage with an activist slant. All are free and widely available (look out for copies in street boxes, gay and lesbian bars and stores). A number of popular, locally produced blogs and websites feature attitude-filled thoughts on the queer scene. Among the best sites are sexy and occasionally gossipy Queerty (www.queerty.com), news-focused Joe.My.God (www.joemygod.com) and the wide-ranging Towleroad (www.towleroad.com). Gender-free store the **Phluid Project** (*see p133*) hosts regular events such as parties, poetry readings and talks.

Bluestockings

*172 Allen Street, between Rivington & Stanton Streets, Lower East Side (1-212 777 6028, www.bluestockings.com). Subway F to Lower East Side-Second Avenue. **Open** 11am-11pm daily. **Map** p111 F29.*

This radical bookstore, fair-trade café and activist resource centre stocks LGBT literature and regularly hosts queer events (often with a feminist slant), including dyke knitting circles, trans-politics forums and women's open-mic nights.

❤ Best LGBT venues

Alibi Lounge *p307*
Classy space for cocktails and mingling.

Club Cumming *p303*
Alan Cumming's permanent entertainment-party space.

The Eagle *p306*
The city's premier fetish bar.

Metropolitan *p307*
Refreshingly unfancy bar.

The Rosemont *p307*
Kick off a night out in Brooklyn at this laid-back spot.

Stonewall Inn *p304*
National gay rights landmark.

Lesbian, Gay, Bisexual & Transgender Community Center

208 W 13th Street, between Seventh & Eighth Avenues, West Village (1-212 620 7310, www. gaycenter.org). Subway A, C, E, 1, 2, 3 to 14th Street; L to Eighth Avenue. **Open** *9am-10pm Mon-Sat; 9am-9pm Sun.* **Map** *p137 D29.*

Founded in 1983, the Center provides information and a support network for residents and visitors. It's used as a venue by more than 400 groups, and public programming includes everything from book signings and film screenings to comedy nights and theatrical performances. It's also home to the city's only LGBT bookstore, the Bureau of General Services – Queer Division, plus a cyber centre and outpost of ethically conscious Think Coffee. The National Archive of Lesbian, Gay, Bisexual and Transgender History and the Pat Parker/Vito Russo Library are also based here. Don't miss the erotic Keith Haring mural, *Once Upon A Time*, that adorns a former bathroom.

Lesbian Herstory Archives

484 14th Street, between Eighth Avenue & Prospect Park West, Park Slope, Brooklyn (1-718 768 3953, www.lesbianherstoryarchives.org). Subway F to 15th Street-Prospect Park. **Open** *hrs vary; see website calendar.* **Map** *p232 M38.*

The Herstory Archives contain more than 12,000 books (cultural theory, fiction, poetry, plays), 1,300 periodicals, more than 1,000 films and videos, plus assorted memorabilia. The cosy brownstone also hosts screenings, readings and social gatherings, plus an open house in June (during Brooklyn Pride) and December.

Alibi *p307*

Leslie-Lohman Museum of Gay & Lesbian Art

26 Wooster Street, between Canal & Grand Streets, Soho (1-212 431 2609, www. leslielohman.org). Subway A, C, E to Canal Street. **Open** *noon-6pm Wed, Fri-Sun; noon-8pm Thur.* **Admission** *suggested donation $9.* **Map** *p87 E30.*

Formerly the Leslie-Lohman Gay Art Foundation, this institution was granted museum status by the state of New York in 2011. Founded in 1990 by Fritz Lohman and Charles Leslie, it seeks to preserve and highlight the contributions of LGBT artists throughout history and up to the present. In addition to changing exhibitions, the museum has a large permanent collection and library, and hosts events such as book signings, panel discussions and low-key parties.

BARS & CLUBS

'It ain't what it used to be,' grumble veterans of New York's gay nightlife. And they're right. The West Village is still home to long-running nightspots, including the historic **Stonewall Inn**, and piano bars such as the **Duplex** (*see p325*) and **Marie's Crisis** (*see p324*), but the scene is continually morphing – sometimes for the better, sometimes not. Twice a month, **Hot Rabbit** (www.hotrabbit.com) takes over East Village venue **Drom** (85 Avenue A, between 5th & 6th Streets, East Village, 1-212 777 1157, www.dromnyc.com) with its huge Friday-night LGBTQ residency, and hosts other events around the city for women-identifying revellers and their queer buddies. Those looking to gawk at outrageous looks, irresistible beats and boundary-pushing drag should head to Ladyfag's monthly **Battle Hymn** (www.battlehymn.club) on Sundays. And join NYC's community of colour at spectacular monthly bashes such as 'Slaysian' party Bubble_T (www.facebook.com/bubbletpresents) and the wild mixer Papi Juice (www.papijuice.com).

East Village

♥ Club Cumming

505 E 6th Street, between Avenues A & B (1-917 265 8006, www.clubcummingnyc.com). Subway F to Lower East Side-Second Avenue. **Open** *7pm-3am Mon-Fri; 3pm-4am Sat, Sun. Admission free-$10.* **Map** *p123 G28.*

Inspired by the impromptu bashes in his dressing room during the run of *Cabaret*, theatre and TV star Alan Cumming teamed up with some NYC nightlife vets to open this now-essential bar. Broadway types mingle with burlesque divas, go-go boys

LGBT

In the know
Movie night

Once a month, the **IFC Center** (see p297)
hosts Queer|Art|Film, a curated screening
series of beloved and lesser-known
classics. Drag queens and queer filmmakers
introduce films such as 9 to 5, To Wong Foo,
Thanks for Everything, and Split.

and underground queer comedians on a
nightly basis, and entertainment ranges from
showtunes to stripteases.

The Cock

*93 Second Avenue, between 5th & 6th Streets
(no phone, www.facebook.com/thecocknyc).
Subway F to Lower East Side-Second Avenue.*
Open *9pm-4am Mon, Tue; 6pm-4am
Wed-Sun.* **Admission** *free-$10.* **No cards.**
Map *p124 F28.*

This grungy hole-in-the-wall still holds the
title of New York's sleaziest gay hangout, but
nowadays it's hit-and-miss. At weekends,
it's a packed grind-fest, but on other nights
the place can often be depressingly under-
populated. It's best to go very late when the
cruising is at its peak.

No Bar

*The Standard, East Village, 25 Cooper
Square, between 5th & 6th Streets (1-212
228 3344, www.nobar.nyc). Subway R, W to
Eighth Street-NYU; 6 to Astor Place.* **Open**
5pm-4am daily (varies). **Map** *p123 F28.*

Over the past few years, the Standard's
fabulously tacky bar has become a hub for
upscale queers to watch *RuPaul's Drag Race.*
Now, No Bar is a full-time gay venue all week,
hosting drag bingo and debauched parties.
Look out for *Drag Race* veterans and NYC
nightlife fixtures lounging on the chintzy
furniture, sipping creative cocktails with
names such as Rim Job and Feel the Beet.

Nowhere

*322 E 14th Street, at First Avenue (1-212 477
4744, www.nowherebarnyc.com). Subway
L to First Avenue.* **Open** *3pm-4am daily.*
Map *p123 F27.*

Low ceilings and dim lighting create a
speakeasy vibe at this subterranean bar. It
attracts everyone from young lesbians to
bears, thanks to an entertaining line-up of
theme nights and dance parties. The pool
table is another big draw.

Phoenix

*447 E 13th Street, at Avenue A (1-212 477
9979, www.phoenixbarnyc.com). Subway
L to First Avenue.* **Open** *3pm-4am daily.*
Map *p123 G27.*

An inevitable stop on any East Village crawl,
the Phoenix never disappoints. With trivia
nights, pop dance parties and lively viewings of
RuPaul's Drag Race, this dark little dive knows
how to keep a crowd around late into the night.

West Village

Cubbyhole

*281 W 12th Street, between W 4th Street &
Greenwich Avenue (1-212 243 9041, www.
cubbyholebar.com). Subway A, C, E to 14th
Street; L to Eighth Avenue.* **Open** *4pm-4am
Mon-Fri; 2pm-4am Sat, Sun.* **No cards.**
Map *p137 D29.*

This minuscule spot is filled with flirtatious
girls (and their boy pals), with the standard
Melissa Etheridge or kd lang soundtrack
blaring. Chinese lanterns, tissue-paper fish
and old holiday decorations emphasise the
festive, homespun charm.

Henrietta Hudson

*438 Hudson Street, at Morton Street
(1-212 924 3347, www.henriettahudson.
com). Subway 1 to Houston Street.* **Open**
*5pm-midnight Mon; 5pm-2am Tue; 4pm-4am
Wed-Sat; 2pm-2am Sun.* **Admission** *free-$12.*
Map *p137 D30.*

A much-loved lesbian hangout, this glam
lounge is slightly off the beaten path, and
attracts women from all over the city and
the 'burbs. Every night is different, with hip
hop, pop, soul, Latin and karaoke among the
musical offerings.

❤ Stonewall Inn

*53 Christopher Street, at Waverly Place (1-212
488 2705, www.thestonewallinnnyc.com).
Subway 1 to Christopher Street-Sheridan Square.*
Open *2pm-4am Mon-Wed; noon-4am Thur-
Sun.* **Map** *p137 D29.*

This National Historic Landmark is the
site of the 1969 gay rebellion against police
harassment, and has since become a cultural
bastion for the community. Special nights range
from dance soirées and drag shows to burlesque
performances and bingo gatherings.

▶ *While you're here, check out George Segal's
sculptures in nearby Christopher Park; see p143.*

Chelsea & Flatiron District

Barracuda

*275 W 22nd Street, between Seventh & Eighth
Avenues (1-212 645 8613, www.facebook.com/
barracudalounge). Subway C, E, 1 to 23rd
Street.* **Open** *4pm-4am daily.* **No cards.**
Map *p153 D26.*

This much-loved, slightly divey Chelsea
institution is a reliably bustling spot. Some of

Bushwiggin' Out

New-style drag stars are making waves – especially in Brooklyn

Lady Bunny. RuPaul. Bianca Del Rio. New York has served as an incubator for some of the most beloved and influential drag stars of all time. So it's no surprise that a new breed of gender-smashing performer has emerged here. Arty, punkish and occasionally hirsute drag artists are building a kingdom in Brooklyn.

The new generation of drag queens on the rise in Bushwick eschews old-school girlie glamour in favour of a more rock 'n' roll aesthetic, turning up onstage with beards, shaved heads and runway-ready wearable art. 'In the '90s, it was the East Village drag scene that pushed boundaries, making drag more of an art form,' says scene queen Simon Leahy. 'And now it's Bushwick, because all the young, broke artists live here.'

Much of the neo-drag action is focused on the annual **Bushwig** festival, which takes place in early September (bushwig.com/nyc). Organised by Leahy (aka Babes Trust) and Horrorchata, the two-day party serves as a showcase for alt-drag stars including Untitled Queen, Merrie Cherry and Charlene. Even the Manhattan establishment has taken notice: drag pioneers Lady Bunny and Linda Simpson

have made appearances at Bushwig, along with *RuPaul's Drag Race* alumni such as Latrice Royale and Alyssa Edwards.

But the Bushwig drag scene (which spills into other neighbourhoods such as Park Slope) isn't confined to one weekend a year. These radical queens regularly host and perform at Brooklyn venues such as **Macri Park** (462 Union Ave, between Conselyea Street & Metropolitan Avenue, Williamsburg, 1-718 599 4999, www.macripark.com), **Littlefield** (635 Sackett Street, between Third & Fourth Avenues, Gowanus, littlefieldnyc.com) and **Bizarre** (12 Jefferson Street, between Jefferson Street & Myrtle Avenue, Williamsburg, 1-347 915 2717, www.bizarrebushwick.com). You'll even occasionally find them on the other side of the river at Village boîtes such as **Pieces** (8 Christopher Street, between Greenwich Avenue & Waverly Place, West Village, 1-212 929 9291, www.piecesbar.com). Subscribe to Gayletter (www.gayletter.com) for updates on where you can find these artistes, who, as Leahy puts it, 'want to showcase that there's more to drag than just lip-synching to Britney songs.'

Bushwig

the city's most talented drag queens perform here nightly. Drinks are on the pricey side, but you'll often get a great show with no cover, so it balances out.

💜 The Eagle
554 W 28th Street, at Eleventh Avenue (1-646 473 1866, www.eagle-ny.com). Subway C, E to 23rd Street. **Open** *10pm-4am Mon-Sat (opens early for some events); 5pm-4am Sun.* **No cards.** **Map** *p153 C26.*

You don't have to be a kinky leather daddy to enjoy this manly spot, but it certainly doesn't hurt. The fetish bar is home to an array of beer blasts, foot-worship fêtes and leather soirées, plus simple pool playing and cruising nights. In summer, the rooftop is a surprising oasis.

NYC LGBT Pride March *p302*

Theater District & Hell's Kitchen
Atlas Social Club
753 Ninth Avenue, between 50th & 51st Streets (1-212 262 8527, www.atlassocialclub. com). Subway C, E to 50th Street. **Open** *4pm-4am Mon-Sat; 3pm-4am Sun.* **Map** *p175 C23.*

This drinkery, designed to look like a cross between an old-school athletic club and a speakeasy, is one of the more relaxed options on the HK strip – at least when it's not packed to the gills, which it can be at weekends. Be sure to check out the bathrooms, which are brightly papered with vintage beefcake and sports magazines.

Boxers HK
742 Ninth Avenue, between 50th & 51st Streets (1-212 951 1518, www.boxersnyc.com). Subway C, E to 50th Street. **Open** *4pm-2am Mon-Thur; 4pm-4am Fri; noon-4am Sat; noon-2am Sun.* **Map** *p175 C23.*

The second location of this local gay sports bar chainlet is a massive three-level funhouse packed with polo-shirted HK boys and happy hour commuters on their way to the nearby Port Authority Bus Terminal. Cheap beer is on tap, machines churn out frozen drinks and it's all served by hunky (and usually topless) bartenders and waiters. In the summer months, the roof deck is one of the prettiest spots in the neighbourhood. **Other location** 37 W 20th Street, between Fifth & Sixth Avenues, Chelsea (1-212 255 5082).

Flaming Saddles
793 Ninth Avenue, at 53rd Street (1-212 713 0481, www.flamingsaddles.com). Subway C, E to 50th Street. **Open** *3pm-4am Mon-Fri; noon-4am Sat, Sun.* **No cards.** **Map** *p175 D23.*

City boys can party honky-tonk-style at this country and western gay bar. It's outfitted to look like a Wild West bordello, with red velvet drapes, antler sconces and rococo wallpaper. Performances by bartenders dancing in cowboy boots add to the raucous vibe.

Industry
355 W 52nd Street, between Eighth & Ninth Avenues (1-646 476 2747, www.industry-bar.com). Subway C, E to 50th Street. **Open** *5pm-4am daily.* **No cards.** **Map** *p175 D23.*

Pretty boys flock to this appropriately named garage-like industrial-chic boîte, which has a stage for regular drag shows and other performances, a pool table, and couches for lounging. DJs spin nightly to a sexy, fashionable crowd.

Therapy
348 W 52nd Street, between Eighth & Ninth Avenues (1-212 397 1700, www.therapy-nyc. com). Subway C, E to 50th Street. **Open** *5pm-2am Mon-Thur, Sun; 5pm-4am Fri, Sat.* **Map** *p175 D23.*

Therapy is just what your analyst ordered. The dramatic two-level space hosts comedy and musical performances, there are some clever cocktails (including the Freudian Sip) and a crowd of well-scrubbed boys. You'll find good food and a cosy fireplace to boot.

Brooklyn
$3 Bill
260 Meserole Street, between Bushwick Place & Waterbury Street , Bushwick (1-718 366 3031, www.3dollarbillbk.com). Subway L to Montrose Avenue. **Open** *2pm-4am daily.* **Admission** *varies.* **Map** *p249 M28.*

This massive, multi-purpose queer temple boasts a state-of-the-art sound system (used to full effect by circuit queens every weekend), a backyard space and a richly decorated honky-tonk bar. Gay men from Manhattan, Jersey City and beyond show up to party with Bushwick locals. Prepare for a long night.

Ginger's Bar

*363 Fifth Avenue, between 5th & 6th Streets, Park Slope (no phone, www.facebook.com/ gingersbar). Subway F, G, R to Fourth Avenue-9th Street. **Open** 5pm-4am Mon-Fri; 2pm-4am Sat, Sun. **Map** p232 K36.*

The front room of Ginger's, with its dark-wood bar, looks out onto a bustling street. The back, with an always-busy pool table, evokes a rec room, while the patio feels like a friend's yard. This casual hangout is full of all sorts of dykes, many with their dogs – or favourite gay boys – in tow.

❤ Metropolitan

*559 Lorimer Street, at Metropolitan Avenue, Williamsburg (1-718 599 4444, www. metropolitanbarny.com). Subway G to Metropolitan Avenue; L to Lorimer Street. **Open** 3pm-4am daily. **Map** p249 J28.*

Some Williamsburg spots are a little pretentious, but not this refreshingly unfancy bar, which resembles a 1960s ski lodge, complete with a brick fireplace. Guys dominate, but there's always a female contingent, and even some straight folks. There are Sunday barbecues on the patio in summer.

❤ The Rosemont

*63 Montrose Avenue, at Lorimer Street, Williamsburg (1-347 987 3101, www. therosemontnyc.com). Subway G to Broadway; J, M to Lorimer Street. **Open** 5pm-4am Mon-Fri; 3pm-4am Sat, Sun. **Map** p249 L29.*

The founders of the popular, now-shuttered Sugarland club opened this charming Williamsburg space as a chill pre-game spot. Enjoy cocktails on the patio, witness stellar Brooklyn drag on the stage, or just relax by the bar during viewing parties of *RuPaul's Drag Race*.

The Vault

*248 McKibbin Street, between Seigel & McKibben Courts, Bushwick (www.facebook. com/thevaultbk). Subway L to Montrose Avenue. **Open** 4pm-4am daily. **Admission** free-$10. **Map** p249 M28.*

Step down into this basement nook for a wide variety of queer delights. The bar space gives Brooklynites a low-key spot to catch up, but those looking for drama can hit the dancefloor, which perches the DJ on a loft and gives subversive drag acts stairs to make a full entrance. Every night packs plenty of activities, from drag shows to bingo.

Harlem
❤ Alibi Lounge

*2376 Adam Clayton Powell Jr Boulevard (Seventh Avenue), at 139th Street (1-917 472 7789, www.alibiharlem.com). Subway B, C, 2, 3 to 135th Street. **Open** 6pm-4am daily. **Map** p223 D11.*

Founded in 2016 by a former human rights attorney, this classy space aims to provide a hub for Harlem's gay community. It may not be home to ragers, but you can expect a chill time getting to know well-dressed men over champagne-based cocktails with names such as 'Elegance is Attitude'.

Queens
Albatross Bar

*3619 24th Avenue, at 37th Street, Astoria (1-718 204 9707, www.albatrossastoria. com). Subway N, W to Astoria Boulevard. **Open** 5pm-4am Mon-Sat 1pm-4am Sun. **Map** p259 L17.*

Astoria's growing LGBTQ community convenes at this cosy bar, which hosts nightly events, such as TV-viewing parties, bingo and karaoke nights. The old-school stage gives every drag act a heightened sense of panache.

Club Evolution

*76-19 Roosevelt Avenue, at 77th Street, Jackson Heights (1-718 457 3939, www.clubevonyc. com). Subway E, F, M, R to Jackson Heights-Roosevelt Avenue. **Open** 5pm-4am daily.*

This lively gay Latin dance club offers a souped-up sound system, plenty of light effects and video screens, friendly staff and an endless supply of pop, reggaetón, salsa, merengue, bachata and hip-hop beats. Saturday nights draw the biggest crowd, but Mexican-themed Lunes Picantes on Mondays and competitive dance battles on Fridays still host more than enough shirtless men on the dancefloor to start or end the week with a bang.

In the know
Same-sex sports

It's almost an NYC rite of passage for gay men to belong to a dodgeball or kickball league at some point in their dirty thirties, but queer women have just as many options for organised play. Meetup group **Girl Social** (www.meetup.com/girl-social) organises sold-out events such as Lezzertag, LezBowl and activities including movie viewings and tours. Men looking for all-ages athletic fun can check out **Guy Social** (www.guysocial. com) for roller- and ice-skating, bowling, dinner nights and more.

Nightlife

From underground warehouse parties and intimate comedy clubs to iconic concert halls, the city's after-dark options are dazzling

Over the years, the nightlife scene has survived such buzz-killing trends as four-figure bottle service, 5am sober raves and celebrity iPod DJs. But Gotham has got its groove back. New clubs and roving parties – especially in Brooklyn, but also slipping beyond the border to Queens – are revitalising the after-dark landscape.

Williamsburg is still a hotspot for clubbing and indie-rock gigs, but the scene increasingly extends to neighbouring Bushwick, home to sprawling culture and party hubs House of Yes and Elsewhere. Manhattan's music scene recently got a boost with the reopening of landmark venue Webster Hall, with upgraded acoustics, facilities and acts courtesy of indie giant Bowery Presents.

Comedy, meanwhile, is killing it with thriving venues across the city. Even better, some of the best weekly shows are free or cheap, which makes going out for a few laughs an inexpensive night on the town.

Slipper Room p314

♥ Best night out

Club Cumming *p303*
Catch eclectic acts while mingling with
the Broadway set at Alan Cumming's East
Village hotspot.

Comedy Cellar *p314*
Envelope-pushing laughs and big names in
intimate quarters.

Good Room *p311*
A friendly and affordable alternative to
mega clubs.

House of Yes *p312*
Creative, costume-encouraged club nights.

Slipper Room *p314*
Retro variety shows mix risqué comedy,
burlesque and circus arts.

CLUBS

Legendary former pleasure zones such as
Studio 54, Paradise Garage, Limelight and
Area are embedded in nightlife's collective
consciousness as near-mythic ideals, but
today's scene is the strongest it's been in
years. This is largely thanks to numerous
nomadic shindigs, often held in out-of-
the-way warehouses, lofts and converted
whatever-you-can-finds that have sent the
energy of NYC nightlife where it belongs:
underground. In addition to the venues
and parties listed below, a visit to www.
timeout.com/newyork will always help to
clue you in. Recent years have seen a burst
of new permanent spaces, especially in
Williamsburg and Bushwick in Brooklyn,
plus bordering neighbourhoods in Queens.
    Many music venues, including **Baby's
All Right**, the **Bell House**, **Brooklyn Bowl,**
the **Knockdown Center** and **Le Poisson
Rouge**, also host DJ sets. *See p317-321.*

Le Bain

*The Standard, High Line, 444 W 13th Street,
at Washington Street, Meatpacking District
(1-212 645 7600, www.standardhotels.
com). Subway A, C, E to 14th Street; L
to Eighth Avenue. **Open** 4pm-midnight
Mon; 4pm-4am Tue-Thur; 2pm-4am
Fri, Sat; 2pm-3am Sun. **Admission** free.
Map p153 C27.*

Although an EDM-driven club scene is filling
bigger and bigger venues, for a more intimate
night out, head to this penthouse club and
terrace atop the Standard, High Line hotel.
The swanky space offers spectacular Hudson
River views from floor-to-ceiling windows

and a spacious rooftop with artificial grass
and a hot tub in the summer. And you can
get within hugging distance of underground
superstars that have included disco daddy
Dimitri from Paris, deep-house kingpin
Marques Wyatt and the aurally anarchic
DJ Harvey.

Black Flamingo

*168 Borinquen Place, between Keap & South
2nd Streets, Williamsburg, Brooklyn (1-718
387 3337, www.blackflamingonyc.com).
Subway G to Metropolitan Avenue; J, M, Z
to Marcy Avenue; L to Lorimer Street. **Open**
6pm-midnight Tue, Wed, Sun; 6pm-4am
Thur-Sat. Admisson free ($10 after midnight
Fri, Sat). **Map** p249 J29.*

In just a few years, this self-described
'plant-based taqueria and discotheque' has
established itself as an essential part of the
increasingly crowded Brooklyn nightlife
scene. A vinyl-friendly setup with wooden
analogue Klipsch La Scala speakers lures
regulars of the local electronic underground
to the charming throwback space, which
features a disco ball anchoring a cork-tile
ceiling. Its intimate rooms can quickly get
packed, due in no small part to big-name DJs
who pop in unannounced, such as seminal
spinner Eli Goldstein (Soul Clap).

Bossa Nova Civic Club

*1271 Myrtle Avenue, at Hart Street,
Bushwick, Brooklyn (1-718 443 1271, www.
bossanovacivicclub.com). Subway J to
Kosciuszko Street; M to Central Avenue.
Open 7pm-4am daily. **Admission** free-$10.*

This 'tropical fantasy dance club' has the edge
over its competitors in the thriving Bushwick
scene with a legitimate sound system
and consistently hot line-ups of under-
underground house and techno DJs. Since
opening in 2012, the nightspot has made a big
name for itself in the community, curating
its own stage at Sustain-Release (an upstate
New York micro-festival from Aurora Halal
of Mutual Dreaming) and hosting original
techno pioneer Adam X on his *Irreformable*
album tour.

In the know
Wallet essentials

Most clubs operate an over-21 policy,
and even if you're in the running for the
World's Oldest Clubber award, you'll need
government-issued ID (such as a passport
or driving licence) to gain admission. It's also
worth carrying cash, as most clubs won't
accept credit cards at the door.

Where's the Party?

All over the city, if you know where to look

New York has a number of regular, peripatetic, season-specific and often long-running bashes – sometimes they even evolve into permanent nightspots, as in the case of **Nowadays** (*see p313*), a venue from the DJ duo behind Mister Saturday Night and Mister Sunday.

Before the **Bunker** (www.thebunkerny.com), there were very few nights in New York devoted to envelope-pushing electronic dance music. Now we've got oodles of 'em. Coincidence? We think not – the party blazed the trail, and it's done so with an uncompromising attitude, paying little heed to commercial trends and concentrating on sheer quality. Big guns, mainly from its own label, regularly pack venues such as all-ages event space the Market Hotel (1140 Myrtle Avenue, at Broadway, Bushwick, Brooklyn). The bash is busier than ever despite running since the early noughties.

Blkmarket Membership (www.facebook.com/Blkmarketmembership) competes with the Bunker for the unofficial title of NYC's best techno party, hosting bashes in the city's established clubs as well as out-of-the-way warehouse spaces. **ReSolute** (www.resolutenyc.com) makes up the third side of the isosceles techno triangle of NYC. It's a fiercely underground affair, which has been bringing the deeper and darker sides of international DJs to town whenever, wherever and however they can since 2007.

Fixed (www.fixednyc.com), a roving party thrown by Dave P and JDH, has been running since 2004, but definitely doesn't look its age. Fixed has outlasted many venues and even more expectations simply by booking the best electronic talent, unbound by genre. It doesn't hurt that the hosts are also terrific DJs themselves, who know exactly what an opening slot should sound like and rarely miss their mark.

If you're looking for something away from the dark corners of clubland, **Tiki Disco** (www.tikidisco.com), an all-inclusive and incredibly popular party, typically spins a mix of disco and house classics interspersed with popular faves such as Lionel Richie. Then there's the **Warm Up** series (*see p289*) at MoMA PS1 in Queens. Since 1997, the museum's courtyard has played host to one of the most anticipated, resolutely underground summer clubbing events in the city.

Elsewhere

599 Johnson Avenue, between Gardner & Scott Avenues, Bushwick, Brooklyn (www.elsewherebrooklyn.com). Subway L to Jefferson Street. Open hrs vary. Admission free-$30. Map p249 N27.

Brooklyn's DIY scene gets a neon-lit glow at this sprawling music and culture complex tucked away in a burgeoning nightlife district off the Jefferson Avenue strip. The spacious main hall features a sensory-overloading laser-and-LED light show, and the venue also has a smaller side room, an upstairs DJ lounge called the Loft, plus a large rooftop deck. The talent's decidedly left of the dial, featuring indie-rockers and DJs with a foot still in the underground as well as mega raves, such as the queer Latinx party Papi Juice, demimonde empress Susanne Bartsch's extravaganza, KUNST, and high-energy dance institution Tiki Disco.

♥ Good Room

98 Meserole Avenue, between Lorimer Street & Manhattan Avenue, Greenpoint, Brooklyn (1-718 349 2373, www.goodroombk.com). Subway G to Nassau Avenue. Open 10pm-4am Thur-Sat. Admission free-$25. Map p249 K26.

Located in the home of former glitzy Polish venue Club Europa, Good Room was reinvented by nightlife impresario Steve Lewis in autumn 2014. The main room was designed with the DJ in mind, with a centrally placed booth and solid sound system, an ample dancefloor and a small raised stage for performances. Another room houses the massive square bar, where friendly bartenders mix surprisingly reasonably priced drinks. A third, smaller room – 'the Bad Room' – contains a massive wall of vinyl and another DJ set-up for separate tunes.

Marquee

289 Tenth Avenue, between 26th & 27th Streets, Chelsea (1-646 473 0202, www.marqueeny.com). Subway C, E to 23rd Street. Open 11pm-4am Wed, Fri, Sat. Admission varies. Map p153 D26.

After shutting down for major renovation, this one-time models-and-bottles club re-emerged... as a models-and-bottles club! In fairness, Marquee 2.0 is an entirely different – and far better – beast than it was in its original incarnation, with more open space, all manner of disco lights and enough razzle-dazzle to make your head spin. Look out for appearances by international house superstars such as Erick Morillo and KSHMR on the calendar.

❤ House of Yes

NIGHTLIFE

2 Wyckoff Avenue, at Jefferson Street, Bushwick, Brooklyn (1-646 838 4937, houseofyes.org). Subway L to Jefferson Street. **Open** *hrs vary; usually 7pm-4am Wed-Sat; 3-9pm Sat, Sun (June-Aug only).* **Admission** *Variety shows $20-$30; club nights $40-$50 ($15-$30 booked online; free entry before 11pm with RSVP usually available).* **Map** *p249 N27.*

House of Yes started life as a ramshackle Brooklyn live-in loft space for artists, musicians and circus folks, who hosted skill-sharing nights where devotees practised juggling, aerial arts and drumming. This punky utopian idyll was destroyed by a massive fire, but that didn't stop the plucky arts collective, which raised enough money to move into a rundown former ice house that was double the size of the original. The new space became a hub for spectacular shows, creative bashes and classes. The group was made homeless a second time in 2013 – this time by rising rents – and the search for a new space began again. But since its resurrection in December 2015, House of Yes has been firing on all cylinders with a jam-packed roster. The venue's upgraded Bushwick home – a nearly 22,000-sq ft teal warehouse identifiable by a giant YES painted on the side – is spacious enough to accommodate all sorts of revelry, from indie shopping markets, variety shows and yoga sessions to visually stunning, immersive film parties and costumed DJ raves with acrobats and stilt walkers. During one shindig that was billed as a sensual celebration of food and flesh, attendees kicked off the night by eating a meal off women's nude bodies with their hands before a programme of interactive erotic performances. Just say yes.

Nowadays

56-06 Cooper Avenue, at Irving Avenue, Ridgewood, Queens, (1-347 523 8535, www. nowadays.nyc). Subway L to Halsey Street. **Open** *4pm-midnight Mon-Thur; 4pm-4am Fri; noon-6am Sat; 3pm-midnight Sun (varies seasonally).* **Admission** *free-$25.*

Two of clubland's stalwart DJs, Justin Carter and Eamon Harkin, opened this indoor-outdoor venue for their hugely popular parties Mister Saturday Night and Mister Sunday, plus other club nights with some of the underground's top names and events such as free outdoor film screenings in summer. The music runs the gamut from deep disco and jacking house to outer-fringes dubstep and techno. At daytime Mister Sunday, expect to find DJs spinning highly danceable jams in a 16,000-sq ft lot. In addition to the dancefloor, the area is furnished with picnic tables and grassy knolls for lounging, food and drink vendors, and games such as bocce and ping-pong. The Kickstarter-financed indoor space features a custom sound system by SBS Designs, specially outfitted for the team and its eclectic dance-music selections.

Nublu Classic

62 Avenue C, between 4th & 5th Streets, East Village (no phone, www.nublu.net). Subway F to Lower East Side-Second Avenue. **Open** *8pm-4am daily (sometimes closed Mon, Sun).* **Admission** *$10.* **Map** *p123 G29.*

Since Swedish-Turkish musician and promoter Ilhan Ersahin opened Nublu in 2002, the club has evolved from a late-night hangout and jam session spot for musicians to a club and small performance space that hosts bands and DJs of all stripes. At the nexus of funk, soul, bossa nova and instrumental hip hop, the bar also holds acts in its orbit such as In Flagranti, Brazilian Girls, Norah Jones, Forro in the Dark and Kudu, as well as Ersahin's band/project Wax Poetic. **Other location** 151 Avenue C, between 9th & 10th Streets, East Village.

Schimanski

54 North 11th Street, between Kent & Wythe Avenues, Williamsburg, Brooklyn (1-718 486 2299, schimanskinyc.com). Subway L to Bedford Avenue. **Open** *hrs vary.* **Admission** *$20-$30.* **Map** *p249 J23.*

The curiously monikered Schimanski – named after a fictional character from a 1981 German crime series – regularly hosts big-name house, techno and bass DJs, plus live gigs. The modern-industrial main room features an expansive dancefloor, while the side room serves as a showcase for less well-known DJs and a sometime restaurant and lounge. Check the calendar to find veterans such as Danny Krivit, Carl Cox and Robert Hood spinning alongside rising talents.

Trans-Pecos

915 Wyckoff Avenue, between Hancock & Weirfield Streets, Ridgewood, Queens (no phone, www.thetranspecos.com). Subway L to Halsey Street. **Open** *hrs vary.* **Admission** *$8-$30.*

As NYC's nightlife moves outward from Manhattan, even Williamsburg can get a bit stuffy. Look then to this cosy, adventurous music spot in Ridgewood, Queens, a few blocks from Bushwick. Intrepid local booker Todd P, the granddaddy of the Brooklyn DIY scene, oversees the show space and community hub. Exciting electronic acts, experimental DJs and outré indie bands regularly visit the venue.

BURLESQUE

New York's burlesque scene is a winking throwback to the days when the tease was as important as the strip. Much of the scene tends to revolve around specific revues rather than dedicated venues; good bets include shows produced by **Dances of Vice** (www. dancesofvice.com), **Thirsty Girl Productions** (www.thirstygirlproductions.com), 'Italian Stallionette' **Angie Pontani** (www. angiepontani.com) and **Calamity Chang**, 'the Asian Sexation' (www.calamitychang.com).

Duane Park

308 Bowery, between Bleecker & E Houston Streets, East Village (1-212 732 5555, www. duaneparknyc.com). Subway F to Lower East Side-Second Avenue; 6 to Astor Place. **Shows** *vary; usually 8pm Tue-Thur; 9.30pm Fri; 7.45pm, 10.30pm Sat.* **Admission** *varies.* **Map** *p123 F29.*

The former Bowery Poetry Club now operates as Southern-inflected supper club Duane Park, though Bowery Poetry (www. bowerypoetry.com) still holds events on Sundays and Mondays. Get dinner and a show – burlesque, jazz, vaudeville or magic – in decadent surroundings featuring crystal chandeliers and Corinthian-topped columns.

Nurse Bettie

106 Norfolk Street, between Delancey & Rivington Streets, Lower East Side (1-212 477 7515, www.nursebettie.com). Subway F to Delancey Street; J, Z to Delancey-Essex Streets. **Open** *6pm-4am daily.* **Admission** *free.* **Map** *p111 G30.*

The '50s-pin-up-inspired venue – named after Bettie Page, one of the 20th century's premier hotsy-totsies – is a natural setting for burlesque. Weekly shows include Spanking the Lower East Side, produced by Calamity Chang, which usually includes six or seven acts, as well as pre-show go-go dancers. Prepare to get up close and personal in the intimate space.

❤ Slipper Room

*167 Orchard Street, at Stanton Street, Lower East Side (1-212 253 7246, www.slipperroom. com). Subway F to Lower East Side-Second Avenue. **Shows** vary. **Admission** $10-$25. **Map** p111 F29.*

After being closed for extensive renovations for more than two years, the Slipper Room reopened with a better sound system, new lighting and a mezzanine, among other swank touches, and reclaimed its place as the city's premier burlesque venue. Among the jam-packed weekly schedule are such long-running shows as Mr. Choade's Upstairs Downstairs (which began in 1999).

COMEDY

New York is one of the greatest cities in the world for comedy – be it stand-up, sketch or improv. On top of scheduled shows at the best venues, anyone from Chris Rock to Amy Schumer could drop by unannounced. In addition to the spaces listed below, the basement performance space in Brooklyn bar **Union Hall** (*see p322*) hosts cutting-edge new work from local acts and favourites from TV shows such as *Broad City*, *High Maintenance* and *Saturday Night Live* (advance booking recommended).

Carolines on Broadway

*1626 Broadway, between 49th & 50th Streets, Theater District (1-212 757 4100, www.carolines.com). Subway N, R, W to 49th Street; 1 to 50th Street. **Shows** vary. **Admission** varies (2-drink minimum). **Map** p175 D23.*

Even comics who are regulars at the city's other stand-up rooms have to work extra hard to get stage time at this venerable institution. Carolines is the best place to see marquee names, including sitcom-ready stars, familiar

---

In the know
Live from New York...

Seminal NYC comedy-sketch show *Saturday Night Live* has been running since 1975. For a chance to score tickets to a dress rehearsal (8pm) or live show (11.30pm) taping, check the website (www.nbc.com/snl) for information in August. You'll need to enter the draw by email during that month for the upcoming season. Alternatively, you can try the standby lottery on the day. Line up by 7am (but to have a chance, you'll need to get there much earlier) under the NBC Studio marquee (on the 48th Street side of 30 Rockefeller Plaza). You must be over 16 with photo ID.

---

faces from the '80s comedy boom and cable-special ravers. You'll never see anything less than professional here.

❤ Comedy Cellar

*117 MacDougal Street, between Bleecker Street & Minetta Lane, Greenwich Village (1-212 254 3480, www.comedycellar.com). Subway A, B, C, D, E, F, M to W 4th Street. **Shows** 7.30pm, 9.30pm, 11.30pm Mon-Thur, Sun; 7pm, 8.45pm, 10.30pm, 12.15am Fri, Sat. **Admission** $14-$24 (2-item minimum). **Map** p137 E30.*

Claustrophobes, beware: it gets crowded down here, especially at weekends, thanks to the immense popularity of this Village standby. Big names from Dave Chappelle to Amy Schumer may drop by for a set, and on any given night you can expect to see local greats whose acts are more X-rated than at other clubs (and who will distract you from your bachelorette-partying neighbours). **Other location** Comedy Cellar at the Village Underground, 130 W 3rd Street, between Sixth Avenue & MacDougal Street, Greenwich Village (1-212 777 7745).

The Creek & the Cave

*10-93 Jackson Avenue, at 11th Street, Long Island City, Queens (1-917 806 6692, www. creeklic.com). Subway G to 21st Street, 7 to Vernon Boulevard-Jackson Avenue. **Shows** daily, times vary. **Admission** free-$5. **Map** p259 J23.*

This Long Island City spot is the gem of the Queens comedy scene. Owner Rebecca Trent programmes shows seven nights a week, and at times you can catch up to five free shows on a busy weekend night. Among its features: cheap, serviceable Mexican food, a ramshackle theatre hosting larger events, a smaller space downstairs for intimate stand-up or storytelling and a bar with adjoining patio for pre- or post-show chilling.

Dangerfield's

*1118 First Avenue, between 61st & 62nd Streets, Upper East Side (1-212 593 1650, www.dangerfields.com). Subway N, R, W to Lexington Avenue-59th Street; 4, 5, 6 to 59th Street. **Shows** 8.30pm Mon-Thur, Sun; 8.30pm, 10.30pm Fri, Sat. **Admission** $25 (2-item minimum). **Map** p209 F22.*

Inside Dangerfield's, it's 1969. The waiters wear matching maroon jackets, and red lamp shades glow on each tabletop in the lounge. The club opened because its namesake, Rodney Dangerfield, wanted a home base to work out new material. Although the room was a talent magnet in its heyday, hosting the likes of Jerry Seinfeld and Chris Rock, today's line-ups are a mix of solid NYC scene fixtures and emerging comics.

Gotham Comedy Club
208 W 23rd Street, between Seventh & Eighth Avenues, Chelsea (1-212 367 9000, www. gothamcomedyclub.com). Subway F, M, R, W to 23rd Street. **Shows** *vary.* **Admission** *varies (2-drink minimum).* **Map** *p153 D26.*

Chris Mazzilli's vision for his club involves elegant surroundings, professional behaviour and mutual respect. That's why the talents he fosters, such as Jim Gaffigan, Tom Papa and Ted Alexandro, keep coming back here after they've found national fame.

Greenwich Village Comedy Club
99 MacDougal Street, between Bleecker Street & Minetta Lane, Greenwich Village (1-212 777 5233, www. greenwichvillagecomedyclub.com). Subway A, B, C, D, E, F, M to W 4th Street. **Shows** *vary; usually 7.30pm, 9.45pm Mon-Thur, Sun; 8pm, 9.45pm, 11.45pm Fri; 6pm, 8.30pm, 10.30pm, 12.30am Sat.* **Admission** *$20-$25 (2-drink minimum).* **Map** *p137 E30.*

Al Martin, the longtime owner of both the New York Comedy Club and Broadway Comedy Club, follows the same basic tenets of those ventures in this intimate basement space below a halal burger joint. Although a few pillars in the 60-seat venue interfere with sightlines, the pub grub, extensive cocktail selection and long list of stars who just might do a spot while passing through town draw crowds every night.

Magnet Theater
254 W 29th Street, between Seventh & Eighth Avenues, Chelsea (1-212 244 8824, www. magnettheater.com). Subway A, C, E to 34th Street-Penn Station; 1 to 28th Street. **Shows** *daily, times vary.* **Admission** *free-$10.* **Map** *p153 D26.*

This comedy theatre exudes a distinctly Chicago vibe, from its DIY aesthetic to the performers, some of whom are from the Windy City. Even the local players here prefer theatrical to premise-based improvisation, and their shows give the impression they're not just seeking fame or commercial exposure, but pursue the craft simply for the joy of being on stage.

Peoples Improv Theater
123 E 24th Street, between Park & Lexington Avenues, Flatiron District (1-212 563 7488, www.thepit-nyc.com). Subway 6 to 23rd Street. **Shows** *daily, times vary.* **Admission** *free-$16.* **Map** *p163 E26.*

After inhabiting a black box in Chelsea for eight years, the PIT leapt across town into the former Algonquin Theatre. The improv and sketch venue has a beautiful proscenium stage, an additional basement space for experimental shows or sketch comedy, and an elegant (if cluttered) full-service bar.

Stand Up New York
236 W 78th Street, at Broadway, Upper West Side (1-212 595 0850, www.standupny. com). Subway 1 to 79th Street. **Shows** *vary; usually 8pm, 10.15pm Mon-Thur, Sun; 6pm, 8pm, 10pm Fri; 5pm, 8pm, 10pm, 11.45pm Sat.* **Admission** *$15-$20 ($18 drink min).* **Map** *p195 C19.*

After some managerial shifts, this musty uptown spot is garnering attention again. The line-ups (including stalwart club denizens such as Jay Oakerson and Godfrey) keep things pretty simple, but there's almost always one performer on the bill that makes it worth the trip.

Tribeca Comedy Lounge
22 Warren Street, between Broadway & Church Street, Tribeca (1-646 504 5653, www.tribecacomedylounge.com). Subway A, C, 1, 2, 3 to Chambers Street; R, W to City Hall. **Shows** *vary; usually 9pm Fri, Sat.* **Admission** *$25 (2-drink minimum).* **Map** *p71 E32.*

The atmosphere in this spot is congenial. The brick walls and makeshift stage remind you that you're in a basement, but the doting waitstaff, haute Italian menu and roomy layout will please fans of creature comforts. Adam Strauss, the owner-booker and a burgeoning comic, makes sure that his programming is packed with young, funny next-wave talent while also saving stage time for himself.

▶ *The club has also expanded to nearby Dark Horse Comedy Club (17 Murray Street, between Broadway & Church Street, 1-646 504 5653, www.darkhorsecomedyclub.com).*

Upright Citizens Brigade Theatre
555 West 42nd Street, at Eleventh Avenue, Hell's Kitchen (1-212 366 9176, www. ucbtheatre.com). Subway A, C, E to 42nd Street-Port Authority; N, Q, R, S, W, 1, 2, 3, 7 to 42nd Street-Times Square; 7 to 34th Street-Hudson Yards. **Shows** *daily, times vary.* **Admission** *free-$14.* **No cards.** **Map** *p153 D26.*

UCBT is the most visible catalyst in New York's current alternative comedy boom. The improv troupes and sketch groups here are some of the best in the city. Stars of *Saturday Night Live* and writers for late-night talk shows gather on Sunday nights to wow crowds in the long-running ASSSSCAT 3000. Celebrity guests have included Tina Fey, Keegan-Michael Key and Ilana Glazer. The late show is free, but you need to reserve tickets in advance. Other premier teams include the Stepfathers (Friday) and the Curfew (Saturday). **Other location** at SubCulture (*see p324*).

ROCK, POP & SOUL MUSIC

Increasingly, forward-looking venues, such as National Sawdust, Le Poisson Rouge, Joe's Pub and recently opened arts centre **The Shed** (*see p179*), offer eclectic line-ups that mix genres and disciplines. Gigs are also busting out of their usual club and concert hall confines: bowling alley-music venue hybrid **Brooklyn Bowl** hosts a smattering of high-profile acts as well as regular dance parties, and indie-music megastore **Rough Trade** (*see p250*) stages free and ticketed concerts.

Information & tickets

Tickets are usually available from clubs in advance and at the door, but bear in mind that if you purchase your ticket on site you may have to pay cash. For larger events, buy online through the venue's website or via **Ticketmaster** (www.ticketmaster.com, 1-800 745 3000) or **TicketWeb** (www.ticketweb.com). Phone ahead for information and show times, which can change without notice.

Major arenas

Barclays Center
*620 Atlantic Avenue, at Flatbush Avenue, Prospect Heights, Brooklyn (1-917 618 6100, www.barclayscenter.com). Subway B, D, N, Q, R, 2, 3, 4, 5 to Atlantic Avenue-Barclays Center. **Box office** noon-6pm Mon-Fri; noon-4pm Sat (varies on event days). **Tickets** vary. **Map** p232 K34.*

The city's newest arena, home of the rechristened Brooklyn Nets basketball team, opened in 2012 with a series of concerts by native son and Nets investor Jay Z. It quickly proved to be a success. Staff are efficient and amiable, the acoustics are excellent, and there's a top-notch view from nearly every one of the 19,000 seats. But, most importantly, the venue has attracted an unexpectedly cool list of acts as diverse as The Weeknd, Drake and Ariana Grande gracing its stage.

Madison Square Garden
*Seventh Avenue, between 31st & 33rd Streets, Garment District (1-212 465 6741, www.thegarden.com). Subway A, C, E, 1, 2, 3 to 34th Street-Penn Station. **Box office** 10am-6pm Mon-Sat (extended hours on show days). **Tickets** vary. **Map** p153 D25.*

Some of music's biggest acts – Billy Joel, Cher, Jonas Brothers – come out to play at the

---

💙 Best music venues

Apollo Theatre *p317*
Newcomers and veterans alike take to the stage at this legendary venue.

Bowery Ballroom *p317*
Elegant stage for indie bands and eclectic acts with great sightlines and sound.

Joe's Pub *p319*
Notable emerging talent and alt cabaret.

Rockwood Music Hall *p321*
Sample several emerging acts across three stages.

Village Vanguard *p324*
Soak up the nostalgia in this old-school jazz joint.

Webster Hall *p322*
Revamped historic venue with the biggest names in electronic, indie, hip hop and more.

Joe's Pub

world's most famous basketball arena, home to the Knicks and also hockey's Rangers. Whether you'll actually be able to get a look at them depends on your seat number or the quality of your binoculars. While the storied venue is undoubtedly a part of the fabric of New York, it's too vast for a rich concert experience. However, a three-year renovation restored the striking circular ceiling and brought new seating and food from top New York City chefs, among other improvements.

Venues

❤ Apollo Theater

253 W 125th Street, between Adam Clayton Powell Jr Boulevard (Seventh Avenue) & Frederick Douglass Boulevard (Eighth Avenue), Harlem (1-212 531 5300, www. apollotheater.org). Subway A, B, C, D, 1 to 125th Street. **Box office** *10am-6pm Mon-Fri; noon-5pm Sat.* **Tickets** *vary.* **Map** *p223 D13.*

This 1914 former burlesque theatre has been a hub for African-American artists for decades, and launched the careers of Ella Fitzgerald and D'Angelo, among many others. The now-legendary Amateur Night showcase has been running since 1934. The venue, known for jazz, R&B and soul, mixes veteran talents such as Dianne Reeves with younger artists like Janelle Monae and Esperanza Spalding.

Baby's All Right

146 Broadway, at Bedford Avenue, Williamsburg, Brooklyn (1-347 599 5800, www.babysallright.com). Subway J, M, Z to Marcy Avenue. **Open** *6pm-2am Mon-Fri; 11am-4am Sat, Sun. Shows vary.* **Tickets** *free-$35.* **Map** *p249 K29.*

This eatery, bar and stage, located on a happening little Williamsburg strip, is well on its way to becoming a local musical institution with its lively schedule of au courant acts and DJs that range from experimental (Pharmakon) to vogueish (Mac DeMarco). The buzzy spot always seems to have something interesting on deck: it's not unusual to find three bills crammed into the same night.

Barbès

376 9th Street, between Sixth & Seventh Avenues, Park Slope, Brooklyn (1-347 422 0248, www.barbesbrooklyn.com). Subway F to Seventh Avenue. **Open** *5pm-2am Mon-Thur; 2pm-4am Fri, Sat; 2pm-2am Sun.* **Tickets** *suggested donation $10.* **Map** *p232 L37.*

Show up early if you want to get into Park Slope's global-bohemian club – it's tiny. Run

by musically inclined French expats, this boîte brings in traditional swing and jazz of more daring stripes: depending on the night, you could catch Colombian, Brazilian, African or French music or acts that often defy categorisation.

Beacon Theatre

2124 Broadway, between 74th & 75th Streets, Upper West Side (1-212 465 6500, www. beacontheatrenyc.com). Subway 1, 2, 3 to 72nd Street. **Box office** *11am-7pm Mon-Sat (varies on event days).* **Tickets** *vary.* **Map** *p195 C20.*

This spacious former vaudeville theatre hosts a variety of popular acts, from comedian John Oliver to jazz-rock legends Steely Dan. While the vastness can be daunting to performers and audience alike, the baroque, gilded interior and uptown location make you feel as though you're having a real night out on the town.

The Bell House

149 7th Street, between Second & Third Avenues, Gowanus, Brooklyn (1-718 643 6510, www.thebellhouseny.com). Subway F, G, R to Fourth Avenue-9th Street. **Shows** *vary.* **Tickets** *free-$30.* **Map** *p232 K37.*

This pioneering venue offers a plethora of cool events each week, including concerts, nerdy lectures and dance parties. In addition to gigs by the likes of the Legendary Shack Shakers, schedule fixtures include off-the-cuff storytelling slam the Moth, National Public Radio trivia show *Ask Me Another*, and the Rub, a funky long-running affair tossed by DJs Ayres and Eleven.

❤ Bowery Ballroom

6 Delancey Street, between Bowery & Chrystie Street, Lower East Side (1-212 260 4700, www.boweryballroom.com). Subway B, D to Grand Street; J, Z to Bowery; 6 to Spring Street. **Box office** *at Mercury Lounge (see p319).* **Tickets** *$15-$125.* **Map** *p111 F30.*

Bowery Ballroom is probably the best venue in the city for seeing indie bands, either on the way up or holding their own. But it also brings in a diverse range of artists from home and abroad, and you can expect a clear view and bright sound from any spot in the venue. The spacious downstairs lounge is a great place to hang out between sets.

Brooklyn Bazaar

150 Greenpoint Avenue, between Franklin Street & Manhattan Avenue, Greenpoint, Brooklyn (no phone, bkbazaar.com). Subway G to Greenpoint Avenue. **Shows** *vary (usually Wed-Sun).* **Tickets** *free-$30.* **Map** *p249 J26.*

A onetime 1930s Polish banquet hall is now a buzzing three-storey venue for concerts and events, with four bars and an outpost of contemporary Tibetan restaurant Dawa's. The weekly gig schedule is eclectic – expect anything from indie rock and electronic to punk and metal, plus karaoke, DJ parties, film nights, comedy shows and curated markets.

Brooklyn Bowl

61 Wythe Avenue, between North 11th & 12th Streets, Williamsburg, Brooklyn (1-718 963 3369, www.brooklynbowl.com). Subway L to Bedford Avenue. **Shows** *vary.* **Tickets** *$5-$35.* **Map** *p249 K27.*

This bowling alley and music venue fully embraces the mania for local nostalgia. The place takes its design cues from Coney Island with old freak-show posters and carnival-game relics, and most of the beer sold on-site is made in the borough. The 600-capacity concert space hosts a smattering of high-profile acts (Trey Anastasio Band, Robert Plant) as well as tribute bands and DJ dance parties.

Brooklyn Steel

319 Frost Street, at Debevoise Avenue, Williamsburg, Brooklyn (www. bowerypresents.com). Subway L to Graham Avenue. **Shows** *vary.* **Box office** *at PlayStation Theater (see p320), or at Rough Trade (see p250) noon-6pm Fri, Sat.* **Tickets** *$20-$75.* **Map** *p249 L26.*

Part of the Bowery Presents stable, Brooklyn Steel is larger than its Brooklyn sister venue Music Hall of Williamsburg (*see right*), boasting an audience capacity of 1,800 in a converted steel fabrication warehouse. Retaining industrial elements such as scrap metal and gantry cranes, the building has three bars, 40 restrooms and a mezzanine for an above-the-fray view. Look for larger indie-rock acts such as PJ Harvey and Hot Chip to fill the vast space.

Forest Hills Stadium

1 Tennis Place at Burns Street, Forest Hills, Queens (no phone, www.foresthillsstadium. com). Subway E, F, M, R to Forest Hills-71st Avenue; LIRR to Forest Hills. **Box office** *usually Apr-Oct noon-8pm Fri (10am for new ticket releases). At Rough Trade (see p250): noon-6pm Fri, Sat.* **Tickets** *$35-$100.*

After extensive renovation, this storied tennis stadium, which hosted memorable matches and concerts from the 1920s through to the '80s, including the Beatles, Stones and others, reopened its doors in 2013 with a rowdy Mumford & Sons gig. These days, the outdoor venue presents a wide variety of artists ranging from My Morning Jacket to Morrissey during its season (usually Apr-Oct).

Kings Theatre

Gramercy Theatre

127 E 23rd Street, between Park & Lexington Avenues, Gramercy Park (1-212 614 6932, venue.thegramercytheatre.com). Subway R, W, 6 to 23rd Street. **Box office** *(show days only) 12.30pm until showtime Mon-Fri; 1hr before doors open until showtime Sat, Sun.* **Tickets** *$15-$50.* **Map** *p163 E26.*

The Gramercy Theatre looks exactly like what it is, a run-down former cinema, but it has a decent sound system and good sightlines. Concert-goers can lounge in raised seats on the top level or get closer to the stage at ground level. Bookings have included such Baby Boom underdogs as Loudon Wainwright III and Todd Rundgren, and the occasional hip-hop show, but tilt towards niche metal and emo.

Hammerstein Ballroom

Manhattan Center, 311 W 34th Street, between Eighth & Ninth Avenues, Garment District (1-212 279 7740, Ticketmaster 1-800 745 3000, www.mcstudios.com). Subway A, C, E to 34th Street-Penn Station. **Tickets** *vary.* **Map** *p175 D25.*

Queues can wind across the block, drinks prices are high, and those seated in the balcony should bring binoculars. Still, this cavernous space regularly draws big performers in the limbo between club and arena shows, and it's ideal for theatrical blowouts; Beck, Nick Cave and Sleater-Kinney have all packed the house.

❤ Joe's Pub

Public Theater, 425 Lafayette Street, between Astor Place & E 4th Street, East Village (1-212 539 8778, www.joespub.com). Subway R, W to 8th Street-NYU; 6 to Astor Place. Box office 2-10pm daily. Tickets $15-$50 ($12 food or 2-drink minimum). Map p123 F28.

One of the city's premier small spots for sit-down audiences, Joe's Pub brings in impeccable talent of all genres and origins. While some well-established names play here, Joe's also lends its stage to up-and-comers (this is where Amy Winehouse made her US debut), drag acts and cabaret performers (Justin Vivian Bond is a mainstay). The food menu – a mix of snacks, shareable plates and main courses – comes courtesy of prominent chef Andrew Carmellini.

Kings Theatre

1027 Flatbush Avenue between Duryea Place & Tilden Avenue, East Flatbush, Brooklyn (Ticketmaster 1-800 745 3000, www.kingstheatre.com). Subway B, Q, 2, 5 to Church Avenue. Box office noon-5.30pm Mon-Sat. Tickets vary.

A gilded movie palace and vaudeville stage when it debuted in 1929, the Kings Theatre closed in the 1970s and sat empty for 37 years. You wouldn't know it today, gazing at the intricately adorned ceilings and gargoyles of the interior. The venue underwent a two-year, $93 million restoration and reopened in 2015. Its stellar line-ups reflect the diversity of the borough, with headlining appearances from salsa singer Gilberto Santa Rosa, moody rock legends Nick Cave & the Bad Seeds and indie-rock staples such as the Pixies and the Raconteurs.

Knitting Factory Brooklyn

361 Metropolitan Avenue, at Havemeyer Street, Williamsburg, Brooklyn (1-347 529 6696, www.knittingfactory.com). Subway L to Lorimer Street; G to Metropolitan Avenue. Open 6pm-midnight Mon-Thur, Sun; 6pm-4am Fri, Sat. Shows vary. Tickets free-$30. Map p249 K28.

Once a downtown Manhattan incubator of experimental music (of both the jazz and the indie-rock variety), Knitting Factory now has

---

In the know
Local guitar heroes

Hometown band the Strokes began their fantastically quick rise with a residency at the modest Lower East Side rock club **Mercury Lounge** (*see right*) in 2000 (the Moldy Peaches opened).

---

outposts across the country. Its New York base, which relocated to Williamsburg, is a professional, well-managed club, with a happening front-room bar, and solid indie-rock and hip-hop bills designed to suit its hipster clientele.

Knockdown Center

52-19 Flushing Ave at 54th Street, Maspeth, Queens (1-718 489 6285, knockdown.center). Subway L to Jefferson Street, then 15-minute walk. Open hrs vary. Basement 10pm-5am Fri, Sat. Admission $15-$35.

Housed in a glass-manufacturing plant built in 1903, Knockdown Center is an adventurous multimedia arts space. Make the trek to Queens, and you'll be rewarded with exploratory music and performance art of all stripes, from DJs traversing the most outré margins of club music to avant-garde dance theatre soundtracked by experiments in harsh noise. Subterranean sister venue Basement (basementny.net) fashions a no-nonsense techno venue out of a network of brick tunnels once used to heat the industrial space.

Mercury Lounge

217 E Houston Street, between Essex & Ludlow Streets, Lower East Side (1-212 260 4700, www.mercuryeastpresents.com). Subway F to Lower East Side-Second Avenue. Box office noon-6 pm Thur-Sat. Tickets $8-$20. Map p111 G29.

The unassuming, boxy Mercury Lounge is an old standby, with solid sound and sightlines (and a cramped bar in the front room). There are multiple band bills most nights, although they can seem stylistically haphazard and set times are often later than advertised. (It's a good rule of thumb to show up half an hour later than you think you should.) Some of the bigger shows sell out in advance; young hopefuls from years gone by to take the stage here include Mumford & Sons.

Music Hall of Williamsburg

66 North 6th Street, between Kent & Wythe Avenues, Williamsburg, Brooklyn (1-718 486 5400, www.musichallofwilliamsburg.com). Subway L to Bedford Avenue. Box office at PlayStation Theater (see p320), or at Rough Trade (see p250) noon-6pm Fri, Sat. Tickets free-$35. Map p249 J28.

The Music Hall of Williamsburg was originally launched as a mirror-image outpost of the similarly sized Bowery Ballroom, though both venues have undergone complicated changes of ownership over the past decade. With elevated areas on either side of the space, the Brooklyn venue upped its Manhattan counterpart with improved sightlines and a bit more breathing room.

Rockwood Music Hall

And like its precursor, well-curated bookings, from indie-rock bands to hip-hop acts, make it one of the best rooms in the city to see a show.

National Sawdust

*80 North 6th Street, at Wythe Avenue, Williamsburg, Brooklyn (1-646 779 8455, www.nationalsawdust.org). Subway L to Bedford Avenue. **Box office** noon-6pm daily and during shows. **Tickets** vary. **Map** p249 J28.*

Brooklyn design studio Bureau V rebuilt the interior of this former sawdust factory as a showcase for both acoustic and electric music. The space can accommodate 170 people seated or 350 standing and includes a bar. With composer and co-founder Paola Prestini as the artistic director – and a host of curators that span classical and indie-rock spheres – there's little doubt the non-profit space is in good hands.

Pete's Candy Store

*709 Lorimer Street, between Frost & Richardson Streets, Williamsburg, Brooklyn (1-718 302 3770, www.petescandystore.com). Subway L to Lorimer Street. **Open** 5pm-2am Mon-Thur; 4pm-4am Fri; 3pm-4am Sat; 3pm-2am Sun. Shows vary. **Admission** free. **Map** p249 J27.*

An overlooked gem tucked away in an old candy shop, Pete's is beautifully ramshackle, tiny and almost always free. The performers are generally unknown and crowds can be thin, but it can be a charming place to catch a singer-songwriter testing out new material.

Pianos

*158 Ludlow Street, between Rivington & Stanton Streets, Lower East Side (1-212 505 3733, www.pianosnyc.com). Subway F to Delancey Street; J, M, Z to Delancey-Essex Streets. **Open** 2pm-4am daily. Shows vary. **Admission** free-$10. **Map** p111 F29.*

In recent years, a lot of the cooler bookings have moved to Brooklyn. But while the sound is often lousy and the room can get uncomfortably mobbed, there are always good reasons to go back to Pianos – very often the under-the-radar, emerging rock bands that make local music scenes tick.

PlayStation Theater

*1515 Broadway, at 44th Street, Theater District (1-212 930 1950, www. playstationtheater.com). Subway N, Q, R, S, W, 1, 2, 3, 7 to 42nd Street-Times Square. **Box office** noon-6pm Mon-Sat. **Tickets** $20-$80. **Map** p175 D24.*

This large, corporate club begs for character but finds redemption in its creature comforts. The sound and sightlines are both good. Those who wish to look into a musician's eyes can stand in the ample front section; foot-weary fans can sit in the cinema-like section at the back. It's a comfortable place to see a well-known band that hasn't (yet) reached stadium-filling fame.

Le Poisson Rouge

*158 Bleecker Street, at Thompson Street,
Greenwich Village (1-212 505 3474, www.
lepoissonrouge.com). Subway A, B, C,
D, E, F, M to W 4th Street.* **Box office**
5pm-close on show days. **Tickets** *$15-$30.*
Map *p137 E30.*

Tucked into the basement of the long-gone
Village Gate, a legendary performance space
that hosted everyone from Miles Davis to
Jimi Hendrix, this cabaret-style space was
opened in 2008 by a group of young music
enthusiasts with ties to both the classical and
the indie-rock worlds. The booking policy
reflects both camps, often on a single bill.
A wide range of great music might span a
feverish Saharan guitarist (Bombino), noisy
art-rock luminaries (Deerhoof) or young
classical stars (pianist Simone Dinnerstein).

Radio City Music Hall

*1260 Sixth Avenue, at 50th Street, Midtown
(1-212 247 4777, www.radiocity.com). Subway
B, D, F, M to 47th-50th Streets-Rockefeller
Center.* **Box office** *10am-6pm daily.* **Tickets**
vary. **Map** *p175 E23.*

Few rooms scream 'New York City!' more
than this gilded hall, which in recent years
has drawn The xx, Diana Ross and Wilco as
headliners. The greatest challenge for any
performer is to not be upstaged by the awe-
inspiring art deco surroundings, although
those same surroundings lend historic heft to
even the flimsiest showing. The venue is home
to high-kicking precision dance company the
Rockettes and their seasonal 'spectaculars'.

❤ Rockwood Music Hall

*196 Allen Street, between E Houston &
Stanton Streets, Lower East Side (1-212
477 4155, www.rockwoodmusichall.com).
Subway F to Lower East Side-Second
Avenue.* **Open** *5.30pm-1.30am Mon-Thur;
5.30pm-2.30am Fri; 2.30pm-3am Sat;
2.30pm-1.30am Sun.* **Tickets** *free-$15
(1-drink minimum per set).* **Map** *p111 F29.*

The cramped quarters are part of this club's
appeal: there are no bad seats (or standing
spots) in the house. You can catch multiple
acts every night of the week on three separate
stages, and it's likely that many of those
performers will soon be appearing in much
bigger halls. Multi-genre polymath Gabriel
Kahane is a regular, as is bluegrass great
Michael Daves.

Saint Vitus

*1120 Manhattan Avenue, between Box &
Clay Streets, Greenpoint, Brooklyn (no
phone, www.saintvitusbar.com). Subway G
to Greenpoint Avenue.* **Open** *6pm-2am Mon-
Thur, Sun; 6pm-4am Fri, Sat.* **Shows** *vary.*
Tickets *free-$25.* **Map** *p249 J25.*

Once a mainstay of NYC's downtown scene,
true rock 'n' roll clubs feel like a dying breed
in the post-Giuliani era. But this Greenpoint
drinkery – moodily decorated with all-
black walls and dead roses hanging above
the bar – reinvigorates the tradition with
a Brooklyn twist. Metal-heads and rockers
will be delighted to find both veteran groups
(Pentagram, Monstrosity) and local talent
taking to the stage.

SOB's

*204 Varick Street, at Houston Street,
Tribeca (1-212 243 4940, www.sobs.com).
Subway 1 to Houston Street.* **Shows** *vary.*
Tickets *$10-$30.* **Map** *p137 D30.*

The titular Sounds of Brazil (SOB, geddit?) are
just some of the many global genres that keep
this venue hopping. Soul, hip hop, reggae and
Latin beats figure in the mix, with Cardi B,
Khalid and Post Malone appearing in recent
years. The drinks are expensive, but the
sharp-looking clientele don't seem to mind.

Sony Hall

*235 W 46th Street, between Seventh & Eighth
Avenues, Theater District (1-212 997 5123,
www.sonyhall.com). Subway A, C, E to 42nd
Street-Port Authority; N, R, W to 49th Street.*
Box office *11am-5pm daily.* **Shows** *vary.*
Tickets *vary.* **Map** *p175 D23.*

From 1938 to 1951, the Diamond Horseshoe in
the basement of midtown's Paramount Hotel
was one of the most prominent nightclubs in
New York, with theatrical producer Billy Rose
presiding over revues stuffed with showgirls.
In 2014 it was revived as a space for the site-
specific immersive production *Queen of the
Night*. Fast forward to 2018, when Sony and
Blue Note Entertainment renovated the
historic digs into a futuristic concert hall,
fitted top to bottom with cutting-edge audio
technology. Expect anything from reggae
to speed metal to blues, and count on the
biggest names in each.

Terminal 5

*610 W 56th Street, between 11th & 12th
Avenues, Hell's Kitchen (1-212 582 6600,
www.terminal5nyc.com). Subway A, B, C, D,
1 to 59th Street-Columbus Circle.* **Box office**
*at PlayStation Theater (see p320), or at
Rough Trade (see p250) noon-6pm Fri, Sat.*
Tickets *$20-$90.* **Map** *p175 B22.*

This three-floor, 3,000-capacity venue is part
of the Bowery Presents empire. Bookings
include bands that only a short time ago were
playing in the promoter's smaller clubs, plus
bigger stars and veterans with loyal fan bases
(Marilyn Manson, Dido). It's great for dancey
acts (Chromeo, Matt & Kim), but be warned:
sightlines from the T5 balconies are among
the worst in the city.

Town Hall

123 W 43rd Street, between Sixth Avenue & Broadway, Theater District (1-212 997 6661, www.thetownhall.org). Subway B, D, F, M to 42nd Street-Bryant Park; N, Q, R, S, W, 1, 2, 3, 7 to 42nd Street-Times Square; 7 to Fifth Avenue. **Box office** *noon-6pm Mon-Sat (plus Sun if show day).* **Tickets** *vary.* **Map** *p175 D24.*

Acoustics at the 1921 'people's auditorium' are superb, and there's no doubting the gravitas of the surroundings – the building was designed by illustrious architects McKim, Mead & White as a meeting house for a suffragist organisation. Melissa Etheridge, Sharon Van Etten and Joe Jackson have performed here, and smart indie songwriters such as the Magnetic Fields have set up shop for a number of nights.

Union Hall

For listings, see p245. **Tickets** *free-$20.*

This spacious Brooklyn bar has a garden, food service and a bocce ball court. Tucked in the basement is a comfortable space dominated by the more delicate side of indie rock, plus indie comedy nights and other events.

Union Pool

484 Union Avenue, at Meeker Avenue, Williamsburg (1-718 609 0484, www.union-pool.com). Subway L to Lorimer Street; G to Metropolitan Avenue. **Open** *4pm-4am Mon-Fri; 2pm-4am Sat, Sun.* **Tickets** *free-$15.* **Map** *p249 J28*

Wind through the kitschy backyard space of this modest but super-cool Williamsburg bar (which featured in the movie *Nick and Norah's Infinite Playlist*) and you'll find yourself back indoors, facing a small stage. Local stars check in from time to time (members of Yeah Yeah Yeahs have shown off their side projects here), but it's dominated by well-plucked smaller indie acts. For a rowdy, amusing Monday night, check out Reverend Vince Anderson and his Love Choir.

❤ Webster Hall

125 E 11th Street, between Third & Fourth Avenues, East Village (no phone, www.websterhall.com). Subway L to Third Avenue; L, N, Q, R, W, 4, 5, 6 to 14th Street-Union Square; 6 to Astor Place. **Admission** *varies.* **Map** *p123 F28.*

Built in 1886, Webster Hall has been through several iterations (and names) before settling into its tenure as a high-calibre concert venue. In the 1950s, performers such as Tito Puente and Woody Guthrie graced the stage, and when it was known as the Ritz in the '80s, the same venue hosted rock legends including U2, Eric Clapton and Guns N'

Roses. After closing for nearly two years to restore its faded art deco splendour and improve acoustics, the grand venue now has a line-up of indie acts, metal bands and hip-hop artists programmed by Bowery Presents. Just be sure to show up early if you want a decent view.

WORLD, COUNTRY & ROOTS MUSIC

Among the cornucopia of live entertainment programmes at the **Brooklyn Academy of Music** (*p336*), **BAMcafé Live** presents free world music, among other genres, in the Peter Jay Sharp Building's Lepercq Space bar on Friday and Saturday nights for much of the year. Excellent barbecue joint **Hill Country** (*see p166*) offers a full schedule of unpretentious roots, rockabilly and country music in its downstairs bar. Other venues featuring acts defined by these styles include **Barbès** (*p317*), **Nublu** (*p313*) and **SOB's** (*p321*).

JAZZ, EXPERIMENTAL & BLUES

Ever since Duke Ellington urged folks to take the A train up to Harlem, New York has been a hotbed of improvisational talent. While Harlem is no longer the centre of the jazz scene, you can soak up the vibe at clubs in the Village that once provided a platform for the virtuoso experiments of Miles Davis, John Coltrane and Thelonious Monk. Boundaries are still being pushed in eclectic avant-garde venues such as **Roulette**, **Spectrum** (for both, *see p334*) and the **Stone**. For well-known jazz joints such as the **Village Vanguard** and **Birdland**, booking ahead is recommended.

55 Bar

55 Christopher Street, between Seventh Avenue South & Waverly Place, West Village (www.55bar.com). Subway 1 to Christopher Street-Sheridan Square. **Open** *3pm-4am daily.* **Tickets** *free-$10 (2-drink min). No cards.* **Map** *p137 D29*

This tiny Prohibition-era dive presents emerging talent almost every night at its usually free early shows. Ticketed sets regularly feature established artists such as Mike Stern, Wayne Krantz and David Binney.

92nd Street Y

For listings, see p330.

Best known for the series Jazz in July and spring's Lyrics & Lyricists, this multidisciplinary cultural centre also

Jazz at Lincoln Center

Established in 1981, Blue Note spotlights jazz titans such as Chris Botti, David Sanborn and Chick Corea. An extensive dinner and late-night menu enhances the daily performances, while the Sunday brunch series is one of the best show deals in the city ($40 including food and one drink).

Iridium

*1650 Broadway, at 51st Street, Theater District (1-212 582 2121, www. iridiumjazzclub.com). Subway N, R, W to 49th Street; 1 to 50th Street. **Shows** vary, usually 8pm, 10pm daily. **Tickets** $20-$85 ($15 food/drink minimum). **Map** p175 D23.*

Iridium lures upscale crowds with a line-up that's split between household names and those known only to the jazz-savvy. The sightlines and sound system are superb.

Jazz at Lincoln Center

Frederick P Rose Hall *Broadway, at 60th Street, Upper West Side. Subway A, B, C, D, 1 to 59th Street-Columbus Circle (1-212 258 9800, www.jazz.org). **Map** p195 C21.*

Rose Theater & Appel Room *(CenterCharge 1-212 721 6500). **Box office** 10am-6pm Mon-Sat; noon-6pm Sun. **Shows** vary. **Tickets** Rose Theater $20-$120. Appel Room $55-$65.*

Dizzy's Club *1-212 258 9595. **Shows** vary; usually 7.30pm, 9.30pm Mon-Thur, Sun; 7.30pm, 9.30pm, 11.15pm Fri, Sat. **Tickets** $10-$45 ($5-$10 food/drink minimum).*

The jazz arm of Lincoln Center, Frederick P Rose Hall, is located several blocks away from the main campus, high atop the Time Warner Center. It includes three rooms: the Rose Theater is a traditional mid-size space, but the crown jewels are the Appel Room and the smaller Dizzy's Club, with stages that are framed by enormous windows looking onto Columbus Circle and Central Park. The venues feel like a Hollywood cinematographer's vision of a Manhattan jazz club. Some of the best players in the business regularly grace the spot; among them is Wynton Marsalis, Jazz at Lincoln Center's artistic director.

Jazz Gallery

*5th Floor, 1160 Broadway, between 27th & 28th Streets, Flatiron District (1-646 494 3625, www.jazzgallery.org). Subway R, W to 28th Street. **Shows** 7.30pm, 9.30pm Thur-Sat. **Tickets** $15-$30. **Map** p163 E26.*

This beloved haunt, one of the city's premier incubators for progressive-jazz talent, relocated from its former Soho digs to a gallery-like space near the Flatiron Building. It's a place to witness true works of art from

offers cabaret, mainstream jazz and singer-songwriters. The small, handsome theatre provides a fine setting for the sophisticated fare.

Birdland

*315 W 44th Street, between Eighth & Ninth Avenues, Theater District (1-212 581 3080, www.birdlandjazz.com). Subway A, C, E to 42nd Street-Port Authority. **Open** 5pm-1am daily. **Tickets** $20-$50 ($10 food/drink minimum). **Map** p175 D24.*

The flagship venue for midtown's jazz resurgence, Birdland takes its place among the neon lights of Times Square seriously. That means it's a haven for great jazz musicians (Joe Lovano, Kurt Elling) as well as performers such as John Pizzarelli, and Broadway cabaret night Jim Caruso's Cast Party. The club is also notable for its roster of bands-in-residence. Sundays feature the long-running Arturo O'Farrill Afro Latin Jazz Orchestra.

Blue Note

*131 W 3rd Street, between MacDougal Street & Sixth Avenue, Greenwich Village (1-212 475 8592, www.bluenote.net). Subway A, B, C, D, E, F, M to W 4th Street. **Shows** 8pm, 10.30pm Mon-Thur, Sun; 8pm, 10.30pm, 12.30am Fri, Sat. **Tickets** $10-$75 ($5 food/drink min). **Map** p137 E30.*

sometimes obscure but always interesting jazzers (Henry Threadgill and Vijay Iyer, to name a couple).

Jazz Standard

116 E 27th Street, between Park Avenue South & Lexington Avenue, Flatiron District (1-212 576 2232, www.jazzstandard.com). Subway 6 to 28th Street. Shows 7.30pm, 9.30pm daily. Tickets $25-$35. Map p163 E26.

In the jazz den below restaurateur Danny Meyer's Blue Smoke barbecue joint, the room's marvellous sound matches its splendid sightlines. The jazz is of the groovy, hard-swinging variety, featuring such acts as trumpeter Dave Douglas, stick man EJ Strickland and regular Monday-night fixture Mingus Big Band.

Smalls Jazz Club

183 W 10th Street, between Seventh Avenue South & W 4th Street, West Village (no phone, www.smallslive.com). Subway 1 to Christopher Street-Sheridan Square. Open 7.30pm-4am Mon-Fri; 4pm-4am Sat; 1pm-4am Sun. Admission $20 (sometimes 1-drink min). Map p137 D29.

A relatively recent arrival on the Village jazz scene, Smalls convincingly channels an old-school hole-in-the-wall jazz joint in its cosy, bare-bones basement space. The booking also skews retro, yet not stubbornly so. You'll hear classic hardbop as well as more adventurous, contemporary approaches. During the week, the cover charge also gains you admittance to nearby Mezzrow, another intimate subterranean room, outfitted with a gleaming Steinway piano.

Smoke

2751 Broadway, between 105th & 106th Streets, Upper West Side (1-212 864 6662, www.smokejazz.com). Subway 1 to 103rd Street. Shows vary; usually 7pm, 9pm, 10.30pm, 11.45pm daily. Admission varies ($20 food/drink minimum at bar, or dinner at tables). Map p194 C16.

Not unlike a swanky living room, Smoke is a classy little joint that acts as a haven for local jazz legends and touring artists looking to play an intimate space. Early in the week,

evenings feature jam sessions and Hammond organ jazz. On weekends, renowned jazzers hit the stage, relishing the chance to play informal gigs uptown.

The Stone

Glass Box Theater, The New School, 55 W 13th Street, between Fifth & Sixth Avenues, Greenwich Village (no phone, www.thestonenyc.com). Subway F, M to 14th Street. Shows 8.30pm Tue-Sat. Admission $20. No cards. Map p137 E28.

Sax star John Zorn ran the Stone out of a small East Village storefront for 13 years before it took up residence at the New School's Glass Box Theater. In addition, the not-for-profit, avant-garde organisation has expanded its programming to other venues, including National Sawdust (*see p320*). Experimentally minded shows, booked by artist-curators, showcase local and international talent.

SubCulture

Lower level, 45 Bleecker Street, between Bowery & Lafayette Street, East Village (1-212 533 5470, www.subculturenewyork.com). Subway B, D, F, M to Broadway-Lafayette Street; 6 to Bleecker Street. Shows vary. Tickets vary. Map p123 F29.

A cross between a cabaret venue and a black box theatre, this subterranean space hosts performances across a range of genres, including jazz, singer-songwriters, classical and musical theatre. It's also a second NYC location for premier improv organisation Upright Citizens Brigade Theatre (*see p315*). With a vibe that's casual yet respectful to artists, it has proved an excellent setting for residencies by Tony Award-winning composer and lyricist Jason Robert Brown, with starry special guests.

♥ Village Vanguard

178 Seventh Avenue South, at Perry Street, West Village (1-212 255 4037, www.villagevanguard.com). Subway A, C, E, 1, 2, 3 to 14th Street; L to Eighth Avenue. Shows 8.30pm, 10.30pm daily. Tickets $35 (1-drink min). Map p137 D29.

Promoter Max Gordon opened this legendary club in 1935, initially featuring an eclectic roster of folk and blues before switching to heavier jazz bills in the late '50s. The hallowed room welcomed Eddie Heywood Jr as the house pianist, along with the likes of Miles Davis, Cecil Taylor and Bill Evans. You can catch glimpses of the venue's history on the walls, which are covered with black and white photos, as you settle in for one of the intimate shows. Staples include Grammy Award-winning Vanguard Jazz Orchestra, which has performed on Mondays since 1966.

In the know
Have a crisis!

If you fancy belting out some show tunes or jazz standards yourself, head to **Marie's Crisis** (59 Grove Street, between Bleecker Street & Seventh Avenue South, no phone). The beloved West Village institution (a former brothel) offers an old-school piano-bar experience (cash only).

CABARET

In an age of globalism, cabaret is a fundamentally local art: a private party in a cosy club, where music gets stripped down to its bare essence at close range. The intense intimacy of the experience can make it transformative if you're lucky, or awkward if you're not. Expect consistently high-grade entertainment at Manhattan's fanciest venues, the swank **Café Carlyle** and the more theatre-oriented **Feinstein's/54 Below**. Local clubs such as **Don't Tell Mama** and the **Duplex** are cheaper and much more casual. **Pangea** and the **Laurie Beechman Theatre** fall between these two poles, and **Joe's Pub** (*see p319*) attracts many exciting alt-cabaret stars, such as Justin Vivian Bond and Bridget Everett.

Feinstein's/54 Below

254 W 54th Street, between Broadway & Eighth Avenue, Theater District (1-646 476 3551, www.54below.com). Subway B, D, E to Seventh Avenue; C, E, 1 to 50th Street; N, Q, R, W to 57th Street. **Shows** *vary.* **Admission** *$15-$145 ($20-$30 food/drink minimum).* **Map** *p175 D22.*

This killer supper club below the legendary Studio 54 space offers an evocative speakeasy atmosphere, excellent tech and a calendar stuffed with major talents. The schedule is dominated by Broadway stars (such as Patti LuPone, Chita Rivera and Ben Vereen), but there's also room for emerging performers and songwriters – not to mention Great American Songbook standard bearer Michael Feinstein, whose name was added to the venue's in 2015.

Café Carlyle

The Carlyle, 35 E 76th Street, at Madison Avenue, Upper East Side (1-212 744 1600, www.thecarlyle.com). Subway 6 to 77th Street. **Shows** *vary.* **Admission** *$75-$220 ($75 dinner or $25 food/drink minimum).* **Map** *p209 E19.*

With its airy murals by Marcel Vertes, this elegant boîte in the Carlyle hotel remains the epitome of New York class, attracting such top-level singers as folk legend Judy Collins, Broadway star Sutton Foster and married cabarettists John Pizzarelli and Jessica Molaskey. Lately, the roster has also included pop stars from the '80s and '90s. Woody Allen often plays clarinet with Eddie Davis and his New Orleans Jazz Band on Monday nights.

▶ *Bemelmans Bar, across the hall, has an excellent pianist for those who want to drink in the atmosphere at a somewhat lower price; see p211.*

Don't Tell Mama

343 W 46th Street, between Eighth & Ninth Avenues, Theater District (1-212 757 0788, www.donttellmamanyc.com). Subway A, C, E to 42nd Street-Port Authority. **Open** *Piano bar 9pm-2.30am Mon-Thur, Sun; 9pm-3.30am Fri, Sat. Shows vary.* **Admission** *$10-$25 (2-drink minimum). Piano bar free (2-drink minimum).* **Map** *p175 D23.*

Showbiz pros and piano-bar buffs adore this dank but homey Theater District stalwart, where acts range from the strictly amateur to potential stars of tomorrow. The line-up may include pop, jazz and musical-theatre singers, plus comedians and drag artists.

The Duplex

61 Christopher Street, at Seventh Avenue South, West Village (1-212 255 5438, www. theduplex.com). Subway 1 to Christopher Street-Sheridan Square. **Open** *Piano bar 4pm-4am daily.* **Shows** *vary.* **Admission** *$10-$30 (2-drink minimum). Piano bar free.* **Map** *p137 D29.*

This narrow, brick-lined upstairs room, located in the heart of the West Village, is a chummy testing ground for emerging talent as well as local favourites such as retro belter Molly Pope. The eclectic offerings often come served with a generous dollop of camp. The no-cover downstairs piano bar provides an often-rollicking open mic until the wee hours.

Laurie Beechman Theatre

407 W 42nd Street, at Ninth Avenue, Theater District (1-212 695 6909, www.westbankcafe. com). Subway A, C, E to 42nd Street-Port Authority. **Shows** *vary.* **Admission** *$15-$45 ($20 food/drink minimum).* **Map** *p175 C24.*

Tucked away beneath the West Bank Café on 42nd Street, the Beechman provides a stage for singers from the worlds of musical theatre and cabaret, and some of the country's best drag entertainers (including multiple alumni of *RuPaul's Drag Race*). On Saturday nights it hosts the long-running burlesque show Le Scandal.

Pangea

178 Second Avenue, between 11th & 12th Streets, East Village (1-212 995 0900, www. pangeanyc.com). Subway L to Third Avenue. **Shows** *vary.* **Admission** *free-$25 ($20 food/ drink minimum).* **Map** *p123 F28.*

An East Village staple for decades, this artsy Mediterranean restaurant has expanded the concert offerings in its back room, with an adventurous list of regulars that puts Great American Songbook singers alongside eccentric artists such as Carol Lipnik, Tammy Faye Starlite and Raven O.

Performing Arts

Get a spot of culture, whether in venerable concert halls, experimental dance spaces or on Broadway

An omnivorous approach to the arts is increasingly common on New York's cultural scene. Multidisciplinary and genre-crossing performance venues such as The Shed, Roulette and Spectrum serve as laboratories for exciting new works, and major museums, including the Whitney Museum of American Art and the Met, offer music and dance programmes alongside visual arts. Change is in the air in the most established quarters, with fresh ideas and faces at Lincoln Center, while the theatre scene is booming both on and off Broadway. For current cultural listings, check out *Time Out New York* magazine or www.timeout.com/newyork.

Wicked *p342*

♥ Best performing arts venues

Ars Nova *p344*
Innovative multidisciplinary shows
and festivals.

Bargemusic *p331*
A magical riverside spot for chamber music.

Brooklyn Academy of Music *p330*
Fresh programming from a venerable
institution.

Carnegie Hall *p330*
Luminaries and emerging stars shine in this
grand setting.

Lincoln Center *p332*
The city's top orchestra, opera and ballet
companies are based here.

Joe's Pub & Public Theater *p319 and p346*
Ground-breaking plays and alt-cabaret
under one landmark roof.

In the know
Backstage passes

It's possible to go behind the scenes at
several of the city's major concert venues.
**Metropolitan Opera Guild Backstage
Tours** (1-212 769 7028, www.metguild.org,
$35, $25 reductions) show you around the
famous opera house from late September
through April. A tour of **Carnegie Hall** (1-212
903 9765, $19; $16 reductions, Sept-July)
ushers you through what is perhaps the
world's most famous concert hall. For $22,
you can also watch an open rehearsal of the
New York Philharmonic at **Lincoln Center**
(1-212 875 5656, Oct-June).

CLASSICAL MUSIC & OPERA

At the big institutions, such as the
Metropolitan Opera and **Carnegie Hall**,
confident artistic leaders such as Peter
Gelb and Clive Gillinson are embracing
new productions, living composers and
innovative approaches to programming.
And the New York Philharmonic's recently
appointed music director Jaap Van Zweden
continues in the progressive vein of his
predecessor Alan Gilbert, albeit with his
own experimental touch.

Outside of **Lincoln Center** (*see p332*)
and **Carnegie Hall**, some of the most
exciting work is happening at smaller
venues downtown and in Brooklyn. New
music groups such as the International
Contemporary Ensemble, Alarm Will
Sound and So Percussion have grown from
promising upstarts to become influential
pillars of the artistic community. Genre-blind
venues, including **Le Poisson Rouge** (*see
p321*), **Spectrum** and **National Sawdust**
(*see p320*) are happy to give them space to
do their thing. These days, it's not rare for a
Baroque opera to be followed by a DJ set or
for an orchestra to interpret music by Mos
Def or Sufjan Stevens. Taking creative cross-
pollination a step further, recently opened
cultural centre **The Shed** (*see p179*) mixes
disciplines such as music and visual art
within a single piece. This is the postmodern
aesthetic in full bloom and there's no better
place to experience it than New York.

The standard New York concert season
lasts from September to June, but there are
plenty of summer events and performances
(*see p288*). Box office hours may change in
summer, so phone ahead or check websites
for times.

The Shed *p179*

Sacred Music

From heavenly choirs to superb secular sounds, NYC churches host a variety of performances

Excellent acoustics, out-of-this-world choirs and serene surroundings make these houses of worship particularly attractive venues. A bonus is that some concerts are free or very cheap.

In Midtown, the magnificent **St Bartholomew's Church** (325 Park Avenue, at 51st Street, Midtown East, 1-212 378 0248, www.stbarts.org) presents a Choral Feast, featuring music from a specific composer – the likes of Palestrina or Mendelssohn – or on a theme, at its 11am Sunday service. In addition to performances by resident ensembles and guests, the church also hosts free Thursday lunchtime concerts from September to June.

Similarly, historic **Trinity Church Wall Street** (75 Broadway, at Wall Street, Financial District,1-212 602 0800, www. trinitywallstreet.org) offers gratis Thursday afternoon recitals in its Concerts at One series (returning in 2020; see website for schedule). Also look out for Bach at One at its satellite **St Paul's Chapel** (209 Broadway, between Fulton & Vesey Streets). Trinity has an ambitious music series and is home to

one of the city's finest choirs, which regularly performs here and sometimes visits Carnegie Hall and Lincoln Center.

The **Church of the Ascension** (12 W 11th Street, between Fifth & Sixth Avenues, Greenwich Village, 1 212 358 1469, tickets 1-212 358 7060, www.voicesofascension.org) is also home to a first-rate professional choir, the Voices of Ascension, and its home turf is the best place to hear it.

The choir, organist and period-instrument chamber orchestra of **Holy Trinity Lutheran Church** (65th Street & Central Park West, Upper West Side, 1-212 877 6815, www. holytrinitynyc.org), located near Lincoln Center, perform free concerts of Baroque music every Sunday from October through April as part of the venerable Bach Vespers series.

On the Upper East Side, the concert series at **Church of St Ignatius Loyola** (980 Park Avenue, between 83rd & 84th Streets, Upper East Side, 1-212 288 2520, ignatius. nyc) is a cultural high point, taking full advantage of the fine acoustics and opulent Baroque-influenced setting.

PERFORMING ARTS

Trinity Church Wall Street

Carnegie Hall

America's oldest performing arts academy continues to present some of the freshest programming in the city. Every year, typically from September through December, the Next Wave Festival showcases avant-garde music, dance and theatre. The nearby BAM Harvey Theater offers a smaller and more atmospheric setting for multimedia creations by composers and performers such as Tan Dun, Meredith Monk and So Percussion. The newest facility, BAM Fisher, has an intimate performance space and studios.

♥ Carnegie Hall
154 W 57th Street, at Seventh Avenue, Midtown (1-212 247 7800, www. carnegiehall.org). Subway N, Q, R, W to 57th Street-Seventh Avenue. **Box office** *11am-6pm Mon-Sat; noon-6pm Sun. Phone bookings 8am-8pm daily.* **Tickets** *vary.* **Map** *p175 D22.*

Artistic director Clive Gillinson continues to put his stamp on Carnegie Hall. The stars – both soloists and orchestras – still shine brightly inside this renowned concert hall in the Isaac Stern Auditorium. But it's the spunky upstart Zankel Hall that has generated the most buzz, offering an eclectic mix of classical, contemporary, jazz, pop and world music. Next door, the Weill Recital Hall hosts intimate concerts and chamber music programmes. Keep an eye out for Ensemble Connect, which consists of some of the city's most exciting young musicians and also performs at the Juilliard School, among other venues.

Tickets

You can buy tickets directly from most venues, whether by phone, online or at the box office. A surcharge is generally added to tickets not bought in person. For more on tickets, *see p339 and p342* In the know.

Major concert halls

For details of the manifold venues at **Lincoln Center**, including the Metropolitan Opera House, *see p332.*

♥ Brooklyn Academy of Music
All *1-718 636 4100, www.bam.org. Subway B, D, N, Q, R, 2, 3, 4, 5 to Atlantic Avenue-Barclays Center; C to Lafayette Avenue; G to Fulton Street.* **Box office** *Sept-June noon-6pm Mon-Sat; July, Aug noon-6pm Mon-Thur; noon-2pm Fri. Phone bookings Sept-June 10am-6pm Mon-Fri; noon-6pm Sat; noon-4pm Sun (show days); July, Aug 10am-6pm Mon-Thur, 10am-2pm Fri.* **Tickets** *vary.* **Map** *p232 K34.*

Peter Jay Sharp Building *30 Lafayette Avenue, between Ashland Place & St Felix Street, Fort Greene, Brooklyn.*

Harvey Theater, *651 Fulton Street, at Rockwell Place, Fort Greene, Brooklyn.*

Richard B Fisher Building, *321 Ashland Place, between Ashland Place & Lafayette Avenue, Fort Greene, Brooklyn.*

Other venues
92nd Street Y
1395 Lexington Avenue, at 92nd Street, Upper East Side (1-212 415 5500, www.92y. org). Subway 6 to 96th Street. **Box office** *6-8.30pm on show days.* **Tickets** *$15-$100.* **Map** *p209 E18.*

The Y has always stood for performances of solidly traditional orchestral, solo and chamber masterpieces. But the organisation also fosters the careers of young musicians and explores European

---

In the know
Outdoor opera

Metropolitan Opera tickets can run well into three figures, but if you find the prices too steep, snag a seat for one of the high-definition movie-screen broadcasts outside the opera house in Lincoln Center Plaza (typically in late August).

and Jewish-American music traditions, with innovative results. Concerts and recitals feature artists such as pianist Jonathan Biss, violinist Jennifer Koh and the New York Philharmonic String Quartet. Discount tickets to premium programmes are available to those age 40 and younger.

❤ Bargemusic

*Fulton Ferry Landing, between Old Fulton & Water Streets, Dumbo, Brooklyn (Brown Paper Tickets 1-800 838 3006, www.bargemusic.org). Subway A, C to High Street; F to York Street; 2, 3 to Clark Street. **Tickets** $35; $20-$30 reductions. **Map** p232 G32.*

This former coffee bean barge presents several chamber concerts a week, set against a panoramic view of lower Manhattan. It's a magical experience (and the programming has grown more ambitious in recent years), but be sure to dress warmly in winter. In less chilly months, admire the view from the upper deck during the interval.

Frick Collection

*For listings, see p210. **Tickets** $45.*

Concerts in the Frick Collection's exquisite circular music room are a rare treat, generally featuring both promising debutants and lesser-known but world-class performers. Concerts are broadcast live in the Garden Court, where tickets aren't required.

Gilder Lehrman Hall

*The Morgan Library & Museum, 225 Madison Avenue, at 36th Street, Murray Hill (1-212 685 0008, www.themorgan.org). Subway 6 to 33rd Street. **Tickets** $25-$55. **Map** p175 E25.*

This elegant, 264-seat gem of a concert hall is a perfect venue for song recitals and chamber groups. The St Luke's Chamber Ensemble was quick to establish a presence here.

Merkin Concert Hall

*Kaufman Music Center, 129 W 67th Street, between Amsterdam Avenue & Broadway, Upper West Side (1-212 501 3330, www.kaufman-center.org). Subway 1 to 66th Street-Lincoln Center. **Box office** noon-7pm Mon-Thur, Sun; noon-4pm Fri (reduced hrs in summer). **Tickets** $15-$100. **Map** p194 C21.*

On a side street in the shadow of Lincoln Center, this 449-seat treasure offers a robust mix of early music and avant-garde programming, plus a healthy amount of jazz, folk and some more eclectic fare. The Ecstatic Music Festival, featuring the latest generation of composers and performers, typically heats up the space from January through March, while the New York Festival of Song regularly presents outstanding singers in appealingly quirky themed programmes.

Metropolitan Museum of Art

*For listings, see p214. **Tickets** vary.*

When it comes to established virtuosos and revered chamber ensembles, the Met's year-round schedule is rich and full (and ticket prices can be correspondingly high). Under the leadership of Limor Tomer, the museum's programming has taken a turn towards genre-flouting performers and intriguing artistic juxtapositions. The museum's Temple of Dendur has been the atmospheric backdrop to music by Alarm Will Sound and Rhiannon Giddens, and the Shanghai Peking Opera has performed in the Astor Court, a recreation of a 17th-century Chinese garden.

▶ *At Christmas and Easter, early music concerts are held in the Fuentidueña Chapel at the Cloisters; see p229.*

Miller Theatre at Columbia University

*2960 Broadway, at 116th Street, Morningside Heights (1-212 854 7799, www.millertheatre.com). Subway 1 to 116th Street-Columbia University. **Box office** noon-6pm Mon-Fri (closed in summer). **Tickets** $50-$100. **Map** p195 C14.*

Columbia University's Miller Theatre has been at the forefront of making contemporary classical music sexy in New York City. Executive director Melissa Smey builds on the work of her predecessor, George Steel, who proved that presenting challenging fare in a casual, unaffected setting could attract young audiences – and hang on to them. Programmes range from early music to contemporary, such as Ensemble Signal and International Contemporary Ensemble (ICE). The long-running Composer Portraits series offers a curated introduction to innovative artists' work.

Roulette

*509 Atlantic Avenue, at Third Avenue, Boerum Hill, Brooklyn (1-917 267 0363, www.roulette.org). Subway B, D, N, Q, R, 2, 3, 4, 5 to Atlantic Avenue-Barclays Center. **Box office** 1hr before performance. **Tickets** vary. **Map** p232 K37.*

This legendary experimental music institution traded dingy Soho digs for a spectacularly redesigned art deco theatre in Brooklyn. The setting may have changed, but Roulette continues to offer

❤ Lincoln Center

*Columbus Avenue, between 62nd & 65th Streets, Upper West Side (1-212 875 5456, www.lincolncenter.org). Subway 1 to 66th Street-Lincoln Center. **Box offices** 10am-6pm or 8pm Mon-Sat; noon-6pm Sun. **Map** p194 C21.*

Built in the early 1960s, this massive complex is the nexus of Manhattan's – in fact, probably the whole country's – performing arts scene. The campus, which is just over 16 acres and home to 11 arts organisations, has undergone a major revamp in recent years, providing new performance facilities as well as more inviting public gathering spaces and restaurants. The main entry point is from Columbus Avenue, at 65th Street, but venues are spread out across the square of blocks from 62nd to 66th Streets, between Amsterdam and Columbus Avenues, plus **Jazz at Lincoln Center** further south (*see p323*). Tickets to most performances are sold online, by phone through **CenterCharge** (1-212 721 6500, 10am-9pm daily) or box offices at individual Lincoln Center venues. A central box office (open noon-7pm Tue-Sat; noon-5pm Sun) at the **David Rubenstein Atrium** (between W 62nd & W 63rd Streets, Broadway & Columbus Avenues) sells discounted tickets to same-week performances. The space is also a venue for frequent free performances (see www.lincolncenter.org/atrium for details).

Big stars, such as conductor Valery Gergiev and pianist Emanuel Ax, are Lincoln Center's musical meat and potatoes. Lately, though, the divide between the flagship Great Performers season (late Oct-mid May), featuring top international soloists and ensembles, and the more audacious (and free), multidisciplinary **Lincoln Center Out of Doors** summer festival (*see p290*) continues to narrow. The **Mostly Mozart Festival**, formerly a moribund four-week summer staple, has been thoroughly reinvented as a showcase of up-and-coming conductors and innovative performers, while **Midsummer Night Swing** (*see p288*) lets participants strut their stuff to a diverse lineup of live music. Each autumn, the **White Light Festival** blends high-quality classical performers with world and popular musicians, all of whom angle to tap into the spiritually transcendent qualities of music. An 18-month renovation turned the cosy home of the Chamber Music Society of

Lincoln Center (www.chambermusicsociety. org), **Alice Tully Hall**, into a world-class, 1,096-seat theatre. A contemporary foyer with an elegant (if a bit pricey) café is immediately striking, but, more importantly, the revamp brought dramatic acoustic improvements. Though its $500-million renovation was scrapped, the comfortable 2,700-seat **David Geffen Hall**, remains a landmark institution, as the headquarters of the renowned New York Philharmonic (1-212 875 5656, www.nyphil.org). The Juilliard School (www.juilliard.edu) is also based at Lincoln Center, and its talented students, faculty and artists-in-residence frequently perform for free or at low cost.

The grandest of the Lincoln Center buildings, the **Metropolitan Opera House,** hosts the Metropolitan Opera (1-212 362 6000, www.metopera.org) from late September to early May. Audiences are knowledgeable and fiercely devoted, with subscriptions remaining in families for generations. Canadian-born conductor Yannick Nézet-Séguin became the Met's first new music director in more than 40 years when he took up the baton in 2018.

Dance Theatre of Harlem, Out of Doors festival

The Met had already started becoming more inclusive before general manager Peter Gelb arrived in 2006. Today, it places a priority on creating novel theatrical experiences with visionary directors (Robert Lepage, Bartlett Sher, David McVicar) and physically graceful, telegenic stars (Anna Netrebko, Sonya Yoncheva, Peter Mattei).

In spring and summer, the majestic space is home to American Ballet Theatre, which presents full-length traditional story ballets, contemporary classics by Frederick Ashton and Antony Tudor, and new works by the company's stellar artist-in-residence, Alexei Ratmansky. The acoustics are wonderful, but the theatre is immense: bring along binoculars or get as close to the stage as you can afford.

The neoclassical New York City Ballet headlines at the opulent **David H Koch Theater** (1-212 496 0600, davidkochtheater. com), which Philip Johnson designed to resemble a jewellery box. During its spring, autumn and winter seasons, ballets by George Balanchine are performed by a wonderful crop of dancers, including the luminous Sara Mearns; there are also works by Jerome Robbins and resident choreographer Justin Peck. The company offers its popular *Nutcracker* from the end of November into the new year. Also look for performances by the revered Paul Taylor Dance Company.

The majestic and prestigious **Lincoln Center Theater** complex (Telecharge 1-212 239 6200, www.lct.org) has a pair of amphitheatre-style drama venues. Its Broadway house, the 1,080-seat **Vivian Beaumont Theater**, is home to star-studded and elegant major productions. Downstairs is the 299-seat **Mitzi E Newhouse Theater**, an Off Broadway space devoted to new work by the upper layer of American playwrights. In an effort to shake off its reputation for stodginess, Lincoln Center launched **LCT3**, which since 2012 has presented the work of emerging playwrights and directors at the **Claire Tow Theater**, built on top of the Beaumont.

Cinephiles frequent the **Walter Reade Theater** and the **Elinor Bunin Munroe Film Center**, programmed by **Film at Lincoln Center** (*see p296*) and site of the prestigious New York Film Festival.

Midsummer Night Swing

Metropolitan Opera House *p332*

a gold mine of far-out programming that could include anything from a John Cage Musicircus, where the audience is invited to wander through a forest of musical acts all playing at once, to rising composers and vocalists who incorporate projections and electronic elements.

Spectrum

70 Flushing Avenue, at Cumberland Street, Garage A, Fort Greene, Brooklyn (no phone, www.spectrumnyc.com). Subway A, C to High Street, then 20min walk; F to York Street, then 20min walk or B62 bus; A, C, F, R to Jay Street-MetroTech, then B57 bus. **Tickets** *$15; $10 reductions. No cards.* **Map** *p232 J32.*

This contemporary-classical laboratory, founded by a neuroscientist and an engineer, harks back to the days when the city's most innovative work was done in private lofts and similar spaces. The venue, a former ball-bearings factory, repurposed for high-fidelity acoustics, relies largely on word of mouth and social media to publicise its ambitious chamber music, progressive jazz and avant-garde rock events.

Symphony Space

2537 Broadway, at 95th Streets, Upper West Side (1-212 864 5400, www.symphonyspace. org). Subway 1, 2, 3 to 96th Street. **Box office** *1-6pm Tue-Sun.* **Tickets** *vary.* **Map** *p194 C17.*

Despite the name, programming at Symphony Space is anything but orchestra-centric: recent seasons have featured jazz trios, Chinese chamber music, a cappella ensembles and HD opera simulcasts from Europe. The annual Wall to Wall marathons (usually held in spring) provide a full day of music free of charge, all focused on a particular theme (for instance, a composer or period).

Opera companies

The **Metropolitan Opera** (*see p332*) may be the leader of the pack, but it's not the only game in town. Contact the individual organisations or check their websites for information and prices, schedules and venues.

American Opera Projects

*South Oxford Space, 138 S Oxford Street, between Atlantic Avenue & Hanson Place, Fort Greene, Brooklyn (1-718 398 4024, www.operaprojects.org). Subway B, D, N, Q, R, 2, 3, 4, 5 to Atlantic Avenue-Barclays Center; C to Lafayette Avenue; G to Fulton Street. **Tickets** vary (average $25). **Map** p232 L34.*

AOP is not so much an opera company as a living, breathing workshop that lets you follow a new work from gestation to completion. Shows, which can be anything from a table reading of a libretto to a complete orchestral production, are staged around the city and beyond.

Amore Opera

*The Riverside Theatre, 91 Claremont Avenue, between 120th & 122nd Streets, Morningside Heights (OvationTix 1-866 811 4111, www.amoreopera.org). Subway 1 to 116th-Columbia University or 125th Street. **Tickets** $20-$40. **Map** p195 B16.*

One of two successors to the late, great Amato Opera Company, the Amore literally inherited the beloved former company's sets and costumes. Many of the cast members migrated as well to keep the feisty Amato spirit alive. In previous seasons, they've presented US premières of lesser known or forgotten works and, more recently, a family-friendly version of Gilbert and Sullivan's comic opera *H.M.S. Pinafore*.

New York City Opera

*Jazz at Lincoln Center and various venues (1-646 981 1888, www.nycopera.com). **Tickets** $20-$150.*

After declaring bankruptcy in 2013, the 'people's opera' returned three years later, revitalised but cautious, with a mix of crowd favourites, revivals, New York premières and chamber operas. Under the guidance of general director Michael Capasso, and with the appointment of composer-in-residence Tobias Picker, the company moves forward with its mission to bring rarities, new works and classics to NYC's opera-loving masses. Productions are staged at the Rose Theater at Jazz at Lincoln Center (*see p323*) and other venues, including Bryant Park in the warmer months.

DANCE

With its uptown and downtown divide, New York dance includes both luminous tradition and daring experimentation. While **Lincoln Center** (*see p332*) remains the hub for traditional balletic offerings, with annual seasons by American Ballet Theatre and New York City Ballet, the **David H Koch Theater** has opened itself up to modern dance too. The deeper downtown you travel, the more you will encounter a younger generation – and it's not limited to Manhattan. In Brooklyn, Williamsburg, Bushwick and Bedford-Stuyvesant have sparked a new generation of dancers and choreographers, and Long Island City, Queens, is also pulsing with movement. Increasingly, museums, such as MoMA and the Whitney, are broadening their reach from the visual arts to showcasing dance and performance.

Notable names & events

The companies of modern dance icons such as Martha Graham, Alvin Ailey, Trisha Brown, Paul Taylor and Mark Morris are still based in the city, alongside a wealth of contemporary choreographers who create works outside the traditional company structure. The downtown performance world is full of singular voices, including Sarah Michelson, Trajal Harrell, Raja Feather Kelly, Maria Hassabi and Beth Gill.

Just as museums are giving dance room to branch out, multidisciplinary festivals such as **Crossing the Line** in autumn, presented by the French Institute Alliance Française (22 E 60th Street, between Madison & Park Avenues, 1-212 355 6100, www.fiaf. org), and **Performa** (1-212 366 5700, www. performa-arts.org), a November biennial, showcase the latest developments in dance and performance. Autumn also brings **Fall for Dance** at **City Center**, which focuses on eclectic mixed bills.

Major venues

For details of the **Metropolitan Opera House** and **David H Koch Theater**, *see p332* Lincoln Center.

Baryshnikov Arts Center
450 W 37th Street, between Ninth & Tenth Avenues, Hell's Kitchen (1-646 731 3200, www.bacnyc.org). Subway A, C, E to 34th Street-Penn Station; 7 to 34th Street-Hudson Yards. Tickets free-$25. Map p175 C25.

Mikhail Baryshnikov, former artistic director of American Ballet Theatre, is something of an impresario. His home base, on a stark overpass near the Lincoln Tunnel, includes several studios, the 136-seat Howard Gilman Performance Space and the 238-seat Jerome Robbins Theatre, which is both intimate and refined. Baryshnikov's background aside, the centre hosts an array of cultural events and operates a robust residency programme; throughout the year, BAC Space artists, who have included Beth Gill, Rashaun Mitchell and Liz Santoro, show works-in-progress.

Brooklyn Academy of Music
For listings, see p330.

With its Federal-style columns and carved marble, the 2,100-seat Howard Gilman Opera House is BAM's most regal dance venue, and has showcased the talents of Mark Morris and William Forsythe, as well as the Mariinsky Ballet. The 834-seat Harvey Theater hosts contemporary choreographers from New York and Europe. Annual events include the DanceAfrica Festival, held each Memorial Day weekend (late May), and the Next Wave Festival, which runs in autumn and winter and features established groups from New York and abroad.

Joyce Theater
175 Eighth Avenue, at 19th Street, Chelsea (1-212 242 0800, www.joyce.org). Subway A, C, E to 14th Street; 1 to 18th Street; L to Eighth Avenue. Tickets $10-$120. Map p153 D27.

This intimate space houses one of the finest theatres – we're talking about sightlines – in town. Among the major companies and choreographers that present work here are Ballet Hispánico, Pilobolus, Complexions Contemporary Ballet, Parsons Dance, Doug Varone and the tap sensation Dorrance Dance. The Joyce is also a popular landing spot for regional ballet troupes, such as Philadelphia's BalletX and Aspen Santa Fe Ballet.

New York City Center
131 W 55th Street, between Sixth & Seventh Avenues, Midtown (1-212 581 1212, www. nycitycenter.org). Subway B, D, E to Seventh Avenue; F to 57th Street; N, Q, R, W to 57th Street-Seventh Avenue. Box office noon-8pm Mon-Sat; noon-7.30pm Sun. Tickets $25-$250. Map p175 M5.

Before Lincoln Center changed the city's cultural geography, this was the home of the American Ballet Theatre, the Joffrey Ballet and the New York City Ballet. Built in 1923, the Moorish Revival building was a Shriners meeting hall before being converted to a performing arts centre two decades later. The lavish decor is golden, as are the companies that perform in the opulent mainstage theatre, including Dance Theater

of Harlem and Alvin Ailey American Dance Theater. The popular Fall for Dance festival, in autumn, features mixed bills for just $15.

Other venues

Abrons Arts Center
466 Grand Street, at Pitt Street, Lower East Side (1-212 598 0400, www.abronsartscenter. org). Subway B, D to Grand Street; F to Delancey Street; J, M, Z to Delancey-Essex Streets. **Tickets** *free-$30.* **Map** *p111 G30.*

This venue, which has a beautiful proscenium theatre, focuses on a wealth of contemporary dance; past artists have included Miguel Gutierrez, Jonah Bokaer, Ann Liv Young and Fitzgerald & Stapleton.

Brooklyn Arts Exchange
421 Fifth Avenue, between 7th & 8th Streets, Park Slope, Brooklyn (1-718 832 0018, www. bax.org). Subway F, G, R to Fourth Avenue-9th Street. **Tickets** *$10-$16.* **Map** *p232 L37.*

Brooklyn Arts Exchange holds classes and performances in its intimate theatre; the space hosts more than 50 performance evenings each season. Artists in residence have included choreographers Yasuko Yokoshi, Dean Moss and Jillian Peña. It's a great place to witness the creative process up close.

Chocolate Factory Theater
5-49 49th Avenue, at Vernon Boulevard, Long Island City, Queens (1-718 482 7069,

www.chocolatefactorytheater.org). Subway G to 21st Street; 7 to Vernon Boulevard-Jackson Avenue. **Tickets** *$15-$20.* **Map** *p259 H23.*

Brian Rogers and Sheila Lewandowski founded this 5,000sq ft performance venue in 2005, converting a one-time hardware store into two spaces: a low-ceilinged downstairs room and a loftier, brighter upstairs white box that caters to the interdisciplinary and the avant-garde. Past choreographers have included Jillian Peña, Big Dance Theater and Tere O'Connor. Rogers, an artist in his own right, also presents work here.

♥ Danspace Project

*St Mark's Church in-the-Bowery, 131
E 10th Street, at Second Avenue, East
Village (OvationTix 1-866 811 4111, www.
danspaceproject.org). Subway L to Third
Avenue; 6 to Astor Place.* **Tickets** *free-$25.*
Map *p123 F28.*

A space is only as good as its executive
director, and Judy Hussie-Taylor has
injected new life into Danspace's
programming by creating the Platform
series, in which artists curate seasons
based on a particular idea. Moreover, the
space itself – a high-ceilinged sanctuary
– is very handsome. Ticket prices are
reasonable, making it easy to take a
chance on unknown work.

Dixon Place

*161A Chrystie Street, at Delancey Street,
Lower East Side (1-212 219 0736, www.
dixonplace.org). Subway F to Lower East
Side-Second Avenue; J, Z to Bowery.* **Tickets**
free-$20. **Map** *p111 F30.*

Ellie Covan started hosting experimental
performances in her living room in the
mid 1980s; two decades later, the plucky
organisation finally opened this state-
of-the-art space. Along with a mainstage
theatre, there's a cocktail lounge, perfect for
post-show discussions. Dixon Place supports
emerging artists and works in progress;
summer events include the annual Hot!
festival of queer arts.

Gibney Dance: Agnes Varis Performing Arts Center

*280 Broadway (entrance at 53A Chambers
Street), Tribeca (1-646 837 6809, www.
gibneydance.org). Subway A, C, J, Z to
Chambers Street; R, W to City Hall; 4, 5, 6
to Brooklyn Bridge-City Hall.* **Tickets** *free-
$40.* **Map** *p87 E31.*

Choreographer and entrepreneur Gina
Gibney reclaimed the former Dance New
Amsterdam, housed in the historic Sun
Building, and renovated it to include
theatre spaces, studios and rehearsal space.
Programming is varied, with an emphasis on
contemporary dance and performance.

Harlem Stage at the Gatehouse

*150 Convent Avenue, at W 135th Street,
Harlem (1-212 281 9240, www.harlemstage.
org). Subway 1 to 137th Street-City College.*
Box office *10am-3pm Mon-Fri.* **Tickets** *free-
$35.* **Map** *p223 C12.*

Performances at this theatre, formerly an
operations centre for the Croton Aqueduct
water system, celebrate African-American life
and culture. Companies that have graced the
flexible space, designed by Frederick S Cook

and a designated New York City landmark,
include the Bill T. Jones/Arnie Zane Dance
Company and Kyle Abraham. Each spring,
the space hosts the E-Moves Festival.

♥ The Kitchen

*512 W 19th Street, between Tenth & Eleventh
Avenues, Chelsea (1-212 255 5793, www.
thekitchen.org). Subway A, C, E to 14th
Street; L to Eighth Avenue.* **Box office** *2-6pm
Tue-Sat; 11am-6pm on show days.* **Tickets**
free-$25. **Map** *p153 C27.*

The Kitchen, led by Tim Griffin, offers some
of the best experimental dance around:
inventive, provocative and rigorous. Some
of the artists who have presented work
here are the finest in New York, such as
Sarah Michelson (who has served as a guest
curator for specific programmes), Dean
Moss and Jodi Melnick.

Movement Research at the Judson Church

*55 Washington Square South, at Thompson
Street, Greenwich Village (1-212 598 0551,
www.movementresearch.org). Subway A, B,
C, D, E, F, M to W 4th Street.* **Tickets** *free.*
Map *p123 G29.*

This free dance series is a great place to
check out experimental works and up-and-
coming artists. Performances are usually
held on Monday evening at 8pm, from
September to June, but it's best to check
the website. The group's week-long autumn
and spring festivals feature shows in venues
across the city. Movement Research also
offers classes and other events around town.

New York Live Arts

*219 W 19th Street, between Seventh & Eighth
Avenues, Chelsea (1-212 924 0077, www.
newyorklivearts.org). Subway 1 to 18th
Street.* **Box office** *5-9pm Mon-Fri; 1-9pm Sat,
Sun.* **Tickets** *free-$65.* **Map** *p153 D27.*

In 2010, the Dance Theater Workshop
and the Bill T. Jones/Arnie Zane Dance
Company merged to form New York Live
Arts, which is dedicated to contemporary
dance under Bill Jones. The company
performs here regularly, along with local
and international choreographers.

Skirball Center for the Performing Arts

*566 LaGuardia Place at Washington Square
South, Greenwich Village (1-888 611 8183,
www.nyuskirball.org). Subway A, B, D, C, E,
F, M to W 4th Street.* **Box office** *noon-6pm
Tue-Sat (closed Sat in summer).* **Tickets** *free-
$85.* **Map** *p137 E30.*

Under the artistic direction of Jay Wegman,
this 860-seat venue is owned and staffed by

New York University, but lends its stage to an eclectic schedule of dance, opera, music and theatre. Its ambitious multidisciplinary programming in recent years has included works by Milo Rau, Mette Ingvartsen, Jan Fabre and Elevator Repair Service, as well as a festival celebrating Karl Marx.

THEATRE

Bette Midler, Denzel Washington, Bryan Cranston and Daniel Radcliffe are among the many boldface names that have shone on Broadway marquees in recent years. Major musicals tend not to have big stars above the title, but favour the familiar in a different way – many are now adapted from pop-culture sources (such as *Harry Potter* and *The Lion King*) or built around existing catalogues of popular songs.

Tickets

Nearly all Broadway and Off Broadway shows are served by one of the city's 24-hour ticketing agencies. For cheap seats (mostly half price), your best bet is one of the **TKTS** discount booths run by TDF, a non-profit performing arts service organisation. If you plan to see an Off-Off Broadway show or dance event, consider purchasing an $11 ticket (plus $1 service fee) from TDF. Register at www.tdf.org, where you'll also find a list of eligible shows. For more ticket tips, *see p330* and *p342* In the know.

TKTS

Father Duffy Square, Broadway & 47th Street, Theater District (no phone, www.tdf.org). Subway N, Q, R, S, W, 1, 2, 3, 7 to 42nd Street-Times Square; N, R, W to 49th Street; 1 to 50th Street. **Open** *Evening tickets 3-8pm Mon, Wed-Sat; 2-8pm Tue; 3-7pm Sun. Same-day matinée tickets 10am-2pm Wed, Thur, Sat; 11am-3pm Sun.* **Map** *p175 D22.*

At Times Square's architecturally striking TKTS base, you can get tickets on the day of the performance for as much as 50% off face value. Although there's often a queue when it opens for business, this has usually dispersed one to two hours later, so it's worth trying your luck an hour or two before the show. The other TKTS branches, which are much less busy, also sell matinée tickets the day before a show; the indoor Lincoln Center outpost is an especially appealing option (see website for hours). Never buy tickets from anyone who approaches you in the queue as they may have been obtained illegally. You can check what's on the boards at all locations on the website before setting out, or download the free app for real-time info. **Other locations** Lincoln Center, David

Rubenstein Atrium, Broadway, between 62nd & 63rd Streets, Upper West Side; South Street Seaport, corner of Front & John Streets, Financial District.

Broadway

Technically speaking, 'Broadway' is the theatre district that surrounds Times Square on either side of Broadway (the actual avenue), between 41st and 54th Streets (plus the Vivian Beaumont Theater, uptown at Lincoln Center). This is where you'll find the grandest theatres in town: wood-panelled, frescoed jewel boxes, mostly built between 1900 and 1930 (*see p340* Broadway theatres). Officially, 41 of them – those with more than 500 seats – are designated Broadway houses. Full-price tickets can easily set you back more than $100; the very best (so-called 'premium') seats cost far more at the most popular shows.

The blockbusters are hard to miss, but at any given point, there are also a handful of new plays, as well as serious revivals of classic dramas ranging from Shakespeare to the works of Tennessee Williams, Eugene O'Neill and August Wilson. Each season also usually includes several small, artistically adventurous musicals to balance out the rafter-rattlers.

Broadway

💜 Broadway theatres

In 2017, the number of officially designated Broadway theatres rose from 40 to 41, when the **Hudson Theatre** (139-141 West 44th Street, www.thehudsonbroadway.com) reopened with its first full production since 1968. The venue retains many of the architectural and decorative features that first greeted patrons in 1903: ornate Greco-Roman motifs on the walls and ceilings; oases of colourful Tiffany glass; a black-marble box office featuring bronze heads of Hermes. During the half-century when it wasn't presenting legitimate theatre, it served as a porn cinema, a nightclub and an event space.

Nearly all the Broadway houses were built in the first three decades of the 20th century, and they are works of art in themselves. To appreciate them properly, arrive a few minutes before curtain time and take stock of the elaborate and lovingly maintained murals, friezes and carvings that help make seeing a show a special occasion.

The Lyceum and the New Amsterdam, which also opened in 1903, are even more remarkable than the Hudson. The limestone Beaux Arts façade of the **Lyceum Theatre** (149 W 45th Street, between Sixth & Seventh Avenues, www.shubert.nyc) features six imposing Corinthian columns; inside, its beautiful wood panelling, suggestive of an Old World library, gives it an intimate air. The **New Amsterdam Theatre** (214 W 42nd Street, between Seventh & Eighth Avenues, www.disneytheatricalsales.com) was home to the legendary Ziegfeld Follies before falling out of use in the 1930s. Sixty years later, its long-dilapidated Art Nouveau interior, a paradisiacal garden of floral and botanical motifs, was painstakingly restored to breathtaking splendour by Disney Theatrical Productions.

Built in 1907, the **Belasco Theatre** (111 W 44th Street, between Broadway & Sixth Avenue, www.shubert.nyc) doesn't seem like much from its staid, neo-Georgian façade. But walk inside and you'll find yourself in an Edwardian fantasy of theatrical magic, with decorative marvels wherever you look. The eccentric stage impresario David Belasco was friends with glassmaker Louis Comfort Tiffany, and his theatre bears the fruit of that friendship: Bunches of purple grapes burst from the room's exquisite stained-glass column capitals. Octagonal panels of Tiffany glass, 22 in all, are set in the coffered ceiling; carved dark wood and elegant murals add to the theatre's cosy, quasi-gothic splendour. David Belasco is rumoured to haunt the building, and who could blame him? It's the kind of place you never want to leave.

To see one of Broadway's loveliest venues, however, you don't need to buy a ticket to a show. The **Mark Hellinger Theatre** (237 West 51st Street, between Broadway & Eighth Avenue), built as a lavish movie house in 1930, is an architectural stunner in red and gold, whose soaring ceilings are decorated with a dozen murals in the style of 18th-century French painting. Considered by many to be the most sumptuous of all Broadway houses, the Hellinger was home to the original production of *My Fair Lady* in 1956. During the lean times of the early 1990s, however, it was sold to the Times Square Church (www.tscnyc.org), which has preserved it carefully and opens it to the public several days a week for religious services.

New Amsterdam Theatre

Come from Away

Long-running shows

Straight plays can provide some of Broadway's most stirring experiences, but they're less likely than musicals to enjoy long runs. Check *Time Out New York* magazine or www.timeout.com/newyork for current listings and reviews. (The shows listed here are subject to change.)

The Book of Mormon

Eugene O'Neill Theatre, 230 W 49th Street, between Broadway & Eighth Avenue, Theater District (Ticketmaster 1-877 250 2929, www.bookofmormonbroadway.com). Subway C, E, 1 to 50th Street; N, Q, R, S, W, 1, 2, 3, 7 to 42nd Street-Times Square; N, R, W to 49th Street. **Box office** *10am-8pm Mon-Sat; noon-7pm Sun.* **Tickets** *$99-$477.* **Map** *p175 D23.*

This gleefully obscene and subversive satire may be the funniest show to grace the Great White Way since *The Producers* and *Urinetown*. Writers Trey Parker and Matt Stone of *South Park*, along with composer Robert Lopez (*Avenue Q*), find the perfect blend of sweet and nasty for this tale of mismatched Mormon proselytisers on a mission in Uganda.

Come from Away

Gerald Schoenfeld Theatre, 236 W 45th Street, between Broadway & Eighth Avenue, Theater District (Telecharge 1-212 239 6200, www.comefromaway.com). Subway A, C, E to 42nd Street-Port Authority; N, Q, R, S, W, 1, 2, 3, 7 to 42nd Street-Times Square; N, R, W to 49th Street. **Box office** *10am-8pm Mon-Sat; noon-6pm Sun.* **Tickets** *$49-$197.* **Map** *p175 D24.*

Irene Sankoff and David Hein's swelling heart of a musical tells a true story from the aftermath of 9/11, when 38 flights were forced to land in the small town of Gander, Newfoundland. Under Christopher Ashley's fluid direction, 12 versatile actors play dozens of roles. The show makes a persuasive case for the value of good intentions; for this kind of uplift you don't need planes.

Dear Evan Hansen

Music Box Theatre, 239 W 45th Street, between Broadway & Eighth Avenue, Theater District (Telecharge 1-212 239 6200, www. dearevanhansen.com). Subway N, Q, R, S, W, 1, 2, 3, 7 to 42nd Street-Times Square. **Box office** *10am-8pm Mon-Sat; noon-6pm Sun.* **Tickets** *$119-$499.* **Map** *p175 D24.*

An awkward and unpopular high school student gets thrust into social relevance after a classmate's suicide in this captivating, Tony Award-winning original musical, which delivers a direct electric jolt to the heart. Benj Pasek and Justin Paul's score combines well-crafted lyrics with an exciting pop sound, and Steven Levenson's book gives all the characters shaded motives.

Hamilton

Richard Rodgers Theatre, 226 W 46th Street W, between Broadway & Eighth Avenue, Theater District (Ticketmaster 1-877 250 2929, www.hamiltonbroadway.com). Subway N, Q, R, S, W, 1, 2, 3, 7 to 42nd Street-Times Square; N, R, W to 49th Street. **Box office** *10am-8pm Mon-Sat; noon-6pm Sun.* **Tickets** *$179-$967.* **Map** *p175 D23.*

Composer-lyricist Lin-Manuel Miranda forges a ground-breaking bridge between hip hop and musical storytelling with this sublime collision of radio-ready beats and an inspiring immigrant slant on Founding

Hamilton *p341*

Dear Evan Hansen *p341*

Father Alexander Hamilton. A brilliant, diverse cast takes back American history and makes it new. Good luck getting tickets: even with a top price climbing towards $1,000, the highest in Broadway history, it's still the hottest show in town.

Harry Potter and the Cursed Child

Lyric Theatre, 214 W 43rd Street, between Seventh & Eighth Avenues, Theater District (Ticketmaster 1-877 250 2929, www. harrypottertheplay.com). Subway A, C, E to 42nd Street-Port Authority; N, Q, R, S, W, 1, 2, 3, 7 to 42nd Street-Times Square. **Box office** *10am-8pm daily.* **Tickets** *$138-$593 per half.* **Map** *p175 D24.*

In the know
Cheap seats

Buzzed-about shows, especially those with big stars on the bill, sell out fast and can cost a small fortune. But many of them, including *Hamilton*, offer daily online or mobile lotteries that give you a shot at winning cheaper tickets. It doesn't cost anything to enter these draws, so look into the details online. Some of the cheapest tickets on Broadway are known as 'rush' tickets, purchased on the day of a show at a theatre's box office (not all theatres have them). On average, they cost $25, and some shows now offer digital rush tickets instead of making you line up at the box office. The **Metropolitan Opera** (see *p332*) operates a lottery for rush tickets on its website (noon Mon-Sat for evening performances; 4hrs before performances for matinees).

The world of Harry Potter has arrived on Broadway, Hogwarts and all, and it is a triumph of theatrical magic. Set two decades after the final chapters of JK Rowling's world-shaking kid-lit heptalogy, Jack Thorne's two-part epic (richly elaborated by director John Tiffany) combines grand storytelling with stagecraft on a scale heretofore unimagined. It leaves its audience awestruck, spellbound and deeply satisfied.

The Lion King

Minskoff Theatre, 200 W 45th Street, between Broadway & Eighth Avenue, Theater District (Ticketmaster 1-866 870 2717, www. lionking.com). Subway A, C, E to 42nd Street-Port Authority; N, Q, R, S, W, 1, 2, 3, 7 to 42nd Street-Times Square. **Box office** *10am-8pm Mon-Sat; noon-6pm Sun.* **Tickets** *$132-$277.* **Map** *p175 D24.*

Director-designer Julie Taymor surrounds the Disney movie's mythic plot and Elton John-Tim Rice score with African rhythm and music. Through elegant puppetry, Taymor populates the stage with a menagerie of African beasts; her staging has expanded a simple cub into the pride of Broadway.

Wicked

Gershwin Theatre, 222 W 51st Street, between Broadway & Eighth Avenue, Theater District (Ticketmaster 1-877 250 2929, www. wickedthemusical.com). Subway C, E, 1 to 50th Street. **Box office** *10am-8pm Mon-Wed; 10am-8.30pm Thur-Sat; noon-6pm Sun.* **Tickets** *$89-$242.* **Map** *p175 D23.*

Harry Potter and the Cursed Child

Wicked

Based on novelist Gregory Maguire's 1995 riff on *The Wizard of Oz*, *Wicked* is a witty prequel to the classic children's book and movie. The show's combination of pop dynamism and sumptuous spectacle has made it the most popular show on Broadway. Teenage girls, especially, have responded to the story of how a green girl named Elphaba comes to be known as the Wicked Witch of the West.

Off Broadway

As the cost of the vast majority of shows on Broadway continues to soar, serious playwrights are opening their shows in the less financially arduous world of Off Broadway, where many of the theatres are not-for-profit enterprises. Venues have between 100 and 499 seats; tickets usually run from $30 to $100. Here, we've listed some of the best theatres and repertory companies, plus a couple of reliable ongoing productions.

Long-running shows

Blue Man Group

Astor Place Theatre, 434 Lafayette Street, between Astor Place & 4th Street, East Village (1-800 258 3626, www.blueman. com). Subway R, W to 8th Street-NYU; 6 to Astor Place. **Box office** *11am-curtain daily.* **Tickets** *$39-$245.* **Map** *p124 F28.*

Three deadpan men with extraterrestrial imaginations (and head-to-toe blue body paint) carry this long-time favourite, which may be the world's most accessible piece

of multimedia performance art. A weird, exuberant trip through the trappings of modern culture, the show is as smart as it is ridiculous.

Sleep No More

McKittrick Hotel, 530 W 27th Street, between Tenth & Eleventh Avenues, Chelsea (Ovation Tix 1-866 811 4111, www.sleepnomorenyc. com). Subway 1 to 28th Street; C, E to 23rd Street; 7 to 34th Street-Hudson Yards. **Tickets** *$120-$325.* **Map** *p153 C26.*

A multitude of searing sights awaits at this dazzling and uncanny installation by the English company Punchdrunk. Your sense of space is blurred as you wander through more than 90 discrete spaces, from a cloistral chapel to a ballroom floor. A Shakespearean can check off allusions to *Macbeth*; others can just revel in the haunted-house vibe.

Repertory companies & venues

For details of **Lincoln Center Theater**, *see p332* Lincoln Center.

59E59 Theaters

59 E 59th Street, between Madison & Park Avenues, Upper East Side (1-212 753 5959, Ticket Central 1-212 279 4200, www.59e59. org). Subway N, R, W to Lexington Avenue-59th Street; 4, 5, 6 to 59th Street. **Box office** *noon-6pm daily.* **Tickets** *$25-$70.* **Map** *p209 E22.*

This chic, state-of-the-art venue, which comprises an Off Broadway space and two smaller theatres, is packed with worthy

In the know
Understudy refunds

If you've come to see a particular performer on Broadway, you may be able to cash in your ticket if that star doesn't show up. As a general rule, you are entitled to a refund if the star's name appears above the title of the show. A card on the wall of the lobby will announce any absences that day – go to the box office if you want your money back.

offerings, including intimate music events. It's also where you'll find the annual Brits Off Broadway festival (www.britsoffbroadway. com), which imports some of the UK's best work for brief runs.

❤ Ars Nova
27 Barrow Street, between Seventh Avenue South & W 4th Street, West Village (1-212 352-3101, OvationTix 1-866 811 4111, www. arsnovanyc.com). Subway 1 to Christopher Street-Sheridan Square. **Box office** *30mins before show.* **Tickets** *$15-$50.* **Map** *p175 C22.*

Committed to presenting innovative new theatre, music and comedy, this offbeat company has been a boon to developing artists since it opened in 2002. In 2019, it moved into the 1917 Greenwich House Theater. Along with smart full productions, Ars Nova also presents an eclectic monthly special called Showgasm and the annual ANT Fest for emerging talents. **Other location** 511 W 54th Street, between Tenth & Eleventh Avenues, Hell's Kitchen.

Atlantic Theater Company
336 W 20th Street, between Eighth & Ninth Avenues, Chelsea (1-212 691 5919, Ticket Central 1-212 279 4200, www.atlantictheater. org). Subway C, E to 23rd Street. **Box office** *noon-6pm Tue-Sat & 1hr before curtain.* **Tickets** *$35-$85.* **Map** *p153 C27.*

Created in 1985 as an offshoot of acting workshops led by playwright David Mamet and actor William H Macy, the dynamic Atlantic Theater Company has presented dozens of new plays, including Steven Sater and Duncan Sheik's rock musical *Spring Awakening* and Conor McPherson's *The Night Alive*. The Atlantic also has a smaller second stage deep underground at 330 W 16th Street.

Brooklyn Academy of Music
For listings, see p330.

BAM's beautifully distressed Harvey Theater – along with its grand old opera house in the Peter Jay Sharp Building – is the site of the Next Wave Festival and other international events. The spring season usually features high-profile productions of classics by the likes of Chekhov and Shakespeare, often shipped over from England with major actors attached.

Classic Stage Company
136 E 13th Street, between Third & Fourth Avenues, East Village (1-212 677 4210, www. classicstage.org). Subway L, N, Q, R, W, 4, 5, 6 to 14th Street-Union Square. **Box office** *noon-6pm Mon-Fri, noon-3pm, 5-8pm Sat; noon-3pm Sun (hrs vary in summer).* **Tickets** *$20-$125.* **Map** *p123 F28.*

With a purview that runs from medieval mystery plays and Elizabethan standards to early modern drama and even the occasional Stephen Sondheim musical, Classic Stage Company is committed to making the old new again. Its artistic director is John Doyle, who made his name in New York with stripped-down Broadway stagings of *Sweeney Todd* and *Company*.

Irish Repertory Theatre
132 W 22nd Street, between Sixth & Seventh Avenues, Chelsea (1-212 727 2737, www. irishrep.org). Subway F, M, 1 to 23rd Street. **Box office** *noon-6pm Mon, Sun ; noon-7pm Tue, Thur; noon-8pm Wed, Fri, Sat (extended hours on show days).* **Tickets** *$50-$70.* **Map** *p153 D26.*

Set in a cosily odd, L-shaped venue, the Irish Repertory Theatre puts on compelling shows by Irish and Irish-American playwrights. Fine revivals of classics by the likes of Oscar Wilde and George Bernard Shaw alternate with Irish-themed musicals and plays by lesser-known modern authors.

Manhattan Theatre Club
Samuel J Friedman Theatre, 261 W 47th Street, between Broadway & Eighth Avenue, Theater District (Telecharge 1-212 239 6200, www.manhattantheatreclub.com). Subway N, Q, R, S, W 1, 2, 3, 7 to 42nd Street-Times Square. **Box office** *noon-6pm Mon-Sat (extended hours on show days).* **Tickets** *$30-$170.* **Map** *p175 D23.*

One of the city's most important non-profit companies, Manhattan Theatre Club spent decades as an Off Broadway outfit before moving into the 622-seat Friedman Theatre in 2003. But it still maintains a smaller space at New York City Center (*see p336*), where it presents some of its best material – such as Lynn Nottage's 2009 Pulitzer Prize winner, *Ruined*. Younger audience members can sign up for the 30 Under 35 programme to get tickets at both theatres for $30.

New Victory Theater
209 W 42nd Street, between Seventh & Eighth Avenues, Theater District (1-646 223

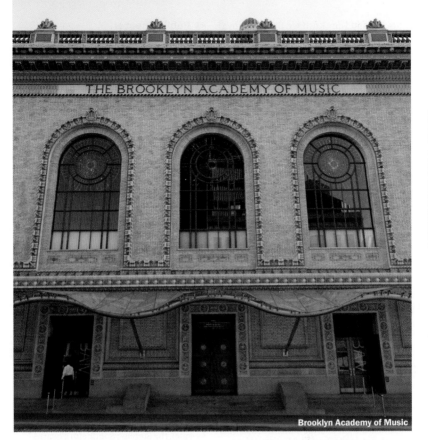

Brooklyn Academy of Music

3010, www.newvictory.org). Subway N, Q, R, S, W, 1, 2, 3, 7 to 42nd Street-Times Square. **Box office** 11am-5pm Mon, Sun; noon-7pm Tue-Sat. **Tickets** $17-$42. **Map** p175 D24.

New York's only full-scale young people's theatre stages innovative productions from around the world. Offerings span everything from reworkings of classic plays and puppetry to contemporary circus troupes and hip hop-inspired dance. The New Victory often collaborates with Autism Friendly Spaces on special adaptations, ensuring all can enjoy the experience of live theatre. Shows often sell out, so buy tickets well ahead.

New World Stages

340 W 50th Street, between Eighth & Ninth Avenues, Theater District (1-646 871 1730, Telecharge 1-212 239 6200, www. newworldstages.com). Subway C, E, 1 to 50th Street. **Box office** 1-7pm Tue; 1pm-curtain Mon, Wed, Fri; 10am-curtain Thur, Sat, Sun. **Tickets** $55-$150. **Map** p175 D23.

Formerly a movie multiplex, this centre – one of the last bastions of commercial Off Broadway in New York – boasts a shiny, space-age interior and five stages, presenting everything from family-friendly spectacles (Gazillion Bubble Show, for example) to downsized transfers of Broadway musicals, such as Jersey Boys.

New York Theatre Workshop

79 E 4th Street, between Bowery & Second Avenue, East Village (1-212 460 5475, www.nytw.org). Subway F to Lower East Side-Second Avenue; 6 to Astor Place. **Box office** noon-6pm Mon-Fri (noon-7pm or 8pm on show days). **Tickets** $25-$85. **Map** p123 F29.

Founded in 1979, the New York Theatre Workshop works with directors eager to take on challenging pieces, including iconoclastic Belgian Ivo van Hove and Tony Award winners Sam Gold and Rachel Chavkin. Besides presenting plays by world-class artists such as Caryl

Churchill and Tony Kushner, the company also premièred *Rent*, Jonathan Larson's seminal 1990s musical.

Pershing Square Signature Center

480 W 42nd Street, at Tenth Avenue, Hell's Kitchen (1-212 244 7529, www. signaturetheatre.org). Subway A, C, E to 42nd Street-Port Authority. Box office 11am-6pm Tue-Sun. Tickets $25-$65. Map p175 C24.

The award-winning Signature Theatre Company, founded by the late James Houghton in 1991, focuses on exploring and celebrating playwrights in depth, with whole seasons devoted to works by individual living writers. Over the years, the company has delved into the oeuvres of August Wilson, John Guare, Horton Foote and many more. Special programmes are designed to keep prices low. Today, the troupe is based in a theatre complex designed by Frank Gehry, with three major spaces and ambitious long-term commission programmes, cementing it as one of the city's key cultural institutions.

Playwrights Horizons

416 W 42nd Street, between Ninth & Tenth Avenues, Theater District (1-212 564 1235, Ticket Central 1-212 279 4200, www. playwrightshorizons.org). Subway A, C, E to 42nd Street-Port Authority. Box office noon-8pm daily. Tickets $59-$109. Map p175 C24.

Hundreds of important contemporary plays have had premières here, including dramas (*Driving Miss Daisy*, *The Heidi Chronicles*) and musicals (Stephen Sondheim's *Assassins* and *Sunday in the Park with George*). More recent seasons have included new works by Taylor Mac, Lucas Hnath, Sarah Ruhand and Craig Lucas, as well as Bruce Norris's Pulitzer Prize winner *Clybourne Park*.

In the know
Summer savings

The best time for a budget break in NYC is summer, when you can take advantage of a wealth of free outdoor cultural events, from big-name **SummerStage** concerts (see *p287*) to gratis dance and music at **Lincoln Center** (see *p290*). Attending one of the star-studded **Shakespeare in the Park** productions (see *opposite*) requires some forward planning, since you generally have to queue in Central Park before the box office opens to obtain your freebie ticket, but the al fresco theatre experience is magical and spending a few hours reading, napping and picnicking in the park while you wait isn't so bad.

❤ Public Theater

425 Lafayette Street, between Astor Place & 4th Street, East Village (1-212 539 8500, tickets 1-212 967 7555, www.publictheater. org). Subway R, W to 8th Street-NYU; 6 to Astor Place. Box office 2-6pm daily (extended hrs on show days). Tickets $15-$95. Map p123 F28.

Under the guidance of civic-minded artistic director Oskar Eustis, this local institution – dedicated to producing the work of new American playwrights, but also known for its Shakespeare in the Park productions – has regained its place at the forefront of the Off Broadway world. The ambitious, multicultural programming ranges from new works by major playwrights to the annual Under the Radar festival for emerging artists. The company's home building, a renovated Astor Place landmark, has five stages.

▶ *The building is also home to Joe's Pub, see p319.*

Roundabout Theatre Company

American Airlines Theatre, 227 W 42rd Street, between Seventh & Eighth Avenues, Theater District (1-212 719 1300, www. roundabouttheatre.org). Subway N, Q, R, S, W, 1, 2, 3, 7 to 42nd Street-Times Square. Box office 10am-6pm Mon, Sun; 10am-8pm Tue-Sat. Tickets vary. Map p175 C23.

Devoted mostly to revivals, the Roundabout often pairs beloved old chestnuts with celebrity casts. In addition to shows at its Broadway flagship, the company also mounts productions at Studio 54 (254 W 54th Street, between Broadway & Eighth Avenue), the Stephen Sondheim Theatre (124 West 43rd Street, between Sixth & Seventh Avenues) and the Harold and Miriam Steinberg Center for Theatre (111 W 46th Street, between Sixth & Seventh Avenues), home to Off Broadway's Laura Pels Theatre. Also here is the Black Box Theatre, where the company helps emerging talent develop new works.

St Ann's Warehouse

45 Water Street, at Old Dock Street, Dumbo, Brooklyn (1-718 254 8779, www. stannswarehouse.org). Subway F to York Street; 2, 3 to Clark Street. Box office noon-6pm Mon-Fri (call for extended hours). Tickets $25-$75. Map p232 H32.

A haven for adventurous theatregoers, St Ann's offers an eclectic lineup of plays and music; recent shows have included high-level work by the Wooster Group and National Theatre of Scotland. In 2015, it moved to its impressive premises in the converted 19th-century Tobacco Warehouse on Dumbo's waterfront.

Second Stage Theatre

305 W 43rd Street, at Eighth Avenue, Theater District (1-212 246 4422, www.2st. com). Subway A, C, E to 42nd Street-Port Authority. Box office noon-6pm daily. Tickets $30-$129. Map p175 D24.

In a beautiful Rem Koolhaas-designed space near Times Square, Second Stage Theatre specialises in American playwrights, and hosted the New York première of Edward Albee's *Peter and Jerry*. It also provides a stage for serious new musicals, such as the Pulitzer Prize-winning *Next to Normal* and the Broadway hit *Dear Evan Hansen*.

Shakespeare in the Park at the Delacorte Theater

Enter park at Central Park West, at 81st Street, and walk east (1-212 539 8500, www. shakespeareinthepark.org). Subway B, C to 81st Street-Museum of Natural History. Tickets free. Map p194 D19.

The Delacorte Theater in Central Park is the fair-weather sister of the Public Theater. When not producing Shakespeare in the East Village, the Public offers the best of the Bard outdoors during Shakespeare in the Park (typically late May-Aug). Free tickets (two per person) are distributed at the Delacorte at noon on the day of the performance.

Around 8am is usually a good time to begin waiting, although the queue can start forming as early as 6am when big-name stars are on the bill. There's also a digital lottery for tickets (see website for details).

❤ Soho Rep

46 Walker Street, between Broadway & Church Street, Tribeca (TheaterMania 1-212 352 3101, www.sohorep.org). Subway A, C, E, N, Q, R, W, Z, 6 to Canal Street; 1 to Franklin Street. Tickets $35-$55. Map p87 E31.

A few years ago, this Off-Off mainstay moved to an Off Broadway contract, but tickets for most shows have remained cheap. Artistic director Sarah Benson's programming is diverse and audacious: recent productions include Jackie Sibblies Drury's 2019 Pulitzer Prize winner, *Fairview*, and plays by Branden Jacobs-Jenkins, Christopher Chen and Aleshea Harris.

Theatre for a New Audience

Polonsky Shakespeare Center, 262 Ashland Place, between Fulton Street & Lafayette Ave-nue, Fort Greene, Brooklyn (OvationTix 1-866 811 4111, www.tfana.org). Subway B, D, N, Q, R, 2, 3, 4, 5 to Atlantic Avenue-Barclays Center; C to Lafayette Avenue; G to Fulton Street. Box office 1-6pm Tue-Sat. Tickets $90-$125. Map p232 K34.

Founded in 1979, TFANA has become New York's most prominent classical-theatre company. In 2013, it moved into its new home, the Polonsky Shakespeare Center, in Brooklyn's cultural district. The flashy, glass-fronted 299-seat venue, designed by Hugh Hardy, has a versatile show space that permits imaginative stagings of works by the Bard, as well as more modern masters such as Samuel Beckett and Thornton Wilder.

Theatre Row

410 W 42nd Street, between Ninth & Tenth Avenues, Theater District (Telecharge 1-212 239 6200, www.theatrerow.org). Subway A, C, E to 42nd Street-Port Authority. **Box office** *noon-6pm daily (until curtain on show days).* **Tickets** *$25-$100.* **Map** *p175 C24.*

Comprising five main venues of various sizes, Theatre Row hosts new plays and revivals by scores of assorted theatre companies. Among the groups that regularly perform here are Keen Company and Mint Theater Company.

Vineyard Theatre

108 E 15th Street, at Union Square East, Union Square (1-212 353 0303, www. vineyardtheatre.org). Subway L, N, Q, R, W, 4, 5, 6 to 14th Street-Union Square. **Box office** *1-6pm Mon-Fri (extended hrs on show days).* **Tickets** *$20-$100.* **Map** *p163 E27.*

The Vineyard produces some excellent new plays and musicals. Past productions have included *The Scottsboro Boys*, the Tony Award-winning *Avenue Q*, and Paula Vogel's haunting *Indecent*, all of which transferred to Broadway.

Off-Off Broadway

Technically, the term Off-Off Broadway denotes a show presented at a theatre with fewer than 100 seats, with tickets usually less than $25. It's where a lot of inexperienced artists pay their dues, but it's also where some of the most daring writers and performers – who aren't necessarily card-carrying union professionals – create their edgiest work. Summer's **New York Musical Theatre Festival** (www.nymf.org) has become an important testing ground for composers and lyricists.

Repertory companies & venues

For multidisciplinary **Dixon Place**, *see p338*.

The Brick

575 Metropolitan Avenue, between Lorimer Street & Union Avenue, Williamsburg, Brooklyn (1-718 285 3863, OvationTix 1-866 811 4111, www.bricktheater.com). Subway G to Metropolitan Avenue; L to Lorimer Street. **Box office** *15-30mins before curtain.* **Tickets** *$15-$20.* **Map** *p249 J28.*

This spunky, brick-lined venue presents a variety of boundary-pushing work. Prominent fringe-scene figure Theresa Buchheister is artistic director as of January 2020. Founder of the experimental and often zany Exponential and !?:New Works festivals (in winter and summer, respectively), she will be working with a team of collaborators.

The Bushwick Starr

207 Starr Street, between Irving & Wyckoff Avenues, Bushwick, Brooklyn (1-866 811 4111, www.thebushwickstarr.org). Subway L to Jefferson Street. **Box office** *30mins before doors open.* **Tickets** *$15-$25.* **Map** *p249 N28.*

As small companies continue to be priced out of Manhattan, everyone's looking to Brooklyn to pick up the slack. This funky black box is one good option: some of the city's fiercest experimental artists and troupes have made the Starr shine brightly.

HERE

145 Sixth Avenue, between Broome & Spring Streets, Soho (1-212 647 0202, TheaterMania 1-212 352 3101, www.here.org). Subway C, E to Spring Street. **Box office** *5-9pm Tue-Sat; noon-5pm Sat, Sun.* **Tickets** *free-$45.* **Map** *p87 E30.*

Dedicated to not-for-profit arts enterprises, this theatre complex has been the launch pad for such well-known shows as Eve Ensler's *The Vagina Monologues* and *Arias with a Twist*, drag diva Joey Arias's collaboration with puppeteer extraordinaire Basil Twist. HERE is also involved in numerous multidisciplinary development programmes.

La MaMa Experimental Theater Club

74A E 4th Street, between Bowery & Second Avenue, East Village (OvationTix 1-212 352 3101, www.lamama.org). Subway F to Lower East Side-Second Avenue; 6 to Astor Place. **Box office** *(at 66 E 4th Street) 1hr before showtime.* **Tickets** *$10-$35.* **Map** *p123 F29.*

Founded by the late Ellen Stewart, La MaMa has been a bastion of the Off-Off scene for more than half a century. The complex has helped to nurture such innovators as Sam Shepard, Charles Ludlam, Lanford Wilson and Ping Chong, and it continues to be an important rung in many rising artists' ladders.

IT'S SHOWTIME

Book the best of Broadway, from
big-hitting musicals to brand-new
shows and all of our critics' top picks.

 TIMEOUT.COM/
NEWYORK/THEATER

THE BEST OF THE CITY

Understand

New York Public Library *p184*

History

The seeds of the Big Apple

In 1609, Henry Hudson, an English explorer in the service of the Dutch East India Company, sailed into New York Harbor, triggering events that would lead to the creation of the most dynamic and ethnically diverse city in the world. The densely layered character of the metropolis intertwines the cultural legacies of successive waves of fortune-seekers, from early Dutch settlers to the fabled tired, poor, huddled immigrant masses of the 19th and 20th centuries. From its beginnings, this forward-looking town has been shaped by a cast of ambitious and sometimes colourful characters, and it continues to be so today.

Little Italy c.1900

Native New Yorkers

The area's first residents were the indigenous Lenape tribe. They lived among the forests, meadows and farms of the land they called Lenapehoking, pretty much undisturbed by outsiders – until the 16th century, when their idyll was interrupted by European visitors. The first to cast his eyes upon this land was Giovanni da Verrazano in 1524. An Italian explorer commissioned by the French to find a shortcut to the Orient, he found Staten Island instead. Recognising that he was on the wrong track, Verrazano hauled anchor nearly as quickly as he had dropped it, never setting foot on dry land.

Eighty-five years later, Henry Hudson, an Englishman in the service of the Dutch East India Company, discovered New York Harbor in the same way. After trading with the Lenape, he ventured up the river that now bears his name, thinking it offered a north-west passage to Asia, but halted just south of present-day Albany when its shallowness convinced him it didn't lead to the Pacific. Hudson turned back, and his tales of the lush, river-crossed countryside captured the Dutch imagination. In 1624, the Dutch West India Company sent 110 settlers to establish a trading post here, planting themselves at the southern tip of the island called Mannahata and calling the colony Nieuw (New) Amsterdam. In many battles against the local Lenape, they did their best to drive the natives away from the little company town. But the tribe was immovable.

In 1626, Peter Minuit, New Amsterdam's first governor, thought he had solved the Lenape problem by pulling off the city's very first real-estate rip-off. He made them an offer they couldn't refuse: he 'bought' the island of Manhattan – all 14,000 acres of it – from the Lenape for 60 guilders' worth of goods. Legend famously values the purchase price at $24, but modern historians set the amount closer to $500. It was a slick trick, and one that set a precedent for countless future self-serving business transactions.

The Dutch quickly made the port of New Amsterdam a centre for fur trading. The population didn't grow as fast as the business, however, and the Dutch West India Company had a hard time finding recruits to move to this unknown island an ocean away. The company instead gathered servants, orphans and slaves, and other more unsavoury outcasts such as thieves, drunkards and prostitutes. The population grew to 400 within ten years, but drunkenness, crime and squalor prevailed. If the colony was to thrive, it needed a strong leader. Enter Dutch West India Company director Peter Stuyvesant.

Peg-leg Pete

A one-legged, puritanical bully with a quick temper, Stuyvesant – or Peg-leg Pete, as he was known – may have been less than popular, but he was the colony's first effective governor. He made peace with the Lenape, formed the first policing force (consisting of nine men), cracked

The Fall of New Amsterdam (Jean Leon Gerome Ferris)

down on debauchery by shutting taverns and outlawing drinking on Sunday, and established the first school, post office, hospital, prison and poorhouse. Within a decade, the population had quadrupled, and the settlement had become an important trading port.

Lined with canals and windmills, and dotted with gabled farmhouses, New Amsterdam slowly began to resemble its namesake. Newcomers arrived to work in the fur and slave trades, or to farm. Soon, a great variety of languages could be heard in the streets – a fact that made Stuyvesant nervous. In 1654, he attempted to quash immigration by turning away Sephardic Jews who were fleeing the Spanish Inquisition. But, surprisingly for the time, the corporate honchos at the Dutch West India Company reprimanded him for his intolerance and overturned his decision, leading to the establishment of the earliest Jewish community in the New World. It was the first time that the inflexible Stuyvesant was forced to mend his ways. The second time put an end to the 40-year Dutch rule for good.

British invasion

In late August 1664, English warships sailed into the harbour, set on taking over the now prosperous colony. To avoid bloodshed and destruction, Stuyvesant surrendered quickly. Soon after, New Amsterdam was renamed New York (after the Duke of York, brother of King Charles II) and Stuyvesant quietly retired to his farm. Unlike Stuyvesant, the English battled with the Lenape; by 1695, those members of the tribe who hadn't been killed off were sent packing upstate, and New York's European population shot up to 3,000. Over the next 35 years, Dutch-style farmhouses and windmills gave way to stately townhouses and monuments to English royals. By 1740, the slave trade had made New York the third-busiest port in the British Empire. The city, now home to more than 11,000 residents, continued to prosper for a quarter-century. But resentment was beginning to build in the colony, fuelled by the ever-heavier burden of British taxation.

Fearing revolution, New York's citizenry fled the city in droves in 1775, causing the population to plummet from 25,000 to just 5,000. The following year, 100 British warships sailed into the harbour of this virtual ghost town, carrying with them an intimidating army of 32,000 men – nearly four times the size of George Washington's militia. Despite the British presence,

Washington organised a reading of the Declaration of Independence, and American patriots tore the statue of King George III from its pedestal. Revolution was inevitable.

The battle for New York officially began on 26 August 1776, and Washington's army sustained heavy losses; nearly a quarter of his men were slaughtered in a two-day period. As Washington retreated, a fire – thought to have been started by patriots – destroyed 493 buildings, including Trinity Church, the city's tallest structure. The British found a scorched city, and a populace living in tents.

The city continued to suffer for seven years. Eventually, of course, Washington's luck turned. As the British forces left, he and his troops marched triumphantly down Broadway to reclaim the city as a part of the newly established United States of America. A week and a half later, on 4 December 1783, the general bade farewell to his dispersing troops at Fraunces Tavern (*see p74*).

Alexander Hamilton laid the groundwork for city institutions that remain to this day, including the New York Stock Exchange

Alexander Hamilton was instrumental in the rebuilding effort. The ultimate self-made man, he was born on the Caribbean island of Nevis in 1755, the illegitimate son of a Scottish nobleman. After the death of his mother, he became an apprentice at a counting house before moving to New York to attend King's College (now Columbia University), but left to volunteer for service. He rose through the ranks and was promoted to lieutenant colonel at age 21 by George Washington. After the war, he laid the groundwork for New York City institutions that remain to this day. He established the Bank of New York, the city's first bank, in 1784. When Washington was inaugurated as the nation's first president in 1789, at Federal Hall on Wall Street, he brought Hamilton on board as the first secretary of the treasury. Thanks to Hamilton's business savvy, trade in stocks and bonds flourished, leading to the establishment in 1792 of what would eventually be known as the New York Stock Exchange.

Destruction of the Colored Orphan Asylum in 1863

The city takes shape...

New York continued to grow and prosper for the next three decades. Maritime commerce soared, and Robert Fulton's innovative steamboat made its maiden voyage on the Hudson River in 1807. Eleven years later, a group of merchants introduced regularly scheduled shipping (a novel concept at the time) between New York and Liverpool on the Black Ball Line. A boom in the maritime trades lured hundreds of European labourers, and the city, which was still entirely crammed in below Houston Street, grew more and more congested. Manhattan real estate became the most expensive in the world.

The first man to tackle the city's congestion problem was Mayor DeWitt Clinton, a protégé of Hamilton. Clinton's dream was to organise the entire island of Manhattan in such a way that it could cope with the eventual population creep northwards. In 1807, he created a commission to map out the foreseeable sprawl. It presented its work four years later, and the destiny of this new city was made manifest: it would be a regular grid of crossing thoroughfares, 12 avenues wide and 155 streets long. Then Clinton overstepped the city's boundaries. In 1811, he presented a plan to build a 363-mile canal linking the Hudson River with Lake Erie. Many of his contemporaries thought it was an impossible task: at the time, the longest canal in the world ran a mere 27 miles. But Clinton pressed on and raised a staggering $6 million for the project.

Work on the Erie Canal began in 1817 and was completed in 1825 – three years ahead of schedule. It shortened the journey between New York City and Buffalo from three weeks to one, and cut the shipping cost per ton from about $100 to $4. Goods, people and money poured into New York, fostering a merchant elite that moved northwards in Manhattan to escape the urban crush. Estates multiplied above Houston Street – all grander and more imposing than their modest colonial forerunners. Once slavery was abolished in New York in 1827, free blacks became an essential part of the workforce. In 1831, the first public transport system began operating, with horse-drawn omnibuses.

... And so do the slums

As the population multiplied (swelling to 240,000 by 1830 and 700,000 by 1850), so did the city's problems. Tensions bubbled between immigrant newcomers and those who could trace their American lineage back a generation or two. Crime rose and lurid tales filled the 'penny press', the city's proto-tabloids. While wealthy New Yorkers were moving as far 'uptown' as Greenwich Village, the infamous Five Points neighbourhood – the city's first slum – festered in the area now occupied by City Hall, the courthouses and Chinatown. Built on a fetid drained pond, Five Points became the ramshackle home of poor immigrants and blacks. Brutal gangs with colourful names such as the Forty Thieves, Plug Uglies and Dead Rabbits often met in bloody clashes in the streets, but what finally sent a mass of 100,000 people scurrying from lower Manhattan was an outbreak of cholera in 1832. In just six weeks, 3,513 New Yorkers died.

Compared to the major Southern cities, New York emerged nearly unscathed from the Civil War

In 1837, a financial panic left hundreds of Wall Street businesses crumbling. Commerce stagnated at the docks, the real-estate market collapsed, and all but three city banks closed. Some 50,000 New Yorkers lost their jobs, while 200,000 teetered on the edge of poverty. The panic sparked civil unrest and violence. In 1849, a xenophobic mob of 8,000 protesting the performance of an English actor at the Astor Place Opera House was met by a militia that opened fire, killing 22. But the Draft Riots of 1863 were much worse. After a law was passed exempting men from the draft for a $300 fee, the (mostly Irish) poor rose up, forming a 15,000-strong force that rampaged through the city. Fuelled by anger about the Civil War (for which they blamed blacks), the rioters set fire to the Colored Orphan Asylum and vandalised black homes. Black people were beaten in the streets, and some were lynched. A federal force of 6,000 men was sent to subdue the violence. After four days and at least 100 deaths, peace was finally restored.

On the move

Amid the chaos of the mid 19th century, the pace of progress continued unabated. Compared to the major Southern cities, New York emerged nearly unscathed from the Civil War. The population ballooned to two million in the 1880s, and new technologies revolutionised daily life. The elevated railway helped New Yorkers to move into what are now the Upper East and Upper West Sides, while other trains connected the city with upstate New York, New England and the Midwest. By 1871, regional train traffic had grown so much that rail tycoon Cornelius Vanderbilt constructed the original Grand Central Depot (it was replaced in 1913 by the current Grand Central Terminal).

One ambitious project was inspired by the harsh winter of 1867. The East River froze over, halting ferry traffic between Brooklyn and Manhattan. Brooklyn, by then, had become the nation's third most populous city, and its politicians and businessmen realised that the boroughs had to be linked. The New York Bridge Company's goal was to build the world's longest bridge, spanning the East River between downtown Manhattan and south-western Brooklyn. Over 16 years (four times longer than projected), 14,000 miles of steel cable were stretched across the bridge, which has a main span of 1,595 feet and a total length of 5,989 feet, while the towers rose a staggering 276 feet above the river. The Brooklyn Bridge opened on 24 May 1883.

The greed of Tweed

As New York recovered from the turmoil of the mid 1800s, William M 'Boss' Tweed began pulling the strings. Using his ample charm, the six-foot, 300-pound bookkeeper, chair-maker and volunteer firefighter became one of the city's most powerful politicians. He had been an alderman and district leader; he had served in the US House of Representatives and as a state senator; and he was a chairman of the Democratic General Committee and leader of Tammany Hall, a political organisation formed by local craftsmen ostensibly to keep the wealthy classes' political clout in check. But even though Tweed opened orphanages, poorhouses and hospitals, his good deeds were overshadowed by his and his cohort's gross embezzlement of city funds. By 1870, members of the 'Tweed Ring' had created a new city charter, granting themselves control of the City Treasury. Using fake leases and inflated bills for city supplies and services, Tweed and his cronies may ultimately have pocketed as much as $200 million.

Tweed was eventually sued by the city for $6 million, and charged with forgery and larceny. He escaped from debtors' prison in 1875, but was captured in Spain a year later and died in 1878. But his greed hurt many. As he was emptying the city's coffers, poverty spread. Then the stock market took a nosedive, factories closed and railways went bankrupt. By 1874, New York estimated its homeless population at 90,000. That winter, *Harper's Weekly* reported, 900 New Yorkers starved to death.

Immigrant dreams

In September 1882, a new era dawned brightly when Thomas Alva Edison lit up half a square mile of lower Manhattan with 3,000 electric lamps. One of the newly illuminated offices belonged to financier JP Morgan, who played an essential part

Top Five NYC Inventions

They made it here

1 Toilet paper

In 1857, Joseph C Gayetty began selling packs of 'medicated paper for the water closet' out of his wholesale shop at 41 Ann Street. The paper was made from pure Manila hemp and treated with aloe to assure patrons it was healthier than their old standby: shreds of used newspaper. Best (or worst) of all, each sheet was watermarked with his name.

2 Pneumatic railway

Inventor Alfred Ely Beach unveiled the first air-propelled train (and technically New York's first subway) in 1870. Pushed by a 20-ton fan, the fancy cylindrical car had plush seats and zirconia lamps and cost a quarter to ride. Sadly, the Panic of 1873 financial crisis blew away any future for this marvel of 19th-century technology, which ran only one block under Broadway from Warren to Murray Streets.

3 Teddy bear

In 1902, political cartoonists poked fun at President Theodore Roosevelt for refusing to shoot an injured black bear while on a hunt. Inspired by the story, Morris and Rose Michtom, Russian-Jewish candy-store owners from Brooklyn who also sold soft toys, sewed a plush bear and displayed it with the label 'Teddy's bear'. It proved so popular, the couple gave up candy and opened a factory to make the cuddly critters.

4 Scrabble

Out-of-work architect and anagram lover Alfred Mosher Butts conceived this wordy board game in 1931 while living in Jackson Heights, Queens. Hoping to sell the game idea, he made hand-cut tiles and obliged family and friends to help develop the basic rules; the game has since sold more than 150 million copies worldwide. The street sign on Butts' corner on 35th Avenue in Queens now pays homage to his invention with number scores punctuating the letters.

5 Remote control

Nikola Tesla, the Serbian-American New Yorker remembered as the archetypal mad scientist, conceived of a radio-controlled boat back in 1898. The idea was so novel that no one believed such technology could exist, particularly New York's patent officers. Tesla went on to become a hero to future generations of couch surfers – once TV was invented. Today, the electric car company, Tesla, is named after this pioneering scientist.

Pneumatic Railway

in bringing New York's, and America's, economy back to life. By bailing out a number of failing railways, then merging and restructuring them, Morgan jump-started commerce in New York once again. Goods, jobs and businesses returned to the city, and very soon such aggressive businessmen as John D Rockefeller, Andrew Carnegie and Henry Frick wanted a piece of the action. They made New York the HQ of Standard Oil and US Steel, corporations that went on to shape America's economic future.

A shining symbol for less fortunate arrivals also made New York its home around that time. To commemorate the centennial of the Declaration of Independence, the French gave the United States the Statue of Liberty, which was dedicated in 1886. Between 1892 and 1954, the statue ushered more than 12 million immigrants into New York Harbor, and Ellis Island processed many of them. The island had opened as an immigration centre in 1892 with expectations of accommodating 500,000 people annually, but the number peaked at more than a million in 1907. In the 34-building complex, crowds of would-be Americans were herded through examinations, inspections and interrogations. About 98 per cent got through, turning New York into what British playwright Israel Zangwill optimistically called 'the great melting pot where all the races of Europe are melting and reforming'.

Many of these newcomers crowded into dark, squalid tenements on the Lower East Side, while millionaires such as Vanderbilt and Frick constructed huge French-style mansions along Fifth Avenue. Jacob A Riis, a Danish immigrant and police reporter for the New York Tribune, made it his business to expose this dichotomy, scouring filthy alleys and overcrowded tenements to research and photograph his 1890 book, *How the Other Half Lives*. Largely as a result of Riis's work, the state passed the Tenement House Act of 1901, calling for drastic housing reforms.

Soaring aspirations

On 1 January 1898, the boroughs of Manhattan, Brooklyn, Queens, Staten Island and the Bronx consolidated to form New York City, the largest metropolis in America with over three million residents. More and more companies started to move their headquarters to this new city, increasing the demand for office space. With little land left to develop in lower Manhattan, New York embraced the steel revolution and grew steadily skywards. By 1920, New York boasted more than 60 skyscrapers (*see p364*).

If that weren't enough to demonstrate New Yorkers' unending ambition, the city burrowed below the streets, starting work on its underground transport system in 1900. The $35-million project took nearly four and a half years to complete. Less than a decade after opening, it was the most heavily travelled subway system in the world, carrying almost a billion passengers on its trains every year.

Changing times

By 1909, 30,000 factories were operating in the city, churning out everything from heavy machinery to artificial flowers. Mistrusted, abused and underpaid, factory workers faced impossible quotas, had their pay docked for minor mistakes and were often locked in during working hours. In the end, it took a tragedy to bring about real changes in employment laws. The Triangle Shirtwaist Fire was one of the worst industrial disasters in New York City history. On 25 March 1911, fire broke out on the eighth floor of the ten-storey Greenwich Village building on the corner of Greene Street and Washington Place. The top three floors were occupied by the Triangle Shirtwaist Company and, fed by the fabrics, the flames spread rapidly up the building. As the roughly 500 garment workers – many of them teenage girls – rushed to escape, they confronted locked exits. The single flimsy fire escape melted in the heat and fell away from the building. A total of 146 perished. Tried for manslaughter, the factory owners were acquitted, but the fire spurred labour and union organisations to seek major reforms. The Factory Commission of 1911 was established, and spawned the Fire Prevention division of the Fire Department, which enforced the creation of fire escape routes in the workplace. The incident also garnered much-needed support for the Ladies Garment Workers Union.

Between 1910 and 1913, New York City was the site of the largest women's suffrage rallies in the United States. Harriet Stanton Blatch (the daughter of famed suffragette Elizabeth Cady Stanton, and founder of the Equality League of Self-Supporting Women) and Carrie Chapman Catt (the organiser of the New York City Women's Suffrage Party) arranged attention-grabbing demonstrations intended to pressure the state into authorising a referendum on a woman's right to vote. The measure's defeat in 1915 only steeled the suffragettes' resolve. Finally, with the support of Tammany Hall, the law was passed in 1919, challenging the male stranglehold on voting throughout the country. With New York leading the nation, the 19th Amendment was ratified in 1920.

In 1919, as New York welcomed troops home from World War I with a parade, the city also celebrated its emergence on the global stage. It had supplanted London as the investment capital of the world, and had become the centre of publishing, thanks to two men: Joseph Pulitzer and William Randolph Hearst. The *New York Times* had become the country's most respected newspaper; Broadway was the focal point of American theatre; and Greenwich Village had become an international bohemian nexus, where flamboyant artists, writers and political revolutionaries gathered in galleries and coffeehouses.

The more personal side of the women's movement also found a home in New York City. A nurse and midwife who grew up in a family of 11 children, Margaret Sanger was a fierce advocate of birth control and family planning. She opened the first ever birth-control clinic in Brooklyn on 16 October 1916. Finding this unseemly, the police closed the clinic soon after and imprisoned Sanger for 30 days. She was not deterred, however, and, in 1921, formed the American Birth Control League – the forerunner of the organisation Planned Parenthood – which researched birth-control methods and provided gynaecological services.

All that jazz

Forward-thinking women such as Sanger set the tone for an era when women, now a voting political force, were moving beyond the moral conventions of the 19th century. The country ushered in the Jazz Age in 1919 by ratifying the 18th Amendment, which outlawed the distribution and sale of alcoholic beverages. Prohibition turned the city into the epicentre of bootlegging, speakeasies and organised crime. By the early 1920s, New York boasted an estimated 32,000 illegal watering holes – twice the number of legal bars before Prohibition.

In 1925, New Yorkers elected the magnetic James J Walker as mayor. A charming ex-songwriter (as well as a speakeasy patron and skirt-chaser), Walker was the perfect match for his city's flashy style and hunger for publicity. Fame flowed in the city's veins: home-run hero Babe Ruth drew a million fans each season to baseball games at the newly built Yankee Stadium, and sharp-tongued Walter Winchell filled his newspaper columns with celebrity titbits and scandals. Alexander Woollcott, Dorothy Parker, Robert Benchley and other writers met up daily to trade witticisms round a table at the Algonquin Hotel; the result, in February 1925, was *The New Yorker*.

The Harlem Renaissance blossomed at the same time. Writers Langston Hughes, Zora Neale Hurston and James Weldon Johnson transformed the African-American experience into lyrical literary works, and

white society flocked to the Cotton Club to see genre-defining musicians such as Bessie Smith, Cab Calloway, Louis Armstrong and Duke Ellington. (Blacks were allowed into the club only if they were performing on the stage, they could not be part of the audience.)

Downtown, Broadway houses were packed with fans of George and Ira Gershwin, Irving Berlin, Cole Porter, Lorenz Hart, Richard Rodgers and Oscar Hammerstein II. Towards the end of the 1920s, New York-born Al Jolson wowed audiences in *The Jazz Singer*, the first talking picture.

After the crash

The dizzying excitement ended on 29 October 1929, when the stock market crashed. Corruption eroded Mayor Walker's hold on the city: despite a tenure that saw the opening of the Holland Tunnel, the completion of the George Washington Bridge and the construction of the Chrysler and Empire State Buildings, Walker's lustre faded in the growing shadow of graft accusations. He resigned in 1932, when New York, in the depths of the Great Depression, had one million unemployed inhabitants.

In 1934, an unstoppable force named Fiorello La Guardia took office as mayor, rolling up his sleeves to crack down on mobsters, gambling, smut and government corruption. La Guardia was a tough-talking politician known for nearly coming to blows with other city officials; he described himself as 'inconsiderate, arbitrary, authoritative, difficult, complicated, intolerant and somewhat theatrical'. His act played well: he ushered New York into an era of unparalleled prosperity over the course of his three terms. The 'Little Flower', as La Guardia was known, streamlined city government, paid down the debt and updated the transport, hospital, reservoir and sewer systems. New highways made the city more accessible, and North Beach (now LaGuardia) Airport became the city's first commercial landing field.

Helping La Guardia to modernise the city was Robert Moses, a hard-nosed visionary who would do much to shape – and in some cases, destroy – New York's landscape. Moses spent 44 years stepping on toes to build expressways, parks, beaches, public housing, bridges and tunnels, creating such landmarks as Lincoln Center, the United Nations complex and the Verrazano-Narrows Bridge, which connected Staten Island to Brooklyn in 1964.

Protest and reform

Despite La Guardia's belt-tightening and Moses's renovations, New York began to fall apart financially. When World War II ended,

800,000 industrial jobs disappeared from the city. Factories in need of more space moved to the suburbs, along with nearly five million residents. But more crowding occurred as rural African-Americans and Latinos (primarily Puerto Ricans) flocked to the metropolis in the 1950s and '60s, to meet with ruthless discrimination and a dearth of jobs. Moses's Slum Clearance Committee reduced many neighbourhoods to rubble, forcing out residents in order to build huge, isolating housing projects that became magnets for crime. In 1963, the city also lost Pennsylvania Station, when the Pennsylvania Railroad Company demolished the site over the protests of picketers to make way for a modern station and new sports and entertainment venue Madison Square Garden. It was a wake-up call for New York: architectural changes were hurtling out of control.

But Moses and his wrecking ball couldn't knock over one steadfast West Village woman. Architectural writer and urban-planning critic Jane Jacobs organised local residents when the city unveiled its plan to clear a 14-block tract of her neighbourhood to make space for yet more public housing. Her obstinacy was applauded by many, including an influential councilman named Ed Koch (who would become mayor in 1978). The group fought the plan and won, causing Mayor Robert F Wagner to back down. As a result of Jacobs's efforts in the wake of Pennsylvania Station's demolition, the Landmarks Preservation Commission – the first such group in the US – was established in 1965.

Allen Ginsberg and Jack Kerouac gathered in Village coffeehouses, and tiny clubs showcased folk musicians such as Bob Dylan

At the dawning of the Age of Aquarius, the city harboured its share of innovative creators. Allen Ginsberg, Jack Kerouac and others gathered in Village coffeehouses to create a new voice for poetry. A folk music scene brewed in tiny clubs around Bleecker Street, showcasing musicians such as Bob Dylan. A former advertising illustrator named Andy Warhol turned images of mass consumerism into deadpan, ironic art statements. And in 1969, the city's long-closeted gay communities came out into the streets, as patrons at the Stonewall Inn on Christopher Street demonstrated against a police raid. The protests, known as the Stonewall riots, gave birth to the modern gay rights movement.

Mean streets

By the early 1970s, deficits had forced heavy cutbacks in city services. The streets were dirty, and subway cars and buildings were scrawled with graffiti; crime skyrocketed as the city's debt deepened to $6 billion. Despite the huge downturn, construction commenced on the World Trade Center; when completed, in 1973, its twin 110-storey towers were the world's tallest buildings. Even as the WTC rose, the city became so desperately overdrawn that Mayor Abraham Beame appealed to the federal government for financial assistance in 1975. Yet President Gerald Ford refused to bail out the city.

Times Square had degenerated into a morass of sex shops and porn theatres, drug use rose and subway travel hit an all-time low due to a fear of crime. In 1977, serial killer Son of Sam terrorised the city with six killings, and a blackout one hot August night that same year led to widespread looting and arson. The angst of the time fuelled the punk culture that rose in downtown clubs such as CBGB. At the same time, celebrities, designers and models converged on Midtown to disco their nights away at Studio 54.

The Wall Street boom of the 1980s and fiscal petitioning by Mayor Ed Koch brought money flooding back into New York. Gentrification glamorised neighbourhoods such as Soho, Tribeca and the East Village, but deeper societal ills lurked. In 1988, a protest against the city's efforts to impose a strict curfew and displace the homeless from Tompkins Square Park erupted into a violent clash with the police. Crack use became endemic in the ghettos, homelessness rose and AIDS emerged as a new scourge.

By 1989, citizens were restless for change. They turned to David N Dinkins, electing him as the city's first black mayor. A distinguished, softly spoken man, Dinkins held office for only a single term, marked by a record murder rate, flaring racial tensions in Manhattan's Washington Heights and Brooklyn's Crown Heights and Flatbush neighbourhoods, and the explosion of a bomb in the basement parking garage of the World Trade Center in 1993 that killed six and injured 1,000.

Deeming the polite Dinkins ineffective, New Yorkers voted in former federal prosecutor Rudolph Giuliani. An abrasive leader, Giuliani used bullying tactics to get things done, as his 'quality of life' campaign cracked down on everything from drug dealing and pornography to unsolicited windshield washing. As cases of severe police brutality grabbed the headlines and racial polarisation was palpable, crime plummeted, tourism soared and New York became cleaner and safer than it had been in decades. Times Square was transformed into a family-friendly tourist destination, and the dot-com explosion brought young wannabes to the Flatiron District's Silicon Alley. Giuliani's second term as mayor would close, however, on a devastating tragedy.

21st-century trauma

On 11 September 2001, terrorists flew two hijacked passenger jets into the Twin Towers of the World Trade Center, collapsing the entire complex and killing nearly 3,000 people. Amid the trauma, the attack triggered a city-wide sense of unity, as New Yorkers did what they could to help their fellow citizens – from feeding emergency crews to cheering on rescue workers en route to Ground Zero.

Two months later, billionaire Michael Bloomberg was elected mayor and took on the daunting task of repairing not only the city's skyline but also its battered economy. The stock market revived, downtown businesses re-emerged and plans for rebuilding the World Trade Center were drawn. True to form, however, New Yorkers debated the future of the site for more than a year until architect Daniel Libeskind was awarded the redevelopment job in 2003. The 9/11 Memorial opened on 11 September 2011 and, in autumn 2013, the WTC's centrepiece tower, 1 World Trade Center, was officially declared the tallest building in the Western Hemisphere. With the opening of the 9/11 Memorial Museum in spring 2014, and the removal of the barriers surrounding the site, the new World Trade Center finally became fully accessible to the public.

While Mayor Bloomberg ushered in many reforms to make NYC a cleaner, healthier metropolis – from the 2003 smoking ban to a major plan to reduce greenhouse emissions – as his second term neared its end, he became increasingly frustrated that some of his pet proposals hadn't been realised. In the midst of 2008's deepening financial crisis, the mayor proposed a controversial bill to extend the tenure of elected officials from two four-year terms to three. The bill was narrowly passed by the New York City Council, and the incumbent won the subsequent elections with just 51 per cent of the vote to become the fourth mayor in New York's history to serve a third term. In October 2010, in a remarkable display of chutzpah, Bloomberg voted to restore the two-term limitation. Three years later, the city elected its first Democratic mayor in a generation, Bill de Blasio.

In June 2011, New York celebrated yet another civil rights milestone when it became the largest state in the US to legalise same-sex marriage.

Just before Halloween 2012, the city was rocked by Hurricane Sandy, a disaster without modern precedent that flooded the subway system, plunged lower Manhattan and other parts of the metropolis into darkness and left thousands of New Yorkers homeless. The fallout was still being felt years later; many businesses and landmarks – including the Statue of Liberty and Ellis Island – remained closed for months, others never recovered from the damage.

When Queens native Donald Trump was elected President of the United States in November 2016, Trump Tower became a magnet for anti-Trump protestors. Mayor de Blasio has since become a frequent opponent of the brash real estate developer and former reality TV star, calling for him to reveal his tax returns and criticising his immigration policies. The commitment of the Mayor of New York to protecting the rights of undocumented residents honours the history of what he has aptly termed 'a city of immigrants'.

Protesters outside Trump Tower

TRUMP MAKE AMERICA HATE AGAIN

Key Events

New York in brief

1524 Giovanni da Verrazano sails into New York Harbor.

1624 First Dutch settlers establish Nieuw Amsterdam.

1626 Peter Minuit purchases Manhattan for goods worth 60 guilders.

1639 The Swedish-born Broncks settle north of Manhattan.

1646 Village of Breuckelen founded.

1664 Dutch rule ends; Nieuw Amsterdam renamed New York.

1754 King's College (now Columbia University) founded.

1776 Battle for New York begins; fire ravages the city.

1783 George Washington's troops march triumphantly down Broadway.

1784 Alexander Hamilton founds the Bank of New York.

1785 City becomes nation's capital.

1789 President Washington inaugurated at Federal Hall.

1792 New York Stock Exchange opens.

1804 New York becomes country's most populous city, with around 80,000 inhabitants.

1811 Mayor DeWitt Clinton's grid plan for Manhattan introduced.

1827 Slavery officially abolished in New York State.

1851 *The New-York Daily Times* (now *The New York Times*) launched.

1873 Central Park is completed.

1880 Metropolitan Museum of Art opens.

1883 Brooklyn Bridge opens.

1886 Statue of Liberty unveiled.

1891 Carnegie Hall opens.

1892 Ellis Island launches as an immigration centre.

1898 The five boroughs are consolidated into the city of New York.

1900 Electric lights replace gas along lower Broadway.

1902 The Fuller (Flatiron) Building becomes the world's first skyscraper.

1904 New York's first subway line opens.

1908 First ball dropped in Times Square to celebrate the new year.

1911 Fire in the Triangle Shirtwaist Company kills 146.

1913 Woolworth Building completed; Grand Central Terminal opens.

1923 The first Yankee Stadium opens.

1929 Stock market crashes; Museum of Modern Art opens.

1931 George Washington Bridge completed; Empire State Building completed; Whitney Museum opens.

1934 Fiorello La Guardia elected mayor.

1939 New York hosts the World's Fair.

1950 United Nations complex finished.

1953 Robert Moses spearheads building of the Cross Bronx Expressway.

1957 Brooklyn Dodgers baseball team move to LA; New York Giants move to San Francisco.

1962 New York Mets debut at the Polo Grounds; Philharmonic Hall, first building in Lincoln Center, opens.

1964 Verrazano-Narrows Bridge completed; World's Fair held in Queens.

1970 First New York City Marathon.

1973 World Trade Center completed.

1975 On verge of bankruptcy, city is snubbed by federal government.

1977 Studio 54 opens; 4,000 arrested during city-wide blackout.

1989 David N Dinkins elected city's first black mayor.

1993 Bomb explodes in World Trade Center, killing six and injuring 1,000.

2001 Hijackers fly two jets into World Trade Center, killing nearly 3,000.

2004 Statue of Liberty reopens for first time since 9/11.

2009 Yankees and Mets move into new state-of-the-art stadiums.

2010 Mayor Michael Bloomberg is inaugurated as the fourth mayor in the city's history to serve a third term.

2011 Gay marriage is legalised in New York State; the 9/11 Memorial debuts.

2012 The Barclays Center, home to Brooklyn's first pro sports team since 1957, opens; Hurricane Sandy hits, paralysing the city.

2014 1 World Trade Center, the Western Hemisphere's tallest skyscraper, completed.

2016 Donald Trump is elected President of the United States, becoming the second native New Yorker to hold highest office (the first was Teddy Roosevelt in 1901).

Architecture

Tall stories

Manhattan, of course, is synonymous with skyscrapers. Following advances in iron and steel technology in the middle of the 19th century, and the pressing need for space on an already overcrowded island, New York's architects realised that the only way was up. The race to reach the heavens in the early 20th century was supplanted by the minimalist post-war International Style, which saw a rash of towering glass boxes spread across Midtown. That race has picked up pace today with a crop of freshly minted cloudbusters.

However, those with an architectural interest and an observant eye will be rewarded by the fascinating mix of styles and unexpected details closer to the ground in virtually every corner of the metropolis, from gargoyles crouching on the façade of an early 20th-century apartment building to extravagant cast-iron decoration adorning a humble warehouse. And it's worth remembering that under New York's gleaming exoskeleton of steel and glass lies the heart of a 17th-century Dutch city.

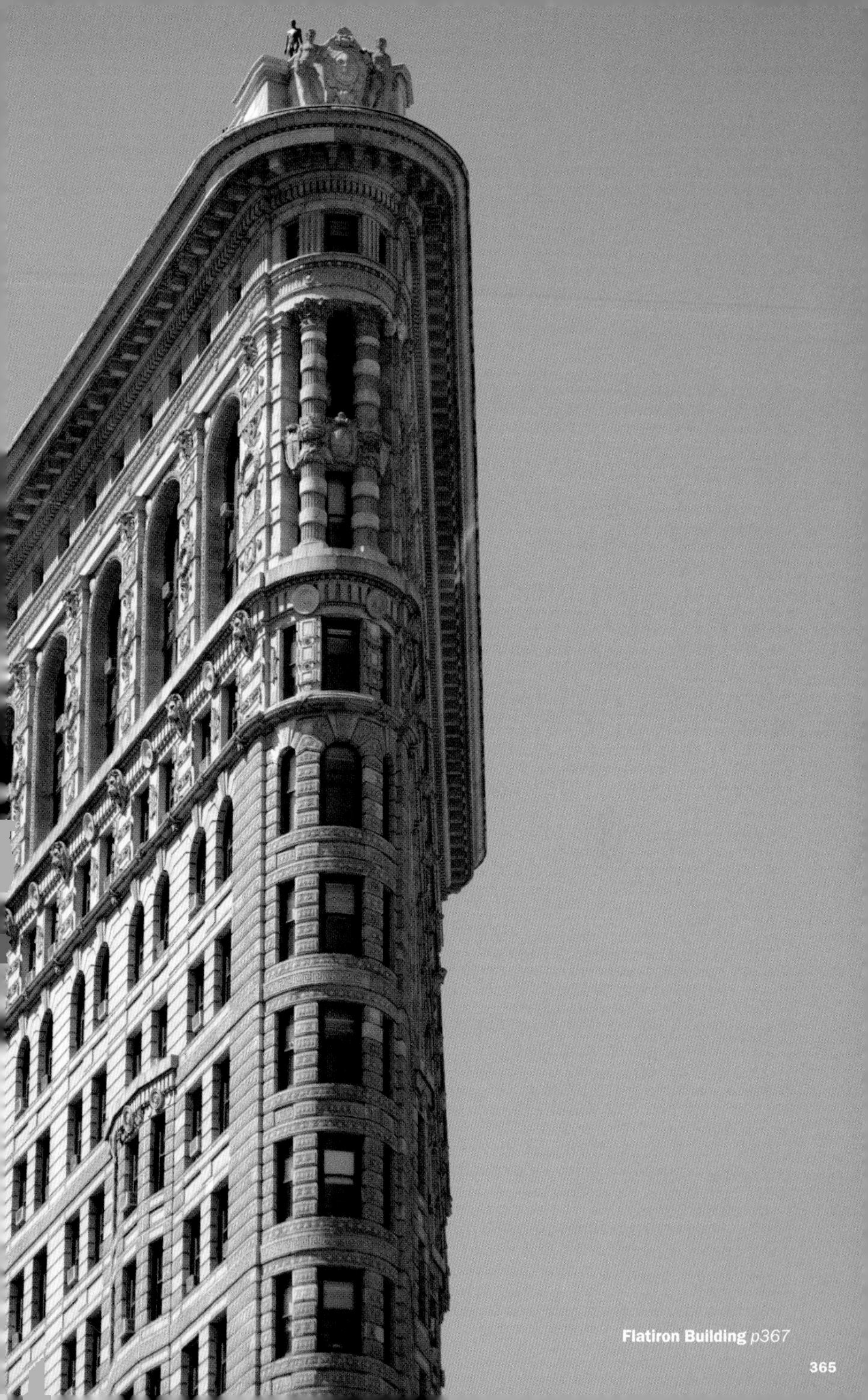

Flatiron Building *p367*

Lowland legacy

The Dutch influence is still traceable in the downtown web of narrow, winding lanes. Because the Cartesian grid that rules the city was laid out by the Commissioners Plan in 1811, only a few examples of Dutch architecture remain, mostly off the beaten path. One is the 1785 **Dyckman Farmhouse Museum** (4881 Broadway, at 204th Street, 1-212 304 9422, www.dyckmanfarmhouse. org; 11am-4pm Thur-Sat; 11am-3pm Sun; reduced hours in winter) in Inwood, Manhattan's northernmost neighbourhood. Its decorative brickwork and gambrel roof reflect the fashion of the late 18th century. The oldest house still standing in the five boroughs, however, is the **Wyckoff House Museum** (5816 Clarendon Road, at Ralph Avenue, Flatbush, Brooklyn, 1-718 629 5400, wyckoffmuseum.org; tours 1-3.30pm Fri, Sat). Erected around 1652, it's a typical Dutch farmhouse with deep eaves and roughly shingled walls.

In Manhattan, the only building left from pre-Revolutionary times is the stately columned and quoined **St Paul's Chapel** (*see p72*), completed in 1766 (a spire was added in 1796). George Washington, a parishioner here, was officially received in the chapel after his 1789 presidential inauguration. The Enlightenment ideals upon which the nation was founded influenced the church's non-hierarchical layout. **Trinity Church** (*see p72*) of 1846, one of the first and finest Gothic Revival churches in the country, was designed by Richard Upjohn. Its crocketed, finialed 281-foot spire held sway for decades as the tallest structure in Manhattan.

Holdouts remain from each epoch of the city's architectural history. An outstanding example of Greek Revival from the first half of the 19th century is the 1842 **Federal Hall National Memorial** (*see p72*), the mighty marble colonnaded structure on the site where George Washington took his oath of office. A larger-than-life statue of Washington by the sculptor John Quincy Adams Ward stands in front. The city's most celebrated blocks of Greek Revival townhouses, built in the 1830s, are known simply as the Row (1-13 Washington Square North, between Fifth Avenue & Washington Square West, Greenwich Village); they're exemplars of the more genteel metropolis of Henry James and Edith Wharton.

Greek Revival gave way to Renaissance-inspired Beaux Arts architecture, which itself reflected the imperial ambitions of a wealthy young nation during the Gilded Age of the late 19th century. Like Emperor Augustus, who boasted that he had found Rome a city of brick and left it a city of marble, the firm of McKim, Mead & White built noble civic monuments and *palazzi* for the rich. The best-known buildings of the classicist Charles Follen McKim include the main campus of **Columbia University** (*see p204*), begun in the 1890s, and the austere 1906 **Morgan Library** (*see p190*). His partner, socialite and bon vivant Stanford White (scandalously murdered by his mistress's husband in 1906 on the roof of the original Madison Square Garden, which he himself designed), conceived more festive spaces, such as the **Metropolitan Club** (1 E 60th Street, at Fifth Avenue) and the luxe Villard Houses of 1882, now part of the **Lotte New York Palace Hotel** (455 Madison Avenue, between 50th & 51st Streets).

Downtown, the old Alexander Hamilton US Custom House, which now houses the **National Museum of the American Indian** (*see p70*), was built by Cass Gilbert in 1907 and is a symbol of New York Harbor's significance in Manhattan's growth (before 1913, the city's chief source of revenue was customs duties). Gilbert's domed marble edifice is suitably monumental – its carved figures of the Four Continents are by Daniel Chester French, the sculptor of the Lincoln Memorial in Washington, DC. Another Beaux Arts treasure is Carrère & Hastings' sumptuous white marble **New York Public Library** of 1911 (*see p184*), built on the site of a former Revolutionary War battleground. The 1913 travertine-lined **Grand Central Terminal** (*see p188*) remains an elegant transport hub, thanks to preservationists who saved it from the wrecking ball.

Vertical reality

Cast-iron architecture peaked in the latter half of the 19th century, coinciding with the Civil War. Iron and steel components freed architects from the bulk, weight and cost of stone, and allowed them to build taller structures. Cast-iron columns – cheap to mass-produce – could support enormous weight. The façades of many Soho buildings, with their intricate details of Italianate columns, were manufactured on assembly lines and could be ordered in pieces from catalogues. This led to an aesthetic of uniform building façades, which had a direct impact on later steel skyscrapers and continues to inform the skyline today. To enjoy one of the most telling vistas of skyscraper history, gaze north from the 1859 **Cooper Union Building** (*see p122*) in the East Village, the oldest steel-beam-framed building in America.

The most visible effect of the move towards cast-iron construction was the way it opened up solid-stone façades to expanses of glass. In fact, window-shopping came

New York Public Library

into vogue in the 1860s. Mrs Lincoln bought the White House china at the **Haughwout Store** (488-492 Broadway, at Broome Street). The 1857 building's Palladian-style façade recalls Renaissance Venice, but its regular, open fenestration was also a portent of the future. (The cast-iron elevator sign is a relic of the world's first working safety passenger elevator, designed by Elisha Graves Otis in 1852.)

Once engineers created the interlocking steel-cage construction that distributed the weight of a building over its entire frame, the sky was the limit

Once engineers perfected steel, which is stronger and lighter than iron, and created the interlocking steel-cage construction that distributed the weight of a building over its entire frame, the sky was the limit. New York has one structure by the great Chicago-based innovator Louis Sullivan:

the 1898 Bayard-Condict Building (65-69 Bleecker Street, between Broadway & Lafayette Street). Though only 13 storeys tall, Sullivan's building, covered with richly decorative terracotta, was one of the earliest to have a purely vertical design rather than one that imitated the horizontal styles of the past. Sullivan wrote that a skyscraper 'must be tall, every inch of it tall... From bottom to top, it is a unit without a single dissenting line.'

The 21-storey **Flatiron Building** (*see p162*), designed by fellow Chicagoan Daniel H Burnham and completed in 1902, is another standout of the era. Its height and modern design combined with traditional masonry decoration was made possible only by its steel-cage construction.

The new century saw a frenzy of skyward construction, resulting in buildings of record-breaking height. When it was built in 1899, the 30-storey, 391-foot **Park Row Building** (15 Park Row, between Ann & Beekman Streets) was the tallest building in the world; by 1931, though, Shreve, Lamb & Harmon's Empire State Building (*see p182*) had more than tripled its record. (For more on the battle for the city's tallest building, *see p369*). Although they were retroactively labelled art deco (such buildings were then simply called 'modern'), the Empire State's setbacks were actually a response to the zoning code of 1916, which required a building's upper storeys to be tapered in order not to block out sunlight and air circulation to the streets. The code engendered some of the city's most fanciful architectural designs, such as the ziggurat-crowned 1926 **Paramount Building** (1501 Broadway, between 43rd & 44th Streets) and the romantically slender spire of the former **Cities Service Building** (70 Pine Street, at Pearl Street), illuminated from within like an enormous rare gem.

Outside the box

The post-World War II period saw the rise of the International Style, pioneered by such giants as Le Corbusier and Ludwig Mies van der Rohe. The International Style relied on a new set of aesthetics: minimal decoration, clear expression of construction, an honest use of materials and a near-Platonic harmony of proportions. The style's most visible symbol was the all-glass façade, similar to that found on the sleek slab of the **United Nations Headquarters' Secretariat Building** (*see p188*).

Designed by Gordon Bunshaft of Skidmore, Owings & Merrill, **Lever House** (390 Park Avenue, between 53rd & 54th Streets) became the city's first all-steel-and-glass structure in 1952. It's almost impossible to imagine the radical vision this glass construction represented on the all-masonry corridor of Park Avenue, because nearly every building since has followed suit. Mies van der Rohe's celebrated bronze-skinned **Seagram Building** (375 Park Avenue, between 52nd & 53rd Streets), which reigns in isolation in its own plaza, is the epitome of the architect's cryptic dicta that 'Less is more' and 'God is in the details'. The detailing on the building is exquisite – the custom-made bolts securing the miniature bronze piers that run the length of the façade must be polished by hand every year to keep them from oxidising and turning green. With this heady combination of grandeur and attention to detail, it's the Rolls-Royce of skyscrapers.

High modernism began to show cracks in its façade during the mid 1960s. By then, New York had built too many such structures in Midtown and below. The public had never fully warmed to the undecorated style, and the International Style's sheer arrogance in trying to supplant the traditional city structure didn't endear the movement to anyone. The **MetLife Building** (200 Park Avenue, at 45th Street), originally the **Pan Am Building** of 1963, was the prime culprit, not so much because of its design (by Walter Gropius of the Bauhaus) but because of its presumptuous location, straddling Park Avenue and looming over Grand Central. There was even a plan to raze Grand Central and construct a twin Pan Am in its place. The

International Style had obviously reached the end of its life when Philip Johnson, instrumental in defining the movement with his book *The International Style* (co-written with Henry-Russell Hitchcock), began disparaging the aesthetic as 'glass-boxitis'.

A different approach was provided by Boston architect Hugh Stubbins's triangle-topped **Citigroup Center** (601 Lexington Avenue, between 53rd & 54th Streets), which utilised contemporary engineering (the building cantilevers almost magically on high stilts above street level) while harking back to the decorative tops of yesteryear. Sly old Johnson turned the tables on everyone with the heretical Chippendale crown on his tower at 550 Madison Avenue (between 55th & 56th Streets), a bold throwback to decoration for its own sake.

Postmodernism provided a theoretical basis for a new wave of buildings that mixed past and present, often taking cues from the environs. Some notable examples include Helmut Jahn's 425 Lexington Avenue (between 43rd & 44th Streets) of 1988; David Childs's retro diamond-tipped **Worldwide Plaza** (825 Eighth Avenue, between 49th & 50th Streets) of 1989; and the honky-tonk agglomeration of Skidmore, Owings & Merrill's **Bertelsmann Building** (1540 Broadway, between 45th & 46th Streets) of 1990. But even postmodernism became old hat after a while: too many architects relied on fussy fenestration and passive commentary on other styles, and too few were creating vital new building façades.

The electronic spectacle of **Times Square** (*see p177*) provided one possible direction for architects. Upon seeing the myriad electric lights of Times Square in 1922, British wit GK Chesterton remarked: 'What a glorious garden of wonder this would be, to anyone who was lucky enough to be unable to read.' The Crossroads of the World continues to be at the cybernetic cutting edge, with the 120-foot-tall, quarter-acre-in-area NASDAQ sign; the real-time stock tickers and jumbo TV screens; and the news ticker wrapping round the original 1904 *New York Times* HQ, 1 Times Square (between Broadway & Seventh Avenue).

Shifting cityscape

New York City is in the midst of a 21st-century building boom that was briefly halted by the recession. In a reversal of the city's historical pattern of development, there has been significant new construction downtown. The **Blue building** (105 Norfolk Street, between Delancey & Rivington Streets), Bernard Tschumi's multifaceted, blue glass-walled condominium, is a startling breakaway from the low-rise brick

Race to the Top

How NYC's architects egged each other onwards and upwards

For nearly half a century after its 1846 completion, the 281-foot steeple of Richard Upjohn's Gothic Revival **Trinity Church** (*see p72*) reigned in lonely serenity at the foot of Wall Street as the tallest structure in Manhattan. The church was finally topped in 1890 by the since-demolished, 348-foot **New York World Building**. But it wasn't until the turn of the century that New York's architects started to reach for the skies. So began a mad rush to the top, with building after building capturing the title of the world's tallest.

When it was completed in 1899, the 30-storey, 391-foot **Park Row Building** (15 Park Row, between Ann and Beekman Streets) enjoyed that lofty distinction. However, its record was shattered by the 612-foot **Singer Building** in 1908 (which, in 1968, became the tallest building ever to be demolished); the 52-storey, 700-foot **Metropolitan Life Tower** (*see p162*) of 1909; and the 793-foot **Woolworth Building** (*see p83*), Cass Gilbert's Gothic 1913 masterpiece.

The Woolworth stood in solitary splendour until skyscraper construction reached a crescendo in the late 1920s, with a famed three-way race. The now largely forgotten former **Bank of Manhattan Building** at 40 Wall Street was briefly the record-holder, at 71 storeys and 927 feet in 1930. Soon after, William Van Alen, the architect of the **Chrysler Building** (*see p188*), unveiled his secret weapon: a 'vertex', a spire of chrome nickel steel put together inside the dome and raised from within, which brought the building's height to 1,046 feet. But then, 13 months later, Van Alen's homage to the Automobile Age was itself outstripped by Shreve, Lamb & Harmon's 1,250-foot **Empire State Building** (*see p182*). With its broad base, narrow shaft and needled crown, it remains the quintessential skyscraper, and one of the most famous buildings in the world. (The ESB's lightning rod/broadcasting antenna, which officially brings the structure's height up to 1,454 feet, was added in 1950.)

Incredibly, there were no challengers for the distinction of New York's – and the world's – tallest building for more than 40 years, until the 110-storey, 1,362- and 1,368-foot **Twin Towers** of Minoru Yamasaki's World Trade Center were completed in 1973. They were trumped by Chicago's **Sears Tower** a year later, but the **World Trade Center** (*see p80*) has since regained the title. With the 1,776-foot 1 World Trade Center, NYC beat the Windy City as home to America's tallest skyscraper.

1 World Trade Center

buildings of the Lower East Side. Also noteworthy is the Japanese firm SANAA's **New Museum of Contemporary Art** (*see p113*); its asymmetrically staggered boxy volumes covered in aluminium mesh shake up the traditional street front of the Bowery. A block north, Norman Foster's slender gallery building for Sperone Westwater art dealers – complete with a 12- by 20-foot lift that doubles as a moving exhibition space – occupies a narrow gap at 257 Bowery (between Stanton & Houston Streets). On the West Side, the **Urban Glass House** (330 Spring Street, at Washington Street), one of Philip Johnson's last designs, sprang up in 2006 amid Tribeca's hulking industrial edifices. The mini-skyscraper is a multiplication of his iconic **Glass House** in New Canaan, Connecticut. Just south of City Hall, the curled and warped stainless-steel façade of 2011's 76-storey **New York by Gehry** (8 Spruce Street, between Nassau & William Streets) has the unmistakable stamp of its creator.

432 Park Avenue

Midtown is seeing the rise of innovative structures and a new era of green, eco-conscious architecture

By 2008, the redevelopment of the World Trade Center, conceived by Daniel Libeskind, was years behind schedule and billions of dollars over budget. However, the **9/11 Memorial Plaza** opened in time for the tenth anniversary of the Twin Towers' fall and David Childs' 1,776-foot 1 World Trade Center (*see p80*) is now the tallest building in the Western Hemisphere. Santiago Calatrava's subterranean **World Trade Center Transportation Hub**, with its cavernous main hall topped by the dramatic winged Oculus structure, debuted in 2016, and with the completion of a fourth tower, the site finally has the feel of a cohesive public space rather than a work in progress.

New heights

While it may seem extraordinary in such an already-dense urban area, Midtown is seeing the rise of innovative structures and a new era of green, eco-conscious architecture. With torqued, glass facets reaching 54 storeys, Cook + Fox's 2010 **Bank of America Tower** at 1 Bryant Park (Sixth Avenue, between 42nd & 43rd Streets) has a thermal storage system, daylight dimmers, green roofs and double-wall construction

to reduce heat build-up. Renzo Piano's 2007 tower for the *New York Times* at 620 Eighth Avenue (between 40th & 41st Streets) also offers such green amenities as automatic shades that respond to the heat of the sun.

After years of setbacks, Pritzker Prize-winner Jean Nouvel's **53 West 53** (53 W 53rd Street), next to the Museum of Modern Art, finally reached its full 82-storey height. The sloped, crystalline structure, with an exoskeleton of irregularly crossing beams, was initially proposed to reach 1,250 feet, but the tower was opposed by activists who feared that its shadow would loom over Central Park, and it was rejected by the city's Planning Commission. After 200 feet were snipped off the top, the plan received the green light.

Several notable cloud-piercers have sprung up on West 57th Street. An east–west walk from Park Avenue will take you past Rafael Viñoly's 1,396-foot **432 Park Avenue** – briefly the tallest residential building in the Western Hemisphere, but soon to be overtaken by under-construction giants nearby – and Christian de Portzamparc's 1,000-foot **One57**. Both of these recent additions to the strip dwarf the **Hearst Tower** (300 W 57th Street, at Eighth Avenue), which was enhanced in 2006 with Norman Foster's elegant 46-storey crystalline addition to the art deco base. The structure is a breathtaking combination of old and new, with the massive triangular struts of the tower penetrating the façade of the base and opening up great airy spaces within. On the street's far western stretch, the eye-popping tetrahedron apartment building **Via 57 West** (625 W 57th Street, between 11th & 12th Avenues), by buzzed-about Danish architect Bjarke Ingels, is a bold addition to the skyline and home to restaurants and a Landmark cinema.

If you build it...

Ambitious new projects have changed the character of entire neighbourhoods, notably on the once-industrial far West Side. The development of the **High Line** (*see p156*) led to an explosion of striking (and not so striking) residential structures in the suddenly desirable blocks alongside the linear park, including Annabelle Selldorf's 19-storey apartment building at 200 Eleventh Avenue and 24th Street, which even has a car elevator. Renzo Piano's **Whitney Museum of American Art** (*see p147*) anchors the southern end, while a curvy, futuristic condo building designed by late Pritzker Prize-winning architect Zaha Hadid is in the northern stretch at 28th Street. Now largely obscured from view from the elevated park by newer structures, Frank Gehry's 2007 **IAC Building** (555 W 18th Street, at West Side Highway) is a ten-storey, white-glass mirage of a building comprising tilting glass volumes that resemble a fully rigged tall ship.

Best-laid plans

Spring 2019 saw the opening of the eastern section of the graceful if grandiose 28-acre

Hudson Yards, the city's largest private real-estate development since Rockefeller Center. The Eastern Yards comprise commercial and residential buildings and a public square connected to the top of the High Line at West 30th Street. The park's centrepiece is an eight-level, climbable, honeycomb-esque installation by British architect Thomas Heatherwick. Designed by Diller Scofidio + Renfro in collaboration with the Rockwell Group, the complex's cutting-edge arts centre, **The Shed**, has a show-stopping party trick. An enormous shell covered in translucent panels of a Teflon-based polymer can be pulled up over the entire eight-storey structure or rolled out to turn the spacious outside courtyard into a massive enclosed space. But there is more razzle-dazzle to come in 2020 with the opening of the outdoor observation deck on lead architect William Pedersen's super-tall 30 Hudson Yards tower. The vertiginous ledge juts out 65 feet from the building, 1,100 feet above the ground. The only constant in New York is constant change.

To keep up with what's going up, visit the **AIA Center for Architecture** (*see p138*), the **Skyscraper Museum** (*see p79*) and the **Storefront for Art and Architecture** (97 Kenmare Street, between Mulberry Street & Cleveland Place, Nolita, 1-212 431 5795, www.storefrontnews.org, closed Mon & Sun), a non-profit organisation that hosts exhibitions, talks, screenings and more.

Hudson Yards

Plan

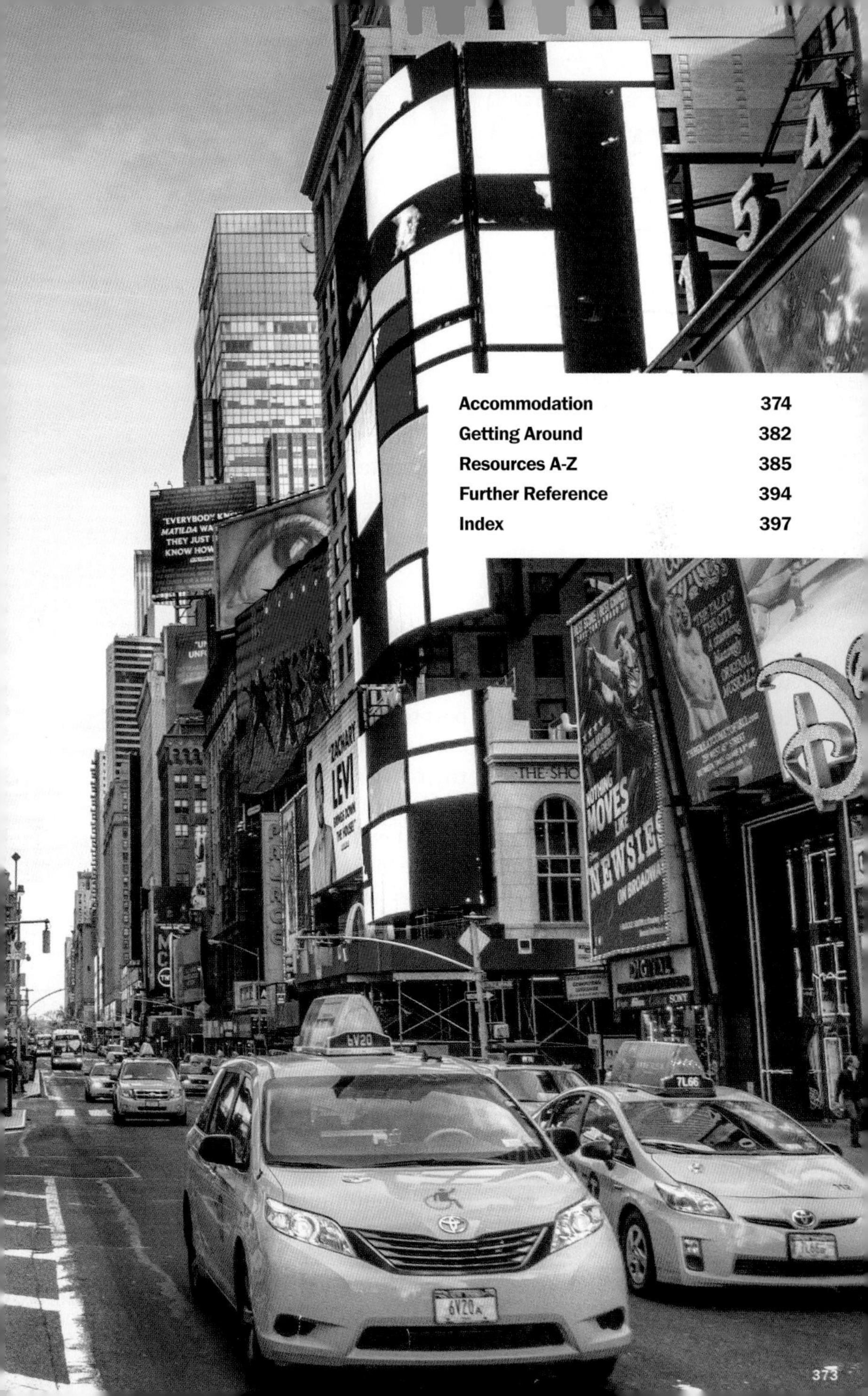
ZACHARY
LEVI
NOTHING MOVES LIKE
NEWSIES
ON BROADWAY

Accommodation

New York's hotel business is booming – the official tourism board reports that more than 125 new properties have opened during the past five years. And despite an average room rate of more than $300 a night in the autumn high season, hotels are nearly full most of the year, according to data and analytics specialist STR. There is now more choice than ever in popular areas such as the Flatiron District, Soho and the Lower East Side. But a significant percentage of new development is in the outer boroughs, especially Brooklyn.

Information and prices

In response to the competition, hotels increasingly offer perks such as guest bikes, free Wi-Fi and local calls, and enhanced in-room technology such as tablets. The best time to get a bargain is during the frigid months of January and February, when rates are at their lowest, according to STR's data, but deals can also be had in high summer, especially August, when high temperatures and humidity drive locals who can afford it to nearby resort areas such as

Sister City p380

In the know
Price categories

Our price categories are based on hotels' standard prices (not including seasonal offers or discounts) for one night in a double room with en suite shower/bath. Bear in mind that, at many properties, pricing veers from budget to expensive, depending on the time of year.

Luxury	$500+
Expensive	$300-$500
Moderate	$150-$300
Budget	up to $150

Ace Hotel New York *p379*

the Hamptons. You may also find reduced prices on individual hotel websites or reservation sites such as Booking.com. Peak season is September and October, when high-profile events such as Fashion Week draw hordes of visitors and the autumn cultural calendar is in full swing.

Building regulations, accommodation taxes and a law prohibiting rentals of less than 30 days in buildings with three or more units makes hosting B&Bs challenging in New York City, but long-established agency **City Sonnet** (1-212 614 3034, www.citysonnet.com) can arrange stays in Manhattan or Long Island City, Queens, starting at around $175 a night. For longer periods, the agency offers stylish, individually decorated one- and two-bedroom lofts, starting at $3,000 a month. Rates include all fees. Alternatively, you can rent a Brooklyn loft space for 30 days or more at **Habitat 101** (1-718 349-2200, www. habitat101brooklyn.com), a converted factory in hip Greenpoint with locally crafted furniture and artwork, from around $4,000 for a studio.

We've listed our favourite places to stay in the city in each price category, but you can find additional listings at www.timeout.com/newyork. Rates can vary wildly according to the season or room category, but our price categories (*see* p374) provide a general guide. Note that most NYC accommodation is non-smoking.

Boro Hotel *p379*

In the know
Taxing times

When budgeting for accommodation, don't forget to factor in 14.75 per cent tax, plus an extra $3.50 per night for most rooms.

Luxury
The Beekman
123 Nassau Street, between Ann &
Beekman Streets (1-212 233 2300,
www.thompsonhotels.com).
Subway A, C, J, Z, 2, 3, 4, 5 to
Fulton Street; R, W to City Hall, 4,
5, 6 to Brooklyn Bridge-City Hall.
Rooms *287.* **Map** *p71 E32.*
During a stay at the Beekman
Hotel, you'll keep returning to one
thing: its breathtaking nine-storey
Victorian atrium, capped by a
pyramidal skylight. Not only are
most of the rooms located off the
galleries surrounding it, but the
image of that dramatic
centrepiece will linger in your
mind. Originally built in 1881, the
early skyscraper was in a state of
neglect when it was acquired by
Thompson Hotels and restored.
The airy, high-ceilinged guest
quarters mix period detail with a
contemporary sensibility: wooden
floors, custom-designed oak beds
with leather headboards and
luxurious Sferra linens, eclectic
vintage pieces, and sleek marble-
tiled bathrooms. Flanking the
atrium bar, the hotel's two
restaurants, chef Tom Colicchio's
Temple Court (*see p83*) and
period-perfect French bistro
Augustine, draw a chic crowd that
keeps the common areas buzzing.

Gramercy Park Hotel
2 Lexington Avenue, at 21st Street,
Gramercy Park (1-212 920 3300,
1-866 784 1300, www.gramercy
parkhotel.com). Subway 6 to
23rd Street. **Rooms** *190.* **Map**
p163 E26.
Other NYC hotels have guest-only
rooftops or gardens, but only one

In the know
Secret garden

The **Gramercy Park Hotel's**
greatest amenity is guest
access to nearby **Gramercy
Park** (see *p170*) – one
of the most exclusive
outdoor spaces in the city. A
member of staff will escort
you there and unlock the
gate. If you want to linger,
you'll either have to wave to
the door staff, or call or text
the hotel to be let out.

---

boasts access to the city's most
storied private outdoor space:
Gramercy Park. The hotel's
interior resembles a baronial
manor occupied by a rock star,
with rustic wooden beams and a
roaring fire in the lobby; an art
collection worth more than $65
million, including works by Jean-
Michel Basquiat, Damien Hirst
and Andy Warhol; and studded
velvet headboards and mahogany
drink cabinets in the bedrooms.
Get a taste of the Eternal City in
Maialino, Danny Meyer's tribute
to Roman trattorias, and end the
evening with a nightcap at the
exclusive Rose Bar.

Greenwich Hotel
377 Greenwich Street, between
Franklin & North Moore Streets,
Tribeca (1-212 941 8900, www.
thegreenwichhotel.com). Subway 1
to Franklin Street. **Rooms** *88.*
Map *p87 D31.*
The design inspiration at this
Tribeca retreat, co-owned by
Robert De Niro, is as international
as the jet-set clientele.
Individually decorated rooms
combine custom-made English
leather seating, Tibetan rugs and
gorgeous Moroccan or Carrara-
marble-tiled bathrooms, most
outfitted with capacious tubs that
fill up in a minute flat (bath salts
from Nolita spa Red Flower are
provided). In the tranquil
subterranean spa, the pool is
beneath the frame of a 250-year-
old Kyoto farmhouse. For dinner,
there's no need to rub shoulders
with the masses at the busy house
restaurant, Locanda Verde – have
your meal delivered to the
cloistered courtyard.

New York EDITION
5 Madison Avenue, at 24th
Street (1-212 413 4200, www.
editionhotels.com).
Subway R, W, 6 to 23rd Street.
Rooms *273.* **Map** *p163 E26.*
Fancy spending the night in one
of the city's most iconic buildings,
overlooking Madison Square
Park? The Metropolitan Life clock
tower is home to a hotel from Ian
Schrager-Marriott brand
EDITION. Inside the 1909
skyscraper, the clean-lined rooms
are light and luxurious, done up

with blond-wood floors and
creamy linen seating, offset by
walnut headboards. You'll find
products with an exclusive scent
by cult perfumer Le Labo in the
minimalist stone-accented
bathrooms. The Clocktower
restaurant – helmed by Michelin-
starred London chef Jason
Atherton – pays homage to the
building's period with clubby
mahogany panelling, a billiards
room and 24-carat-gold bar.
Among the attractions of the new
Times Square EDITION are a fine-
dining restaurant from acclaimed
chef John Fraser and a decadent
nightspot with dinner theatre
courtesy of artsy collective House
of Yes (*see p312*). **Other location**
20 Times Square, 701 Seventh
Avenue, Theater District (1-212
398 7017).

The Plaza
768 Fifth Avenue, at Central Park
South, Midtown (1-212 759 3000,
1-888 850 0909, www.theplazany.
com). Subway N, R, W to Fifth
Avenue-59th Street. **Rooms** *282.*
Map *p175 E22.*
The closest thing to a palace in
New York, this 1907 French
Renaissance-style landmark
reopened in 2008 after a two-year,
$400-million renovation.
Although 152 rooms were
converted into private condo
units, guests can still check into
one of 282 elegantly appointed
quarters with Louis XIV-inspired
furnishings and white-glove
butler service. The opulent vibe
extends to the bathrooms, which
feature mosaic baths, 24-carat
gold-plated sink fittings and even
chandeliers – perhaps to make the
foreign royals feel at home.
Embracing the 21st century, the
hotel has equipped every room
with an iPad. The legendary Oak
Room and Oak Bar, both
designated landmarks, are now
open only for private events, but
you can still take afternoon tea in
the restored Palm Court. There's
also a luxurious Guerlain spa and
an upscale food hall conceived by
celebrity chef Todd English,
which includes both old and new
cult NYC purveyors, such as
William Greenberg Desserts and
No. 7 Sub.

COME LIE WITH US

From five-star stays to budget beds and brilliant boutiques, we've hand-picked the best hotels for you to book online.

 TIMEOUT.COM/ NEWYORK/HOTELS

THE BEST OF THE CITY

The Ludlow

The Surrey

20 E 76th Street, between Fifth & Madison Avenues, Upper East Side (1-212 288 3700, 1-888 419 0052, www.thesurreyhotel.com). Subway 6 to 77th Street. **Rooms** *189.* **Map** *p209 E20.*

Occupying an elegant 1920s building given a $60 million overhaul, the Surrey updates the grand hotel model. The coolly elegant limestone and marble lobby showcases museum-quality contemporary art, and guestrooms are dressed in a refined palette of cream, grey and beige, with the addition of luxurious white marble bathrooms. But the centrepiece is undoubtedly the incredibly comfortable DUX by Duxiana bed, swathed in sumptuous Sferra linens. The hotel is flanked by top chef Daniel Boulud's Café Boulud and his chic cocktail destination, Bar Pleiades (see p211). There's also a luxurious spa.

Expensive

The Broome

431 Broome Street, between Broadway & Crosby Street, Soho (1-212 431 2929, www.thebroome nyc.com). Subway 6 to Spring Street. **Rooms** *14.* **Map** *p87 E30.*

The Broome takes the boutique concept to new bijou levels. Set in a five-storey 1825 building and co-owned by four long-time local restaurateurs, it has just 14 rooms, furnished with residential pieces from chic interior stores such as Mitchell Gold & Bob Williams and Design Within Reach. Many guestrooms overlook the open-air interior courtyard, where Moroccan tiles, flower boxes, and classic French café tables create a tranquil setting for the complimentary continental breakfast in warm weather – croissants are baked on-site. With a one-to-one staff-to-room ratio, you can expect personal attention and nice touches such as lavender-and-bergamot-infused sheets, free local calls and movies.

Chambers Hotel

15 W 56 Street, between Fifth & Sixth Avenues, Midtown (1-212 974 5656, www.chambershotel.com). Subway E, M to Fifth Avenue-53rd Street. **Rooms** *77.* **Map** *p175 E22.*

Room design at this small boutique hotel takes its cue from upscale New York loft apartments, combining designer furniture with raw concrete ceilings, exposed pipes, floor-to-ceiling windows and polished walnut floorboards or Tibetan wool carpeting. Guest quarters also feature some of the 500-piece art collection. Everything is designed to make you feel at home, from the soft terrycloth slippers in bright colours to the architect's desks stocked with a roll of paper and coloured pencils should creative inspiration hit.

The Ludlow

180 Ludlow Street, between Houston & Stanton Streets, Lower East Side (1-212 432 1818, www. ludlowhotel.com). Subway F to Lower East Side-Second Avenue. **Rooms** *175.* **Map** *p111 G29.*

With a prime spot on the buzzing Lower East Side, this purpose-built red-brick boutique property has an artfully aged interior, but the design is eclectic. An oak-panelled lobby leads to a sprawling living room with a salvaged limestone fireplace and a bar that spills out on to an ivy-clad patio. Rooms mix classic and contemporary elements: big factory-style windows, rustic ceiling beams, Indo-Portuguese four-poster beds and petrified-wood nightstands. Bathrooms are fitted with brass rain showers or soaking tubs and Maison Margiela robes. The hotel restaurant, Dirty French, is helmed by the team behind Carbone (see p138).

NoMad New York

1170 Broadway, at 28th Street, Flatiron District (1-212 796 1500, www.thenomadhotel.com). Subway R, W to 28th Street. **Rooms** *168.* **Map** *p163 E26.*

As with nearby hipster hub the Ace Hotel, the NoMad is a self-contained microcosm encompassing destination dining – courtesy of Daniel Humm and Will Guidara, of the Michelin-three-starred Eleven Madison Park (see p166) – and a buzzing bar. Jacques Garcia, designer of Paris celeb hangout Hôtel Costes, transformed the interior of a 1903 New York office building into this convincing facsimile of a grand hotel. The chic rooms, furnished with vintage Heriz rugs and distressed-leather armchairs, are more personal – Garcia based the design on his old Paris apartment. Many feature old-fashioned claw-foot tubs for a scented soak in Côté Bastide bath salts.

Standard, High Line

848 Washington Street, at 13th Street, Meatpacking District (1-212 645 4646, www.standardhotels. com). Subway A, C, E to 14th Street; L to Eighth Avenue. **Rooms** *338.* **Map** *p137 C29.*
The lauded West Coast mini-chain arrived in New York in 2009. Straddling the High Line, the retro 18-storey structure has been configured to give each room an exhilarating view, either of the river or a Midtown cityscape. Quarters are compact (from 230sq ft) but the combination of floor-to-ceiling windows, curving tambour wood panelling and 'peekaboo' bathrooms (with Japanese-style tubs or huge showerheads) give a sense of space. Eating and drinking options include an upscale grill, a beer garden and a swanky top-floor bar with 360-degree vistas. Nightspot Le Bain (see p310) has a massive jacuzzi in the middle of the dance floor. **Other location** 25 Cooper Square, between 5th & 6th Streets, East Village (1-212 475 5700).

Wythe Hotel

80 Wythe Avenue, at North 11th Street, Williamsburg, Brooklyn (1-718 460 8000, www.wythehotel. com). Subway L to Bedford Avenue. **Rooms** *70.* **Map** *p249 J27.*
A 1901 cooperage near the waterfront topped with a three-storey glass-and-aluminium addition, the Wythe embodies

In the know
Hotel Art

The **Wythe Hotel**'s 50-foot-tall 'hotel' sign was created from salvaged tin signage by local artist Tom Fruin. Some of the rooms look out on to an exterior wall decorated with a Steve Powers graffiti mural that recreates vintage Brooklyn advertising.

Brooklyn industrial-artisan chic. Heated concrete floors, exposed brick, reclaimed-timber beds and witty, custom-designed wallpaper create a rustic-industrial vibe, offset by fully plugged-in technology: a cable by the bed turns your iPhone into a surround-sound music system. In many of the rooms, floor-to-ceiling windows offer a Manhattan skyline panorama. There's also an airy, all-day restaurant, Reynard (see p251).

Moderate
Ace Hotel New York

20 W 29th Street, at Broadway, Flatiron District (1-212 679 2222, 1-212 991 0551, www.acehotel. com). Subway R, W to 28th Street. **Rooms** *272.* **Map** *p163 E26.*
Founded in Seattle by a pair of DJs, this cool chainlet has expanded beyond the States to London and Kyoto. In its New York digs, the musical influence is clear: select rooms in the 1904 building have functioning turntables, stacks of vinyl and gleaming Martin guitars. And while you'll pay a hefty amount for the sprawling loft spaces, there are options for those on a smaller budget, outfitted with vintage furniture and original art. In the buzzing lobby, the bar is set within a panelled library salvaged from a Madison Avenue apartment, and DJs or other performers add to the atmosphere almost every night. On-site dining options include chef April Bloomfield's Breslin Bar & Dining Room, and there's an outpost of Opening Ceremony (see p91) if you haven't a thing to wear. A Brooklyn location is in the works.

Boro Hotel

38-28 27th Street, at 39th Avenue, Long Island City, Queens (1-718 433 1375, www.borohotel.com). Subway N, W to 39th Avenue. **Rooms** *108.* **Map** *p259 J21.*
There's one thing you can't get in a Manhattan hotel room: the spectacular skyline views that are only possible from the other side of the water. But the interior of this boutique hotel will also catch your eye. Exposed concrete ceilings and cinderblocks, nods to the area's industrial roots, are softened with white oak flooring. Guest rooms with floor-to-ceiling windows are sparsely furnished with cool contemporary pieces such as custom-made leather chairs, Jasper Morrison for Vitra cork stools and, in some quarters, deep freestanding soaking tubs. Many rooms include balconies, and you can also take in the view from the seasonal rooftop bar. The library-lounge has books curated by NYC institution Strand Book Store, and there's a hip pizza restaurant, Beebe's.

citizenM New York

218 W 50th Street, between Broadway & Eighth Avenue, Theater District (1-212 461 3638, www.citizenm.com). Subway C, E to 50th Street; N, R, W to 49th Street; 1 to 50th Street. **Rooms** *230.* **Map** *p175 D23.*
The fast-growing citizenM brand aims to democratise the luxury-hotel experience. With rates starting at around $200 a night, guests can kick back on a $10,000 Vitra armchair in the eclectic lobby and admire the 26ft-tall installation *Walking in Times Square* by Julian Opie. Catering to a time-zone-crossing, tech-savvy clientele (the M stands for 'mobile'), the Amsterdam-based company has devised a new model informed by its founders' travel frustrations, cutting high-overhead amenities such as room service in the process. The 24-hour canteenM dispenses cocktails (until 2am), coffee, all-day breakfast and other dishes. The compact rooms focus on the essentials: an extra-large king-size bed and a powerful rain shower (in a cool cubicle with coloured ceiling lights). You can control the

hue, and everything else in the room – from the blinds to the smart TV– using a tablet.

Duane Street Hotel

130 Duane Street, at Church Street, Tribeca (1-212 964 4600, www.duanestreethotel.com). Subway A, C, 1, 2, 3 to Chambers Street. Rooms 43. Map p87 E31.

Opened on a quiet Tribeca street in 2007, this boutique property takes its cues from its well-heeled residential neighbourhood, offering loft-inspired rooms with high ceilings, oversized triple-glazed windows, hardwood floors and a chic, monochrome colour scheme. Free Wi-Fi, L'Occitane products in the slate-tiled bathrooms, plus bike loan and complimentary passes to a nearby gym cement the value-for-money package – a rare commodity in this part of town.

The Marlton

5 W 8th Street, between Fifth & Sixth Avenues, Greenwich Village (1-212 321 0100, www.marltonhotel.com). Subway A, B, C, D, E, F, M to W 4th Street; R, W to 8th Street-NYU. Rooms 107. Map p137 E29.

Hip hotelier Sean MacPherson transformed a former low-rent lodging into this affordable boutique hotel. The 1900 building has plenty of local history – Beat

---

In the know
TWA Hotel

The words 'airport hotel' and 'fashionable' may seem a contradiction in terms, but in spring 2019, Eero Saarinen's landmark 1962 Trans World Airlines terminal at JFK Airport reopened as the retro-chic **TWA Hotel** (1-212 806 9000, www.twahotel.com), complete with a Jean-Georges Vongerichten restaurant, a rooftop pool overlooking the runways and even a museum showcasing vintage TWA travel posters, uniforms and more. Layovers have never been so glamorous.

---

icon Jack Kerouac wrote a couple of novellas there, and the place put up would-be Andy Warhol assassin Valerie Solanas – but the lobby's deceptively lived-in-looking interior, with broken-in leather armchairs and an espresso bar, has largely been created from scratch. The on-site Mediterranean restaurant and wood-panelled cocktail bar also have vintage looks. Measuring up at between 110sq ft and 175sq ft, the standard rooms are mini versions of those you might find in a Paris grand hotel, with gilt-edged velvet headboards, crown mouldings, and petite marble sinks and Côté Bastide products in the bathrooms.

Sister City

225 Bowery, between Rivington & Stanton Streets, Lower East Side (1-646 343 4500, www.sistercitynyc.com). Subway B, D, F, M, 4, 6 to Broadway-Lafayette Street. Map p111 F29.

In contrast to the raucous streetscape outside, this sleek Ace Hotel sibling exudes head-clearing calm. In the airy lobby, with its chequerboard marble floor and plants, a shifting 'soundscape' designed by electronic musician Julianna Barwick sonically reflects cloud patterns picked up by a rooftop camera. Self-service check-in kiosks reduce any anxiety-inducing encounters. High-ceilinged guest rooms continue the slightly retro, stripped-down aesthetic with custom Italian cherry-wood furnishings, wall-mounted valets and chic striped bedlinen, and many feature original Noguchi lanterns. The 11th floor bar, Last Light, offers panoramic downtown-skyline views.

Yotel New York

570 Tenth Avenue, at 42nd Street, New York, Hell's Kitchen (1-646 449 7700, www.yotel.com). Subway A, C, E to 42nd Street-Port Authority. Rooms 713. Map p175 C24.

The international team behind this futuristic hotel is known for airport-based capsule accommodation that gives travellers just enough space to get horizontal between flights. Yotel

---

New York has ditched the 75sq ft cubbies in favour of 'premium cabins' more than twice the size. Adaptable furnishings (such as motorised beds that fold up futon-style) maximise space, and the bathroom has streamlined luxuries such as a heated towel rail and monsoon shower. If you want to unload excess baggage, the 20ft tall robot (or Yobot, in the hotel's playful lingo) will stash it for you in a lobby locker. In contrast with the compact quarters, the sprawling public spaces include a massive wraparound terrace bar. A Long Island City, Queens, location is scheduled to open in late 2020.

Budget

The Bowery House

220 Bowery, between Prince & Spring Streets, Nolita (1-212 837 2373, www.theboweryhouse.com). Subway J, Z to Bowery. Rooms 126. Map p111 F29.

Two young real-estate developers transformed a 1927 Bowery flophouse into this stylish take on a hostel. Corridors with original wainscoting lead to cubicles (singles are a cosy 35sq ft) with latticework ceilings to allow air circulation, although some of the 'cabins', as they're called, have windows. Quarters with double or queen-size beds are also available. It might not be the best bet for light sleepers, but the place is hopping with pretty young things attracted to the hip aesthetic and the location. Cabins are decorated with vintage prints and historical photographs, and Egyptian cotton robes are provided in the double-occupancy options. The (gender-segregated) communal bathrooms have rain showerheads and products from local spa Red Flower. When you want more breathing room, hang out in the guest lounge, outfitted with chesterfield sofas and a huge LCD TV, or on the large roof terrace.

Carlton Arms Hotel

160 E 25th Street, at Third Avenue, Gramercy Park (1-212 679 0680, www.carltonarms.com). Subway 6 to 23rd Street. Rooms 54. Map p163 F26.

Pod 39

The Carlton Arms Art Project started in the late 1970s, when a small group of creative types brought fresh paint and new ideas to a run-down shelter. Today, the site is a bohemian backpackers' paradise and a live-in gallery – every room, bathroom and hallway is festooned with outré artwork, including a room and a couple of early stairwells by Banksy. Eye-popping themed quarters include the Money Room and a tribute to the traditional English cottage. New works are introduced regularly and artists return to restore their creations. About a third of the rooms have private bathrooms; the rest are shared.

Harlem Flophouse
*242 W 123rd Street, between Adam Clayton Powell Jr Boulevard (Seventh Avenue) & Frederick Douglass Boulevard (Eighth Avenue), Harlem (1-347 632 1960, www.harlemflophouse. com). Subway A, B, C, D to 125th Street. **Rooms** 5. **Map** p223 D14.*
The dark-wood interior, moody lighting and lilting jazz make musician René Calvo's uptown inn feel more like a 1920s speakeasy than a 21st-century lodging. The airy guest quarters, which are named after jazz greats and prominent Harlem figures, have restored tin ceilings and

working sinks in antique cabinets, and are furnished with a quirky mix of junk-store finds and period knick-knacks. Four of the rooms are on the top two floors and each pair shares a bathroom. The ground-floor Ellington room has private facilities and a garden.

The Jane
*113 Jane Street, at West Street, West Village (1-212 924 6700, www.thejanenyc.com). Subway A, C, E to 14th Street; L to Eighth Avenue. **Rooms** 171. **Map** p137 C29.*
Opened in 1908 as the American Seaman's Friend Society Sailors Home and Institute, the six-storey landmark was a residential hotel when hoteliers Eric Goode and Sean MacPherson took it over. The Jane's wood-panelled, 50sq ft rooms were inspired by vintage train sleeper compartments: there's a single or bunk bed with built-in storage and brass hooks for hanging up your clothes – but also iPod docks and wall-mounted TVs. Alternatively, opt for a more spacious, wainscoted Captain's Cabin with private facilities – many have terraces or Hudson River views. If entering the hotel feels like stepping on to a film set, there's good reason. Inspiration came from various celluloid sources, including *Barton Fink's* Hotel Earle for the lobby.

Pod 39
*145 E 39th Street, between Lexington & Third Avenues, Murray Hill (1-212 865 5700, www. thepodhotel.com). Subway S, 4, 5, 6, 7 to 42nd Street-Grand Central. **Rooms** 366. **Map** p175 F24.*
The Pod's contemporary budget-hotel concept has spread to four locations across the city, including a brand-new Brooklyn outpost. Pod 39 occupies a 1918 residential hotel for single men – you can hang out by the fire in the redesigned gents' sitting room. As the name suggests, rooms are snug, but not oppressively so. A range of configurations includes single or queen-size beds, or stainless-steel bunk beds equipped with individual TVs and bedside shelves inspired by airplane storage. But you should probably know your roommate well since the utilitarian, subway-tiled bathrooms are partitioned off with sliding frosted-glass doors. Chef Alex Stupak's on-site Mexican bar-eaterie, Al Pastor, supplies margaritas, local beer and snacks at the sprawling seasonal rooftop bar. **Other locations** Pod 51, 230 E 51st Street, between Second & Third Avenues (1-212 355 0300); Pod Times Square, 400 West 42nd Street, at Ninth Avenue (1-844 763 7666); Pod Brooklyn, 247 Metropolitan Avenue, at Driggs Avenue, Williamsburg, Brooklyn.

Getting Around

ARRIVING & LEAVING

By air
John F Kennedy International Airport *1-718 244 4444, www. jfkairport.com.*
The **subway** (*see p383*) is the cheapest option. The **AirTrain** (www.airtrainjfk.com, $5, plus $1 for a MetroCard if required) links to the A train at Howard Beach or the E, J and Z trains at Sutphin Boulevard-Archer Avenue ($2.75-$3).

The **NYC Express Bus** 1-718 777 5111, www.nycairporter.com; (one way $19, round trip $35) connects JFK and Manhattan, with stops near Grand Central Terminal, Penn Station and Port Authority Bus Terminal. Buses run from 11am to 7pm daily, every 30mins from JFK and hourly to JFK.

SuperShuttle (1-800 258 3826, www.supershuttle.com) vans offer shared door-to-door services between NYC and the major airports, but can be time-consuming if there are multiple drop-offs.

A **yellow cab** to or from Manhattan will charge a flat $52.80 fare, plus toll (usually around $10), a $4.50 rush-hour supplement weekdays between 4pm and 8pm, and tip (15 per cent is the norm). If you're travelling to or from the outer boroughs the fare will be on the meter (*see p384*).

LaGuardia Airport *1-718 533 3400, www.panynj.gov/airports/ laguardia.html.*
Seasoned New Yorkers take the **M60 Select Bus Service** ($2.75), which terminates at W 106th Street at Broadway in Morningside Heights. The ride takes 40-60mins, depending on traffic, and buses run 24hrs daily. The route crosses Manhattan at 125th Street in Harlem. Get off at

Lexington Avenue for the 4, 5 and 6 trains; at Malcolm X Boulevard (Lenox Avenue) for the 2 and 3; or at St Nicholas Avenue for the A, B, C and D trains.

Less time-consuming options include the **NYC Express Bus** (one way $16, round trip $30). **Taxis** and **car** services charge about $30-$40, plus toll and tip.

Newark Liberty International
Airport *1-973 961 6000, www. panynj.gov/airports/newark-liberty.html.*
The best bet is the $13, half-hour trip via New Jersey Transit to or from Penn Station. The airport's monorail, **AirTrain Newark** (www.airtrainnewark.com), is linked to the NJ Transit and Amtrak train systems.

Bus services operated by **Coach USA** (1-877 894 9155, www.coachusa.com) run to Manhattan, stopping at three Midtown locations: Grand Central Terminal, Bryant Park and Port Authority Bus Terminal (one way $17, round trip $30); buses leave every 15-30mins. A **car** or **taxi** will run at $50-$75, plus toll and tip.

By bus
Most out-of-town buses come and go from the Port Authority Bus Terminal. **Greyhound** (1-800 231 2222, www.greyhound.com) runs long-distance travel to US destinations. The company's **BoltBus** (1-877 265 8287, www.boltbus.com), booked online, serves several East Coast cities. **New Jersey Transit** (1-973 275 5555, www.njtransit.com) runs services to most of New Jersey and parts of New York State. Finally, **Peter Pan** (1-800 343 9999, www.peterpanbus.com) runs extensive services to cities across the north-east.

Port Authority Bus Terminal *625 Eighth Avenue, between 40th & 42nd Streets, Garment District (1-212 564 8484, www.panynj.gov/ bus-terminals/port-authority-bus-terminal.html). Subway A, C, E to 42nd Street-Port Authority.* **Map** *p398 S13.*

By rail
America's national rail service is run by **Amtrak** (1-800 872 7245, www.amtrak.com). Nationwide routes are slow and infrequent (yet full of character), but there are some good fast services linking the eastern seaboard cities. (For commuter rail services, *see p383*).

Grand Central Terminal *42nd to 44th Streets, between Vanderbilt & Lexington Avenues, Midtown East. Subway S, 4, 5, 6, 7 to 42nd Street-Grand Central.* **Map** *p175 E24.*
Grand Central is home to Metro-North, which runs trains to more than 100 stations in New York State and Connecticut.

Penn Station *31st to 33rd Streets, between Seventh & Eighth Avenues, Garment District. Subway A, C, E, 1, 2, 3 to 34th Street-Penn Station.* **Map** *p175 D25.*
Amtrak, Long Island Rail Road and New Jersey Transit trains depart from this terminal.

PUBLIC TRANSPORT

Changes to schedules can occur at short notice, especially at weekends – check the MTA's website before travelling and pay attention to the posters on subway station walls and announcements on trains and subway platforms.

Metropolitan Transportation Authority (MTA) *511 local, 1-877 690 5116 outside New York State,*

*1-212 878 7000 international,
www.mta.info.*
The MTA runs the subway and bus lines, as well as services to points outside Manhattan. News of service interruptions and MTA maps are on its website. Be warned: backpacks, handbags and large containers may be subject to random searches.

Fares & tickets
Although you can pay with exact change (no dollar bills) on buses, to enter the subway system you'll need either a single-ride ticket ($3, available from station vending machines only) or a **MetroCard**. You can buy MetroCards from booths or vending machines in the stations, from the New York Transit Museum in Brooklyn (*see p235*) or Grand Central Terminal (*see p188*).

The standard base fare across the subway and bus network on a MetroCard is $2.75. Up to three children 44 inches tall and under can ride for free on subways and local buses when accompanied by a fare-paying adult. Free transfers between the subway and buses are available only with a MetroCard (for bus-to-bus transfers on cash fares, *see p383*). Up to four people can use a pay-per-ride MetroCard, sold in denominations from $5.50 to $80. (There is an additional $1 for a new MetroCard.) If you put $5.50 or more on the card, you'll receive a five per cent bonus, reducing the cost of each ride. However, if you're planning to use the subway or buses often, an Unlimited Ride MetroCard is great value. These cards are offered in two denominations, available at station vending machines but not at booths: a seven-day pass ($33) and a 30-day pass ($127). Both are good for unlimited rides within those periods, but you can't share a card with your travelling companions.

The MTA is currently rolling out a new payment system, OMNY, using contactless credit cards, reloadable cards and digital wallets, but MetroCards will also be accepted until it's completed in 2023. For details, visit www.omny.info.

Subway
Cleaner and safer than it has been for decades, the city's subway system is one of the world's largest and cheapest. For fares and payment options, *see left*. Trains run around the clock. If you are travelling late at night, board the train from the designated off-peak waiting area, usually near the middle of the platform; this is more secure than the ends of the platform, which are often less populated in the wee hours.

Stations are most often named after the street on which they're located. Entrances are marked with a green and white globe (open 24 hours) or a red and white globe (limited hours). Many stations have separate entrances for the uptown and downtown platforms – look before you pay. Trains are identified by letters or numbers, colour-coded according to the line on which they run. Local trains stop at every station on the line; express trains stop at major stations only. Bear in mind that on some lines the local and express services change at weekends and late at night – for example the local W service is replaced by the usually express N. We've provided weekday transport information in our listings and on the maps, so be sure to check www.mta.info for weekend updates.

The most current subway map is reprinted at the back of this guide; you can also ask MTA staff in service booths for a free copy, or refer to enlarged maps displayed in each subway station.

City buses
White and blue MTA buses are usually the best way to travel crosstown and a pleasant way to travel up- or downtown, as long as you're not in a hurry. They have a digital destination sign on the front, along with a route number preceded by a letter (M for Manhattan, B for Brooklyn, Bx for the Bronx, Q for Queens and S for Staten Island). Maps are posted on most buses and at all subway stops; they're also available from the Official NYC Information Center (*see p392*).

All local buses are equipped with wheelchair lifts.

The fare is payable with a MetroCard (*see left*) or exact change ($2.75 in coins only; no pennies or dollar bills). MetroCards allow for an automatic transfer from bus to bus, and between bus and subway. If you pay cash, and you're travelling uptown or downtown and want to go crosstown (or vice versa), ask the driver for a transfer when you get on – you'll be given a ticket for use on the second leg of your journey, valid for two hours. Select Bus Service (SBS) on some busy routes offer faster travel at the same fare with self-service ticket machines at bus stops. Insert your MetroCard or coins and a receipt will be issued. You can then board the bus via any door and there's no need to show the receipt unless asked to do so by an inspector. The MTA's express buses head to the outer boroughs for a $6.75 fare.

Rail
The following commuter trains serve NY's hinterland.

Long Island Rail Road *511 local, 1-718 217 5477 outside New York State, www.mta.info/lirr.* Provides rail services from Penn Station, Brooklyn and Queens to towns throughout Long Island.

Metro-North Railroad *511 local, 1-212 532 4900 outside New York State, www.mta.info/mnr.* Commuter trains serve towns north of Manhattan and leave from Grand Central Terminal.

New Jersey Transit *1-973 275 5555, www.njtransit.com.* Service from Penn Station reaches most of New Jersey, some points in New York State and Philadelphia.

PATH Trains *1-800 234 7284, www.panynj.gov/path.* PATH (Port Authority Trans-Hudson) trains run from six stations in Manhattan to various New Jersey destinations, including Hoboken, Jersey City and Newark. The 24-hour service costs $2.75.

Boat

Operated by cruise company Hornblower, the **NYC Ferry service** (www.ferry.nyc) launched in 2017, offering routes between Manhattan (East 34th Street in Midtown or Wall Street in the Financial District) and popular outer borough destinations including Dumbo, Williamsburg and Red Hook in Brooklyn, and Long Island City, Astoria and Rockaway Beach in Queens. A one-way fare costs $2.75 and the fleet is equipped with free Wi-Fi and a boutique news stand that sells coffee and booze. However, boats can be over-crowded at popular times such as summer weekends.

In addition to sightseeing tours, the **New York Water Taxi** (1-212 742 1969, www.nywatertaxi. com) offers a hop-on hop-off All Day Access Pass ($37, $31 reductions) between stops at W 42nd Street in Midtown, near the World Trade Center and Wall Street in the Financial District, and Dumbo in Brooklyn, which cruises close to the Statue of Liberty and the Brooklyn Bridge.

Taxis

If the centre light atop the taxi is lit, the cab is available and should stop if you flag it down. Get in and then tell the driver where you're going. (New Yorkers generally give cross-streets rather than addresses.) By law, taxis cannot refuse to take you anywhere inside the five boroughs or to New York airports. Green Boro Taxis serving the outer boroughs can be hailed on the street in the Bronx, Queens (excluding airports), Brooklyn, Staten Island and Manhattan north of West 110th and East 96th Streets. Use only yellow or green medallion (licensed) cabs.

Taxis will carry up to four passengers for the same price: $2.50 plus 50¢ per fifth of a mile or per minute idling, plus 80¢ in standard surcharges, an extra $1 during rush hour (4-8pm Mon-Fri) and a $2.50 congestion surcharge for routes below 96th Street. The average fare for a three-mile ride is about $15, but this varies depending on the time and traffic.

If you have a problem, take down the medallion and driver's numbers, posted on the partition. Always ask for a receipt – there's a meter number on it. To complain or to trace lost property, call 311 or visit www. nyc.gov/taxi. Tip 15-20 per cent, as in a restaurant. All taxis now accept major credit cards.

Car services

Car services are regulated by the Taxi & Limousine Commission. Unlike cabs, drivers can make only pre-arranged pickups. Don't try to hail one, and be wary of those that offer you a ride. Companies such as **Carmel** (1-212 666 6666, www. carmellimo.com) and **Dial 7** (1-212 777 7777, www.dial7.com) will pick you up anywhere in the city for a set fare. Popular ride-matching services booked via mobile app, such as **Uber** (www.uber.com) and **Lyft** (www.lyft.com), typically offer lower prices.

DRIVING

Car hire

You need a credit card to rent a car in the US, and usually must be at least 25 years old. Car hire is cheaper in the city's outskirts and further afield than in Manhattan. NYC companies add around 20 per cent in taxes. If you just want a car for a few hours, **Zipcar** (US: 1-866 494 7227, www.zipcar.com; UK: 0333 240 9000, www.zipcar. co.uk) is cost effective.

Alamo *US: 1-844 354 6962, www.alamo.com. UK: 0800 028 2390, www.alamo.co.uk.*
Budget *US: 1-800 218 7992, www.budget.com. UK: 0808 284 3455, www.budget.co.uk.*
Enterprise *US: 1-855 266 9289, www.enterprise.com. UK: 0800 800 227, www.enterprise.co.uk.*
Hertz *US: 1-800 654 3131, www. hertz.com. UK: 0843 309 3099, www.hertz.co.uk.*

Parking

Make sure you read parking signs and never park within 15 feet of a fire hydrant (to avoid a $115 ticket and/or having your car towed). Parking is off-limits on most streets for at least a few hours daily. The Department of Transportation provides information on daily changes to regulations (dial 311). If precautions fail, call 1-212 971 0771 for Manhattan towing and impoundment information; go to www.nyc.gov for phone numbers in other boroughs.

CYCLING

While biking on NYC's streets is only recommended for experienced cyclists, the **Citi Bike** system (www.citibikenyc. com, 1-855 245 3311) gives you temporary access to bikes at hundreds of stations in Manhattan, Brooklyn and Queens. Visitors can purchase a 24-hour ($12) or three-day ($24) pass at a station kiosk with a credit or debit card. You'll then receive a 'ride code' that will allow you to undock and ride for 30 minutes at a stretch. A longer trip will incur an extra fee.

Unlimited Biking (1-212 749 4444, www.unlimitedbiking. com) offers cycle hire at seven locations, including Central Park, South Street Seaport and Pier 78 on the Hudson River (some are closed Nov-Mar). Rates (including helmet) start at $15 for an hour ($12 for kids' bikes), plus $8.75 for each additional hour. The company also runs cycling tours.

The Manhattan Waterfront Greenway, a 32-mile route that circumnavigates the island of Manhattan, is a fantastic asset: you can ride, uninterrupted, along the Hudson River from Battery Park to Upper Manhattan's Fort Tryon Park, as well as along stretches of the East River. The free NYC Bike Map, covering cycle lanes in all five boroughs, is available from the **Department of City Planning Bookstore** (120 Broadway, at Cedar Street, 31st floor, Financial District, 1-212 720 3667). It's open limited hours so call before visiting. Alternatively, you can download the map from www. nyc.gov/planning.

WALKING

One of the best ways to take in NYC is on foot. Most of the streets are laid out in a grid pattern and are relatively easy to navigate.

Resources A-Z

Travel Advice

For up-to-date information on travel to a specific country – including the latest on safety and security, health issues, local laws and customs – contact your government's department of foreign affairs. Most have websites with useful advice for would-be travellers.

Australia
www.smartraveller.gov.au

Republic of Ireland
foreignaffairs.gov.ie

Canada
www.voyage.gc.ca

UK
www.fco.gov.uk/travel

New Zealand
www.safetravel.govt.nz

USA
www.state.gov/travel

ACCIDENT & EMERGENCY

Emergency numbers
In an emergency only, dial **911** for ambulance, police or fire department. For hospitals, *see below*; for helplines, *see p387*; for the police, *see p390*.

You will be billed for any emergency treatment. Call your travel insurance company before seeking treatment to find out which hospitals accept your insurance. The following hospitals have emergency rooms:

New York Presbyterian/Lower Manhattan Hospital *170 William Street, between Beeckman & Spruce Streets, Financial District (1-212 312 5000). Subway 2, 3 to Fulton Street; 4, 5, 6 to Brooklyn Bridge-City Hall. **Map** p71 F32.*

Mount Sinai Hospital *Madison Avenue, at 100th Street, Upper East Side (1-212 241 6500). Subway 6 to 103rd Street. **Map** p209 E16.*

Mount Sinai West *1000 Tenth Avenue, at 59th Street, Upper West Side (1-212 523 4000). Subway A, B, C, D, 1 to 59th Street-Columbus Circle. **Map** p175 C22.*

New York-Presbyterian Hospital/Weill Cornell Medical Center *525 E 68th Street, at York Avenue, Upper East Side (1-212 746 5454). Subway 6 to 68th Street. **Map** p209 F21.*

ADDRESSES

Addresses follow the standard US format. The room, apartment or suite number usually appears after the street address, followed on the next line by the name of the city and the zip code.

AGE RESTRICTIONS

Buying/drinking alcohol 21.
Driving 16.
Sex 17.
Smoking 18.

ATTITUDE & ETIQUETTE

New Yorkers have something of a reputation for being rude, but 'outspoken' is more apt: they are unlikely to hold their tongues in the face of injustice or inconvenience, but they can also be very welcoming and will often go out of their way to offer advice or help. Some old-fashioned restaurants and swanky clubs operate dress codes (jacket and tie for men, for example, or no baseball caps or ripped jeans), but on the whole, anything goes sartorially. Still, it doesn't hurt to phone to check.

CUSTOMS

US Customs allows foreigners to bring in $100 worth of gifts (the limit is $800 for returning Americans) without paying duty. One carton of 200 cigarettes (or 100 cigars) and one litre of liquor (spirits) are allowed. Plants, meat and fresh produce of any kind cannot be brought into the country. You will have to fill out a form if you are carrying more than $10,000 in currency. You will be handed a white form on your inbound flight to fill in, confirming that you haven't exceeded any of these allowances.

If you need to bring prescription drugs into the US, make sure the container is clearly marked, and bring your doctor's statement or a prescription. Marijuana, cocaine and most opiate derivatives, along with a number of other drugs and chemicals, are not permitted: the possession is punishable by a stiff fine and/or imprisonment. Check in with the US Customs and Border Protection Service (www.cbp.gov) before you arrive if you're unsure.

HM Revenue & Customs allows returning visitors to the UK to bring £390 worth of 'gifts, souvenirs and other goods' into the country duty-free, along with the usual duty-free goods.

DISABLED

Under New York City law, facilities constructed after 1987 must provide complete access for the disabled – restrooms, entrances and exits included. In 1990, the Americans with Disabilities Act made the same requirement federal law. Many older buildings have added disabled-access features. There has been widespread compliance with the law, but call ahead to check facilities.

Since only about a quarter of subway stations are equipped with lifts, getting around by public transport can present a challenge for wheelchair users. The MTA lists accessible stations on its website (https://new.mta.info/accessibility); all city buses have elevators or ramps. All

Local Weather

Average temperatures and monthly rainfall in New York

	Temp High (°C/°F)	Temp Low (°C/°F)	Rainfall (mm/in)
January	3 / 38	-4 / 24	84 / 3.3
February	4 / 40	-3 / 26	78 / 3
March	9 / 49	1 / 34	98 / 3.75
April	16 / 61	6 / 43	103 / 4
May	22 / 71	12 / 54	107 / 4
June	27 / 81	17 / 63	90 / 3.5
July	29 / 85	20 / 68	106 / 4
August	28 / 83	19 / 67	102 / 4
September	24 / 76	15 / 59	95 / 3.75
October	18 / 65	9 / 48	84 / 3.3
November	12 / 53	4 / 39	104 / 4
December	6 / 42	-1 / 30	93 / 3.6

RESOURCES A-Z

Broadway theatres are equipped with devices for the hearing-impaired and many offer sign language interpretations, closed captioning, or live or prerecorded audio descriptions. Theatre Access NYC (www.theatreaccess.nyc) offers a search function for specific facilities by show on its website.

Lighthouse International *111 E 59th Street, between Park & Lexington Avenues, Upper East Side (1-212 821 9200, 1-646 874 8384 store, www.lighthouse.org). Subway N, R, W to Lexington Avenue-59th Street; 4, 5, 6 to 59th Street. Open 10am-5pm Mon-Fri. Store 10am-5pm Mon-Fri. Map p209 E22.*
In addition to running a store that sells handy items for the vision-impaired, Lighthouse provides helpful information for blind people (residents and visitors).

Mayor's Office for People with Disabilities *2nd Floor, 100 Gold Street, between Frankfort & Spruce Streets, Financial District (1-212 788 2830, www.nyc.gov/mopd). Subway J, Z to Chambers Street; 4, 5, 6 to Brooklyn Bridge-City Hall. Open 9am-5pm Mon-Fri. Map p71 F32.*
This city office provides a broad range of services for the disabled.

Society for Accessible Travel & Hospitality *1-212 447 7284, www.sath.org.*
This non-profit group educates the public about travel facilities for people with disabilities, and promotes travel for the disabled. Membership, which costs $49/yr ($29 reductions) includes access to an information service, discounts to events, and a quarterly newsletter.

DRUGS

Possession of small amounts of marijuana has been decriminalised, but is still a misdemeanour. Recent legislation reduced the penalty for possession of less than 1oz to a $50 fine, or $200 for possession of 1-2oz.

Possession of 'controlled substances' (cocaine, ecstasy, heroin, etc) is not taken lightly, and charges come with stiff penalties – especially if you are convicted of possession with intent to sell. Convictions carry anything from a one-year prison sentence plus a fine to 20 years' incarceration.

ELECTRICITY

The US uses a 110-120V, 60-cycle alternating current rather than the 220-240V, 50-cycle AC used in Europe. The transformers that power or recharge newer electronic devices such as laptops are designed to handle either current, and may need nothing more than an adaptor for the wall outlet. Other appliances may also require a power converter. Adaptors and converters can be purchased at airport shops, pharmacies and electronics chains such as Best Buy (www.bestbuy.com).

EMBASSIES & CONSULATES

See also p385 **Travel Advice**.

Australian Consulate-General *34th Floor, 150 E 42nd Street, between Lexington & Third Avenues, Midtown East (1-212 351 6500, www.newyork.usa.embassy.gov.au). Subway S, 4, 5, 6, 7 to 42nd Street-Grand Central. Open 9am-5pm Mon-Fri. Map p175 F24.*

British Consulate General *1 Dag Hammarskjold Plaza, 885 Second Avenue, at 48th Street, Midtown East (1-212 745 0200, www.gov.uk/world/organisations/british-consulate-general-new-york). Subway E, M to Lexington Avenue-53rd Street; 6 to 51st Street. Open by appointment only. Phone enquiries 9am-4pm Mon-Fri. Map p175 F23.*

Consulate General of Canada
*20th Floor, 466 Lexington Avenue,
at 42nd Street, Midtown East
(1-212 596 1628, www.canada.ca/
Canada-In-New-York). Subway
S, 4, 5, 6, 7 to 42nd Street-Grand
Central. Open 9am-5pm Mon-Fri.
Map p175 F24.*

Consulate General of Ireland
*17th Floor, 345 Park Avenue,
between 51st & 52nd Streets,
Midtown East (1-212 319 2555,
www.dfa.ie/irish-consulate/
newyork). Subway E, M to
Lexington Avenue-53rd Street; 6 to
51st Street. Open 10am-2pm Mon,
Tue, Thur, Fri. Map p175 E23.*

New Zealand Consulate-General
*41st Floor, 295 Madison Avenue, at
41st Street (1-212 832 4038, www.
mfat.govt.nz). Subway S, 4, 5, 6,
7 to 42nd Street-Grand Central.
Open 9am-12.30pm Mon-Fri.
Map p175 F24.*

HEALTH

Public health care is virtually
nonexistent in the US, and
private health care is very
expensive. Make sure you
have comprehensive medical
insurance before you travel.
For HIV testing and HIV/AIDS
counselling, *see right* **Helplines**.
For a list of hospitals, *see p385*.

Contraception

**Planned Parenthood of New York
City Margaret Sanger Center,** *26
Bleecker Street, at Mott Street,
Greenwich Village (1-212 965
7000, www.plannedparenthood.
org). Subway B, D, F, M to
Broadway-Lafayette Street; R,
W to Prince Street; 6 to Bleecker
Street. Open 8am-6.30pm Mon-
Tue, Thur, Fri; 8am-8.30pm
Wed; 8am-4.30pm Sat. Map
p123 F29.*
The best-known network of
family-planning clinics in the
US. Counselling and treatment
are available for a full range
of needs, including abortion,
contraception, HIV testing and
treatment of STDs.
   Other locations throughout
the city.

Dentists
**New York County Dental
Society** *1-212 573 8500, www.
nycdentalsociety.org. Open
9am-5pm Mon-Fri.*
Can provide local referrals. An
emergency contact line at the
number listed above runs outside
office hours; alternatively, use
the search facility on the society's
website.

Opticians
Morgenthal Frederics *399 W
Broadway, at Spring Street,
Soho (1-212 966 0099, www.
morgenthalfrederics.com).
Subway C, E to Spring Street.
Open 11am-8pm Mon-Fri;
11am-7pm Sat; noon-6pm Sun.
Map p87 E30.*
The house-designed, handmade
frames on display in Morgenthal
Frederics' David Rockwell-
designed shops exude quality
and subtly nostalgic style.
Frames start from around $365
for plastic, but the buffalo
horn and gold ranges are more
expensive.
   Other locations throughout
the city.

Pharmacies
The fact that there's a **Duane
Reade** pharmacy on almost every
corner of Manhattan is lamented
among chain-deriding locals;
however, it is convenient if you
need an aspirin pronto. Several
branches of Duane Reade and
its parent company Walgreens,
including the one at 145 Fourth
Avenue, at 14th Street, Union
Square 1-212 677 0214, www.
walgreens.com), are open 24
hours. Also widespread are **CVS**
(with one of several 24-hour
locations at 241 West 57th Street,
at Eighth Avenue (1-212 247 5848,
www.cvs.com) and **Rite Aid** (with
one of several 24-hour branches
at 301 W 50th Street, at Eighth
Avenue, 1-212 247 8384, www.
riteaid.com). For New York's
oldest apothecary, **CO Bigelow**,
see p142.

STDs, HIV & AIDS
For the National STD & AIDS
Hotline, *see right* **Helplines**.
GMHC *446 W 33rd Street,
between Ninth & Tenth Avenues,*

*Hell's Kitchen (1-212 367 1000,
1-800 243 7692 hotline, gmhc.
org). Subway A, C, E, 1, 2, 3 to
34th Street-Penn Station; 7
to 34th Street-Hudson Yards.
Open 9am-6pm Mon-Fri. Hotline
2-6pm Mon-Fri; recorded
information at other times.
Map p175 C25.*
GMHC is the nation's leading
provider of HIV/AIDS care,
prevention services and
advocacy. The organisation also
offers free HIV and STD testing
at 224 West 29th Street, between
Seventh & Eighth Avenues,
Chelsea (1-212 367 1100). Visit
the website for walk-in and
appointment-only hours.

Riverside Sexual Health
Clinic *160 W 100th Street,
between Amsterdam & Columbus
Avenues, Upper West Side (no
phone). Subway B, C, 1, 2, 3 to 96th
Street; 1 to 103rd Street. Open
walk-in 8.30am-3.30pm Mon-Fri
(closed 2nd Tue of each mth). Map
p153 C26.*
Call 311 or visit www.nyc.gov for
other free clinics.

HELPLINES

All numbers below are open 24
hours unless otherwise stated.

**NYPD Sex Crimes Report
Line** *1-212 267 7273.*

**NY State National HIV/AIDS
Hotline** *1-800 541 2437. Open
10am-8pm daily.*

Samaritans *1-212 673 3000.*
Counselling for suicide
prevention.

**SAMHSA (Substance Abuse
and Mental Health Services
Administration) National
Helpline** *1-800 662 4357*

ID

Always make sure you carry
picture ID: even people well
over 18 or 21 may be carded
when buying tobacco or alcohol,
ordering drinks in bars, or
entering clubs.

INSURANCE

Non-nationals and US citizens
should have travel and medical
insurance before travelling. For
a list of New York urgent-care
facilities, *see p385.*

INTERNET

New York City's public payphones are being replaced by **LinkNYC** (www.link.nyc) connection points offering free Wi-Fi. You can also charge your phone and use the built-in tablet to access maps and city services, or make calls (*see p392*). Many cafés and other businesses, parks and public spaces in the city offer free Wi-Fi, including branches of Starbucks (www.starbucks.com). The website has a search facility featuring a Wi-Fi filter.
FedEx Office *1-800 463 3339, www.fedex.com.*
Outposts of this ubiquitous and efficient computer and copy centre are peppered throughout the city; many are open 24 hours a day.

New York Public Library *1-917 275 6975, www.nypl.org.*
Branches of the NYPL are great places to get online for free, offering both Wi-Fi and computers for public use (45mins-1hr computer limit per day). Out-of-towners with official ID and proof of address can get a guest pass to use library facilities. The Science, Industry & Business Library (188 Madison Avenue, at 34th Street, Midtown East), part of the public library system, has more than 50 computers.

LEFT LUGGAGE

There are luggage-storage facilities at arrivals halls in **JFK Airport** (Terminal 1: 7am-11pm, $4-$16 per bag per day; call 1-718 751 2947); (Terminal 4: 24hrs, $4-$16 per bag per day; call 1-718 751 4020). At **Penn Station**, Amtrak offers checked baggage services for a small fee for some of its ticketed passengers. Due to heightened security, luggage storage is not available at the Port Authority Bus Terminal, Grand Central Terminal, LaGuardia or Newark airports.

One Midtown alternative is to leave bags with the private firm, located between Penn Station and Port Authority, listed below. Some hotels may allow you to leave suitcases with the front desk before check-in or after check-out; if so, be sure to tip the concierge.

Schwartz Luggage Storage *357 W 37th Street, at Ninth Avenue, Garment District (1-212 290 2626, www.schwartztravel.com).* **Open** *24 hrs. Rates $2.50 per bag per hour or $5-$10 per bag per day (depending on size).* **No cards.** *Map p175 C24.*

LEGAL HELP

If you need a lawyer in NYC, contact the **New York City Bar Association** (1-212 626 7373; www.nycbar.org), which can provide referrals to attorneys practising in almost every area of the law, from personal injury to criminal defence. Outside the city, contact the New York State Bar Association Lawyer Referral & Information Service (1-800 342 3661, www.nysba.org). If you're arrested and held in custody, call your insurer's emergency number or contact your embassy or consulate (*see p386*).

LGBT

For more gay and lesbian resources, including the Lesbian, Gay, Bisexual & Transgender Community Center, *see p303*.
Gay, Lesbian, Bisexual & Transgender National Hotline *1-888 843 4564, www.glbtnationalhelpcenter.org.* **Open** *4pm-midnight Mon-Fri; noon-5pm Sat.*
This phone service offers excellent peer counselling, legal referrals, details of various gay and lesbian organisations, and information on bars, restaurants and hotels. Younger callers can contact the toll-free GLBT National Youth Talk Line (1-800 246 7743, 4pm-midnight Mon-Fri; noon-5pm Sat).

LIBRARIES

See p184 **New York Public Library**.

LOST PROPERTY

For lost credit cards or travellers' cheques, *see p390*.
Grand Central Terminal *Lower level, near Track 100. 1-212 532 4900.* **Open** *7am-6pm Mon-Fri.* You can call 6am-10pm daily to submit an enquiry if you've left something on a Metro-North train.

JFK Airport *1-718 244 4225, or contact your airline.*

LaGuardia Airport *1-718 533 3988, or contact your airline.*

Newark Liberty International Airport *1-973 961 6243, or contact your airline.*

Penn Station *Long Island Rail Road: between tracks 13 & 14. 1-718 217 5477.* **Open** *7.20am-7.20pm Mon-Fri. New Jersey Transit: 1-973 275 5555.* **Open** *6am-11pm Mon-Fri; 7am-11pm Sat, Sun. Report items lost on Amtrak trains at www.amtrak.com/reporting-lost-items.*

Subway & Buses *New York City Metropolitan Transit Authority, 34th Street-Penn Station, near the A-train platform, Garment District (call 511).* **Open** *8am-3.30pm Mon, Tue, Fri; 11am-6.30pm Wed, Thur.*

Taxis *311, www.nyc.gov/taxi.*

MEDIA

Newspapers
Founded in 1801 by Alexander Hamilton, the **New York Post** is the nation's oldest continuously published daily newspaper. It has swerved sharply to the right under owner Rupert Murdoch, it includes more gossip than any other local paper, and its headlines are often sassy and sensational.

The **Daily News** has drifted politically from the Neanderthal right to a more moderate but always tough-minded stance.

Despite recent financial woes, The **New York Times** remains the city's, and the nation's, paper of record. Founded as the *New-York Daily Times* in 1851, it has the broadest and deepest coverage of world and national events and, as the masthead proclaims, it delivers 'All the News That's Fit to Print'. The hefty Sunday edition includes a well-regarded magazine, as well as arts, book review, travel, real-estate and various other sections.

The **New York Amsterdam News**, one of the nation's longest-running black newspapers, offers a trenchant African-American viewpoint. New York also supports a

Spanish-language daily: **El Diario La Prensa**. Free tabloids **AM New York** and **Metro New York** offer locally slanted news, arts and entertainment listings.

Magazines

New York magazine is part news weekly, part lifestyle reporting and part listings. Since the 1920s, the **New Yorker** has been known for its fine wit, elegant prose and sophisticated cartoons. It has also evolved into a respected forum for serious long-form journalism.

Based on the tried and trusted format of its London parent magazine, **Time Out New York** is an irreverent, critical weekly guide to what's going on in the city: arts, restaurants, bars, events and more. It's distributed free every two weeks on Wednesdays.

Since its launch in 1996, the bimonthly **BlackBook Magazine** has covered New York's high fashion and culture with intelligent bravado. Glossy monthly **Manhattan** focuses on celebrities and luxury lifestyle content. Since the mid-1980s, **Paper** has offered the buzz on bars, clubs, downtown boutiques and more.

Commercial radio

American commercial radio is rigidly formatted, which makes most pop stations extremely tedious and repetitive during the day. Tune in on evenings and weekends for more interesting programming. Always popular, **WQHT-FM 97.1**, 'Hot 97', is a commercial hip hop station with all-day rap and R&B. **WKTU-FM 103.5** is the premier dance music station. **WWPR-FM 105.1**, 'Power 105', plays top hip hop and a few old-school hits. **WBLS-FM 107.5** showcases classic and new funk, soul and R&B. **WBGO-FM 88.3**, based in Newark, NJ, is strictly jazz, and **WAXQ-FM 104.3** offers classic rock.

WNYC-FM 93.9 (*see also below*) and **WQXR-FM 105.9** serve up a range of new and classical music. **WXNY-FM 96.3** and **WQBU-FM 92.7** spin Spanish and Latin sounds.

Public & college radio

The city's excellent National Public Radio-affiliated station, **WNYC-FM 93.9/AM 820**, provides news and current-affairs commentary and broadcasts the BBC World Service. **WBAI-FM 99.5** is a left-leaning community radio station.

College radio is innovative and commercial-free, but reception is often compromised by Manhattan's high-rise topography. **WNYU-FM 89.1** and **WKCR-FM 89.9** are, respectively, the stations of New York University and Columbia.

Talk radio & sports

WABC-AM 770, **WCBS-AM 880** and **WINS-AM 1010** offer news, plus traffic and weather reports. **WFAN-AM 660** airs Giants, Nets, Devils and Yankees games. **WCBS-AM 880** is the flagship radio station of the Mets.

Television

Due to skyscraper density, it's virtually impossible to get decent TV reception in Manhattan without a cable service. There are hundreds of cable channels, but the following major networks broadcast nationwide. **CBS** (Channel 2 in NYC) has the top-rated investigative show, *60 Minutes*, on Sundays at 7pm; overall, programming is geared to a middle-aged demographic, but CBS also screens shows such as *CSI*, *Elementary* and the reality series *Survivor*. **NBC** (4) is the home of *Law & Order* and the long-running sketch-comedy series *Saturday Night Live*. **Fox-WNYW** (5) is popular with younger audiences for shows such as *Family Guy* and *The Simpsons*. **ABC** (7) is the king of daytime soaps, family-friendly sitcoms and hits like *Modern Family*, *Grey's Anatomy, The Bachelor* and *American Idol*.

NYC's main public TV station is **WNET** (13). Documentaries, arts shows and science series alternate with *Masterpiece* (Anglo costume and contemporary dramas packaged for a US audience) and reruns of British sitcoms.

For channel numbers for cable TV providers, check a local newspaper or the web. **MSG** (Madison Square Garden), **ESPN** and **ESPN2** are all-sports stations. **Comedy Central** is all comedy, airing *South Park* and *The Daily Show*. **Cinemax**, the **Disney Channel**, the **Movie Channel**, **HBO** and **Showtime** are often available in hotels. They show uninterrupted feature films and exclusive specials; the latter two offer popular series such as *Westworld, Homeland* and *Billions*.

MONEY

Over the past several years, much of American currency has undergone a subtle facelift, partly to deter increasingly adept counterfeiters; all denominations except the $1 bill have been updated by the US Treasury. (However, 'old' money remains in circulation.) Coins include copper pennies (1¢) and silver-coloured nickels (5¢), dimes (10¢) and quarters (25¢). Half-dollar coins (50¢) and the gold-coloured dollar coins are less common.

All paper money is the same size, so make sure you fork over the right bill. It comes in denominations of $1, $2, $5, $10, $20, $50 and $100 (and higher, but you'll never see those bills). $2 bills are quite rare. Try to keep some low notes on you because getting change may be a problem with anything bigger than a $20 bill.

ATMs

The city is full of ATMs – in bank branches, delis and many small shops. Most of them accept Visa, MasterCard and major bank cards, but some charge a fee for transactions. It's also wise to check with your bank about its fees for foreign transactions. Most ATM cards double as debit cards, if they bear the Maestro or Cirrus logo.

Banks & bureaux de change

Banks are generally open from 9am to 6pm Monday to Friday, though some stay open longer and/or on Saturdays. You need photo ID, such as a passport, to cash travellers' cheques. Many banks will not exchange foreign currency and some bureaux de change close at around 6pm or 7pm. In emergencies, most large hotels offer 24-hour exchange facilities, but the rates won't be great.

Travelex *1578 Broadway, at 47th Street, Theater District (1-212 265 6063, www.travelex.com). Subway N, R, W to 49th Street.* **Open** *9am–10pm Mon-Sat; 9am-7pm Sun (hrs vary).* **Map** *p175 D24.*

Travelex offers a complete range of foreign-exchange services, with locations in visitor-heavy areas and airports.

Other locations throughout the city.

Credit cards & travellers' cheques

Credit cards are essential for renting cars and booking hotels, and handy for buying tickets over the phone and the internet. The five major cards accepted in the US are **American Express**, **Diners Club**, **Discover**, **MasterCard** and **Visa**. MasterCard and Visa are the most popular; American Express is also widely accepted. Thanks to a deal between MasterCard and Diners Club, all businesses that accept the former can now in theory accept the latter, though in practice many business are unaware of this and may not comply.

If your cards or travellers' cheques are lost or stolen, call the following numbers:

American Express *1-800 528 4800 1-800 221 7282 travellers' cheques.*

Diners Club *1-800 234 6377.*

Discover *1-800 347 2683.*

Mastercard *1-800 627 8372.*

Visa *1-800 847 2911.*

Tax

Sales tax is 8.875 per cent in New York City, and is applicable to restaurant bills, services and the purchase of just about anything, except most store-bought foods, clothing and shoes under $110.

In the US, sales tax is almost never included in the price of the item, but added on to the final bill at the till. There is no tax refund option for foreign visitors.

Wire services

Moneygram *1-800 666 3947, www.moneygram.com.*

Western Union *1-800 325 6000, www.westernunion.com.*

OPENING HOURS

Banks and government offices, including post offices, close on federal holidays. Retail in the city shuts down on Christmas Day and New Year's Day, although movie theatres and some restaurants remain open. Some museums are closed on Mondays, but may open when a public holiday falls on a Monday. New York's subway runs 24 hours a day, 365 days a year, but always check station signs for track or schedule changes, especially during weekends and holidays.

Banks *9am-6pm Mon-Fri; generally also Sat mornings.*

Businesses *9am or 10am to 5pm or 6pm Mon-Fri.*

Post offices *9am-5pm Mon-Fri (a few open as early as 7.30am and close as late as 8.30pm); some are open Sat until 3pm or 4pm.* The James A Farley Post Office (see right) is open 24 hours daily for automated services.

Pubs & bars *4pm-2am Mon-Thur, Sun; noon-4am Fri, Sat (but hours vary widely).*

Shops *9am, 10am or 11am to 7pm or 8pm Mon-Sat (some open at noon and/or close at 9pm). Many are also open on Sun, usually from 11am or noon to 6pm.*

POLICE

In an emergency only, dial **911**. The NYPD stations below are in central, tourist-heavy areas of Manhattan. For the location of your nearest police precinct or information about police services, call 1-646 610 5000 or visit www.nyc.gov.

17th Precinct *167 E 51st Street, between Third & Lexington Avenues, Midtown East (1-212*

826 3211). Subway E, M to Lexington Avenue-53rd Street. **Map** *p175 E23.*

Central Park Precinct *86th Street & Transverse Road, Central Park (1-212 570 4820). Subway 4, 5, 6, B, C to 86th Street.* **Map** *p209 D18.*

Sixth Precinct *233 West 10th Street, between Bleecker & Hudson Streets, West Village (1-212 741 4811). Subway 1, 2 to Christopher Street.* **Map** *p137 D31.*

Seventh Precinct *19½ Pitt Street, at Broome Street, Lower East Side (1-212 477 7311). Subway F, J, M to Delancey Street-Essex Street.* **Map** *p111 G29.*

Midtown North Precinct *306 W 54th Street, between Eighth & Ninth Avenues, Hell's Kitchen (1-212 767 8400). Subway 1, 2, , C, E to 50th Street; N, Q, R, W to 57th Street.* **Map** *p175 C22.*

Midtown South Precinct *357 W 35th Street, between Eighth & Ninth Avenues, Garment District (1-212 239 9811). Subway 1, 2, 3 to 34th Street-Penn Station; A, C, E to 42nd Street-Port Authority Bus Terminal.* **Map** *p175 C25.*

POSTAL SERVICES

It costs 55¢ to send a 1oz letter within the US. Each additional ounce costs 15¢. Postcards mailed within the US cost 35¢. The Global Forever Stamp ($1.15) can be used to send a postcard or 1oz letter anywhere in the world. Faster Priority Mail and Priority Express Mail options are available for both domestic and international destinations. Call 1-800 275 8777 or see www.usps.com for more information.

James A Farley Post Office *421 Eighth Avenue, between 31st & 33rd Streets, Garment District (1-212 330 3296, 1-800 275 8777 24hr information, www.usps.com). Subway A, C, E to 34th Street-Penn Station.* **Open** *24 hrs daily. Counter service 7am-10pm Mon-Fri; 9am-9pm Sat; 11am-7pm Sun.* **Map** *p175 D25.*

In addition to operating a counter service, NYC's general post office has automated self-service machines for buying stamps and posting packages.

PUBLIC HOLIDAYS

New Year's Day *1 Jan*
Martin Luther King, Jr Day *3rd Mon in Jan*
Presidents Day *3rd Mon in Feb*
Memorial Day *last Mon in May*
Independence *Day 4 July*
Labor Day *1st Mon in Sept*
Columbus Day *2nd Mon in Oct*
Veterans Day *11 Nov*
Thanksgiving Day *4th Thur in Nov*
Christmas Day *25 Dec*

RELIGION

Here are just a few of New York's many places of worship. Check online or the telephone book for more listings.

Abyssinian Baptist Church *See p227.*

Cathedral Church of St John the Divine *See p204.*

Church of St Paul & St Andrew United Methodist *263 W 86th Street, between Broadway & West End Avenue, Upper West Side (1-212 362 3179, www. stpaulandstandrew.org). Subway 1 to 86th Street.* **Map** *p195 C18.*

Islamic Cultural Center of New York *1711 Third Avenue, between 96th & 97th Streets, Upper East Side (1-212 722 5234, www.icc-ny. us). Subway 6 to 96th Street.* **Map** *p209 F17.*

Madison Avenue Presbyterian Church *921 Madison Avenue, between 73rd & 74th Streets, Upper East Side (1-212 288 8920, www. mapc.com). Subway 6 to 72nd Street.* **Map** *p209 E20.*

New York Buddhist Church *331-332 Riverside Drive, between 105th & 106th Streets, Upper West Side (1-212 678 0305, www. newyorkbuddhistchurch.org). Subway 1 to 103rd Street.* **Map** *p195 B16.*

St Patrick's Cathedral *See p186.*

UJA Federation of New York Information & Referral Center *1-877 852 6951, www. ujafedny.org.* **Open** *9am-5pm Mon-Thur; 9am-4pm Fri.* This hotline provides referrals to temples, synagogues, other Jewish organisations and groups.

SAFETY & SECURITY

New York's crime rate, particularly for violent crime, is at its lowest since the 1950s. Most crime occurs late at night and in low-income neighbourhoods. Still, a bit of common sense won't hurt. Don't flaunt your money and valuables, keep phones and other electronic gadgets out of sight, and try not to look obviously lost. Avoid deserted and poorly lit streets, walk facing oncoming traffic so no one can drive up alongside you undetected, and close to or on the street. Muggers prefer to hang back in doorways and shadows. If you are threatened, hand over your valuables at once, then dial 911.

Be extra alert to pickpockets and street hustlers – especially in crowded areas like Times Square.

SMOKING

The 1995 NYC Smoke-Free Air Act makes it illegal to smoke in virtually all indoor public places, including the subway. As of May 2011, smoking is also prohibited in NYC parks, pedestrian plazas (such as the ones in Times Square and Herald Square) and on beaches. Violators could face a $50 fine.

STUDY

Those who study in NYC have access to an endless extracurricular education, as well as a non-stop playground. Foreign students should get hold of an International Student Identity Card (ISIC) in order to secure discounts. These cards can be purchased from your local student-travel agent (go to www. isic.org or ask at your student union or an STA Travel office).

Manhattan's main universities include: the **City University of New York**'s 25 colleges (1-212 997 2869, www.cuny.edu); **Columbia University** (116th Street & Broadway, Morningside Heights, 1-212 854 1754, www.columbia. edu); the **Cooper Union** (30 Cooper Square, between 5th & 6th Streets, East Village, 1-212 353 4100, www.cooper.edu); **Fordham University**, which has campuses in the Bronx and on the Upper West Side (1-718 817 1000, 1-212 636 6000, www. fordham.edu); the **New School** (66 W 12th Street, between Fifth & Sixth Avenues, Greenwich Village, 1-212 229 5150, www. newschool.edu); **New York University** (70 Washington Square South, Greenwich Village, 1-212 998 1212, www.nyu.edu); and performing arts school **Juilliard** (60 Lincoln Center Plaza, at Broadway, Upper West Side, 1-212 799 5000, www. juilliard.edu).

TELEPHONES

Dialling & codes

As a rule, you must dial 1 + the area code before a number, even if the place you are calling is in the same area code. The area codes for Manhattan are **212** and **646**; Brooklyn, Queens, Staten Island and the Bronx are **718** and **347**; **917** is reserved mostly for mobile phones and pagers. Numbers preceded by **800**, **877** and **888** are free of charge when dialled from within the US.

In an **emergency**, dial 911. All calls are free (including those from pay and mobile phones).

For the **operator**, dial 0. If you're not used to US phones, then note that the ringing tone is long; the engaged tone, or 'busy signal', consists of much shorter, higher pitched beeps.

Collect calls are also known as reverse-charge calls. To make one, dial 0 followed by the number, or dial AT&T's 1-800 225 5288.

For **directory assistance**, dial 411 or 1 + area code + 555 1212. Doing so may cost nothing, depending on the pay phone you are using; carrier fees may apply. Long-distance directory assistance may also incur long-distance charges. For a directory of toll-free numbers, dial 1-800 555 1212.

For **international calls**, dial 011 + country code (Australia 61; New Zealand 64; UK 44), then the number (omitting any initial zero).

Mobile phones

US visitors should check with their provider whether they need to unlock a roaming option. Visitors from other countries will need at least a tri-band handset or a smartphone, plus an international roaming agreement or SIM card. Prepaid SIM cards can be purchased at mobile phone company shops and electronics chains such as Best Buy (www.bestbuy.com) for around $10 or less.

If you carry a mobile phone, turn it off in museums and restaurants, and at plays, movies and concerts. New Yorkers are quick to show their annoyance at an ill-timed ring.

Public phones

New York City's old-school payphones are being replaced by **LinkNYC** (www.link.nyc) connection points, offering free US calls as well as Wi-Fi and access to maps and city services on a built-in tablet. To make a call, dial the number on the keypad or tablet touch screen and talk into the speaker or plug in your personal headphones. If you need to make long-distance calls, use a phone card, available from phone company shops, supermarkets, many convenience stores and chain drug stores such as Duane Reade, Rite Aid and CVS (*see p387*).

TIME & DATES

New York is on Eastern Standard Time, which extends from the Atlantic coast to the eastern shore of Lake Michigan and south to the Gulf of Mexico. This is five hours behind Greenwich Mean Time. Clocks are set forward one hour in early March for Daylight Saving Time (Eastern Daylight Time) and back one hour at the beginning of November. Going from east to west, Eastern Time is one hour ahead of Central Time, two hours ahead of Mountain Time and three hours ahead of Pacific Time.

In the United States, the date is written as month, day and year; so 8/6/20 is 6 August 2020. Forms that foreigners may need to fill in, though, are often the other way round.

TIPPING

In restaurants, it's customary to tip at least 15 per cent, and since NYC tax is 8.875 per cent, a quick way to calculate the tip is to double the tax. In many restaurants, when you are with a group of six or more, the tip will be included in the bill. For tipping on taxi fares, *see p384*.

TOILETS

The media had a field day when the first pay toilet to open in the city since 1975 received its 'first flush' by officials in a special ceremony in 2008. 'Public Toilet No.1', as the *New York Post* christened it, is in Madison Square Park (Madison Avenue, between 23rd & 24th Streets, Flatiron District) and was due to be followed by around 20 across the city, but more than a decade later only a few more had been installed. It costs 25¢ to enter the large stainless steel and tempered glass box (beware: the door opens after 15 minutes). Below is a list of other convenient rest stops; for more options, see www.nyrestroom.com.

Downtown

Battery Park Castle Clinton *Subway 1 to South Ferry; 4, 5 to Bowling Green.*

Tompkins Square Park *Avenue A, at 9th Street. Subway L to First Avenue; 6 to Astor Place.*

Washington Square Park *Thompson Street, at Washington Square South. Subway A, B, C, D, E, F, M to W 4th Street.*

Midtown

Bryant Park *42nd Street, between Fifth & Sixth Avenues. Subway B, D, F, M to 42nd Street-Bryant Park; 7 to Fifth Avenue.*

Grand Central Terminal *42nd Street, at Park Avenue, Lower Concourse. Subway S, 4, 5, 6, 7 to 42nd Street-Grand Central.*

Penn Station *Seventh Avenue, between 31st & 33rd Streets,*

Subway A, C, E, 1, 2, 3 to 34th Street-Penn Station.

Uptown

Charles A Dana Discovery Center *Central Park, north side of Harlem Meer, 110th Street at Malcolm X Boulevard (Lenox Avenue). Subway 2, 3 to 110th Street-Central Park North.*

David Geffen Hall *Broadway, at 65th Street. Subway 1 to 66th Street-Lincoln Center.*

Delacorte Theater *Central Park, midpark, at 81st Street. Subway B, C to 81st Street-Museum of Natural History.*

TOURIST INFORMATION

Official NYC Information Center *Macy's Herald Square, 151 W 34th Street, between Broadway & Seventh Avenue, Garment District (1-212 484 1222, www. nycgo.com). Subway A, C, E, 1, 2, 3 to 34th Street-Penn Station; B, D, F, M, N, Q, R to 34th Street-Herald Square.* **Open** *10am-10pm Mon-Sat; 11am-9pm Sun.* **Map** *p175 D25.*

Located on the mezzanine of Macy's, the city's official (private, non-profit) visitors' information centre offers advice, maps, leaflets and coupons, and sells tour tickets and discount passes.

VISAS & IMMIGRATION

Visas

The **Visa Waiver Program** (VWP; www.cbp.gov/esta) allows citizens of 38 countries, including Australia, Ireland, New Zealand and the UK to visit the US for up to 90 days (for business or pleasure) without a visa. Visitors must have a machine-readable passport (e-passport) valid for the full 90-day period, a return ticket, and authorisation to travel through the ESTA (Electronic System for Travel Authorization) scheme. You must fill in the ESTA form at least 24 hours before travelling (72 hours is recommended) and pay a $14 fee; the form can be found at https://esta.cbp.dhs.gov/esta.

If you do not qualify for entry under the VWP, you will need a visa; leave plenty of time to check before travelling.

Immigration

Your airline will give all visitors an immigration form to be presented to an official when you land. Fill it in clearly and be prepared to give an address at which you are staying (a hotel is fine).

Upon arrival in the US, you may have to wait an hour or, if you're unlucky, considerably longer, in Immigration, where, owing to tightened security, you can expect slow-moving queues.

You may be expected to explain your visit; be polite and prepared. Note that all visitors to the US are now photographed and electronically fingerprinted on arrival on every trip.

WEIGHTS & MEASURES

Despite attempts to bring in metric measurements, you'll find imperial used in almost all contexts in New York and throughout the US. People think in ounces, inches, gallons and miles.

WORK

Non-nationals can't work in the US without the appropriate visa; these are hard to get and generally require you to prove that your job could not be done by a US citizen. Contact your local embassy for further details. Some student visas allow part-time work after the first academic year.

UK students who want to spend a summer vacation working in the US should contact **BUNAC Travel Services** for help in securing a temporary job and also the requisite visa (Priory House, 6 Wrights Lane, London W8 6TA, 033 3999 7516, www.bunac.org).

Further Reference

BOOKS

Architecture

Richard Berenholtz *New York, New York* Miniature panoramic images of the city through the seasons.

Stanley Greenberg *Invisible New York* A photographic account of hidden architectural triumphs.

New York City Landmarks Preservation Commission *Guide to New York City Landmarks*

Karl Sabbagh *Skyscraper* How the tall ones are built.

Kevin Walsh *Forgotten New York* Discover overlooked architectural gems and anachronistic remnants.

Norval White & Elliot Willensky *The AIA Guide to New York City* A comprehensive directory of important buildings.

Culture & recollections

Irving Lewis Allen *The City in Slang* NYC-bred words and phrases.

Joseph Berger *The World in a City* The *New York Times* columnist explores the communities located within the five boroughs.

Andrew Blauner (ed) *Central Park: An Anthology* Writers reflect on the city's most celebrated green space.

Anatole Broyard *Kafka Was the Rage: A Greenwich Village Memoir* Vivid account of 1940s Village bohemia and its characters.

George Chauncey *Gay New York* Gay culture from 1890 to 1940.

Martha Cooper & Henry Chalfant *Subway Art* A definitive survey of city graffiti.

Josh Alan Friedman *Tales of Times Square* Sleaze and decay in the old days.

Nelson George *Hip Hop America* The real history of hip hop, from Grandmaster Flash to Puff Daddy.

Bill Helmreich *The New York Nobody Knows: Walking 6,000 Miles in the City* Observations and interviews from an epic trek across the five boroughs.

Jane Jacobs *The Death and Life of Great American Cities* A hugely influential critique of modern urban planning.

Chuck Katz *Manhattan on Film 1 & 2* On-location walking tours.

Gillian McCain & Legs McNeil *Please Kill Me* An oral history of the punk scene.

Joseph Mitchell *Up in the Old Hotel* Quirky recollections of New York from the 1930s to the 1960s.

Thurston Moore & Byron Coley *No Wave* Musicians reminisce about the downtown post-punk underground scene in this nostalgia trip co-edited by the Sonic Youth frontman.

Adrienne Onofri *Walking Brooklyn* Thirty tours illuminate the culture and history of the borough.

Patti Smith *Just Kids* The punk poet recalls the 1960s/'70s scene with artist Robert Mapplethorpe.

Sam Stephenson *The Jazz Loft Project: Photographs and Tapes of W Eugene Smith from 821 Sixth Avenue, 1957-1965* Images and conversation transcripts from the jazz-obsessed photographer's loft, which became a rehearsal space for some of the era's greatest musicians.

EB White *Here is New York* A clear-eyed love letter to Gotham.

History

Herbert Asbury *The Gangs of New York: An Informal History of the Underworld* A racy journalistic portrait of the city at the turn of the 19th century.

Robert A Caro *The Power Broker* A biography of Robert Moses, New York's mid 20th-century master builder, and his chequered legacy.

Federal Writers' Project *The WPA Guide to New York City* A wonderful evocation of the 1930s by writers who were employed under FDR's New Deal.

Sanna Feirstein *Naming New York* The origins of Manhattan place names.

Tom Folsom *The Mad Ones: Crazy Joe Gallo and the Revolution at the Edge of the Underworld* Engaging ride though the world of the Mafia during the 1960s.

Eric Homberger *The Historical Atlas of New York City* Through maps, photographs, illustrations and essays, this hefty volume charts the metropolis's 400-year heritage.

Clifton Hood *722 Miles: The Building of the Subways and How They Transformed New York* The birth of the world's longest rapid transit system.

Kenneth T Jackson (ed) *The Encyclopedia of New York City* An ambitious and useful reference guide for the city.

David Levering Lewis *When Harlem Was in Vogue* A study of the Harlem Renaissance.

Jonathan Mahler *Ladies and Gentlemen, the Bronx is Burning* A gritty snapshot of NYC in 1977.

Mitchell Pacelle *Empire* The story of the fight to build the Empire State Building.

Clayton Patterson (ed) *Resistance* A collection of essays reflecting on the Lower East Side's history as a radical hotbed.

Luc Sante *Low Life* Opium dens and brothels in New York from the 1840s to the 1920s.

Russell Shorto *The Island at the Center of the World* How the Dutch colony shaped Manhattan – and America.

Mike Wallace & Edwin G Burrows *Gotham: A History of New York City to 1898* The area's history from native settlements to the consolidation of the five boroughs of NYC.

Mike Wallace *Greater Gotham: A History of New York City From 1898 to 1919* The long-awaited sequel to the Pulitzer Prize-winning chronicle covers 20 formative years of the modern city's development.

Fiction & poetry

Kurt Andersen *Turn of the Century* Millennial Manhattan as seen through the eyes of media players.

Paul Auster *The New York Trilogy: City of Glass, Ghosts* and *The Locked Room* A search for the madness behind the method of Manhattan's grid.

Kevin Baker *Dreamland* A poetic novel about Coney Island's glory days.

James A Baldwin *Another Country* Racism under the bohemian veneer of the 1960s.

Michael Chabon *The Amazing Adventures of Kavalier and Clay* Jewish comic-book artists battling with crises of identity in the 1940s.

Jennifer Egan *Manhattan Beach* During WWII, a young woman joins a team of divers at the Brooklyn Navy Yard and learns about her missing father's murky past.

Ralph Ellison *Invisible Man* Epic examination of race and racism in 1950s Harlem.

Jack Finney *Time and Again* An illustrator travels back to 19th-century New York City.

Larry Kramer *Faggots* A devastating satire of gay NYC.

Rachel Kushner *The Flamethrowers* A gritty evocation of the lives of artists and anarchists in the '70s.

Jonathan Lethem *Chronic City* The author of *The Fortress of Solitude* packs this Manhattan-set novel with pop-culture references.

Phillip Lopate (ed) *Writing New York* An excellent anthology of short stories, essays and poems.

Colum McCann *Let the Great World Spin* Interconnected stories set in 1970s New York.

Patrick McGrath *Trauma* A first-person account of psychic decay that floats a critique of post-9/11 social and political amnesia.

Tim McLoughlin (ed) *Brooklyn Noir 1, 2 & 3* Second-borough crime tales.

Frank O'Hara *The Collected Poems of Frank O'Hara* The great NYC poet found inspiration in his hometown.

Richard Price *Lush Life* A contemporary murder story set on the Lower East Side.

David Schickler *Kissing in Manhattan* The lives of quirky tenants in a teeming Manhattan block.

Hubert Selby Jr *Last Exit to Brooklyn* Dockland degradation, circa 1950s.

Edith Wharton *Old New York* Four novellas of 19th-century New York City.

Colson Whitehead *The Colossus of New York: A City in 13 Parts* A lyrical tribute to city life.

Tom Wolfe *The Bonfire of the Vanities* Rich/poor, black/white – an unmatched slice of 1980s NYC.

Film

The Amazing Spider-Man *(2012)* The reboot of the comic book web-slinger franchise features Andrew Garfield as the ultimate New York superhero and nods to the city's cinematic history. Sequels followed.

Annie Hall *(1977)* Woody Allen and Diane Keaton in this valentine to Manhattan.

Breakfast at Tiffany's *(1961)* Audrey Hepburn as the cash-poor, time-rich socialite Holly Golightly.

Can You Ever Forgive Me? *(2018)* A real-life tale of literary misadventure focuses on a couple of down-on-their-luck dreamers in wintry 1991 Manhattan.

Dog Day Afternoon *(1975)* Al Pacino is a Brooklyn bank robber in Sidney Lumet's classic.

Do the Right Thing *(1989)* Racial strife in Brooklyn's Bedford-Stuyvesant in Spike Lee's drama.

The French Connection *(1971)* As detective Jimmy 'Popeye' Doyle, Gene Hackman chases down drug traffickers in William Friedkin's much-imitated thriller.

The Godfather *(1972)*, **The Godfather: Part II** *(1974)* Francis Ford Coppola's brilliant commentary on capitalism in America is told through the violent saga of Italian gangsters.

Mean Streets *(1973)* Robert De Niro and Harvey Keitel shine as small-time Little

Italy hoods in Martin Scorsese's breakthrough film.

Midnight Cowboy *(1969)*
Street creatures 'Ratso' Rizzo and Joe Buck face an unforgiving Times Square in John Schlesinger's darkly amusing classic.

A Most Violent Year *(2014)*
JC Chandor's absorbing no-bull drama chronicles the trials of an immigrant gas-company owner in scrappy Koch-era New York.

Superfly *(1972)*
Blaxploitation classic, propelled by legendary Curtis Mayfield soundtrack.

The Taking of Pelham 123 *(2009)*
The plot premise may be flawed – in this Denzel Washington/John Travolta remake, as well as in the 1974 original – but it stirs up strap-hangers' darkest fears.

Taxi Driver *(1976)*
Robert De Niro is a crazed cabbie who sees all of New York as a den of iniquity in Scorsese's drama.

Music

Beastie Boys *No Sleep Till Brooklyn*
The hip-hop troupe's on-the-road anthem exudes local pride.

Leonard Cohen *Chelsea Hotel #2*
Of all the songs inspired by the Chelsea, this bleak vision of doomed love is on a level of its own.

Billie Holiday *Autumn In New York*
Holiday's yearning version of the 1934 jazz standard evokes Central Park colours and 'shimmering clouds in canyons of steel'.

Jay-Z with Alicia Keys *Empire State of Mind*
The Brooklyn rapper's ode to NYC is a 21st-century rival to Sinatra's classic anthem.

Billy Joel *New York State of Mind*
This heartfelt ballad exemplifies the city's effect on the souls of its visitors and residents.

LCD Soundsystem *New York, I Love You but You're Bringing Me Down*
An ambivalent critique of the city New Yorkers love to hate.

Charles Mingus *Mingus Ah Um*
Mingus brought the gospel to jazz and created an NYC masterpiece.

Public Enemy *It Takes a Nation of Millions to Hold Us Back*
A ferociously political tour de force from the Long Island hip-hop group whose own Chuck D once called rap 'the CNN for black America'.

The Ramones *Ramones*
Four Queens roughnecks, a few buzzsaw chords, and musings on turning tricks and sniffing glue – it transformed rock 'n' roll.

Frank Sinatra *Theme from New York, New York*
Ol' Blue Eyes' bombastic love letter melts those little-town blues.

Bruce Springsteen *My City of Ruins*
The Boss praises the city's resilience post-September 11 with this track from *The Rising*.

The Strokes *Is This It*
The effortlessly hip debut of this hometown band garnered praise and worldwide attention.

The Velvet Underground *The Velvet Underground & Nico*
Their first album is still the gold standard of downtown cool.

Wu Tang Clan *C.R.E.A.M.*
This hot cut from a landmark debut album (the title stands for 'cash rules everything around me') paints a gritty portrait of urban survival over an eerie, endlessly circling piano-and-organ backdrop.

Websites

www.clubplanet.com
Follow the city's nocturnal scene.

www.forgotten-ny.com
Discover old New York here.

www.manhattanusersguide.com
An insiders' guide to what's going on around town.

www.mta.info
Subway and bus service news.

www1.nyc.gov
City Hall's official New York City website has lots of useful links.

www.nycgo.com
The official New York City tourism organisation provides information on sights, attractions, hotels, restaurants, shops and more.

www.nytimes.com
'All the News That's Fit to Print' from The *New York Times* (limited access for non-subscribers).

www.timeout.com/newyork
The Time Out New York website covers the best of the city, from upcoming museum exhibitions, shows and events to the latest film releases, sample sales and thousands of restaurant and bar reviews written by our critics.

Apps

Arro *(free)*
Find a yellow taxi, get a fare estimate and pay all via the app.

Exit Strategy NYC *($3.99)*
Helps you navigate the subway like a canny local, showing which carriage is most convenient for the exit you want.

MTA Subway Time *(free)*
Official real-time arrival info for selected lines (more routes are added periodically until complete).

ShopDrop *(free)*
Discount-fashion hounds consolidate info from nearly a dozen websites in this sample-sale locator.

SitOrSquat *(free)*
Find nearby restrooms on a map with a 'sit or squat' rating to avoid unsanitary situations.

Time Out *(free)*
Our indispensable guide to what's happening in New York (and other cities), plus integrated Uber transportation and daily deals.

TKTS *(free)*
See which Broadway and Off-Broadway shows are on the boards at the discount ticket booths before you join the queue.

Index

INDEX

Picture credits

Pages 2 (top) Victoria Lipov/Shutterstock.com, 2 (bottom) pisaphotography/Shutterstock.com, 3, 23 (top), 164 Songquan Deng/Shutterstock.com, 5, 15 (top) IM_Photo/Shutterstock.com, 6 lazyllama/Shutterstock.com, 11 (top Ingus Kruklitis/Shutterstock.com, 11 (bottom) Marc Venema/Shutterstock.com, 12 (top) S. Borisov/Shutterstock.com, 12 (bottom) BiksuTong/Shutterstock.com, 13 (top) Michael Urmann/Shutterstock.com, 13 (bottom), 342 Disney, 14 (top), 215 (bottom) Anton_Ivanov/Shutterstock.com, 14 (bottom) Spinel/Shutterstock.com, 15 (bottom), 25 (bottom), 312 Kenny Rodriguez/House of Yes, 16 (top) Iñaki Vinaixa for Lincoln Center, 16 (middle), 29, 198, 205, 269 Felix Lipov/Shutterstock.com, 16 (bottom), 155 (top) Farzad Owrang - ©Simone Leigh; Courtesy of the artist and Luhring Augustine, New York, 17 (bottom), 219 ItzaVU/Shutterstock.com, 18 (top), 54, 104 Mark Wickens/Oroboro, 18 (bottom), 45 (bottom) Nitzan Rubin, 20 Dr. Alan Lipkin/Shutterstock.com, 21 (top) Viktor Fuchs/Shutterstock.com, 21 (bottom) Andrey Bayda/Shutterstock.com, 22, 40 (centre), 48 (bottom) Courtesy of Major Food Group, 23 (bottom) Miune/Shutterstock.com, 24 (top), 369 Christopher Penler/Shutterstock.com, 24 (middle) ©AMNH/D. Finnin, 24 (bottom) Ritu Manoj Jethani/Shutterstock.com, 25 (top) DW labs Incorporated/Shutterstock.com, 26 (top) Linda Harms/Shutterstock.com, 26 (bottom) pio3/Shutterstock.com, 27 (top) Iourli Tcheka/Shutterstock.com, 27 (bottom) f11photo/Shutterstock.com, 30, 35 (bottom) SCOOTERCASTER/Shutterstock.com, 31, 270 lev radin/Shutterstock.com, 32 (top) Ron Adar/Shutterstock.com, 32 (bottom) mariakray/Shutterstock.com, 33, 121 Warren Eisenberg/Shutterstock.com, 34 shu2260/Shutterstock.com, 35 (top) Stef Ko/Shutterstock.com, 36 Malgosia S/Shutterstock.com, 37 (top) T Photography/Shutterstock.com, 37 (bottom), 272 (right) littlenySTOCK/Shutterstock.com, 39 ©Evan Sung/Uncle Boon's, 40 (left) Diane Kang/Atomix, 40 (right) STARR Restaurants, 41 Linda Facci/JG Melon, 42 Katie Burton/Red Rooster Harlem, 43 Jack's Wife Freda, 44 (top) Clinton Street Baking Company, 45 (top), 244, 306 Filip Wolak , 46 Wendy Connett, 47 (top) Zandy Mangold, 47 (bottom) BlackTail, 48 (top) Daniel Krieger, 49 Roxana Marroquin, 50 Attaboy, 53 Feng Sway, 56 ©Fredrika Stjarne, 57, 133 John Muggenborg/muggphoto.com, 58 (top) Magpie, 58 (bottom), 106 Courtesy of Hesperios, 59 Printed Matter, 61 Shutterstock.com, 63 Stephan Guarch/Shutterstock.com, 66 Steven Bostock/Shutterstock.com, 69 eric8669/iStock.com, 72 agsaz/Shutterstock.com, 73 RoBenatti/Shutterstock.com, 74, 238 Edi Chen/Shutterstock.com, 75 Phil Maddocks/Shutterstock.com, 76 Gabi Porter, 77 JJFarq/Shutterstock.com, 78, 207 Kamira/Shutterstock.com, 81 Scott Rudd, 85 valeriy eydlin/Shutterstock.com, 86 Neilskliim/Shutterstock.com, 89, 100, 116, 130, 145 Paul Wagtouicz, 91 Kirna Zabête, 92 Robert Wright/Roman and Williams Guild, 94 Mmuseumm, 97 Vladimir Mucibabic/Shutterstock.com, 98 Courtesy of Museum of Chinese in America (MOCA), 103 Robyn Lehr/Pasquale Jones, 105 Depop Space NY, 109, 260, 345 Osugi/Shutterstock.com, 110, 255 Leonard Zhukovsky/Shutterstock.com, 112 ©Peter Aaron/Esto, 114, 115 (top) Katz's Deli, 115 (bottom) Frankel's, 117, 170 Teddy Wolff, 122 The Phluid Project, 125 Courtesy Merchant's House Museum, 127, 128 Time Out, 135 Inolas/Shutterstock.com, 136 PnPy/Shutterstock.com, 138 Andre Baranowski/Blue Hill, 139 Bokic Bojan/Shutterstock.com, 140 S Freihon/Dante, 143 mervas/Shutterstock.com, 146 Brian Logan Photography/Shutterstock.com, 147 ©Whitney Museum of American Art, 148 High Street on Hudson, 149 CHNT/Shutterstock.com, 151 Oscity/Shutterstock.com, 152 Eileen Costa/The Museum at FIT, 154 Courtesy Damián Ortega and Gladstone Gallery, New York and Brussels - Photography by David Regen, 155 (middle) Farzad Owrang - Courtesy of Luhring Augustine, New York, 155 (bottom) Farzad Owrang - ©Christina Forrer; Courtesy of the artist and Luhring Augustine, New York, 156 Albachiaraa/Shutterstock.com, 157 PnPy/Shutterstock.com, 159 Artists & Fleas, 161, 173 eric laudonien/Shutterstock.com, 162 haeryung stock images/Shutterstock.com, 165 Museum of Sex, 167 Cayla Zahoran, 169 ABC Carpet & Home, 174 ADRIAN WILSON/WWW.INTERIORPHOTOGRAPHY.NET, 177 Manu Padilla/Shutterstock.com, 179, 328 Iwan Baan/The Shed, 183 Vitezslav Valka/Shutterstock.com, 185, 393 Bumble Dee/Shutterstock.com, 186 Richard Caden/FAO Schwarz, 188 Kantapit Tanadkarn/Shutterstock.com, 193, 257 robert cicchetti/Shutterstock.com, 196 mikhail/Shutterstock.com, 199, 215 (top) Diego Grandi/Shutterstock.com, 200 ©2017 Corrado Serra/New-York Historical Society, 202 George Apostolidis/Mandarin Oriental New York, 204, 210 EQRoy/Shutterstock.com, 208 ApinBen4289/Shutterstock.com, 212 itoodmuk/Shutterstock.com, 213 Courtesy of Veronica Beard, 214 Mia2you/Shutterstock.com, 221 James Kirkikis/Shutterstock.com, 222 StefanoT/Shutterstock.com, 224 poludziber/Shutterstock.com, 226 © Driely S. 2014 – www.peladopelado.com, 229 Trish Mayo/Morris-Jumel Mansion, 231 H.J. Herrera/Shutterstock.com, 235 Courtesy of the New York Transit Museum, 237 Salvador Maniquiz/Shutterstock.com, 242 (top) Jonathan Dorado/Brooklyn Museum, 242 (bottom) Sarah DeSantis/Brooklyn Museum, 245 Inna_liapko/Shutterstock.com, 247 solepsizm/Shutterstock.com, 248 The City Reliquary Museum, 252 Feng Sway, 254 Martina Badini/Shutterstock.com, 258 Olya Vysotskaya/Self-Taught Genius Gallery, 263 Nicholas Knight/©The Isamu Noguchi Foundation and Garden Museum, New York, 265 Melissa Sinclair, 266 quietbits/Shutterstock.com, 267 goofyfoottaka/Shutterstock.com, 272 (left) Norman McGrath/Bronx Museum of the Arts, 275 Wave Hill, 277 PT Hamilton/Shutterstock.com, 278 cpaulfell/Shutterstock.com, 280 Elzbieta Sekowska/Shutterstock.com, 282, 288 Jazz Age Lawn Party, 285 Ryan Purcell/Afropunk, 287 Smorgasburg, 289 (top), 332, 333 Kevin Yatarola/Lincoln Center, 289 (bottom), 362 a katz/Shutterstock.com, 290 Nellie Oh Honey Beavers, 292 Hoover Tung/Shutterstock.com, 295 Jeremy Liebman/Metrograph LLC, 296 World History Archive/SuperStock.com, 297 mrk movie/Marka/SuperStock.com, 298 Nitehawk Cinema, 301 Bushwig, 302, 303 Alibi Lounge, 305 Maro Hagopian/@marohagopian, 309 John Goddard/Slipper Room, 316 David Andrako/Joe's Pub, 318 Whitney Cox/King's Theatre, 320 Manish Gosalia/Rockwood Music Hall, 323 Lawrence Sumulong/Jazz at Lincoln Center, 327, 343 (right) Joan Marcus/Wicked, 329 Juan Salmoral Franco/Shutterstock.com, 330 Chris Lee/www.chrisleephotographer.com, 335, 365 Sean Pavone/Shutterstock.com, 337 Paula Court, courtesy of The Kitchen, 339 SpeakingPix/Shutterstock.com, 341 Matthew Murphy/Come from Away, 342 (left) Hamilton, 342 (right) Matthew Murphy/Dear Evan Hansen, 343 (left) Harry Potter and the Cursed Child, 347 Francis Dzikowski/Esto, 350 GagliardiPhotography/Shutterstock.com, 353 Everett Historical/Shutterstock.com, 354 Jean Leon Gerome Ferris/Wikimedia Commons, 356 NYPL/Wikimedia Commons, 358 Wikimedia Commons, 367 MACH Photos/Shutterstock.com, 370 Roman Tiraspolsky/Shutterstock.com, 371 Mariusz Lopusiewicz/Shutterstock.com, 373 Luciano Mortula - LGM/Shutterstock.com, 374 Adrian Gaut/Sister City, 375 (top) Ace Hotel, 375 (bottom) Floto + Warner/Boro Hotel, 378 Annie Schlechter/The Ludlow, 381 Annie Schlechter/The Pod Hotels.

CREDITS

Credits

Crimson credits
Editor Lisa Ritchie
Listings researchers Claudia Bloom, Lisa Brown, Olivia Simonds, Jasmine Ting
Cartography Gail Armstrong

Series Editor Sophie Blacksell Jones
Production Manager Kate Michell
Production Designer Emilie Crabb
Print Manager Patrick Dawson
Design Mytton Williams

Chairman David Lester
Managing Director Andy Riddle

Advertising Media Sales House
Marketing Sophie Shepherd
Sales Lyndsey Mayhew

Contributors
Itineraries Lisa Ritchie. **New York Today** Lisa Ritchie. **Eating & Drinking** Dan Q Dao, Christina Izzo. **Shopping** Lisa Ritchie. **Explore** Lisa Ritchie and contributors to *Time Out New York* magazine. **Events** Olivia Simonds and contributors to *Time Out New York* magazine. **Film** Joshua Rothkopf, Lisa Ritchie and contributors to *Time Out New York* magazine. **LGBT** David Goldberg and contributors to *Time Out New York* magazine. **Nightlife** Andrew Frisicano, Ro Samarth, Christopher Tarantino and contributors to *Time Out New York* magazine (Clubs); David Goldberg and contributors to *Time Out New York* magazine (Comedy); Andrew Frisicano, Ro Samarth and contributors to *Time Out New York* magazine (Music); Adam Feldman (Cabaret). **Performing Arts** Andrew Frisicano, Ro Samarth and contributors to *Time Out New York* magazine (Classical Music & Opera); Adam Feldman and contributors to *Time Out New York* magazine (Dance & Theatre). **History** Joseph Alexiou, Richard Koss, Kathleen Squires. **Architecture** Eric P Nash. **Accommodation** Lisa Ritchie and contributors to *Time Out New York* magazine.

Photography credits
Front cover J. Banks/AWL-images
Back cover left: EQRoy/Shutterstock.com; centre: Miune/Shutterstock.com; right: Warren Eisenberg/Shutterstock.com.
Interior Photography credits, *see p404.*

Publishing information
New York City Guide 25th edition
© TIME OUT ENGLAND LIMITED 2019
November 2019

ISBN 978 1 78059 270 1
CIP DATA: A catalogue record for this book is available from the British Library

Published by Crimson Publishing
21d Charles Street, Bath, BA1 1HX (01225 584 950, www.crimsonpublishing.co.uk) on behalf of Time Out England.

Distributed by Grantham Book Services
Distributed in the US and Canada by Publishers Group West (1-510-809-3700)

Printed by Replika Press, India

While every effort has been made by the authors and the publishers to ensure that the information contained in this guide is accurate and up to date as at the date of publication, they accept no responsibility or liability in contract, tort, negligence, breach of statutory duty or otherwise for any inconvenience, loss, damage, costs or expenses of any nature whatsoever incurred or suffered by anyone as a result of any advice or information contained in the guide (except to the extent that such liability may not be excluded or limited as a matter of law).

All rights reserved. No part of this publication may be reproduced, stored in a retrieval system, or transmitted in any form or by any means, electronic, mechanical, photocopying, recording or otherwise, without prior permission from the copyright owners.

Plan Ahead Online
Use Trip Planner+
at www.mta.info
for subway & bus directions

Manhattan
Bus Map
February 2019

© 2019 Metropolitan Transportation Authority. Unauthorized duplication prohibited.

LEGEND

Full-time Service
(Every day 7 a.m.–10 p.m.)

Part-time Service

Select Bus Service bus stop.
Fare is paid before boarding

Direction of Service (two-way
service has no arrows)

Full-time Terminal

Part-time Terminal

+selectbusservice